Table of Contents

Mandate for Leadership II

Continuing the Conservative Revolution

Stuart M. Butler is Director of Domestic Policy Studies at The Heritage Foundation. He has a Ph.D. in American economic history from St. Andrews University in Scotland. He is the author of *Enterprise Zones: Greenlining the Inner Cities* and *Privatizing Federal Spending* (forthcoming).

Michael Sanera is an Assistant Professor of Political Science at Northern Arizona University. A Ph.D. in Political Science from the University of Colorado, he has served as the Assistant Director for Planning and Evaluation in the U.S. Office of Personnel Management, and is the author of "Review of Discretionary Grant Administrative Procedures at the Department of Education," a consulting study for the Department of Education.

W. Bruce Weinrod is Director of Foreign Policy and Defense Studies at The Heritage Foundation. Mr. Weinrod, whose work focuses on East-West relations, arms control, and Latin America, has a J.D. from Georgetown University School of Law and an M.A. in International Affairs from the University of Pennsylvania. His previous professional experience includes the White House staff, Capitol Hill and the Foreign Policy Research Institute. Mr. Weinrod has published numerous articles on foreign policy and defense issues and is a member of the International Institute for Strategic Studies.

Library of Congress Catalog Card No. 84-062539
ISBN 0-89195-036-2

Composition: Unicorn Graphics
Washington, D.C.
Cover Design: Sparkman & Bartholomew Assoc.
Washington, D.C.

PART 3: INSTITUTIONAL REFORMS

PART 4: IMPLEMENTING THE MANDATE
Michael Sanera

Foreword

When the original *Mandate for Leadership* was released, just weeks after Ronald Reagan's first presidential election victory, the U.S. was engulfed by problems and the new President was confronting challenges unparalleled in nearly a half-century. *Mandate* was designed to be a detailed road map to help the fledgling Reagan Administration steer the nation into a sound future, guided by conservative principles. In looking back on those early months, Ronald Reagan was to say that *Mandate* gave him and his Administration "special substantive help we'll never forget. . . . We've been using *Mandate* to our and the country's advantage." By the end of the President's first year in office, nearly two-thirds of *Mandate*'s more than 2,000 specific recommendations had been or were being transformed into policy.

As Ronald Reagan now approaches his second inauguration, basking in an unprecedented electoral mandate, he and the nation have come far from the dismal days of 1980. Just as American voters have begun to realign themselves politically, so the nation has been realigning itself. Its economy is healthier, its arsenal is stronger, its government meddles less in everyone's lives and its political system and society once again are the envy of the world. Much has been achieved in the past four years.

Yet there are tough challenges confronting the second Reagan Administration. Not all the old problems have been solved, and some have not even been tackled. More important, policies must be fashioned to ensure the continuation and permanence of the Reagan Revolution. It is toward this end that The Heritage Foundation submits to the President, the Members of his Cabinet, Members of Congress, and our fellow Americans across the land this volume, *Mandate for Leadership II, Continuing the Conservative Revolution.*

Marshalling the talents and experience of more than 150 experts, *Mandate II* examines nearly every major policy center of the federal government. It offers nearly 1,300 specific proposals to make the federal government leaner, the economy stronger, the nation safer, and the individual American freer.

In prescribing policies for domestic issues, *Mandate II* is guided by several basic principles, including the need to 1) restructure incentives to encourage the efficient use of resources; 2) return control of government programs to those most directly affected by them; 3) expand the economy; and 4) turn over to the private sector a myriad of government services.

In foreign policy and defense issues, *Mandate II* is guided by a conviction that 1) the U.S. must develop a defense that actually defends the nation rather than merely deters Soviet attack; 2) U.S. alliances must be strengthened, as must ties with the nation's friends in Europe, the Pacific Basin, the Middle East, and Latin America; 3) democratic pluralism must be promoted in the Third World and in Soviet-dominated states; and 4) the Soviet Union must be challenged ideologically, diplomatically, and politically and must not be led to assume that the U.S. accepts as permanent the destruction of democratic institutions in Central Europe.

Perhaps one of the most formidable and underrated challenges faced by the first Reagan Administration was the reflexive opposition to Reagan policies by the entrenched federal bureaucracy. It soon became apparent that oftentimes "personnel is policy." Drawing on lessons from the experience of the first Reagan Administration, *Mandate II* outlines a program for implementing the policies put forward by the Administration. This program examines the problems that appointees face in working their policies through the bureaucracy and lays out a plan of action for ensuring success.

The policies prescribed by *Mandate II* may not all be endorsed in each specific by the Board of Trustees, the officers or the staff of The Heritage Foundation. They are primarily the views of the authors who have signed each of *Mandate II*'s chapters. Yet they all reflect The Heritage Foundation's deep commitment to the virtues of the free enterprise system, to a leaner government, and to a stronger defense. They are based, too, on The Heritage Foundation's appreciation of traditional American values. And they all are intended to ensure that Americans get what they voted for in 1980 and 1984—the benefits, hopes, and challenges of an American opportunity society.

While acknowledgements are mentioned elsewhere in this volume, I would like to give special thanks to two of my valued colleagues: Burt Pines, our Vice President of Research whose keen eye oversaw the policy recommendations; and Phil Truluck, our Executive Vice President and Chief Operating Officer, whose overall supervision of *Mandate II* made it possible.

Edwin J. Feulner, Jr.
President
The Heritage Foundation

Acknowledgements

A project of this scale involves many people, without whose time and skills the final product would be impossible. Central to *Mandate II*, of course, were the task force chairmen, and the task force members, who provided the reports that comprise this volume. These reports were transformed into the final product with the generous assistance of Greerson McMullen, who coordinated the work of the task forces and the preparation of each chapter; Burton Yale Pines, who provided valuable comments on the manuscript; and Richard Odermatt and Gordon Jones, who guided the production process. In addition, thanks should go to Alison Horton and her assistants, who prepared the manuscript for editing and publication, and to Jane Cocking, John O'Hara, and Jean Savage.

For their work on Part 4 of *Mandate II*, the author thanks Cora Montoya, Jennifer Apfelgrun, and Ed Hurley. Helpful comments on early drafts were provided by several close associates; especially useful were the detailed comments of Charles Heatherly. Special thanks go to Robert Rector, who made major contributions to the research, organization, and writing of Part 4 of *Mandate II*. Any credit for its success must be shared with Robert. Its inadequacies and imperfections, of course, are the author's alone.

Stuart M. Butler
Michael Sanera
W. Bruce Weinrod

Acknowledgments

Part 1

Domestic Agencies

Overview—Domestic Agencies

by
Stuart M. Butler

As the Reagan team prepares for another four years in the White House, it faces a very different challenge than it did in January 1981. Four years ago, conservatives came to Washington with a firm sense of direction and a clear set of goals. The task at hand was straightforward: Use the levers of executive power and the new President's strong support in the Congress to begin moving toward those goals. What the new Administration needed at that time was a set of tactics and near-term objectives to switch the Washington policy-making machine into the conservative gear. The detailed recommendations of Heritage's *Mandate for Leadership* helped provide that blueprint.

Today, the situation is quite different. The challenges are greater and so is the potential magnitude of success. The second term Reagan team must take stock of the last four years and set realistic objectives for the next four—objectives which, when reached, will become an indelible imprint on the nation. This is no simple task. It is much easier for a team to be focused when it is not burdened by the day-to-day pressures of governing. Power generally distorts and diffuses the initial clear vision. The Reagan Administration has been no exception. After a seeming invincibility in the first year of the term, when dramatic victories were chalked up in the Congress and bold policy initiatives kept the momentum firmly with the White House, Reagan officials gradually appeared to lose their edge.

There were several reasons for this, as the following chapters explain in detail. Congress and the Washington bureaucracy, for example, began to get the measure of the new conservative appointees. After the initial shock of the Reagan victory had faded, the bureaucracy began to dig in, while the opposition in Congress organized more effectively. Reagan officials began to find themselves on the defensive when they went to Capitol Hill, and their own civil service staffs were increasingly successful in persuading them to put "practicality" before "ideology." So chastening and frustrating was this experience that many of the President's most committed supporters left Washington in disgust or succumbed to"Potomac Fever"—thinking like a bureaucrat rather than a political official.

The Reagan game plan also came under mounting pressure as the congressional budget process was used to thwart the President's strategy of reducing the scale of federal government activities in American society. The intricacies of the budget process allowed legislators to block White House budget proposals and whittle away

Reagan's early spending victories. While growth in federal taxes was brought under control in the 1981 Tax Act, therefore, the Administration's poor batting average in either winning or sustaining budget cuts led to growing deficits. The gusher of red ink made the President's congressional supporters increasingly nervous.

The Administration's solid victory in the polls this November, therefore, masks a disturbing loss of momentum and sense of direction within the government. Indeed, the overriding importance of the election itself made it difficult for officials to project their thinking beyond November 6th. Consequently, the Administration's efforts must be refocused and clear objectives and strategies formulated if the Reagan Agenda is to be fulfilled. The alternative is a drift toward mediocrity which betrays the confidence of the tens of millions of Reagan voters

The pages that follow, addressing each department of government, sketch a conservative strategy for the Second Reagan Administration. Specific goals are proposed which, the authors believe, can be reached by 1988. Also detailed are initiatives for 1985 which should be important steps toward those objectives. In many cases these are the second stage of a two-term program, building upon Reagan's successes; but in other cases, they are "unfinished business" from the first term agenda.

The Administration's specific policy objectives must not be pursued in isolation, separate from an overall strategy. A successful strategy requires policy initiatives in all areas of government that are compatible with general approaches or themes. The themes for the Second Reagan Administration should move the operation of government and the body of law further toward the conservative vision of society chosen by the American people in 1980 and again in 1984. These are:

THEME 1: Restructure incentives in federal programs to foster the efficient use of resources and to encourage self-improvement.

The Administration made progress during its first term in reducing expenditures by changing the incentive structures contained in federal programs so that the excessive use of federal or private resources is discouraged. Example: User charges have been applied in a number of programs. A change in the incentive structure should be an even stronger theme during the second term. In many instances, the incentives in programs still invite waste and dependency. By altering these incentives, the Administration could meet the twin conservative goals of providing federal assistance where it is needed while reducing the burden which government places on the economy.

A number of recommendations in the following chapters provide such improved incentives. Examples: financial assistance to students should be linked to academic performance; elderly Americans with chronic illnesses should be allowed to receive care in their own homes while receiving federal assistance, rather than being forced to go to expensive hospitals and nursing homes to qualify for federal reimbursements for health costs; the tax deductibility of group health plans needs to be capped and increased copayments imposed for hospital stays under Medicare to discourage excess in demand and bring down costs; greater use should be made of road and waterway tolls; and peak period fees should be placed on corporate jets that choose to land at busy airports during rush hour and impose enormous costs on the air traffic control system. Reforming incentives in this way to save resources is not a question of ideology, it is common sense and sound management.

THEME 2: Put the control of programs back into the hands of those affected by them.

One of the greatest successes of the Administration, largely overlooked by commentators, has been the decentralizing of federal programs by transferring responsibility for detailed administration to the states. The various block grant programs, for instance, have provided states with the flexibility they need to use resources wisely and within a system of rules that reflect social conditions.

Such decentralization must continue as a central theme of the Second Reagan Administration. Transferring responsibilities to the states subjects programs more to the watchful eye of the voter. It also encourages innovation and experimentation, enabling states to benefit from each other's experiences. And when funding responsibilities are transferred to the state, it restrains total spending because programs are paid for by those who are more immediately affected by them, and not by the national taxpayer—it is much harder to obtain funding for a pork-barrel water project when the entire tab has to be picked up by the state businesses and residents who are affected by it, than when it is spread thinly across all the country's taxpayers.

Decentralization can be fostered in a number of ways. Encouraging the use of vouchers for housing and various social services, for instance, would make these services reflect more accurately the needs of those they are intended to serve, and the providers would have to take careful account of the costs of alternative suppliers. Similarly, shifting responsibilities firmly to the states for providing infrastructure would lead to a long-overdue reappraisal of the need for projects. Declaring the federal interstate highway system complete, for instance, and transferring to the states the full responsibility for collecting and spending gasoline taxes, would reduce sharply the clamor for unnecessary road construction—driven at the moment by the prospect of "free" federal grants.

THEME 3: Stimulate enterprise in the economy by creating competitive open markets and a more favorable system of regulation and taxation.

The Administration made significant progress in its first term with tax and regulatory changes designed to encourage risk-taking, hard work and tough competition. An expanding economy, the President argued, is not only important as a means of creating jobs and prosperity, but it is vital if tax revenues are to be generated to pay for programs which assist the less fortunate for programs in the national interest.

Further steps are needed to enable the country to harvest the fruits of an efficient competitive economy. Action is needed, for instance, to dismantle trade barriers that reward inefficient producers at the expense of the consumer and to push for reductions of such barriers in international forums. Similarly, further steps need to be taken to deregulate financial institutions to speed the flow of capital to new businesses, more off-shore federal lands should be opened up to oil exploration, and the tax system should be modified to encourage capital formation by excluding savings from taxable income—even if this means rejecting "flat" taxes which reduce rates by taxing savings.

THEME 4: Reform decision-making, rule-making and the structure of programs in order to achieve conservative goals.

To attain conservative objectives, the Reagan team must continue to make changes in the operation of government programs. Food assistance, for instance, can be targeted better to those in genuine need by disentangling the many overlapping food programs. Similarly, a secure income for retired Americans could be insured by providing the elderly with a Social Security Bond, thereby making it unconstitutional for Congress to tamper with benefits.

THEME 5: Examine ways of privatizing federal programs.

The central theme of the Second Reagan Administration's approach to budget cutting must be privatization—shifting government functions to the private sector.

During its first four years, the Reagan Administration met with defeat after defeat in Congress on budget votes because it took the position that the only way to reduce government spending was to reduce services. It is not the only way. Private firms, for instance, can provide many government services —either under contract or completely within the private sector—much less expensively than federal workers. The Reagan Administration thus must offer the American people the alternative prospect of a reduction in spending with the same, or even better, levels of service. By taking this position, the Administration would not be forced into the position of denying that certain essential or useful services should be provided. Instead, the White House merely could argue that it is inefficient for such services to be funded and operated from Washington.

Several privatization steps should be taken. Greater use should be made of private contractors to provide commercial services to government itself. Vouchers in housing, Medicare, Medicaid and education should be adopted or extended to stimulate more efficient provision of services. Programs should be redesigned to foster private sector mass transportation and municipal services. And the Individual Retirement Account system should be expanded as a private sector option that provides disability, health insurance, and other elements of the current Social Security system.

* * *

By adopting the five themes, the Second Reagan Administration could pursue specific policy objectives within a framework that provided an approach readily comprehensible to the American people. The privatization theme would spur a fundamental debate: Should a service be guaranteed by government; if so, is it better to provide it directly by government or through the private sector? If it is apparent that government should indeed provide it, the incentive theme implies that methods should be sought to deliver it as efficiently as possible while discouraging excessive use or dependency. The decentralization theme would also appeal strongly to citizens, because it means that the services should be operated by levels of government as close as possible to the nation's voters, so that they have more direct control over programs. And designing programs in keeping with conservative principles, while stimulating the private economy to bring prosperity and revenue for government, fits the conservative mood of the country.

Success depends too on challenging Congress to put its house in order. The congressional budget process has become a fiasco in which fiscal responsibility is ignored and agreements between the White House and Capitol Hill on budget objectives are undermined by committee maneuvering. A thorough overhaul of the budget process is overdue, and essential if rational budget decisions are to be made.

The Reagan Administration has brought America to an historic crossroads. The federal sector had grown rapidly since the 1930s, taking a steadily increasing proportion of national resources and exercising even greater political power. Ronald Reagan came to Washington in 1981 and pledged to halt that growth in federal power and then reverse it. In four years some modest steps have been taken. But government has continued to grow and the reforms introduced are still politically fragile and incomplete. The Administration, moreover, too often seems confused and without direction. If Ronald Reagan moves decisively to give a clear sense of purpose to his government, and a coherent strategy to achieve his agenda, he has within his grasp the opportunity to take America down a new path toward smaller federal activity, responsible programs locally managed, and a robust economy. He has an opportunity to insure that the U.S. becomes once again an opportunity society. If, instead, the White House is content merely to bask in the glow of good feeling generated by Ronald Reagan, without entrenching its past successes and building upon them, the Reagan Administration will be no more than an interesting footnote in the growth of federal government.

1

The Department of Agriculture

by
George S. Dunlop*

The U.S. Department of Agriculture (USDA) employs a staff of more than 109,000 in 30 different bureaus, and provides services costing more than $34 billion annually.

The original mission of the Department of Agriculture, dating from its beginning in 1862, was to engage in research and education on behalf of farmers, helping them to increase production and improve efficiency. With the Great Depression came a second mission, to increase farm prices by restricting production through federal regulation. The idea was to treat agriculture much like a public utility—trying to guarantee profitable prices to farmers in return for their surrendering much of their freedom to develop their own planting and marketing strategies. These kinds of "public utility" farm pro-

SECRETARY
John Block, 1981-Present

PERSONNEL: 109,773

BUDGET (In Billions of Dollars)

1985 Estimate	$38.4
1984 Estimate	$34.8
1983 Actual	$46.4
1982 Actual	$36.2
1981 Actual	$26.0
1980 Actual	$24.5
1975 Actual	$ 9.7

Established: 1862

Major Programs:
- Forest Service
- Farmers Home Administration
- Soil Conservation Service
- Commodity Credit Corporation
- Agricultural Research Service
- Food and Nutrition Service

* Task Force members included Hyde Murray, Mary Fereber, D. Gale Johnson, E. C. Pasour, Jr., and Tom Boney.

grams grew increasingly costly and ineffective during the 1950s and 1960s, and with the exception of tobacco and peanuts, more market-oriented farm programs were put into place.

A third mission was created for the Department during the 1960s: transferring income and resources from taxpayers to those considered by Congress to be disadvantaged. Rural development programs and food assistance programs were the principal manifestations of this new mission. Resources committed grew at a phenomenal pace, until they dwarfed the first two missions. The dollar amounts spent for these programs continued to grow during the Reagan Administration, reaching new highs.

The major functions in UDSA are:

Science and Education: The Land Grant College system of research, teaching, and extension is a federal-state partnership that forms one of the strongest elements of the U.S. agricultural infrastructure. Research is a traditional USDA mission; its own research is conducted by the Agricultural Research Service, employing about 8,300 persons in 140 locations. USDA spends about $750 million each year in agricultural research through ARS and by cost sharing with the states through the Cooperative State Research Service.

International Affairs and Commodity Programs: Agricultural Stabilization and Conservation Service state and county committees are responsible for local administration of the full range of commodity support and conservation programs dealing directly with farmers and ranchers. This agency has an operating budget of some $300 million, plus additional annual outlays ranging between $5 and $19 billion for commodity programs funded through the Commodity Credit Corporation. Such outlays operate as entitlements for those qualified, and are generally related to the previous crop year. Unusual weather conditions or changes in the world economic situation can cause large fluctuations in outlays from year to year. The Foreign Agricultural Service is responsible for export expansion programs. About $5 billion in various kinds of credit guarantees for leveraging private sector export sales, plus about $1.3 billion in humanitarian food assistance, is used for this purpose each year.

Natural Resources and Environment: With 40,000 employees and an annual budget of $2.1 billion, the U.S. Forest Service manages 190 million acres of federal national forests for multiple use purposes of timber, watershed, wildlife, other natural resources, and recreation. Timber harvests from Forest Service lands account for 20 percent of the annual U.S. timber harvest. The Soil Conservation Service, with 13,500 employees and annual outlays of about $1 billion, provides technical assistance, soil surveys, and research and analysis on soil conservation problems in virtually every county in the U.S. Together, these two agencies account for half of USDA's employees.

Small Community and Rural Development: The Farmers' Home Administration administers federal lending and grant programs for farm credit, rural development and rural housing. The agency has annual outlays of $4.7 billion, and is responsible for more than two million loans totaling $69 billion. The Federal Crop Insurance Corporation administers the nationwide all-risk crop insurance program with federal outlays of $600 million. The Rural Electrification Administration makes direct loans and guarantees loans for the purpose of extending and improving electric and telephone service in rural areas, and in subsidizing rates. This activity is "off budget."

Food and Consumer Services: The Food and Nutrition Service administers the Food Stamp Program, the School Lunch and other child nutrition programs, such as the feeding program for Women, Infants and Children (WIC), the Special Milk Program, Supplemental Food Programs, and other food assistance programs, with annual outlays of $17.7 billion.

Marketing and Inspection Services: The principal objective of the Animal and Plant Health Inspection Service is to protect the animal and plant resources of the nation from dangerous diseases and pests. The Food Safety and Inspection Service insures that meat and poultry products meet legal standards. The Agricultural Marketing Service promotes orderly and efficient marketing and distribution of agricultural products from the nation's farms. Other agencies performing marketing and other services are the Federal Grain Inspection Service, the Agricultural Cooperative Service, the Office of Transportation, and the Packers and Stockyard Administration.

Economics: The Statistical Reporting Service provides crop and livestock estimates for domestic production. The World Agricultural Outlook Board provides estimates on foreign agricultural production. The Economic Research Service studies the components of the agricultural production system.

THE FIRST TERM EXPERIENCE

Farm Policy in Disarray

Agriculture is the largest industry in the United States. Farm assets are equal to about 70 percent of the capital assets of all manufacturing corporations. Over 20 percent of the nation's jobs and more than 20 percent of the Gross National Product come from agriculture. Farm exports total more than $38 billion annually and contribute a positive $20 billion to the international trade balance sheet.

Agriculture is the most unpredictable business in America. Farmers, ranchers, and others in the food and fiber production system are at the mercy of events beyond their control—including weather, disease, pests, and changing markets. Because of this inherent unpredictability, there are very few governments in the world that have not established some measure of food security and farm security programs. The challenge for U.S. policymakers has been for American programs to operate within a free market economy. That has proven difficult under the best of circumstances. In recent years, conditions have been particularly rough on the farm.

By 1980, farm income had plummeted to its lowest comparable level since the Great Depression. Farmers' costs of production were increasing by 18 percent annually, and because there were tremendous surpluses of almost every commodity, prices received for crops had little prospect for keeping up with costs. Farm indebtedness had increased 75 percent over the previous four years, and that meant farmers and ranchers were sustaining their businesses with borrowed money, rather than the profits that drive the free enterprise system.

When President Reagan took office in 1981, he assumed responsibility for managing public policy for an agriculture industry reeling from the triple shock of spiralling inflation, the highest interest rates in a century, and the devastating impact of Jimmy Carter's 1980 grain embargo. These factors were staggering in their effect on the agricultural production system. Much of the agriculture industry seemed panicked.

In early 1981, therefore, the conditions for managing agricultural policy were far from optimal, especially for an Administration that wanted to reduce the size and scope of federal involvement in the private sector. In fact, the Reagan Administration found itself forced by specific provisions of law—that is, under the direction of Congress—to deal with excess capacity in ways that assured a continued and prominent federal presence in virtually every detail of farm production.

In the 1981 farm bill, Congress greatly restricted the discretionary authority of the Secretary of Agriculture and removed much of the flexibility in his management of the federal farm programs. Of course, this meant that Congress would now tinker constantly with Agriculture. Indeed, there have been farm bills in every year of the Reagan Administration. This has tended to make the commodity programs even less sensitive to market forces, and has strengthened their "public utility" bias in statute. It has not improved the economic outlook for agriculture. Even with a decrease in production cost inflation to the three percent from the 18 percent range, and the reduction in interest rates by more than eight points under the Reagan Administration, real farm income has not improved very much, while farm program costs have tripled.

Congress has responded to this by trying to turn farm programs into income transfer mechanisms. Some of the crop production control mechanisms mandated by Congress in 1983 and 1984 have less to do with production control management than in ensuring that the "diversion payments" to eligible farmers arrived in time for election day.

Excessive growth in the USDA budget has occurred mainly in the last eight years. From 1975 to 1983, USDA outlays doubled in real terms, from $7.6 billion to $19.7 billion—an increase of 159 percent. Analysis of the USDA budget indicates that this growth can be attributed primarily to the expansion of nutrition programs and commodity price support programs. Annual outlays for the Department of Agriculture grew considerably under the Carter Administration, increasing in nominal terms from $16.7 billion in FY 1977 to $26 billion in FY 1981.

This 56 percent increase in four years was followed by a slower rate of increase under the Reagan Administration. Outlays increased by 31 percent from FY 1981 thru FY 1983, from $26 billion to $34 billion.

In the face of a USDA budget out of control, the Reagan Administration failed to develop a comprehensive plan for what it wanted to accomplish in agricultural policy and food assistance reform. It appeared unwilling—or unable—to assign a sufficiently high priority to USDA problems. Reagan stalwarts at USDA, including Agriculture Secretary John Block, made earnest efforts to keep USDA intervention and the USDA budget at the lowest level consistent with the entitlement nature of the programs mandated by Congress. But they often found their policy and reform initiatives negotiated away by other officers of the Administration as part of efforts to obtain sufficient votes in Congress to achieve other urgent policy objectives. It is vital to the success of the next administration that high priority be given to devise sensible USDA policies. If the Administration will not carry out the reform necessary in food assistance and farm programs, the dynamic for making transfers of authority to the states in food assistance programs will be lost and the bountiful U.S. agricultural industry could be seriously impaired by world-wide over-production induced by excessive subsidies in farm prices for income transfer reasons.

THE NEXT FOUR YEARS

USDA's first function—collection and dissemination of information and the protection of the health and safety of the nation's food supply—is well run, conceptually sound, and a bargain for the taxpayers. If anything, more effort in research and information processes would be desirable if America is to keep its competitive edge and comparative advantage in agriculture.

The USDA function of specific farm commodity programs, however, needs urgent and immediate attention in five categories:

1) Reform of farm commodity programs;
2) Reform of U.S. trade policy for agriculture;
3) Reform of soil and water conservation policy;
4) Reform of agricultural credit policies;
5) Reform of nutrition programs.

The first two should receive immediate priority by the Administration. Failure in these areas would have tremendous adverse impact on the entire U.S. economy. These problems thus need the President's personal attention. Items three and four are critical for the long run, and are related to the health of the overall agriculture production system. They can be handled best along with the first two in the 1985 farm bill.

The USDA function of food aid assistance has been converted into little more than income transfer. So the government should do one of two things. Either it should ensure that the nutrition rationale is returned to the programs, or they should be scrapped and replaced by the more efficient method of just sending out the money without even pretending it is solely for food assistance. To the extent that direct food assistance is desirable and necessary, it best can be handled at the local level. Such food assistance reforms should be given high priority.

Reform of Farm Commodity Programs

Farm commodity programs generally do not need urgent attention. While all of agriculture is suffering from the effects of macroeconomic and geopolitical events and situations—including the strength of the dollar and embargoes—most farm programs are operating within the parameters of reasonably sound policy and with relatively little cost to the taxpayers. Important reforms have been undertaken in the dairy program, for instance, and seem to be having their intended effect. The peanut and tobacco programs, while not without problems in their internal operation and while criticized, operate with less federal control and less cost to the taxpayers than in the past. Livestock and poultry producers never have enjoyed federal programs, and show no sign of desiring them.

There are, however, significant federal commodity programs for wheat, feedgrains, cotton, and rice. These are very market sensitive commodities, vital to the health of the U.S. agricultural production system and extremely export oriented. Virtually all of the rest of agriculture is affected by the supply, demand, and price characteristics of these four commodities.

By any measure, the supply and demand of these commodities is now out of balance, and the distress increases daily for those who produce them and are affected by them. The imbalance results from direct federal actions and the Reagan Administration's inability to correct problems caused by Congress and preceding Administrations.

The roots of current overproduction and surplus go back to the early 1970s, when farmers were given the green light to open up their production capability full throttle. At the time there was widespread concern about food shortages. In the short run, the farm legislation seemed to work well; farm income soared to new highs. But Congress continually increased production incentives. Farmers responded with enthusiasm. Harvested crop acreage grew by about 55 million acres, livestock production jumped, and farm production assets more than tripled.

Then Carter embargoed grain sales to the Soviet Union. In an effort to "help" farmers overcome the disastrous effects of the embargo the Carter Administration increased the "loan rates," which serve as the essential inducement to production for farmers worldwide. Not to be outdone, the Congress further increased the price supports until they were above market clearing levels. Predictably, this encouraged further production and surpluses. Add to that the double-digit inflation and double-digit interest rates facing farmers in 1981. This led to a 1981 farm bill that increased income protection mechanisms and granted ever higher price supports. By 1983, these policies had produced a massive, mounting grain surplus and depressed prices.

Policymakers then decided to slam on the brakes, without taking their foot of the accelerator. Congress pressed for programs to pay farmers to reduce their planted acreage. This induced farmers to take these payments and use them to purchase the materials to obtain increased yields on the acres they kept in production. Paid diversion programs have characterized policy since the Carter years, and 1983 brought acreage diversion in the form of PIK—payment in kind. Faced with massive surpluses and literally nowhere to store the 1983 crop, USDA removed some 80 million acres from production with payment in kind—which originally cost the taxpayers $9 billion. PIK probably would not have resulted in reduced production because of more intense cultivation of remaining acres, but the worst drought in 50 years took care of that.

Despite all this "help" for farmers, the results have been discouraging: Exports are down, farm income is down, and taxpayer costs are up. The bottom line is: U.S. farm policy for the principal farm commodity program crops is not working. The 1985 farm bill must put agriculture policy back on course.

The new farm bill must address four principal elements of farm commodity programs that operate in a manner inimical to the long-term health of the economy. They are:

1) The "loan rate." This device operates as a free "put option" for farmers. That is, loan rates protect farmers from downward price movement. Farmers throughout the world know that the U.S. loan rate is the lowest possible price for a commodity. For this reason, U.S. loan rates are the principal factor determining prices and influencing the world's farmers when they make planting and marketing decisions.

2) The "target price." This is an arbitrary value assigned by Congress for each covered commodity. If the nationally determined market price for a commodity is less than this level after the end of the marketing season, the government sends an income transfer payment for the difference to eligible farmers. This is called a "deficiency payment."

3) "Farmer held reserve." Here, the government extends a loan to farmers for their commodities and pays farmers to store the commodity on the farm. The rationale for this is that America should have a food security reserve under the control and influence of market forces.

These three mechanisms are inherently sound in concept and serve to add elements of predictability and income protection based on market forces in an inherently unpredictable business. When these three programs operate within price support levels that balance supply and demand, they are benign and distort the market very little. However, when they are operated in such a way as to serve as inducements to production, they are perverse. Overproduction results in oversupply, which results in depressed prices for everyone, often reaching levels below the cost of production for virtually everyone except the most efficient farmers and ranchers. Eventually all market prices are driven down and only those protected by government subsidies survive in business.

This is precisely what is happening to the world agriculture production system, and it must be corrected, lest production control begin to so dominate the policy scene as to destroy the U.S. agricultural economy and impoverish other agricultural exporting nations that depend on agriculture for their national existence.

4) Production Control. Government control over farm planting and marketing—and hence prices—enables bureaucrats and regulators to determine production.

The first three elements of U.S. farm policy are now out of balance, leading to global overproduction; and foreign nations are dumping their surpluses thanks to predatory export subsidies. This is having devastating impacts on U.S. agriculture. Congress has turned to production control as the key element of U.S. farm policy because it can use the mechanism to transfer income in a politically beneficial way. But the long-term effect of this market policy will be reduced U.S. capacity. America's share of international markets will be the first to be hit, since those markets will be subject to expanding foreign production (which is taking place faster than the U.S. is reducing acreage). Ultimately, pressure will build up for import quotas and protectionism, to halt the erosion of the nation's trading position.

To avoid all of these things, the new Administration must utilize the strength of the market, not thwart it. The policy prescriptions to make the necessary transition to market-oriented agricultural policy are relatively simple. First, the Administration should restore to the three farm commodity program mechanisms—the loan rate, the target price, and the farmer-held reserve—levels of price supports that will balance supply and demand at the prevailing world price.

Then this market-clearing formula should be enacted into law that does not have to be reauthorized every few years. This would discourage Congress from tampering with the formula regularly, and protect the formula with a presidential veto.

The loan rates should be flexible enough to respond to unanticipated future market events. The precise figure for each commodity would need to be determined, but the range would probably best be 70 to 85 percent of the average market price for the last five years, with the high and the low years removed to take out unusual events in any one year, such as drought, flood, or disease. Unless the loan rate is significantly below the world market price, however, it will be destructive to U.S. agriculture in the long run.

The farmer-held reserve could operate on the same principle, and the target price really should operate in the same fashion. But it is not reasonable to expect the Administration to expend its limited political capital on selling farmers a "pig in a poke." A market-based system will not be sustainable politically unless farmers feel it will give them cash flow to sustain the very high level of indebtedness that many now carry. There will also be costs to the Treasury and the taxpayers. The policy should be to leave the target price where it is for two or three years, gradually making it compatible with the loan rate, or even eliminating it entirely in the future.

The value of the loan rates and other programs is capitalized into the value of farmland. As such, significant reductions in these price supports would have an adverse impact on farmland value, which serves as the equity base for financing virtually all agricultural operations. Land values are already falling in some areas, and that would make it difficult for Congress to reduce price supports to market clearing levels. So it would be prudent to shift to a market oriented farm policy in a gradual manner. Retaining a target price on other income transfer mechanisms in law may be the best way to facilitate that. There would need to be some payment limitation (currently set at $50,000 for each farmer) so that income transfers are not made to the wealthy. And it may be that other tools to target available funds to those in greatest distress would be necessary.

Action also needs to be taken to end the government's ability to control the industry. The law should be repealed that allows the Secretary of Agriculture to impose production control and acreage limitation mechanisms for the principal production agriculture commodities. They do not work. And with the increased likelihood of continual breakthroughs in agricultural production technology, through biotechnology, improved crop yield and animal reproductive research, production controls will never work in a free society. Quotas on a per farm basis for commodities that can be produced virtually anywhere in the world are unthinkable and unmanageable.

These recommendations involve relatively simple adjustments to already existing programs; they require viewing farm programs' performance in the long run, something Congress has not been doing. If the new Administration is not willing to expend the political capital and resources needed to make this a top priority for the legislative agenda for 1985, it should simply try to get the lowest possible budget for agricultural programs, leaving it to Congress to haggle over how to divide up the money.

In the course of the legislative schedule, Congress will likely pass a 1985 farm bill so late in the year that the President will have little choice but to sign it. In the event of a deadlock or a veto of the 1985 farm bill, present authorizations would expire and there would be a reversion to the underlying permanent law, often referred to as the 1938 and 1949 Acts. This is not really workable as a farm policy; the prospect of it taking effect has made Presidents sign farm bills they do not like.

The only way to overcome that built-in institutional dynamic favoring Congress is for the President to strike first. He should call the bluff of legislators on Capitol Hill, forcing them to allow a system of controls to go into place if they will not accept a market-based alternative—just as he has allowed government departments to shut down when Congress refused to enact budget cuts. To prepare for this, the President should announce early in 1985 the creation of a "Permanent Law Implementation Task Force," composed of USDA officers who would begin immediately to make the necessary plans and announcements for the imposition of full production control of agriculture in the U.S. if Congress gave the Administration no alternative. This should be linked to a plan to enable farmers to vote in referenda during the summer and fall of 1985 on whether they want to operate under such quotas and allotments.

Farmers would almost surely not vote for such production controls, and this would put enormous pressure on Congress to adopt the President's proposals. Only by taking a bold initiative in this way to break down the institutional roadblocks that Congress has so effectively employed in the past, can the President leverage the kind of policy he wants.

This approach would force Congress and the public to debate the issue of whether America is willing to make a transition to market-oriented agriculture, or whether it was determined to keep farmers dependent upon a public utility type agriculture, where all the price, production, and marketing decisions would be made in Washington.

Reform of U.S. Trade Policy for Agriculture

The U.S. leads the world in agricultural trade. American agriculture is organized to operate in a world market, and the health of the farm economy is dependent on the ability to export farm products at competitive prices and on having access to foreign markets. The United States supplies 80 percent of all the soybeans, 60 percent of all the feed grains, 40 percent of all the wheat and cotton, and 20 percent of the tobacco and rice moving in world trade.

More than one-fourth of U.S. farm income is derived from exports, and two of every five acres of crop land in the United States is devoted to exports. More than 60 percent of U.S. wheat production, nearly half of the soybean and rice production, more than half of all cotton grown and about one-third of the corn production are exported. The value of all these exports is expected to exceed $38 billion in 1984, making agriculture sales the largest single positive item in the U.S. balance of international payments. For every $1 billion worth of agricultural exports, 30,000 jobs are created in the private sector. In short, if the U.S. is to prosper it must have an agricultural policy that will enable it to export agricultural products.

Yet, it is impossible for a market-oriented agricultural policy to benefit U.S. farmers and the U.S. economy if American farmers cannot obtain access to foreign markets. In recent years, subsidies by nations, primarily the European Economic Community, to their farmers have increased markedly. In 1976, $2 billion in subsidies brought the Europeans sales of $12 billion in agricultural products. By 1984, their export subsidies had increased to the $10 to $12 billion range, leveraging more than $30 billion in export sales. Through the use of these massive subsidies, the European Community displaces products in markets where farmers in America and other nations would otherwise enjoy a comparative advantage.

American farmers cannot compete with the European treasuries. Strong action on the part of the U.S. government is necessary to ensure that world trading moves quickly toward being truly free.

If the new Administration is not prepared to invoke a full range of measures to force predator nations to end their massive subsidies to agricultural exports, it can hardly ask U.S. farmers to move toward a market-oriented system and be underbid by subsidized West European agriculture. To date, the U.S. response to this has been far too measured.

The new Administration should:

1) Develop a Cabinet consensus that the use of predatory export subsidies and other unfair trade practices in agriculture is intolerable for the U.S.

2) Make it clear to the foreign countries that the U.S. will no longer accept subsidized attacks on its export markets and that, as a last resort, it will impose the countermeasures in carefully calibrated steps against the offending nations.

3) Call for a new round of multilateral trade negotiations under the General Agreement on Tariffs and Trade, to draw up new rules of free trade. If—and only if—an acceptable agreement is forthcoming, it should pursue vigorously a market orientation for U.S. farm commodity programs.

Reform of Soil and Water Conservation Policy

Current U.S. farm commodity programs have side effects associated with bringing fragile acres into full-scale production. Of the eight million acres of farmland brought into production between 1977 and 1982, for instance, at least half is highly erodible land. Production on this marginal cropland not only contributes to surplus production, but also to serious soil erosion.

This direct connection between farm program policies that induce overproduction and the nation's conservation needs was identified by the Administration since 1981. Congress must recognize that the core problem of agricultural production on marginal cropland is price supports above market clearing levels.

The best government action to reduce soil erosion would be to reduce production incentives where they are above market clearing levels. However, Congress is more inclined to want to keep the farm price supports as high as possible, and treat the soil erosion problem as a separate, unrelated farm program. Indeed, the most recent scheme in Congress is a plan to create a new mechanism to transfer income to farmers under the guise of a multi-billion dollar soil conservation "reserve" program. This would pay farmers to take fragile lands out of production.

The connection between farm policy and conservation policy must be demonstrated in a number of ways.

1) Support the "sodbuster" concept.

Pending legislation in Congress would deny participation in farm programs erodible land brought into production for the first time in ten years, unless the farmer places an appropriate conservation practice on that land. This is called the "sodbuster bill," and is backed by the Reagan Administration.

The Administration should continue working to expand the sodbuster idea beyond erodible land being brought into production for the first time in ten years to all erodible cropland. Such a policy would make the farm programs consistent with a conservation effort and would establish an Administration policy of discouraging poor farming practices that contribute to soil erosion.

2) Improve the Administration of the Conservation Programs.

The federal government is spending approximately $1 billion each year on soil and water conservation. These funds provide technical assistance to farmers and share the cost of applying conservation practices, such as terracing, reduced tillage and contour farming. Some cost-sharing conservation practices contribute primarily to reducing soil loss. However, many practices whose costs are now shared by the federal government may not have erosion reduction as a primary goal. For example, a 1981 Agricultural Stabilization and Conservation Service report found that over one-half of the conservation practices applied with funds spent through the Agricultural Conservation Program were installed on lands eroding at less than the five tons per acre per year—considered an acceptable rate of erosion.

3) Emphasize the federal research and educational role in conservation.

Conservation tillage has been successful in this country. Its use has increased from an estimated 29 million acres in 1973 to over 110 million acres in 1983—approximately one-third of the national crop land. The USDA has sought aggressively to expand the use of conservation tillage. The Soil Conservation Service, the Agricultural Stabilization and Conservation Service and the Extension Service have played an important part in disseminating and educating farmers on the benefits of conservation tillage. However, of the 110 million acres of cropland tilled by conservation tillage practices in 1983, less than 1 million acres received any federal cost-sharing.

4) Highlight the private sector's role in conservation.

The Administration should continue to encourage private conservation initiatives, such as those in conservation tillage. Federal programs to share the cost of installing government spending for cost-sharing conservation equipment should be scrutinized.

5) Reform of Agricultural Credit Programs.

During the last eight years, farm indebtedness has soared. Between 1977 and 1981, it increased by $78 billion, some 75 percent. Farmers' annual food and fiber production costs rose by $46 billion, or 55 percent. Inflationary policies pursued at that time led to spiraling land values and to the illusion of greater wealth. This paper wealth was converted into very real debt, which has grown since 1981 by an additional $33 billion to almost $215 billion. As long as interest rates stay at their present level, profitability for most farming operations will be difficult—and unattainable for many. This will mean even greater indebtedness and reliance on federal farm lending programs as operators struggle to stay in business. The Farmers Home Administration (FmHA) is the primary federal source of agricultural credit. Although FmHA currently underwrites only about 12 percent of all farm loans, it has become the focus of continual attempts over the past few years for congressional action to assist troubled farm borrowers.

Proposals to help agricultural borrowers have included moratoria on repayment of loans, debt restructuring plans, lowering interest rates and legislation to enable FmHA to provide easier repayment conditions to delinquent borrowers. Legislation enacted in April 1984 gave FmHA servicing authority to assist troubled borrowers.

Abnormally high borrower delinquency rates and farm foreclosures and bankruptcies have been cited as proof that farmers need congressional assistance to overcome financial difficulties. Yet, the situation is not nearly as grim. Surveys show that most of the farm debt is held by a relatively small number of the largest farm operators. Generally, the larger the farm, the larger the percentage of heavy debt. In fact, debt ranges from 11 percent for small farms to about 44 percent for farms with over $200,000 annual sales.

The distress felt today stems in large part from seeds sown in the 1970s. High inflation was then encouraging many producers to borrow large sums for real estate acquisition. Many producers who did not exercise prudent management now find that their operations cannot support the debt service. The Farmers Home Administration, moreover, was very eager to provide credit; a significant number of today's delinquencies are on loans made during the late 1970s.

Other factors also contribute to the financial problems farmers now face. The grain embargo significantly reduced commodity prices, while many foreign markets still have not been recovered. Further, the drought of 1983 brought additional hardship to producers not covered with adequate crop insurance or who had not signed up with PIK.

As a greater number of farmers are refused credit from commercial lenders, they are turning to FmHA for credit assistance. In 1970, 46,657 borrowers were lent a total of $275 million by FmHA for annual operating expenses. In FY 1984, Congress appropriated $1.91 billion for loans to 58,360 farmers, and in August 1984, a supplemental appropriation of $650 million was added. On the other hand, the farm ownership program loan level has decreased somewhat in recent years due to lower levels of real estate acquisition.

Potentially, the most costly program is FmHA's disaster emergency loan program. Since this program is appropriated on a "such sums as may be necessary" basis, there is no limit to the loans made as a result of losses from natural disasters. These loans, moreover, carry highly subsidized interest rates. These loans have totalled as much as $5.1 billion in 1981 and are expected to be around $2 billion for FY 1984.

To avoid massive costs to the taxpayers by FmHA, several steps are necessary:

1) Tighten eligibility requirements.

FmHA programs generally are designed to serve small family farmers who cannot obtain credit elsewhere. The notable exception is the emergency disaster program. To preserve the integrity of these programs, a strict enforcement of the "credit elsewhere" test must be maintained. Current law clearly indicates this is the intent of Congress, but the volume of loans being processed may inhibit thorough reviews to ensure compliance with this requirement.

2) Encourage graduation to other lenders.

Current law requires a regular review of each FmHA borrower's financial situation to ensure that credit is continued only when other sources are not available. This requirement appears to be loosely enforced, with many borrowers receiving subsidized loans long after they have the ability to turn to private sector lenders. FmHA credit should be available only until the borrower can "graduate" to other lenders. Legislation or a change in the regulation is needed to clarify this procedure—possibly to the point of mandatory graduation after a specified number of years of receiving FmHA loan assistance.

3) Improve financial records.

There is a need for better record-keeping by borrowers to enable FmHA loan officers to assess the condition of farm operations.

4) Improve the crop insurance programs.

The Federal Crop Insurance program was enacted to replace ineffective federal disaster programs. Once the insurance program reaches its full potential it will eliminate the huge costs to the taxpayers covering farm losses due to natural disasters. More emphasis is needed to offer Federal Crop Insurance Corporation disaster protection for crops in all counties. Currently, farmers not participating in the federal crop insurance program can turn to FmHA for deeply subsidized loans to cover crop losses due to natural disasters. Where possible, FmHA requires these borrowers to take crop insurance to guard against future losses. Once a fully comprehensive national crop insurance program is implemented the FmHA disaster emergency loan program can be eliminated.

The increased demand for agricultural credit from the federal government must be controlled. The taxpayers cannot continue to bear the burden of subsidized lending programs that should be handled by the private sector. The availability of government agricultural lending programs has a class of farmers who maintain eligibility for low cost government loans for years and compete with other producers who are forced to obtain credit at market rates. This is unfair. In most cases FmHA borrowers are the heaviest credit risks. Their continued subsidization with taxpayers' money—often for years after all reasonable chances for successful operations are gone—requires close scrutiny.

Reform the Food Stamp and Food Assistance Programs

One of the greatest disappointments of the Reagan Administration was its inability to persuade Congress to correct the structural weaknesses in food assistance programs, particularly food stamps. Savings were achieved mainly by reducing program growth. Significant savings still are possible by altering program operations, retargeting tax dollars, and eliminating overlapping benefits.

The primary weakness in the current food stamp program is that it is funded mainly by the federal government, but administered by states and localities. With the federal government providing 96 percent of the total cost of the food stamp program, state and local governments have little incentive to uncover fraud or to improve administration. For example, about $1 billion in stamps each year is provided to ineligible recipients by state and local administrators. This represents eight percent of the food stamp program cost. There has been some modest improvement in eligibility errors within certain states, as a result of pressure from the Reagan Administration, but more improvement is necessary.

Several structural changes could be made. Among them: The provision of food assistance currently provided through the food stamp program could be transferred to the states as a part of a redistribution of federal-state responsibilities.

The states could be given greater flexibility in administering a food assistance program while the federal cost could be limited to a fixed amount. Such amount could, but need not, be indexed to respond to changing economic conditions such as higher unemployment in particular states. This state option block grant would provide states with incentive to improve program administration and provide them the opportunity to structure their programs to meet the needs of their citizens. This is the approach recommended by the President's Task Force on Food Assistance in January 1984.

For those states not opting for the block grant approach, the food stamp program should be changed by:

1) Restoring the purchase requirement.

Before 1979, recipients had to pay a share of the value of food stamps. The poorest households were exempted. Since the Carter Administration eliminated this purchase requirement, there has been an increase in participation and program costs, while the nutritional focus of the program has declined. Essentially, food stamps have become yet another income transfer program.

2) Institute workfare for able-bodied recipients.

The work ethic originally included in many "New Deal" programs has been lost in newer federal welfare programs, including food stamps. Workfare would require able-bodied recipients of food stamps to do community service work. Workfare would help eliminate from the program those who had other unreported jobs and would encourage those who could get jobs to do so. Those who are able to work, but in need, could be assisted through job search training and actual work experience in community service work.

3) Eliminate overlapping federal benefits.

Many food stamp recipients enjoy other federally subsidized programs such as school lunch, school breakfast, the child care food program, and the special supplemental food program for women, infants, and children. Components of several other federal programs, such as Aid to Families with Dependent Children and Supplemental Security Income, presume a portion for food assistance. Food stamp benefits for families receiving other assistance should be adjusted to reflect such assistance. Alternative methods for doing this have been suggested by the General Accounting Office and Grace Commission.

4) Target benefits based on actual household composition.

Currently food stamp benefits are based on a legislatively established "typical" household consisting of a man and a woman (age 20 to 54), and two children (ages 6 to 8 and 9 to 11). This does not reflect the actual composition of the average food stamp household. Consequently some households receive too little; most receive too much, based on their actual household composition relative to the food stamp allotment. Food stamp benefit allotments should be adjusted to reflect actual conditions. Again, alternative formulas have been suggested by the General Accounting Office and the Grace Commission, either of which would improve the present method.

5) Assure greater accountability by states for errors.

About $1 billion is misspent on food stamps to ineligible recipients. The Reagan Administration's "error rate sanction system" has provided some incentive for increased state attention to reducing these errors by improving program administration. However, the food stamp sanction system is considerably weaker than that used for AFDC, reported the General Accounting Office in 1984. There is no reason for a more lenient error rate standard for food stamps than for AFDC, especially when food stamps are totally federally funded while the AFDC benefits are only partially funded by the federal government. None of the money, moreover, owed by states that failed to meet the existing sanction levels has been collected. Strict enforcement must be begun to collect the millions of dollars owed by states.

6) Improve verification of need.

Congress passed legislation in 1984 that will require improved verification of income and assets for various welfare programs, including food stamps. These changes must be effected quickly and thoroughly. Existing regulatory restraints should be revised to permit or even require greater verification. It is especially important that verification procedures be taken before individuals are permitted to participate in the food stamp program. While detection of fraud is desirable, prevention of fraudulent participation is far preferable.

Child Nutrition Programs

In child nutrition, several reforms are needed. As with food stamps, the matter should be considered in terms of whether federal programs should continue, or whether these functions should be assumed by the states as part of a major redistribution of current federal programs. At a minimum, state option block grants should be established so that each state can establish its own form of assistance to provide nutrition assistance to those now covered by these federal programs.

Efforts also are needed to target federal dollars more effectively. Among them:

1) Eliminate subsidies to students from higher income families.

Currently about $500 million is spent each year to subsidize school meals for children from families with incomes above 185 percent of poverty, over $18,870 for a family of four.

2) Contract out school food services.

The school food service programs represent the fourth largest food service "business" in the country. Some states prohibit local school authorities from hiring private firms to provide food services, even though other public institutions have saved tax dollars doing this. Federal legislation may be required to enable schools to utilize the private sector if they wish.

3) Reinstate a means test for day care homes in the child care food program.

During the Carter Administration the income eligibility, or "means" test was eliminated for families of children attending day care homes. Since then, the program predictably has grown rapidly, primarily because of the mounting participation among children from non-poor families. The USDA Office of Inspector General and the President's Task Force on Food Assistance recognize the need for change. Currently over half of the meals subsidized by the federal government, at a cost of $80 million annually, go to children from families over the poverty line, which is $18,870 for a family of four.

4) Target WIC program benefits to most needy.

In the Women, Infants and Children program, regardless of the amount of money designated for the program, targeting of benefits to those most in need of supplemental foods should be increased. Recent statistics from the Department of Agriculture indicate that less than half of the program's participants are in the highest priority categories, pregnant women, breastfeeding women, and infants who are at nutritional risk.

Commodity Distribution Program

In 1983, Congress mandated the distribution of surplus commodities even though discretionary authority existed, and remains, for the Secretary of Agriculture to distribute commodities when they are in surplus. The new authority mandated by the Congress is unnecessary, and costs $50 million in distribution costs, which previously had been paid for by state and local governments and charitable organizations.

INITIATIVES FOR 1985

1) Seize the initiative on the 1985 Farm Bill.

Early in 1985 the President should inform Congress of the Administration's intentions for future farm policy. The announcement should include the President's intention to veto any farm bill that does not conform to that plan for policy. To back up this threat, USDA should quickly establish a "Permanent Law Implementation Task Force" of USDA officials, to set in motion the lengthy bureaucratic procedures and farmer referenda necessary for the implementation of permanent law, should congressional inaction require that course to be followed.

2) Make commodity programs market-oriented.

The Administration should send to the Hill a legislative proposal for the reauthorization of the basic farm program that expires in 1985. This should take the form of a new farm bill that is unequivocally market-oriented.

3) Reform U.S. trade policy for agriculture.

The next Administration must develop an immediate consensus that strong action in measured steps is necessary to assure a free and open world trading system so vital to world prosperity. In particular, the world trading system is desperately in need of a new round of multi-lateral trade negotiations under the General Agreement on Tariffs and Trade (GATT). The Administration cannot expect American farmers to accept a market-oriented agriculture system if other countries use the resources of their central banks and national treasuries to subsidize exports. Consequently, steps should be taken to force countries subsidizing their farm exports to enter into serious negotiations to end unfair trade practices.

4) Reform soil and water conservation policy.

Several steps are necessary to resolve the increasingly serious problem of soil erosion and water resource degradation, stemming in large part from policies that encourage overproduction. All of these recommendations require statutory change, and should be part of the next Administration's 1985 farm bill proposal. They include a reduction in production incentives, aggressive pursuit of the "sodbuster" concept, which prohibits federal farm subsidies for crops grown on fragile lands, better targeting of the $1 billion being spent annually on soil and water conservation programs to the most fragile lands, and an increase in resources for disemminating information to farmers on the benefits and efficiencies of conservation tillage and other newly developed conservation practices.

In addition, the Administration should oppose the establishment of new programs designed to transfer income to farmers under the guise of "soil conservation."

5) Reform Farmers Home Administration lending policies.

The farm credit picture will not improve until farm commodity programs become market-oriented. However, a number of basic changes in the manner many FmHA program operate also are necessary and urgent. Almost all of these require changes in statutes, and should be part of the next Administration's 1985 farm bill proposal. They include tightening eligibility requirements, by strict enforcement of the "credit elsewhere" tests already in law; encouraging farmers to use private sector lenders; improving the financial records required of borrowers, so they can establish whether they are actually in profitable businesses or not, and improving the crop insurance program, by insisting that FmHA borrowers participate in those counties where crop insurance is available.

6) Reform the food stamp and food assistance programs.

The Administration should provide for two simultaneous sets of reform. The first would restore the nutrition function. The second would transfer authority and responsibility for the design and administration of food assistance programs to the states through the mechanism of state-option block grants.

To counter opposition to reform in the Congress, the President should announce that he is prepared to exercise his veto of food assistance programs. And in anticipation of Congress holding back legislation until the last minute, so that it can wring concessions from the White House, the President immediately should form a Food Assistance Implementation Task Force of USDA officials to design a federal food assistance program under his general authority laid out in Section 32 of the Agricultural Adjustment Act. This task force would work simultaneously with the legislative schedule, and its mere existence would discourage Congress from trying to blackmail the President. The President's use of Section 32 authority means no one in America would go hungry if the Congress refused his reforms.

2

The Department of Commerce

by
Edward L. Hudgins and Richard B. McKenzie*

The U.S. Department of Commerce was established in 1903 as the Department of Commerce and Labor, and became a separate department in 1913. The *U.S. Government Manual* states that "The Department of Commerce encourages, serves, and promotes the Nation's international trade, economic growth, and technical advancement." It adds that these ends are sought "with a policy of promoting the national interest through the encouragement of the competitive, free enterprise system. . . . " With over 35,000 employees and a budget of about $2 billion, the Commerce Department consists of several offices and bureaus, often only distantly related to one another. Commerce is concerned with three major goals: 1) to promote

SECRETARY
Malcolm Baldrige, 1981-Present

PERSONNEL: 32,715

BUDGET (In Billions of Dollars)

1985 Estimate	$ 2.2
1984 Estimate	$ 2.2
1983 Actual	$ 1.9
1982 Actual	$ 2.0
1981 Actual	$ 2.3
1980 Actual	$ 3.8
1975 Actual	$ 1.6

Established: 1913

Major Programs:
- National Oceanic & Atmospheric Administration
- Bureau of the Census
- International Trade Administration
- National Bureau of Standards
- Economic Development Admin.

* Task Force members included Robert Okun and Thomas DiLorenzo.

domestic economic growth, productivity and competitiveness; 2) to promote international trade and U.S. exports, while controlling the export of items that may be of strategic or military use to the enemies of the U.S.; and 3) to provide a variety of information on such topics as population, business productivity, and even the weather. Commerce also protects patents and trademarks and provides other special services.

The principal offices within the Department are:

The Bureau of the Census: This is the government's largest statistical agency. It collects figures not only on population but also on housing, agriculture, state and local government, foreign trade, manufacturing, construction, mineral industries, and retail, wholesale and service trades. In addition to taking the national decennial census, the Bureau conducts special censuses at the request, and expense, of state and local governments.

Bureau of Economic Analysis: This Bureau develops and interprets the economic data of the United States. It focuses on national income and product accounts, interrelationships among industrial markets, regional economic information, the U.S. balance of payments, and indicators tracing economic trends.

Bureau of Industrial Economics: This office conducts analyses and research on a wide range of industrial economic matters. It develops data on producer goods, consumer goods, and consumer services for several federal agencies.

National Bureau of Standards: The goal of the National Bureau is to maintain and improve the nation's measurement capabilities. The Bureau is concerned with the uniformity and accuracy of physical and technical measures for length, weight, temperature, time, electricity, and so forth.

National Oceanic and Atmospheric Administration: NOAA establishes policy for the nation's oceanic, coastal and atmospheric resources. This office in recent years has moved away from research and information functions toward active policy-making.

Patent and Trademark Office: The U.S. Constitution gives Congress the power "To promote the Progress of Science and useful Arts, by securing for limited Times to Authors and Inventors the exclusive Right to their respective Writings and Discoveries." The Patent and Trademark Office protects inventions, discoveries, and trademarks for the exclusive use of their creators or owners. Nearly 106,000 patent applications were filed in 1983.

Office of Economic Affairs: The Office of Economic Affairs analyzes economic developments and attempts to generate policy options. It studies such matters as U.S. competitiveness in international markets, the supply and demand for strategic minerals, industrial policy and business capital investment. Since the Chrysler Loan Guarantee Act of 1979, a special office has been established to coordinate, analyze and develop federal policy toward the U.S. auto industry.

Office of Productivity, Technology and Innovation: The Office identifies and seeks to eliminate barriers to productive growth, provides business information and analysis to the private sector, and seeks ways to increase incentives for the commercialization of federally funded basic and applied research. Its task of promoting private research and development through tax incentives, changes in antitrust and other laws is especially important.

Economic Development Administration: EDA was created in 1965 to generate jobs, help protect existing jobs in economically depressed areas, and enhance the capacities of states and localities to plan and conduct economic development programs. With a budget of approximately $300 million, EDA pours much effort and money into public works programs and other assistance to the unemployed, including those rendered jobless because of alleged foreign competition.

Minority Business Development Agency: This agency, established in 1969, seeks to promote and expand the activities of minority businesses in the private sector. It provides information, technical assistance, loan procurements and similar support. In recent years this agency has moved in the direction of aid to larger rather than smaller minority businesses.

International Trade Administration: ITA executes non-agricultural U.S. trade policy and coordinates it with the Office of the Trade Representative. ITA promotes exports, controls and sometimes restricts imports, administers trade adjustment assistance, monitors international trade agreements, licenses exports and monitors strategic trade.

Under ITA, the U.S. and Foreign Commercial Service deals primarily with promoting exports. The office of International Economic Policy develops regional and multilateral economic policies and performs such tasks as monitoring the implementation of trade agreements and representing the U.S. at certain international trade policy meetings. The Trade Administration enforces U.S. import and export laws. It carries out initial investigations of cases brought by U.S. companies alleging unfair trade practices by foreign companies. It also monitors compliance of foreign exporters with U.S. trade restrictions. It processes licenses for U.S. exports and recommends and implements strategic trade policy. There are other special offices under the ITA, such as an office of Trade Information and Analysis, and an office on Textiles and Apparel, which restricts and monitors imports of these items.

United States Travel and Tourism Administration: This agency promotes travel to the U.S. by foreign tourists. It produces promotional literature and information, and maintains six foreign offices.

THE FIRST TERM EXPERIENCE

The incoming Reagan Administration accepted the broad conservative position that Commerce's goals of promoting economic growth and international trade best could be furthered by generally leaving businesses and individuals free to conduct their affairs as they saw fit. The Administration also felt that in recent decades the government has taken actions that have impeded economic growth and trade. Overregulation hindered entrepreneurship and creativity, thus slowing U.S. economic growth, efficiency and competitiveness, while overtaxation created a disincentive for individuals and companies to work and strive harder. Attempts to compensate for this situation through direct aid or the targeting of specific industries for help, Reagan officials maintained, simply distorted the market and had been counterproductive.

The Reagan Administration's record in promoting economic growth and international trade reflects movement in the right direction. However, the record contains a number of black marks and there is a great deal of room for improvement.

On the domestic front, the Administration took a number of positive steps to promote industrial growth and competitiveness. Most important was the three-year tax cuts. By reducing income taxes and various business taxes, the Economic Recovery Act of 1981 provided the capital for the strong economic expansion begun in late 1982. Further, the Administration attempted to reduce economically unwise regulations on business. It attempted to shift the general task of investment, job creation, increased productivity and economic growth away from government and to the market, the only arena in which these goals can be realized. For example, the Administration recommended zero funding for the Commerce Department's Economic Development Administration for FY 1983. Congress, however, appropriated $198.5 million for this wasteful and unnecessary agency.

The Administration created a President's Commission on Industrial Competitiveness. Rather than focusing on a national industrial policy—government-initiated actions to direct such things as investment and production—it wisely has concentrated on strengthening the healthy increase in U.S. entrepreneurial activity. This attention could help to break the habit of looking to government and large corporations for the answers to economic problems. Rather it is the innovation and hard work spurred by economic freedom that ignite economic growth.

In the area of international trade, the Administration's performance has been mixed. U.S. Trade Representative William E. Brock has performed well in a very difficult job. He erred when he imposed auto import quotas in 1981, but has indicated that he does not plan to renew the quotas when they expire in 1985. Brock and the White House have taken a bold stand by opposing so-called domestic content legislation. This legislation would mandate that all cars sold in the U.S. be manufactured with a high percentage of U.S.-made parts.

The Administration opposed steel quota legislation. However, in response to an International Trade Commission split decision, finding that the U.S. steel companies deserve "protection" from foreign steel, the Administration says it will seek new "voluntary" restrictions on steel imports.

The Administration pushed for a Free Trade Area with Israel. Under such an arrangement the U.S. and Israel would drop all trade restrictions against one another. With this initiative, the Administration took the offensive, not only opposing protectionism but promoting a positive, reciprocal arrangement. It received bipartisan support in Congress. Legislation giving the U.S. Trade Representative power to negotiate this agreement was passed this year and later signed by President Reagan. A Free Trade Area could set an example and make it easier to promote free trade policies.

The Administration and Trade Representative Brock have resisted a great deal of pressure to increase restrictions on international trade. At times, the Administration has bent to the pressure, for example, by further restricting textile imports. Free trade will remain an important policy area for years. The record shows that the Administration must strengthen its stand for free trade and against protection; once concessions are made to any industry, others are quick to demand equal treatment.

While Brock has been fairly consistent in defending free trade, the Commerce Department itself, under Commerce Secretary Malcolm Baldrige, has been more receptive to protectionist arguments. These conflicting tendencies are unfortunate. Equally unfortunate has been the Administration's proposal to create a cabinet-level Department of International Trade and Industry. It would consolidate all trade matters into one department—a seemingly sensible proposal—yet the chances are that the proposed department would make the government far more susceptible to protectionist lobbying pressure than is currently the case.

THE NEXT FOUR YEARS

International Trade Policy

Free international trade plays an important role in the promotion of U.S. economic prosperity and low consumer prices. Yet over the last year industries such as automobiles, steel and textiles, and even firms handling tuna, tomatoes, and dehydrated onions have sought import restrictions. So-called voluntary quotas already restrict the supply of automobiles coming into the U.S., while domestic content legislation currently before Congress would in effect just about eliminate imports of foreign cars.

Similarly, steps are being taken to restrict the import of steel and textiles. Protectionism proponents promise that it would increase U.S. exports, raise employment, and revitalize the U.S. economy. Experience teaches that protection painfully has the opposite effect. The Administration, therefore, should ignore calls for new protectionism, and instead move to dismantle existing barriers.

1) End the use of quotas, "voluntary" restrictions, orderly marketing agreements, and other such restriction on the importation of foreign goods into the U.S.

The historic reductions in protective tariffs achieved by the free, industrialized countries since World War II are being rapidly offset by import quotas. These restrictions pacify powerful political interest groups but they work to the detriment of the economy of a country in a number of ways.

First, import restrictions cost the U.S. consumer billions of dollars in higher prices. Limiting the supply of goods, allows prices to increase. Limiting the import of Japanese cars to 1.85 million per year, for example, has allowed the average price of an American car to rise $400 in 1984; it caused the price of each Japanese car to rise by about $1000. This means that American consumers will pay over $5 billion more in 1984 for cars because of quota restrictions. Similarly, the Congressional Budget Office (CBO) estimates that the proposal before Congress to limit foreign steel to a 15 percent share of the U.S. market would by 1989 add $7.7 billion to annual steel costs. These higher costs, of course, ultimately reach consumers in the form of higher prices for goods containing steel.

Second, trade restrictions reduce the competitive pressures felt by domestic industries. This means that domestic industries can remain more complacent in adjusting their products to meet consumer needs, confident that the American government will help them buy more time to adjust through import restrictions.

Third, protection of one industry, or a part of an industry, harms other industries. Higher prices for raw steel, for example, harm the metalworking industry.

Fourth, while trade restrictions may temporarily maintain or increase the level of employment in protected industries, they create new unemployment elsewhere in the economy. For example, increased costs for companies that are forced to buy overpriced, protected steel would hold down demand for their products and thus increase unemployment in such companies. Further, the billions of extra dollars that consumers are forced to pay for protected, overpriced goods, such as cars or clothes, are billions of dollars they do not have to spend on other goods and services. The Congressional Budget Office, for instance, estimates that cutting off foreign imported cars by domestic content legislation, while increasing immediate employment among unionized American auto workers, would result in a minimum net loss of 66,000 jobs nationwide.

Fifth, trade restrictions invite retaliation by other countries. This would hurt American exports and the world economy in general. The Great Depression of the 1930s was prolonged and deepened by countries competing to be more protectionist than their neighbors. The world today seems teetering on the brink of a new international trade war. To prevent it, the various recommendations for further U.S. trade restrictions must be resisted.

2) Initiate a new round of talks of the General Agreement on Tariffs and Trade (GATT).

To help stem protectionism, the Administration should propose a new GATT round. Past rounds have led to important reductions in trade barriers. Quotas and so-called non-tariff barriers, such as licensing and inspection requirements, need to be tackled. In addition, the GATT should be expanded to cover the export of services and investments, two areas of growing international importance in which the U.S. has a dominant and growing stake. A new GATT round focusing on these areas would help increase international trade, making it easier for American firms to export their goods without facing barriers thrown up by foreign governments.

3) Drop the proposal to create a Department of International Trade and Industry.

While the Reagan Administration proposal for a Department of International Trade and Industry, or DITI, seems to be dead at this time, the recent increase in protectionist pressures could easily breath life back into the idea. Contrary to the Administration's arguments, a U.S. DITI would not meet the alleged challenge of Japan's MITI (Ministry of International Trade and Industry). Rather, it would encourage protectionist policies, cost U.S. consumers and taxpayers billions of dollars, and threaten thousands of American jobs.

The proposed new department is meant to increase bureaucratic efficiency by consolidating the government's work on international trade issues, currently divided between the Department of Commerce and the Office of the U.S. Trade Representative. The aim is also to present a united front on trade matters when dealing with other countries. But a DITI would foster further protectionism. Currently, industries are putting a great deal of pressure on the Commerce Department and the U.S. Trade Representative to promote protection against foreign imports. If the handling of international trade were turned over to one department, it would be far easier for industries to lobby for protection and costly subsidies for exports. A strong, unified department probably would turn much of its power towards gaining such ends, to the detriment of the U.S. consumer, the U.S. worker, and ultimately to the detriment of U.S. exports and trade.

4) Promote Free Trade Areas as a means of liberalizing world trade.

A Free Trade Area (FTA) is an agreement between two countries whereby both drop all trade restrictions against the other. Recent legislation allows the U.S. Trade Representative to negotiate such an agreement with Israel. The FTA concept should be promoted by the U.S. as an excellent way to promote free trade worldwide. Besides the general benefits of free trade already discussed in this section, FTAs possess special virtues.

First, a FTA is a mutual agreement. Many industries justify protectionist policies by noting that the markets of many U.S. trading partners are not as open to American exports as U.S. markets are to them. A FTA eliminates this problem. No one could complain that a FTA is not "fair" to one country or the other.

Second, the certainty of a FTA allows businesses in each country to make long-range business and investment plans, secure in the knowledge that trade regulations will not change unpredictably from year to year depending on the power of given pressure groups—as is the case today with quotas, for instance.

Third, FTAs create a political momentum toward free trade. Part of the reason why the U.S. has moved towards a FTA with Israel is because the European Economic Community recently has made such an agreement, giving European goods an advantage in the Israeli market. An FTA sets in motion competition between nations to reduce protectionist barriers.

FTAs should not, however, be thought of as substitutes for multilateral trade agreements such as the GATT. Rather they should be used in tandem with GATT, allowing nations to move ahead quickly to establish free trade with each other, while creating pressure for multicountry agreements.

5) End restrictions on the export of American goods to foreign buyers, where no foreign policy considerations are involved.

Federal laws currently place needed restrictions on the export of technology and other strategic goods that might benefit a potential enemy. Other export restrictions have no relation to foreign policy and in fact harm the U.S. economy. For example, special interest groups have managed to ban the export of western timber in order to "protect" the U.S. against higher prices or shortages of supplies. Similarly, there is a ban on the export of U.S. oil. Both of these bans harm the economy more than they help. If a good is truly of strategic importance to the U.S., it would be better to create stockpiles of the commodity, as is done currently with strategic metals.

The current Export Administration Act contains the Group N list of short supply items upon which are imposed export restrictions—not for security reasons, but for questionable economic reasons. Group N should be abolished, as should the bans on exporting lumber, oil and all other goods and commodities the export of which are restricted for economic reasons.

6) Repeal export restrictions based on other U.S. regulatory laws.

Regulatory policies dealing with product development can promote worthy social goals. But regulatory excess not only can be costly for U.S. firms but can actually prohibit U.S. exports. For example, the Food and Drug Administration (FDA) has moved beyond regulating products in this country. It now seeks to prevent drug companies from manufacturing and exporting drugs that are approved in foreign countries but not approved in the U.S. This exceeds the FDA's job of protecting the American public. Not only does FDA meddle in the affairs of foreign countries, but it puts U.S. firms at a disadvantage in competing for foreign markets. The law should be amended to prohibit such restrictions.

In another regulatory practice that impairs U.S. trade, the U.S. is the only major trading country that extends its domestic antitrust laws to its export trade. This extraterritorial extension of antitrust laws is widely believed to reduce the competitiveness of U.S. exports in international markets. Often the problem stems from uncertainty surrounding the application of the law to international transactions. Companies may abandon or curb some operations, or engage in unduly restrictive transactions, that would not be necessary if the antitrust laws were clearer. Rather than the size of the firm, the level of competition in the world market should be the criterion for triggering antitrust laws. Many export opportunities potentially are being missed by the inability of U.S. firms to combine their export efforts.

7) The International Trade Commission should place greater emphasis on protecting U.S. patents. If necessary, amend Section 337 of

Tariff Act of 1930 (19 U.S.C. Sec. 1337) to facilitate this.

One important function of the ITC is to protect the property rights of U.S. companies against patent trademark violation by foreign concerns. When a foreign company illegally expropriates a U.S. patent or trademark and uses it to produce goods for export to the U.S., the U.S. company can appeal to the ITC for action against the illegally produced goods.

Vice-Chairman of the ITC, Susan Liebeler, seems to be sensitive to the importance of such property rights, but others seem confused. For example, sometimes the ITC requires that a U.S. company not simply prove that its patent has been stolen but also that its business is adversely effected by the importation of illegally produced goods. Such an injury test is entirely inappropriate in such cases. The issue is property rights. If an unscrupulous author took another man's published work, replaced the true author's name with his own, published it, and tried to market it as his own work, the case clearly would be one of theft—no one would ask about the effects of the plagiarized work on the sales of the original.

The protection of U.S. firms in cases of patent and trademark theft is an important function of the ITC. If need be, Section 337 should be amended to make clear that an injury test is not required and that theft alone is grounds for relief against a foreign company.

8) Eliminate the trade adjustment assistance program.

The Administration has made cuts, but the program still continues to exist. Under this program, workers who are unemployed due to increased foreign imports are given more generous unemployment benefits.

It is said that workers displaced by changes in imports tend to be regionally concentrated and deserve special assistance. There are a number of objections, however, to paying extra compensation for those displaced by changing trade patterns. It is not clear, for instance, why compensation should be extended to one group and not to other groups. Similarly, it is often difficult to determine whether the demise of a given industry is primary the result of increased imports or of incompetent management.

9) Amend or abolish Section 201 of the Trade Act of 1974.

Under Section 201 of the Trade Act of 1974 a company that suffers damages from foreign imports can seek protection relief supposedly to facilitate an orderly adjustment to the new market situation. Such cases are handled by the International Trade Administration of the Commerce Department and by the International Trade Commission (ITC). These offices determine whether and why damage has occurred and what remedies, if any, are appropriate.

It is questionable, of course, whether business should be protected from foreign competition, even if such protection is only "temporary." "Temporary" protection, moreover, has an unfortunate habit of becoming permanent. A number of recent ITC rulings point to the inadequacies of Section 201. For example, the problem of whether an American company is harmed primarily by imports—or primarily by its own mismanagement, high wages, and failure to invest—often receives inadequate attention.

If the abolition of Section 201 is not possible, amendments should be added to moderate its adverse effects. An amendment could make it clear that companies seeking relief must demonstrate that foreign imports are a greater cause of their difficulties than demand changes and increased costs taken together. A consumer and employment "impact statement" could be prepared by the ITC for each case, and this statement taken into account when remedies are proposed. Requiring a consumer and employment impact statement would balance the interests of consumers and workers in other industries against the interests of industries seeking protection.

East-West Trade

The Commerce Department also deals with matters of East-West trade, attempting to keep items of strategic importance out of the hands of the Soviet Union and its allies. (See the chapter on Strategic Trade elsewhere in this volume.)

One recent development deserves mention here. In May 1984, the Soviet Union and Poland concluded a new 15-year bilateral economic agreement that ties the Soviet and Polish economies closer together. Among the provisions: the Poles agree to pay for Soviet goods and perhaps loans in part with goods produced in Polish factories. This means that American and Western credits extended to Poland to help develop its industries will be of direct aid to the Soviets. In July, the Communist government of Poland announced an amnesty for many political prisoners and a loosening of some restrictions, in large part in the hope of establishing closer economic ties with the West. But the new USSR-Polish agreement means that closer Western economic ties to Poland will benefit the Soviets, and thus har the West, much more than would have been the case before the new agreement and before martial law.

The U.S. should extend no new credit, loan guarantees, or IMF membership to Communist Poland in light of its new economic arrangement with the Soviets.

Protecting Patents

At the basis of American liberty and the free market system is the right to private property. Protection of property is one of government's fundamental tasks. Of special economic importance is the right to one's own ideas and the right to reap the profits of one's inventions. The protection of patents is specifically listed in the Constitution as one of the powers of Congress. The Commerce Department has the duty of executing this function. The incentive provided by the right to profit from one's innovations is crucial to America's continuing industrial and technological progress. Several reforms would help assure adequate protection of intellectual property rights. Among them:

1) Tighten the Freedom of Information Act to ensure the confidentiality of entrepreneurial information.

The Freedom of Information Act (FOIA) of 1974 was meant to ensure citizen access to information on them that the government might have and to facilitate scrutiny of the decision making process of government and regulatory agencies. However, the major users of the FOIA have not been public interest groups and journalists but businesses. Many businesses seek to discover the industrial secrets of their competitors via the FOIA. Businesses dealing with the federal government, for instance, are often required to provide detailed information about the composition and production of their goods. Such information can then be secured by competing businesses through the FOIA. Such requests often come from foreign businesses seeking information on American firms, or on foreign companies that do business with the U.S. Communist countries also make full use of the FOIA to secure trade secrets. A recent Supreme Court ruling upheld the right of a government agency, in this case the Environmental Protection Agency, to release a company's trade secrets. This illustrates the seriousness of the current situation. If competitors are allowed to expropriate the results of other companies' R & D in this way, the economic incentive for research is reduced. This means fewer new products and fewer new areas of economic growth. Unless the FOIA is reformed, the long-term growth of the American economy could be slowed.

The problem can be (imperfectly) resolved in three ways: First, by imposing legislative restrictions on the types of information government agencies can demand from firms to satisfy regulatory functions; second, by imposing legislative restrictions on the types of information government agencies can release on demand in the absence of a court order; and third, by giving firms providing information the right to charge for information released by government agencies.

2) Enforce domestic process patents against products made in a foreign country by a patented process without proper authority.

Foreign companies currently can use U.S. process patents abroad without authorization, and then sell the resulting products in the U.S. Such legalized theft creates a strong economic disincentive for innovative companies. This problem can be resolved by improving the enforcement of domestic process patents against foreign products made by such processes without proper authority.

3) Modify anti-trust and intellectual property right laws to allow freer licensing by the patent holder.

Often the most efficient way to introduce new products into the market is by licensing the technology upon which the products are based. This enables intellectual property owners, especially in smaller or newer businesses, to employ the resources of established enterprises in order to produce and market new products quickly and at lower cost. Unfortunately the courts often rule that such licensing agreements violate anti-trust laws, basing their opinions on the form of such agreements rather than their effects on competition. A modification of intellectual property right and anti-trust laws, to require courts to consider the effects on competition, would help promote economically beneficial licensing, and so promote technological innovation.

Promoting Research and Training

America's prosperity and competitive advantage owe much to continuing scientific discoveries and technical innovations. Traditionally America has been in the forefront of such advances. Yet basic research and the training of a new scientist are costly and long-term enterprises. In light of the rapid scientific and technological advances over the last decade, basic research is more important than ever.

Better incentives for research are necessary—but not in the form of government grants controlled by inefficient government bureaucracies. Closer cooperation is needed between universities and business.

The following would promote these ends.

1) Make permanent the suspension of Treasury Regulation Section 861.8, which currently makes R & D more expensive and will potentially drive R & D offshore.

Section 861.8 requires U.S. firms with overseas operations to allocate a percentage of their U.S. R & D expenditures against their foreign source income for tax purposes. The effect of this complex tax formula is to deny U.S. firms the full tax benefits of conducting R & D in the U.S. This would make U.S.-based R & D marginally more expensive and potentially force R & D offshore. The current moratorium on Section 861.8 lapses soon. Some businesses already are studying the possibility of moving their R & D operations out of the U.S. The moratorium on Section 861.8 should be made permanent.

2) Make permanent the Research and Development (R & D) tax credit and make it applicable to software and start-up companies.

The Economic Recovery Act of 1981 granted a 25 percent tax credit on increases in research and development expenditures. This has triggered increased R & D investments. However, the credit effectively excludes start-up companies and computer software. Further, the credit expires at the end of 1985. Since most R & D projects are long term, this deadline will soon act as a severe disincentive to future R & D. The credit should be made permanent and applied to start-up companies and computer software.

3) Allow tax credits and enhanced deductions for corporations contributing state-of-the-art scientific equipment and related support services to universities and colleges.

Currently the demand for qualified engineers, scientists and technicians far outstrips the supply. Part of this problem arises from the expense of education, which in these fields requires costly equipment and laboratories. The rapid pace of technological change means that students trained on old equipment often find their education partially irrelevant to the requirements of modern industry. Tax credits and enhanced deductions for corporate contributions of state-of-the-art equipment and support services for educational purposes would foster up-to-date training and promote closer cooperation between universities and the private sector without expanding the federal budget or bureaucracy.

4) Allow a 25 percent tax credit for corporate funding of research in universities and other non-profit institutions.

Such credits would promote basic research and more. University research would become more relevant to market needs. Tax credits for corporate contributions, meanwhile, would help reduce the enormous dependence of universities and colleges on federal funds, thus easing the pressure for more federal spending on education.

Institutional Changes

Several institutional changes at the Department of Commerce would allow it better to promote economic growth and efficiency. Among them:

1) Abolish the Economic Development Administration.

The Reagan Administration was wise not to request funds for this agency in 1983; the Congress was wasteful to grant the agency $198.5 million. EDA typifies those agencies that waste public money pursuing goals that the market achieves much more efficiently. The jobs programs operated by the agency are especially useless. Over the last decade the U.S. private sector has produced 20 million new jobs. Experience shows that reducing tax and regulatory barriers is the best way for government to aid private sector job creation. The Administration should continue to seek the abolition of this agency.

2) Abolish the Minority Business Development Agency and merge its functions with the Small Business Administration.

MBDA has contributed little to the creation of minority businesses. It duplicates a number of the tasks currently performed by the Small Business Administration. Worse still, it has moved toward helping larger minority businesses that in fact do not need help, making them more dependent on the federal government.

The promotion of minority businesses is a worthy policy goal. Government places numerous barriers in the way of individuals and new businesses entering the market. Typical of these barriers are licensing requirements, labor laws, and health and safety rules that do not take account of the reality of running a small firm. These barriers especially harm minorities, who begin lower on the economic ladder and have much further to climb. Minority businesses should be promoted by removing such governmental obstacles.

Other Measures

Numerous other steps involving deregulation, changes in federal laws, and the activities of other departments should be taken by the next Administration. These, however, go beyond the jurisdiction of the Commerce Department. Few measures, for example would unleash economic activity and innovation more than continued reduction and simplification of taxes. If Commerce is to fulfill its charter, it should support those advocating such tax initiatives.

Similarly, Commerce should urge the Federal Trade Commission to act where possible against restraint of trade by local municipal authorities. In the past, the FTC has acted more to restrain trade—in the name of some unclear conception of "fairness"—than to protect the consumer against truly fraudulent practices of restraint of trade. However, under Chairman James C. Miller, the FTC has adopted a more reasonable approach and has even broken new ground in protecting the public against restraint of trade.

The FTC acted against the cities of Minneapolis and New Orleans, for instance, maintaining that these cities' regulation of the taxicab business constituted restraint of trade. The Supreme Court upheld this ruling. This case clearly illustrates that the only real monopoly that restrains entry into the market is one backed by the state. This case sets an important precedent. Commerce should endorse it and, whenever appropriate, should press the FTC to remove local regulations that in effect act as a restraint on trade and create a state backed monopoly.

International Monetary Fund

The international debt crisis has adversely effected U.S. trade. The riskiest debt is $350 billion concentrated in Latin America. Partially because of this debt, U.S. exports to Latin America fell from $39 billion in 1981 to $22.6 billion in 1983.

Much of the responsibility for the debt problem must be attributed to the International Monetary Fund (IMF). The IMF acted in the 1970s to attract private money into developing countries, to be lent to governments for questionable state enterprises. This lending took place with the assurance that if a government got in financial trouble and could not meet its loan payments, the IMF would step in and advance the necessary funds. But by encouraging private loans to governments, the IMF helped guarantee that imprudent lending would occur. These loans allowed Third World governments to engage in reckless economic policies. And the IMF was not able to head off or deal adequately with the inevitable crisis.

The IMF offers loans to debtor countries under certain economic conditions. Some of the IMF conditions, such as reducing inflation and budgets, are economically useful; but others threaten to harm debtor nations in the long run. Mandated reductions of imports, for instance, can help a country's balance of payments. But such restrictions can also harm debtor nations by cutting off goods that are essential for economic recovery. And such import restrictions certainly harm U.S. exports.

At this point there is no simple solution to the debt crisis. But it is clear from this crisis that the International Monetary Fund has outlived its original function and that its activities over the last decade are questionable. The U.S. should reexamine its support of IMF activities.

The U.S. Trade Representative

Each year the leaders of the United States, Japan, the United Kingdom, West Germany, France, Italy, and Canada meet to deal with pressing international economic issues. The U.S. Trade Representative usually does not attend these meetings. The absence of the Trade Representative, to counsel the President and to confer with officials from the other participating nations, no doubt accounts for many lost opportunities to improve world trade. When then-U.S. Trade Representative Robert Strauss accompanied President Carter to the 1979 Tokyo summit, for example, there was progress in trade liberalization. In the future, it should be standard practice for the U.S. Trade Representative to attend the annual economic summits.

INITIATIVES FOR 1985

While all of the above recommendations should and can be implemented during the life of an Administration, several steps should be taken immediately.

1) Take a firm stand against protectionism.

The President should declare that the U.S. will place no further barriers in the way of international trade, and that instead it will actively seek the removal of trade barriers by other countries, through the GATT, through Free Trade agreements, and through any other means necessary. The President should devote a major section of the State of the Union address, and other speeches, to explaining to the American people the serious economic dangers of protectionism and the benefits of free trade. There is much misunderstanding concerning the relative merits of protectionism and free trade and this needs to be corrected. Many still believe, for instance, over 200 years after Adam Smith refuted the theory, that national strength is acquired by keeping out foreign goods and relying as much as possible on domestic industries. History shows that such a policy leads to weakness and poverty.

2) Give priority to tax reform during the next session of Congress.

The President should make it clear that just as the 1981 tax cuts were the primary cause of the economic expansion, a general reform of the tax system, including a flatter rate structure and lower corporate and capital gains taxes, is the recipe for economic growth—not Commerce Department programs.

3) Focus attention on the importance of entrepreneurship to economic growth, and seek to remove barriers to entrepreneurs.

The key role played in the economy by individual and corporate initiative and innovation is beginning to come to the attention of policymakers. The Joint Economic Committee of Congress recently held a series of hearings on economic entrepreneurship. The President's Commission on Industrial Competitiveness has also examined the issue.

There is a great resurgence in the U.S. of entrepreneurial activity, which has created more jobs and new products and inventions. The number of firm creations is breaking records. The President should point out that it is private initiative, not government that is responsible for this.

3

The Department of Education

by
Eileen M. Gardner*

The Cabinet-level Department of Education was established by Congress in 1979. Previously, its functions had been housed within the Department of Health, Education and Welfare—HEW (thereafter renamed Health and Human Services). Proponents of a separate department argued that it would provide greater efficiency and accountability. Because education is of vital national concern, these proponents argued, it was imperative that there be a separate federal education department, which, they insisted, would be more responsive to the school districts, parents, and Congress.

The bulk of the programs transferred to the new Department had

SECRETARY
Terrel Bell, 1981-NN. 1984

PERSONNEL: 5,360

BUDGET (In Billions of Dollars)

1985 Estimate	$16.0
1984 Estimate	$16.1
1983 Actual	$14.6
1982 Actual	$14.1
1981 Actual	$15.1
1980 Actual	$13.1
1975 Department did not exist	

Established: 1979

Major Programs:
- Office of Elementary & Secondary Education
- Office of Special Education & Rehabilitation Services
- Office of Vocational & Adult Education
- Office of Postsecondary Education

* Many people helped in preparing this chapter. Regrettably, they are not in positions to be named.

been housed in the Education Division of HEW. After some streamlining and reorganization, the new Department was structured to accommodate several broad program areas. The three most important of these were civil rights, research, and education programs.

The mission of the Office for Civil Rights has been to enforce statutes prohibiting discrimination in federally assisted education programs or activities: Title VI of the Civil Rights Act of 1964, Title IX of the Higher Education Amendments of 1972, Section 504 of the Rehabilitation Act of 1973, and the Age Discrimination Act of 1975. The charge to the Office of Education Research and Improvement (OERI) was to build an effective research and improvement system through applied research; demonstration, technical assistance, and dissemination; and professional and institutional development. Functions grouped under OERI include those of the National Institute of Education (NIE), and the National Center for Education Statistics (NCES). The role of NIE and NCES—the heart of federal education research activities—is to furnish hard, reliable data, statistical projections, and research reports that educators at all levels can utilize.

The major offices established to oversee federal education programs were the Offices of Special Education and Rehabilitative Services (OSERS), Bilingual Education and Minority Language Affairs (OBEMLA), Elementary and Secondary Education (OESE), Vocational and Adult Education (OVAE), and Postsecondary Education (OPE). The Office of Special Education and Rehabilitative Services was established to assist in the education of handicapped children and adult rehabilitation and to conduct research. The Office of Bilingual Education and Minority Language Affairs, authorized under Title VII of the Elementary and Secondary Education Act, was established to improve the English speaking ability of limited English-proficient students by supporting bilingual education projects in local school districts.

The Office of Elementary and Secondary Education was established within the Department to assist local and state education agencies and to promote equal educational opportunities and educational excellence for public and private pre-elementary, elementary and secondary school children. This Office, one of the Department's largest, includes programs for compensatory education, educational support, equal educational opportunity, and school improvement. Many of the smaller OESE programs were later folded into the 1981 Chapter 2 Block Grant.

The Office for Vocational and Adult Education was established to train youth and adults for work and to help adults obtain a high school diploma or its equivalent. Because the states and localities provide 90 percent of the funds for vocational education, a major function of OVAE has been to provide states with technical assistance. The Adult Education program, among other things, provides federal financial support for state-administered programs, assists refugees and immigrants, offers technical assistance to states, disseminates information and originally supported community education (this last function was folded into the 1981 Chapter 2 Block Grant).

Through its Office of Postsecondary Education, the Department provides a wide variety of federal support for postsecondary education, including student financial assistance, student and institutional development, college housing and facilities, and veterans affairs.

THE FIRST TERM EXPERIENCE

The Reagan Administration advanced a number of major education legislative initiatives during its first term. Tuition tax credits and vouchers were proposed to afford parents greater control over education and to stimulate competition for an ailing education monopoly. The credits would have allowed parents to subtract from the amount of tax owed up to half of private school tuition costs. The Administration also proposed a voucher (The Equal Educational Opportunity Act of 1983) which would have allowed school districts to convert Chapter 1 allocations into vouchers that could be used to purchase educational services in either public or private schools.

The Administration pressed for a School Prayer Constitutional Amendment to remove any suggestion that the Constitution prohibits prayer in schools, requires participation in prayer, or prohibits composed prayer.

The incoming Reagan team made it clear that one of its top priorities was the abolition of the Department of Education, to break the stranglehold of centralized special interest control over education policy and to return responsibility for education to its rightful place: the states and localities. In addition, it urged the adoption of education block grants, to free the state and local levels of crippling regulatory burdens and high administrative costs and to end the preemption of the education process by the federal government. The Chapter 2 Block Grant of the 1981 Omnibus Reconciliation Act was to contain most of the elementary and secondary educational programs.

Improvements in the higher education funding system were also requested to limit federal help to those individuals truly needing assistance, to reduce federal subsidization of interest rates, and to require students receiving College Student Grants to help pay for a portion of their expenses.

The Reagan Administration sought clarification of the term "recipient" (as applied to Title IX of the Higher Education Amendments of 1972) to mean only the program or activity receiving direct or indirect federal funds—this limitation to curtail federal regulatory reach and to protect the integrity of private schools.

The Administration also pledged a redefinition of the federal role in education to one of leadership: that is, defining and encouraging excellence, making available the most up-to-date and well-proven methods of its attainment, and recognizing people and programs that exemplify excellence in education with presidential excellence awards.

These initiatives were successfully realized in direct proportion to the degree to which the Administration had control of decision making. The greatest success, therefore, was at the executive level. The bi-partisan Commission on Excellence in Education was established by Secretary Terrel Bell. Its timely analysis in 1983 of the education malaise and its prescriptions for cure triggered widespread affirmative response: A national consensus on certain education principles emerged—core competencies for all students, higher standards, better teacher preparedness. Education task forces were set up in all the states that did not already have them. By Spring 1984, 44 states were raising their graduation requirements, 42 were reforming their curricula, 42 were revising their teacher certification and preparation requirements, and 35 were assessing policies for the evaluation and testing of students. The Education Department's January 1984 State Education Statistics report, which presented performance outcomes, resource inputs, and population characteristics of the states in 1972 and 1982, shattered some long held illusions (such as that more money automatically improves academic performance) and laid the groundwork for additional analysis. Finally, the Department's Secondary School Recognition Program (which awards principals of outstanding high schools) and the President's Academic Fitness Awards Program (which awards outstanding students) have proven to be effective stimulants of educational excellence.

Success at the judicial level, however, has been limited and possibly short-lived. The Justice Department, arguing on behalf of the Department of Education, apparently won a major victory with the Supreme Court's ruling in *Grove City College v. Bell (1984).* In this ruling, the Court held that current legislation limits the scope of Title IX (prohibiting sex discrimination) of the 1972 Higher Education Amendments to an institution's specific program or activity receiving direct or indirect funds. It cannot be applied to the entire institution. The Administration's victory may be short-lived: In response, congressional liberals drafted the so-called Civil Rights Act of 1984, which would mandate unprecedented and devastating intrusion by the federal government into the activities of the states and private institutions. Although the bill failed in the closing days of the pre-election session, renewed efforts to pass a new version can be expected.

Administration efforts at the legislative level failed almost completely. The tuition tax credit legislation was tabled in the Republican Senate in 1983 by a vote of 59-38. The dilatory manner in which the Secretary of Education and the White House (with the notable exceptions of President Reagan and Counselor Edwin Meese) dealt with this proposal may have contributed to its defeat. No action at all was taken on the Administration's proposal to convert Chapter 1 allocations into vouchers.

The School Prayer Constitutional Amendment did not do much better. Although it received an impressive majority of 56-44 in the Senate in March 1984, it fell 11 votes short of the two-thirds necessary for passage of a Constitutional Amendment. Efforts to abolish the Department of Education were abandoned after Administration officials failed to garner support for an Education Foundation proposal. Indeed, the procrastinating manner in which the Administration dealt with the proposal sent signals to the Hill that the Administration was less than serious about the venture. Although some streamlining was completed (most recently in September 1983), the Department is more deeply entrenched than ever and enjoys increasing funding.

Congress took little action on the Administration proposals to reform student financial aid. The Block Grant proposal, however, enjoyed modest success: The 1981 Omnibus Budget Reconciliation Act folded 42 narrow, categorical education programs into the Chapter 2 Block Grant. This has given state and local education agencies greater discretion over the application of federal funds and has saved them an estimated $1.8 million in administrative costs and 191,000 man-hours in paper work. In addition, case studies indicate that state agencies have been careful and responsible in applying the grants.

Several of the incomplete initiatives of the last four years might have succeeded if an early, unified effort had been focused on the task of winning congressional and public support. In some cases, factions within the Administration either failed to act at crucial points or acted counterproductively, thereby ensuring defeat of the effort. A carefully designed game plan and a Secretary dedicated to President Reagan's agenda and to working with the conservatives in the Department to implement it were often lacking.

The Commission on Excellence in Education rallied the nation, which has begun the long, arduous journey back to world pre-eminence in education. Thanks to the Commission, far-reaching reform has been generated without additional federal money or mandates. The response to the report on Excellence and the Chapter 2 Block Grant is prophetic: Americans are proving themselves capable and willing to take on the responsibility for educating their children through state and local initiatives—initiatives that were stymied by the growing federal control.

THE NEXT FOUR YEARS

The establishment of a Cabinet-level Department of Education was an historic blunder, a combination of overweening federal ambition and pandering to interest groups. Still, the Department exists. The question now becomes: How can it be turned into an agency of minimum nuisance, modest scope and yet positive moral influence on the nature and quality of American education.

A suitably reformed Department of Education would resemble a three-room schoolhouse. The Department has only three proper functions; if well done, each would be a reasonable accommodation of the nation's interest in education to the fact that the national government should itself have little to to with running schools and colleges.

The first room would house a check-writing machine and teller's window. It is the room from which federal funds are disbursed to states and localities, occasionally to schools and colleges, and very occasionally to individual recipients. The goal would be to issue only a small number of checks—though the amounts involved might be substantial. Essentially all elementary and secondary education aid should take the form of block grants to states and localities. These should be for stated, but generally broad purposes, and it will be the obligation of the recipients, not federal bureaucrats, to decide exactly how to spend the funds. Because there would be few "strings" attached to the block grants, the process of issuing them could be simple, swift, and staightforward.

Postsecondary financing is more complex because of the tradition of federal aid to individual students. But here, too, there is no compelling reason why funds cannot be "wholesaled" to the colleges and universities for them to "retail" to qualified, needy students. In the process of reorganizing the college student aid programs, one broad policy goal should be pursued: the concentration of subsidies on qualified needy individuals. They should no longer be available to students who can, perhaps with the help of their families, pay for their own educations, or to students who are not interested in attending college but are wooed by student-hungry institutions holding out the lure of federal assistance. Federal student aid has only one purpose: to enable qualified low-income students interested in attending college to do so. Its purpose is not to increase the fiscal comfort level of the upper middle class, to relieve parents of their responsibility to educate their offspring, or to assist otherwise non-competitive colleges to keep their classrooms full of otherwise uninterested students. Loans of convenience for non-needy students are fine, and federal guarantees for such loans are acceptable, but they must entail no net subsidy, and very serious penalties should apply to borrowers—many of whom move into high-paying professions—who do not repay their loans.

The second room of the future Department of Education would house a small but outstanding statistical bureau. It would gather, analyze and distribute the information with which the nation can determine "how it's doing" in education. This was the first federal responsibility in education, dating back to the 1860s, and it should be the last to be eliminated even if the Department of Education ever were abolished. Indeed, this function should be strengthened.

The federal government has the capacity and special obligation to collect education data of high quality and reliability and to issue reports on the condition and progress of American education at all levels. As states institute tuition tax credit and voucher programs, it will be important to have a thorough, impartial system of accountability to accompany the change. This second "room," then, should direct the administration of professionally designed achievement tests, conducted under controlled conditions. In this way the country could guard itself against the manipulation of test scores by school personnel and the watering down of the test by companies seeking to please the marketplace. Rather, honest comparisons based on high standards could be obtained and promptly publicized to gain insights into how to improve the quality of the education enterprise and to give parents the information they need to make responsible choices.

The third room of a remodeled Department of Education would house a "bully pulpit." From there the Department's leaders and other Americans with sound ideas would assist in the effort to improve schools and colleges. Ideas would issue forth, with serious talk of values and curricular content, and "moral pressure" for school reform could be mobilized. Save for the National Commission on Excellence in Education, the Department of Education has been derelict in projecting a vision of what citizens might reasonably expect from their children's schools, teachers, textbooks and colleges. Weak leadership explains part of this dereliction, as does a disinclination to rile the education profession. But perhaps most pervasive is the curious view, widely held in the present Department, that every sound idea must be accompanied by a federal program of regulation.

One of the messages from this Department of Education should be that there is no automatic relationship between national leadership in education and federal programs, spending, or regulations. The American people do not need Washington to run their schools. All they need is a sense that excellence is legitimate and achievable, some suggestions about what standards to set for their own schools, the relevant questions to ask their teachers and local administrators, and some information on how the schools are doing and what seems to work around the country.

The missing room of the future Department of Education is the dungeon. It should be missing. The Department ought not be viewed as an enforcement agency. Today, however, the Department engages in two broad types of enforcement activity. The first seeks to protect individuals against discrimination. This may be a proper federal role, but it is not a proper role for the Department of Education. It is a proper role for the Department of Justice. All civil rights enforcement activities of the Department of Education should be transferred to the Department of Justice. There, enforcement action should proceed only from private suits or suits filed by the Justice Department and not through compliance reviews.

The other type of enforcement now undertaken by the Education Department entails the tracking of federal funds, to ensure that they are spent in accord with the myriad rules and regulations attached to them. This obligation would automatically ease, however, as more federal aid is converted into block grants. As for documenting that federal funds are spent only for approved purposes, that is the work of accountants, auditors, and inspectors—of which every federal agency has its share. Their assignment could be straightforward: if funds are misspent, they must be returned or subtracted from the next block grant.

Decentralization

Centralization has failed American education. Capitulating to the demands of special interest groups, the federal government has imposed upon the nation's schools false dogmas that have undermined the education process and distorted education's primary mission—the search for truth, the acquisition of academic skills, the development of a responsible citizenry. The issue of centralized versus decentralized education must be brought before the American people. Documented results of federal education programs should be debated on their merits. President Reagan's charge to the National Institute of Education to assess Chapter 1—compensatory education—is a positive step. The President should appoint a national commission of public-at-large representatives to hold hearings, to review the evidence, and to publish a report to the nation. Then, initiatives to reverse the downward trend in American education resulting from its centralization should be advanced.

Two decentralizing initiatives that should be stressed are tuition tax credits and vouchers, and block grants.

Tuition Tax Credits and Vouchers

Tuition tax credits and vouchers are viable antidotes to education's present problems. The Secretary of Education should travel widely, stressing the importance and necessity of parental choice, and indicating that credits and vouchers can facilitate choice for parents of all income levels. He should point out that the present public school monopoly, buttressed by the iron control of the teachers unions, lacks incentive to change. To improve American education, he should emphasize, this monopoly must be opened up to competition via tuition tax credits or vouchers.

Because Congress consistently has refused to pass tuition tax credit and voucher legislation and because vouchers are best instituted at the state level, state initiatives in this area should be encouraged and publicized by the Department of Education. The Minnesota Tax Deduction law typifies a successful state initiative. In California, a voucher proposal that tries to accommodate the difficult issues of state regulatory control, discrimination, and the higher cost of educating children in the public schools also warrants close attention.

An issue that will assume great importance as tuition tax credit and voucher legislation are debated is that of standards. Vouchers present a dilemma. They enable parents to make a real choice. But, it can be argued, a system of alternate schooling will be preferable only to the degree that the guiding principles of the new schools are an improvement over those that have guided the old. No improvement will be made if, for example, the alternate schools pursue distorted or antisocial objectives. One option that should be considered is that of publicly debating the purpose of schooling in the United States, and the values this nation represents, and the feasibility of instituting broad, reasonable agreed-upon guidelines at the state level.

Block Grants

The Chapter 2 Block Grant has helped to free states from the paperwork and restrictions of federal mandates, allowing those who work closest with children to apply funds in ways that further the education process. This freedom is a great boon for quality administrators. Indeed, local control was a persistent theme voiced by the secondary school principals who were honored in 1983 by the U. S. Department of Education for excellence in education.

Early assessment of the Chapter 2 Block Grant has shown that it has been well received. The incoming Administration should build on this to increase Chapter 2 funding by 50 percent and to fold into it such additional categorical programs as the Women's Educational Equity Act, Follow Through, Training and Advisory Services, General Aid to the Virgin Islands, Territorial Teacher Training, and Ellendor Fellowships. As the political climate becomes more favorable, legislation should be introduced to fold the remaining federal educational programs into Chapter 2.

The Courts and Civil Rights

The Administration needs actively to seek clarification or redefinition of several key civil rights issues that affect education.

School Prayer

The Reagan Administration's request of the Supreme Court to use the Alabama moment of silence case, *Wallace v. Jaffree*, to help clarify these issues is an important beginning toward alleviating what had become the state's hostility to religion. Meanwhile, school prayer referenda are being proposed at the state level. Given the resistance at the federal level to amending the U.S. Constitution, state referenda are central to maintaining the political momentum. To encourage this trend, state efforts should be publicized by the new Administration.

Busing

Discrimination is wrong. Yet neighborhood schools where one race predominates are not in and of themselves discriminatory. On the other hand, busing has caused upheavals, high financial costs, and resegregation. Understandably, both black and white parents oppose it. By law, once a school has 1) "fully and faithfully implemented a constitutionally acceptable desegregation plan designed by the court," and 2) "subsequently engaged in no intentionally segregative acts," it is considered "unitary" and should no longer be subject to remedial supervision by the courts. Neither should the school have to submit plans concerning the future adminstration of the school district. Control of the district should be left in the hands of the school board, parents, and other local education agencies.

The Adminstration should move to obtain unitary declarations from school districts that can pass the two-part test. Even if the districts are composed of a majority of one race, they should be free of harassment.

Office for Civil Rights

Regulations and Enforcement Procedures

The definition of discrimination embedded in the Office for Civil Rights regulations has worked against true civil rights. A practice is considered discriminatory if it has the effect—not the intent—of excluding a disproportionate number of legally protected groups.

The affirmative action regulations that flow from this definition have created resentment in the majority who are unfairly excluded from a program or activity and in the minority who are placed in situations they neither picked nor often are prepared to handle competently. In some cases the "protected" minorities have shunned the "protection" of the Civil Rights agency. In other cases, members of protected groups have sought to exploit the laws at the expense of the general welfare, and have been backed by the Office for Civil Rights—the very Office that should protect the laws from such misuse.

One complaint lodged against OCR concerns its primary method of ensuring compliance with civil rights statutes and regulations. These are seldom enforced by direct suits against an institution or by fund termination. Rather, OCR polices recipients of federal aid via a compliance review process which uses effects-based judgments to target institutions for compliance review—even when no complaint of discrimination has been filed. Institutions, especially state schools that rely most heavily on federal aid, agree to these intrusive and costly reviews and investigations in order to avoid the termination of funds and negative publicity.

The Secretary of Education should order a thorough review of such civil rights regulations with the goal of eliminating the effects-test wording. This could be undertaken by the Office of General Counsel's Division of Regulation Management. Investigations and enforcement proceedings should be limited to concrete, specific acts of discrimination; practices should not be considered discriminatory if they have the effect, but not the intent of leading to an imbalance of legally protected groups.

Affirmative action and numerical quotas should not be considered acceptable methods of achieving parity. The schools should be free to do their job, which is to educate the nation's youth. No subsidiary agenda should be added to this already formidable task.

Higher Education

Financing

Federal funds for higher education are poorly targeted and misused by too many of those who receive them. A 1981 General Accounting Office Report chronicled shocking cases of student misuse of federal funds. The report was strongly critical of institutions for not having or enforcing adequate standards. A second problem concerns the receipt of fixed interest Guaranteed Student Loans (GSL) by those who do not need federal assistance, and inadequate payback safeguards. The GSL default rate is more than 15 percent and the program has debts of more than $1 billion. In 1985 the Administration should support legislation that would require students receiving federal financial assistance to adhere to minimum academic standards. In addition, the Administration's proposal to replace the Pell Grants with the College Work Study Program should be considered seriously, since it requires the student to make a tangible contribution toward his or her education. Interest rate subsidies should be phased out and middle- and high-income students should be required to pay interest on their loans immediately upon graduation.

The third and perhaps most important issue in higher education concerns the need to define its very purpose. Traditionally, that purpose has included the preservation of the values of civilization, the pursuit of truth, the transmission of knowledge, and the development of active, disciplined minds. Much of this was accomplished through the core curriculum: philosophy develped an understanding of justice; art and literature refined the sensitivities and elevated the thoughts; history taught mankind's lessons; mathematics and science taught exactitude.

During the last quarter-century, however, the purpose of higher education has been altered radically. Egalitarianism has replaced elitism; social mobility has replaced social responsibility; job training has replaced leadership training; value relativity has replaced Judeo-Christian principles. The core curriculum in most universities has been abandoned and an understanding of its purpose has been lost.

The result has been woefully unprepared college graduates, fit for little of anything, least of all responsible leadership.

To address this dismal situation, the President should appoint a commission on higher education to pose the question, "What is the Purpose of Higher Education?" and to suggest ways to address that purpose. In addition, the Department of Education should consider using the higher education initiative of the National Endowment for the Humanities—the Chairman's Study Group on the State of Learning in the Humanities in Higher Education—as a model for its own future efforts. Grants should be awarded to those institutions trying to restore excellence to their schools through core curricula or other methods that would bring coherence to the curriculum. In addition, the Administration should take the bully pulpit role and raise the important question of value, and of its function in institutions of higher education.

Streamlining the Department of Education

Congressional critics, the Office of Management and Budget (OMB), and the Office of Personnel Management (OPM) long have been urging the Department of Education to reorganize more efficiently. The Department has taken small, but incomplete, steps to comply since the beginning of Reagan's term. The latest (1983) reorganization, although sound, involved only the Office of Elementary and Secondary Education. More steps need to be taken.

The principles embodied in the 1983 reorganization should be applied to all offices within the Department. Secondly, Department of Education positions should be reclassified by OPM standards. OPM's 1983 audit of four offices showed that 50 to 80 percent of the positions in the Department are overgraded. A possible $15 million in savings could be realized from reclassification.

Steps should be taken to reduce administrative top-heaviness. Specifically, (a) the Office of Management should be merged with the Office of Planning, Budget, and Evaluation, and headed by one presidential appointee; (b) the Office of Intergovernmental/Interagency Affairs should be merged with the Office of Legislation and Public Affairs and headed by one presidential appointee; and (c) the Regional Offices should be abolished or consolidated.

Data collection and research also should be overhauled. The National Institute of Education and the National Center for Education Statistics (NIE and NCES) were intended to depoliticize research. With the benefit of hindsight, that was clearly futile: They merely have been isolated from larger policy concerns and left captive to education data collection and research interest groups.

NIE and NCES must be integrated into the organizational life of the Department of Education. This is possible under the terms of existing statute. NIE (and its policy council, NCER), NCES, and the Office of Education Research and Improvement (OERI) should be abolished and recombined into a new Office of the Assistant Secretary for Research. An individual of distinction and demonstrated accomplishment should be recruited to head this new office.

INITIATIVES FOR 1985

1) ***Appoint a national commission to examine the effectiveness of federal education programs.***

2) ***Encourage state initiatives to establish tuition tax credits and education vouchers.***

3) ***Publicize state efforts to allow prayer in school.***

4) ***Obtain unitary declarations from school districts that can pass the two-part test on discrimination—do not harass such districts if they pass the test, even if they are composed of a majority of one race.***

5) ***Review civil rights regulations affecting education, with the goal of eliminating the effects test wording.***

6) ***Enact legislation that would require students receiving federal financial assistance to adhere to minimum academic standards.***

7) ***Appoint a Presidential Commission on Higher Education, to examine the purpose of higher education and to suggest ways of achieving that purpose.***

8) ***Merge the Office of Management with the Office of Planning, Budget and Evaluation.***

9) ***Merge the Office of Inter-Governmental/Inter-Agency Affairs with the Office of Legislation and Public Affairs.***

10) ***Abolish or consolidate the Regional Offices.***

11) ***Abolish the National Institute of Education, the National Center for Education Statistics, and the Office of Education Research and Improvement, and combine their functions into a new Office of the Assistant Secretary for Research.***

4

The Department of Energy

by
Milton R. Copulos*

Created in 1977, the U.S. Department of Energy (DOE) was to be a key element in President Carter's plan to move energy to the head of the national agenda. Assembled from components of existing federal agencies, such as the Federal Energy Administration, Energy Research and Development Administration, and Federal Power Commission (now Federal Energy Regulatory Commission), the Department was intended to provide a centralized focus for the coordination of energy research and regulation.

The initial emphasis was on energy regulation, especially enforcement of price and allocation controls on crude oil and refined products. Early emphasis also was on the development of so-called

SECRETARIES
James Edwards, 1981-Nov. 1982
Donald Hodel, Nov. 1982-Present

PERSONNEL: 16,984

BUDGET (In Billions of Dollars)

1985 Estimate	$ 9.4
1984 Estimate	$ 8.8
1983 Actual	$ 8.4
1982 Actual	$ 7.6
1981 Actual	$ 7.8
1980 Actual	$ 6.5
1975 Department did not exist	

Established: 1977

Major Programs:
- Atomic Energy Defense Activities
- Federal Energy Regulatory Commission
- Power Marketing Administration

* Task force members included Jan Vlcek, Hon. Mark Rowden, John Grey, Tom Kuhn, and Jack Carney.

commercial demonstration projects such as synthetic fuels plants and the Clinch River Breeder Reactor. In addition, DOE engaged in extensive research on commercial demonstrations of alternate energy systems, and the development of mandatory energy conservation programs.

The Reagan Administration has shifted DOE's programmatic emphasis; certain of its missions have been eliminated through the expiration of legislation or by executive action. DOE now is focusing mainly on three areas: energy security, basic energy research, and management of the production of special nuclear materials.

The energy security programs include the stockpiling and management of the Strategic Petroleum Reserve, the creation of contingency plans for various types of energy emergencies, and the coordination of U.S. efforts with its allies. Research includes a wide range of programs including all forms of energy, from solar power to oil and gas, and some research related to nuclear safety. The special nuclear materials aspects of DOE include the operation of a number of facilities that produce nuclear fuel, and other forms of refined uranium products.

THE FIRST TERM EXPERIENCE

The first years of the Reagan Administration have been marked by successes and failures. More than anything else, however, they have been marked by a dramatic shift in the market environment within which the Department must function. In 1980, the world was still concerned about an energy crisis—despite the advice from some free market economists that the crisis fears were greatly exaggerated. Today, it is concerned about an energy glut. Then, the continuing rise of oil prices was widely viewed as a certainty. Today, their gradual decline appears just as sure. In 1980, the scope and dimension of the federal regulations strangling energy production seemed sure to increase with each passing day. Today, regulatory growth has been largely arrested, and in some cases even reversed. Much of the credit for the good news on energy goes to the market, but some also is deserved by the Reagan Administration's efforts to ensure that the market operates and so brings benefits to the consumer.

The 1980 Heritage Foundation energy task force focused largely on how DOE could be reorganized and, eventually, abolished. Experience has now demonstrated, however, that no matter how desirable this goal, it seems unattainable without the expenditure of extraordinary amounts of political capital. In any case, many of DOE's most objectionable programs have been eliminated or reduced to tolerable limits under the Reagan Administration. It thus seems that the

Department will exist for the foreseeable future. The challenge is to ensure that it attains its newly stated goal of fostering "adequate supplies of energy at reasonable prices."

On a number of fronts, the Reagan Administration has had notable successes in energy policy. Among the most important was the President's move during his first month in office to eliminate the remaining price controls from crude oil and petroleum products.

Despite scare stories promising rapidly rising prices, decontrol brought enormous benefits to consumers and stimulated new production. When the higher federal taxes are taken into account, retail gasoline prices have dropped 7.8 percent. The fall is even more dramatic when adjustments are made for inflation. Another area of progress has been the increased Strategic Petroleum Reserve. With over 400 million barrels in the SPR, the U.S. now has the capacity to offset a total loss of imports for over 90 days.

The Administration also obtained enactment of comprehensive legislation to deal with the management of nuclear wastes. This thorny problem had eluded resolution by previous administrations, and was of vital importance to maintaining nuclear power as a realistic energy option.

The Reagan Administrations has cut DOE's personnel and funds for "commercial demonstration" projects. It has eliminated a significant portion of the energy regulatory burden and, perhaps most important, has reversed the adversarial relationship with the private sector that had existed during the Carter years. Still, despite the Department's generally high marks under Reagan, there remain a number of problem areas.

One of the most serious was DOE's initial reluctance to move aggressively on issues. While to some degree this reflected the Administration's primary desire to abolish DOE, it meant that energy policymaking was abdicated to the Congress in many vital areas, squandering the legislative advantage normally enjoyed by a new President. As a result, policies of the previous Administration, which generally were at odds with the Reagan philosophy, were continued by default. Worse, some of those policies were even accepted without question, largely because some initial appointees to key DOE slots did not in fact agree with the President's positions.

Among the leading examples of this was DOE's advocacy of continued funding for the Great Plains Gasification Plant, a synthetic fuels project. Despite strong evidence that the facility was unlikely to be able to produce natural gas cheaply enough to compete in the energy market, and the virtual certainty that it would need further federal assistance, a $2.2 billion loan guarantee was granted to the project.

To some extent, DOE's position on the synthetic fuels projects reflects another of the agency's weak spots: its tendency to bow too easily to congressional pressure. Although the agency has met with considerable success in lobbying on some issues, on others it has given in far too quickly. This was particularly true with regard to natural gas decontrol, where the DOE's initial failure to act effectively greatly increased the difficulties in obtaining new legislation. It was also apparent in the DOE conservation budget, where congressional demands for greater than necessary funding were accepted.

Another worrisome DOE deficiency has been its failure to move expeditiously to settle claims under the expired petroleum price and allocation rules. This is especially disturbing given the President's recognition of the inherent unfairness of those rules.

Still, while there remains room for improvement, DOE under Ronald Reagan has been vastly better than DOE under Jimmy Carter. Great strides have been made in making the Department more efficient, instituting major management reforms, reducing unnecessary personnel and programs, and reversing the adversarial relationship which had evolved between DOE and its nominal constituency. This, if nothing else, must be acknowledged as a major accomplishment, and a basis for a strategy for the second Administration

THE NEXT FOUR YEARS

The fundamental concern transcending specific energy issues is the question of redefining DOE's role so that the Department enhances the nation's energy security. The Secretary must be an advocate of sound energy policy—before Congress and as a member of the Cabinet Council on Energy and Natural Resources. More than any specific program or act, the continued emphasis on market-oriented solutions to energy problems by the Secretary can have a major effect in ensuring that reliance on the market is the primary tool for dealing with energy issues—not only at DOE but throughout the federal government.

In addition, a number of specific policy objectives should be pursued. Among the key areas are:

Oil and Gas

The central thrust of Administration policy over the next four years should be to complete the return to a free market in energy. Among the most important short-term goals are the elimination of the vestiges of price controls on various energy forms. Decontrol of natural gas is critical, as is the resolution of outstanding cases under the old price and allocation rules. Important too are reforms of the nuclear industry, the careful crafting of market-oriented responses to energy emergencies, and the matter of the International Energy Agency, with its potential for imposing an international regulatory regime over the U.S. domestic energy market.

Natural Gas Decontrol

The Administration is to be commended for proposing comprehensive natural gas legislation that would have removed all price controls from the wellhead, encouraged more competition through contract carriage (that is, allowing natural gas producers to sell directly to gas consumers and contract with pipelines to transport it), and repealed such federal restraints on gas use as the Power Plant and Industrial Fuel Use Act. The Administration and Secretary of Energy Donald Hodel made a strong but unsuccessful effort to secure passage of this legislation; they should continue to pursue comprehensive natural gas legislation in 1985. Deregulation of substantial portions of natural gas in January 1985 under the Natural Gas Policy Act's schedule only continues the difficulties that stem from the part-regulated and part-unregulated natural gas market imposed by the Act.

Thus, the Administration should ask the next Congress to remove all wellhead price controls as soon as possible. The Administration also should encourage competition by requiring pipelines to allow natural gas producers to purchase space on pipelines to transport gas directly to consumers.

The Power Plant and Industrial Fuel Use Act of 1978 and Natural Gas Policy Act incremental pricing provisions have seriously curtailed industrial and electric utility markets for natural gas. These laws should be repealed to allow all energy users to make fuel choices on the basis of economic factors, not government fiats. Repeal would allow U. S. industry to use domestic gas at a lower cost than other energy alternatives, thereby improving their products' competitiveness in international markets as well as improving the quality of the environment.

The Secretary of Energy also should spur competition in the gas marketplace. To do this he could invoke Title IV of the DOE Organization Act and intervene before the Federal Energy Regulatory Commission (FERC) to urge it to modify current policy, and require the transportation of gas, often priced lower than pipeline gas, that is sold directly by producers to consumers.

DOE should stick by its plans to use the Strategic Petroleum

Reserve almost immediately in the event of an interruption of foreign supplies. It is important that the growing size of the Reserve be publicized to assure Americans that their nation has a secure energy supply. The 1984 crisis in the Straits of Hormuz illustrated how such publicity can quell a potential panic, and keep oil prices from reacting to psychological factors that do not reflect actual economic conditions.

The Department also should run a full-scale test of the Reserve, including the actual sale of oil. Congressional action may be required for this, but there appears to be ample support for it on Capitol Hill. DOE should also study the feasibility of developing a system of options through which SPR oil could be contracted for in advance of an emergency.

Settlement of Price and Allocation Violation Claims

One of the Administration's major accomplishments was the removal of remaining price and allocation controls from crude oil and refined products. However, the Administration has not been successful in resolving outstanding compliance disputes under those rules. Although Reagan's Energy Secretaries have professed support for such settlements, more than three years after the termination of controls, there has been only one major settlement. The Department has failed to implement its professed pro-settlement policy, in part because of divided authority between DOE's Office of the General Counsel and the Special Counsel. More significant however, DOE has been intimidated by partisan criticism of its settlement procedures.

Emergency Preparedness

The term "emergency preparedness" has become a Washington code-word to describe policies intended to deal with oil interruptions, including policies involving the Strategic Petroleum Reserve. The Reagan Administration rightly vetoed the Standby Petroleum Allocation Act. The veto signaled that market mechanisms, not federal controls, are the optimum means for dealing with oil supply interruptions. DOE must continue to block attempts to establish direct or indirect federal controls.

The International Energy Agency

The International Energy Agency was established a decade ago to create a system whereby its members could share oil supplies in the event of a major oil interruption. Since its creation, however, the international oil market has changed fundamentally in terms of the number of sources of petroleum, the size of national stockpiles, the availability of surplus capacity outside the Organization of Petroleum Exporting Countries, and overall consumption patterns. Consequently, many of the premises of the IEA agreement no longer are valid.

The IEA agreement allows for a review of its status after ten years. It thus is now appropriate to re-examine the agreement and revise it to reflect the new realities of the international oil market. This re-examination should consider, among other things, the abolition of the International Energy Agency, since experience indicates that political considerations make it virtually impossible for the agency to perform its primary mission—the sharing of oil supplies during an oil interruption. During the 1973 and 1979 oil crises, for instance, many nations signatory to the IEA agreement bought heavily in the oil "spot market" without regard to the consequences of their actions for world prices or supplies. As a result, panic buying drove prices to levels far higher than necessary. More important, many nations bought and hoarded far more than they needed, further adding to the unnecessary price hike. It is unlikely that member nations will act any differently in the event of a future interruption, if they believe that large spot market purchases are in their national interest.

Conservation Programs

While the basic notion of mandatory conservation contradicts the empirical evidence, there remains a strong constituency for such efforts within the Congress. The Department of Energy should reduce outlays for such programs. In particular, the Secretary of Energy should seek repeal of the laws mandating the Residential Conservation Service (RCS) and the Commercial and Apartment Conservation Service (CASC). Neither of these programs will achieve their stated goal of helping low-income energy users. They merely provide a subsidy for upper-income users, at the expense of the poor.

Inter-Agency Issues

There are a number of issues relating to oil and gas that are not the direct responsibility of the Department of Energy, but to which the Secretary of Energy can make a major contribution as an advocate. Among the most important of these are 1) off-shore leasing of oil and gas tracts, and 2) access to federal lands.

Off-shore Leasing: In July 1982, the Department of the Interior announced an accelerated five-year leasing program for off-shore oil and gas. Among the most important aspects of this plan was the use of so-called area-wide lease offerings that allowed firms to pick the most attractive prospects. Congress, however, moved rapidly to restrict the lease offering by withdrawing large tracts from consideration. As of 1984, congressional withdrawals included more than 52 million acres—areas closed to leasing now encompass three times the land actually under lease.

If America is to avoid again becoming hostage to oil imports, the off-shore leasing program must proceed without interference. Off-shore acreage holds many of the most promising prospects for oil and gas development. The Secretary of Energy should continue to act as a strong proponent of off-shore lease offerings, and resist congressional pressures to close acreage to explorations.

Access to Federal Lands: Increasingly, Congress has banned oil and gas exploration in federal enclaves, although such areas hold great promise for a host of mineral resources—particularly oil and natural gas. As of 1984, some 82 million acres of on-shore federal lands were designated as "wilderness areas," closing them forever to oil and gas exploration. Another 50 million are under consideration at the Bureau of Land Management and Forest Service for the same classification.

Coal Issues

As with oil and natural gas, federal regulation of coal has been reduced over the last four years. This trend should accelerate. DOE's emphasis on basic research in coal-related areas should continue. The Secretary of Energy's strong advocacy of sound coal policies in the Cabinet Council on Energy and Natural Resources should continue.

Coal-related policies over the next four years should be designed to increase reliance on market mechanisms in the leasing process, eliminate federal regulations that inhibit the use of coal, and foster greater competition in coal transportation.

Coal Research

The first four years of the Reagan Administration significantly reduced federal funding for coal-related research. The nature of research, moreover, shifted from demonstrations of commercial technologies and other types of applied research to more basic and less mature technology.

The shift of DOE research dollars away from commercialization programs for coal might have been viewed as hindering the fuel's long-term prospects. In fact, the opposite is true. Federal commercialization programs act as magnets, attracting scarce engineering and scientific talents with their subsidies. But because they are generally selected on political rather than economic criteria, these programs do not use engineering and scientific talent in the most efficient manner. False signals are sent to the marketplace. It really does not matter what type of fuel is involved; the result is the same: wasted dollars and wasted effort.

Eliminating federally subsidized commercialization programs, therefore, would allow industry to redirect its commercial research in ways that truly reflect the needs of the market. Generic research on basic scientific questions related to the use of coal, on the other hand, is a proper activity of government, and should continue.

The primary criterion for experiments involving intermediate-sized test plants should be to prove technological feasibility, not to demonstrate economic viability. In addition, approaches should be emphasized that do not involve direct funding. There should, for instance, be greater reliance on patent protection, and tax incentives to encourage the private sector to take the initiative in the selection and development of projects.

Synthetic Fuels Corporation

The Synthetic Fuels Corporation has provided neither the necessary basic research nor applied research to accomplish its stated goals. While further research into the broader uses of coal is desirable, it cannot be accomplished through the SFC. The Corporation should be abolished, with the administration of its existing contractual obligations transferred to an appropriate federal agency.

Power Plant and Industrial Fuel Use Act (PIFUA)

The Reagan Administration has modified PIFUA's regulations significantly, providing the flexibility Congress originally intended, and reducing the draconian nature of the program that emerged during the Carter Administration. In addition the Reagan Administration supported partial repeal of PIFUA in the Omnibus Budget Act of 1981 and urged the repeal of remaining demand-restraint provisions on natural gas. It should, however, retain the provision that provides exemption from the new source performance standards of the Clean Air Act—a valuable incentive for additional coal use.

Issues Not Directly Under DOE Jurisdiction

There are two coal-related issues confronting DOE that are essentially inter-governmental: 1) acid rain, and 2) coal slurry pipelines. These need close attention from the new Administration.

Acid Rain: The most critical issue facing the coal industry is acid rain. Ironically, there is not even general agreement among scientists as to the cause of acid rain—or indeed if it even exists—let alone what to do about it. Still, there are moves in Congress to impose a harsh regulatory regime on the Midwest's coal burning plants. The assumption is that these plants are the principal cause of acid precipitation. Given the growing body of information suggesting that other sources may be responsible for the environmental problems currently attributed to acid rain, the Reagan Administration is right to demand further study of the issue. Therefore the Secretary of Energy should oppose current acid rain legislation and push for further research.

Coal Transportation: Coal is a classic high bulk, low value commodity for which transportation costs define markets. As such, the coal industry gains through increased competition in transportation. But despite the broadening deregulation of the transportation industry, the coal industry has yet to benefit. Coal transportation rates have increased by 40 percent in the past eight years, while the mine mouth price of coal has declined by 20 percent. The net effect of this price shift has been to make most coal hauling railroads financial success stories while many coal companies are in serious financial difficulties.

The principal reason for the continuing increase in coal hauling rates is that about 65 percent of the nation's coal mines are "captive"; they have only one means of transportation. In the West, the figure exceeds 95 percent. Legal barriers are preventing development of alternative methods of coal transportation. These barriers can be removed by granting federal eminent domain to firms wishing to construct coal slurry pipelines. A major priority of the Administration in the next Congress should be the enactment of legislation authorizing federal eminent domain for coal slurry pipelines.

Reviving the Nuclear Option

From the end of World War II to the mid-1960s, demand for electricity in the U.S. grew rapidly. During the 1970s, however, the increased costs resulting from rising oil prices and stringent environmental regulations markedly slowed energy growth. At the same time, growth in electricity generating capacity also slowed. In part this was because of the slowdown in demand; but it was due also to mounting governmental barriers to construction. Increasingly, local utility commissions simply refused to allow the rate increases necessary to finance new power plants. At the same time, environmental, and safety regulations lengthened the time needed to complete them. These factors discouraged the financial community from underwriting new utility plant construction, virtually bringing it to a halt.

While the potential effects of the slowdown of new plant construction—shortages—were mitigated by the decline in the growth of demand, the respite is certain to be temporary. Utilities anticipate serious electricity shortages before the end of the decade. This would penalize the economy severely. To avert this, new generating capacity needs to be built. A significant proportion of this must consist of nuclear powered units.

In some regions of the country, large fossil-fired plants cannot be used because of environmental constraints, such as air quality regulations, or because there is no ready access to sufficient supplies of coal. Moreover, in many cases nuclear plants enjoy a sizeable cost advantage over fossil fuel alternatives. The key point is that the nation cannot afford to forego any of its options for generating electricity if the nation's future power needs are to be met.

As was the case four years ago, there are three basic requirements for the survival of the U.S. nuclear power option: 1) completion and timely licensing for safe operation of the nuclear power plants under construction or on order; 2) a more timely and predictable licensing process for future plant orders; and 3) the orderly completion of the nuclear fuel cycle. Required too is a clear and persuasive articulation by the President of the country's need for nuclear energy.

During the last four years, nuclear power has continued to decline as an energy option for the U.S. No nuclear power plants have been ordered since 1978, and all 39 nuclear plants ordered after 1973 have been cancelled. Since 1972 over 100 plants have been cancelled, at the cost of approximately $9 billion. The Department of Energy predicts that between 10 and 20 plants now under construction also will be cancelled, at a cost of $15 to $20 billion.

The responsibility for revitalizing the nuclear option rests primarily with the private sector. Only the nuclear industry itself can ensure the safe operation of nuclear plants and fashion the private sector institutional reforms necessary if any additional nuclear plant projects are to be mounted.

Yet many of the problems facing nuclear power stem from anachronistic systems of state rate regulation and a regulatory regime. These roadblocks must be removed. The President must:

1. Reaffirm the importance of nuclear energy to the U.S.
2. Press for legislative and administrative reforms to the present

licensing and regulatory process that will allow the timely licensing and operation of plants now under construction and remove obstacles to future plant orders.

3. Seek legislation to replace the Nuclear Regulatory Commission with an agency headed by a single administrator, responsible to the President, for the orderly and effective management of the nuclear regulatory program.

4. Adopt federal tax and rate-setting policies to facilitate private sector financing of nuclear power projects.

5. Support legislation extending the public protection and insurance/indemnity provisions of the Price-Anderson Act, which ensures prompt and reasonable settlements of claims resulting from nuclear accidents.

6. Take steps to reestablish the U. S. as a reliable nuclear trading partner and effective leader in nuclear nonproliferation policy.

The President should appoint a bipartisan Presidential Commission on Nuclear Power to examine the role of this energy source, the problems requiring remedial action and the measures required to redress them.

In 1983, the President's Private Sector Survey on Cost Control (the Grace Commission) estimated that up to $30 billion could be saved by reforming "backfitting"—the imposition of new regulatory requirements on power plants under construction after approval has already been given. The Commission found that a further $10 billion could be saved for the 73 plants then awaiting licenses from the Nuclear Regulatory Commission by adopting rational controls over the imposition of new requirements. The NRC has yet to establish a comprehensive system for the new regulatory requirements.

The Commission must also develop a means of preventing its procedures from being manipulated to delay plant licensing, even where no real health or safety concern exists. Anti-nuclear activists recently have adopted the tactic of seeking out disgruntled former employees of nuclear power installations, and asking them to raise complaints about the plant's design or operation. Although many of the issues raised are completely without merit, it is still necessary to hold full hearings on them. The hearings add needless delays to the licensing process—and millions of dollars to the plant's cost. Some means of dismissing such specious allegations is needed.

The politically motivated refusal of state and local officials to take actions necessary for power plant licensing also should be addressed. This is particularly critical to the development of evacuation plans to be used in the event of a serious nuclear accident. Some state and local officials, for instance, have refused to cooperate in the design of such plans, and have indicated that they will not allow state or local police officials to cooperate in the evacuation. This is clearly irresponsible, and intended merely to prevent the NRC from granting licenses. The responsibility for overseeing evacuation should, in any case, be transferred to the Federal Emergency Management Administration.

Fundamental licensing and regulatory reforms are required if nuclear power plants are to be ordered in the future. Congress must authorize NRC not only to grant approvals to standardized designs developed by the industry, but also to grant early site approvals and to license both the construction and operation of plants.

Industry and the regulators must take joint responsibility for ensuring the safety of nuclear power plants. While, by law, the NRC oversees the safety of licensed nuclear activities, it is the licensees in practice, who have the ultimate responsibility for the safe operation of their facilities. Yet, following the Three Mile Island accident, the Kemeny Commission found that the NRC's preoccupation with prescriptive regulations "tends to focus industry attention narrowly on the meeting of regulations rather than on a systematic concern for safety" and, indeed, "may in some instances have served as a deterrent for utilities or their suppliers to take the initiative in proposing measures for improved safety." Since the Three Mile Island accident, the industry has made substantial progress in establishing credible programs for sound facility management and operational safety.

The NRC must recognize the important contribution made by industry programs and encourage these efforts by providing regulatory incentives for industry safety initiatives. An undue emphasis on detail at the NRC has led to countless unnecessary delays, and diverted the Commission's attention from the more important basic question: "Are nuclear power plants safe?" Moreover, it has provided an opportunity for critics to halt power plant construction by continually raising issues—many of which have been resolved in previous hearings—merely to delay licensing until rising costs force utilities to abandon the projects. Worst of all, the emphasis on detail has eroded overall safety by failing to differentiate between genuine problems that warrant serious concern, and minor concerns that have no real safety consequences.

The NRC therefore should set broad safety goals, and then allow operators to determine how best to meet them. It should focus on the most likely problem areas, rather than so-called worst case scenarios. Finally, it should recognize that the NRC cannot manage the details of the nuclear industry. The Commission's goal should be to ensure that firms act responsibly.

Restructuring the NRC

The Nuclear Regulatory Commission, as it currently is structured, has proved incapable of fulfilling its mission. This appears to be the consensus of officials ultimately responsible for nuclear regulation—the Commissioners themselves.

Virtually all other federal regulatory agencies charged with protecting the public health and safety are headed by a single administrator rather than a commission. The President should seek legislation to replace the present five-member Commission with a single administrator who possesses clear authority and is accountable to the President and the Congress. In addition, the mission of the NRC should be clearly identified as nuclear safety and domestic safeguards—it should be divested of such responsibilities as nuclear export licensing, and other non-nuclear safety functions.

Extending the Price-Anderson Act

The issue of bodily injury or property damage caused by a nuclear accident must be addressed. This is covered by the Price-Anderson Act, which balances the benefits of public protection against a predictable level of financial exposure for the industry. Originally enacted in 1957 for a ten-year period, the Act has twice been extended for additional ten-year periods. Unless Congress acts prior to August l, 1987, the authority of the NRC and the DOE to extend Price-Anderson coverage to licensees and government contractors after that date will expire—although coverage will continue for those already covered on that date.

The legislation strikes a reasonable balance, and protects both the public and the industry. Accordingly, Congress should extend the Price-Anderson Act to cover licenses issued after its current expiration date of August l, 1987.

Managing Nuclear Wastes

In 1982, Congress enacted the Nuclear Waste Policy Act, establishing an institutional framework necessary for the safe, permanent disposal of nuclear wastes. The Administration already has made major strides toward implementing the program and should continue to do so.

Transporting Nuclear Materials

To use nuclear technology, radioactive fuel and waste materials must be transported. Government and industry must work together to assure the continued viability of nuclear materials transportation. The Secretary of Energy should oppose any effort to reverse existing federal law and regulations, which now provide reasonable national radioactive transportation standards.

Nuclear Commerce and Nonproliferation

U.S. nuclear power policy historically has affected other nations through regulation and enrichment services. Recent U.S. decisions on such subjects as the supply of enrichment services, high-level radioactive waste management and reprocessing, however, have signaled U.S. indifference and preoccupation with domestic concerns.

In addition, there is a widespread perception within the international nuclear community—in large part due to the accident at Three Mile Island—that U.S. nuclear plants are not well managed, and that the U.S. regulatory system is irrational. This has contributed to the erosion of America's once dominant position. This not only limits the ability of America to influence policies regarding nuclear power in other nations, but it also undermines the export possibilities for U.S. nuclear safety technology.

Perhaps the most serious consequence of the loss of American leadership in the nuclear power field, however, has been the resultant decline of U.S. influence regarding nuclear proliferation. If the U.S. is to be a leader in efforts to ensure nuclear energy is used for peaceful purposes, then it must be involved in the international nuclear market. But a combination of congressional intransigence and the legacy of Carter Administration policies have made an effective U.S. role in international nuclear commerce very difficult. If the U.S. expects to influence other nations' policies regarding nuclear proliferation, then it must recognize that it cannot remain aloof to the needs of its allies for technical assistance. Nor can it ignore cooperative efforts in areas such as uranium enrichment and reprocessing.

Uranium Enrichment Policy

The United States must regain preeminence as an international supplier of uranium enrichment services. This would lead to lower nuclear fuel costs for electricity customers and assist the nation in meeting its nuclear nonproliferation goals. Until a decade ago, the United States enjoyed a virtual worldwide monopoly in the market for uranium enrichment services provided to non-communist countries. Since then, the U.S. market share has dropped to about 35 percent because of foreign competition and the emergence of a secondary market that resulted from inflexible sales contracting policies that forced customers into take-or-pay arrangements.

DOE has recognized the need for action on this issue. The Department should proceed with three primary actions: (l) implement the new Utility Services Contract as the primary basis for contracting enrichment services; (2) make its choice in the Spring of l985 for the technology of the future and proceed to build production capability using either the Advanced Gas Centrifuge or the Atomic Vapor Laser Isotope Separation process; and (3) operate its current production facilities at the maximum cost efficiency. In sum, DOE must take the results of its new contracting effort and technology decision, and fashion a new long-range strategy that involves business-like behavior and cost efficient operation.

Appoint a Presidential Commission on Nuclear Energy

Transcending all other recommendations is the need to convene a high-level, bipartisan Presidential Commission on Nuclear Energy to examine the role of nuclear power in meeting the nation's future electrical energy needs, to identify the problems preventing nuclear energy from fulfilling its role, and to propose specific solutions to those problems.

The U.S. is in danger of losing the nuclear power option. Unless the rapid deterioration of the option is arrested and promptly reversed, sufficient electrical generating capacity to meet U.S. needs will cease to be available, with severe economic and security consequences. Only a third of the necessary capacity is currently planned. Not only will new plants not be ordered if the current policies persist, but plants now under construction are likely to be cancelled. The cancellation of such plants under construction would cost thousands of jobs, send severe shock waves through the financial community, and lead to higher rates for consumers.

INITIATIVES FOR 1985

There are a number of actions the new Administration could take in its first weeks to move towards creating a free market in energy. The Administration should:

1) Introduce legislation to decontrol all categories of natural gas, and insure competition among suppliers.
2) Settle all outstanding claims under the expired petroleum allocation and price control rules.
3) Introduce legislation authorizing a test sale of Strategic Petroleum Reserve oil.
4) Request Congress to repeal both the Residential Conservation Service, and Commercial and Apartment Conservation Service programs.
5) Introduce legislation to facilitate the construction of coal slurry pipelines.
6) Introduce legislation to reform the nuclear licensing process.
7) Appoint a panel to study restructuring the Nuclear Regulatory Commission.
8) Support explicitly the extension of the Price-Anderson Act.

5

The Environmental Protection Agency

by
Nolan E. Clark*

The Environmental Protection Agency is a regulatory agency created in 1970 to centralize federal environmental enforcement programs. The EPA is involved in pollution research, monitoring, standard-setting, and enforcement. The principal statutes under which the EPA operates include the Clean Air Act, the Federal Water Pollution Control Act as amended by the Clean Water Act of 1977, the National Environmental Policy Act, the Resource Conservation and Recovery Act, the Toxic Substances Control Act, and the "Superfund" statute. The EPA's responsibilities under these statutes include setting ambient standards for air quality that the states are to meet, setting technology-based standards to be met by major emitters of air pollution, assisting in the funding of and setting standards for municipal

ADMINISTRATORS
Anne Burford, Jan. 1981-Mar. 1983
William Ruckelshaus, Mar. 1983-Present

PERSONNEL: 13,042

BUDGET (In Billions of Dollars)

1985 Estimate	$4.1
1984 Estimate	$3.9
1983 Actual	$4.3
1982 Actual	$5.1
1981 Actual	$5.5
1980 Actual	$5.6
1975 Actual	$2.5

MAJOR PROGRAMS:
Enforcement of Clean Air Act
Clean Water Act
Toxic Substances Control Act
Research & Development
Pollution Control
Air, Noise and Radiation Programs
Water and Waste Management
Pesticides and Toxic Substances

* Task Force members included Robert W. Crandall and R. J. Smith.

waste water treatment, setting technology-based standards for major emitters of water pollution, regulating the use of pesticides, setting standards for the testing of new chemical products, regulating the use of hazardous chemicals, setting standards for the disposal of hazardous solid wastes, and funding the clean-up of hazardous waste disposal sites.

Although one of the newest federal regulatory agencies, EPA is the largest non-departmental regulatory agency—and its influence exceeds it size. EPA regulations affect the quality of air and water, the availability of new chemicals and new pesticides, the production and disposal of hazardous waste, and the cost of many of the products that Americans buy. Vast costs are imposed on the public by compliance with federal environmental requirements. According to estimates by the Carter Administration's Council on Environmental Quality, the U.S. spent $37 billion in 1979 on compliance with federal environmental rules—approximately 1.5 percent of the gross national product.

In light of EPA's vast powers, the public could benefit substantially from rational and effective EPA programs. Conversely, flawed EPA decisions impose large costs on the economy offset by no corresponding benefit. Sensible EPA policies must be designed to achieve the goals of environmental protection at the lowest possible cost.

The Rationale for the EPA

The economic rationale for government regulation of pollution is that private transactions result in "too much" pollution. So long as the private costs involved in such transactions are equal to social costs, society as a whole is enriched by private transactions. Problems arise, however, when social costs exceed private costs. For example, a manufacturer's costs of production may be reduced because he is able to emit noxious gases into the air and dump toxic chemicals into the water. If these discharges damage and impose costs on third parties (what economists call externalities), the real social cost of production will be higher than the private cost. Unless the cost is shifted back to the producer, the nation will, from an economic standpoint, use too much of the polluting product or process and too high a level of pollutants discharged into the environment.

Under common law, externalities are generally dealt with through transfer payments, backed up by a judicial system that awards damages to injured parties. That is, the legal system defines rights—such as rights to property, rights to freedom from intentional or negligent infliction of harm. By means of legal steps to protect these rights, the costs of the pollution discharges are shifted back to the manufacturer.

Because of the possibility of making transfer payments, externalities caused by pollution do not necessarily require government regulation. But in some cases, transfer payments are not made because rights are not clearly defined. Then, the correct solution is a clearer governmental definition of rights and duties. The only justifiable rationale for government regulation of environmental pollution must rest on high transaction costs involved in enforcing rights to pollute or to be free of pollution. Search and negotiation transaction costs can be very high in many cases—take, for example, the possible cost of tracing the cause and effect of smog in the Los Angeles Basin. Accordingly, there may also be some basis for certain types of government intervention to deal with the costs of environmental pollution.

Assuming that in a particular case governmental intervention is appropriate, the next and difficult question is when it should be federal government involvement in environmental regulation. From an economic standpoint, federal regulation may be appropriate under several circumstances: when the costs of pollution within one state are imposed on other states; when economies of scale can be realized from centralization; and when uniform regulation is essential to maintain the benefits of a nation-wide common market. From a political standpoint, decentralized decision-making is an important value. It helps to maintain freedom, promote accountability, and ensure that political decisions reflect the desires of the citizens most affected by those decisions.

Generalizing the appropriate environmental regulatory role of the federal government is difficult. It can be presumed, however, that environmental regulation should remain at the state or local level whenever the causes and the consequences of pollution are primarily within the confines of one state.

The Costs of Federal Environmental Regulation

The taxpayer-financed budget of the EPA is the least of the costs arising from federal environmental regulation. The major cost of the EPA is the misallocation of resources that results from inappropriate regulation.

Optimal regulation would place the costs of pollution directly upon the entities responsible for it. But it is impossible for the EPA to achieve such optimal regulation. Measuring the effects of individual pollutants, monitoring discharges, and many other key requirements are extremely difficult. Given limited data, regulators simply do not know the costs that result from particular pollution sources. Consequently, they must find alternative means of regulation. The regulatory method chosen necessarily departs from the theoretical optimum, and may substantially affect the costs and benefits involved.

One regulatory philosophy embodies a zero-risk, zero-discharge, "protect the environment at any cost" approach. This philosophy is epitomized by the Clean Water Act goal of eliminating all discharges of pollutants into navigable waters by 1985. The zero-risk, zero-discharge approach is guaranteed to impose costs higher than economically optimal. A second philosophy involves weighing the costs and benefits of pollution control requirements. This philosophy is reflected, for example, in the Toxic Substances Control Act requirement that if the EPA Administrator finds that use or disposal of a chemical present "an unreasonable risk" he shall apply a variety of requirements "to the extent necessary to protect adequately against such risk using the least burdensome requirements."

Excessive costs also result when regulators use "command and control" regulations (for instance, by dictating technologies) rather than using regulatory systems that permit the flexibility that results from market systems. Regulatory systems can introduce market flexibility by allowing manufacturers to exchange clean-up obligations, so that firms that face a high cost to reduce a given increment of a pollutant can contract with other firms to achieve the same level of clean-up at lower cost. For example, under regulations in place in 1981, the highest incremental cost of particulate removal for electric utilities burning high sulfur coal was approximately $2,600 per ton of particulates, whereas steel industry regulations imposed costs of up to $27,000 per ton of particulates removed.

Resources are always wasted when environmental regulations require uniformity. For ease of administration, however, regulations frequently mandate uniformity. Millions of dollars have been spent needlessly, for instance, because coal-burning plants have been required to install stack scrubbers, when environmental clean-up could have been achieved much more economically merely by allowing the plants to burn cleaner coal.

Government programs to reduce pollution also waste resources by distorting incentives of state and local governments. When a state or local government determines how environmental clean-up money is spent, but a portion of the financing comes from the federal government, the state and local governments almost inevitably will spend too much money. From the perspective of the state or local government, the costs appear lower than they actually are. This problem pervades federal environmental programs. Millions of dollars have been wasted because cities built "gold-plated" sewage treatment plants with federal dollars. Millions more may be wasted when federal dollars are used to clean up hazardous waste sites designated by states.

Finally, resources may be wasted when private sector mechanisms could be used in place of command and control regulations. In some cases, governments could reduce costs by defining rights more clearly or by helping to facilitate less expensive transfer payments, such as by facilitating insurance compensation systems.

THE FIRST TERM EXPERIENCE

In view of these parameters of proper environmental policy, the Reagan Administration has made some steps in the right direction. Top appointees at EPA expressed a commitment to "good science" and the Administration was philosophically committed to decentralization through an increased role for state governments and through privatization. The Administration also wanted to reduce the direct costs of environmental clean-up—by cutting the EPA budget.

In addition, the Reagan Administration sought to trim the indirect costs of regulation. Indeed, one of its earliest acts was the promulgation of Executive Order 12291, mandating that regulatory agencies apply cost-benefit analysis to each rule-making action, and that they adopt the least costly regulatory alternative unless prohibited by the requirements of a particular statute. Executive Order 12291 was backed up by Office of Management and Budget review of proposed regulatory changes.

Although the Reagan Administration had the right intentions, its accomplishments at EPA have been modest. Direct regulatory costs were reduced by means of budget cuts, and EPA, prompted in part by the OMB aid, began to look more closely at costs. Delegating responsibility to the states also increased. Modest steps were taken to increase the use of market incentives and private initiatives: the "bubble" policy was expanded; solid waste disposers were required to obtain liability of insurance or otherwise demonstrate ability to pay for future claims.

Yet, on balance, the Reagan Administration has failed badly at EPA. At the start of the Administration, the public was prepared to accept reduced environmental protection costs as long as it could feel certain that the environment still was being protected. The political climate appeared to be ready for substantial legislative changes to reduce regulatory costs. By 1983, however, the credibility of the EPA had been shattered and the public had serious doubts about the Administration's commitment to protecting the environment. Efforts to reduce costs were henceforth viewed with suspicion, and the prospects of enacting cost-cutting legislation shrank to zero.

The Administration's failure at EPA has several causes. Broadly speaking, it waited too long before it articulated concern about the environment and had no program for legislative reform. The Administration's plan for the EPA seemed to consist of two elements: budget cuts and regulatory relief. Both backfired. If legislative reforms had first reduced the workload of the EPA, budget cuts would have aroused no concern. Instead, budget cuts raised questions about the Administration's commitment to environmental protection. And, while regulatory relief cut costs, the business community's access to OMB suggested that regulatory relief was driven by business' ability to make its view known to OMB, rather than on the merits of the particular case.

Distrust increased because many top political appointees failed to communicate effectively with EPA's professional staff, with the environmental community, or, in many cases, even with the business community. Questionable decisions were made at the EPA, only to be reversed after a public backlash. The credibility of the agency declined and doubts grew as to whether the political appointees were even commited to "good science."

Concern about possible misuse or political manipulation of the Superfund program developed when the Justice Department instructed EPA not to provide certain documents to Congress, based on a claim of executive privilege. The ensuing congressional hearings, an outpouring of critical press articles, and potential contempt proceedings against the Adminstrator destroyed any remaining credibility of the EPA. Only through a purge of top political appointees was the collapse in credibility arrested. The political price, however, had already been paid. The chance for sensible legislative changes had disappeared.

THE NEXT FOUR YEARS

The fundamental issue facing EPA is the need for new legislation. Virtually all of the statutes enforced by EPA require reauthorization. Rational legislative changes will not be won easily, thanks in large part to the legacy of the first four years. Legislative success must be built upon a foundation of credibility, solid research, sound analysis, and improved monitoring and enforcement.

Improved Research

Because of economies of scale, environmental research belongs at the federal level. The Reagan Administration mistakenly reduced EPA's research efforts. Yet increased and improved research is essential for a rationalization of current regulations and for improved legislation. Evidence suggests that some current regulatory and legislative standards are overly stringent. Research is necessary for intelligent change. Further, EPA cannot possibly achieve all of its current legislative mandates. To set a realistic agenda, EPA must expand its research and integrate its research with the design of new regulation.

Improved Monitoring and Enforcement

Monitoring of individual sources and ambient levels of pollution is weak. Improved monitoring is essential to evaluate whether existing regulations are rational. It also is critical for a sensible enforcement program. Solid enforcement, moreover, is essential to EPA's credibility. For example, the Superfund program eventually should be returned to the states. In the meantime, EPA needs to ensure vigorously that the most hazardous waste sites are cleaned up. In its first years, the Administration focused too much on negotiations. Business willingness to take private steps to clean up sites depends largely upon the knowledge that the alternative is litigation that will impose greater costs on the polluters than would private clean-ups.

Decentralization

It is imperative to seek legislative changes that sort out the environmental responsibilities of appropriate levels of government. Much of the current environmental legislation creates a complex and convoluted inter-relation between federal and state responsibilities. Authority and responsibility should not be segmented. Responsibility should be vested explicitly either in the federal government or in the state governments. When the causes and consequences of pollution are entirely intrastate, states should set regulatory standards, not the federal government.

Pork-Barrel Programs

Central to much of the current legislative superstructure regulating environmental clean-up is the illusion that federal contributions are cost-free. The Administration must teach the American people that this is not true. Pork barrel programs masquerading as environmental programs should be eliminated. Just as millions of federal tax revenue dollars were wasted building extravagant local sewage treatment plants, additional millions may be wasted in financing "gold-plated" hazardous waste site clean-ups—enriching the companies that engage in the clean-up, but impoverishing the rest of Americans, with no comparable environmental improvement. Sewage waste treatment and hazardous waste clean-up is a local problem. The Administration should seek legislation to turn these programs back to the states.

Development of a Property Rights Approach

Since the justification for environmental regulation diminishes as property rights are more clearly defined and as transaction costs are reduced, the Administration should, when feasible, take steps to obviate the need for regulation. It may be possible, for instance, to eliminate the need for regulation of solid waste disposal, because the location of the waste is generally concentrated, allowing costs and effects to be clearly determined. The use of manifest systems to document producers of the waste, combined with insurance obligations, may facilitate liability suits, and thereby permit a solution in the private courts instead of through regulation.

The EPA should work with states to assist them in defining rights of victims in a manner that makes private litigation feasible when injuries occur. If rights are defined and enforceable, and waste disposers are required to obtain insurance, the insurance underwriters will take steps to police the disposal of solid waste, thereby obviating the need for federal regulations dictating means of disposal.

The Administration should explore the prospects for a property-rights approach in other areas, such as water pollution. Experience shows that on small streams where property rights are clearly defined, common-law suits have been adequate to maintain fishable streams. The EPA should explore whether, with governmental assistance, such an approach can work for larger bodies of water. It could work with states, for instance, to define property rights more clearly. The EPA also could research on cause and effect relationships of water pollution so that owners of property rights could better identify discharges that diminish the value of their property rights. For example, EPA might ascertain the feasibility of introducing tracer elements into plant outflows to ease the problems of proving cause and effect.

Flexibility and Trading Risks

Even if the Administration reduces the need for federal regulation, a federal role remains. In such areas, it is critical that the Administration seek legislation that will allow flexibility and the trading of risks.

The Administration should seek to dispel the illusion that all risks and all discharges can be eliminated. Often one risk is traded for another. Reduced use of pesticides may increase food prices. Decreased discharges of airborne emissions may mean increased solid waste in dangerous landfills. Attempts to eliminate totally the risk that air pollution poses for jogging asthmatics may mean eliminating the automobile.

Thus, when regulation is necessary, the Administration should seek authority to allow the flexibility to balance costs and benefits. If there are cases where it is impossible to measure costs and benefits, Congress needs to specify the levels of risks that it considers acceptable. But legislation should be sought that would allow flexibility regarding the means by which that level of risk is achieved.

Flexibility is best achieved by expanding market incentives. In particular, the Administration should seek legislative changes that would allow new factories to trade emissions reduction credits, rather than mandating specific technology for new plants. Such market rights would provide the flexibility that would protect the environment at a reduced cost.

INITIATIVES FOR 1985

1) Issue an annual presidential report on the state of the environment.

Through substantive speeches, the President can help satisfy the legitimate public concern about the state of the environment. These addresses could be combined with awards recognizing private initiatives to protect and enhance the environment.

2. Force responsible parties to clean up the most dangerous hazardous waste disposal sites or to pay for such clean-ups (including punitive damages.)

The EPA Administrator's steps to obtain voluntary clean-ups of hazardous waste sites are commendable, but they will be much more effective when responsible parties know that the threat of punitive damages is real.

3. Seek amendments to the Clean Air Act that will allow balancing of costs and benefits and expanded use of market incentives.

The Clean Air Act has imposed inordinate and unproductive costs. The environment can be protected at a much lower cost if these two basic legislative changes are made.

4. Appoint a task force that includes state and local government officials to recommend realignments of environmental responsiblities among various levels of government.

The EPA Administrator should appoint a task force that could begin to identify which programs should be shifted back to the states and which should remain the responsibility of the national government.

5. Resist efforts to turn Superfund into a permanent federal program.

The clean-up of hazardous waste sites is intrinsically a state or local problem. Millions of dollars could be wasted on inefficient clean-ups financed by federal taxes. The national government should provide information and research regarding hazardous waste clean-up, but legislation that would extend Superfund as a federally funded clean-up program should be rejected.

6

The Department of Health and Human Services

by
Ronald F. Docksai*

Considering its size and influence, the Department of Health and Human Services (HHS) is the Pentagon of U.S. domestic policy. The Secretary's formal responsibility is to advise the President on health, welfare and income security policy, direct the Department's staff in carrying out the programs and activities of the Department, and promote general public understanding of the Department's goals, programs and objectives. The Secretary carries out these functions through five Operating Divisions—the Social Security Administration, the Health Care Financing Administration, the Office of Human

SECRETARIES
Richard Schweiker, 1981-March 1983
Margaret Heckler, March 1983-Present

PERSONNEL: 141,715

BUDGET (In Billions of Dollars)

1985 Estimate	$322.1
1984 Estimate	$296.0
1983 Actual	$276.6
1982 Actual	$251.3
1981 Actual	$228.1
1980 Actual	$194.7
1975 Actual	$112.4

Established: 1953 (Formerly HEW)

Major Programs:
Social Security Administration
Health Care Financing Admin.
Human Development Services
Food & Drug Administration
Public Health Service

* Task Force members included Hayden Bryan, Roberta Dunn, Steven A. Grossman, S. Anna Kondratas, and David Sundwall, M.D.

Development Services, the Office of Community Services, and the Public Health Service.

The Social Security Administration (SSA) administers HHS's income security programs for the aged, disabled, and poor. Nearly 67 percent of the HHS budget is for SSA program outlays. These include Old-Age Survivors and Disability Insurance, Supplemental Security Income, Aid to Families with Dependent Children, Child Support Enforcement, Low Income Home Energy Assistance, and Refugee and Entrant Assistance programs.

The Health Care Financing Administration (HCFA) was created in 1977 to oversee Medicare, Medicaid and related federal medical quality care control programs. The Medicare program is funded through Social Security contributions, premiums, and general revenue. HCFA also coordinates with the states to develop programs, activities, and organizations closely related to the Medicare program. It directs the Medicaid program, which through grants to states provides medical services to the needy and the medically needy.

The Office of Human Development Services (HDS) administers grant programs serving the poor, aged, Native Americans and children, including the Social Services Block Grant and Head Start. Its programs comprise the bulk of government "social work" efforts. The Office of Community Services administers the Community Services Block Grant, for which the Administration has requested no funding in FY 1985. The OCS recently has undertaken some food and shelter coordinating activities, but its functions probably would be folded into HDS with the elimination of most of its funding.

The Public Health Service (PHS) is one of the oldest federal offices. Created in 1798 and authorized to oversee marine hospitals for the care of American merchant seamen, it has vastly broadened authority—to protect and advance the nation's physical and mental health. It does this largely by coordination with the states to set and implement "national health policy."

THE FIRST TERM EXPERIENCE

The Reagan Administration has managed to bring some order and economy to health and human resource policy, despite opposition from Congress. Unfortunately, public expectation of government services apparently continues to rise, although perhaps less rapidly than four years ago. Americans generally expect more and better quality health and human services, yet are increasingly unwilling to pay for them.

In 1965, the total U.S. health care expenditures were approximately

$39 billion, representing close to six percent of the gross national product (GNP). By 1983, this had increased to roughly $321 billion, or 10.5 percent of GNP. HHS estimates that total health care expenditures will exceed $750 billion by 1990, accounting for at least 12 to 13 percent of GNP.

American health care rivals U.S. agriculture as the most regulated and centrally directed part of the domestic economic system. New and innovative ways to defederalize the American health care system, and efforts to move toward a "New Federalism" approach to the provision of social services, formed the core of the Reagan Administration's strategy. This remains the broad challenge facing the Department of HHS during the next four years.

The size of HHS outlays, which totalled $276.8 billion in FY 1983, is the world's third largest budget, exceeded only by the entire budgets of the United States and the Soviet Union. It is estimated that outlays will total $296.2 billion in 1984 and $318.1 billion in 1985. Between 1975 and 1985 the HHS budget has grown more than threefold. However, the rate of increase has declined significantly from 17.7 percent in 1981 to 7.4 percent in 1985. The largest growth has been in entitlement programs. Expenditures for such programs could constitute nearly 96 percent of total HHS outlays in 1985. That year, HHS will provide direct benefits to nearly one in every four Americans. The budget provides increased funding for the Department's major entitlement programs for the elderly, disabled and poor, including those in need of medical care; and it maintains or increases support for important discretionary programs.

New Federalism

When Ronald Reagan took office, a politically earnest—although organizationally sparing—effort was launched to implement "New Federalism." With the help of its congressional allies, the Administration was partially successful in transferring much administrative and revenue-generating authority back to the state and local level. The Department of HHS succeeded in defederalizing major portions of the American health care service system.

Health and human services costs escalate wildly, and bureaucracy proliferates, when all issues and problems are focused at the national level in the form of rigid categorical programs. The Reagan Administration took bold steps to correct this approach, but the task is not yet completed. New Federalism, in accordance with America's constitutional principles, meant returning to states and local governments a large measure of responsibility—and flexibility in the exercise of that responsibility—for meeting the varying needs of citizens. There are commonalities in each state population, and in their needs for health and human services. Each state, for instance, has an elderly population, some families with dependent children temporarily unable to support themselves, and possibly some refugees. But there are different shares of these populations within each state, and needs vary within each population group depending on state circumstances. The New Federalism initiative was based on a refusal to impose on these divergencies the uniform straightjacket of nationally administered categorical programs.

The best example of Reagan's cooperative federalism is the transformation of numerous categorical programs into a small number of block grants to the states. This reformulation reflects the legitimate diversity within the federal union. It has encouraged popular government and democratization and has minimized the bias of national special interest groups—while significantly promoting the efficient spending of the taxpayer's dollar. Many health programs were folded into such block grants as the Preventive Health and Health Services Block Grant, the Primary Care Block Grant, and the Maternal and Child Health Block Grant programs. Critical to the Administration's success in achieving this complex restructuring of health entitlement programs were two powerful Republican committee chairmen, Senate Labor and Human Resources Committee Chairman Orrin Hatch, and Finance Committee Chairman Robert Dole.

The first phase of the block grant program, carried out during 1981-1983, represented a major improvement in administrative efficiency and an important step toward the consolidation of programs. Among the now-proven benefits of block grants is that states can exercise discretion in applying federal funds to meet the highest priority needs of their citizens. Most states have used their authority to switch funds between activities and programs—and between block grants—as circumstances dictated. This characteristic of block grants should be explored further and employed where possible in the reauthorization of all block grants. According to the General Accounting Office, most states also utilized their authority to carry over funding to the following fiscal year—enabling funds to be spent in a carefully planned way, not wasted in a year-end spending spree.

Another sign of the improved efficiency, as well as a democratization of the public-funding process, is the increased level of participation by the public at large as funding decisions were moved to the states. States used combinations of advisory committees, informal meetings, as well as sophisticated statistical measures of performance and client-need in the decision-making process.

A significant improvement in efficiency also resulted from the flexibility permitted the states for administrative simplification. The block grants have allowed states to reduce the time and effort required to write grant applications and to report to the federal government on the performance of programs under separate categorical grants. At the same time, states created their own oversight procedures to ensure efficient implementation and appropriate activities by the service providers.

The General Accounting Office also reports evidence of a conscientious effort by the states to adopt various existing management tools to administer the block grant programs, including monitoring techniques, technical assistance, data collection and auditing. The use of standardized techniques within the states is the type of benefit that the Administration sought to encourage by the block grant program.

Perhaps the strongest opposition to the block grant format has been voiced by representatives of special interest groups who had enjoyed greater political clout under the categorical funding structure. Yet, this actually reveals a virtue of block grants: they allow the elected representatives at the state or local level to have greater influence in the allocation of funds.

It was unwise of previous administrations to divest states and local governments of responsibility for health and human services issues, placing that power in Washington. And it would have been similarly unwise to go completely in the opposite direction, denying all federal interest and responsibility. The Reagan Administration so far has and must continue to recognize the importance of this delicate balancing act.

Basic Research

An example of a national interest is basic biomedical and behavioral research. Leaving such activities to private enterprise or state funding probably would reduce them significantly. This is because the investor would be unable to charge for the product of his efforts when the knowledge gained reached the public domain, and was exploited by those who did not risk their money. Reduced funding of local programs and more efficient funding of basic national programs would improve research without boosting total national health costs.

The eleven institutes comprising the National Institutes of Health (NIH) are the world's most productive and successful research institutes in basic medical science. The nearly $5 billion budget for the NIH is the largest of the Public Health Service. Eighty percent of these funds are devoted to grants and contracts awarded on a competitive basis to scientists in medical schools, universities, and private research institutes throughout the country.

The NIH budget proved the most difficult to control during the past four years. Although the Administration indicated its support for basic research by proposing a budget with slight increases to accommodate some inflation, the advocates of basic science research lobbied successfully for boosts of between 10 and 15 percent per year. Congress has reauthorized the two largest institutes at NIH, the National Cancer Institute (NCI), and the National Heart, Lung and Blood Institute (NHLBI). It has also created a new Arthritis Institute. Despite such growth, NIH supporters complain that the scientific community is uncertain about future funding.

An ongoing concern of the Reagan Administration continued to be the amount of research funds spent on institutional support, or "indirect costs." Attempts by the Office of Management and Budget to mandate a 10 percent decrease in this category were vigorously opposed by the academic community, which maintained that such support was essential for their ability to function.

Social Concerns

Although reauthorization bills were drafted in each Congress, passage was frustrated by efforts of some legislators to add to the bills statutory protection for the fetus in research projects. Current regulations prohibit indiscriminate research on fetuses intended for abortion, but a demand was made that such regulations be codified, to end any distinction between the rules governing research on fetuses intended for abortion and those for fetuses carried to term.

Consideration of this issue was blocked in the Senate in 1984, when several liberal legislators objected to an amendment by Senator Jeremiah Denton (R-AL) to the bill reauthorizing the activities of the National Institutes of Health (S.773). The Denton rider made explicit legislatively what so far had been a vague regulatory prohibition of biomedical research methods injurious to a human fetus. The matter is likely to be debated anew in 1985. Most observers expect imminent action in the courts on the issue.

Primary Care

The Primary Care Block Grant, administered by the Health Resources and Service Administration (HRSA), was formed from a number of primary care programs. But unlike the other health blocks established in 1981, the Primary Care Block Grant imposed burdensome and restrictive requirements and conditions on states if they were to receive funding. As a result, only one state (and for one year only) and the Virgin Islands have received funds to operate their community health center programs. Legislation is needed to create opportunities for a new federal-state partnership for the provision of primary care services to medically under-served populations.

Other HRSA programs such as the National Health Service Corps, Health Maintenance Organizations and Health Manpower have also shifted their emphasis toward less federal involvement.

Centers for Disease Control

The traditional role of this agency has been to control infectious diseases. During recent years, however, the CDC has expanded its activities to include management of certain prevention programs unrelated to infectious disease, including screening for hypertension. The New Federalism initiative successfully grouped some of these prevention programs under the Preventive Health Services Block Grant—although strong lobbying for certain programs meant they were kept out of the block grant.

Health Costs

In 1982 the Health Resources Administration and Health Services Administration were combined into the Health Resources and Services Administration (HRSA). This led to more effective administration.

In the wake of a long running battle between HHS and OMB over final regulations allowing Medicare payments to pre-paid health maintenance organizations (HMOs) and competitive medical plans (CMPs), these regulations finally were released and published in Spring 1984. It was the most important step by the 98th Congress toward a more competitive American health care system. As reflected in the Tax Act of 1982 (TEFRA), which these regulations implement, increased reliance on pre-paid "necessary medical services" such as HMOs and other group health plans exerted competitive price pressure on traditional fee-for-service plans. Although it is too early to estimate the cost of the program, most HHS actuarial veterans expect the new HMO regulations to reap significant cost savings to both private and government insurance plans.

Throughout the 1970s, the federal government tried to contain health costs by imposing controls on prices, hospital capital expenditures, and the utilization of health care services. The Reagan Administration recognized that this regulatory approach to controlling health care would fail. Only a greater reliance on market forces would encourage more efficient utilization of health care resources.

Several reforms were enacted in the Administration's early years. The 1982 Tax Act, for example, changed the way Medicare reimburses HMOs, while the 1983 Social Security amendments established a prospective payment system for Medicare reimbursement. Previously, Medicare had used a retrospective cost reimbursement system, paying all "reasonable" costs. This encouraged marginally necessary or totally unnecessary services to be provided, contributing significantly to rapidly rising health costs.

As for Medicaid, the Omnibus Budget Reconciliation Act of 1981 provided incentives for states to control costs by reducing the federal matching rate. In addition, eligibility for the program was reduced somewhat by changes in the Aid to Families with Dependent Children (AFDC) program.

It was not until FY 1984 that the Administration introduced comprehensive legislation to reduce health care cost escalation by encouraging price competition, in contrast with the Carter Administration's reliance on controls. The Reagan proposal included a limit on unlimited tax deductability of employer-provided health insurance, greater cost-sharing for short hospital stays in Medicare (in exchange for catastrophic illness protection), a voucher system for Medicare, and certain cost-sharing requirements in the Medicaid program. The Administration, however, failed to win congressional approval of the package.

Welfare Entitlements

The Reagan Administration's attempts to deal with welfare and other need-based entitlement reform met with partial success. The motive for reform was the inefficiency and poor incentive structure in the major means-tested programs. Spending had mushroomed. In constant dollars, there was an eleven-fold increase in federal means-tested benefits between 1951 and 1984—from $6 billion to $68 billion in 1985 constant dollars. The poverty population, meanwhile, was declining—from 39.5 million in 1959 to approximately 35 million in 1983. The percentage of U.S. population that would be poor without government transfers actually had been rising since the mid-60s. Clearly the system was fostering dependency rather than helping the poor to achieve independence. Taxpayers were spending more and more with less and less impact.

The Administration's main focus was to make welfare programs more efficient and to target benefits to the truly needy. The most controversial change involved reducing Aid to Families with Dependent Children (AFDC) eligibility for families with earned income by limiting "work incentive" benefits. This was done because in many instances the income of such families exceeded the incomes of the non-welfare working poor, creating inequities. In theory, work incentives to help the poor achieve self-sufficiency are desirable; in practice, the AFDC incentives had little effect on the number of welfare mothers who worked. Similarily, their repeal had a negligible effect on the number of mothers who quit work to go back on welfare. The Reagan initiative thus was successful in reducing spending while inflicting very little hardship.

Other AFDC changes included the elimination or reduction of benefits for students beyond high school, and the limitation of benefits for pregnant women with no other children. Mandatory workfare for able-bodied AFDC and food stamp recipients without children under six was proposed by the Administration, but Congress gave the states the option to make it voluntary.

The main change in the Medicaid program was a graduated reduction in federal Medicaid grants to states—unless the states reduced both mistakes in eligibility and benefit growth. The states were also empowered to require copayments from recipients. Eligibility for households with income over 130 percent of the poverty rate was withdrawn, and changes penalized states for excessive error rates in food stamp distribution. Other welfare changes include merging of social service and community service funding into a block grant.

In budget terms, the Administration's efforts to reduce welfare spending have been successful. Estimated 1984 real costs will be lower than in 1981, in real terms. The underlying and unsustainable expansion of welfare programs has stopped. The impact on the poor has been widely debated, but it does not appear that the basic social safety net is threatened. Politically, the success has been mixed. The Administration has changed the terms of the welfare debate, but the inflamed political dialogue on this issue, and the resultant public perception of unfairness, have kept the Administration on the defensive and threatens further reform.

THE NEXT FOUR YEARS

The new Administration will be faced with a window of opportunity that will be open only briefly. During this period, some substantial and extremely significant proposals should be advanced to improve the states' capacities to provide sensitive, high quality, and cost-efficient social and health services. The major issue facing the Administration will be how to provide adequate health and social services to the nation without costs that mortgage the economic future of the country.

Substantial sums are currently expended by the Health Care Financing Administration (HCFA), the Social Security Administration (SSA), and the Office of Human Development Services (HDS). An aging population benefitting from the technological improvements in care for the elderly and newly-born could strain federal resources severely. The nation's long-term health care problem can only be solved by a two-track approach. First, programs that provide services and financing must be restructured; this will spur the states to be more innovative, sensitive, and efficient. Second, encouragement must be given to free market approaches to support the family and to make that basic institution better able to provide for dependent family members.

Phase Two of Block Grant Program

In the next Administration, HHS should pursue a dual budgetary goal. It should continue 1) reducing the explosive growth in the nation's health and human service costs and 2) streamlining federal spending on these functions. The result should be the greater availability and affordability of higher quality health and human services.

To accomplish these goals, the effort to distinguish clearly what are truly federal responsibilities and to concentrate national resources on these needs must continue. Two particular types of programs deserve a smaller share of the taxpayer dollar: those with a social engineering or interventionist philosophy, distrustful of the individual's capacity to make responsible decisions, and those catering solely to the demands of narrow special interest groups.

To the extent that the national government's role in health and human services is thus redefined, it can also be reduced. Stifling regulation, which often only increases cost, lessens availability, and stimulates excessive utilization, should be minimized. Limiting the immediate and direct involvement of the national government would enable state and local governments and the private sector—including the family, community, philanthropic agencies, and private enterprise—to deliver a variety of necessary services more effectively. Community-based organizations have proven to be particularly successful in providing services to the elderly and the handicapped, and in creating food banks, for example.

In attempting to focus the resources of the federal government more efficiently, the Administration must distinguish between those individuals in need of federal subsidies through accidental or unavoidable circumstances, and those who make a conscious decision to become a financial burden to the taxpayers. Incentives to individuals to seek further taxpayer subsidies should be minimized.

The overall success of the block grant program suggests strongly that the next Administration should expand the use of block grants, and protect the state and local government prerogatives within the existing block grants. Regardless of the level of funding available for block grants, the improved efficiency of administering these funds is an important element of fiscal prudence.

Welfare Entitlements

Federal Medicaid funding to those states with health care costs that are excessive, when compared to nationally established growth rate targets, should be reduced 3 percent by the next Administration. That is a reasonable "carrot and stick" approach. The national government requirements still would be compassionate and reasonable, respecting the diversity of circumstances within the states. And those states with exceptionally high unemployment rates would continue to receive a one percent offset to the reductions imposed for exceeding growth-rate targets.

While the Administration has had some success in encouraging states to reduce Medicaid expenditures, more could be done to provide such incentives to program patients and providers. Income-related vouchers should be adopted for Medicaid. By providing recipients with a fixed amount of money that could only be used to purchase approved health insurance coverage, vouchers would encourage participants to "shop around" and select cost-effective providers.

Under current Medicaid guidelines, beneficiaries can lose complete eligibility if their earnings rise above a certain level. This discourages them from increasing their income. Relating the amount of the subsidy to a beneficiary's income level could alleviate this problem by providing the very poor with protection, but by gradually reducing benefits as income increases.

As in Medicare, program participants should be given the option of taking their benefits in the form of a voucher, which they could supplement if they wished. For example, Medicaid beneficiaries could use their voucher amount to enroll in Health Maintenance Organizations (HMOs), which provide quality care at a cost 10 to 40 percent less than the traditional fee-for-service reimbursement system. HMOs offer individuals a plan that meets all their health needs for one flat fee. The HMO is at risk for the cost of services and therefore has incentives to provide cost-effective care. The savings from HMOs are largely the result of reductions in unnecessary hospital admissions. The voucher would not be limited to HMOs, but would be available for any alternative delivery plan that offers a basic set of services.

The Administration wisely is proposing that all employable AFDC applicants and recipients be required to participate in work programs as a condition of eligibility. States now have the option to establish Community Work Experience programs and mandatory job-search requirements, but only half have done so, even on a limited basis. The Reagan "workfare" proposal would ensure that AFDC recipients are encouraged to find work in the private sector, or perform useful public services when no private job is available. Requiring this in all states, after first allowing the states to design their own programs, would guarantee wise and responsible use of the federal taxpayer's dollar at the state and local level.

The Administration also should reexamine work disincentives across the entire range of welfare programs at its earliest opportunity. Although its AFDC cuts were a budgetary success, it is contradictory to push for workfare on the one hand while increasing work disincentives on the other. A coordinated approach to welfare policy is needed; while welfare should provide for those unable to help themselves, it also should encourage self-sufficiency.

A first step in achieving this would be to measure the effect of overlapping benefits and the impact of in-kind benefits; too often programs are altered in isolation. The next step would be consolidation and simplification of the scores of need-based programs. In addition, welfare reform should consider the impact of the tax code on the poverty population.

Care for the Elderly

In the case of programs for the elderly under the Administration for Aging, the Reagan Administration combined the federal financing role and exercise of some federal authority with greater room for state flexibility and administration. The Administration later proposed that funds for four separate types of grants—services, group meals, home-delivered meals, and administration—be turned into a single but less restrictive grant. The White House also proposed to allow states even more flexibility to allocate the funds as they see fit, but that each of these services be funded and none totally eliminated by the states. These proposals should be approved by Congress.

Home Health Care

The keystone of long-term health care policy should be a comprehensive program fostering home services. By the start of the next century, those citizens aged 65 years and over are expected to increase in number by 35 to 40 percent. Increasing, too, will be chronic and acute illnesses. To temper the cost of building and maintaining new nursing homes, the elderly and disabled should have the option of being cared for in their own homes. To do this, changes must be made in the Medicare/Medicaid and Public Health Service acts. For too many of the nation's elderly, institutionalization is the prelude to an early death. Allowing patients to remain in their own homes is an antidote to an ominous wave of depersonalized institutional medical care. If it is coupled with eligibility controls to prevent such medical care mushrooming into a new entitlement, it will also save money.

A significant improvement could be made by consolidating funds currently expended to provide financing and services for long-term care (LTC). A new LTC block grant, funded at the total levels of program expenditures for LTC components of Medicare, Medicaid and other programs, would be an important step forward. This would give the states increased flexibility to pursue innovative ways of meeting the needs of their disabled populations. Many states have had difficulties matching funding sources with the service needs of the people they desire to serve. Increasing state flexibility and control would result in administrative savings at the federal and state levels. States would be able to make better use of private sector resources—volunteers, philanthropic organizations, and business support.

Family Social Services

The federal government now provides an open-ended entitlement for the payment of foster care and adoption assistance, as well as money for child welfare services and training. There is a consensus that children do better in the family—and if a family is not available, in a permanent family-like setting. Although states have been increasing adoptions and reducing the number of children in foster care, the foster care program could be greatly improved by returning responsibility to where it belongs—the states. The consolidation and level funding of foster care, adoption and child welfare services and training would give the states the flexibility to provide assistance in the most appropriate setting. Such flexibility would permit increased funding of services to prevent children from entering the foster care system. It also would encourage states to move children from foster care into adoptive homes, since adoption payments have been less than foster care payments. The movement from foster care into adoption would also ease administrative burdens within the state.

A good example of initiatives now under discussion concerns an adoption assistance program. A new incentive proposal for 1985 would discourage lengthy and inappropriate foster-care placement, and as a result, constrain program-cost growth.

Private Fiscal Capacity

Recent research shows clearly that private markets provide families with their long-term care needs through insurance and investment. There is market potential, for instance, for private long-term care insurance, pension modifications and private savings. The Administration should propose legislation to encourage private market functioning in innovative financing mechanisms through insurance and pensions, such as allowing tax deductions for disability insurance, retirement health care, and similar requirements. A restructuring of federal programs also would help private markets to function by enabling people to be aware of the limited amount that the public sector will be able to provide.

Adopting a simpler tax system with an increased dependent deduction also would encourage families to provide for themselves. The Administration should consider modifying the IRA law to allow increased contributions, and the establishment of IRAs for disabled dependents and family members. [See section in this volume on "The Social Security System."]

Health Care

The next Administration must stress market-oriented reforms that encourage people to economize on routine services, yet secure adequate protection for serious illnesses.

This means the new prospective payment (or diagnostically-related group [DRG]) must be modified, since it is a price control mechanism which still does not address the underlying problem of the health care industry—that third parties insulate the patient from the true cost of health care. While the approach does contain some incentives to curb waste and inefficiency, controls tend to create new problems.

Only a true market provides the right signals for pricing decisions. It is unlikely that the DRG system will reflect market conditions accurately; it thus will cause distortions and inequities. Since DRGs are applied only to Medicare patients, hospitals may pass on any losses by shifting costs to privately insured patients. In addition, they may lead providers to lower the quality of care and will encourage them to find ways of getting around the controls to maximize their revenues.

Unlike regulation, enhancing market forces would set up a genuine framework for cost reduction based on voluntary exchange. A decentralized marketplace provides the greatest freedom for providers and consumers to meet their needs and desires.

To shift policy in the direction of a more market-based system, the Administration should propose limiting the open-ended tax exclusion of employer-provided health insurance. By artificially reducing the cost of health insurance coverage, current tax law has led employees to demand, and employers to provide, comprehensive first-dollar coverage. These plans often cover costs traditionally paid for by employees themselves, such as dental and eye care. Moreover, once group insurance becomes so comprehensive and tax-supported, individuals lose any incentive they might otherwise have had to seek out the most cost-efficient care.

Setting a limit on the tax deductibility of employer-paid health insurance premium contributions would not lead anyone to drop coverage altogether; it simply would end the subsidy for purchases of health insurance in excess of the limits. The intent of the subsidy should be only to help people purchase insurance that would protect them from large and unexpected medical expenses. It should not encourage them to use tax-free plans for routine services—thereby exacerbating the problem of rapidly rising health care costs. The tax cap would encourage employees to accept more cost-sharing through higher deductibles and copayments, or lead them to select less expensive alternative delivery systems that provide care more cost-effectively, such as Health Maintenance Organizations.

A comprehensive Medicare reform proposal should include protection against catastrophic expenses, yet also promote greater cost consciousness by imposing cost-sharing for routine services. This should be done by imposing a small copayment beginning with the second day of a hospital stay. Beyond 60 days, however, the patient should be provided with complete protection against the costs of illness. Current Medicare policy provides the most protection when it is the least needed, but offers nothing for patients who face skyrocketing costs associated with a catastrophic illness.

Recent legislation now allows Medicare beneficiaries to join qualified Health Maintenance Organizations. The program pays 95 percent of the per capita Medicare costs, adjusted for geographic regions. Greater cost-sharing under Medicare may give greater incentives for enrollees in the program to join such HMOs, which provide cost-effective care by a more prudent use of services. This approach should be promoted.

A voucher proposal for Medicare should again be proposed to allow beneficiaries to select among a variety of alternative delivery plans to enroll in the one they feel offers the best care for the amount spent. Other plans could offer full coverage and require Medicare voucher holders to pay somewhat more than the voucher amount. The reform, however, would maximize consumer choice and enhance participant cost-consciousness. It would be a real step toward a decentralized, market-oriented health care system for the aged.

In the long run, Individual Retirement Accounts (IRAs) could be used to allow individuals to save for the purchase of old-age health insurance. The current Medicare program could be restructured to finance only catastrophic protection. This approach largely would eliminate the government's involvement in most day-to-day health care decisions, while insuring that no person would go bankrupt due to a major illness.

National Institutes of Health

In constant dollars, funding for National Institutes of Health (NIH) biomedical research and training nearly tripled between 1962 and 1982—an annual real growth rate of 5.2 percent. Since 1982, the Reagan Administration has trimmed this to a projected 4.4 percent for 1982 to 1989. In constant dollars, the proposed outlay level would exceed the 1981 peak for NIH biomedical research and training activities. Allowing this increase but holding it below the inflation rate will help keep the long-term growth trend of these activities at a more sustainable level for the remainder of the 1980s, thereby ensuring the nation their continued benefits and encouraging a better use of research funds, including an emphasis on basic research. Those who evaluate federal spending only in terms of increasing amounts of dollars spent on such programs ignore the lesser real value of each dollar spent on these programs in periods of escalating costs and inflation.

INITIATIVES FOR 1985

1) Extend home health care services.

Widening the use of home health programs, included under Medicare/Medicaid, the Public Health Service Act, and other laws, would reduce costs considerably. Home health care is an efficient and yet humane health services program for handicapped citizens and elderly and infirm who do not wish institutionalization. It remains an increasingly popular concept and an alternative policy to institutionalization.

2) Move ahead with reprivatization.

HHS can use "contracting out" and other private sector program initiatives to implement alternative health and human services strategies to counter the costly dominance by the public sector. In particular, licensing and programs rules should be amended to permit churches, community organizations and other "non-industry" providers to deliver services under the auspices of HHS programs.

3) Pursue health care cost containment based on competition.

HHS must find an acceptable compromise on the health care competition omnibus legislative package, which was strongly but unsuccessfully promoted during the last two Congresses. The link between cost containment and health care competition cannot be overstated. In particular, copayments should be built into federal medical programs, and a cap should be placed on the health insurance tax deduction.

To convey the sense of urgency required to make this a top priority for the Administration, the HHS Secretary should ask for the full and active participation of the President in promoting an Administration offensive on behalf of the regulatory and legislative package to implement this strategy.

4) Reform child care policy.

Federal adoption reform to promote placement, protection of the rights of the unborn and newly born, and improved child care services ought to be high among the Department's priorities for 1985-1986.

7

The Department of Housing and Urban Development

by
Peter J. Ferrara*

The Department of Housing and Urban Development (HUD) deals with three broad program areas: aid for low-income housing, community development subsidies, and general housing finance. The Department is also considered broadly responsible for defining the Administration's urban policy.

The major low-income housing programs are Public Housing and Section 8. Public Housing was begun in the 1930s, and for decades was the chief federal housing program. Under this program, local public housing authorities, financed by the federal government, build

SECRETARY
Samuel Pierce, 1981-Present

PERSONNEL: 13,779

BUDGET (In Billions of Dollars)

1985 Estimate	$15.5
1984 Estimate	$15.9
1983 Actual	$15.3
1982 Actual	$14.5
1981 Actual	$14.0
1980 Actual	$12.6
1975 Actual	$ 7.5

Established: 1965

Major Programs:
- Government National Mortgage Assn.
- Solar Energy & Energy Conservation Bank
- Fair Housing & Equal Opportunity
- New Community Development Corp.

* Task Force members included Mary H. Parker, John C. Weicher, Robert L. Woodson, J. French Hill, E. S. Savas, and Mark Frazier.

and operate housing for rental to qualified low-income families, who are charged below-market, subsidized rents related to their incomes.

Section 8 was begun under the Nixon Administration, as an alternative to Public Housing. Until recent changes, it has had two major functioning components—New Construction and Existing Housing. Under Section 8 New Construction, the federal government would contract with private developers to build or rehabilitate, and then manage, rental housing for eligible tenants. The private managers again charge below-market rents related to tenant incomes, in return for government subsidies. Under the Existing Housing Program, eligible tenants are allowed to choose qualified housing on their own, and the federal government pays the difference between the rent charged by the private owner and the income-related rent contributions from the tenant.

The major community development programs are Community Development Block Grants (CDBG) and Urban Development Action Grants (UDAG). Under CDBG, the federal government distributes annual grants to state and local governments for a broad range of possible community development projects. Under UDAG, federal funds are granted or loaned through local governments to business enterprises for commercial, industrial or housing projects in distressed areas.

The major general housing finance programs within HUD are operated by the Federal Housing Administration (FHA) and the Government National Mortgage Association (GNMA). FHA sells insurance against default to issuers of qualified mortgages for low and moderate income home buyers. FHA insurance is also sold to cover mortgages for multi-family residential housing and health care facilities. GNMA buys FHA and VA insured mortgages from lenders and sells securities backed by pools of these loans, creating a secondary mortgage market. The same secondary market function is performed for conventional, non-federally insured mortgages by two technically private (though federally chartered and assisted) corporations outside HUD—the Federal National Mortgage Association (FNMA) and the Federal Home Loan Mortgage Corporation (FHLMC).

THE FIRST TERM EXPERIENCE

For FY 1985, the President's budget included HUD outlays of $15.2 billion, and budget authority of $10.5 billion. The two major low-income housing programs account for 55 percent of all outlays and 46 percent of all budget authority. The two major economic development programs account for 29 percent of outlays and 37 percent of budget authority.

The incoming Reagan Administration sought to reduce HUD spending while targeting available benefits to the most needy. Top ranking Reagan appointees at HUD recognized the substantial drawbacks of new housing construction programs, and the desirability of replacing such programs with vouchers. These officials also sought a new direction for urban policy, emphasizing local leadership and responsibility, the elimination of unnecessary tax and regulatory burdens on local economies, greater reliance on the private sector, and urban improvements based on a general economic recovery. The Department was also committed to the enactment of President Reagan's proposed Enterprise Zone initiative. Another early goal was to reduce the regulatory burdens on state and local governments imposed through HUD-administered programs.

The Results

The Department can boast a string of substantial accomplishments under Reagan. Major steps were taken toward a long-term shift away from new construction housing programs and toward rent vouchers. In particular, planned construction of new units, and the accompanying budget authority, was slashed sharply. The construction of almost 675,000 new units was authorized for FY 1978-FY 1981 under Public Housing and Section 8, while only 84,000 new units were authorized from FY 1982-FY 1985. For FY 1985, only 5,000 new units have been authorized, limited to the Public Housing program. In 1983, authority for new construction under Section 8 was repealed, except for special units built for the elderly and handicapped. As a result of these changes, the budget authority for subsidized housing programs was reduced from $25 billion in FY 1981 to $4.3 billion in FY 1985. At the same time, HUD won congressional approval for a major housing voucher demonstration program, with 15,000 vouchers authorized for FY 1984 and 87,500 requested for FY 1985. HUD still hopes to replace the Section 8 Existing Housing program with such vouchers. Under such a voucher plan, low-income families would receive a certificate with a specific cash value, which they could then use (and supplement if they so desired) to rent housing in the open market. No direct subsidies would be given to landlords or to developers.

The Department targeted its subsidized housing programs more toward those who are actually poor by reducing the maximum income for eligibility to receive aid from 80 percent of the area median income to 50 percent. The cost of these programs was further reduced by increasing rents from 25 percent of household income for each tenant to 30 percent. This change primarily affected higher income beneficiaries, with little impact on those with the smallest incomes, so the Administration was again successful in reaching its goal of focusing aid on those most in need.

These actions, plus cutting and then freezing spending for CDBG and UDAG, are primarily responsible for a dramatic reduction in total HUD budget authority from $33.4 billion in FY 1981 to a proposed $10.5 billion in FY 1985, a reduction of 69 percent. This reduction in budget authority has not translated as rapidly into reductions in outlays, primarily because of continued spending to complete and maintain prior new construction commitments. But HUD outlays under Reagan have been stabilized, increasing from $14.0 billion in FY 1981 to $15.2 billion in FY 1985, an increase only of about 2 percent per year. Over time, the dramatic reduction in budget authority will produce sharper reductions in outlays, if new spending commitments are not developed in the meantime.

Secretary Samuel Pierce is to be commended for his solid accomplishments in management reform at HUD. He consolidated and thoroughly reorganized the Regional and Area offices, achieving significant savings. HUD staff has been reduced across the board by 28 percent. Debt collection practices have been improved and the number of audits has been increased, resulting in dramatic increases in recovery rates for funds owed to the Department. Improved property disposition procedures have also greatly increased receipts from HUD property sales. Strong and fairly successful efforts were also made to eliminate, outdated or ineffective programs, such as the New Community Development Corporation, Self-Help Development, Planning Assistance, and the Solar Energy and Conservation Bank.

Regulatory burdens on state and local governments relating to the CDBG program also have been significantly reduced. HUD Minimum Property Standards for single family homes have been greatly simplified, with significant cost savings for homebuilders to pass on to homebuyers.

The Department's urban policy objectives have also met with some successes. The old pattern of state and local dependence on the federal government and expectations of federal bailouts has been replaced by an emphasis on local self-reliance, long neglected local strengths and advantages, and general economic recovery. Departmental leadership has increased state and local awareness and the utilization of the private sector options for providing traditionally public services. The Department has also emphasized the possibilities for state and local deregulation of their own economies.

Another accomplishment was the development of a comprehensive Enterprise Zone proposal, which properly emphasizes the removal of government burdens on economic activity—instead of government subsidies—as the best means of generating jobs in distressed areas. HUD leadership regarding the program has induced many state and local governments to enact their own programs consistent with the federal concept.

Among the shortcomings of the first term, HUD failed to win congressional approval of Enterprise Zones, and of more than limited substitution of vouchers for low-income housing construction. The Department's campaign for Enterprise Zones can be faulted for not sufficiently involving high-level Administration figures, including Secretary Pierce, at an early stage, and for giving insufficient support to the legislative effort. The Department has also been slow to develop and trumpet an initiative for tenant ownership of public housing, though the idea seems to have caught on within the Department. One lesson from these shortcomings: the Department should have more confidence in the practicality and potential popularity of its own good ideas.

A significant failure has been HUD's uncritical acquiescence to baseless rationales and justifications for economic development subsidy programs such as CDBG and UDAG. These programs have no justification and the Department should stop supporting them.

The Department generally missed the opportunity in the first term to champion grass roots, neighborhood groups seeking to improve their communities. As a result, the Reagan Administration lost an important opportunity to develop strong political ties to such groups. At the same time, the Department showed it was not immune to creating new federal boondoggles, establishing the Rental Rehabilitation program.

THE NEXT FOUR YEARS

The Department has an opportunity in the next four years to build on its considerable successes and to correct its past mistakes. In particular, strategic policy should be based on the following long-run reform goals.

Housing Vouchers

The Department should press for housing vouchers to replace Public Housing, Section 8 and all other HUD low-income housing programs.

Under HUD's demonstration voucher program, families with incomes less than 50 percent of the local median may apply to their local public housing authority to receive a voucher. Available vouchers are distributed to qualifying applicants on a first-come, first-served basis. Each voucher has a monthly dollar value determined by the qualifying family's income and the average local rental cost of basic quality housing. When a family receives a voucher, it can shop for housing in its community and use the voucher's monthly value to help pay the rent for the unit it chooses. The chosen unit must, however, meet HUD's Housing Quality Standards. The voucher's monthly value does not change depending on the actual cost of the chosen unit. A recipient family can choose the lowest cost qualifying housing, minimizing the amount of its own contribution to the rent. Or it can choose higher cost housing, paying the additional cost out of its own pocket.

This is a well-designed voucher program. Compared to federally sponsored construction or rehabilitation of new housing, it has several major advantages. For low-income families, vouchers allow the freedom to choose the style and location of their housing, rather than being assigned to a particular government-developed building. Taxpayers benefit because vouchers can deliver superior housing aid to the poor for far less than new housing construction programs, thanks in part to less delay and red tape compared with government-subsidized construction.

Probably the most important reason for inefficiency of the new construction projects is that they are not subject to the competition and natural incentives of the private market. Public Housing managers have no incentive to operate the project efficiently and maintain quality standards, since the government guarantees tenants and revenue. The managers can make no personal profit by improving standards and efficiency. Moreover, private landlords under Section 8 have an incentive to increase rents as much as HUD will allow, since the government picks up the increase as long as the tenant is already paying 30 percent of income in rent.

With vouchers, by contrast, the government does not interfere with the private market's competition and incentives. Private landlords and developers are offered no guarantees, subsidies, or cost-plus contracts. They are not even guaranteed tenants. They must compete in the private market as usual to attract whatever tenants are available, with or without vouchers.

By eliminating these inefficiencies, vouchers would reduce the cost of providing low income housing assistance. A 1982 Congressional Budget Office study, for instance, found that each unit of newly constructed Section 8 housing cost $6,000 per year, compared to $2,300 for the voucher type Section 8 Existing Housing program.

Basically, the same number of low-income families could be helped through vouchers as new construction programs—at less than half the cost.

To substitute vouchers completely for all current low income housing programs, HUD first should ask Congress to halt funding for new units under such programs except those addressed to the special needs of the elderly and handicapped. These funds should then finance additional vouchers, upgrading HUD's voucher demonstration into a full-fledged program. Funds used to provide assistance to those already participating in the Section 8 Existing Housing program should be used to provide vouchers to these families instead. As commitments for already built Public Housing and Section 8 projects expire, the freed funds should be used to finance further vouchers. After financing was developed in this manner for a reasonable number of new vouchers each year, similar to the number of new units recently authorized annually under current programs, additional savings from the phase-out of current programs should be used for general tax relief.

To accelerate the phase-out of the old programs, HUD should attempt to buy out existing Section 8 contracts with private landlords. For existing Public Housing projects, HUD should first encourage tenant management and then tenant ownership. For projects where tenant ownership is not feasible, all current operating and modernization subsidies should be ended. Instead, the tenants in these projects should be given vouchers and the project managers allowed to raise rents. If a project could not raise enough funds through vouchers and rent payments to continue operation, then the project should be sold to the highest bidder without restrictions, and tenants could use their vouchers to seek housing elsewhere. Local Public Housing authorities selling projects would be required to use the proceeds to improve remaining projects.

Eventually, the voucher program could be made into an entitlement program, with all eligible families receiving a voucher. This should only be done, however, as part of a broad-based overhaul of all federal welfare programs. Through such an overhaul, payment levels under food stamps, Aid to Families with Dependent Children, Medicaid and housing vouchers would be made consistent with each other to provide an overall package of low-income support, not significantly greater for individual recipients than total support under current programs. Consequently, funds for the entitlement vouchers in effect would come from the other reformed, streamlined, rationalized welfare programs. An additional, separate step would be the integration of income, housing, and social services assistance for the elderly and handicapped.

Public Housing Home Ownership Initiative

Wherever possible, HUD should help public housing tenants to become owners of their public housing on feasible terms.

Developing such homeownership would give low-income families a direct financial stake in their residence and neighborhood. This equity stake could change behavior dramatically. Destructive tenants who plague housing projects today would likely mend their ways when they became owners, or be forced to do so by their owning peers. Former tenants turned owners would have clear incentives to operate and maintain their new property efficiently, and could be expected to make special efforts to do so. For example, new owners may well volunteer their labor extensively for their new building, doing such jobs as cleaning and janitorial services, garbage collection, gardening, simple repairs, painting and front door surveillance. This already is happening in public housing projects where residents have been allowed to take over in management functions, such as projects in Washington, D.C., and St. Louis. In these and other cases, residents have achieved remarkable reductions in operating costs, and created jobs within the community—to such a degree that residents once thought too poor to own and maintain their own homes now have the means and skills to do so.

The reduced destructiveness, improved efficiency, and volunteer labor could reduce greatly the costs of operation and maintenance of a building, and improve quality—especially when compared with the performance of current government managers of public housing who face no market competition or incentives. This means reduced costs and better living conditions for the new homeowners. The government would benefit financially since it would no longer be responsible for operating and maintenance subsidies for sold buildings.

The Heritage Foundation already has published a proposal for such a homeownership opportunity initiative, based on a legislated "Public Tenants' Right to Buy." Moreover, HUD has announced plans for a demonstration program for homeownership, and homeownership legislation has been introduced in Congress by Rep. Jack Kemp (R-N.Y.) and Sen. Steve Symms (R-Idaho). Under the Heritage proposal, public tenants would have the right to form tenant associations to take over management of each residential building. When the tenant association achieved a record of competent and effective building management, the tenants would have the right to buy the building through the association as a cooperative. The price would be 30 percent of the assessed market value, with no down payment required.

Tenants turned owners thus would immediately have a deep and powerful 70 percent equity interest in their buildings. To ensure that the new owners did not make a quick profit by selling their interests immediately, each owner who sold his share in the first year would have to repay the entire 70 percent discount to the local public housing authority. This repayable share would decline 10 percentage points each year after that, so that an owner would have to wait seven years until he could sell his share and keep the full market value. For the government, even selling the buildings at 30 percent of value would produce net financial gains because of the savings in operating and maintenance subsidies that would not have to be provided to sold buildings.

Local public housing authorities would have to grant below-market mortgages to the purchasers to cover the remainder of the purchase price and to compensate for the fact that low-income families cannot benefit significantly from the tax deductions involved in homeownership.

With the low purchase price, below-market interest rates, and the steep savings in operating and maintenance costs, many public housing tenants would be able to become homeowners through this "Right to Buy" program. Experimental efforts with public housing tenant management associations across the country have indicated strongly that tenant management can be successful. The American Enterprise Institute and the National Center for Neighborhood Enterprise report that in a dozen experimental tenant management housing projects crime rates have fallen, administrative costs have been reduced, resident employment has increased, rent collections are up sharply, and vacancies and evictions are down. The American Enterprise Institute reports that within one year of tenant management taking over a project in Washington, D.C., administrative costs were cut 63 percent and maintenance by 26 percent. Improved rent collections and reduced vacancies increased rental income significantly, producing an overall operating surplus for the project.

Proper Economic Development Policies

The Department's long-term economic development strategy should be based on the encouragement of private initiatives and the creation of freer markets, with state and local governments taking greater responsibility for public services and infrastructure. A true Enterprise Zone program is fully consistent with this goal and should be pushed hard by the Department.

CDBG and UDAG, however, are not consistent, and should be phased out. The Community Development Block Grant provides national funds for local public services and infrastructure. Unfortunately, it also invites misallocation, because state and local governments tend to undertake projects eligible for the "free" funds, rather than those which, dollar for dollar, would be more beneficial. The Urban Development Action Grant assists business enterprises that supposedly could not make it in the marketplace on their own. It pulls private investment into these projects and so denies it to more worthy, viable projects elsewhere in the economy. Moreover, despite its intent, UDAG money often has gone to enterprises that probably would have gone ahead without a grant, and thus has only given extra profit to the already successful. The poor are supposed to benefit indirectly from the projects the wealthy undertake with these funds—an alleged example of trickle-down economics. In practice, substantial benefits to the poor are difficult to find. UDAG funds often have been used to subsidize downtown hotels and luxury housing, with the poor benefitting only through a few jobs as bellhops, maids, and doormen.

Moreover, UDAG funds generally have been loaned to businesses rather than granted, and these funds now are being repaid to local governments, which can loan them out again. There is no reason why the federal government must keep expanding each year an existing UDAG fund pool in the face of large federal deficits.

CDBG spending should be cut immediately. There is little sense in a deficit-ridden federal government providing development funds to state and local governments now enjoying surpluses running at over $50 billion annually. If the Administration proposes another New Federalism package with a group of federal programs to be taken over the states, CDBG should certainly be included in the package. Otherwise, the Department should aim to zero out CDBG funding within four years. As for UDAG, the Department should propose the immediate elimination of all new funds.

A properly structured Enterprise Zone program is consistent with conservative principles of economic development. Within such zones, a more open, free market environment would be created through federal, state and local relief from taxes, regulations, and other government burdens on economic activity. The reduction of these burdens would create and expand economic opportunity within the zone areas, allowing private-sector entrepreneurs to create jobs and expand economic activity. The zones should not involve any new government spending for business subsidies or loans, or any new federal subsidies for local services or infrastructure.

State and local governments already have established Enterprise Zones in about 300 communities across the country. While not all such zones are entirely consistent with the ideal, there is already considerable evidence of success. The Washington-based Sabre Foundation estimates that by the end of this year the zones will have created or saved over 60,000 jobs, and stimulated almost $2 billion in new investment in the zone areas.

The Department has proposed a federal Enterprise Zone program and it should press Congress to enact the measure. This proposal, however, lacks the best tax incentives for stimulating small businesses—originally intended as the backbone of the program. These would center on incentives to encourage investment in small zone businesses, such as allowing investors to deduct from taxes all or part of their investment in a small zone firm in the first year. Moreover, HUD seems to have abandoned the important idea of encouraging state and local governments to focus on reducing government burdens rather than providing traditional economic development subsidies. To make the Enterprise Zone program a national success, the Department must remain faithful to the original concept behind it, and must assign staff to administer the program, when enacted, who understand this concept and are committed to it.

Privatizing Housing Finance

As a long-term goal, the Department should seek to shift the functions of the Federal Housing Administration and the Government National Mortgage Association, as well as the non-departmental Federal National Mortgage Association and Federal Home Loan Mortgage Corporation, to the private sector.

FHA home mortgage insurance guarantees to the lender that he or she will be repaid the full value of a covered mortgage in return for a fee of one-half of 1 percent of the amount of the mortgage. Such FHA insurance is only available for low and moderate income homebuyers. Today, private mortgage insurance has developed for conventional mortgages above the FHA limits. For about half the FHA fee, private insurance covers part of the top portion of a mortgage, where the greatest risk lies.

At the very least, FHA should restrict its activities to mortgages issued to truly low and moderate income homebuyers. This can be done by reducing maximum mortgage limits for FHA insurance. The rest of the market should be left for private insurance. By insuring larger mortgages through FHA, the government is squeezing out private insurers, and contributing to inflation of housing prices. When a function can be performed in the private sector, it should not be usurped by a government bureaucracy. Indeed, if private insurance can serve low and moderate income homebuyers without a substantial increase in cost or a reduction in availability of mortgages, there is no reason why the FHA cannot yield the function entirely to the private sector.

FHA also currently insures mortgages issued for low-income housing erected under HUD new construction programs. If these programs are replaced with housing vouchers, FHA will no longer need to perform this function. FHA also insures mortgages on nursing homes and apartment buildings. But such businesses should be left to buy insurance in the private sector. FHA consequently should stop issuing such insurance and subsidizing commercial enterprises.

GNMA, FNMA and FHLMC buy mortages from lenders and resell them to investors, creating a secondary mortgage market. This is accomplished by packaging the mortages in an investment pool, and selling securities which pass on a share of the principal and interest payments in each pool. Recently, some private companies have begun to buy and pool mortages and sell their own security interests in such pools. Many lenders have themselves begun purchasing mortages as well. A vibrant and widespread secondary mortgage market consequently has now developed. The existence of this market greatly increases the flexibility and hence attractiveness of mortgage investments which attracts more funds into mortgages, leading in turn to lower mortage interest rates.

GNMA is a wholly federally owned corporation which deals only in FHA and VA insured mortgages and mortgages issued for properties involved in government housing programs—particularly new construction programs. FNMA and FHLMC were originally government chartered but now are privately owned corporations, though the FHLMC Board of Directors is appointed by the President. Both deal primarily in conventional, non-FHA mortgages, with FHLMC focusing on mortgages issued by savings and loan associations.

Though technically private, FNMA and FHLMC receive significant federal assistance. The federal government trades their securities along with federal securities, such as treasury bills, creating the aura of federal backing for the agency securities in the market place. This perception is enhanced because FNMA and FHLMC are guaranteed lines of credit from the U.S. Treasury, although neither has used this authority. The securities of these agencies are also exempt for the burdensome requirements of the U.S. securities loans. All of these factors enable these agencies to sell their securities at lower interest reate, since buyers perceive them as less risky.

This federal assistance provides FNMA and FHLMC an unfair competitive advantage, keeping present and potential competitors from competing most effectively and winning bigger market shares. It is clear that they could operate successfully without this assistance, though special consideration may have to be given to FNMA's portfolio of older, low-yielding mortgages to make the corporation viable without federal assistance. All forms of special federal assistance or ties to these two corporations should be eliminated, including the oversight and regulatory functions of HUD and Treasury. FNMA's portfolio of older mortgages could possibly be sold to GNMA on favorable terms as part of the reform.

FNMA and FHLMC should also be allowed to take over the secondary market operations for private, FHA-insured mortgages, now performed by GNMA. This would restrict GNMA to only trading in mortgages related to government housing programs. If new construction programs were replaced by housing vouchers, the remaining role for GNMA would be reduced commensurately. GNMA would still operate for just a few residual housing programs.

Reforms that would enhance the ability of private companies to operate in the secondary mortgage market were adopted in the closing session of the last Congress. These reforms were embodied in two bills proposed by Sen. John Tower (R-Texas)—the Secondary Mortgage Market Enhancement Act (S. 2040) and the Trust for Investment in Mortgages Act (S. 1822). These measures will eliminate obsolete regulations and tax treatment that previously discouraged participation in secondary mortgage markets by private firms. The Administration should study whether any further such reform is possible to ease private participation in secondary mortgage markets.

Empowering People

The key, long-term theme of HUD's urban policy should be to encourage cities to create freer local markets and increase reliance on the private sector. Local markets are freed through state and local tax reduction, deregulation, and reductions in other government burdens on economic activity. This includes providing city services through competitive private-sector institutions rather than bureaucratic, public-sector monopolies. It also means encouraging and accommodating local neighborhood groups seeking to address community problems and social needs. The federal government's proper role is to adopt the policies for general economic growth, the crucial importance of which must be heavily emphasized. An additional, proper and thoroughly consistent theme is local self-reliance and leadership according to the principles of federalism.

HUD advocated these principles during President Reagan's first term, but with widely varying degrees of clarity, conviction, consistency and effectiveness. HUD should promote them with zeal in the future. In addition, HUD should advance a new theme—empowering local citizens to address the problems and needs they face individually and their communities face collectively.

This new theme implies a new perspective and emphasis on the above themes. Local citizens, for instance, could be empowered to take over city services through neighborhood groups and associations wherever feasible. To accomplish this, state and local governments could be encouraged to offer tax rebates to citizens who formed local groups that took responsibility for providing garbage collection, street cleaning and maintenance, snow removal, day care and other neighborhood services. Recent studies by the Sabre Foundation for the Joint Economic Committee indicate the feasibility of encouraging homeowners to turn self-assessing associations and assume complete responsibility for many basic services.

The general concept of providing public services through the competitive private sector rather than through monopolistic government bureaucracies should be heavily reemphasized by HUD in the future. Numerous studies and extensive experience confirm that sharp improvements in service quality and major cost savings result from such approaches. HUD should promote this aggressively to state and local governments and provide funding for demonstration projects. HUD also should seek to eliminate the bias in favor of governmental service delivery created by the fact that state and local taxes are deductible for federal tax purposes, but fees for private services are not.

The idea of empowering people leads to new perspectives and emphasis on deregulation. Eliminating unnecessary occupational licensing laws, reducing or eliminating the minimum wage for teenagers, eliminating unnecessary, protectionist restrictions on home work, would empower many of the current unemployed or underemployed to find or create meaningful, financially rewarding jobs. The Department should seek such deregulation in cooperation with the Department of Labor.

Empowering local citizens also prompts new forms of tax relief. Ideas such as allowing the "expensing" (that is, deducting in one year) of investments in small businesses, whether debt or equity, should be examined carefully. This would help the creation of small businesses, which are the key to job creation in low income neighborhoods. As a catalyst for development, tax relief is far more effective, and less subject to arbitrary bureaucratic decisions, than direct cash assistance to businesses or development agencies.

HUD recently has been virtually silent on the subject of general state and local tax relief. It should recognize and forcefully advocate in the future the great power of such relief in freeing local economies and stimulating economic growth.

A focus on the concept of empowering people raises in particular the importance of local neighborhood groups trying to solve local problems. Across the nation, distressed communities are demonstrating through such organizations that they have latent talents and unrecognized ability to perform services, develop their local economies, and address social needs. They do so far more effectively than centralized, bureaucratic, big government programs. In Detroit, for instance, local black citizens established an organization, Homes for Black Children, which in its first year placed more black children in permanent adoption than all 12 of the city's other public and private adoption agencies combined. In Washington, D.C., housing project residents established "College Here We Come," providing tutorial and financial support that has enabled over 400 neighborhood youths to attend college. In Kentucky, "neighborhood enterprise associations" comprised of inner city residents are obtaining ownership of abandoned neighborhood real estate, which they are developing themselves.

HUD should do what it can to empower these groups to achieve their legitimate goals, primarily by breaking down the regulatory barriers that now seriously hinder their activities. Burdensome zoning restrictions, unneeded professional licensing requirements, and outdated, featherbedding building codes are just some examples of the many regulations that today serve to prevent the inner city disadvantaged from acting to better their own condition. Among other things, HUD should seek the appointment of a presidential commission to examine and publicize regulatory barriers that foreclose local community service initiatives. HUD could also sponsor conferences to feature and publicize successful neighborhood-based action, and bring together successful neighborhood leaders for cross-fertilization and personal recognition.

Direct government funding of such groups (on the other hand) often can destroy them by creating dependence and stifling innovation, replacing entrepreneurship with grantsmanship. In the past, much funding has been commandeered by ideological rather than service groups, resulting in taxpayer support for partisan advocacy rather than practical, real world accomplishments. Indeed, legitimate neighborhood groups often can be helped simply by eliminating funding for the local partisan groups, and stifling central planning bureaucracies that erect additional barriers to effective neighborhood action. Through these efforts, HUD can build true links to real, inner city people, and create a meaningful political competition for their loyalties.

Finally, using vouchers to assist the needy and deliver services further empowers local citizens. Housing vouchers, for example, give the poor more control over their own housing. General education vouchers would do the same in regard to education for all Americans, doing the most for the poor who have the least choice and control now. HUD should study and advocate feasible and prudent voucher initiatives.

INITIATIVES FOR 1985

In pursuit of the long-term goals, the Administration should advance the following specific proposals in 1985:

1) Press vigorously for substitution vouchers for low income housing programs.

The Administration should ask Congress to eliminate funding for all new units under such programs and seek expansion of the housing voucher demonstration into a full program.

2) Urge legislation for a Home Ownership Program for public housing tenants, and begin a demonstration program under current legislation.

3) Press vigorously for passage of the Administration's Enterprise Zone proposal and ensure that it will be properly administered within the Department.

4) Eliminate any new Urban Development Action Grant funding, and cut substantially Community Development Block Grant money.

5) Encourage Treasury to allow first-year expensing of investments in small businesses, so that investors would have an incentive to risk their money in new, job-creating enterprises in the inner city.

6) Reorient urban policy to emphasize deregulation, to encourage local innovation and self-reliance.

The Administration should form a Presidential Commission to identify regulatory barriers to local initiative, and hold conferences to bring together effective neighborhood leaders committed to self-reliance.

8

The Department of the Interior

by
Gordon S. Jones

The Department of the Interior was created in 1849. It administers over 700 million acres of onshore federal lands and 1 billion acres of the Outer Continental Shelf. It has trust responsibilities for an additional 50 million acres of land, mostly Indian reservations. On these lands, Interior oversees the conservation and development of fuel and non-fuel minerals and water resources, and the conservation, development and utilization of fish and wildlife resources. Interior is responsible for the reclamation of abandoned surface coal mined lands, for those currently being surface mined, and for the reclamation, through irrigation, of arid lands in the West. It also manages hydroelectric power systems.

SECRETARIES
James Watt, 1981-Nov. 1983
William Clark, Nov. 1983-Present

PERSONNEL: 73,451

BUDGET (In Billions of Dollars)

1985 Estimate	$4.5
1984 Estimate	$4.8
1983 Actual	$4.6
1982 Actual	$3.9
1981 Actual	$6.8
1980 Actual	$4.4
1975 Actual	$2.1

Established: 1849

Major Programs:
- Bureau of Land Management
- Bureau of Reclamation
- National Park Service
- Bureau of Indian Affairs
- United States Fish & Wildlife Service

The Department coordinates federal and state recreation programs and preserves and administers the nation's scenic and historic areas. Job Corps Conservation Centers and Youth Conservation Corps Camps also fall into the Department's domain, as does the coordination of other manpower and youth training programs.

The Department of Interior is concerned with the social and economic development of the territories of the United States and the Trust Territory of the Pacific Islands. In addition, it provides services to Indians and Alaska natives.

Over the years, as functions have been added and others removed, the Department's role has changed from that of general housekeeper for the federal government to manager of the nation's natural resources.

THE FIRST TERM EXPERIENCE

When the Reagan Administration took office in January 1981, it inherited a natural resource record that could not have been worse. While the nation suffered through yet another energy shock in 1979—demonstrating once again national vulnerability to foreign disruption—production of energy from federally owned resources continued to decline. America was entering its tenth year of a moratorium on the leasing of federal coal. (Approximately 40 percent of the nation's coal is federally owned.) Less than four percent of the nation's one billion off-shore acres had been made available for leasing for oil and gas exploration; and the backlog of unprocessed onshore oil and gas lease applications had the makings of a national scandal.

Despite congressional calls for action regarding America's dangerous dependence on foreign sources for strategic and critical minerals—such as cobalt, manganese, chromium, platinum and vanadium—the Carter Administration did little to address the problem. At the same time it sought the adoption of legislation placing millions of acres of prospectively valuable mineral land off limits to exploration.

Notwithstanding its predilection toward preservation, the Carter Administration did little to protect the nation's parkland except to seek to bring more private land under federal control. In the fall of 1980, the General Accounting Office disclosed major health and safety defects within many national parks, requiring the expenditure of hundreds of millions of dollars.

The congressionally enacted program under which surface coal mining practices were to be regulated and abandoned coal mined lands were to be reclaimed under state supervision—with ongoing federal oversight—remained in federal hands. In 1981, nearly four years after the statute was signed into law, 88 percent of the coal mines in the nation were under federal, not state, control.

In addition, throughout the West, where massive federal land holdings mean that Interior Department policies have their greatest impact, the "Sagebrush Rebellion" was spreading like wildfire. Initial outrage over the Carter water project "hit list" was soon followed by a general attack on an unresponsive and heavy-handed federal bureaucracy. On a variety of issues, from abandoned coal mined lands to wilderness proposals, the Carter White House found itself seriously out of step with its Western constituency.

Thus the stage was set, in January 1981, for Ronald Reagan, a former Western Governor who was familiar with the responsibilities and activities of the Interior Department, to right the wrongs of the past by appointing a conservative Secretary of the Interior. In the course of his Administration, President Reagan did so twice: James G. Watt and William P. Clark. The record of these two conservatives on the whole, has been very good. To a great extent the agenda has been accomplished and a reasoned approach to natural resource management has returned to the Department of the Interior. In such matters as energy policy, strategic and critical minerals, water policy, the management of national parks, and regulatory reform, there have been significant successes. Yet in other areas, such as privatization, wilderness policy, and the achievement of control over an unwieldy bureaucracy, success has been, at best, very limited. Even the gains achieved by Watt and Clark could easily be lost. Thus, the legacy of President Reagan's first term is uncertain.

Strategic and Critical Minerals

Perhaps the greatest success of the Department of Interior in the first Reagan term was the implementation of a national minerals policy—a strong and effective focusing on American vulnerability in the face of heavy reliance on foreign sources for the building blocks of its civilization. At his confirmation hearing, Secretary Watt indicated his intention to be a leading advocate for that concern. Secretary Clark has followed suit.

From his early outspoken opposition to the Law of the Sea Treaty to his aggressive pursuit of a presidential minerals policy, Watt sought to ensure that minerals were an important national concern—sufficient at times to overwhelm other national issues. President Reagan's 1982 "National Materials and Minerals Program Plan and Report to Congress" was the first such presidential pronouncement since President Eisenhower's in 1954. It was Watt's commitment to mineral matters that ensured that proclamation. While the President's announcement was not a step-by-step delineation of forthcoming Executive actions, it was the highest level endorsement of the view that mineral dependency could have serious implications for national security and economic well-being. The Watt-inspired presidential minerals policy statement, combined with President Reagan's ordered resumption of stockpile purchases (after nearly a twenty-year delay) and together with the efforts of the National Security Council in the establishment of the Emergency Mobilization Planning Board, gave the Administration an excellent start in highlighting the issue of strategic and critical minerals.

The President's minerals message had implications for other agencies throughout the government, since it demonstrated serious commitment to evaluating the ramifications of proposed federal actions from the standpoint of non-fuel minerals. The Department of Interior, in particular, took action to demonstrate its commitment to, and compliance with, the President's objectives. Within these agencies comprising the Department a significant reordering of budget priorities was undertaken and accomplished. However, the one federal agency with what many viewed as statutory responsibility for concern with minerals issues—the Bureau of Mines—fell far short of the high expectations placed upon it. Morever, the recent replacement of "rock in the box" experts within the Bureau with theorists and planners will further dilute the ability of the Bureau to function as an aggressive advocate for the public interest inherent in a healthy and vibrant domestic minerals industry.

Secretary Clark, given his perspective as a former National Security Advisor, has carried forward with Watt's commitment to the strategic and critical minerals issue. One of his first actions, completing an effort begun by Watt, was to appoint a National Strategic Materials and Minerals Program Advisory Committee composed of 26 representatives of the private sector, academia, and state government. This diverse and bipartisan panel should be able to scrutinize the myriad problems confronting the domestic mining and minerals-related industries, and to recommend specific actions to address those difficulties.

One clear problem for the domestic minerals industry, and for the nation, is the continuing removal of increasingly large tracts from availability for the search for future mineral supplies. Watt's efforts to implement the Wilderness Act of 1964—in which Congress clearly mandated mineral exploration and development until December 31, 1983—was met with an outcry by a small but articulate band of wilderness advocates, who conveniently forgot the essence of the 1964 compromise. Watt's effort to make a place in federal land-use decisions for strategic and critical mineral needs was, in large part, thwarted. It was never possible to get Congress to acknowledge that the geological forces that created beautiful scenery also created rich natural resources essential to national survival.

Although frustrated with the apparent unwillingness of the Congress to recognize the minerals value of much of the federal estate, Watt was not similarly restrained regarding the potential of the oceans. An early advocate of a "no" vote on the Law of the Sea Treaty, Watt moved assuredly into oceans issues following the President's decision not to sign the international pact. On August 4, 1982, through his Cabinet Council, Watt initiated the preparation of a presidential ocean policy and the proclamation of an Exclusive Economic Zone. Seven months and six days later President Reagan made both announcements.

Watt had begun his efforts to seek to bring under U.S. jurisdiction an ocean frontier totaling some 3.9 billion acres so that the U.S. could explore and develop discoveries made by the Geological Survey of extremely rich cobalt deposits. Clark, who had moved Watt's initiative through the National Security Council and to the President's desk, has become the greatest exponent of the Exclusive Economic Zone (EEZ). He has carried forward Watt's early efforts to ensure industry exploration of the Juan de Fuca ridge off the coast of Oregon and California as well as the cobalt-rich manganese crusts near Hawaii.

National Energy Policy

Unfortunately, the figures must be repeated once again. The vast majority of the nation's energy resources lie within federal control, namely 40 percent of the coal, 35 percent of the natural gas, 80 percent of the oil, 85 percent of the tar-sands, oil shale and geothermal energy. America now imports as much oil as it did during the 1973-1974 oil embargo, only the cost in terms of dollar-drain and the trade deficit is many times greater. Little wonder that Secretary Watt, with the full support of President Reagan, embarked upon an aggressive program of developing the nation's energy resources.

There can be little question that Watt succeeded. His aggressive, five-year Outer Continental Shelf oil and gas leasing program endorsed by the federal courts, laid out an ambitious but essential program for energy security. The lease offerings conducted under that program were an unqualified success. In case after case, offerings produced bids exceeding CBO estimates by as much as four times.

The federal treasury is not the only beneficiary of these lease offerings. Drilling is now ongoing on the OCS at an unprecedented rate in an effort to recover energy resources. The most significant of the discoveries was in tracts off central California in May 1981, a sale to which vigorous objections were raised. One tract in that sale yielded a bonus bid of $333 million—the highest bid ever received—and in November 1982, the real return came in with the discovery of a massive oil field (the so-called Santa Maria), the largest ever made in the federal OCS. Exploration continues in the Gulf of Mexico, California, Alaska and the Atlantic.

The modifications made by Watt in the OCS program were essential and significant:

- Frontier areas which energy experts long had urged be made available for leasing, were, at last, added to the schedule.
- Through a series of streamlining steps, the time from listing to offering for frontier areas shrunk for 41 months to 21.
- In those areas selected for leasing, all tracts not previously deleted for environmental, national defense, or other reasons were slated for leasing.
- The time-consuming, labor-intensive, and tract-limiting process for determining acceptable bonus bids (ascertaining fair market value) was revised to utilize market oriented acceptance criteria, permitting the offering of all tracts within an area. In the process, the minimum acceptable bid was increased by six times, from $25 an acre to $150 an acre.

It was these changes which allowed the Reagan program to succeed where other efforts to increase the development of offshore energy had failed.

In almost all respects, the Reagan off-shore program was a success: in acres offered, acres leased, revenue received, jobs created, exploration undertaken, discoveries made, regulatory reform achieved. In one area, however, the program was not an overwhelming success: the public perception.

An effective environmental lobby, combined with a largely uninformed and unsympathetic press, created the illusion of a national outcry against the Reagan energy program. The result was an ill-conceived congressional moratorium on off-shore oil and gas leasing off New England, Florida, and California.

Secretary Clark has sought to defuse the media hype surrounding the Administration's off-shore policies. While still committed to the Watt program, including area-wide lease offerings, he has indicated a willingness for earlier deletions from leasing consideration. This has eased some, but not all, state concerns. The essence of Clark's approach remains uncertain, given what amounts to mandatory deletions from recent scheduled offerings due to congressional moratoria, Department of Defense-related withdrawals and international disputes. However, Clark's rhetoric has been extremely strong in recognizing the nation's energy needs, the role now played by off-shore resources (25 percent of the nation's natural gas and 10 percent of its oil), the future prospects for energy recovery (85 percent of energy to be found on federal lands will likely be discovered off-shore) and the post-1971 safety record of off-shore oil and gas exploration and production.

Despite Clark's easygoing, conciliatory style, serious problems still remain: congressional critics have not been stilled; coastal governors still object to the offerings even when they are two to three hundred miles off their shores; other states are upset with the absence of revenue sharing legislation and an agreement on the equitable division of revenue produced from adjoining federal-state tracts. In fact, the program today appears no less controversial than it was in the days of Secretary Watt. The underlying fault of the Reagan Administration has been its failure to inform the American people that their interest and the nation's interest lies in the expeditious development of off-shore oil and gas resources. This must be corrected.

The Reagan Administration has succeeded in returing to multiple use millions of acres of federal land previously withheld from the search for energy. These *de facto* withdrawals, combined with the outrageous backlog of oil and gas lease applications, as well as the failure of the federal government to permit leasing on federal land in the State of Alaska, had frustrated the nation's energy program. Secretary Watt responded to these deficiencies by ordering the revocation of outdated withdrawals and land classifications and by issuing oil and gas leases in the State of Alaska for the first time since 1966. In addition, exploration within the National Petroleum Reserve in Alaska was undertaken by the private sector, replacing the ill-considered, expensive and unsuccessful government exploration program. During a three-year period, Watt leased for on-shore oil and gas exploration twice the acreage leased during the previous three years.

Once again, however, a vocal environmental lobby and an uninformed national press combined to effectively prevent sensible exploration of prospectively valuable federal land. Sensing defeat on other fronts, Watt ceased issuing oil and gas leases on wilderness study lands, "further planning" areas and recommended wilderness areas, thus declaring off limits tens of millions of acres. According to the U.S. Geological Survey, very significant portions of these lands possess hydrocarbon material. The disingenuous nature of the opposition to a free market energy search within the wildlife refuge system is revealed by the fact that the National Audubon Society's Rainey Wildlife Refuge has been producing oil and gas. Preservation and exploration clearly can be compatible.

Eventually the oil and gas leasing program fell victim to a self-imposed moratorium resulting from allegations of impropriety by a participant in the Department's simultaneous leasing program. After an eleven-month delay, Clark announced the resumption of the lottery program with a variety of safeguards.

Secretary Watt moved aggressively to end the decade-long moratorium imposed on the leasing of federally owned coal, leasing 2.5 billion tons of coal—six times the amount leased over the previous decade. This yielded $128.6 million in bonus bids. In doing so, he provoked a storm of controversy that was irrelevant to the true issues in the debate. Critics of the leasing program display a shocking ignorance of economics and an insensitivity to the needs of the nation for a stable supply of low-cost energy.

Regrettably, this meaningless, inconsequential and irresolvable debate has been used by long-time opponents of Western coal leasing to place yet another moratorium upon the program.

Land Withdrawals

A major issue to those concerned about the nation's energy and minerals future is the amount of federal land off-limits to leasing or operation of the mining law. In 1976, Congress required a review of all withdrawn lands except Indian reservations, National Parks, National Wildlife Refuges, National Wild and Scenic Rivers, National Trails, and U.S. Forest Service Wilderness Areas. The total was in excess of a quarter-billion acres, or 12 percent of the land area of the United States.

In 1981, that withdrawal review program, the revocation of withdrawals, and the subsequent opening of lands to mining and mineral leasing began in earnest. Since January of that year, the Bureau of Land Management has reviewed nearly 20 million acres and has opened 6 million acres to the operation of the mining law and 6.3 million acres (there is some overlap) to mineral leasing. Before 1981, just 850,000 acres had been reviewed, only 525,000 acres opened to the mining law, and a mere 18,000 acres opened to mineral leasing.

Unfortunately the Reagan Administration's impressive performance was derailed by the decision, made under congressional pressure, to withdraw 36 million acres of National Forest Service lands and 25 million acres of wilderness study areas. By 1984, 320 million acres, or 43 percent of the total federal mineral estate, remained closed to mineral activity. Only 7 million fewer acres were closed to mineral leasing in 1984 than at the start of the Administration.

Royalty Management

For nearly twenty years, the General Accounting Office and various congressional committees faulted the manner in which the Department of the Interior accounted for the revenues it received from energy and mineral production on federal and Indian lands. Despite the dramatically increasing sums involved—approximately $5 billion in 1980—previous administrations did little to address this issue.

Secretary Watt was not so lethargic. In fact, his record on royalty management is nothing short of phenomenal. In a little over two years he:

- involved the governors of all Western states as well as tribal leaders in a cooperative effort to seek solutions;
- brought in the Federal Bureau of Investigation and the Inspector General to address allegations of oil theft on the federal estate;
- doubled the number of federal inspectors, while ordering a training program for their benefit;
- instituted a cooperative federal-state audit program for the recovery of unpaid royalties yielding, to date, over $100 million in revenues;
- established a blue-ribbon panel to recommend solutions, and on receipt of those recommendations immediately ordered their implementation; and
- submitted to Congress, in accordance with the panel recommendations, a proposed statute that was later signed into law.

In the course of his royalty management efforts, Secretary Watt reorganized the mineral leasing activities within the Department. He removed from the research-oriented U.S. Geological Survey its predominantly regulatory Conservation Division, establishing that division as the Mineral Management Service (MMS). Subsequently, the Outer Continental Shelf oil and gas leasing program—previously divided among three Assistant Secretaries—was placed within MMS. Later, all on-shore mineral functions—except those strictly related to royalty accounting—were removed from MMS and placed within the Bureau of Land Management. For the first time, one entity within the Department of Interior was solely responsible for on-shore mineral activities, thus facilitating congressional oversight, and increasing accountability and public access. Secretary Clark later place both mineral-related functions under one Assistant Secretary.

The royalty management effort was a major accomplishment of the

Reagan Administration. In the face of a serious national issue, Secretary Watt moved aggressively, decisively, and with unqualified success—a success recognized by all those familiar with the program but by few others. The reorganization that resulted from the focus on the royalty program was long overdue.

Regulatory Reform

A key Reagan objective was regulatory reform. To a great extent, that goal was accomplished by Secretary Watt's Department of the Interior. Perhaps the greatest indicator of that success was the Office of Surface Mining, established in 1977 to ensure the regulation, by states, of surface coal mining activities within their jurisdictions. As previously noted, 88 percent of the coal mines in the country were still under federal control in 1981. During Secretary Watt's tenure, 92 percent of the regulations affecting those mines were revised and brought into accordance with federal statute. As a result, governors felt comfortable making their states part of the regulatory scheme. Thus when Watt left the Department, all but four of the 10,000 coal mines in the country, were under a state regulatory program. In addition, the "abandoned mined land" programs for twenty-two states were approved, permitting the channeling to those states of more than $450 million to reclaim land subject to past environmental abuses. Prior to 1981, only two states had approved programs, and had received $2.6 million.

Unfortunately, despite the unqualified success of the Office of Surface Mining program, its support among all 25 coal mining states, its consistently effective appearances before congressional committees, and its continuing vindication in court challenges, a recent retrenchment has taken place. Shortly after Watt's departure, the Department took control of the regulatory program of two coal mining states, in what appeared to be an effort to demonstrate regulatory toughness in the face of a challenge to Interior's oversight role by environmental organizations. Such lack of faith in the concept of federalism should not be repeated and efforts to take the Office back to the old days of regulatory overkill should be avoided.

Water Policy

In perhaps no other area were Western expectations of Reagan Administration change greater than in the matter of water policy. Disillusionment gave way to outrage over the approach of Secretary Cecil Andrus to this, the most vital issue to westerners. President

Carter's water project hit list, combined with his national water policy, followed by the Interior Solicitor's infamous water rights opinion, effectively had destroyed any confidence there might have been in Carter water policy. The Solicitor, Leo Krulitz, decided unilaterally that all unreserved water in Western rivers belonged to the federal government.

Not suprisingly, the arrival of President Reagan and Secretary Watt on the scene was greeted with enthusiasm by Western water experts, particularly when one of Watt's first actions was the withdrawal of the Krulitz opinion. Unfortunately, an intra-Administration dispute over the matter of cost-sharing long frustrated efforts to initiate critical "new start" water projects.

It took Secretary Clark, through his long friendship with the President, to break the logjam, and implement the Watt policy on water projects: to seek construction financing for each new start at a level consistent with the ability of the non-federal sponsors to participate financially and to honor prior commitments made by the United States. Cost sharing arrangements are now to be established on a case-by-case basis.

Parks, Fish, and Wildlife

No other activity within the Department of the Interior more clearly demonstrates the needless defensiveness of the Reagan Administration on environmental issues than the area of parks, fish, and wildlife. The Administration was on the defensive from the start regarding its commitment to the care of the National Park System—despite Watt's decision to retain as Director of the National Parks Service a career park employee and Carter appointee. Watt found himself required consistently to deny that he had any intention to mine, timber, or drill on National Park lands. Yet the controversy continued, fueled by professional opponents of the Administration, and the press.

It was not James Watt who initiated the effort to tighten the budget for parkland acquisition at a time of fiscal constraint, but Jimmy Carter's Secretary of Interior, Cecil Andrus. From a high of $366.8 million in Fiscal Year 1978 to a low of $65.4 million in Fiscal Year 1981, the Andrus budget for increasing the size of the park system dropped each year. Yet it was Watt who took the political heat. His initial request for $36.6 million for fiscal year 1982 was quadrupled by a Congress that sought to have it both ways—fiscally prudent, but against Watt and for the parks.

While seeking a more sensible budget at a time of growing deficits, Watt was not opposed to increasing the size of the national recreation system if it could be done in a prudent manner. Thus, over a three-year period Watt added over 1.6 million acres to the park and refuge system by trades and donations. In 1983, over 1.4 million acres of park and wildlife were added to the federal estate—more than any year since Alaska was purchased in 1867.

Unquestionably the major environmental success of the Reagan Administration, however, was Secretary Watt's commitment to a $1 billion Park Restoration and Improvement Program intended to protect the natural resource base and restore the physical facilities in the national parks, and to bring them to acceptable health and safety standards. An analogous program was initiated to address maintenance and rehabilitation needs at refuges, fish hatcheries and research laboratories.

During the Reagan Administration, and in response to legislation supported and signed into law by the President, private investment in historic preservation increased five-fold from 1981-1983. Approval of rehabilitation projects expanded from 1,761 projects certified from 1977 to 1980, representing $786 million in investment, to 5,177 projects, representing $3.8 billion in private investment approved between 1981 and 1983.

Secretary Watt endorsed, supported, and later implemented the Coastal Barrier Resources Act, which prohibits the use of federal loans, grants, and subsidies for development in the delicate coastal barrier ecosystem. This statute will save both taxpayers' dollars and precious natural resources.

Secretary Clark's recent announcement of a joint Ducks Unlimited/U.S. Government program to restore wetlands in five states is one of the most ambitious cooperative public and private efforts to improve and develop wildlife habitats in United States conservation history.

Each of these initiatives is positive, supportable, and the essence of good public, environmental and conservative policy. Unfortunately the Administration has yet to receive adequate credit for these actions. Notwithstanding the dearth of public acclaim for such undertakings—whether from the "environmental" community or from members of the press—there is no reason to depart from conservative principles to seek to gain converts from either group. No action will ever be enough. The Administration should remember this while preparing the park acquisition budget for the next fiscal year.

Privatization

Ownership and use of the 740 million acres of federal lands became a highly controversial and difficult political issue for the Reagan

Administration. During the Carter years, the "Sagebrush Rebellion" voiced the demands of several Western states that federal lands should be ceded to state control. Candidate Ronald Reagan made it clear in the summer of 1980 that the West should "count me in as a rebel." He later pledged his administration to ensuring that the states would obtain an equitable share of the public lands.

While Secretary Watt publicly announced his intention to defuse the rebellion rather than to accede to its wishes for massive federal land sales, he did move to make more land available to state and local governments in the case of need and in accordance with pre-exisiting agreements. Thus 40.1 million acres were conveyed to the State of Alaska and native corporations between 1981 and 1983, in fulfillment of the 1959 Alaska Statehood Act and the 1971 Alaska Native Claims Settlement Act. From 1981 to 1983, Interior increased by four times the number of acres transferred to state and local governments for parks and public purposes over the 1980 total. In addition, in a three-year period, Watt transferred to eight Western states over 328,000 acres promised those states on their entry into the Union. Only 3,859 acres had been transferred to the states from 1977 to 1980.

Watt's preference for more responsible federal ownership rather than a change of ownership was at least partially responsible for the collapse of the Administration's modest efforts to sell, or "privatize," some surplus federal land. President Reagan had been persuaded by members of his economic advisory staff that the only way to improve the efficiency of public lands and resolve disputes over their use was to transfer them to private ownership. In February 1982, the President signed an Executive Order establishing a Property Review Board, reporting directly to the President, to identify appropriate lands for sale. Office of Management and Budget Director David Stockman indicated that the five-year target for such sales was $17 billion.

The program ran into heavy opposition, however, as journalists and environmentalists accused the Administration of letting private interests "pillage" the nation's land. In addition, ranchers and other private interests benefitting from access to public land had little incentive to support the idea of paying the market price for that privilege, especially when the nature of their "informal property rights" had in many cases been capitalized into the price they paid for their adjoining private tracts. At the same time, they began to question whether their access would be protected under state control. State leaders soon began to wonder whether the costs of ownership might not outweigh the benefits. Watt responded by recommending that only small parcels of land be sold, and that the total be well below that urged by the privatizers in the White House.

By summer 1983, Watt had prevailed. Land sales were removed

from the purview of the Property Review Board. The net effect of four years of public land policy, therefore, has been to ignore demands for the decentralization of government, to placate private commercial interest, to irritate so-called environmentalists, and to continue the costly inefficiencies of federal land ownership. From this experience, privatization advocates should have learned: (1) Success of their policy requires a Secretary of the Interior who does not merely wish to be a better federal manager than his predecessors; and (2) privatization can only succeed if informal property rights are considered carefully and if coalitions are assembled to counter them.

U.S. Territories

The incoming Reagan Administration was urged to review the federal organizational scheme, and the current and alternative economic assistance programs for the nation's overseas territories. Unfortunately, no progress has been made on this task. In fact, there are indications of a further fragmentation of policy. Progress on the examination of alternative economic assistance programs for territories and their inhabitants, for instance, has been limited to technical assistance, and to efforts to attract investment.

The Interior Department has failed to make a compelling case for taxing the territories differently from the mainland. On the contrary, the major decisions over economic policy in the territories have been left with the Treasury Department, whose interests are in raising revenue and not in encouraging development and self-sufficiency.

The results of this approach can be seen in the Caribbean Basin Initiative, which represents a missed opportunity, thanks to organizational deficiencies and a lack of policy direction. It is also evident in a failure to consider U.S. Territorial Policy in the Treasury Department's resolution of tax administration. Similarly, the proposal to permit Guam to assume the role of the United States' Hong Kong generally has been ignored by most officials of the Interior Department, to the detriment of the island itself, to the rest of the United States, and to the possible future refugees from Hong Kong.

Three separate interagency groups on territorial policy have been created, further fragmenting administration and policy formulation. In addition, by switching the Micronesian status review to the national security side of the Office of Management and Budget, the limited coordination achieved by OMB in the past has been eliminated.

The Lessons

On balance, the record of Secretary Watt and Secretary Clark is exceptional. Generally the conservative policy objectives of President Reagan have been set in motion. That is not to overlook a number of setbacks, but these are to be expected when one is seeking a fundamental transformation of the manner in which government conducts its business. What is important is that the Administration continue on course to its destination. What cannot be permitted is a substantial reordering of priorities, a lowering of goals or an abandonment of political commitment.

Even the accomplishments of Secretaries Watt and Clark could be quickly reversed in imperceptible ways. Substantive changes too easily are disguised as mere stylistic modifications. A change in tone can quickly become a policy reversal. Keeping policy on course requires a dedicated team, loyal to President Reagan and his philosophy and committed to its implementation. That is why agencies are staffed by both political appointees and career civil servants. It is the obligation of the former to ensure that the goals and objectives of their President are carried out to the fullest extent possible. And it is the responsibility of the latter to assist in the accomplishment of the mission, while providing technical assistance and professional advice.

With this in mind it is important to reflect upon the Department of the Interior. For nearly two years the Assistant Secretary for Policy, Budget and Administration and the Deputies for Budget and Policy have been career bureaucrats. There is hardly a more important area within the Department than the budget and policy office, yet it is operating devoid of political direction except that furnished by the Secretary. How much of his effort can he devote to ensure that every aspect of that budget is in conformance with the President's programs?

When the position of Director of the Office of Policy Analysis within PBA recently became vacant, the career bureaucrat acting as Assistant Secretary replaced him with another career bureaucrat. Thus the Office is without the guidance of a political appointee, though it is busily churning out policy papers. Certainly such talent needs to be harnessed, focused and directed not toward just any objective, but toward the objectives of President Reagan.

Already within the Department under William Clark there is slippage, as there was during Secretary Watt's later days. One can see the slow but sure movement back to the old ways because they are more comfortable and familiar: the study of coal leasing rather than leasing itself because that is what the Department has done for a decade; the utilization of tract selection in OCS leasing because it is more labor intensive and makes such good use of the models and efforts of generations of economic geologists.

Despite some comments to the contrary, Secretary Clark has not succeeded where Watt failed. In fact the issues merely have been set aside for later consideration. The challenges that faced Watt remain unresolved: leasing of energy-rich near-shore OCS tracts in the face of state opposition and national need; leasing of Western federal coal reserves in response to market demand at a time of low coal prices; energy and mineral exploration in highly promising wilderness study area or RARE II, III, or IV areas; convincing Congress to forego wilderness creation in the face of evidence of hydrocarbon or strategic and critical minerals potential; refusing to purchase more park land in the face of skyrocketing costs and an increasing deficit; and more.

Differences in Secretarial style have not taken the issues off the Department's plate—they have merely taken them out of the newspapers. While some resolution is possible in the quiet tones now spoken at the Department, nevertheless what is at issue is fundamental disagreement regarding an approach to natural resource policy. It is not an argument that can be won on another's terms. Thus a national discussion and debate is critical and long overdue.

Perhaps one of the most significant achievements of Secretary Watt was simply that he raised, for the first time, the real essence of the natural resource debate. It is important to remember that Watt's departure from Interior was not due to substance but to style; his policies remain a most successful legacy. He organized and directed the Department as perhaps no other Secretary in history. He did indeed succeed in his mission of bringing change to the Department of Interior—not as fully as he wished, but more than anyone could have ever hoped.

Secretary Clark has brought to the natural resource arena a low-keyed, judicial approach while moving forward with the initiatives of Secretary Watt. Clark's national security background gives added strength to his dedication to energy and minerals production. It is important that he continue to seek to fufill the unfinished agenda that brought President Reagan to Washington.

THE NEXT FOUR YEARS

For the new Administration to succeed in implementing a balanced natural resource policy it is vital that the American people be informed and involved. To date, the debate over the future of the nation's vast resource base has been left to a small band of active, aggressive and articulate proponents of the failed policies of the past. No truly serious effort has ever been undertaken to inform the American people of their very real interest in natural resource policy and the wisdom of a conservative approach to that issue area. Conservatives need today to seize the high ground.

Contrary to the view held by some, no press is not good press. No press is exactly what most conservatives traditionally have received when it comes to natural resources. No press leaves the issue to those with whom conservatives disagree, allowing them to select the vocabulary and the terms of the debate. The Department of the Interior—in fact the entire Administration—should embark upon an effort to fulfill an important aspect of its statutory and constitutional responsibility by informing the American people of what is at stake in the natural resource debate.

One indispensable requirement for that effort is the placement throughout the bureaucracy of committed conservatives capable of joining the debate while effectively implementing the policies and philosophy of the President.

One reason the bureaucracy is often so unwieldy is a narrow tunnel vision on the part some bureau managers, who see themselves not as Department of the Interior employees, but as employees of the National Park Service or the Geological Survey. One initiative of Secretary Watt that deserves at least another try is the cross-fertilization of the Department's agencies by the fluid movement of Senior Executive Service (SES) managers among the various bureaus. It is unlikely that the National Parks would have been allowed to deteriorate so significantly had such a program been in place years ago.

In addition to these general management initiatives, there are a number of specific areas which should be addressed in the next four years:

Energy and Mineral Resources

The first requirement in the search for energy and minerals is access. The Reagan Administration has had only spotty success in opening lands to mineral exploration. Concerted efforts by policy officers of the Bureau of Land Management, Forest Service, and Minerals Management Service are thus needed to improve access to publicly-owned energy and mineral resources. Access decisions that fully take into account the needs of the private sector, rather than the whims of bureaucrats, must be the rule rather than the exception.

The policy of placing vast areas of public land off-limits to America's mineral exploration efforts has been ludicrous—only a fraction of one percent of the total land area of the U.S. has ever been affected by mining. In addition, massive new wilderness designations constitute essentially a step backward from the realization of the need for multiple use. The Department should stand as an aggressive and powerful advocate—particularly in light of the expertise represented by the U.S. Geological Survey and the Bureau of Mines—in opposition to wilderness designation when potentially in conflict with energy and mineral exploration efforts. This is not an issue on which responsible public officials can afford to be silent.

Financial planning and budgeting for exploration and mineral development outlays is risky enough without the cyclical swings of government policies. The next Administration should make as permanent and steady as possible government requirements and opportunities for the energy and minerals industry. One aspect of such policies concerns the matter of regulatory reform. Great strides were made early in the Reagan Administration in streamlining the rules governing the leasing, mining, and reclamation of coal lands. Similar progress must be made in reforming rules affecting offshore oil and gas operations, and in simplifying the labyrinth of regulations covering mineral exploration and development on publicly owned forests and grasslands.

The Department of the Interior must retain a market approach to the development of energy and mineral resources. The marketplace must be allowed to determine the amount and timing, within the requirements of statute, of the utilization of America's natural resources—not some isolated public official several stages removed from the operation of the marketplace. Thus the advances achieved during Secretary Watt's tenure must be retained, particularly in the area of off-shore oil and gas and federal coal leasing. Many of the recommendations made by the congressional coal commission already had been instituted by Secretary Watt. One can hope that on the the coal environmental impact statement will be completed quickly and that program will move forward aggressively in response to market forces. In addition, further tinkering with the on-shore oil and gas leasing program should be avoided in order that the private sector can move forward in its search for domestic energy.

In the Outer Continental Shelf oil and gas leasing program, Secretary Clark's efforts to resolve expeditiously the division of revenues accruing from adjoining federal-state offshore tracts has been an important step forward and should be pursued. However, Administration opposition to off-shore revenue sharing makes little sense. Coastal communities need to have a greater stake in off-shore development. Revenue sharing offers that opportunity. The Administration should endorse a version of that legislation that would ensure that such funds are returned to the state and local communities and not some quasi-federal entity that will continue to oppose off-shore development.

Implementation of the President's Exclusive Economic Zone (EEZ) should continue on the same aggressive path which Secretaries Watt and Clark have chosen. However, the private sector is anxious to assume a large part of the exploratory workload in the vast EEZ. It makes little sense to expand the federal bureaucracy when private enterprise could undertake such programs.

The domestic mining industry continues to have serious difficulty. One aspect of its problems concerns foreign competition. While the domestic mining industry subscribes to the principles of free trade, the industry's steady decline is in part the result of foreign trade practices which are not fair. For example, the U.S. currently is a participant in loans to foreign nations with government-supported minerals operations. Such loans, whether to the mining activity itself, to the infrastructure essential to the mining effort, or to other unrelated activities that free up that country's capital for assisting the mining operation, in the end hurt U.S. operations. One can hope that Secretary Clark's minerals advisory panel will provided assistance in offering solutions to these and other problems now vexing that industry.

During the term of the new Adminstration steps, should be taken to facilitate the orderly utilization of the nation's natural resources:

1. The Secretary of the Interior should exercise his authority under existing law to formulate an action plan to reverse the trend of public land withdrawals that inhibit or preclude the domestic mining industry's ability to explore, develop, and produce strategic and critical minerals or other non-fuel minerals from the nation's public lands. Legislation is not needed to take this step.

2. In the leasing of fuel minerals the Administration must seek to persuade Congress that the regimen of environmental statutes passed in the 1960s and 1970s is more than adequate to protect the environment. Indeed, these laws in many instances go beyond the reasonable and extract a price—higher costs for consumers and lost jobs.

Water Policy

Some steps have been taken toward rationalizing water policy by introducing the discipline of the marketplace. Additional steps should be taken over the course of the next few years. The policies adopted under Secretary Watt require that electric power purchasers bear the total costs of their share of planned projects, and that their contribution be made up front. That was a useful reform, which should be followed up immediately by a similar requirement for irrigation water consumers. It is a bit more difficult to internalize flood control benefits, but it is not impossible. Recreational users should be required to pay market rates for their benefits.

Costs will never be allocated fairly as long as arbitrary water shares are written into long-term contracts for agricultural and M&I (municipal and industrial) uses. New contracts do have more flexibility than older ones did, but the allocation itself makes it impossible to arrive at a "market" price for water. Over the long run, elimination of the allocation formula will make the contracts more flexible and responsive to changing demographic and industrial patterns, and permit the determination of market prices for water.

During the last Congress, the Administration connived with the Congress in the renewal of a power sale contract between the government and power users in Arizona, Nevada, and California, for power generated at Hoover Dam. This contract, which permits existing users to buy power at rates far below market value, and which excludes from access the growing population areas of Southern California, is an outrageous rip-off of the American taxpayer. There will be other, similar contract renewals coming due. The Interior Department should stiffen its lip in a non-election year, and renew these contracts only at market rates.

In addition, the Bureau of Reclamation operates power generating facilities at many of its Western reclamation projects. These facilities could be operated by private industry, and BuRec should make another attempt at selling them off. The failure of its initial attempt, in the first Reagan Administration, should not be considered the final decision of the marketplace on this effort.

There are three federal agencies building dams and water projects: the Bureau of Reclamation, the Army Corps of Engineers, and the Soil and Conservation Service of the Department of Agriculture. This duplication of expertise is wasteful and inefficient. It is time to consolidate the dam-building function in one agency.

Such a move should be accompanied by a separation of the planning phase from the construction phases of projects. The planning function should be carried out by a different agency from the agency carrying out the construction. The present system leads to over-design, because construction then means an increase in the total budget of the agency doing the planning. Separation of the functions now would also make it more likely, down the road, that the entire construction function could be contracted out to private enterprise.

Privatization

To break the impasse on privatization, the Administration should introduce a modified privatization program consisting of:

1. Range land sales that include a proposal to protect the interests of ranchers who now hold grazing rights. Ranchers holding permits would be able to exercise the option of buying the rights at the discounted present value of the projected annual fees. This would mean, in effect, that the rancher would receive the difference between the bill and the option price. In this way, the rangeland would benefit from the improvements encouraged by private ownership, the taxpayer would gain from sales, and existing users would be protected.

2. Non-sensitive timberlands in the West should be sold on the open market(with public hunting rights and easements built into the contract), so that private companies would no longer be subsidized by the taxpayer, and firms would have an incentive to manage the land carefully to protect their investment—just as they do in the East.

U.S. Territories

1. The Administration must treat assistance to the territories, especially for infrastructure, as an investment. It should begin an ambitious program to complete a basic infrastructure program.

2. Immediate attention should be given to Puerto Rico and the Virgin Islands as important elements of the Caribbean Basin Initiative. The St. Croix airport should receive priority attention, as should an Eastern Caribbean Center at the College of the Virgin Islands and the English-speaking Caribbean. Steps should be taken to encourage the development of the Caribbean countries using transportation, machinery and other resources and of Puerto Rico and the Virgin Islands.

3. As an essential element of its study of the tax system, the Administration should develop a separate schedule for source income in the territories, to enable them to compete effectively in the regional economies. Questions of tax administration should not be permitted to dictate territorial policy.

4. The application of federal laws and regulation to the territories should be reviewed, and action taken to eliminate unnecessary constraints. Amendments to the Clean Air Act could serve as a model, by preserving the objectives of the Act while permitting the EPA Administrator to make such waivers as are appropriate. The blanket subjection of the territories to continental U.S. standards subordinates policy objectives to administrative convenience.

5. Attention should be given to the situation of the Guam Power Authority. The Administration immediately should convene a meeting with Guam's leaders, Guam Power Authority and the Navy, with the objectives of establishing Guam Power as a financially viable entity and terminating the power pool agreement with Navy.

INITIATIVES FOR 1985

1) Appoint a second Public Land Law Review Commission to examine the system of federal ownership and management of huge areas of the Western United States.

Since the first Commission reported in 1977, and since the enactment of the Federal Land Policy Management Act in 1976, there has been plenty of opportunity to judge the workability of the system. A new Commission should include prominent representatives of the movement to privatize natural resources, economists, and state government, as well as environmentalists and land managers.

2) Play a more active role as spokesman for the domestic mining industry in matters of policy that affect the industry's competitive posture in the world markets.

3) Delay submitting names to fill the three member National Critical Materials Council until the recently established 26 member National Strategic Materials and Minerals Program Advisory Committee has had an opportunity to fulfill its mandate.

If the mandate cannot be accomplished, and the NCMC is filled in a hasty manner, the question of funding for both groups should be raised.

4) Submit proposals to Congress for the completion of school lands exchanges in Western states, permitting the states to consolidate their lands for effective management.

Similarly, the checkerboard ownership of federal lands in such Western states as Utah and Nevada should be eliminated speedily. The on-going debate over acre-for-acre and dollar-for-dollar equivalencies is debilitating and unproductive.

5) Initiate experiments in alternative wilderness management.

Designation of wilderness by Congress should not automatically mean perpetual federal management of the resource. Local governments and even private enterprise should be given the option of bidding on management to federal specifications.

6) De-authorize water projects that remain on the books, but which, by common consent, will never be built.

Such a request to Congress would generate trust and respect in the environmental community, would not cost money, and would permit a concentration of planning resources on projects which are more worthy of construction.

7) Consolidate three interagency policy review groups concerned with the territories into a single organization at the White House.

This step would establish a single policy for the political, social, and economic development of the off-shore areas and to co-ordinate and incorporate such policy within foreign policy, national security, and domestic policy.

8) Give careful consideration to unifying all line agency responsibilities for off-shore areas, including program or other assistance to the free associated states.

This unified responsibility should be within the existing arrangement in the Department of the Interior, or as a separate interagency office. The Administration should require all agencies, including the Department of State and the U.S. Trade Representative, to co-ordinate their activities with the office.

The Administration should involve the territorial leaders in formulating and conducting foreign policy, and strengthening the relations between the territories and their neighbors.

9

The Department of Justice

by
Paul D. Kamenar*

Despite its small size, the Justice Department shoulders some of the federal government's most important responsibilities. The Department prosecutes all federal crimes, defends the United States in almost all lawsuits brought against the government, is a principal source of legal counsel to the President and Congress, and in its frequent appearances before the courts—in particular the Supreme Court—it is a major force in shaping law. It also manages federal prisons, guards the nation's borders, handles most matters concerning immigration, and its Drug Enforcement Administration (DEA) polices trafficking in controlled substances. The Federal Bureau of Investigation (FBI), yet another component of the Department, investigates all federal crimes, is responsible for domestic security investi-

SECRETARY
William French Smith, 1981-Present

PERSONNEL: 55,686

BUDGET (In Billions of Dollars)

1985 Estimate	$3.5
1984 Estimate	$3.4
1983 Actual	$2.8
1982 Actual	$2.6
1981 Actual	$2.8
1980 Actual	$2.6
1975 Actual	$2.1

Established: 1870

Major Programs:
- Federal Bureau of Investigation
- Immigration and Naturalization Service
- Drug Enforcement Administration
- Federal Prison System

* Task Force members included Patrick B. McGuigan, Randall R. Rader, and Michael B. Wallace.

gations, conducts background checks on many federal employees, and plays a significant role in improving the administration of criminal justice on the state and local level.

The Department's principal functions are discharged by about a dozen components, many of which are engaged principally in field operations. Criminal investigation primarily is performed by the FBI and the DEA, which between them have a budget of about $1.5 billion and 25,000 employees—accounting for over one-third of the Department's resources. The Immigration and Naturalization Service has a budget of $574.5 million in FY 1985 and over 11,000 employees. The Bureau of Prisons and the United States Marshals Service manage the federal prison system and the federal judiciary, respectively.

Although the bulk of the Department's resources enforce federal law in the field, it is the remaining components of Justice that have the greatest importance in shaping legal policy. For one thing, these sections are staffed at their highest levels by political appointees charged with pursuing legal policies reflecting the agenda of the incumbent Administration. For another, these components administer statutory programs that allow for broad interpretation. And then, in what may be Justice's most critical function, these sections appear in court to press the Administration's interpretation of federal law.

The central policy-making component of the Justice Department is the Office of the Attorney General. It establishes the guidelines for five key sections:

1) The Office of the Solicitor General, a group of twenty or so lawyers, supervises federal appellate litigation, including that before the Supreme Court;

2) The Office of Legal Policy develops and analyzes a broad range of legal policy initiatives, particularly affecting the administration of justice and the operation of the federal courts;

3) The Office of Legal Counsel is, in essence, Justice's "general counsel," responsible for interpreting federal law and for rendering legal advice to the Attorney General and other Executive agencies on the full range of legal questions;

4) The Office of Legislative Affairs is the liaison between the Justice Department and Congress and, in principle, is responsible for securing congressional enactment of the Department's legislative initiatives; and,

5) The Office of Public Affairs deals with the news media and brings the Department's policy initiatives to the public's attention.

There are also six major litigating divisions — antitrust, criminal, civil, civil rights, land and natural resources, and tax.

THE FIRST TERM EXPERIENCE

The 1980 Republican Platform set out the principal objectives of the Reagan Administration. The goals tasked to the Justice Department included a reduction of crime and drug trafficking; the elimination of quotas in employment and housing; immigration reform; and judicial appointments of those who respect traditional family values. In addition, Justice plays a critical role in promoting and implementing almost all the Administration's policy objectives, be they constitutional issues, federalism as a system of government, or other economic, environmental or regulatory matters.

Personnel

Attorney General William French Smith publicly has championed the objectives of the Reagan Administration. While he has had a personal interest in such notable successes as tougher drug enforcement, other Reagan objectives have not been attained. This is due in part to the Attorney General's failure to gain "hands-on" control of the Department and in part to the personnel and structural problems which have made cohesive policy development difficult. The management problem has been exacerbated by the leadership hiatus caused both by the congressional delay in confirming Edwin Meese as the new Attorney General, and by delays in filling other high posts. Many of Justice's shortcomings are the fault of some of the Attorney General's chief assistants and of the simple fact that most of the Department's staff lawyers do not share, or even are hostile to, the Reagan agenda.

As the Assistant Attorney General for Legislative Affairs, Robert A. McConnell is responsible for formulating and coordinating legislative policy for the Department. He has had a difficult time handling this tough and extremely important task partially attributable to a recalcitrant House Judiciary Committee chaired by Democrat Peter Rodino. Legislative successes, such as congressional enactment of bankruptcy reform, often have occurred, but there have been significant legislative failures.

There was a notable lack of strong support from the Department's legislative team during many of the most vital judicial issues battles central to the Reagan agenda, such as the crime reform package, the proposed constitutional amendments for a balanced budget, or the effort to overturn the *Roe v. Wade* pro-abortion decision, or to permit voluntary school prayer.

The Solicitor General is primarily responsible for representing the legal position of the United States, and thus the Reagan Administration, before the Supreme Court. The Solicitor General's office under the guidance of Rex Lee appears to have had more successes than failures. However, there have been too many instances in which the principles inherent in the Reagan agenda were not argued by the Solicitor General's Office, or were advocated timidly. In some cases, in fact, arguments contradicted the Administration's philosophy. There is concern that some short-term victories were achieved at the expense of laying a more solid foundation upon which future cases could be decided.

According to jurist James McClellan, the Solicitor General has made it clear that he views his role not so much as an advocate of the Administration, but rather as an adjunct of the Supreme Court itself. This deferential attitude has been reflected in many of Lee's briefs and by his failure to file briefs at all in other cases. He has not sought to reverse any prior decisions nor has he directly challenged the validity of the Court's analysis in establishment clause cases. Nor did he dispute the flimsy basis of the *Roe v. Wade* decision in his brief and argument in the *City of Akron* case, which was lost by a 6-3 decision.

Lee seemed at times oddly out of step with the Reagan principles when he took the side of centralized government and opposed federalism in his arguments in *FERC v. Mississippi*, and *EEOC v. Wyoming*. The assault on states' rights and *National League of Cities v. Usery* continues in the brief filed in the important case of *Garcia v. San Antonio Metropolitan Transit Authority*. In another states' rights case, Lee's interpretation of the Eleventh Amendment in *Pennhurst State School and Hospital v. Halderman* was so extreme that it forced Justice Lewis Powell, writing for the majority, to remark that the dissent, echoing Lee's argument, "rests on fiction," "is wrong on the law, and, most important, would emasculate the Eleventh Amendment."

As Assistant Attorney General of the Civil Rights Division, William Bradford Reynolds, and his deputy, Charles J. Cooper, have done an outstanding job to achieve the Reagan goal of pursuing "color blind" policies in enforcing civil rights laws. Reynolds also has pointed out the flaws and dangers in the Civil Rights Act of 1984.

The Justice System Improvement Act Agencies have scored some gains in the last two years. For example, Alfred Regnery, head of the Office of Juvenile Justice and Delinquency Prevention, redirected his office's resources to solve serious problems, such as missing children, crime in the schools, and chronic juvenile offenders. Director Steven R. Schlesinger, of the Bureau of Justice Statistics, has compiled new and very revealing statistical information concerning the criminal justice system that is useful in formulating policy as well as in measuring the policy's success.

Apart from any personnel weaknesses, Justice's structural problems have inhibited cohesive policy development. Aside from the Attorney General or Deputy Attorney General themselves, no officer of the Department has authority for policy development and implementation. Although the Attorney General created an Office of Legal Policy (OLP) shortly after taking office, it has not enjoyed the authority needed to lead on policy issues or to arbitrate policy differences. When the Attorney General personally assumed responsibility for crafting new policies—as he did in the case of immigration reform—the Department's performance has been impressive. However, Justice's top officers cannot neglect their other responsibilities to arbitrate among the competing priorities, claims, and bureaucratic prerogatives of the many components with policy-making authority.

This confusion has been exacerbated because OLP's policy-making prerogatives generally have been confined to only certain areas. Much of the policy-making authority in antitrust, civil rights, criminal law reform, and elsewhere is vested outside of the Office of Legal Policy. Moreover, because there is no clear demarcation of responsibilities, there is often a scramble for authority when new policy initiatives arise. The lesson is that OLP should be abolished and that all policy development be consolidated under one position within the Department.

Crime Reform

Public support for fighting crime is undeniably strong. Opinion polls invariably rank crime right behind economic prosperity as the subject of most concern to the average American. Those on the lower rungs of the economic ladder are hardest hit by crime.

In the closing days of the 98th Congress, significant crime reform legislation was at last enacted. This legislation, originally passed by the Senate as S.1762, was added by the House to the Continuing Resolution and signed into law by the President. The difficult passage of this crime reform package suggests a history of failure at the Justice Department to use its resources effectively, as well as providing a lesson how to succeed legislatively. If this victory had been achieved much earlier, as it could have been, the Justice Department would have been in a position to press its case at the end of the 98th Congress to have the additional crime reform measures enacted, or at least placed that much further ahead on the legislative agenda.

At first the Department had tried to persuade Congress to enact the long pending comprehensive Criminal Code Reform Act. When movement on this seemed unlikely, Justice wisely separated the Code's most controversial sections and introduced a revised crime package. Liberals on the Senate Judiciary Committee, as expected, objected to some of the most important provisions of the new legislation, namely those restoring capital punishment, reforming the exclusionary rule, preventing widespread abuse of habeas corpus, and restructuring the Federal Tort Claims Act. These opponents vowed to strangle the bill by filibustering or by offering numerous amendments.

The Reagan Administration should have taken the offensive at that time. Instead, the Justice Department capitulated and dropped these four important provisions from its crime package. The remaining bill, passed by Congress, was still an improvement over current law in many significant respects, covering the areas of bail reform or preventive detention; sentencing reform; forfeiture of profits from criminal enterprises; insanity defense reform; drug enforcement; and violent crime reforms. The opportunity to fulfill the Reagan mandate on the crime front, however, was substantially and unnecessarily delayed.

Drug Enforcement

One of the Department's successes with respect to its field operations has been the Drug Enforcement Administration's crackdown on illegal drug trafficking. The Attorney General's initiative to maximize the resources of both the FBI and DEA to tackle this problem has been successful for the most part despite certain bureaucratic turf squabbles. One indication of the effectiveness of this program is that the heroin retail price has gone up as the supply has gone down. Nevertheless, more resources and efforts are needed to stem the tide of the importation of drugs, especially from or through Cuba, Nicaragua, and other Latin countries.

Prison Construction

The Administration has funded the largest prison construction project in the history of the federal system. Some 6,000 additional cell beds will be available in the near future.

Pornography

When he signed the Child Protection Act of 1984, President Reagan announced plans for creating a Task Force on Pornography. Despite a promising start, the idea became mired in bureaucratic lethargy. The role of organized crime in pornography as well as its societal impact seems to elude those at Justice who could move more aggressively on this problem.

Smith Guidelines

On March 21, 1983, the Justice Department promulgated the revisions to the Attorney General's Guidelines for Domestic Security Investigations by the FBI—the so-called Levi guidelines. These revisions were needed to enhance the FBI's ability in the areas of foreign counterintelligence and counterterrorist activities. While some civil libertarian groups criticized these changes, the Smith guidelines strike a proper balance between society's duty to protect itself from subversion and the rights of its citizens in a free society. The Administration also proposed its National Security Decision Directive 84 (NSDD-84) to require government officials with access to the highest classified information to have certain of their public writings reviewed for inadvertent disclosure of government secrets. Strong liberal and media opposition forced the Department to withdraw the directive. The directive should be reintroduced.

Civil Rights

For 20 years, the most important battle in the civil rights field has been for control of the language. It is the rhetoric of civil rights that justifiably appeals to Americans' admirable inherent sense of fairness. The battle for the hearts and minds of Americans largely had been won by the time of the passage of the Civil Rights Act of 1964 and the Voting Rights Act of 1965. While later legislation would extend government protection to new areas, such as housing and credit, and new conditions, such as sex, age, and handicap, the basic vocabulary had already been written into law. Americans and their laws oppose "discrimination," "segregation," and "racism"; they favor "equality," "opportunity," and "remedial action." The secret to victory, whether in court or in Congress, has been to control the definition of these terms.

The legislative battles of 1964 and 1965 were won by persuasive arguments that racial justice consists of color-blindness. Race must not be a factor in those political, economic and administrative decisions affecting the most important aspects of an individual's life. Despite these laws, however, color-blindness had been disappearing from civil rights enforcement. Indeed, judicial battles were being won by the argument that racial justice actually consists of race-consciousness—and that the law must favor some races over others. This momentum, however, has been halted by the Reagan Administration's Justice Department. It has returned to the original vision of color-blind justice. Elsewhere in the Reagan Administration, however, officials have undercut this policy. For example, when the Justice Department attacked minority set-asides in public contracts in Miami, Florida, the White House reserved part of the work for minority contractors. When the Justice Department eliminated employment racial quotas in Memphis, the Labor Department required racial "goals" and timetables for public contractors. When the Justice Department succeeded in limiting government regulation of educational programs accepting federal aid, the White House staff went along with Congress in its attempts to legislate further regulation.

Employment

This Administration's greatest victories in the cause of color-blind justice may have come in the field of employment. In the *Stotts* case, involving layoffs of fire-fighters in Memphis, the Supreme Court agreed with Justice that federal courts should be barred from discriminating on the basis of race. The lower courts had held that fire department layoffs should be imposed on a racial basis to preserve the existing ratio of whites to blacks, thereby protecting less senior blacks hired pursuant to a consent decree. The Supreme Court, citing the arguments of the sponsors of the 1964 Civil Rights Act, struck down the layoff quotas and upheld the original system of layoffs based on seniority.

The Civil Rights Division has moved swiftly to apply the nondiscrimination principles of *Stotts* to other employment contexts. The Division takes a broad reading of the decision, concluding no person may be given an advantage over another unless he or she has been proven to be an actual victim of discrimination.

The Department's stance against quotas in any form bumped into a White House strategy to woo minority businessmen. Reacting to criticism of the Department's attacks on minority set-asides in Dade County, the White House press office seemed to undercut Justice by announcing that the Administration favored set-asides in general, and took exception only to unspecified particulars of the Dade County scheme. This endorsement of the principle of racial discrimination further complicated the task of the defenders of the Administration's civil rights policies.

Probably the most significant employment discrimination issue of 1984 was the momentum of the "comparable worth" theory of sex-based pay discrimination. This doctrine would require employers to pay a female-dominated job the same wage as a male-dominated job whenever a "job evaluation study" determined that such jobs are "comparable" in intrinsic value. If enacted into law, this would lead to a flood of litigation, massive wage redistribution, a distortion of free market principles, and ultimately, widespread job dislocation.

The comparable worth movement received dramatic impetus from a 1984 decision by a U.S. District Judge in the case of *AFSCME v. State of Washington*, ordering the state to pay nearly $1 billion to female employees based upon the job evaluations prepared by a consulting firm. The Administration did not participate in the appeal of the decision. Yet there has been forceful Administration opposition to the dangers of comparable worth. It has come from Civil Rights Commission Staff Director Linda Chavez. The Justice Department, on the other hand, has voiced only cautious and low-key opposition to legislative efforts to apply the comparable worth doctrine to federal employment. The fight against comparable worth must become a top priority for the next Administration.

Housing

The fact that quotas can damage minorities has been demonstrated clearly in the area of housing. The complaint filed in 1984 by Justice against the Starrett City housing project in New York City is a step in the right direction and may well determine whether the law guarantees minority access to housing or forces integration by quota. The policy of Starrett City is to maintain racial integration through "controlled tenant selection on the basis of race." In short, the policy establishes a quota. According to press accounts, Starrett City seeks to preserve a ratio of 65 percent whites to 35 percent minorities, even though more minorities desire to rent there.

No other case so starkly presents the potential conflict between forced integration and equal opportunity. Minorities lucky enough to get into Starrett City get the benefits of multi-racial housing. Minorities who would exceed the quota are forced to seek housing elsewhere. Justice quite properly is defending minority rights to equal access to housing, as Congress intended.

Busing

The relentless pursuit of racial quotas has damaged public education enormously. Forced integration through busing for racial balance has accelerated "white flight" from the public schools and diminished public willingness to support those schools. Majorities of both blacks and whites have opposed busing for many years, and a group of black parents recently persuaded a federal judge in Norfolk, Virginia to end the busing of elementary school students. Civil rights groups will appeal the decision, but as columnist William Raspberry, a leading black spokesman, asks, "Isn't it time for those black leaders who care about the education of black children to stop pursuing policies that enhance neither integration nor education?"

The Reagan Administration took office committed to stopping those policies. Although the Supreme court rebuffed the Justice Department's support of a petition for *certiorari* seeking to reduce mandatory busing in Nashville, the Department is continuing its efforts to bring relief to Denver and St. Louis.

The Department's *amicus* brief in the Denver case argued that the role of a federal court is not to produce racial balance, but to remedy the effects of intentionally discriminatory governmental conduct. A court has no authority to engage in an ever-changing, open-ended effort to reconstruct a school system to its own liking. Once the court has devised a plan to remedy past discrimination, a school system's job is to comply with it. After this has been done, the court must release the schools from its grip. This principle of limiting the remedy to the scope of the proven violation also appears in the Department's support for the *certiorari* petition of the State of Missouri from the St. Louis busing settlement.

Justice, nonetheless, must do more to limit busing orders to achieve a favorable landmark decision on busing similar to that of the *Stotts* decision.

Federal Programs

The Department's concern about the over-intrusive reach of federal authority is best reflected by its victory in the *Grove City College* case. The Civil Rights Act of 1964 and the Education Amendments of 1972 prohibit discrimination in programs receiving federal assistance. Over the years, the natural tendency of courts and bureaucracies to expand their jurisdiction led to an attempt to regulate all institutions receiving federal aid. Grove City College, a church school in Pennsylvania, receives no direct federal aid, but does admit students with federal loans and grants. The Supreme Court agreed with Justice that the statutory prohibition against discrimination extended only to programs dealing with student financial aid, and not to other programs of the college.

Overturning this decision and expanding substantially federal interference in state, local and private matters has been the misguided goal of those backing the proposed Civil Rights Act of 1984. This bill has been stalled thanks to objections by Reynolds, Chavez, and the President himself.

Voting Rights

After the Supreme Court had held that plaintiffs challenging the legality of electoral schemes had to prove discriminatory intent, civil rights attorneys asked Congress to eliminate the intent requirement. The Justice Department, however, correctly opposed a test based on discriminatory results and thereby forced a legislative compromise. This seemed to satisfy Justice, but there remain important problems with the judicial interpretation of the Voting Rights Act.

One problem is that the idea of discriminatory results is insufficiently defined in the law to restrain the activist courts. For example, a Texas federal court approved two 40 percent black congressional districts because both were represented by Democrats "sensitive" to minority needs; a Mississippi court, however, struck down an identical plan where a Republican held one of the seats. In most cases, the courts have treated the new statute as a mandate for judicial gerrymandering to insure the election of black politicians.

The Justice Department has supported most of this racial gerrymandering, although it has not intervened against run-off primaries in the South. The Department does not accept the view that every adverse impact on minorities is illegal. However, after rejecting the intent standard, it has yet to develop a rational intermediate standard.

Antitrust

During the Reagan Administration, Justice has repudiated many of the Carter Administration's antitrust policies. The Carter Justice Department, for instance, backed legislative attempts to bar all mergers between large corporations if those combinations involved assets over $100 million, even though the merger would lead to no demonstrable anticompetitive restraints. The effort to prevent, by new legislation, so-called conglomerate mergers was accompanied by a misguided enforcement effort by the Carter Justice Department. The Department also sought to punish businesses criminally for certain vertical distribution practices that were previously believed to be of only marginal concern to federal antitrust enforcers.

In contrast to these policies, the Reagan Justice Department has argued that "bigness is not necessarily badness." It made efforts to ensure that antitrust law enforcement was influenced primarily by economic analysis and not social or political concerns. The Justice Department signaled that it would no longer support legislation prohibiting conglomerate mergers. Instead, Baxter announced that he would revise the Justice Department's Merger Guidelines, published in 1968, with an eye toward permitting greater merger activity. He halted prosecution by the Antitrust Division of "shared monopoly" cases and announced that not only would he not prosecute certain vertical practices criminally, but he would encourage the courts to judge their legality under a less severe test. The drawn-out, complicated and expensive antitrust cases concerning AT&T and IBM (the latter dropped in 1982 after 14 years) demonstrated in part that new enforcement policies were needed to keep pace with technology development. In speeches and congressional testimony, Attorney General Smith and Antitrust Chief Baxter made it clear that big business would no longer unjustifiably be the whipping boy of government officials.

When the first revision of the merger guidelines was issued in June 1982, Smith said that the "new Merger Guidelines should reduce much . . . uncertainty by delineating the general principles and specific standards used by the Antitrust Division" in evaluating mergers. While they lasted, the "Baxter" guidelines were an extremely useful indicator of likely governmental action by which the business community could plan their conduct. Much of this progress was lost, however, when Baxter's successor, J. Paul McGrath, revised the guidelines on June 14, 1984. The McGrath rules restore uncertainty about which mergers will be challenged because they give too much discretion in the Assistant Attorney General for Antitrust to challenge particular mergers.

The McGrath guidelines, moreover, were not needed. The Herfindahl-Hirschman Index thresholds measuring the degree of market control exercised by a firm were not greatly different from the concentration ratios that were used previously by the Department to judge mergers. The Baxter guidelines were gaining the kind of broad acceptance in academic literature that eventually would have made it difficult for future Administrations to discard them. Not only did the 1984 McGrath guidelines make it easier to challenge mergers, but frequent guideline revision has now been established. Why should future Administrations hostile to mergers be bound by the McGrath guidelines when McGrath did not feel constrained by Baxter?

THE NEXT FOUR YEARS

Criminal Justice

While the Comprehensive Crime Control Act (S. 1762) was enacted belatedly, there are a number of other important weapons in the fight against crime that were not but should be enacted:

1) Capital Punishment. One of the satellite bills to S.1762 that was not enacted by Congress would reestablish a constitutional death penalty at the federal level for certain heinous homicides, treasons or espionage cases.

2) Federal Tort Claims Act Reform. This bill would make the United States, rather than individual law enforcement officers, liable for torts stemming from errors and wrongdoing by the government.

3) Habeas Corpus Reform. This bill requires federal courts to give "full and fair" deference to state court judgments and limits the time during which a judgment by a state court may be challenged in federal court.

4) Insanity Defense Reform. S. 1762 merely limits the scope of the insanity defense and shifts the burden of establishing it to the defendant. Previously, the Justice Department had supported a bill repealing the defense altogether except where mental state of the accused was so deranged that he lacked the requisite state of mind for there to be an offense. This position should be reversed to eliminate the defense.

5) Drug Enforcement. More effective coordination of the drug war is still sorely needed. Passage of legislation akin to S. 1787 would at least give the Attorney General the needed, additional leverage to coordinate the various components in the drug enforcement effort, including not only the U.S. Customs Service, the Coast Guard and the Drug Enforcement Agency, but also the Defense Department and the CIA.

Antitrust

The Administration should abolish the treble damages provisions for antitrust violations and adopt the "rule of reason" in assessing damages. Although controversial, this would discourage questionable private antitrust litigation and ensure that any economic injury suffered was compensable. The model for this proposal can be found in the National Cooperative Research Act of 1984, signed into law on October 11, 1984. That law applies the rule of reason test to joint venture technological research and allows only single damages.

The Administration also should continue opposing initiatives to establish a "national industrial policy." While there is little consensus among advocates on the elements of industrial policy, it is clear that it leads to enormous government intrusion into business decision-making.

Attorney Fees Reform

Over 100 vague and sketchy laws permit litigants against the government to be awarded very high legal fees, paid by the taxpayer. Court-awarded fees under these statutes have soared to more than $2.2 million for a single case. Some courts even have used "multipliers" or "bonuses" to double or triple an attorney's customary hourly rate when computing an award. For example, a Harvard law professor recently requested $331,441 in fees at an effective hourly rate of $412.50 for litigating a case in his spare time.

To end this abuse, the Congress passed an amendment to the Comprehensive Crime Control Act to set these hourly rates at $40 and $60 per hour. This reform should be implemented immediately.

Judicial Appointments

The Justice Department plays an important role in screening candidates for federal judgeships and advising the White House on judicial selection. Reagan appointments to the Supreme Court and the Court of Appeals have helped to strengthen conservative legal jurisprudence.

Less encouraging has been the appointment of district judges. These judges form the great majority of all judicial appointments and, because of their enormous equitable powers and fact-finding responsibilities, often dictate the outcome of litigation to a greater extent than the higher courts. The White House must work closely with the Justice Department to appoint conservative judges at the district level, to redress the liberal imbalance.

INITIATIVES FOR 1985

1) Create a chief policymaker.

The next Administration should create a single position, with the rank of Associate Attorney General, responsible for all policy development over the Office of Legal Policy, the Office of Legislative Affairs, and a new office of public information that would be constituted from the personnel and functions of the existing Office of Public Affairs. If the Justice Department is to play a policy-making role, the structural impediments to success must be removed. At the same time, there should be personnel changes to ensure that the Reagan agenda is implemented vigorously rather than timidly.

Criminal Initiatives

2) Seek passage of the companion bills to the Comprehensive Crime Control Act.

3) Seek repeal of provisions of the Gun Control Act of 1968 that make a regulatory nightmare out of the legal ownership of firearms.

The proposed Federal Firearm Owners Protection Act of 1984 which recognizes the merits of lawful self defense, and was approved by the Senate Judiciary Committee, should also be part of the overall crime reform effort.

4) Direct all U.S. Attorneys to seek maximum penalties for violent criminals and those convicted of drug trafficking and dealing.

5) Require U.S. Attorneys to utilize "victim impact statements" to assist the court in sentencing and to provide for victim restitution where appropriate.

6) Reissue the mandate creating the pornography commission so that the Department can focus on prosecutions in this area heavily controlled by organized crime.

Civil Rights Initiatives

7) The* Stotts *decision should be implemented in the Executive Branch and in the courts.

The Labor Department's new discrimination regulations for federal contractors under the Office of Federal Contract Compliance Programs have been held up for four years by the dispute over goals and timetables. After *Stotts,* such disguised quotas should be outlawed and nondiscrimination mandated. Similar reforms should be made in the guidelines of the Equal Employment Opportunity Commission. All federal support for set-aside programs should be ended. The Department should continue its effort to extend the *Stotts* principle to hiring, promotion, and all aspects of the employment relationship.

8) Continue to resist attempts to increase the scope of federal regulation under the guise of civil rights—such as recent congressional moves to pass legislation stemming from the* Grove City *decision.

9) Oppose legislation imposing an "effects test" for housing discrimination.

Such legislation would change the focus from equal access to the forced maintenance of integrated neighborhoods.

10) Adopt a more forceful position in opposing the doctrine of comparable worth in the courts and Congress.

Comparable worth represents another manifestation of the "equality of results" philosophy that distorts the true civil rights principle of equal opportunity. It ignores the myriad of factors that affect wage rules, and would lead inevitably to complete federal—or judicial—control of the labor market.

11) Support the "intent" standard in voting rights cases.

The current confusion in the voting rights cases before the lower courts should persuade the Department that only the "intent" standard is really feasible. The Department at least should extend the principle of avoiding race-conscious remedies in voting rights. The cure for gerrymanders against minorities is not gerrymander against whites; rather, it is the use of neutral criteria like compactness in redistricting remedies.

Immigration Reform

12) Overhaul the INS.

Reform of the immigration laws is a legislative issue that must have a high priority. Unfortunately, the Administration's four year-lobbying effort led by Justice has been massive, but ineffective. Separate from the need for legislative reform, however, lies perhaps the most ailing agency in the government. Study after study shows that the Immigration and Naturalization Service (INS) continues to wallow in its backwater of antiquated managerial practices and hopelessly outdated data storage and retrieval equipment. Thus, the President and new Attorney General must confront and solve the bureaucratic disaster that is the INS.

10

The Department of Labor

by
Steven M. Antosh*

The Department of Labor has the task of enhancing and protecting the position of American wage earners. The Department's activities fall into two major categories: 1) the Department is responsible for affirmative programs that have the stated goal of assisting wage earners through job training and placement services; and 2) the Department administers a myriad of laws that regulate what may be termed as "substantive" labor relations affecting employees. This includes laws regulating wage rates, conditions and hours of work, employee unemployment and disability insurance, and private pension programs.

SECRETARY
Raymond Donovan, 1981-Present

PERSONNEL: 18,968

BUDGET (In Billions of Dollars)

1985 Estimate	$26.7
1984 Estimate	$27.1
1983 Actual	$38.1
1982 Actual	$30.7
1981 Actual	$30.1
1980 Actual	$29.7
1975 Actual	$17.6

Established: 1913

Major Programs:
- Employment & Training Administration
- Employment Standards Administration
- Occupational Safety & Health Administration
- Mine Safety & Health Administration
- Bureau of Labor Statistics

* Task Force members included Michael Avakian, Michael Arif, Edward Hughes, and Dan Heldman.

The National Labor Relations Board (NLRB) is an independent regulatory agency created by and responsible for enforcing the National Labor Relations Act. The NLRB's principal function is to regulate "procedural" labor relations—that is, the process by which employee rights are adjudicated, including unionization and collective bargaining agreements. The Board consists of five members serving five year terms, who hear disputes brought by the General Counsel. The General Counsel and his field personnel of 33 regional directors and their staffs handle all initial phases of labor disputes.

THE FIRST TERM EXPERIENCE

Headed by Secretary Raymond Donovan, the Department of Labor initiated major changes during the Reagan Administration. Among them:

1) Donovan cut Labor's budget—-more than any other cabinet department. One third of the 1981 Reagan budget cuts came from Labor. Its staff was slashed from 23,000 to 18,000 employees.

2) Donovan ended the wasteful and corrupt Comprehensive Employment Training Act (CETA). This was replaced by the Job Training Partnership Act (JTPA), which spends 73 percent of its funds for training, compared to less than 20 percent under CETA. JTPA's reliance on the private sector for job training, and on state and local governments for administration, has cut waste and corruption drastically. The JTPA program budget of $3.6 billion in Fiscal Year 1985 contrasts with CETA's $9.5 billion at its zenith in Fiscal Year 1978.

3) Donovan made drastic improvements at the Occupational Safety and Health Administration (OSHA). Once the bane of employers everywhere, OSHA developed a targeting program for safety inspections that focuses enforcement efforts on high-risk work places with below-average safety records. As a result, the rate of workdays lost due to interruptions actually has declined and small employers are not pestered by OSHA inspectors over trivial and irritating regulations, such as the rule requiring split toilet seats. Furthermore, the agency has secured increased numbers of settlement agreements. In 1980, 22 percent of all OSHA citations were contested. The rate is now down to 3 percent.

The Administration was not equally successful in all its undertakings. Opponents have stalled two of Donovan's most important initiatives to increase employment opportunities.

Donovan proposed a youth employment opportunity wage that would help create jobs among youth under 22 years old by establishing a summer seasonal minimum wage of $2.50 per hour—75 percent of the current adult minimum wage. Legislation for this has been stalled in Congress, even though it has the support of business, economists, youth, and the National Conference of Black Mayors.

Donovan also proposed regulatory changes to legalize home-based businesses in several crafts. This was opposed primarily by organized labor, despite the potential it has for helping female-headed families. A 1984 AT&T study found that 13 percent of the households in the United States conduct some sort of business enterprise from home. Over half of these enterprises provide the principal source of family income. It has been estimated that by 1990 twenty million new jobs could be created in the home computing or "telecommuting" industry alone. This does not even include myriad possibilities of other home-based occupations conducted by the disabled, the elderly, women with infant children, and families in rural communities.

Efforts to legalize "homework" have been stalled by extensive litigation with the International Ladies Garment Workers Union. Meanwhile Senator Orrin Hatch (R-Utah) has proposed legislation to end the government's authority to ban homework. The litigation and the legislation should be pursued vigorously by the next Administration to expand job opportunities for women and the disabled.

The National Labor Relations Board

The Board is charged with enforcing the right of employees in the private sector to refrain from or engage in self-organization, and with policing practices by employers and labor unions that would interfere with these rights. Under Chairman Donald L. Dotson and a Reagan-appointed majority, the Board became the object of great public scrutiny and criticism, primarily from organized labor and the liberal-controlled House of Representatives.

Board decisions have had three major effects:

1) Sensitivity to the fact that labor disputes involve individuals with choices that may not be reflected in the desires of either the union or management. For example, Carter's NLRB decreed that the Conair Corporation had seriously violated the National Labor Relations Act. As punishment, Carter's Board required the company to bargain with the union with which it had a dispute. The result was that innocent workers were forced into union representation because of the alleged misdeeds of their employer. The District of Columbia Court of Appeals subsequently denied enforcement in *Conair*. In contrast to Carter's NLRB, the Dotson Board took the position in the *Gourmet Foods* case that it does not have the authority to issue

"minority bargaining orders" as punishment for employer misconduct.

2) Simplification of the operation of labor relations. It has refused to read into union contracts provisions not obtained in bargaining *(Milwaukee Springs II* and *Otis Elevator II)* or to invent remedies that do not exist in the statute *(Meyers Industry)*—practices regularly indulged in by the Carter Board.

3) A refusal to decide at taxpayer expense minor labor disputes that can be handled through private arbitration *(United Technologies* and *Olin Corporation).* This, combined with the Board's decision not to hear cases unrelated to concerted activity, should help cut the backlog of cases.

The Board has suffered, however, from neglect by the White House. Given the importance of Board appointments, filling vacancies was bound to be controversial. But the Administration has been far too cautious. No successor has been announced for Board member Howard Jenkins, whose term expired August 27, 1983. The Administration's appointment of Rosemary Collyer as General Counsel was announced just two weeks before her predecessor's term ended. The President should exercise his appointment power to keep the Board positions filled with recess or permanent appointments at all times.

The Reagan Administration has moved far ahead of previous administrations in recognizing the rights of individual workers. Conservatives can take encouragement from the appointment of a Secretary of Labor and Chairman of the National Labor Relations Board who have recognized the difference between "labor" and "labor unions."

Unfortunately, sound philosophy and good appointments did not always lead to effective action. Though some progress has been made administratively, there was a serious lack of legislative accomplishment.

In many cases much could have been accomplished even through unsuccessful attempts at legislative initiatives. It is hard to imagine that the AFL-CIO and the NEA could have opposed President Reagan any more vociferously than they did. Yet the Administration gave its supporters few reasons to get involved in legislative battles. There were virtually no votes on labor issues in either House of Congress around which the President's supporters could rally. Moreover, White House inaction was made worse by the activities of Senator Lowell Weicker (R-CT), who delayed or killed every Administration measure before the Senate Labor Committee. If the next Administration is to make any major legislative gains, steps should be taken to secure more supportive Labor Committee membership in the next Congress.

President Reagan proved himself quite proficient in speaking directly to the interests of union members despite the different agenda of the union hierarchy. He must rid his staff of their inordinate fear of union leadership and move ahead forcefully on his program.

THE NEXT FOUR YEARS

Developing a Cohesive National Labor Policy

Perhaps the key Reagan Administration failure was the lack of a genuine national labor policy. No official at the White House seemed to understand labor relations or the need for a cohesive labor policy.

The core of the national labor policy should be the solid commitment that every employee must be allowed to express his or her free choice. From the union perspective, the difficulty with this concept is that employees increasingly have been exercising free choice to decide that they do not want union representation. Although the same rules apply now that applied twenty years ago, and the National Labor Relations Board is holding elections within the same amount of time as before, unions are winning a declining proportion of elections.

The Administration must take seriously the need for a national labor policy that recognizes employee rights.

Promote union responsibility to members: The Administration should protect the rights of those workers who freely choose to join a labor organization. It is time to consider changes to the Landrum-Griffin Act to protect such individual rights. Congress enacted this important piece of legislation twenty-five years ago. It was designed to curb labor union corruption and racketeering by forcing democracy upon the unions. An elaborate framework of union member rights, reports, election rules, and safeguards was installed. Yet union officials have continued to insulate their power from member control. These leaders have been helped by a Labor Department that had abdicated its powers of enforcement.

The next Administration must address this problem. For one thing, the statute needs amending. Congress envisaged that the individual member would act in his own behalf and file lawsuits in federal court to rectify abuses of his rights. However, the Teamster, Mine Worker and Steelworker elections in the past twenty years prove that a lone union member has difficulty taking action either where organized crime is in control of his union or where entrenched union leaders systematically abuse their power. In these cases, the Secretary of Labor must be able to sue union officers to protect the public interest in free unions. This is the very reason why the law was enacted.

Although the Secretary currently cannot protect individual rights, he can and should use his present power of investigation under Section 601 to the fullest extent possible to ensure that union member rights are not violated.

Second, regaining procedural and financial integrity is only part of the problem. The law must also ensure democratic union elections. Recently, in *Local No. 82, Furniture & Piano Movers v. Crowley*, the Supreme Court split the enforcement remedies for Title I (member rights) and Title IV (union election) violations. In *Crowley*, union members who were not permitted to vote for officers in a union election, a clear Title I violation, sued for an injunction. Yet, because the remedy involved setting aside an election the case was thrown out by the Supreme Court, since it constituted a Title IV action that may be brought only by the Secretary of Labor. The particularly frustrating aspect of this decision was that the Labor Department's official position is not to undertake investigation prior to an election, on the ground that it might be deemed undue intervention in internal union affairs.

Even if the Department turns its position around, union members still must be able to bring their Title I suits that affect election activity covered by Title IV. Legislation to reverse the decision in *Crowley* should be introduced.

Anti-racketeering legislation also should be pushed by the next Administration. Recent federal court decisions demonstrate that organized crime still exerts power in many local unions. Legislation against racketeering has passed the Senate (S.336), but it has been blocked in the House. Since this particular bill and its objectives have been endorsed by AFL-CIO President Lane Kirkland, the Administration ought to be able to pressure those House leaders who are keeping this legislation from becoming law. Such a law would bar union officials from specified offices immediately upon conviction. It would extend the period of debarment from five to ten years. These measures are particularly necessary in light of abuses that have surfaced regarding union pension funds. The Labor Department's Inspector General reports that "millions and millions of dollars are being passed through these funds." The documented violations of the Employee Retirement Income Security Act (ERISA) to date are not isolated instances of union misconduct—they represent broad-based practices and involve many unions. American workers deserve well-run pension funds that maximize growth to keep ahead of inflation.

Legitimate questions concerning the use of pension money for promoting private union "social" objectives have also been raised under ERISA. The Department has generally avoided the issue and has ignored its own studies raising serious questions of legality. However, a "socially desirable" investment should be limited not only by the normal standards of responsibility expected of fund managers, but also by whatever investment performance standards a union deems desirable. A judge reviewing a sour financial investment might find it difficult to support an investment chosen solely on distinctions based upon personal political ideology, such as wholesale avoidance of stable defense industries in favor of investment in highly competitive unionized textile companies. The concept of a socially desirable investment should be made illegal under ERISA.

The Department's Labor Management Standards Administration (LMSA) has audited union finances under the reporting provisions of Landrum-Griffin. This is long overdue. In fiscal 1980, there were 212 audits compared to a projected 1,900 audits for 1984. This effort must continue. Union assets belong to members, not to union officials. Prior to 1980, LMSA was severely criticized by the General Accounting Office for failing to audit union financial records as required by law.

Halt compulsory support for the political choices of union leaders: The Helms Amendment to the Federal Election Campaign Act would prohibit the use of compulsory dues for political purposes. The administration should support this strongly.

Stop the coercion of workers: In June 1984, the Administration endorsed Senator Charles Grassley's amendment (S.462) to the Hobbs Act—the federal anti-extortion statute—to prohibit extortionate behavior by unions and employers. This would reverse the Supreme Court's 1973 decision in *United States v. Emmons*, that the Hobbs Act does not outlaw a union's use of violence to achieve its "legitimate" objectives. Protecting the free choices of individual workers demands an atmosphere free from violence and coercion. It must be recognized that violence, including picket line violence, is more of a problem for employees and those desiring to work than for employers. It should be banned. The Department should give this legislation its strong support in the new Congress.

Another major initiative for the next Administration is to use labor policy to promote fairness and efficiency in federal contracts. This would consist of several steps. Among them:

Repeal the Davis-Bacon Act: The Davis-Bacon Act is a 50-year-old law requiring the Department of Labor to pay "prevailing" wages on virtually all federally financed construction projects. Over the years, as the economy and the nature of the construction industry have changed, Davis-Bacon has caused considerable waste in tax resources. The Reagan Administration has been reluctant to request outright repeal of the Act. In 1983, the Administration did revise Davis-Bacon regulations. The changes are the first step towards complete repeal of the Act. While pushing for repeal, the next Administration should concurrently initiate reforms possible within the original intent of the law that would prevent further waste.

A Congressional Budget Office study has concluded that repeal would save taxpayers approximately $1 billion annually, by lowering construction costs for the federal government.

Short of repeal, the Secretary of Labor could save money by allowing government contractors unlimited use of helpers; this could save about $600 million annually; a limited use of two helpers for every three journeymen would result in annual savings in excess of $400 million. Moreover, changing the narrow definition of prevailing wages in a locality to the average wage in the area should save more than $100 million annually.

Raising the statutory threshold at which the Act takes effect would lead to additional savings. For example, raising the threshold contract to $250,000 from its present $2,000 would save more than $230 million annually. Raising it to $1 million would exempt only 15 percent of total federal construction dollars and lift the competitive burden of the Act from small businesses. Raising the threshold also would reduce the costly $100 million paperwork burden on all contractors.

Repeal the Service Contract Act: Another costly governmental intrusion into the free market is the Service Contract Act. It is to the service industry what Davis-Bacon is to construction. Estimates vary on just how much money the government could save if the Service Contract Act were repealed, but General Accounting Office computations estimate annual savings of about $500 million. The purpose of the Act, passed in 1965, was to eliminate wage rates from the competitive bidding process for government contracts. The Service Contract Act requires the payment to service employees of certain minimum wages and fringe benefits on every federal service contract or subcontract in excess of $2,500. Each service employee must be paid not less than the wage rate and fringe benefits prevailing in the locality for similar labor classifications. A service contract for less than $2,500 requires contractor compliance with the Fair Labor Standards Act of 1938.

Congress amended the Act in 1972, adding a new section 4(c)—the successorship clause. This provides that, when one contractor had been subject to a union collective bargaining agreement, a subsequent or successor contractor must pay his employees not less than the wages and fringe benefits paid by the predecessor under that union contract. The successor also must pay any wage and fringe benefit increases included in the former union contract. The successorship provision inflates costs when government work is performed by private firms ("contracting out") because the contractor loses the incentive to hold down labor costs, since the taxpayer absorbs the cost of any wage and benefit package agreed to with the union. Moreover the provision encourages union representation since rejecting collective bargaining would subject employees to pay based on generally lower prevailing wage scales.

The Service Contract Act should be abolished. Until then, however, several modifications could reduce costs to the taxpayer. Among them:

1) the Service Contract Act should be amended to raise the minimum levels for contract coverage from the current $2,500 to $1 million;

2) the Act should be amended to repeal the successor contractor clause, which encourages unionization and cost escalation, and expand the number of job classifications permitted on those contracts.

Eliminate duplicative functions at the OFCCP: Every pay period, businesses with federal contracts must file wage reports with the Office of Federal Contract Compliance Programs. OFCCP is the Department of Labor's version of the Equal Employment Opportunity Commission (EEOC). Its function is to assure, by contractual requirements, that contractors doing business with the federal government do not discriminate in hiring. The EEOC, however, already prohibits such discrimination by any employer with fifteen or more employees. The EEOC coordinates anti-discrimination policies of most federal agencies.

Thus there is an almost total overlap of functions between OFCCP and EEOC. Many contractors must file forms with both agencies. The staff of each agency performs almost identical screening functions seeking out instances of employment discrimination. By abolishing OFCCP and transferring its non-duplicative functions to EEOC, the federal government could save almost the entire OFCCP budget—$48 million in FY 1983.

Promote contracting out of federal services: Significant savings are possible by "contracting out" those federal functions where the government competes with the private sector, or where there exists no justifiable reason for having the function performed by any branch of the federal government. Contracting out means that private firms perform part of the government's work under contract. Maintenance work on a motor pool, for instance, would be undertaken by a local private repair shop, or office cleaning and catering might be provided by outside firms.

The government should contract out non-necessary governmental functions because such contracting out: 1) is more efficient; 2) utilizes specialized skills existing in the marketplace that do not exist in the government; 3) permits work force reduction or expansion necessary to complete the contract; 4) permits quick responses to new and changed needs; 5) permits control of capital outlays—spreading out costs over time at relatively constant and predictable levels; 6) offers a means by which to compare the cost of services; 7) reduces the dependence on monopoly suppliers to the government and so reduces the public's exposure to crippling strikes and slowdowns; 8) reduces the size of the government; 9) spurs competition; and 10) widens the tax base.

The Reagan Administration took a step toward contracting out when it updated Office of Management and Budget Circular A-76. Its numerous exceptions, however, make it unworkable. The circular, in theory, requires federal departments to compare the cost of providing a commercial good or service "in house" with bids by private companies. The agency must choose the less expensive alternative.

A 1984 study of contracting out, conducted by the Office of Management and Budget, reveals that despite the deficiencies of A-76, considerable savings have been achieved in many agencies. On average, agencies have cut costs by 20 percent when commercial services have been privatized in this way, leading to potential savings of over $1 billion a year by 1988. Even the threat of contracting out has encouraged in-house work to become more efficient.

Many federal activities have been contracted out through the program. The submarine base at Bangor, Maine, for instance, awarded a $36 million contract to private firms for grounds maintenance, trash collecting, mail services, photographic services and several other functions, with significant savings in operating costs. In 1983 the National Oceanic and Atmospheric Administration decided to hire a private firm to store and distribute charts. The fee was $1 million—less than half the cost of doing the job in house. Other jobs contracted out include vehicle maintenance, data processing, janitorial services and catering services.

The issues involved in the 1981 Professional Air Traffic Controller Organization (PATCO) strike illustrate the merits of contracting out. PATCO gave Washington long and convincing notice that a strike was inevitable. A private company would not have ignored such an alert. Yet absolutely nothing was done to prepare for or to prevent the walkout. A private sector contractor would have been prepared, otherwise he would simply lose the contract and be replaced.

Although Circular A-76 now mandates contracting out as the general rule, it bars the competitive practice from activities with ten or fewer employees, where the savings from private provision are less than ten percent, for certain work of the Department of Defense, or where no "meaningful" private sector competition is available. Unfortunately the exceptions have become the rule.

Reform at the National Labor Relations Board

Amend the Board's Jurisdictional Standards: The U.S. Supreme Court has declared that, in passing the Wagner Act, Congress intentionally gave the NLRB the fullest jurisdictional breadth constitutionally permissible. Congress left to the Board the authority to ascertain whether certain labor practices or representation questions would, in particular situations, adversely affect commerce.

In this regard, the Board adopted a $500,000 figure for retail industries and a $50,000 figure for non-retail industries as jurisdictional thresholds. Presumably these dollar volume benchmarks were intended to change as inflation either increased or decreased. In the Landrum-Griffin Act of 1959, Congress enacted section 14(c) of the National Labor Relations Act. That section affirmed the authority of the Board to decline to act in specific labor disputes and representation matters when it deemed their impact on commerce to be insufficient. At the same time, however, Congress specifically prohibited the Board from declining jurisdiction over firms that met its discretionary jurisdictional requirements at the time of enactment. In other words, these requirements became a minimum that the Board could not later alter.

Since the Landrum-Griffin Act, the consumer price index (CPI) has risen nearly 250 percent. This has expanded Board jurisdiction in the retail sector alone by an extra 15 percent. Ensnared within the Board's spreading authority are many small businesses. In 1970 and 1974, Congress gave the Board new jurisdiction over approximately 660,000 postal workers and thousands of employees of nonprofit hospitals. Add to this the fact that the Board has asserted jurisdiction in such new areas as religious secondary schools and proprietary hospitals and the result has been a skyrocketing caseload.

The next Administration should press for Amendments to section 14(c) of the Landrum-Griffin Act. Specifically, Congress should allow the Board to raise its thirty-year-old jurisdictional dollar standard to account for inflation. In the retail industry, this would set the jurisdictional floor in 1984 at an annual sales level of about $2,000,000. Drawing from the lessons of the Small Business Act and the Equal Employment Opportunity Act, the legislation should also preclude Board jurisdiction over firms with fourteen or fewer employees.

Reform the NLRB Office of the General Counsel: The Taft-Hartley

Act created an independent Office of the General Counsel to investigate charges, issue complaints, and prosecute such complaints before the Board. As such, the Counsel has plenary authority for all labor litigation from initiation to final resolution before the Board itself. If the General Counsel interprets cases differently from the Board, he can blunt policy changes by controlling the acceptance of cases. Since the General Counsel's term is not coincident with presidential terms, the Counsel can be politically and ideologically opposed to an Administration. This was the case until April 1984 when the term of the Carter-appointed General Counsel finally expired.

Two changes could reduce the possibility of conflict between the General Counsel and the Board.

First, the Advice Division in the General Counsel's office should be abolished. This Division writes memos to the field staff "explaining" Board decisions on questions of law. The NLRB regional offices have enough attorneys of their own to do the same job. They should simply read Board opinions and act. This would lessen the possibility of the kind of confusion that occurred in *Milwaukee Springs II* where the Board refused to imply anti-plant closing provisions into collective bargaining agreements.

Abolishing the Advice Division would reduce substantially the time needed to obtain regional action on unfair labor practice complaints, since it now takes at least six to eight weeks to get a decision from the Advice Division. In this time, the Board's ability to act may become moot if the situation is urgent, such as in the case of Section 10(j) and Section 10(l) injunctions.

Second, the Enforcement Litigation Division should be put under the authority of the Board, rather than the General Counsel. Currently the General Counsel has dual and contradictory roles. He must serve as an advocate in cases he has selected to bring before the Board while also serving as the Board's attorney in cases brought to the U.S. Court of Appeals for review or enforcement of Board orders, even in cases where the Board has overruled the General Counsel's earlier position. The Board itself should control the attorneys who defend the Board's decision on appeal. This process has already begun at the Board and should be fully implemented.

The Board's staff must be responsive to Board decisions. Of prime importance are the 33 Regional Directors. Many of them have shown great independence from the Board's direction. These posts should be transformed from career civil service positions into political appointees or non-career Senior Executive Service positions serving at the Board's pleasure. Currently, the General Counsel's office has only one such position. This is insufficient to ensure that the NLRB field staff (now more than 3,000) reflects the Board's policies.

The General Counsel should instruct the Director of Personnel to advertise and recruit more positions from outside the agency. This will bring into government service more people with "hands on" experience in labor relations. The General Counsel's office has become virtually a closed shop—-hiring few people from outside the agency or even the region in which a vacancy occurs.

INITIATIVES FOR 1985

1) Appoint a White House staff member with a technical understanding of labor issues to coordinate labor policy and agency appointments.

2) Replace OMB Circular A-76 with instructions more favorable to contracting out of federal services.

3) Issue regulations repealing all prohibitions of home-based enterprises.

4) Step up audits of union finances by the Labor Management Standards Administration.

5) Issue regulations clarifying that the only acceptable criteria for pension fund investment are safety and return on investment.

6) Extend regulations permitting more job classifications on contracts involving the Service Contract Act.

7) Extend regulations permitting helpers on contracts involving the Davis-Bacon Act.

8) Step up Section 601 investigations of union election activity under the Landrum-Griffin Act.

9) Abolish the Advice Division of the General Counsel's office of the National Labor Relations Board, and transfer these functions to the NLRB Solicitor.

10) Pass the Youth Employment Opportunity Wage.

11) Amend the Hobbs Act to make union and corporate extortion a crime.

12) Pass anti-racketeering legislation (S. 336).

13) Introduce, endorse, and secure up-or-down votes to force debate on amending the Landrum-Griffin Act, to give the Secretary of Labor the concurrent power to enforce Title I rights.

14) Amend the Federal Election Campaign act to prohibit the use of union dues for political purposes.

15) Repeal the Service Contract and the Davis-Bacon Acts.

11

The Department of Transportation

by
Fred L. Smith, Jr.*

The Department of Transportation (DOT) is organized into agencies dealing with each form of transport. These agencies finance and oversee to various degrees all aspects of the U.S. transportation system. The highway system is managed by the Federal Highway Administration (FHWA), the airport and airway system by the Federal Aviation Administration (FAA), the passenger and freight rail system by the Federal Railroad Administration (FRA) and mass transit activities by the Urban Mass Transportation Administration

SECRETARIES
Andrew Lewis, 1981-Feb. 1983
Elizabeth Dole, Feb. 1983-Present

PERSONNEL: 61,752

BUDGET (In Billions of Dollars)

1985 Estimate	$26.6
1984 Estimate	$25.3
1983 Actual	$20.6
1982 Actual	$19.9
1981 Actual	$22.5
1980 Actual	$18.9
1975 Actual	$ 9.7

Established: 1966

Major Programs:
- Federal Highway Administration
- Federal Railroad Administration
- Urban Mass Transportation Administration
- Federal Aviation Administration
- Coast Guard

* Task Force members included Frank Wilner, Gabriel Roth, Stan Sender, George Aste, Al Pisarski, and Robert Okun.

(UMTA). Ports and waterways and the shipping industry are dealt with by the U.S. Army Corps of Engineers and the Department of Transportation's Maritime Administration (MARAD). DOT recently gained a role in space transportation in its Office of Space Commercialization.

Transportation also is influenced by a number of non-DOT federal regulatory agencies. These include the Interstate Commerce Commission (ICC), with regulatory powers over most surface transportation; the Federal Maritime Commission (FMC) for ocean shipping; the Civil Aeronautics Board (CAB)—due to go out of existence December 31, 1984—for airlines; and the National Transportation Safety Board (NTSB) for transportation related safety matters. The Department of Justice and the Federal Trade Commission, meanwhile, share in administering the antitrust regulations that play a significant role in transportation.

THE FIRST TERM EXPERIENCE

The Reagan Administration has espoused a pro-market transportation policy. For example, the FY 1983 federal budget states that the Administration will place "... maximum reliance on the private sector and, secondarily, on state and local governments." This implies that many federal transportation activities should be transferred to the private sector and other responsibilities to state or even local control. Carrying out such a policy would reverse a two century pattern of growing federal control over transportation. The federal government now provides some transportation services directly, finances to some degree almost all transportation activities, regulates to some extent almost every aspect of transportation, and blocks the evolution of private sector alternatives by managing collectively resources that could and should be privatized.

The market-oriented restructuring of national transportation policy planned by the Reagan Administration would have had the government establish the institutional framework—property rights and liability rules—but would have eliminated the top-down, hands-on centralized planning approach ingrained in the current system. The time was ripe in 1981 for such restructuring. The problem of making government work had brought many policymakers to reconsider whether the mere existence of public goods and natural monopolies really justifies a major governmental role—and if so, whether that role need be federal.

Practical politics also made the timing right. The interstate highway system, the largest DOT budget item, was nearing completion;

Congress had already proposed defederalizing the nation's airports; national discontent with federal preemption of state highway policies (the 55 mph speed limit, for example) was growing; transportation deregulation was moving apace; support for transportation user fees was increasing; and mounting labor unrest provided the opportunity to privatize the nation's air traffic control system. On all fronts, the time seemed appropriate for a major restructuring of national transportation policy.

Initially, the Administration did promote elements of a pro-market program. The Corps of Engineers, for instance, led Administration efforts to enact a cost-based user fee system to finance the nation's inland waterways and ports. The Administration also, as part of its New Federalism initiative, proposed to transfer about half of all federal highway management responsibilities to the states. Unfortunately, these actions were the exceptions.

By the end of its second year, however, a business-as-usual attitude had reconquered DOT. The agency's budget was up by over 40 percent, financed by sharply higher fuel and other excise taxes—deceptively labelled as "user taxes." This legislation also required highway users to subsidize mass transit systems (one cent of the five cents per gallon gas tax hike was dedicated to mass transit) and this weakened the wise policy that all user groups should pay their own way. DOT budget growth outpaced state and local transportation spending and led to further federalization of the nation's transportation system. The new Chairman of the Interstate Commerce Commission adopted a go-slow approach on deregulation; while the Administration, by forcing all states to raise their drinking ages, further abandoned its federalist principles.

Rhetorically, the Administration continues to support free-enterprise transportation policies. In practice, it has surrendered to the traditional belief that all roads start and end in Washington. Reagan's senior transportation officials, like most of their predecessors, seem to believe that the primary role of the private sector is to pay taxes and obey regulations; while that of the states and localities is to implement federal policies.

The Administration's failures reflect a lack of preparation, planning, and purpose. Those charged with transportation policy had no vision of a defederalized, market-oriented transportation policy. Thus, they were easily caught up and swept along by events. Having no plans of their own, in each crisis they were vulnerable to the traditional nostrums of increasing federal transportation spending, expanding regulations, and further centralizing the system.

The management and leadership skills of these officials are not at issue. Indeed, they have been extremely effective in dealing with

Congress and conducting campaigns to win enactment of their policies. Unfortunately, they also have sold the policies of Congress to the Administration, rather than the Administration's policies to America.

Charting a new course will be difficult. Existing policies enjoy vested constituencies that have a long history of working closely with the DOT and congressional committees. These groups predictably will resist change. To implement the Reagan agenda, new coalitions and new alliances must be forged.

The time is ripe for a redesign of the political landscape. Most Americans would benefit from transportation privatization, defederalization, or deregulation. Moreover, most Americans are discontented with excessive federal rules and regulations. Yet, this majority remains unorganized, unlike the champions of the status quo. New political alignments rarely occur spontaneously; leadership and work will be required to organize the general public to support transportation policy reform.

THE NEXT FOUR YEARS

The federal government has played an increasingly significant role in the overall financing and management of transportation infrastructure. The rationale for this involvement owes more to history than to logic. Private firm "bail-outs," national defense, traditional pork barrel politics and bureaucratic concern over the growth of toll roads all led to an expanded federal role.

The net result is that DOT has become the manager of one of the world's largest enterprises—the U.S. transportation infrastructure. This infrastructure is worth hundreds of billions of dollars and rivals the assets owned by the governments of some of the largest socialist nations in the world. And like any socialist manager, the DOT bureaucrats face two extremely difficult problems: how to invest in new plant and equipment, and then how to manage that plant. In the absence of the information provided by a market, their decisions are made politically.

As Adam Smith noted long ago, political decisions often seem to result in the construction of roads that go nowhere. Experience validates this observation. The government land grants to the railroads encouraged over-investment in Western railroads in the nineteenth century, and under-utilized waterway, port and airport facilities in the decades since. More recently, the federal government has expanded urban mass transit massively with little attention to the formal cost benefit analyses that supposedly discipline such investments. The absence of a profit and loss test creates a vacuum into which politics moves, and politics is concerned with granting favors—not achieving efficiencies.

Government does little better as a manager. Efforts to price transportation services via user fees have been tried in very few cases, and have been disappointing even then. The lack of a market forces an agency to rely on an analytic exercise to determine "fair," "equitable," and "reasonable" prices. Although this employs many economists for years, there is little evidence that they have improved transportation efficiency.

There are many reasons why administrative efforts to set prices are unlikely to work. One main reason is that many costs in transportation systems are shared costs, joint costs, and so forth. Any allocation of these costs is arbitrary. Lacking a defensible and objective allocation procedure, the agency must assign such costs on political grounds. Thus, politics will always play a key role in pricing government-supplied services. Even when analysis demonstrates that a specific user group imposes greater costs and thus should pay more for the facility, the results are all too likely to be ignored in the political decision process. For example, numerous federal and highway cost allocation studies have found that heavily loaded trucks are the major cause of avoidable highway deterioration. These results suggest that trucks should pay some form of damage-related weight-distance charge. Nonetheless, no such charge has ever been levied at the federal level and only a handful of states employ such fees.

Highways and Bridges

A well-orchestrated program to persuade Americans that their highway system was collapsing—and needed expensive repair—gained much attention. This effort was conducted by the construction industry and its public works allies. It was intended to convince the media and the politicians that America's roads were falling apart and taxes must be raised immediately to fix them. In fact, there was little overall data on road quality. The most comprehensive data source—that collected by the Federal Highway Administration (FHWA) of DOT—suggested a system gradually maturing, experiencing no overall deterioration and certainly not in danger of imminent collapse.

DOT leadership unfortunately ignored its own findings and led the charge to impose higher fuel taxes and expand the federal transportation role. Thus the Surface Transportation Assistance Act of 1982 was enacted. That bill raised the federal gasoline tax by five cents and increased the DOT budget by $5 billion annually.

Money, however, is not the solution to the highway problem. To be sure, the highway system does face serious problems. These problems have little to do with the amounts being spent and much to do with how the road system is managed. With the notable exception of private and toll road segments, the U.S. highway system is not managed in any coherent fashion. Investment decisions reflect the availability of funds and the disparate objectives of federal, state and local authorities, while operating decisions reflect centralized regulatory policies. There is little reliance on pricing to ensure that users consider the consequences of the services they consume—again with the exception of toll facilities. Although users pay various "user taxes," these have no relation to the costs of road use and have no positive incentive value. Current federal policies provide neither road managers nor users with adequate incentives to improve the productivity of the road system.

The federal government's ability to encourage efficient road use by pricing policies is limited. There are only two types of costs that might be reduced by changes in highway use: those associated with congestion and those associated with road damage. Congestion costs are low for most roads at most times. As a result, only systems of pricing that vary with the time and place of use can influence users to consider these costs. Reducing the efficiency losses associated with congestion would require greater reliance on local-level fees or tolls. Federal policies, however, discourage such pricing experiments.

Charging tolls is prohibited on any federally financed highway and discouraged on any federally funded bridge or tunnel. Thus, the public policy laboratories of America—the state and local governments—have had little opportunity to explore road pricing. Instead, road authorities have relied upon regulation and capacity expansion to "manage" rush-hour traffic. For example, many jurisdictions restrict road use during rush-hour on special HOV (high occupancy vehicle) lanes. However, there has been little experimentation with pricing policies.

More experimentation is needed. Current policies should be revised to encourage localities to test alternative ways of making more efficient use of the current highway system. Environmental and other factors ensure that expansion of existing capacity will be extremely difficult; this makes progress on the management front extremely important. Pricing is the most attractive method that has not yet been tried.

Road damage, the second type of avoidable cost, is overwhelmingly caused by heavily loaded axles. To take account of this, some form of damage-based distance charge is needed to encourage truckers to consider such alternatives as more lightly loaded vehicles or rigs with a larger number of axles. The appropriate per mile charge might well vary widely because of many factors, such as the weather and the road design. These variations suggest again the superiority of regional or segment-specific fees over federal uniform taxes.

Another type of problem arises from the fragmentation of management responsibilities and the perversities of current highway aid formulas. The federal government raises somewhat more than 25 percent of all highway revenues and then disburses these funds to the states and localities by politically determined distribution formulas. Current federal aid formulas also favor construction or major reconstruction over maintenance. As a result, the road authority is encouraged first to overdesign the road, to take advantage of the "cheap" federal funds, and then to under-maintain the road to advance the date when "cheap" reconstruction financing will become available. Under the current federal aid formulas, the road authorities have little incentive to consider more efficient lifetime highway maintenance policies. Indeed, given the current financing policies make efficient road management irrational.

Another series of problems arises because of the growing tendency of Congress to impose requirements in all federal legislation that funds be spent in specified ways. Examples include minority hiring requirements and labor-preference legislation. These cross-cutting requirements raise the price of federally funded programs, but have little to do with transportation.

Cross-cutting requirements conflict with the American system of federalism. If the federal government is to play a limited role in the transportation area, it should allow states and localities discretion in using the funds—which, after all, are largely paid by users in their jurisdictions. This argues for making all cross-cutting requirements conditional on funding. That is, Congress might recommend various policies, but these would not become mandatory unless Congress appropriated the funds necessary for their implementation.

More generally, highway management would be improved if financial and management responsibility were assigned to the same level of government or private organization, and roads were managed on a segment-specific basis. That suggests private or toll management would be preferable to government operation, and state and local management superior to federal management.

The current highway legislation expires in 1986, so the new Administration will have the opportunity to reconsider highway policy. In doing so it should:

1) Encourage Toll/Private Roads.

Current laws exempt fuel consumed on private roads from taxation, but collect the fuel tax from all toll facility users, even when those tolled segments receive no federal aid. The Administration should eliminate or reduce the exemption and make any provider of road services—private or government—eligible for a pro-rata share of the highway taxes paid by its customers. This would eliminate the current bias against private and toll roads and do much to encourage further pricing and management experimentation.

2) Reduce Barriers to Charging Tolls.

As an interim step, consideration should be given to extending to all highways the funding flexibility afforded bridges, tunnels, and approaches. The latter can receive federal funds while still relying on tolls. Even for these facilities, however, current legislation requires that a facility receiving federal funding discontinue its tolls as soon as its initial bond is paid. Given the need for maintenance, reconstruction, and congestion pricing on such facilities, this policy makes no sense. All restrictions to a more extensive use of tolls should be eliminated.

3) Disentangle Management Responsibilities.

The Administration should propose legislation to assign sole financial and management responsibility for each portion of the nation's highway system to some specific level of government. The New Federalism initiative was a step in this direction. That program failed in part because the Administration was trying to force local governments to take over the least attractive components of the system, and to do so without any federal transfer of taxing authority. The Administration should renew its efforts, this time lowering the federal gasoline tax, to provide state and local governments the option of raising their own fuel taxes. The Administration also should consider a one-time transfer payment to groups accepting facilities not expected to generate revenue adequate for self-financing.

4) Place Tolls on Interstate Highways.

The interstate highway system—particularly the inter-city links—should be considered a possible candidate for imposition of tolls. The system is particularly valuable to commercial trucking. This industry could improve productivity significantly if it could employ larger rigs on the roads. Of course, these would cause more traffic congestion and interference, and inflict greater damage. To compensate for this, the interstate system—or part of it—could be designated a National Truck Highway System. Commercial vehicles using this system might be required to install special meters and pay a rate based on their loadings, mileage and axle configuration. Automobiles and light vehicles might be exempted from the toll or be required to purchase a special medallion.

Oregon is now exploring the use of a remote metering device that could be used to bill commercial vehicles for highway travel. Such devices reduce the delays and administrative costs associated with conventional tolling.

5) Declare the Interstate Highway System Complete.

The interstate highway system long has been "nearly" complete. However, the current aid formulas encourage states to hold back on final completion since every state that has not completed its interstate work is entitled to at least one-half percent of all revenues distributed under this program. There is little of the Interstate yet to complete, and even less that is worth completing. Recent Congressional Budget Office studies suggest that as much as 70 percent of the uncompleted portion of the interstate system has no national significance. Such roads are better left to local discretion and funding.

Airports and Airways

The Administration has done little to introduce market-oriented programs into the federal airways and airport program. The Federal Aviation Administration (FAA) finances all civilian air traffic control (ATC) services and employs most air traffic controllers directly. The FAA also finances a portion of airport construction via the Airport Improvement Program. These programs are financed from the Airport and Airways Trust Fund, which receives the 8 percent ticket tax on commercial airline tickets and a fuel tax on non-commercial aviation fuel.

The air travel system has three components: the airliner, the airspace management system, and the airport. Only the first of these is managed by the private sector. Federal control of key elements of air travel has become an important problem of its own. Firms always have been free to purchase airplanes, and under deregulation they are free to fly wherever they wish. However, that freedom is severely limited by the availability of landing slots, determined by the FAA, and ground capacity assessed by local airport managers.

In the current system, the airlines cannot directly invest their resources to expand capacity in either of these areas. Airspace and airport investment and operating decisions are resolved outside the market—largely on political grounds. The deregulation of the airlines has made the rigidities in the remainder of the system far more obvious. Deregulation has led to major changes in the way airlines do business. Airlines have sought to discount fares and this has led them to seek cost savings. One major trend occasioned by this has been a move away from direct flights and toward a hub-and-spoke distribution system. Passengers are picked up from a number of airports, brought to a "hub" for that airline, and then transported to their final destinations. That system offers great efficiencies, but places far greater stress on the air traffic and airport capacity. And since these two portions of the air transportation system remain outside the market system, the change in airline operations has not brought about a corresponding redeployment of resources. In particular, the FAA cannot readily reassign its controllers to reflect changing demand patterns and this rigidity is largely responsible for the growing significance of flight delays.

Unfortunately, many have assumed these problems reflect a failure of airline deregulation. In fact, air traffic delays reflect both inadequate capacity and inefficient federal management. They are unlikely to be resolved as long as the air travel business continues to change in response to consumer demand. The FAA and, to a lesser extent, the local airport managers are largely outside the market system. They have little incentive to act upon these demands, since airlines cannot simply purchase additional airport or airspace capacity.

The Air Traffic Control System

The federal role in air traffic control is unusual, made familiar only by its long duration. Local or toll authorities manage traffic on the nation's highways. The rail industry controls its own traffic flows, even though the rail grid includes many grade crossings that involve important international safety issues.

Public management of the air traffic control system has led to serious lags in introducing safety and cost-reduction technologies. Airspace users have had great difficulty in planning for change. Decisions on expansion, resource deployment and operating policies all are subject to political debate. Further, the monopolization of the ATC system by the FAA reduces the information needed to determine optimal investment and operating decisions. Finally, FAA operates under civil service regulations, which provide management little flexibility to reward good and to penalize poor performance. The 1981 controllers' strike, and the labor problems now reemerging, are merely symptoms of these inherent problems.

Private operation of the air traffic control system would resolve many of these problems. Although air traffic control typically has been subject to government oversight, several European nations contract out all or part of their system to private firms. In fact, the existing policy of the Office of Management and Budget (specifically the productivity comparison requirement of OMB Circular A-76) would require the FAA to contract out existing ATC centers whenever the private sector might perform these functions more efficiently. Since the data suggest that this will be the rule, the FAA should consider transferring the entire ATC activity to the private sector.

Since the experience of many small U.S. airports and foreign countries has been so successful, OMB should push for an expansion of the contracting-out program. An active demonstration program would provide important information on the value of privatization and could encourage communities now lacking ATC facilities to petition FAA to expand the program still further. It is important, moreover, to develop comparable experience with major air traffic control. A large enroute or regional control center should be selected for this demonstration effort. The DOT should submit a report detailing how the ATC system might be privatized and what legislative and administrative changes would be necessary to achieve that result.

To facilitate such a changeover, the Administration should modify the current financing arrangements for air traffic control. The FAA's computerization of its overall operation should allow individual aircraft to be billed according to their use of the system. The ability to price usage on such a time/route basis would allow more precise pricing policies, which might improve system efficiency. As such pricing policies are introduced, the existing ticket and fuel taxes should be reduced.

The Landing Slot Issue

The problems of the ATC system were highlighted by the Professional Air Traffic Controllers' strike and the FAA "solution" to that crisis. After the 1981 strike, the FAA shifted from its earlier policy of simply controlling landings to a "flow control" policy. Under flow control, an airplane departing from, say, Philadelphia and scheduled to arrive at Atlanta at a certain time must possess a landing slot authorizing such a landing. This has made slots at congested airports extremely valuable. Even if the aircraft has a slot, it will not be allowed to depart until calculations indicate that it will be able to proceed to a direct landing. FAA believes that the inexperience of its workforce prevents the former "stacking" procedures which allowed airplanes to circle in holding patterns if there was congestion at their destination airport.

The flow control concept creates problems. Delays encountered anywhere in the system require aircraft throughout the nation to defer departure until the system "catches up." The ban on stacking means that the system will not be able to take advantage of last-minute breaks in traffic. An efficient system would probably require buffer capacity at several points in the system.

Landing slot restrictions also threaten to restrict competition. The Civil Aeronautics Board (CAB) limited the number of airlines allowed to compete along any specific route. However, the same effect would be achieved by an FAA-imposed limitation on the number of slots.

The privatization of the ATC system would ensure that slot capacity was adjusted rationally. This process might occur by establishing regional corporations to take over existing airspace management in each congested airspace region. These Airspace Management Corporations would examine the available capacity and determine what fraction of that capacity could be marketed—capacity would be retained by the management group to handle nonscheduled airlines, general aviation, and emergencies. The marketable airspace would be auctioned to commercial airlines on a competitive basis. The funds made available could be devoted to expanding capacity. Pending that resolution, however, the FAA should allow the existing slots to be used as efficiently as possible. For a brief period in 1983, the FAA did allow the slots for landing at Washington's National Airport to be traded. This demonstrated the practicality of slot markets. Since then however, the FAA has blocked market allocation of slots. The FAA again should allow the sale of all slots in the nation.

Federal Role In Airport Management

The federal government has played a significant role in constructing airports. Federal funds have financed from 30 to 40 percent of airport construction costs. Airports finance other costs through landing fees and rents on their facilities. Privatization and defederalization promise increased efficiency in this element of the air transportation system. Moreover, current federal policies limit the options available to airport managers to deal with congestion. Congestion is the result of excessive peak period demand, but airport managers are discouraged under current FAA policy from imposing fees that might encourage off-peak usage.

These restrictions limit the ability of the airport manager to manage airport demand through pricing. "Head" taxes or other passenger facility fees would help manage capacity problems. Landing fees reflecting opportunity cost and pavement damage would encourage airlines to adjust their scheduling and choice of equipment, employ less-used airports, and would enable airport managers to calculate the commercial value of new capacity.

Most experts believe that environmental and other concerns will limit airport expansion for the remainder of this century. It is critical that means be found to do more with the existing facilities. A recent Congressional Budget Office study found that pricing policies could improve significantly the utilization of existing facilities. Simply imposing peak-period fees on general aviation aircraft (that is, small private airplanes) might extend the capacity life-span of many airports by three to five years. The charges need not be large; relatively minor charges on general aviation aircraft (which are primarily business aircraft) at New York's LaGuardia Airport resulted in major shifts in usage.

There is a significant lack of private sector experience in managing large airports. A first step towards acquiring such experience would be for the federal government to privatize the two facilities it now operates in the Washington area: National Airport and Dulles International Airport. These airports should be auctioned to the highest bidder and allowed maximum flexibility to solicit business. A commission recently has been established to review the status of these airports; the Administration should encourage the commission to explore privatization.

At the very minimum, the Administration should reintroduce a defederalization proposal to transfer all major airports to local control, and reduce the current ticket and fuel tax accordingly. A portion of the funds now in the airport trust fund should be made available to those airports willing to leave the federal system.

National Waterway Policies

Waterways and ports long have been a favored area for government spending, while subsidies for ship building have almost as long a record. In the infrastructure area, the Reagan Administration initially proposed that the operating and investment costs of each facility be financed by its users. But the White House quickly retreated. The full-cost requirement was reduced under pressure from the waterway interests, while the requirement that operating costs be recovered on a facility-specific basis was dropped in favor of a system-wide uniform fee recovery program.

Even these partial steps are worthwhile. Waterway users could be expected to recognize the cross-subsidy implications of any uniform pricing policy. Users of low-cost waterways can be expected to protest the "unfair" charges they must pay to subsidize users navigating high-cost segments. Thus a move toward full cost recovery might undermine the political unity of the waterway users and allow further steps to rationalize the system.

The Administration should continue insisting that all use-related costs of waterway construction, maintenance, and operation be paid by users. Ideally, each user group should pay its specific costs.

Even crude pricing rules, however, will be subject to intense political attack. Consequently, waterways may be an ideal candidate for a quasi-privatization strategy. Users should be encouraged to form Cooperative Management Associations that would work with the Corps of Engineers to maintain, operate, and finance specific facilities. As users assume the financial burdens, it is appropriate that they be given such management responsibilities. Moreover, under such a system, users are more likely to support efforts to improve the productivity of the waterway system. Guidelines to encourage such cooperative efforts should be developed.

Railroads

Federal intervention in the railroad sector has emphasized regulation. Since the creation of the Interstate Commerce Commission (ICC) in 1887, government has sought to manage the industry for what it has believed is the "public good". In fact, ICC regulation has harmed the consumer by limiting competition. ICC rate enforcement stabilized cartels, which allowed the industry to raise prices and increase its profits. This pro-industry bias, however, gradually eroded as the ICC began to use its powers to grant favors to specific communities, to shippers, and to labor. The ICC made it increasingly difficult for a railroad to abandon non-economic routes and to achieve productivity improvements. In the early days, the rail industry accepted these constraints and relied on its dominant position in freight and passenger competition to maintain its profitability. The costs of the ICC-mandated inefficiencies could and were passed along to the customers. As long as the railroads dominated freight and passenger transportation, this option was possible. But eventually, highway transportation and air service eliminated rail's competitive advantage in the passenger area, while truck, waterway, and pipeline transportation gradually eroded railroads' competitive advantages in hauling freight.

Passenger Rail

Congress nationalized rail passenger service in 1971 to "save" the service. The Amtrak legislation included significant subsidies to modernize the system and make passenger rail once again competitive. Congress provided funds to upgrade selected track mileage, as in the Northeast Corridor project, and operating subsidies to maintain ridership until these improvements had achieved their impact.

Congressional pressures and good management have encouraged productivity improvements in Amtrak. Both labor and management are aware that Congress might cut off all subsidies if Amtrak fails to make progress. As a result, passenger revenues have begun to cover a larger share of operating costs. However, operating costs are only part of the total costs of passenger train operation. It generally is agreed that Amtrak will never be able to cover its total costs, including depreciation, taxes, and interest.

Thus, the whole premise of the Amtrak program should be reconsidered. The old myth that passenger rail was a sound enterprise suppressed only by the willful neglect of the freight rail industry is difficult to sustain and has all but disappeared. The belief that rail passenger service provides some special value similarly has waned. It has become increasingly clear that rail travel is simply noncompetitive.

Nothing appears likely to change this situation. European and Japanese rail systems are experiencing a similar decline, although their concentrated populations and higher cost alternatives ensure that passenger rail will remain a more important mode for a longer time. Even in the United States, passenger rail may survive along densely populated corridors. Long-haul scenic trips, like ocean liners, may survive on a limited basis; the revival of the Orient Express in Europe suggests this possibility. However, no case exists for the continuation of nationwide subsidized passenger rail service. Amtrak subsidies should be eliminated.

As a first step, DOT should report annually by route on the income distribution of the Amtrak ridership, the impact of Amtrak subsidies on competing modes of transportation, and the likelihood that the current subsidy will increase. Amtrak should be required to make the case explicitly for maintaining the subsidy on each route, and the rules forcing Amtrak to discontinue service on heavily loss-making routes should be tightened.

Amtrak management should be granted additional management flexibility to improve productivity. In particular, management should enjoy the same flexibility in dealing with labor as was granted Conrail. Instead of paying dismissed workers a full salary for six years, Congress allowed management to pay a one-time severance of from $20,000 to $25,000. This is largely responsible for Conrail's dramatic management improvements. Amtrak deserves the same chance to improve its operations.

DOT should educate the public on the comparative strengths and weaknesses of passenger rail. Popular support for Amtrak, in part, reflects ignorance about its environmental, conservation, income distribution, and mobility impacts, and how these relate to the comparable data for bus, automobile, and airline travel. Modifying public policy in this area will require a major educational effort. In this effort, the Administration should solicit the support of those private sector firms adversely affected by subsidized Amtrak competition and consider their problems when formulating policy.

Freight Railroads and Conrail

Freight rail raises different problems. As a result of two major deregulation acts—the 4R Act of 1976 (the Railroad Revitalization and Regulatory Reform Act) and the Staggers Rail Act of 1980—the rail industry gained a large degree of rate freedom. Although the ICC retains final control over rates in several key commodity categories, the industry now can modify its rates within wide ranges for most freight and can reduce non-economic routings. This freedom arrived just in time for an industry that had been suffering a long-term and steady economic decline. The industry is making major use of that new flexibility.

This freedom, however, came too late for some railroads. They were saddled with routes where short line hauls, one or two car pickups, and multiple switching requirements made it hard to take advantage of most technological advances. Moreover, the traffic most suitable for rail haul—non-urgent, heavy bulk commodities traveling long distances—were in decline. To "save" the northern railways, Congress nationalized these railroads, forming a new Consolidated Rail Corporation (Conrail). Congress provided financial assistance to the company and created a special board to oversee the reorganization of the railroad.

As the costs of this bail-out mounted, Congress concluded that it had to provide Conrail management with the flexibility it long had denied the private railroads. Conrail has taken great advantage of this freedom to reduce its workforce and abandon non-economic trackage. As a result, Conrail now is operating in the black and has attracted positive purchase offers from the private sector.

The factors that may lead to the re-privatization of Conrail are instructive. First, the Conrail takeover left most of the U.S. rail system in private hands. Thus, Conrail's policymakers had a free market example to guide their efforts to streamline Conrail, and to demonstrate the viability of the private sector. In contrast, Amtrak and many urban mass transit systems have eliminated competition, and thus made competition more difficult. Their managers cannot determine readily how the private sector might respond to consumer needs. They thus are less ready to consider privatization.

Reforming Mass Transit

In budget size, the Urban Mass Transportation Administration (UMTA) is second within DOT only to the Federal Highway Administration. Moreover, over the last decade, UMTA has grown more rapidly than other federal transportation programs. The current federal role reflects the belief that a modern society requires improved urban mobility and that mass transit offers a more efficient and cleaner alternative to the private automobile. There is also a belief that the private sector had demonstrated its inability to provide an alternative in this area and that therefore federal intervention was essential to realize these benefits. None of these beliefs is well-founded. Any "solution" to the urban mobility problem should concern itself with the full range of options available for travel within the urban community: automobile, private transit, public transit, and even walking or cycling. Mass transit is but one element in the overall urban mobility system, and for most cities mass transit is a small and even declining component of the overall system.

The primary problems of public transit are that use patterns generally peak in the morning and evening; that the poor, the handicapped and the elderly have fewer options; and that current mass transit systems are inefficient and require large and mounting subsidies. These problems have little to do with money and much to do with the nature of the urban transportation system and how it is managed.

As noted earlier, the failure to price highway use means that motorists face few incentives to consider the full costs of driving during rush hour. Pricing urban peak load road travel would have major benefits in greater urban mobility. For instance, a simple two-tier license plate system, with the lower cost plate restricted to non-peak, non-congested streets, would go far toward addressing the problem. A second factor creating the urban mobility problem is the tendency of local governments to suppress private sector transportation options through regulation. This suppression is unfortunate, because a World Bank study of urban transportation policy found that urban mobility might be enhanced significantly if the private sector were allowed to compete. That study found that successful urban transit programs had several things in common; they generally were privately owned; relied on smaller vehicles; had flexible route structures; and faced competition. This study suggests that local regulation may have contributed to the urban mobility problem by forcing private firms from the scene.

If regulation was a major factor in the disappearance of private mass transit, then the solution to the urban mobility problem may have little to do with funding levels and much to do with regulation. In this case, a solution would be to deregulate urban transportation.

Thus, the Federal Trade Commission's efforts to employ the antitrust laws to curb the ability of local governments to restrict competition should be endorsed and expanded. Local restrictions on private transit may constitute the single major barrier to urban mobility. Such restrictions reduce the employment and entrepreneurial opportunities available to minority groups, reduce mobility for the poor and others lacking access to private automobiles, and increase the "need" for urban mass transit subsidies. FTC deserves full support for recognizing that a free economy is threatened by such government monopolies. The argument that such efforts conflict with the New Federalism thrust of the Administration are not well founded. New Federalism means returning power to the people. Individuals have economic rights and these rights should be protected just as strongly as their civil rights.

Productivity improvements are needed in the mass transit sector. Experience with other transportation areas—railroads, airlines, trucking—suggests that productivity improvements result from competition, not improved planning. Thus, the most significant way to encourage more productive transit is to deregulate the private sector.

The distributional impacts of mass transit also deserve closer attention. The assumption that mass transit subsidies help the poor has not been confirmed empirically. By contrast, studies suggest that private transportation services provide opportunities for minority entrepreneurs. Indeed, private sector alternatives—in some cases, illegal transportation options, such as "gypsy taxis"—provide the only services to some less affluent neighborhoods of some American cities. Deregulation would encourage currently illegal services to become legitimate additions to the transportation system.

Proposals to make private firms eligible for public subsidies, on the other hand, should be considered carefully. If the government pays the bill, the private firm may have little incentive to ensure customer satisfaction in any cost-effective fashion. The firms may concentrate on serving political rather than economic objectives to ensure their future contracts.

It should also be recognized that transit costs are not necessarily reduced by attracting new riders. In many urban systems, reduced ridership at rush hour ("peak shaving") would reduce the transit system's work force and lower capital requirements, which might well lower overall trip costs.

The federal mass transit aid formulas should consider the extent to which the local community restricts private sector transportation activities. Mass transit aid is intended to facilitate urban mobility; communities that have crippled their private transportation system with regulation deserve less federal assistance. There is a long record of such formula adjustments in other areas—energy conservation tax breaks are not available to taxis in cities that prohibit ride-sharing, for example.

Current revenue sharing and tax policies also encourage communities to provide services publicly. Supporting private transportation through tax incentives would reduce local tax levels, and this also would reduce the "tax effort" of the community and hence its share of revenue sharing funds. The revenue sharing formula should be revised to neutralize this public sector bias. At the moment, the more a locality taxes its citizens to provide subsidized public services, the more federal assistance it receives. Also, the tax law allows deductions of local tax payments but not fees paid to private transportation providers. The tax laws should be reformed to ensure neutrality with respect to the private-public transportation choice.

Privatizing Space

Space transportation is a new responsibility for the Department of Transportation. After considerable debate, DOT was assigned responsibility for facilitating the commercialization of space, and a new Office of Space Commercialization was created. Today the only significant private sector involvement in space involves space-based telecommunications satellites. To date, the National Aeronautics and Space Administration (NASA) has dominated the delivery of such satellites into orbit. Moreover, NASA now plans to build and manage a space station intended to be an "industrial park" in space. Neither transportation nor laboratory management are inherently governmental functions, yet NASA shows little interest in transferring these activities to the private sector and returning to a research and development mission.

The problem of moving these functions to the private sector, where they belong, has already arisen in the pricing policies adopted by NASA. NASA has placed considerable emphasis on developing the shuttle, a reusable launch vehicle. The argument has been that such a vehicle would be more economical and thus lower the costs of transporting items into space. So far, that hope has not been realized. Full cost pricing of the shuttle, however, would result in sharply higher prices. But NASA uses a promotional pricing policy that recovers only a fraction of the full costs of launching the shuttle. This pricing policy makes it extremely difficult for a private firm to compete. NASA appears to be adopting the predatory pricing practices so often condemned in the private marketplace. NASA should immediately charge full price for all commercial deliveries.

A more basic question, however, is why NASA has assumed responsibility in the first place for what would normally be considered commercial activities—such as transporting freight or managing an industrial park. NASA has moved far from its initial role as a research and development agency. No case has been made for its new role. The commercialization of such demonstrated technology has never been considered a function of government. Activities that have no commercial value or that cannot justify their costs should not be subsidized unless there are offsetting non-economic considerations. The government is not needed to transport freight or to manage commercial laboratories here on Earth; there appears to be even less case for it taking such a role outside the United States in space. The shuttle system and the management of the space station should be transferred to private control as soon as possible. If NASA believes these systems require some basic financial support, then it might become a customer of these new private firms, just as was the U.S. Post Office of the early private airlines.

Commercialization, however, requires that property rights be clearly established. Space is still treated as public property, much like the seabed. Economic activities that might occur if owners could secure the gains attendant on private ownership are foregone. The Reagan Administration took a significant lead in promoting necessary property rights by opposing the centralized management philosophy inherent in the Law of the Sea Treaty. It should now extend that same private property approach into space. Ideally, the U.S. should try to persuade all nations to provide for private ownership of specific slots or even orbits for commercial purposes. However, failing such universal acceptance of capitalism, the U.S. should ensure that those slots controlled by U.S. interests are granted secure tenure rights. These slots now represent the highest value properties in space and thus are most likely to demonstrate the efficiency advantages of private ownership in any event.

Completing the Job of Deregulation

Transportation deregulation is in trouble; re-regulation is a significant threat. The Reagan Administration failed to capitalize on its opportunities in this area, and thereby allowed those favoring polities over markets to regroup and counter-attack. Many in Congress, and even within those groups formerly favoring deregulation, are now pushing for legislation to "fine tune" the deregulation process.

This threat of re-regulation should be addressed in the second term. The Administration should declare firmly that it has no intention of allowing transportation deregulation gains to be reversed, and that the President will veto all re-regulation bills.

The Administration must clarify its stance on other forms of economic and non-economic regulation. Historically, the transportation industry explicitly was placed outside the antitrust regulatory laws. Since the Interstate Commerce Commission, the Federal Maritime Commission and the Civil Aeronautics Board regulated rates and entry, it was believed that they should also regulate the industry's organization and business arrangements. But as these traditional regulatory agencies fade away, the question arises: Should transportation be placed under the antitrust regulatory control of the Federal Trade Commission and the Department of Justice—or should the industry be fully deregulated?

Unlike most forms of economic regulation, the antitrust laws still enjoy much popular and even intellectual support. Whether transportation markets are self-regulating or whether they require explicit regulation remains an issue of some debate. Most antitrust scholars agree that the antitrust laws have been flawed theoretically and have been used in practice to suppress competition. However, there is little agreement on what should be done.

In the area of safety, environment, and energy, the Administration has favored regulating. Non-regulatory means of enhancing safety, environmental quality, or energy conservation have received little consideration. There has been no discussion of the extent to which environmental problems emerge from the failure to establish clear property rights and liability concepts, nor any thought given to the extent to which private insurance has already played a major role in improving the safety of transportation, and might play a greater role if the insurance industry itself were deregulated.

Rather than passively awaiting events, the Reagan team should embark on a policy of further deregulation in several key areas.

Trucking Deregulation

The deregulation of the motor carriage industry for both property and the moving sector has been a dramatic success. Although there has been considerable restructuring of the industry, with firms entering and leaving specific markets, most firms have expanded their operations to enter markets formerly closed to them. As a result, on many routes there are far more competitors than during the regulatory era. Discounting is common and advertising for new business has become more aggressive. Trucking and moving firms have learned much about how to attract and retain customers—and make profits while doing so. The Administration should trumpet that success and use it to push for the elimination of all remaining regulatory restrictions on the industry.

The trucking industry deserves total deregulation and should receive it. To accomplish that objective, it will be necessary to develop a two-part piece of legislation. The first section should sunset all ICC powers over both the trucking industry and the household goods moving industry. The second should legalize all voluntary arrangements within the trucking industry.

Railroad Deregulation

Rail deregulation advanced more slowly than trucking deregulation during the first term, and it owed more to Congress' realization that the industry was failing than to any belief that deregulation would bring about benefits to the consumer. Rail resources cannot be redeployed as readily as trucking resources and thus deregulation generally has taken the form of independent action and flexibility of rates. The ICC has acted responsibly in placing the responsibility for rates with the shippers and carriers; the Commission has refused to second-guess the market. Not suprisingly, that hands-off attitude has proved controversial. Many shippers believe the old system of ICC review would benefit them, and many have sought to reverse rail deregulation by introducing legislation to "fine tune" the existing acts. Such changes would undo many of the gains achieved to date.

The Administration should insist that time be allowed for deregulation to work. Hasty efforts to intervene at this stage would merely reduce the incentives to undertake the painful adjustments now underway within the industry, and encourage a return to the political framework. Those firms that have most aggressively restructured their activities to conform to a market framework would be penalized.

INITIATIVES FOR 1985

The Administration should move decisively in 1985 to signal its commitment to free transportation markets. The Administration should:

1) Privatize the air travel system.

The air transportation system cannot remain half private and half government dominated. The successful deregulation of the airlines has brought the rigidities inherent in bureaucratic control of the air traffic system and a federalized airport system to the fore. The

Administration should convene a working group to privatize one major congested air travel region—Chicago or New York are logical choices. That working group should transfer all current air traffic control functions to a newly established Regional Airspace Management Corporation, draw up plans to de-federalize all regional airports, and recommend legislation ensuring that both the Airspace Corporation and the airports are granted the operating flexibility and pricing freedom required to meet consumer needs safely and efficiently. No single act would more clearly signal the Administration's commitment to free markets in transportation.

2) Introduce legislation to complete the deregulation of trucking.

The motor carrier and moving industry deregulation acts have succeeded. The ICC serves no further purpose and its powers over these transportation sectors should be ended. The reluctance of the carriers to support ICC sunsetting results not from any significant special privileges they obtain from the ICC currently, but rather because eliminating the ICC form of regulation would place them in the hands of the antitrust regulators. On both principled and pragmatic grounds, there is no reason to regulate the voluntary arrangements of the trucking industry. The Administration should introduce legislation to deregulate the industry fully.

3) Complete the Conrail sale and oppose all efforts to re-regulate the railroads.

The only alternative to a free market in rail transportation is a nationalized rail system. Conrail indicates both the inevitability of that course under the old regime and the resiliency possible when shippers and the railroads are required to reach voluntary agreements. The Administration should complete the Conrail sale, and move vigorously to head off any legislative moves to re-regulate the industry. Leadership in this area is essential, since the shipper community is divided. Some shippers believe their interests would be advanced were rail rates subject to greater regulatory control; others have moved to bargain aggressively and adapt their operations to the free market. A clear signal by the President and the DOT leadership that the Administration will oppose any effort to re-regulate the industry would do much to ensure that Conrail will be the first and last nationalized railroad in the nation.

4) De-federalize the highway system.

The Administration should introduce legislation which would transfer full management responsibility and authority for portions of the highway system to state and local governments. The legislation should reduce the current federal highway "user" taxes to provide the states and localities with the opportunity to tax gasoline to finance these new responsibilities. The legislation also should ensure that all legal impediments to tolling and private participation in the road network are removed. It is critical that the Administration signal its commitment to reducing the federal highway role. The President should request a meeting with the nation's governors to discuss this matter and solicit their ideas on what would be necessary to achieve this transfer.

5) Clarify the costs of regulation.

The Administration should estimate the costs of each of the special cross-cutting requirements now incorporated into the various transportation acts, and use that information to develop support for the elimination of these provisions.

6) Introduce legislation to deregulate local transportation.

The Administration should introduce legislation that would encourage local communities to deregulate local transportation services. That legislation should modify current aid formulas to provide incentive grants to communities that take this step. The legislation should encourage the establishment of Transportation Enterprise Zones, similar to the urban Enterprise Zones, in which firms and individuals would be free to offer all transportation services.

7) Educate the public.

Many of the irrational features of current transportation policy result from widespread public misunderstanding over the impact of various policies. This lack of public understanding makes it extremely difficult to eliminate such costly pork-barrel programs as Amtrak, decrease mass mass transit aid, and reduce the federal transportation role. The President should schedule a series of addresses developing the case for free markets in transportation to begin this educational process.

12

The Department of the Treasury

by
Norman B. Ture*

The Department of the Treasury carries major responsibility for carrying out an Administration's economic program. Apart from its immediate involvement and responsibility for tax policy, Treasury is the principal executive branch department concerned with and responsible for financial institution deregulation, improving international financial arrangements, and interaction with the Federal Reserve Board in establishing a sound monetary system. And because of the heavy emphasis in the daily work of the Treasury on projection of economic aggregates and analysis of economic developments, as well as the Treasury Secretary's explicit role as the President's chief economic policy advisor and spokesman—and his membership on the Cabinet's economic policy-making team—the Treasury is an

SECRETARY
Donald Regan, 1981-Present

PERSONNEL: 118,507

BUDGET (In Billions of Dollars)

1985 Estimate	$150.9
1984 Estimate	$137.7
1983 Actual	$116.0
1982 Actual	$110.5
1981 Actual	$ 93.4
1980 Actual	$ 76.7
1975 Actual	$ 41.2

Established: 1789

Major Programs:
- Office of Revenue Sharing
- Internal Revenue Service
- United States Customs Service
- Bureau of Government Financial Operations
- Bureau of Alcohol, Tobacco, & Firearms

* Task Force members included John M. Palffy and Ron Utt.

active and major participant in budget policy-making. Indeed, no other part of the executive branch is so deeply involved in formulation and implementation of the President's economic policies as is Treasury.

This stewardship, to be sure, is severely circumscribed by the operating responsibilities of other Administration agencies, by the White House's own primary involvement in policy-making, and by congressional actions. To the extent, therefore, that the Treasury falls short of achieving the goals set for each of the principal parts of a President's economic program, the responsibility is broadly distributed across the government.

THE FIRST TERM EXPERIENCE

Candidate Ronald Reagan in 1980 called for a drastic reorientation and refocusing of U.S. economic policy. The theme of his policy, summarized in the 1980 election campaign and in the early months of 1981, was "Give the economy back to the American people." Articulated in careful detail was the commitment to reduce dramatically the presence of the federal government in the daily economic life of households and businesses, and to withdraw the government from private economic decision-making to the greatest possible extent. Behind this determination lay the conviction that however well-intentioned federal programs and activities may be, they materially impair the efficient functioning of the free market system and the economy's performance. Giving the economy back to the American people, therefore, required not merely reducing the size of the federal government and the scope of its activities, but also revising the way in which it carries out its activities to minimize interference with the operation of the market system. Achieving these objectives, it was hoped, would permit the market system to operate in a manner spurring vigorous economic growth with much reduced rates of unemployment and inflation.

To achieve these results, the President, in 1981, presented an economic program with four major features.

Reduction of Spending Growth

A key element of the program was to reduce the rate of growth of federal outlays and to alter the content of federal spending programs so that resources would be freed for use by the private sector and that the government's use of such resources would be as economical as possible. The latter goal was particularly important. Transcending considerations of eliminating waste, its attainment required the careful evaluation of all federal spending programs to identify their objectives and to determine that these objectives were pursued appropriately by the federal government; determine whether the content of the program represented the most efficient means for pursuit of the objectives deemed to be appropriate; and decide how much of the nation's real resources or income claims should be allocated to these functions. In short, this aspect of the President's program called for a rigorous reassessment and revision of the spending side of the budget.

Tax Reform

The central objective of tax reform was to reduce, if not eliminate, the excise effects of the tax system in distorting the market's relative price signals. The initial legislative proposals called for equal percentage across-the-board reductions in marginal tax rates in the individual income tax; and replacement of the complex and antique depreciation system with a simple and modern capital cost recovery system.

These two reforms were a major, albeit merely a first, step in an extended program of tax revisions aimed at making the federal income tax as nearly neutral as possible. The initial individual income tax proposals sought to reduce the pervasive income tax bias against saving and investment, and in favor of current consumption, and the bias against productive employment in the market place of one's time, skills, and resources. The replacement of depreciation by cost recovery was aimed at reducing the tax bias against investment in durable production facilities, which had been compounded by the erosion by inflation of the real value of depreciation allowances based on original cost.

It was recognized explicitly that these tax reforms would entail significant revenue losses, particularly in the first several years after their enactment. Reducing income tax liabilities, however, was not the aim of these proposed tax reforms. Their objective was to address the two major distortions resulting from the prevailing income tax, namely the bias against saving and investment and against productive work. For the same reason, the reforms were not aimed at income redistribution, nor were they intended as short-term, anti-recessionary devices. Their focus was on the long term, on providing a tax system which would, far less than the prevailing system, distort the market's relative cost and price signals.

Regulatory Reform

The President called for reform of the federal government's enormously diverse and extensive regulatory systems. The concern was not to dismantle the prevailing regulatory system nor to relinquish the use of the regulatory powers. The objective was to shift regulation's focus from circumscribing, controlling, and constraining household and business entities to improving the effectiveness of markets by internalizing, whenever possible, relevant external benefits and costs.

Monetary Policy Reform and Financial Institution Deregulation

The President's program sought to improve the performance of financial markets, essential to the effective performance of all of the economy's other markets. Achieving this required freeing financial markets from their antiquated regulatory constraints, which imposed artificial restrictions on the ability of financial market participants to diversify their product lines and markets, and which imposed a wide array of controls on the pricing of financial services.

Along with freeing up the financial markets, the President's program also sought to induce the Federal Reserve's Board of Governors to adopt and maintain firmly the monetary policy required for efficient functioning of financial markets. The essential purposes of these markets are to identify the costs and rewards for foregoing current consumption in exchange for future income, and to mobilize the saving of the millions of households and businesses, directing this saving into the most productive capital uses. Monetary policy which results in frequent, erratic, and unpredictable changes in the stock of money greatly increases the cost of efficient portfolio management and distorts and obscures the real terms of trade between current consumption and future income. Excessively rapid money supply growth, in addition, results in inflation. This interacts with the progressive tax system to raise real marginal tax rates, accentuating their adverse effects on saving and investment, work, innovative risk-taking, entrepreneurship—-the sources of economic progress. An imperative for success of the Reagan program in revitalizing the free-market system, therefore, was to achieve a monetary policy that afforded a moderate and steady growth in the stock of money.

A collateral concern was to insure that the change in U.S. monetary policy improved the efficiency of the international exchange markets and enhanced the capacity of financial institutions in other nations to deal with the problems created by a decade of upheaval in world trade and the resulting turbulence in international commodity markets. Achieving these objectives called for more than merely expanding the financial support to international financial agencies, such as the International Monetary Fund and the World Bank. Far more important, it called for reforming the policies, activities, and practices of these institutions.

The Reagan Administration's economic program was intended to provide the institutional setting in which the market system could operate more efficiently over the long run. The results of this more effective operation, it was hoped, would be a larger economy, growing more rapidly and steadily, with more people employed at higher real wage rates, and with a lower inflation rate than would be realized if the program were not pursued. Emphasis was on the performance of the market system, freed from undue constraints and less impeded by government intrusions. In contrast with past program rhetoric, it was not perceived that these results would be the direct outcomes of the economic program itself. The Reagan program was not predicated on the notion that the federal government directly controls the economy's performance or that economic outcomes depend primarily on government action.

In this context, then, the Reagan program is not to be evaluated in terms of economic developments to date. It is far too early to determine whether that program, if fully implemented, will lead to the desired results. Moreover, the program has not been carried out completely. Attempting to identify specific economic developments as the outcomes of the programs, therefore, would be highly misleading, at best, and in fact, simply wrong.

Overall Budget Policies

Many factors, political and otherwise, contributed to limiting the implementation of the Reagan program. The largest proximate impediment was the drastic deterioration in the budget picture. The deficits exploding soon after the beginning of the Reagan Administration were attributable in very large part to the sharp intensification in late 1981 of recessionary forces which had been developing since the end of 1978. It was a serious mischance which befell the new Reagan Administration that it had to initiate its policies just when the accumulation of recessionary forces developing over the preceding several years reached a critical mass, a development which no one in or out of the government had anticipated. The resulting explosion of the deficit reflected these recessionary developments—it did not cause them, and the deficit would have been far worse if the Reagan program had not begun and had it not cushioned the decline.

Neither the Administration nor the Congress saw the budget deficit in this light. Misplacing policy priorities, both the Congress and the

Administration reversed policy direction beginning in late 1981. This eroded the measures that they had cooperated in enacting in the spring and summer of that year. In a vain effort to curtail the prospective budget deficits, Congress cut back on the expansion of defense preparations and enacted in 1982 the largest tax increase in U.S. history, amounting to almost a quarter of a trillion dollars over five fiscal years. More important than the mere magnitude of the tax increase, the Tax Equity and Fiscal Responsibility Act of 1982 (TEFRA) severely cut back on some of the most important features of the Economic Recovery Tax Act of 1981 (ERTA). The repeal of the acceleration of cost recovery write-off, scheduled for properties acquired in 1985, 1986 and thereafter, and the abandonment of safe-harbor leasing were major steps backward in tax policy. The gasoline tax increase in 1982, the Social Security tax increase in 1983, and the tax increases in the Tax Reform Act of 1984 were retreats from the initial goal of reducing the federal government's presence in the economy.

More fundamentally, these measures assigned a higher policy priority to budgetary arithmetic than to the basic goals of creating a fiscal structure more conducive to an efficiently operating market economy. Ironically, the modest improvements in budget deficit prospects are attributable far more to the resurgence of the economy since the third quarter of 1982 than to the largely counterproductive tax increase enacted since 1981. Moreover, the loss of momentum toward the ultimate tax neutrality goals initiated by ERTA has been a high price to pay for the relatively small budget deficit reductions that have been achieved.

Ostensibly, this policy reversal was needed to prevent the deficits from damaging the economy. In fact the budget deficits have not prevented the recovery or slowed its pace, let alone aborted it. More important, the deficits have not "crowded out" private capital formation. Indeed, contrary to the conventional—and demonstrably mistaken—wisdom, private capital formation and household investment in consumer durables have been the primary force propelling economic recovery, with overall consumption expenditures lagging behind the growth in real GNP. By the same token, the vigor of the recovery since late 1982 clearly invalidates the proposition that deficits would act as a drag on the economy's growth, producing a recovery far weaker than most of those in the postwar era.

Tax Policy

The Administration can take pride in persuading the Congress to reduce statutory tax rates for individual income taxpayers, and subsequently for having protected these rate cuts from the repeated efforts of congressional opponents to rescind or cap them. It can also justifiably boast of having introduced at least partial indexation of the individual income tax to mitigate bracket creep, and of having prevented repeal of indexing. The Administration, moreover, is to be commended for having pushed for and achieved liberalization of Individual Retirement Accounts. One of its major achievements was the establishment of the Accelerated Cost Recovery System (ACRS). These and other ERTA reforms are major advances toward the neutrality goal of tax policy—of reducing the government's intrusion into household and business economic behavior by tax distortion of market signals.

On the other hand, the Administration—in particular the Treasury—has not stood firm against efforts to roll back the progress in tax policy. The advance represented by ACRS toward neutral tax treatment of savings used for investments in durable production facilities was substantially undone by the severe limitation on ACRS enacted in 1982 in TEFRA. Nor did the Administration seek to frustrate efforts to raise individual marginal tax rates by the "loophole" closing measures enacted in TEFRA and in the 1984 Tax Reform Act. By widening the definition of taxable income, these measures have pushed many taxpayers into higher tax brackets, thereby increasing the marginal tax rates to which their activities are exposed. The Administration not only failed to prevent these backdoor rate increases, it actively promoted them. Because much of the income added back to the tax base through loophole closing consists of saving or the returns for saving, this kind of tax increase accentuates the income tax bias against saving. By urging such measures, the Treasury has redirected tax policy away from one of the central objectives of the original Reagan tax programs.

In sum, progress has been made toward providing a tax system that is much more nearly neutral—consonant with the requirements of an efficient, free market system—than the system in place prior to 1981. Yet backsliding, impelled primarily by concerns about the deficit, has eroded this progress and weakened the momentum for a continued advance toward a neutral tax system. The goal of a tax system that least distorts market signals about the costs and rewards for alternative uses of resources, a tax system that minimizes government intrusion in the nation's economic life, is still to be achieved.

Spending Policy

In its effort to curb the growth in total government spending, the Reagan Administration has had successes and failures. In current dollars, total federal outlays (on a national income basis) increased at an average annual rate of 11.8 percent in the four years from 1976 through 1980; in the subsequent three and a half years, the annual growth rate was 9.1 percent, on the average. On the other hand, in constant 1972 dollars, federal government purchases of goods and services have increased at an average annual rate of 5.0 percent in the three and a half years from the last quarter of 1980 through the second quarter of 1984—considerably faster than the 3.0 percent average annual growth in total real GNP in the same period, and twice as fast as the 2.4 percent annual rate of increase in federal purchases in the four years from 1976 through 1980.

This comparison however, obscures important compositional changes. In the four years after 1976, real defense purchases grew at an annual rate of 1.9 percent, while in the three and a half years since 1980 the average annual growth in these outlays was 7.4 percent. In contrast, nondefense purchases increased at a rate of 3.4 percent from 1976 through 1980, but they declined at an average annual rate of 0.25 percent from 1980 through the middle of 1984.

Other federal government outlays also show significant compositional shifts. In the four years of the Carter Administration, federal transfer payments, in current dollars, increased at an average annual rate of 11.6 percent; in the three and a half years from the last quarter of 1980, these payments have grown at a much slower pace—-7.4 percent per annum, on the average. Grants-in-aid to state and local governments increased by 9.8 percent a year on the average, from 1976 through 1980, but in the three and a half years ending in the middle of 1984, these outlays decreased at an annual rate of about 0.4 percent. Net interest payments by the federal government had grown at 18.8 percent a year during the Carter Administration; in the three and a half years from the end of 1980 through the middle of 1984, these outlays grew at a moderately faster rate of 21.3 percent a year.

The record shows very clearly that the Reagan Administration has slowed the growth in nondefense federal outlays. It has also, in significant respects, shifted outlay composition. To be sure, the slowing of growth in nondefense purchases, transfer payments, and grants-in-aid has not offset the acceleration in defense spending growth, as President Reagan intended. The accelerating expansion of net interest disbursements, moreover, has offset much of the deceleration in other nondefense spending, so that the rate of growth of federal outlays overall slowed only moderately—to a significantly lesser extent than had been hoped when the economic program was first presented in 1981. This is still a far more substantial achievement than can be shown in the tax policy area.

As emphasized earlier, merely reducing the expansion rate of federal government spending was not—nor should it have been—the sole aim of the Reagan programs in this area. Even more important was reform of spending programs to insure that they served appropriate objectives and were designed to pursue these objectives as efficiently as possible. In this connection, there is little evidence on which to judge the results of the program. It does seem clear, however, that less attention by far has been given, in the Administration and in the Congress, to issues of program objectives and design than to program amounts.

Monetary Policy

Many had thought that the problem of determining the proper course for monetary policy had been resolved in October 1979, when the Federal Reserve appeared serious about achieving a target growth rate for M1 (the base measure of money supply) that was consistent with a gradual deceleration in inflation. In changing its operational procedures in 1979, the Fed implied that it would focus on growth in the monetary aggregates and would eschew interest rate targets and efforts to fine tune the economy. In practice, however, this new policy was never implemented by the Fed. The instability of monetary growth that had prevailed for a decade or more prior to Fall 1979 was accentuated, not moderated, in the years thereafter.

The October 1979 policies were described as "monetarist," but that designation is wrong. The key feature of a monetarist policy is stable, moderate and predictable monetary growth; this is precisely the President's program, articulated early in 1981, urging a steady reduction over a six-year period in the growth rate of the money supply from the double digit rates prevailing in the last half of 1980.

The President's recommendations in this respect were disregarded with a vengeance by the Federal Reserve. The Fed allowed the money supply, as measured by M1, to contract at an annual rate of about 11 percent during the spring of 1980; but from late Spring to early Fall the M1 growth rate soared, reaching an annual rate of more than 20 percent during the third quarter of the year. During the last quarter of 1980, the M1 growth rate plunged, turning negative in January 1981. The monetary roller coaster ride continued in that year: by the middle of the second quarter of 1981, the annual rate of growth of M1 over the prior 13 weeks zoomed up to 14 percent, dropping precipitously to mid-year, climbing moderately during the third quarter, declining during much of the fourth quarter, before zooming upward that December. The pattern, with different timing and amplitude, was repeated in 1982, again in 1983, and has continued through the first seven and a half months of 1984. In 1982, for example, M1 grew at an annual rate of more than 18 percent during the 13 weeks ending in January, at a slightly negative rate over the 13 weeks ending in mid-Spring, at a moderate 3½ to 5½ percent rate through much of the middle of the year, and at double digit rates as high as 17 percent from August throughout the first half of 1983. Since that time, M1 has grown at annual rates (over 13-week periods) ranging from a high of more than 11 percent to a low of less than 2 percent.

Examination of these data leads to two major conclusions: 1) unless one believes in virtually instantaneous response of real economic activity to a slow-down in the growth of the money supply, the Federal Reserve most assuredly did not cause the precipitous decline in real GNP that began in the last quarter of 1981 and continued into the third quarter of 1982; and 2) the enormously volatile and unpredictable pattern of money supply growth prevailing throughout the Reagan Administration's first term—which is antithetical to the policy the President had urged early in 1981—has contributed to uncertainty in the financial markets and impaired the efficiency of their operation.

It is apparent that the Fed has not given up its policies of attempting to manage the economy on a short-run, discretionary basis, using the federal funds rates as a policy instrument. Pegging interest rates is not a sustainable policy, and in the complete absence of an observable policy rule there is no way for market participants to anticipate what will happen next. Fearing either a resurgence of inflation or a draconian monetary restriction, financial markets have become increasingly jittery. These jitters are reflected in extraordinary risk premiums attached to virtually all loan contacts, and this explains a substantial part of the unusually high "real" interest rate levels that have prevailed for several years.

What is apparent in reviewing both the Fed's performance and the deliberations of the Federal Open Market Committee is that the Fed has been acting in a highly discretionary manner, attempting to manage the course of the U.S. economy according to its own judgment of where the economy is and where it will be in the next quarter or two. The Fed seems to have given little thought to the long-run consequences of such a policy on the future rate of inflation. To the Fed, it appears that inflation is caused by "too rapid" growth in the real economy and is to be curbed by monetary actions aimed at keeping the expansion of real economic activity to a noninflationary pace. This Phillips Curve view of inflation disregards the fact that sustained inflation is always and everywhere a monetary phenomenon, and that trends in the real economy, when divorced from changes in money growth, have little bearing on past, present, or future inflation.

This approach to policy leaves the Fed rudderless. It is impossible even for the Fed itself to predict its own future actions. And because the Fed is rudderless, the market has no way to predict the future course of money growth, the price level, interest rates, or the level of economic activity. Moreover, the consequent volatility in financial markets contributes to the financial problems arising elsewhere in the world. It is not the federal deficit that has generated the financial crisis of "third world" nations or caused disarray of foreign exchange and financial markets abroad. The flight of capital from abroad to the U.S., now popularly attributed to high real interest rates in the U.S., allegedly caused by the deficit, was the source of bitter complaint by foreign governments at the very outset of the Reagan Administration, when the budget deficits, actual and expected, were far smaller than those that subsequently emerged.

With respect to this aspect of the President's program, it must regrettably be concluded that not only has the objective not been achieved but that the U.S. is farther than ever from the sound monetary policy which had been sought.

Regulatory Policy: Financial Markets

Considerable progress, on the other hand, has been made in freeing up financial markets from inappropriate and counterproductive regulatory constraints. Relaxing these constraints on how financial institutions may be organized and operate, on the composition of their assets holdings, and on the rates they may charge for loans and services has permitted an increase in the efficiency with which these institutions perform their functions. These reforms have also led to a surge of innovation both in the kinds of services offered and the methods for their delivery. This has been highly constructive.

The difficulties encountered by a number of banks, including giants such as Continental Illinois, have impelled a drive for re-regulation in recent months. This thrust toward reinstituting nonmarket constraints on financial institutions misidentifies the source of the problems these institutions currently face.

Deregulation did not generate the current difficulties; they arose, rather, out of investment policies, developments in the world oil market, and imprudent and excessively exuberant borrowing and development policies by less developed countries when regulation was in full bloom.

Indeed, it is far closer to the truth to identify regulation itself as a major factor contributing to the recent stresses imposed on financial companies. The sources of failure and threat of failure or serious financial reverses of a number of banks arose in the mid-70s when the banks' management decided to invest in volatile high-yield loan portfolios, dangerously concentrated in oil and Latin American obligations.

In the late 1970s rapid technological changes, high interest rates, and intense competition from non-bank financial intermediaries threatened the future viability of the commercial banking and thrift system. Unregulated competitors offered consumers high-yield liquid investments and customer services which bankers were forbidden by federal rules to offer. In 1980 Congress finally succumbed to the inevitable choice: either deregulate banks or watch them go bankrupt as they lose their sources of funds.

As a first step Congress allowed banks to offer depositors market interest rates. When the cost of money to banks consequently increased, they were forced to seek out more profitable endeavors. Their most fundamentally sound options, functional or geographical diversification, were prohibited by federal regulation. But a third and economically less desirable alternative—investing in high-risk, high-yield loans—actually was encouraged by the existing system of federal deposit insurance and regulatory oversight.

In a freely operating bank system, with private insurance instead of insurance by government agencies, insurance premiums would vary according to risk. If a bank were to increase its portfolio risk, the private insurer would raise the premiums it charged the bank. The bank would be forced to bear the cost of its riskier portfolio and would, therefore, confront an objective constraint on the degree of risk it assumed. Instead of varying the insurance premium according to portfolio risk, however, the Federal Deposit Insurance Corporation charges a flat percentage rate. Consequently, bankers can increase the risk of their portfolio, and hence their potential yield, without any corresponding increase in insurance costs. And this is what has occurred.

The appropriate remedy certainly is not to reimpose the kinds of regulatory constraints that have been eliminated in the last few years. Nor is it to be found in enhancing the International Monetary Fund's capacity to impose economic austerity policies on debtor nations. The constructive approach, rather, is to proceed with the freeing up of financial institutions and increasing their exposure to the discipline of the free market.

THE NEXT FOUR YEARS

The limited success of the Reagan Administration in implementing its Economic Recovery Program does not mean that the program was inappropriate or improperly specified. Certainly the central goal of the program—freeing the economy from the intrusion of government—is as warranted today as it was at the beginning of 1981. The reaffirmation of this goal and a rededication to the original four-part program early in the next Administration would go far toward eliminating existing uncertainty about public economic policies.

Tax Policy

The backsliding on tax policy since 1981 has generated doubts about the continuation of specific features of the tax law that were enacted in 1981 with the aim of reducing the tax bias against private saving and capital formation. Putting these doubts to rest would contribute to continuing economic advance.

To allay these doubts, the President should make it clear that the primary objective of his tax policy will be to restore the momentum for a program of tax reform designed to achieve the most nearly neutral tax system. Any such program must reject out of hand the various selective tax increase proposals that have been given currency in recent years and months. Proposals to cap the ERTA income tax rate reductions, to impose income tax surcharges on individuals with incomes above some designated amount, to limit or abolish income tax indexing, to impose new or more severe minimum taxes on corporate taxpayers, and similar tax changes are exercises in demagoguery. They have no redeeming economic merit, and by virtue of their adverse effects on saving and capital formation they would impair the well-being of the great majority of productive Americans.

Similarly, any constructive tax reform program setting neutrality as the principal objective criterion to be served, and greater efficiency and productivity of the economy as its ultimate goal, must eschew the various "flat tax" or "modified flat tax" proposals that have been suggested. The term "flat" tax refers properly only to a tax with a single statutory rate; the term does not delineate any specific base to which that rate is to be applied. In popular usage, however, the term has come to mean an income tax, applied with fewer and possibly lower statutory rates, to a base that has virtually no exclusions, deductions, exemptions, or credits. To the extent that such a tax would, in fact, provide lower rates in a less steeply progressive schedule than at present, this would indeed be a step toward neutrality. But if this reducing and flattening of the rate structure is to be purchased at the price of adopting a tax base which, as in the case of virtually all "flat tax" proposals, would greatly increase the severity of the tax bias against saving, it would be a very bad bargain.

The so-called modified flat taxes do not even carry the small advantage of the "pure" flat taxes in imposing the bias against saving in an even-handed way.

Instead of flirting with these "flat" tax proposals, the Administration should pursue a program of tax changes, to be enacted over the next few years, aimed at providing the most nearly neutral tax system that can be achieved. The fundamental attributes of that system include:

- Confining tax liabilities to individuals, since corporations do not and cannot pay taxes; only individuals can and do pay taxes, whether in their capacity as sellers of productive services or buyers of products or services.
- Imposing its liabilities on the broadest possible income base, with the broadest and most general possible exclusion of current saving and the most complete possible inclusion of all returns on that saving.
- Imposing its liabilities at the lowest and flattest possible statutory rates, relying on a zero-rate bracket and personal exemptions to afford whatever degree of progression in effective tax rates by income level that can be justified against any comprehensible and acceptable standard.
- Imposing its liabilities on the largest possible number of people and in such a manner as to make each of them as aware as possible of his or her tax liability.

A tax system of this character would be vastly simpler and much more nearly uniform in its application than is the existing system. It would, therefore, consist far less than the existing system of what are in fact differential excises on ways of producing and of using income. It would, therefore, introduce fewer distortions into the market system's price and cost signals, and accordingly impair economic efficiency to a much lesser degree. In addition, it would be much fairer than the present system, imposing liabilities at a far more nearly uniform marginal rate on a more clearly understood and acceptable tax base, one substantially devoid of the differentials resulting from arbitrary and arcane special provisions. It would produce each dollar of revenue with less cost of compliance, administration, and enforcement than the present system. It could not be achieved overnight, but its ultimate specifications should be identified at the outset of any tax reform legislation so that legislative missteps and deviations might be minimized.

Spending and the Budget

It is far from clear whether further substantial deceleration in the growth of federal spending is feasible if defense preparation is not to be emasculated and if transfer payment programs—"entitlements"—are deemed untouchable. Whether the spending growth rate can be slowed, the spending policy imperative calls for shifting the priority of budget questions from "how much" to "why; is that an appropriate objective; how can it best be pursued." Only then should the question be raised, "how much of the nation's resources should be devoted to it?" This shift in priorities entails rejecting the amount of the deficit as having any bearing on the determination of budget policy and spending programs. Logic and empirical evidence show clearly that it is the level of government spending that imposes burdens on the private economy, and not the level borrowing. Advocates of "deficit closing" tax increases have failed to show either that tax hikes are less damaging than borrowing or that missing taxes actually will reduce borrowing—since the increases will only weaken the resolve to cut spending.

If followed, this approach would lead to major revisions in so-called entitlement programs. It would have the federal government withdraw from the business of providing retirement annuities under the Social Security system, transferring this function to the private insurance industry. It would also imply privatizing unemployment insurance. A private insurance system with premiums reflecting the differential hazards of unemployment among occupations and industries would help the market to cast up more accurate signals about the risk-adjusted rewards for alternative jobs. The same approach to decision-making in spending would yield comparable results over a broad spectrum of existing programs, very likely with major reductions in outlays, and possibly in tax revenues, as well.

Regulatory Policy

The most important gains in the reform of government regulation during the first term were made in connection with financial institutions. The next Administration should not re-regulate but rather recapture the deregulation momentum, aimed at providing a private market environment for banks and other financial companies [See section in this volume on the Regulatory Process].

Monetary Policy and Monetary Systems

The results of the highly volatile, unpredictable monetary policy which has been pursued for many years have led to an increasingly widespread conviction that fundamental and drastic revision of the

U.S. and international monetary systems is essential. Proposals for reform range from urging a return to some unspecified gold standard to substitution of the price of gold, or that of a basic commodity basket, as the criterion for determining changes in the stock of money by the Federal Reserve. At the extreme, there are even proposals for eliminating all central bank functions of the Federal Reserve, relying instead on banking institutions to create money in response to free market demands for it.

All of these proposals share a conviction that the observed ills in the domestic and international monetary systems are attributable to the Federal Reserve's following the wrong rules. In fact, the problems appear to derive far more from the Fed's failure to apply any approach systematically and consistently. The Fed appears to operate on the conviction that it has both the responsibility and the capability to determine and control the levels and rates of growth of both nominal and real GNP, and hence the inflation rate, and that its actions to control monetary aggregates should be determined on the basis of its forecasts regarding both the short-term course of nominal and real GNP and the price level under alternative monetary aggregate and interest rate scenarios. Its track record, however, reveals that the Fed is more often mistaken than correct, that the connection between its actions and real GNP is minimal, and that the principal result of its policy in recent years has been extreme uncertainty in the domestic and world money markets, and consequently an undue increase in the risk premium in interest rates.

It is not the lack of acceptable and useful rules that is the source of most of the monetary system ills, but the failure of the Fed to follow any one such rule consistently. The Fed should adopt and rigorously adhere to that rule which generates the greatest possible degree of certainty by financial market participants as to the Fed's actions—although not necessarily as to what the consequences of those actions will be. A rule that calls for the Fed to chase after the price of any particular commodity or basket of commodities is likely to prove counterproductive. The probability of actually stabilizing any such price is slight, and the consequences of success or failure in doing so are likely to be insignificant. The pursuit of any such a goal, on the other hand, is certain to require a high degree of discretionary conduct by the Fed, thereby maximizing uncertainty about the results of that conduct for the change in monetary aggregates. This is, of course, the very problem that current Fed policy produces. As long as the Fed continues to perform central bank functions, the most important guiding principle should be that it acts in such a way and according to that rule that minimizes market uncertainty about monetary aggregates.

Even the most nearly optimum Federal Reserve policy and institutional arrangements should not be invested with the promise of resolving the difficulties in the international money market. No monetary rule can be guaranteed to impose a discipline that will overcome the inefficiencies of socialized economies abroad. Nor will any rule preclude the policymakers of many other nations from forming extravagant expectations and pursuing imprudent, unrealistic, free-lunch economic policies. But an appropriate rule, along with the freest possible domestic financial markets, would impose a wholesome discipline on U.S. financial institutions that would contribute over the long run to a sounder, more productive world economy.

INITIATIVES FOR 1985

To set the tone for policy in the next four years the President should take the opportunity, early in 1985, to reaffirm the Administration's commitment to the four components of policy he formulated in 1981: a reduction of the growth of federal spending; tax revisions to reduce distortions of the operations of the free market; regulatory reform; and a steady, moderate growth of the supply of money while freeing financial markets of undue regulatory contraints.

Guided by these objectives, the Administration should move forward in 1985 with a number of proposals setting policy firmly on the course outlined above.

1) Resist deficit hysteria.

Calls for tax increases to "cut" the deficit should be attacked. Tax increases would damage the recovery, introduce new distortions into the economy, and take the pressure off spending reductions.

2) Concentrate on spending reforms and reductions.

The President should press for further spending cuts to reduce the pre-emption of resources by the government. The Administration should carefully examine innovative approaches to budget control, such as privatization, and support proposals to reform the runaway congressional budget process.

3) Improve the tax system.

Tax simplification and the lowering of rates would remove part of the dampening effect of taxes on the economy. On the other hand, flat tax proposals that widen the tax base by increasing taxes on saving should be strongly opposed.

In pursuing the goal of eliminating the tax bias against saving, the Administration should support modifications of the tax code that move in the direction of excluding current saving from the tax base, for example, by extending the IRA exclusion.

4) Encourage consistency in Fed policy.

The Administration should press the Federal Reserve Board to maintain a systematic and consistent rule in its monetary policy. Attempts by the Fed to "fine-tune" the economy have been counterproductive, leading to confusion and higher risk premiums in the financial markets.

Part 2

Defense and Foreign Policy Agencies

Overview-Defense and Foreign Policy

by
W. Bruce Weinrod

The Reagan Administration took office confronting a decade-long accumulation of foreign and defense policy problems. Reduced military spending, unilateral halts in weapons systems, and a reluctance to consider the use of force all contributed to a perception abroad of U.S. retrenchment. Detente, flawed arms control treaties, and loosened strategic trade and credit flow restrictions to the Soviet bloc, meanwhile, helped shift the military balance away from the West.

Vietnam, Watergate, the general leadership failure of the Carter years, and the deliberate muting of the Soviet challenge by Administrations of both parties had led some Americans to conclude that: 1) the threat or actual use of U.S. force, except where narrowly defined vital U.S. interests are clearly at stake, is unwise; 2) the U.S. no longer could influence significantly the course of world events; 3) the U.S. is the primary cause of international tensions and conflict, or at least is as much to blame as Moscow; 4) the expansion of U.S. influence is undesirable; 5) the triumph of leftist or Marxist insurgencies and movements in developing nations is inevitable; and 6) the President's authority to use force overseas should be seriously constrained.

The Reagan Administration has had a profound impact upon international politics. By rebuilding America's arsenal and restoring the lost balance in U.S.-Soviet military power, by moving decisively in Grenada which once again legitimized U.S. use of force and illustrated that Marxist control is not irreversible, by vigorously encouraging democratic evolution in friendly authoritarian and quasi-demo-cratic nations, and by its stated refusal to accept the permanency of totalitarian rule or Soviet imposition of its system in Central Europe, the Administration demonstrated that a decline of the West or a triumph of leftist totalitarianism is not inevitable. The Administration has reinvigorated Americans' traditional optimism and confidence in their own economic system and the U.S. role in the world, as well as in the prospects for the flourishing of Western values elsewhere.

Among the most important developments in national security policy were: 1) modernization of U.S. defenses; 2) offering a vision and a new paradigm for U.S.-Soviet strategic relations through a defensive nuclear strategy; 3) deployment of U.S. intermediate-range ballistic missiles in Europe; 4) the successful working out of agreements and understandings with U.S. allies to tighten restrictions on strategic, trade, and credit flows to the Soviet bloc; 5) the refusal to bargain away U.S. security interests in arms reduction talks in return for short-term domestic political gains.

In foreign affairs, important developments included: 1) maintaining Western alliance unity despite potentially divisive issues; 2) steps toward forging a Pacific community of free nations allied with the West; 3) consolidating democratic institutions in El Salvador and elsewhere; 4) reversal of Communist encroachment in Grenada; 5) halting more than a decade of Soviet expansion; and 6) emphasizing the battle of ideas and the content of broadcasting to Soviet-bloc nations; 7) improvement of U.S. relations with the People's Republic of China without abandoning the traditional U.S. friendship with the Republic of China on Taiwan.

While the Administration's record on balance was quite good, there were problems. Among them: 1) confusion in determining a basing mode for the MX intercontinental ballistic missile, thereby squandering momentum for congressional and public acceptance of the MX; 2) bowing to Congress' demands that the development or deployment of military systems be linked with arms control progress; 3) failure to coordinate adequately strategic trade policy or to give the Department of Defense a clearer role in the process; 4) assignment of a low priority to Central America at the early stages of the Administration, which delayed personnel and other changes needed for a successful U.S. policy in the region; 5) failure to assist adequately the Afghan freedom fighters; 6) committing U.S. forces to Lebanon without sufficient evaluation of its implications. Sharing the blame for some of these shortcomings, of course, is Congress, which often refused to give the Administration the resources it requested to implement its policies.

The Administration also has not conveyed a complete sense of the goals of U.S. foreign and defense policy. This is necessary to provide guidelines for Administration policy makers and to demonstrate cohesion and purpose to the public. The following sections of *Mandate II* offer several themes and a number of specific suggestions, which can serve as a framework for foreign and defense policy in the second Reagan Administration.

THEME 1: Defending America

Historians almost certainly will view Reagan's strategic defense initiative (SDI) as the most important national security development of his first Administration. By seeking a defensive system capable of destroying incoming Soviet or other hostile missiles, SDI is consonant with the proposition that protection of the civilian population is a primary obligation of government. It is also consistent with the moral impulse to avoid or reduce the possibility of mass civilian destruction. Finally, through protecting U.S. retaliatory capability, the SDI would strengthen deterrence by reducing the possibility that the Soviets might believe that a first-strike could succeed. SDI has forced rethinking of strategic doctrines and approaches developed three decades ago, and has sparked efforts to integrate the current strategic balance and advanced technologies into strategic thinking.

The Administration must raise SDI's priority and pursue such objectives as: clarifying the goals and priorities of strategic defense with an emphasis upon technologies that can destroy missiles in their boost-phase; upgrade air defenses, since a defensive system also should protect against incoming bombers and cruise missiles; integrate civil defense planning into the SDI, since population protection would multiply the positive impact of strategic defense; and develop short-term options to protect the vulnerable U.S. retaliatory capability, especially the new MX missile, through ballistic missile defense.

At the same time, the U.S. must continue modernization of strategic offensive forces, strengthening of conventional capabilities, and development of new technologies for NATO to offset Soviet-bloc quantitative advantages. Restrictions on strategic trade with the Soviet bloc should be tightened further and all subsidized credit flows to Moscow and its satellites should be ended. Arms reduction negotiations with Moscow should be approached with great caution and not made the centerpiece or litmus test of U.S.-Soviet relations.

Particular attention should be given to the unique problems created by Soviet and Soviet proxy involvement in the developing world. A new organizational structure should coordinate U.S. policy and actions regarding low-intensity warfare. Terrorism should be viewed as a form of warfare rather than as isolated violence, and therefore, treated as a part of low-intensity conflict policy. U.S. intelligence capabilities must be improved to enable the U.S. to deal with terrorists before they have acted.

The Administration should initiate policies that prod internal Soviet reform and an end to its expansionism abroad. In Central America, pluralism and an end to Soviet-bloc alliances with nations of that region must be pursued. In the Middle East, Soviet efforts to control energy resources, and the adventurism of Libya, must be countered. Security ties with, and racial reform in, South Africa should be pursued, as should the removal of Cuban troops from Angola, where free elections should be held.

THEME 2: Strengthening Alliances and Assisting Friends

The U.S. needs friends around the world to be secure and prosper and to lessen the chances of conflict. Among the ways to strengthen the U.S. alliance structure and its ties with its friends around the world are: increasing NATO's military strength by emphasizing emerging advanced technologies, increased cooperative production and standardization of weapons systems, agreements on sharing responsibility for threats to the alliance from outside of NATO's boundaries, and the creation of a new commission to review unresolved and potential future problems in the U.S.-European relationship.

The effort to develop a Pacific Basin Community and to increase Japanese defense efforts should be a high priority. In the Middle East, the strategic relationship with Israel should grow. Administration efforts, begun in the first term, to stabilize or strengthen friendly governments in the developing nations, and to assist them with military aid when insurgencies threaten their survival, should continue. Economic assistance programs should remain an element of U.S. policy, but must emphasize private sector development, incentives, and the free flow of capital into and out of developing nations.

THEME 3: Promoting Democratic Pluralism

The Reagan years have witnessed a strengthening and spreading of democratic pluralism internationally. Numerous governments with fragile democratic institutions have held successful free elections; other regimes have continued moving toward democracy. Still others have become fully democratic. In the case of Bolivia, for instance, the Administration helped forestall a coup against an elected government.

The Administration should continue this highly important effort. Obviously, the Administration objective should not be to impose exact replicas of the U.S. political system. Each nation's political structure must take into account the unique history and customs of that people. At the same time, the common denominator of Administration efforts should be the development and consolidation of pluralistic institutions and procedures that permit competing centers of power and influence, within the government (an independent judiciary, the rule of law) and in the society at large (independent religious institutions, free press, private enterprise and voluntary unions).

Full observance of human rights is an important part of democratic pluralism. In this regard, the extension of Western influence and democracy and the blocking of Soviet advances are in themselves human rights' victories. At the same time, a number of steps could encourage democratic pluralism, including: assisting friendly nondemocratic regimes threatened by Soviet-backed Marxist insurgencies, since the imposition of leftist totalitarian rule precludes democratic evolution; applying pressure when appropriate on friendly non-democratic governments to commence or continue democratic evolution and to respect human rights; channelling National Endowment for Democracy and other U.S. funds into programs that institute or consolidate democratic institutions.

THEME 4: Challenging the Soviet Union

In public statements, the President and other high Administration officials have emphasized that the U.S. does not accept the current expanse of the Soviet empire as a permanent and irreversible feature of the historic landscape. Regarding Grenada, for example, a Soviet-supported regime was replaced by one which is attempting to build democratic institutions. The U.S. has stated, meanwhile, that it does not accept as permanent the destruction of democratic institutions in Central Europe. As for international Communism itself, that, says President Reagan, will "end up on the ash heap of history."

These premises of the Reagan first term were supported by a number of developments. The Soviet Union seemed to be stagnating, witnessing declines in many indices of economic and material well-being. Events in Central Europe continued to demonstrate that Communism and Soviet domination have not taken root. Mozambique and Angola showed signs of moving away from the Soviet orbit, while the success of the UNITA forces in Angola demonstrated that Marxist governments can face strong indigenous challenges, and the growing strength of the democratic forces within Nicaragua made the full consolidation of Communist control doubtful.

The second Reagan Administration should continue to challenge Moscow. The Soviet empire will not collapse soon. U.S. policies can prod the process of transformation within the USSR and an end to its expansionism.

Most important, Washington must develop a coherent strategy, rather than a series of isolated tactics for dealing with the Soviet challenge. This strategy must take into account the fact that the USSR is an empire with many weaknesses and vulnerabilities, internally and on its periphery.

The U.S. also should expand its efforts at public diplomacy, particularly in broadcasting factual information to Soviet-bloc inhabitants about the nature and extent of internal failings of the Communist system. At the same time, the U.S. must not strengthen or help preserve the Soviet system. As such, Washington must restrict

Moscow's access to Western advanced technologies and to subsidized credit flows. Soviet rulers must be forced to make difficult decisions about the allocation of resources.

* * *

These key themes—defending America, strengthening alliances, promoting democratic pluralism and challenging the Soviet Union—provide the framework for a coherent and consistent U.S. national security and foreign policy for the next four years. Such a framework would provide touchstones for policymakers as they deal with the myriad of daily policy decisions and would convey to the American public a sense of direction in U.S. policy.

Public support is essential to the long-term success of U.S. foreign policy. The Administration, therefore, must ensure public awareness and understanding of the nature of the challenges facing the U.S. as well as the appropriate U.S. response. Part of this effort should be an attempt to recreate a bipartisan consensus for U.S. foreign and national security policy. Ultimately, the public and the Congress must understand and accept the rationale of Administration policy, or there will be difficulties in fulfilling it.

Policy consists not only of objectives and programs, of course, but also of people and process. The Reagan agenda will succeed only if the President appoints individuals who understand and are committed to his worldview. At the same time, changes in the role of the National Security Council and in the structure of the Departments of Defense and State, could boost the chances of Reagan's policies succeeding.

Ronald Reagan achieved much in his first term. But Moscow has a long-term view. For there to be real change in the Soviet system and its international behavior, the new Reagan Administration must resist the temptation of easy or short-term solutions. The President therefore must assemble a foreign policy and national security team that shares his worldview, and proceed with an agenda that offers the hope and vision of a world where tyranny of the left and the right is fading and where democratic pluralism and self-determination flourish.

13

The Department of Defense

STRATEGIC OFFENSIVE FORCES

by
Joseph T. Mayer*

The Reagan Administration has made important progress toward modernizing America's strategic nuclear Triad of land-, air-, and sea-based forces, as well as the crucial network of command, control, communications and intelligence (C³I) systems. Nonetheless, the growing Soviet threat and overall U.S. security requirements demand renewed urgency and commitment to U.S. strategic modernization.

SECRETARY
Caspar Weinberger, 1981-Present

PERSONNEL:		
	Civilian	1,015,779
	Army	780,000
	Air Force	592,000
	Navy	558,000
	Marine Corps	194,000

BUDGET (In Billions of Dollars)

1985 Estimate	$297.8
1984 Estimate	$250.6
1983 Actual	$223.9
1982 Actual	$185.9
1981 Actual	$159.2
1980 Actual	$136.0
1975 Actual	$ 87.1

Established: 1949

Major Programs:
- Department of the Air Force
- Department of the Navy
- Department of the Army
- United States Marine Corps

* Task Force members included Eugene Iwanciw and Dr. Francis P. Hoeber.

The Reagan program recognizes the ultimate significance of the U.S.-Soviet nuclear force competition, without sacrificing the modernization and readiness needs of U.S. general purpose forces. In fact, strategic programs account for only some 10-15 percent of the total Pentagon budget, as compared to a high of over 25 percent under President Kennedy.

The strategic modernization package announced by President Reagan in October 1981 laid the foundation for the long-term recovery of U.S. nuclear forces, but it fell short of providing a short-term response to the Carter-Mondale legacy of strategic neglect. It remains, nonetheless, a useful framework for shaping the strategic forces agenda for the next four years and beyond.

The most serious shortcomings of the Reagan Administration's strategic program are: (1) failure to address adequately the "window of vulnerability," particularly that of U.S. land-based missiles; (2) unwarranted production cutbacks and constraints in proposed modernization programs; and (3) compliance with the unratified SALT II Treaty, despite continuing Soviet violations—a problem exacerbated by congressional attempts to tie U.S. weapons programs to arms control negotiations.

THE NEXT FOUR YEARS

Continue nuclear deterrence based upon force modernization.

A policy of nuclear deterrence will remain central to U.S. national security for the forseeable future. To deter Soviet aggression or terminate it, consistent with preserving the security of the U.S. and its allies, requires a credible nuclear strategy and force structure. U.S. strategy has evolved toward a greater emphasis on the ability to destroy Soviet political and military assets, instead of population centers. What had been absent, until the Reagan Administration, was a commitment to deploy forces capable of executing such a strategy. Yet, to be credible to the Soviets, this strategy must be backed by survivable U.S. nuclear forces, including those capable of accurately striking hardened Soviet targets, such as missile silos and leadership command facilities.

Maintain and strengthen the strategic Triad

The strategic Triad strengthens deterrence through a mutually reinforcing balance of land-, air-, and sea-based weapons. These three components, each with its unique characteristics, complicate the Soviet targeting and defense problems, and safeguard against failure by a specific system or unanticipated technology breakthroughs. The Triad, therefore, continues to be a prudent means of structuring U.S. strategic nuclear forces.

Develop the relationship between strategic offense and strategic defense

Strategic offensive forces alone can no longer carry the sole burden of preserving the nuclear peace. Technological advances now make possible fulfillment of the moral and strategic imperative to shield the U.S. from nuclear attack. This can be accomplished by integrating strategic defensive and offensive forces and should be one of the highest U.S. national security priorities.

To achieve these objectives, the program recommendations detailed below should be implemented during the course of the next four years.

Restructure the Strategic Defense Initiative to provide for defense of MX

The proposal to base MX in existing Minuteman silos does not improve the chances of the land-based element of the strategic Triad to survive a Soviet attack. Therefore, the Strategic Defense Initiative should provide for the defense of the MX. Preferential defense of MX should be achieved, at least initially, by means of a traditional land-based ballistic missile defense system, as a first step toward a more advanced, comprehensive defense. Further silo hardening technology should also be incorporated into the MX basing system as quickly as research allows.

Increase and Improve MX

The decision to reduce the MX program from 200 to 100 missiles, and the failure of Congress to fund fully the Administration's budget requests, has slowed the process of redressing the destabilizing Soviet advantage in prompt, hard-target-capable weapons. A supplemental budget request should restore MX production to the Fiscal Year 1985 request of 40 missiles. In view of significant hardening of the Soviet target structure, the U.S. should also deploy the higher yield MK-21 warhead for MX. Finally, a review of the U.S. nuclear force posture should take place during the MX deployment to consider the potential need for additional missiles beyond the planned force of 100.

Develop Midgetman missile

The Midgetman missile may hold the key to the longer-term future of U.S. land-based forces. Its size will provide greater basing flexibility, thus enhancing its survivability against a Soviet attack. The Defense Department, therefore, should continue to pursue a vigorous research and development (R&D) program for the Small Intercontinental Ballistic Missile (the so-called Midgetman), with the objective of examining the technical feasibility of initial deployment in this decade.

Improve Minuteman

The endurance and flexibility of the Minuteman missile force should be upgraded. The 100 Minuteman III missiles due to be replaced by the MX should be redeployed in Minuteman II silos in order to capitalize on the increased warhead number (3 to 1) and greater capability of the Minuteman III missile. Research and development funding should be allocated to address the potential for deploying light-weight Advanced Inertial Reference Sphere (AIRS) guidance systems on all Minuteman IIIs to improve missile accuracy. Retargetting capabilities from airborne launch control centers should be incorporated into all Minuteman IIIs, and funds should be budgeted to complete an emergency power supply program for the remaining 350 Minuteman III missiles to enhance the endurance and effectiveness of surviving missiles following a Soviet first strike. Finally, serious consideration should be given to the full deployment of MK-12A warheads on all Minuteman IIIs to improve the Minuteman's capability against hardened Soviet targets.

Provide advance procurement funds for additional B-1 bombers

The B-52 bomber fleet is aging, increasingly expensive to operate and maintain, and of decreasing effectiveness against sophisticated Soviet air defenses. To compensate for the ultimate retirement of B-52s, the U.S. needs a robust B-1 bomber force. Therefore, the arbitrary production limit of 100 B-1s should be raised, and advance procurement funds should be requested in FY 1986 to initiate the purchase of an additional 75 to 100 B-1s. This will allow the U.S. to keep open a strategic bomber production line for three to four more years, while work on the Advanced Technology Bomber (ATB) or "Stealth" bomber continues—thus avoiding a gap in strategic bomber production, while also taking advantage of reduced per unit costs for additional B-1s, and maintaining competitive cost and quality incentives for the ATB program.

Production of more than 100 B-1s is an appropriate response to Soviet air defenses and the requirements of deterrence. In addition, it would strengthen the U.S. negotiating position in the Strategic Arms Reduction Talks (START). The B-1's conventional force capabilities also constitute an asset for meeting future U.S. force projection needs in a nuclear conflict. Inland basing of these bombers should be exploited to maximize their survivability against Soviet submarine-launched ballistic missile (SLBM) attack.

Develop Stealth technology

The Advanced Technology Bomber program should remain a high priority to develop and exploit new technologies, such as a reduced radar cross section, in a next-generation aircraft. Major advances in this area already have been incorporated into the current B-1 and cruise missile programs.

Upgrade current air-launched cruise missiles (ALCMs) with improved engine, guidance, and electronic-countermeasure systems

Strong support should be maintained for the "Stealth" or advanced cruise missile (ACM) program which is needed to overcome steadily improving Soviet air-defenses. However, the range and accuracy of current ALCM weapons should also be upgraded with improved engine, guidance, and electronic countermeasure systems.

Safeguard Sea-Based Forces

The survivability of U.S. sea-based strategic nuclear forces long has been considered a major factor in maintaining deterrence. These systems are hampered, however, by their tenuous communication links with national command authorities, their limited hard-target capabilities and their vulnerability to attack while in port (only 40 percent to 60 percent of the fleet is at sea under normal operating conditions). Nor can the U.S. assume that sea-based forces always will remain highly survivable. Considerable attention should be given to assessing Soviet improvements in anti-submarine warfare (ASW) capabilities, as well as potential countermeasures to such developments.

Maintain Submarine Capabilities

Faster, quieter and more survivable Trident submarines should be procured at a pace of at least one boat per year to ensure the timely replacement of older Poseidon subs. Poseidons, nonetheless, continue to make a contribution to deterrence, and the U.S. should not deactivate these boats solely to comply with the unratified SALT II Treaty. Beginning in 1989, Trident subs should be equipped, as planned, with hard-target-capable D-5 missiles essential for preserving the credibility of the U.S. nuclear deterrent.

Deploy nuclear-armed sea-launched cruise missiles (SLCMs)

The deployment of nuclear-armed SLCMs on attack submarines and surface ships will enhance the credibility of the U.S. sea-based deterrent by providing a dispersed, flexible and survivable capability to strike hardened enemy targets at long ranges.

Strengthen Command, Control, Communications and Intelligence

C^3I is the glue that holds the U.S. nuclear deterrent together. It provides for timely warning of attack and allows the National Command Authority to issue orders in response to a nuclear attack. Programs to improve the responsiveness and endurance of U.S. C^3I systems should continue to receive high priority.

Specifically, the submarine communication system (Extremely Low Frequency or "ELF") should be completed, and development of laser communications for subs should be expedited. In addition, the TACAMO submarine communication planes should be replaced with new aircraft, equipped with advanced communications units, to ensure enduring communications with Trident subs capable of operating at extended ranges.

C^3I facilities should be hardened to protect against nuclear effects. The survivability of critical space-based intelligence assets should be improved, and expendable launch vehicles (ELVs) should be procured to provide a standby satellite launch replacement capability. The utilization of new technologies, including fiber optics and very high speed integrated circuits (VHSIC), should also be exploited to the benefit of all three legs of the Triad.

Modernize Nuclear Materials and Warheads

The modernization program outlined above includes requirements for newer, more efficient nuclear warheads. Therefore, great attention should be paid to assuring the timely availability of nuclear materials. This requires the modernization of production facilities and support for vigorous warhead research programs at U.S. national laboratories in Los Alamos, Sandia, and Lawrence Livermore.

Accelerate maneuverable warhead (MARV) program

As a result of Soviet efforts to deploy a comprehensive strategic defense system—aided by violations of the ABM Treaty—there exists an urgent requirement for research and development on means to ensure that U.S. ballistic missile warheads can penetrate Soviet defenses and reach their targets successfully. This effort should emphasize penetration aids and maneuvering re-entry vehicles (MARVs), with the goal of significantly reducing the time required to deploy these systems in the event of a Soviet break-out from the ABM Treaty. The U.S. Strategic Defense Initiative and retaliatory warhead programs also are needed as hedges to protect against a possible Soviet treaty break-out.

INITIATIVES FOR 1985

The Administration should formulate Fiscal Year 1985 supplemental and Fiscal Year 1986 budget requests to ensure funds to:

1) Restore MX production to 40 missiles for Fiscal Year 1985;

2) Structure the Strategic Defense Initiative to provide for the defense of MX;

3) Provide advance procurement monies for additional B-1 bombers;

4) Upgrade current ALCMs with improved engine, guidance and electronic-countermeasure systems; and,

5) Deploy nuclear-armed SLCMs.

STRATEGIC DEFENSE

by
Carnes Lord*

In what must be accounted an historic act, President Reagan announced, on March 23, 1983, that the U.S. would pursue technologies that could offer an alternative to current U.S. reliance on offensive strategic forces for sustaining nuclear deterrence. The rationale behind the Administration's Strategic Defense Initiative (SDI), as it has come to be called, breaks fundamentally with the theory of "mutual assured destruction" that has dominated American thinking about nuclear strategy for the last twenty years. This is a welcome and long overdue development. Subsequent studies of the technologies and the policy implications of ballistic missile defense (BMD) have validated the President's initial confidence in the concept.[1]

A new office has been established immediately under the Secretary of Defense to oversee and coordinate SDI program development, and the Administration has requested modest amounts of additional funding for SDI-related research and development in FY 85. These are important and necessary steps. At the same time, much remains to be done, and there is considerable cause for concern over the scope and pace of the strategic defense effort and the level of commitment to it by the Administration as a whole, and by the Department of Defense in particular.

The true significance of the SDI lies not so much in the promise of particular technologies for defense against Soviet ballistic missiles, but in the recognition that defense of the United States is critical to effective deterrence, an essential mission of American military forces, and provides the possibility of substantial protection for the public should nuclear conflict occur. Intellectual habits and organizational imperatives within the defense establishment continue, however, to work powerfully against such a view. The Administration so far has not done enough to ensure that the SDI has the doctrinal and organizational support it needs if it is to be sustained over the coming decades. It has failed to generate widespread public support for the strategic defense concept or to lay the groundwork for broad and sustained public and congressional backing of substantial increases in funding in future years. The constant drumbeat of politically inspired criticism of the SDI must be countered by a well-conceived and

---

* Task Force members included Colin Gray, Robert Pfaltzgraff, and Joseph Douglass.

[1]The study of defensive technologies long predates the President's initiative. One particular technological concept, proposed by General Daniel Graham's High Frontier project, focused on orbiting satellites and played a key role in rekindling interest in strategic defenses.

coordinated effort of public education and political advocacy by Administration spokesmen.

In the area of doctrine, there is little evidence that the Administration yet has integrated strategic defense fully into American nuclear force planning. Attention has focused on the long-term possibilities of nationwide defense against ballistic missile attack at the expense of near-term options for protection of key military assets such as land-based ballistic missiles. Moreover, virtually no attention appears to have been given to dimensions of strategic defense other than Ballistic Missile Defense. Yet an understanding of the important inter-relationship between BMD and continental air defense, land defense (defense of land-based military assets against special operations and sabotage), and civil defense is crucial to evaluating the promise of a defense-dominant strategic posture.

With respect to organization, the problems posed by Army control of U.S. BMD programs are likely to become increasingly acute as strategic defense lays greater claim to the defense budget. Effective integration of strategic offensive and defensive programs probably will require that the Air Force have executive responsibility in both of these areas. At the level of the Office of the Secretary of Defense and the Joint Staff, effective mechanisms need to be established for coordinating planning and policy across the spectrum of strategic defense activities, including civil defense. At the minimum, this should involve strengthening and expanding the scope of the new SDI office. At the operational level, relationships between the various joint and service commands (as well as the civilian agencies) with responsibilities in this area need to be worked out.

THE NEXT FOUR YEARS

Clarify Strategic Defense Priorities

The fundamental objective of a BMD program should not be "leak proof" defense of the continental U.S. (which no system could guarantee), but deterrence of Soviet attack against the U.S. or its allies by complicating Soviet military planning and minimizing the prospects for successful execution of Soviet nuclear strategy. At the same time, a full-scale strategic defense system could save many millions of American lives should a nuclear conflict occur. There is no conflict between the long-term goal of a boost-phase BMD capability utilizing exotic technologies and the near-term goal of closing the "window of vulnerability" that continues to undermine the deterrent value of U.S. offensive nuclear forces. The U.S. approach to BMD program development should emphasize the development of multiple systems that can destroy missiles in boost-phase, in space, and as they approach U.S. missile bases and other important sites. Defensive systems should be deployed sequentially as the appropriate technologies mature.

Protect retaliatory capability

First priority should be given to defending high-value military targets, particularly the MX (but also the Midgetman when it is deployed) ICBM. Homing Overlay Experiment (HOE) technology, recently tested successfully for the first time, which provides the capability to intercept incoming missile warheads before they re-enter the atmosphere, should be pursued vigorously as the basis for a system to be deployed in the early 1990s. Renewed attention needs to be given to near-term deployment options for the Sentry program (formerly Low Altitude Defense System) for terminal defense of ICBMs. In particular, the option of a modified, less costly Sentry system involving a single stage interceptor missile should be considered. Other possibilities for inexpensive terminal defense of ICBM silos and other critical targets should continue to be explored. ABM Treaty constraints should not be allowed to inhibit planning for non-nuclear BMD capabilities that support essential strategic force requirements, and early, large-scale deployment options should be readied in any event as a response to Soviet treaty non-compliance or deployment of a full defensive system.

Emphasize shorter over longer-term technologies

While it is premature to pronounce in favor of any of the exotic systems for nationwide BMD currently under consideration, it is critical that the research effort not be diverted from pursuing options that would provide some measure of population or area defense by the mid-1990s.

Upgrade air defenses

The U.S. faces a major challenge from rapidly developing Soviet capabilities in long-range bomber aircraft and cruise missiles. In this light, air defense requirements for the continental U.S. and NATO Europe have to be reevaluated radically. There is an urgent need for a new continental air defense doctrine going well beyond the current minimalist posture. Renewed production and procurement of E-2

Airborne Warning and Control System (AWACS) aircraft is critical for effective monitoring of attacking aircraft and cruise missiles. Advanced interceptors dedicated to the continental air defense mission are needed in numbers substantially greater than currently planned. Procurement of the Patriot air defense system also should proceed, but priority should be given to replacing this outdated system with a high-performance missile system with capabilities against cruise and ballistic missiles as well as aircraft. The Joint Anti-Tactical Missile currently under development may fill this role, but a strong effort is needed to persuade the Congress that alleged ABM Treaty constraints should not be permitted to inhibit the military effectiveness of such a system. What is required is a missile comparable to the Soviet SA-12, which is currently believed to have capabilities against U.S. theater and even strategic ballistic missiles.

Rethink role of civil defense

Improved BMD and air defense of the United States will alter fundamentally the terms of the debate over the utility and nature of U.S. civil defense programs. A strong argument can be made for transferring civil defense responsibility from the Federal Emergency Management Agency to the Department of Defense. At the same time, the Department of Defense must be encouraged to view civil defense (as well as land defense of military assets) as a critical element of its mission, and to integrate it fully with strategic defense planning.

INITIATIVES FOR 1985

1) Review Defense Department organization and doctrine to support a comprehensive strategic defense effort.

2) Develop options for near-term defense of MX and other key military targets.

3) Accelerate timetable for deployment of mid-course and boost phase BMD systems to the mid-1990s.

4) Accelerate development of a new high-performance air defense missile system with capabilities against cruise and ballistic missiles.

5) Continue production and procurement of AWACS aircraft.

6) Increase procurement of interceptor aircraft for continental air defense.

7) Consider specific ways in which European and Asian (especially Japanese) technology and other resources can be integrated into the SDI.

ARMS REDUCTION

by
James T. Hackett*

The Reagan Administration took office committed to the urgent restoration of U.S. defense capabilities. The President promised to initiate the speedy modernization of U.S. forces, particularly the strategic deterrent. Substantial progress has been made toward that end, but deployment of many of the new weapons, such as the MX missile and B-1B bomber, will not be complete until the end of the decade. Others, such as the Stealth bomber and Midgetman missile, will not be ready for deployment until the 1990s. Therefore, Reagan's defense modernization must be continued to enable the U.S. to deal from strength in any arms control negotiations. Arms reduction efforts are prudent only in conjunction with defense modernization, not without it.

In 1981, the new Administration committed itself to review the record of SALT II and other arms control negotiations; develop new approaches leading to essential equivalence between U.S. and Soviet forces; assure that arms control negotiations were not divorced from the broader political and military behavior of the parties; negotiate with Moscow only on a basis of strict reciprocity; and conclude no arms control agreement locking the U.S. into military inferiority. As promised, the Administration thoroughly reviewed arms control issues before resuming negotiations. When START (Strategic Arms Reduction Talks) began in June 1982, the U.S. proposed deep reductions in strategic offensive weapons. Despite subsequent U.S. revisions of its position, including a build-down proposal, Moscow kept repeating "nyet" and refused to return to the talks after the December 1983 recess.

While preparing to deploy Pershing II and ground launched cruise missiles (GLCMs) in Western Europe, the U.S. sought to eliminate a whole category of medium-range missiles in the Intermediate Nuclear Force (INF) negotiations. The Soviets used these negotiations to attempt to stop the deployments and to drive a wedge between the U.S. and its NATO allies. This effort failed; in Fall 1983, NATO began deploying Pershing IIs and GLCMs. The Soviets then walked out of the INF talks, declaring them dead unless the West stopped its deployments and removed from Europe the missiles already deployed. Moscow, meanwhile, continued its buildup of missiles aimed at Western Europe. By the end of 1984, the Soviets will have over 750

---

* Task Force members included Michelle Van Cleave and David Sullivan.

SS-20 warheads deployed against Western Europe, compared to only about 50 NATO Pershing II warheads.

The Administration determined to end the official U.S. cover-up of Soviet arms control violations and the practice of misleading the American people about Soviet policies and behavior. In January 1984, in response to a request from Congress, the Administration released an initial list of seven significant Soviet violations of arms control agreements. More comprehensive lists of at least 17 Soviet violations subsequently have become public. No further action, however, has been taken on the Soviet violations, other than fruitless discussions in the U.S.-Soviet Standing Consultative Commission (SCC), the compliance mechanism established under the SALT agreements. Despite years of effort, the SCC has been totally unable to resolve these compliance issues.

Arms control policies based on the hope that negotiations with Moscow will lead to agreements that effectively limit the major instruments of Soviet military and diplomatic power are unrealistic, lead to a false sense of security, and do not protect the American people. A new era in arms control is beginning, based on the development of defensive systems to protect the United States and its allies from Soviet missile attack. It includes a reduction in the destructiveness of offensive weapons made possible through improved accuracy, mobility, and survivability. This can lead to a reduction in the destructive power of nuclear weapons, while providing a more credible deterrent and greater real security for the American people.

THE NEXT FOUR YEARS

Avoid Unilateral Concessions

Negotiations must not be conducted simply for their own sake. The results of past arms control negotiations are not reassuring. The greatest increase in Soviet strategic power vis-a-vis the United States has occurred since 1972, despite alleged constraints on an arms buildup by SALT I, SALT II, and the ABM Treaty. Given the historical record and U.S. experience negotiating with Moscow, future agreements should not be concluded unless they actually prevent weapons increases and are effectively verifiable. History teaches that no agreement is better than an ambiguous or unverifiable one. There is more than one way to achieve arms reductions. Experience has shown that relying on the Soviets to comply with ambiguous signed agreements is not the best way.

Oppose Congressional Constraints

The President and his staff should firmly oppose efforts by Members of Congress to legislate unilateral U.S. arms constraints, or to "require" the executive branch either to engage in arms control negotiations or take certain arms control positions in dealing with the Soviets. Such intrusions into the executive authority of the President should be fought by the Administration in Congress and vetoed if passed.

Educate the Public

The President and his senior advisors should educate the public, Congress, and the allies on the limitations of the arms control process. The Administration should explain the possibilities of achieving genuine arms reductions and improved national security through defensive weapons, and the development of smaller, more accurate and more survivable offensive weapons.

Stand Firm on START and INF

The Administration has made far-reaching and significant proposals in START and in the Intermediate Range Nuclear Force negotiations for genuine, deep reductions in the U.S. and Soviet nuclear arsenals. The U.S. START proposal to "build down" ballistic missile warheads from current levels of 7,400 to 7,800 on each side to 5,000 is a sensible way to limit these destabilizing weapons. The U.S. should stand by these proposals.

Similarly, the original U.S. offer in the INF talks to eliminate an entire class of intermediate-range nuclear weapons still remains a desirable goal. The U.S. subsequently offered to limit deployments in Europe of Pershing IIs and GLCMs in exchange for a reduction in Soviet SS-20s. This remains a fair and prudent approach for reducing these weapons to equal levels, without abandoning the fundamental objective of eliminating them altogether. The U.S. and its allies should not be intimidated by Moscow into offering new concessions in order to get the Soviets back to the bargaining table. These talks on regional weapons should not be merged with the exceptionally complex negotiations on strategic arms.

Reject Limits on Strategic Defenses

The U.S. should reject any Soviet effort to limit the development or deployment of U.S. strategic defenses (the so-called Star Wars program). Reagan's Strategic Defense Initiative (SDI) is a promising new approach to preserving the U.S. nuclear deterrent and restoring strategic stability. SDI is an attempt to move away from the present balance of terror, which holds the American people hostage to the huge Soviet arsenal of strategic nuclear weapons, toward a defense against such weapons.

Soviet objections to the "militarization of space" are hollow and hypocritical in view of existing Soviet military activities in space, extensive Soviet research and development in space weapons and the fact that ballistic missiles already travel through space on their way to their target. The Soviets have built a massive offensive nuclear force, and now fear that advances in U.S. defensive technology will deny them use of that force to intimidate the West. With the allocation of sufficient resources, the U.S. can develop a defense that really—at last—defends. The SDI program should be given high priority. Soviet efforts to block or limit this program through arms control should be rejected as not in the security interests of the United States, except as part of an agreement that would significantly reduce Soviet strategic offensive forces.

Limit ASAT Discussions

Washington should continue to reject Soviet attempts to prevent the testing of a U.S. anti-satellite (ASAT) weapon. An ASAT program is essential to U.S. security and should not be suspended or delayed. The U.S. should discuss improved "rules of the road" for satellites and space vehicles to prevent accidents or incidents in space. But discussion of a limited ban on ASATs should not be undertaken unless careful analysis proves that a limited ban is feasible, verifiable, and would not adversely affect the U.S. Strategic Defense Initiative.

The U.S. is more dependent than the Soviet Union on satellites to perform the vital military functions of early warning, global communications, strategic targeting, and intelligence monitoring. Even small-scale Soviet cheating on an ASAT agreement could have catastrophic consequences for U.S. security. Therefore, ASAT negotiations must not be undertaken until all implications have been thoroughly considered and a determination made that such talks are in the national interest and could lead to desirable results.

Renegotiate or Withdraw from the ABM Treaty

The President should order the development and deployment of U.S. strategic defenses as rapidly as possible, and inform the Soviet Union at the appropriate time that U.S. security will no longer permit the U.S. to remain defenseless under the terms of the 1972 Anti-Ballistic Missile Treaty. There is little disagreement that Moscow has been violating the ABM Treaty by constructing a major ABM radar at Krasnoyarsk, by deploying air defense missiles that can be used against ballistic missiles as well as aircraft, and by developing the components of a nationwide ABM defense. This Soviet build-up of strategic defenses could presage a gradual Soviet "break-out" of the ABM Treaty. The Soviet build-up will erode enormously the credibility of the U.S. strategic deterrent. The President should insist that the Soviets comply with the ABM Treaty and correct their violations so long as the U.S. and U.S.S.R. are still parties to that agreement.

Technological developments, however, already have made the 12 year-old treaty anachronistic. The ABM agreement, in any event, was to have operated in conjunction with significant limits on U.S. and Soviet offensive strategic forces. More than a decade of negotiating has failed to produce a treaty effectively limiting offensive weapons. Without such a limitation, the ABM Treaty is destabilizing and detrimental to U.S. security. By constraining U.S., but not Soviet, strategic defenses, while the Soviets have continued to build up their offensive forces, the ABM Treaty has increased the vulnerability of the U.S. land-based deterrent.

The United States should take full advantage of recent rapid developments in high speed computers, laser weapons, and other advanced technology to develop and deploy defensive systems to protect the U.S. nuclear deterrent. Terminal defense of U.S. ICBM sites should be deployed first, followed by the development and deployment of a layered ABM defense of the United States. The U.S. should offer to renegotiate the ABM Treaty to permit the deployment of such defenses, with the understanding that if the Soviet Union does not agree to prompt renegotiation, the U.S. will withdraw from the Treaty. The constitutional requirement to provide for the common defense is a more compelling national responsibility than continued compliance with an agreement the Soviets are violating extensively.

Reject Unverifiable Nuclear Test Bans

The U.S. should insist on improvements in the verification procedures of the Threshold Test Ban Treaty (TTBT) before submitting it to the Senate for approval. In view of over 14 known Soviet violations of the 1974 Threshold Test Ban Treaty, the Administration has asked the Soviet Union to negotiate improved verification and compliance provisions, including on-site inspection on demand, before submitting it to the Senate. Ten years' experience has shown that current means of seismic verification are inadequate to verify Soviet compliance.

A comprehensive test ban (CTB) is not in the national interest and should not be pursued. The comprehensive nuclear test ban sought by some arms control advocates cannot be verified with existing technology. More important, a comprehensive test ban would be militarily undesirable, since a ban on all underground testing would erode the effectiveness of the U.S. nuclear arsenal, including the current offensive strategic, deterrent, and defensive weapons. Nuclear testing is necessary to develop safe, modern weapons, and to assure operational confidence in the existing stockpile. As long as there are nuclear powers that pose a threat to peace, such weapons will be needed to deter nuclear attack and prevent nuclear blackmail.

Stand Fast with MBFR Position

The U.S. should not make militarily disadvantageous concessions at the Mutual and Balanced Force Reduction negotiations (MBFR), which have been going on in Vienna for eleven years without much sign of agreement. Two major problems remain. One is the discrepancy of some 200,000 between what the West estimates and what Moscow claims are the Warsaw Pact troop levels. The second is the geographic asymmetry of forces. The Soviet heartland is only 300 miles from Central Europe and Moscow thus could reinforce a Warsaw Pact invasion quickly and massively. U.S. reinforcements are more than 3,000 miles away. The U.S. must not jeopardize Western security by making preemptive concessions on these issues.

Chemical Weapons Agreements

Cautiously Congress should approve funding for production of modern binary chemical weapons, which are needed to make the U.S. chemical deterrent safer to store and transport, and more credible. The existence of a substantial Soviet chemical warfare capability with no adequate Western deterrent increases the likelihood of the use of nuclear weapons, since that would be the only credible Western response to the Soviet use of chemical or biological weapons.

Verification of the production of chemical weapons, or the existence of chemical weapon stocks, is virtually impossible. Any chemical plant or laboratory can produce lethal chemical or biological agents. Similarly, militarily significant stockpiles can be hidden anywhere. Despite these major verification problems, the U.S. mistakenly has tabled a draft treaty at the 40-nation Committee on Disarmament (CD) in Geneva that attempts to ban the production of chemical weapons and calls for the destruction of existing stockpiles. Instead of proposing such unverifiable agreements, the U.S. should seek to establish mandatory international reporting, inspection, and compliance mechanisms to monitor the use of chemical and biological weapons. Mandatory international sanctions must be developed for use against nations employing such weapons.

Support Mandatory Confidence-Building Measures

In the Stockholm Conference on Disarmament in Europe (CDE), the U.S. should seek the adoption of useful confidence-building measures (CBMs), while opposing Soviet proposals for meaningless declaratory agreements. This 35-nation conference is an outgrowth of the Helsinki Conference on Security and Cooperation in Europe (CSCE). The Soviets complied with the Helsinki guidelines on confidence building measures only until the Polish crisis. Then the Soviets violated the guidelines. The U.S. should oppose voluntary CBMs and empty statements in support of peace, and press for mandatory measures that genuinely improve Western security. If unsuccessful, the U.S. should not agree to a second phase for this conference.

INITIATIVES FOR 1985

1) Establish a Presidential Arms Control Compliance Commission. The Commission would consist of top-level presidential advisers drawn from two existing bodies, the President's Foreign Intelligence Advisory Board and the President's General Advisory Committee on Arms Control and Disarmament. The Commission should have only two responsibilities: to advise the President on the national security implications of Soviet violations of arms control agreements and to recommend compensatory U.S. actions. The Commission would receive all intelligence pertinent to Soviet compliance and, from the Defense Department, military options for U.S. responses. Consulting with the Secretaries of State and Defense, the National Security

Adviser, and the Directors of Central Intelligence and Arms Control, the Commission would forward options and recommendations for action directly to the President. This would create an effective mechanism for promptly addressing compliance issues at the highest level of government. The existing mechanism is not effective, due to bureaucratic inertia, institutional biases, and conflicts of interest within the government over arms control policy. Without an effective compliance system, the U.S. should neither negotiate nor sign arms control agreements.

2) Designate a Compliance Official in the Department of Defense.

The President should assign a senior Pentagon official the prime responsibility for analyzing and assessing on a continuing basis the impact of Soviet violations on U.S. national security. This official and his staff would be responsible for developing and forwarding through the Secretary of Defense to the Presidential Compliance Commission recommendations on military steps, such as accelerated research and development, changes in weapons procurement, or deployments of forces, as possible compensatory measures in response to Soviet violations of arms control agreements.

3) Transfer the U.S. Standing Consultative Commission (SCC).

The SCC, which is responsible for raising arms control compliance issues with the Soviets, should be transferred from the Arms Control and Disarmament Agency to the White House, where it would report to the Presidential Compliance Commission.

4) Begin ABM Deployment.

Inform the Soviet Union through the SCC that the U.S. intends to reestablish the single ABM site permitted by the ABM Treaty. The site should be changed from Grand Forks, North Dakota, (deactivated since 1976) to the MX base at Cheyenne, Wyoming. A terminal ABM defense should be deployed there as soon as possible.

5) End SALT II Voluntary Observance.

Since the signing of SALT II in 1979, the Soviets have increased the number of nuclear warheads targeted on the United States by 75 percent. Moscow, moreover, has violated at least five key provisions of that agreement. Yet the U.S. continues to hold its strategic forces at levels set by SALT II even though the Senate has never approved the accord and despite Moscow's violations of it.

The Soviet Union is exceeding the overall numerical ceiling of 2,250 strategic nuclear delivery vehicles, the heart of the SALT II agreement. As of January 1, 1984, the Soviets had 2,524 strategic nuclear delivery vehicles covered by SALT II, plus 235 Backfire bombers not covered by SALT. The United States has fewer than 1,900 strategic nuclear delivery vehicles and has been honoring this unratified agreement scrupulously. Soviet statements and actions show clearly that they do not consider themselves bound by its limits; neither should the United States.

In addition to exceeding the numerical limits, the Soviets are violating SALT II by testing a second new-type ICBM (the SS-X-25), encrypting the telemetry from missile tests to conceal violations, and interfering with U.S. satellites and radars monitoring missile tests. They also are violating SALT II's "Common Understanding" that they would not deploy their mobile SS-16 ICBMs, are expanding the pattern of concealment of their strategic weapons, and are testing the engines of a third new type ICBM, the SS-X-26. In view of these Soviet actions, the President should announce at an early date that the U.S. is no longer bound by SALT II.

6) Alert the American People to Soviet Arms Control Violations, and Take Appropriate Compensatory Steps.

The President should inform the public of the full extent of Soviet arms control violations and initiate compensatory actions, including recommendations 4 and 5 above. Other compensatory steps could include the following:

- Deploy an additional 100 Minuteman III missiles now in storage to replace the oldest Minuteman IIs. This action has been approved and funded by Congress. It would increase U.S. ICBM warheads by 200 and require the end of unilateral U.S. observance of SALT II.
- Accelerate the Midgetman mobile ICBM program and assure that Midgetman is deployed in a flexible basing mode that provides true mobility.
- Develop and deploy a dual-capable air defense/ABM missile, to defend against either bombers, or cruise or ballistic missiles.
- Develop advanced penetration aids for U.S. ballistic missiles.
- Begin building a nationwide early warning and battle management radar system, which would require amendment of or withdrawal from the ABM agreement.

THE ARMY

by
Brian Green

The Reagan Administration goals for the Army included the development of a force structure responsive to NATO and non-NATO contingencies; improved readiness to engage in combat; improved ability to sustain U.S. forces once engaged; and a very heavy emphasis on modernization of equipment. Other goals included development of anti-armor and air defense forces; improved command, control, communication and intelligence (C^3I) capabilities; improved mobility; and improved unit training and cohesion.

The Administration has accelerated acquisitions significantly, including the M1 tank, the Bradley fighting vehicle, and the Apache AH-64 attack helicopter. As a result, the Army today is more heavily armed with more capable weapons than it was three years ago.

In force structure, there has been renewed emphasis on special forces, the New Manning System (a program designed to promote unit cohesion and thus better combat performance), and the development of light forces. These changes portend further organizational shifts designed to create more appropriate command and force structures responsive to the full range of military contingencies.

Some problems, however, have persisted. Funding for ammunition, spare parts, fuel, and other consumables that contribute to readiness and battlefield sustainability, has not kept pace with the acquisition of new weapons or the increased size of the force. Serious technological problems have beset some projects, notably the now-cancelled Viper short range anti-tank weapon, and the DIVAD air defense gun for short range protection against enemy air forces. Although cause for concern, such problems are not especially surprising during a period when many new systems are being developed and introduced.

Some problems with the All Volunteer Force concept also have become apparent. The Army is short of skilled technical and medical personnel, and the improving economy and shrinking manpower pool will cause recruiting problems in the near future. Furthermore, while manpower levels in the Selected Reserves have gone up, serious shortages persist in the Individual Ready Reserve (IRR), particularly in medical and combat arms personnel. The shortages in the IRR impair critically the U.S. ability to mobilize and rapidly reinforce the active Army, leaving serious manpower shortages in the event of major hostilities until the time draftees enter into service, six or seven months later. Equipment shortages and aging equipment also plague the Reserves.

Despite some technical setbacks, the Reagan Administration generally has been successful in accelerating urgently needed force modernization. But while the Army is more capable today than when the Reagan Administration took office, it is not as ready or sustainable as it should be.

THE NEXT FOUR YEARS

Emphasize forces that contribute to tactical mobility and coordination

As the Army now recognizes, a relatively static, forward defense based on attrition in a situation of dramatic quantitative inferiority, be it in the European theater, Persian Gulf, or elsewhere, is not viable. Coordinated maneuver that generates surprise and disrupts the enemy is one key to success.

Strengthen programs that improve C^3I and lethality of weapons

Because the U.S. and NATO generally cannot match the Soviet Union in purely quantitative terms, programs that provide superior tactical intelligence and higher kill probabilities (such as target designation and precision-guided munition programs) are vital to success.

Increase funding and implementation of readiness and sustainability programs

Good doctrine and advanced weaponry can have only limited impact unless units are adequately manned and trained, and have adequate stocks of ammunition, spare parts, fuel, and other consumables. Increased funding in these areas is vitally important if the Army is to fight effectively for any length of time. In spite of their importance, these accounts are perennial targets for congressional budget cutters.

Review the Army's electronic warfare (EW) tactics

Electronic warfare includes such activities as jamming communications and detection and destruction of radars. The Soviets place a very strong emphasis on EW. The Army should be more aware of this and should review its EW tactics and correct deficiencies where they are found.

Provide the Army Reserves with more new equipment

Some reserve units would be used to fill out understrength active army units during a mobilization. It is critical, therefore, that the Reserves train with, operate, and maintain the modern equipment that they will be using in combat.

Review methods to resolve manpower and skill shortages in the Individual Ready Reserve

The Army will face urgent shortages of medical and combat arms personnel in the first stages of any major conflict. The IRR, from which trained combat replacements must be drawn, has suffered from manpower problems so persistent that a draft specifically for the IRR may be the only viable solution. A registration or draft may also be necessary for medical personnel.

Maintain the current mix of heavy and light divisions in the active Army

Heavy divisions are more capable than light units of fighting heavy Soviet and Warsaw Pact forces in Europe. Unless increases are made in active manpower strength of the Army, the creation of any more light divisions would come at the expense of existing units.

Light divisions can play a role in a European conflict, defending areas unsuitable for heavy armored forces, such as mountain and urban areas, and defending rear areas. They also can contribute significantly in non-NATO contingencies, where there is little need of heavy armored forces, by rapidly reinforcing Rapid Deployment Forces. To the extent they are needed, more light divisions should be created in the Reserves, where manpower strength is increasing. Light divisions in the Reserves have the advantages of being easier to maintain, train, and transport once mobilized than heavy divisions.

INITIATIVES FOR 1985

1) Accelerate the LHX (experimental light helicopter) program. The helicopter has proven to be a very survivable, mobile platform, effective in anti-armor and intelligence gathering roles. The Army is facing block obsolescence of the bulk of its light helicopter fleet in the 1990s. Replacement of the aging fleet is urgently needed.

The LHX program involves the development of a new generation of light attack, scout, and utility helicopters, all using a common airframe. The program will provide a generational leap in helicopter technology and the potential cost savings of the common air frame are very large. Reprogrammed Fiscal Year 1984 and Fiscal Year 1985 funds for the LHX program that were cut by Congress should be restored. This will allow for a two-year acceleration of the program, from a projected initial operating capability of 1994 to 1992.

2) Consider purchasing a limited number of currently operational Israeli remotely piloted vehicles (RPVs).

The value of RPVs was demonstrated by the Israelis in Lebanon, where they were used to provide information critical for destroying Syrian air defense missile sites. RPVs for the Army could perform such valuable missions as designating targets for precision-guided munitions and providing tactical intelligence of battlefield events as they unfold. The Army RPV program has had technical difficulties. Purchasing some Israeli RPVs could provide the Army with some immediate capabilities and operational experience.

3) Protect the currently programmed increases in readiness and sustainability accounts.

This funding is necessary for more (and more realistic) training, to reduce maintenance backlogs, and to start to correct the current shortfalls in munitions, equipment, and war reserves of secondary items.

4) Hold production of M1 at 720 annually.

Congress has tried to accelerate purchases of the M1 tank. Holding production to 720 annually will avoid premature completion of currently planned procurement and allow time for the development of a turretless, more heavily armored follow-on that is responsive to the most recent Soviet anti-armor measures.

5) Produce the DIVAD short range air defense gun at low rates until the technical problems are solved.

If they cannot be solved at reasonable cost, lower rates will allow for easier program cancellation. Procurement of the West German Gepard short range air defense gun should be considered.

6) Expand the COHORT (Cohesion Operational, Readiness, and Training) program.

The COHORT program promotes unit cohesion which is critical to fighting effectiveness. It is a key component of the New Manning System and has two main elements: long-term assignment of personnel to company-sized units and unit (rather than individual) replacement of forces in duty stations.

Thus far, the COHORT program has been very successful at the small scale on which it has been tried, and it should be expanded. More units should be involved, and battalion sized units (3-5 companies) should be rotated. Unit replacement should be integrated into war plans to prevent problems arising from a war time shift from unit replacement back to individual replacement. Training for COHORT units should be linked to its larger unit affiliation to allow for smoother and safer integration of the COHORT unit into its larger unit.

7) Maintain the health of the All Volunteer Force.

The diminishing manpower pool, the improving economy, and persistent shortages of skilled technical personnel in the Army make steps to improve recruitment imperative. Recruitment funding must be preserved, and the Army (indeed, all the services) should be permitted to retain these funds if not needed immediately. Efforts must be made to appeal to a wider, high quality manpower pool, particularly college bound men and women. This could be done by offering an enlistment option that would provide a relatively short period of service with lower pay and benefits but substantial post-service educational benefits, benefits which could be transferred to the enlistee's dependents should he or she decide to stay in the military.

THE NAVY

by
Lou Kriser

The overriding goal of the Reagan Administration with respect to the Navy has been to increase its size to 600 ships. Other goals included improving the quality of the Navy's ships, improving the Navy's readiness to go to war, and its ability to sustain combat operations. Qualitative advances were necessitated by the relentless qualitative and quantitative improvements in Soviet submarine and naval air forces.

In the past three years, there have been dramatic improvements in Naval capabilities. At the end of 1980, the U.S. Navy had about 460 ships and it was estimated that this would fall to about 350 ships by the mid-1980s due to shipbuilding cuts by the Carter Administration. Now, there are already 525 ships; and those needed to meet the 600-ship goal have been authorized and will be deployed by the late 1980s.

This success can be attributed directly to the Administration's determination and ability to marshall congressional support. Yet more progress is needed in some areas. While the Navy has procured 25 percent of its objectives in war reserve munitions, increased funding for the past several years will continue to improve the Navy's readiness and sustainability. Currently planned further increases in funding, however, are necessary for the Navy to achieve its readiness and sustainability goals and must not be cut.

Furthermore, the Soviet naval threat continues to grow, as indicated by the construction of a new large deck Soviet aircraft carrier and estimates of a planned total of eight. Continued technical improvements in the quality of U.S. ships will be required to counter the Soviet threat as it grows in intensity and diversity.

THE NEXT FOUR YEARS

Continue building approximately 22 ships per year

At this steady pace, the Navy can achieve and maintain its goal of a 600-ship fleet by the late 1980s. Instead of the on-again, off-again programs of the past, the Navy has achieved a steady pace which, in the long run, saves money. It also maintains the defense industrial base, in this case the shipyards, and provides a credible five-year program that permits more rational force planning and budgeting by Congress and the Navy.

Build the new classes of ships in the five-year plan

These include:

- ***New DDG-51 Guided Missile Destroyer:*** In the early 1990s half the destroyer force and 90 percent of the Anti-Air War (AAW) destroyer forces will become obsolete. The DDG-51 class destroyer will be equipped with the Aegis anti-air weapons system. The Aegis system will allow the DDG-51 to defeat a full range of Soviet naval air threats, from sea skimming cruise missiles to the Backfire bomber. As will all new major surface combatants, the DDG-51 will be built significantly more hardened to nuclear blast and electromagnetic pulse effects than the ships of the past, further enhancing its survivability.
- ***New SSN:*** A new nuclear attack submarine is currently planned for the late 1980s. The current new SSN, the 688 Los Angeles class, will have 20-year old technology by the end of the 1980s. A modern, sophisticated submarine will be needed to address the Soviet submarine threat.
- ***New Minesweepers:*** The Soviets have a vast supply of mines but the Navy has virtually no ability to clear those mines from vital harbors, coastlines and chokepoints. After a quarter-century of neglect, the Navy plans to build two new classes of minesweepers, one for ocean operation and another for harbor clearing. The 31 planned are a bare minimum and should be increased.
- ***New Amphibious Ships:*** These are needed to improve U.S. power projection capabilities. Current plans are to build a new class of amphibious assault ship, the LHD-1, that will transport troops, equipment and cargo and can be converted into a helicopter and V/STOL (Vertical and Short Take Off and Landing) aircraft carrier. More new dock landing ships (the LSD-41 class) will be procured, and the older LPD class amphibious assault ships will be modernized.

Plan for the 21st Century's ships

Any ships authorized during the next administration will not be commissioned until the early 1990s; they thus will be steaming well into the 21st century. Two types of new ships should be considered. The first is a cruiser large enough to carry the sophisticated weaponry of the future and tough enough to withstand the weapons of tomorrow. The current CG-47 (the Ticonderoga class cruiser with the Aegis air defense system) has limited growth potential. The second is a smaller, more flexible destroyer-size ship. This should be built to permit ease of upgrading capabilities. The destroyer should be a variable payload ship (VPS) with Ship System Engineering Standards (SSES). With this concept, standardized variable payloads, including anti-submarine warfare, anti-air warfare, shore bombardment, and anti-surface warfare suites, can provide a range of capabilities for standard ships. More important, upgrading capabilities in response to growing threats would be relatively easy because of the ease of replacing or switching these suites.

Build Another Nimitz Class, Large Deck Carrier

This carrier was dropped from the latest Five-Year Defense Plan, but will be necessary to sustain a 15-carrier Navy in the 1990s. To replace the World War II era *Midway* in the 1990s, the new carrier must be started soon. In addition, the Navy should start studying requirements for its next generation of carrier-based airplanes. Today's aircraft probably will not be able to defeat newer, faster, and long range missiles in the 1990s.

INITIATIVES FOR 1985

The Administration should:

1) Provide long lead-time funds for a new Nimitz class carrier with full funding in 1986.

2) Pressure Congress to provide long-lead funds for a new advanced fighter and bomber.

3) Increase readiness and sustainability funding.

Increased funding currently programmed by the Navy must be protected from congressional cuts.

4) Initiate studies for the new surface combatants of the 21st century.

5) Review the Navy's electronic warfare (EW) tactics.

The Navy must be more aware of what Soviets call the "radio-electronic combat environment." U.S. Navy tactics must evolve to defeat increasingly sophisticated Soviet EW capabilities, and a thorough review should identify any current tactical weaknkesses.

THE MARINE CORPS

by
Mackubin Thomas Owens

Over the past four years, the Reagan Administration has attempted to enhance the Marine Corps' performance in a number of important respects. These included improving:

1) Strategic mobility to enhance the Marines' ability to force an entry into hostile territory, and to sustain their presence once ashore;

2) "Tooth-to-tail" ratio, that is, fire power relative to support troops;

3) Tactical mobility, enabling the Marine Air-Ground Task Force (MAGTF) Commander to maneuver his forces once they are ashore;

4) Anti-air and anti-armor capability;

5) Readiness and sustainability.

In addition, the Administration has sought to sustain the recruitment of high quality individuals and to maintain high retention rates.

In most of these areas, there have been substantial successes. While many of these initiatives did not originate during the Reagan Administration, they could proceed primarily because of the increased military expenditures requested. For example, in the area of strategic mobility, the implementation of the Maritime Prepositioning Ships (MPS) concept, which prepositions unit equipment and supplies near potential crisis areas to allow for more rapid supply of forces, has moved ahead speedily. The first of three MPS brigades will be operational this year. The second and third will achieve initial operating capability in 1985 and 1986, respectively. There has been renewed emphasis on amphibious shipping and on tactical mobility programs through the acquisition of the Light Armored Vehicle (LAV) and continued modernization of the Marine helicopter fleet.

Problems remain, however. Most important, the Marine Corps lacks a clear and unambiguous mission. This results, for example, in wasteful competition with the Army in the area of rapid intervention forces. Other problems result from a "bureaucratic" aproach that has affected the Marine Corps as well as the other services. It no longer is the case, for example, that "every Marine is an infantryman first." In an attempt to increase efficiency, the Marine Corps has reduced individual training time and emphasized instead specialized training at the expense of advanced infantry training. This approach is detrimental to a service as small as the Marine Corps.

Officer and Non-Commissioned Officer (NCO) education also is deficient. Officer education in the Marine Corps, from the Basic School to Command and Staff, does not place sufficient emphasis on the art of war. At the same time, promotion to NCO and staff NCO is not based on having achieved certain military educational goals. The result is that officers have become involved too deeply in administrative details while insufficiently educated NCOs are less able to fulfill responsibilities commensurate with their rank.

The "bureaucratic model" also results in micromanagement from higher headquarters, and an emphasis on quantifiable readiness and training standards. This has led to less meaningful and less useful inspections, and has provided incentives for commanders to overmanage subordinates, reducing to a degree the generally high Marine Corps morale.

Initiatives, no matter how brilliant, must be funded to be implemented. But money is not the only consideration. Coherent thinking about strategy leads to improvements in doctrine, operations and tactics, and force structure. Such thought is not enhanced by the bureaucratic model with its emphasis on quantifiable standards.

THE NEXT FOUR YEARS

Develop a clear mission for the Marines

The Marine Corps should concentrate on becoming the key Rapid Deployment Force (RDF), with ground combat responsibility for areas outside of Europe and Korea.

Encourage fundamental re-thinking about force structure and weapons

Developing a clear mission, such as that of the RDF, will require such thought. Possible changes in the force structure might include the creation of light or "mountain" infantry battalions, and light armored/mechanized battalions.[1]

INITIATIVES FOR 1985

1) Ask Congress to fund fully strategic and tactical mobility programs initiated or expanded by the Reagan Administration.

---

[1]These suggestions were offered in: Jeffrey G. Barlow, ed., *Reforming the Military* (Washington, D.C.: The Heritage Foundation, 1981).

These include: strategic sealift propositioning programs (such as MPS), the Light Armored Vehicle (LAV), the Assault Amphibian Vehicle (LVTT), the CH-53H Super Stallion cargo helicopter, and the Joint Services Advanced Vertical Lift Aircraft (JVX).

2) Increase funding of readiness and sustainability accounts.

Special emphasis should be placed on ammunition procurement to more quickly reduce the recently publicized ammunition shortfall.

3) Change the curriculum of Marine Corps schools.

The curriculum should emphasize tactics, operations and military history rather than techniques, procedures and terminology. Wargaming should be promoted as a means of teaching logical, coherent decision-making under pressure. In other words, the schools should emphasize the art of war.

4) Improve the rewards for those selected to the faculty of Marine Corps schools.

Allow the directors to select the best Marine Corps officers as instructors.

5) Emphasize informal "continuing education" for officers between their formal schooling.

6) Develop formal tests that must be passed as a prerequisite to promotion.

7) Revive the Infantry Training Regiment concept.

This used to follow Boot Camp for all recruits. All Marines should be qualified infantrymen regardless of their Military Occupational Specialty.

8) Devote time in every unit to refresher infantry training.

9) Make "free play" tactical and operational exercises a regular part of Marine training.

These require commanders to adapt to changing situations far more effectively than the "by the numbers" unit training that now is emphasized in Combined Arms Exercises.

10) Change unit evaluations.

Unit evaluations should reflect an emphasis on the ability of a unit to respond successfully to tactical and operational exigencies. Current unit evaluation (like MCCRES, the Marine Corps Combat Readiness Evaluation System) stresses meeting a "laundry list" of quantifiable standards. This "laundry list" is helpful but should not be the final measure of unit readiness.

THE AIR FORCE

by
Mark Albrecht*

The overall objective of the Administration for the non-strategic Air Force has been to reverse the perilous decline in U.S. air power as measured by numbers and age of aircraft, and readiness and sustainability.[1] Readiness and sustainability improvements were to come through increased and improved training, and greater stores of spare parts, fuel, munitions and secondary war reserves. Active and reserve components of the Air Force were to be modernized and expanded through additional procurement of new aircraft.

The original Reagan Administration goal was to achieve a force structure with 40 tactical fighter wings by FY 1986. The capabilities of the Air Force were to be expanded further by improving electronic warfare, communications, air defense suppression, target acquisition, surveillance, and warning capabilities. The Administration also sought to achieve a military airlift capability of 66 million ton miles per day by 1995.[2]

In the past several years the Air Force has managed to reverse many of the disturbing readiness and sustainability trends. The Tactical Air Command, for example, has experienced a 78 percent increase in tactical sortie rates and a 44 percent increase in flying hours since 1978. The very successful Red Flag training exercises, utilizing F-5s as "adversary" aircraft, have expanded activity levels by 33 percent since 1980.

The Administration also has accelerated procurement rates for aircraft. Acquisition levels for F-15s and F-16s have exceeded those projected in the final Carter Administration Five Year Defense Plan. The number of F-16 squadrons (24 planes each) has climbed from three in 1980 to 19 today. As for military airlift, five additional C-130 squadrons of 15 planes each have been created (for use primarily as intra-theater transports), while the KC-10 tanker/cargo plane program has been continued.

A number of research and development initiatives are nearing completion and soon will enter production. Among them are: the Advanced Medium Range Air-to-Air Missile (AMRAAM) and the

---

*Task Force members included Gerald Smith.

[1]The non-strategic Air Force is divided operationally into the Tactical Air Command (TAC), with forces responsible for air superiority as well as ground attack, and Military Airlift Command (MAC), responsible for air transport of men and material.
[2]Ton miles are calculated by multiplying the number of tons moved by the number of miles they were transported.

Lantirn (Low-Altitude Navigation and Targeting Infrared System for Night) programs. Both programs will help provide a technical edge to the tactical Air Force.

Among management changes were decentralization of management decision making and the institution of long-range plans and objectives for specific mission requirements. Two successful examples of these techniques are the Combat-Oriented Maintenance Organization (COMO), responsible for the great improvements in sortie rates, and the Airlift Master Plan, at least partially responsible for ensuring progress on acquisition of the badly needed C-17 cargo plane.

While successes have been substantial, the Administration has not met all of its goals. The Air Force has failed to achieve efficient production rates for its fighters, the F-15 or F-16, thus raising the cost per unit. Nor have the production rates been sufficient to reach the 40 wing benchmark by FY 1986; this goal has been deferred until FY 1989. Even then it will not be reached unless production rates are improved significantly over present levels.

There also remains a serious shortfall in airlift capability. The long-term need for dramatically expanded airlift capabilities is due to the need for rapid reinforcement of land forces in many contingencies. The Air Force currently can carry less than half of its stated goal, and currently programmed production will not meet that goal until the turn of the century. Intra-theater airlift is a particular problem, relying heavily on aging C-130s.

Ammunition supplies remain a serious problem. The Air Force currently maintains only about 30 percent of its currently stated sustainability requirements. While older munitions could be used to sustain the Air Force, this would be at significant cost in terms of damaged or lost airplanes and potential combat effectiveness.

The Air Force is confronting an ever-growing threat from Soviet and Soviet-bloc air forces. The Soviets are now deploying a new generation of fighters (the MiG 29 Fulcrum, MiG 31 Foxhound and SU-27 Flanker), a new intercontinental bomber (the Blackjack), and new generations of cruise missiles and surface-to-air missiles. At the same time, the Air Force's F-4(fighter), F-111(bomber), and F-106(interceptor) aircraft are aging and becoming obsolete. The tactical Air Force must fight and survive although outnumbered in a high threat environment. The need for technical superiority over the Soviets, continued modernization, and improved training remains unabated.

THE NEXT FOUR YEARS

Replace aging F-4s and F-111s with the dual-role F-15E

The F-15E will allow one plane to fulfill both air superiority and ground attack roles. In performing its ground attack mission, the F-15E should be supplemented with stand-off air-to-surface missiles. These would be used to attack heavily defended, high priority military targets—such as enemy airfields—whose destruction will be necessary to win the air superiority battle.

Continue development of the Advanced Tactical Fighter (ATF) program

A new generation of tactical fighters, probably incorporating the latest stealth technology (making detection much more difficult), will be required to maintain technological superiority over the Soviets.

Achieve acquisition rates of 260 to 280 tactical aircraft per year

This rate will permit economical production and will allow the Air Force to achieve its goal of 40 tactical wings. An eventual mix of 96 F-15s and 180 F-16s procured annually will provide maximum flexibility in terms of ground attack and air superiority missions, as well as theater and continental U.S. air defense missions. As soon as the Advanced Tactical Fighter becomes available, it should be added to the mix.

Consider the F-20 for the active Air Force

The quick scramble time, high sortie rate, and relatively low cost ($11.4 million) of the F-20 Tigershark make this plane useful in a variety of roles, particularly the defense of high priority military targets such as airfields. If fiscal constraints preclude acquisition of F-15s and F-16s at rates sufficient to achieve 40 fighter wings, the F-20 would be an excellent supplement in a "high-medium-low" mix of fighters. The F-20 should also be considered for Air Force National Guard and Reserve units.

Accelerate the C-17 program

The C-17 will address the inter-theather and intra-theater airlift problems and is the key to future U.S. airlift capability. Its range and ability to utilize short, austere airfields provides the C-17 with great flexibility. It is scheduled to achieve initial operating capability in 1992, but providing additional research and development funds could accelerate the program by a year. If fiscal constraints do not permit this, currently programmed funding must be rigorously defended. The C-5B, an updated version of the inter-theater C-5A transport, is currently in production. Both the C-17 and C-5B programs need to be carried through to completion if the Military Airlift Command is to reach its 66 million ton miles per day goal by the end of the century.

INITIATIVES FOR 1985

1) Purchase the F-20 as the Air Force adversary aircraft.

The Air Force has been using F-5s to simulate enemy aircraft in the Red Flag training exercises, but a new aircraft with higher performance is needed. The F-20 is relatively inexpensive because the manufacturer has funded the development and testing with no government funding.

2) Fully fund the FY 1986 request for the AMRAAM and LANTIRN programs.

These two programs will contribute significantly to the lethality and survivablity of the tactical Air Force. The AMRAAM is a "fire and forget" air-to-air missile. By loading the homing devices on the missile (rather than relying on the launching plane to guide the missile to its target), the launching plane can fire several missiles at different targets and fly to relative safety, thus reducing exposure to enemy fire and improving survivability. The LANTIRN program will allow ground attack aircraft to operate around the clock and in most bad weather conditions.

3) Fully fund the programmed increases in readiness and sustainability.

Readiness and sustainability must remain at the top of the Air Force agenda. Stocks of munitions, spare parts, and fuel must grow at comparable or higher rates than the growth of the tactical Air Force and military airlift aircraft.

4) Resume acquisition of the E-3A AWACS Airborne Warning and Control System.

The AWACS carries long-range, look-down radars, capable of detecting both ground and air targets. It can provide a survivable means of battle management, surveillance, and warning for North American air defense and overseas theater missions. Without further funding, the AWACS production line probably will close in fiscal year 1986.

LOW-INTENSITY CONFLICT

by
Richard Shultz*

Overview

Since 1981 the Reagan Administration has been developing a strategy and the capabilities required to respond to low-intensity threats. However, confusion persists within the Administration over how to define low-intensity conflict (LIC)[1] and how to identify those threats that pose the greatest potential danger to U.S. interests in the 1980s.

The Administration has developed initiatives in all three areas of low-intensity warfare policy: 1) countering Marxist insurgencies against friendly governments—the U.S. Army 1st Special Operations Command (SOCOM) and the Joint Chiefs of Staff (JCS) Special Operations Agency (JSOA) were established to respond to low-intensity threats, especially those requiring a counter-insurgency strategy (e.g., El Salvador); 2) assisting pro-Western insurgencies against Marxist regimes—paramilitary assets of the CIA have been expanded to assist insurgents challenging Soviet-backed regimes (e.g. Nicaragua); and 3) negating the threat of terrorism—important initiatives have been undertaken. Presidential National Security Decision Directive (NSDD) 138 ordered the appropriate agencies to develop an offensively focused anti-terrorist capability.

While each of these is important and does identify the principal low-intensity threats the U.S. is likely to face, they are only first steps. If appropriate policy, strategy, and capabilities are to evolve, the decision to expand and build upon these initial steps has come from the President. The commitment—indeed the resolution—to make the case for this policy must be articulated publicly and frequently by the Administration.

Overall Initiative for 1985

The Administration should establish within the National Security Council a "special group" for LIC.

---

*Task Force members included Hugh Tovar, James Motley, and George Talbot.

[1]Low-intensity conflict includes guerrilla war, revolution, insurgency, civil war, and coup d'etat. Terrorism which often is treated as a separate subject, also can be considered as a type of low-intensity warfare.

This would create a single channel for integrating the appropriate bureaucratic elements involved in LIC operations. Depending on the mission, this could include the military services, Central Intelligence Agency, United States Information Agency, the State Department, and other agencies when appropriate. The special group should be sub-divided into three branches to focus on the most critical LIC threats the U.S. is likely to face: countering insurgency; assisting insurgency; and counter/anti-terrorism. The NSC special group should be supported by a joint center charged with planning and implementing operations. Each of the principal civilian and military elements involved in LIC requires a parallel structure to the NSC special group and joint center, headed by the equivalent of an Assistant Secretary.

What follows are the objectives and means required for each of the three principal low-intensity missions identified above.

* * *

COUNTERING INSURGENCY

In the decades since World War II, the developing world has been beset constantly by insurgency and revolution. Many of these conflicts have been and continue to be stimulated by Moscow. They seek to exacerbate and exploit internal grievances to advance Soviet political interests.

The U.S. has responded to revolutionary insurgency by assisting governments in Central America with a variety of mostly military means. However, if there is truth to the axiom that in insurgent warfare, "the guerrilla wins merely if he does not lose," then offensive operations designed to inflict a decisive military defeat upon the guerrilla's armed force will have a difficult time succeeding, since the asymmetrical nature of guerrilla warfare dictates that the smaller, weaker force avoid decisive military engagements. Further, while a pronounced U.S. military effort is seen frequently as necessary to accelerate the ability of the military of the host country to meet the insurgent challenge, the addition of those necessarily foreign manpower resources frequently has the counter-productive effect of delegitimizing host country political sovereignty. In spite of the best of intentions, U.S. efforts to counter internally destabilizing and hostile armed political movements in developing nations have not met with great success.

LONG-TERM OBJECTIVES

Develop an effective counter-insurgency strategy

The U.S. requires a strategy through which needed assistance programs can be generated and implemented in troubled regions without the damning charge of "military interventionism." Where U.S. geostrategic interests are threatened, it is incumbent upon the United States to provide positive measures to influence the direction and pace of such change.

Devise a comprehensive counter-Marxist strategy

The U.S. should develop strategies and policies to counter revolutionary insurgency by dealing simultaneously with the dynamics of each element of the threatened state; i.e., providing security and self-defense while nation-building and pacification efforts also are underway.

INITIATIVES FOR 1985

The Administration should:

1) Create a country-dedicated Civic Action Force under the NSC "special group" for LIC.

It should include representatives of the intelligence community, the United States Information Agency, and other governmental elements when necessary. The structure of the force would be determined by the nature of the problem.

2) Establish outlines of priorities and suggested methods of implementation using available resources in-country.

Representatives of each agency assigned to the Civic Action Force should task appropriate elements of their parent agency to provide detailed programmatic outlines. Examples might include: 1) a public budget and finance plan that includes measures for the unified collection of and accountability for taxes; 2) training for teachers and nurses aides; 3) vaccination of livestock and soil and nutrition evaluation; 4) strengthening local government through education and training of entry level public servants; 5) a U.S. Information Agency plan for telling the government's story and 6) development of small business programs and cooperatives in rural areas.

3) Devise military and psychological operations.

Developed in tandem with economic and political development

plans to provide satisfactory levels of military performance, such training must include psychological and motivational aspects of "Why We Fight" instead of just "How to Fight."

4) Implement an effective public relations program.

It should be aimed at convincing citizens of both nations that the overall effort is targeted at improving local socio-economic conditions as well as defeating the insurgents.

* * *

ASSISTING ANTI-MARXIST INSURGENCY

Since 1975, security interests of the U.S. have been damaged significantly on two fronts. Communist forces, exploiting guerrilla warfare or outright invasion have taken control of Vietnam, Cambodia, Laos, Angola, Ethiopia, Nicaragua, and Afghanistan. Other countries important to the United States are threatened with similar disruption. Accompanying communist advances on three continents, the turbulent swell of Islamic radicalism has shattered the political fabric of Iran and Lebanon and threatens other countries of great strategic importance to the U.S.

Yet very little has been done over the past decade to counter these challenges to U.S. security. In fact there were several steps backward.

- Legislation was passed by the Congress which made it almost impossible to undertake paramilitary activity. (The Clark Amendment expressly prohibited such activity in Angola; the Hughes-Ryan Amendment effectively shackled all forms of covert action.)
- Congressional investigations and exposures of CIA operations in the mid-1970s intensified public sensitivity regarding covert operations, further dampening professional interest in such activity.

Not until 1980 did this situation begin to ameliorate. There now are some encouraging signs. The cautious, limited effort in Afghanistan probably has enabled the Freedom Fighters to sustain their harassment of the Soviets with greater effectiveness. It has aroused comparatively little public attention and probably will continue at the existing level. The "contra" operation has been moderately effective. The Sandinista government, though not seriously weakened by the "contra" attacks, is disturbed and fearful. On the other hand, the Sandinistas have capitalized on the adverse publicity and congressional sensitivity to the mining of Nicaraguan waters.

THE NEXT FOUR YEARS

Adopt a clear policy

On balance, it is fair to say that current U.S. paramilitary efforts in the countries noted, although moderately effective in the short term, will have no significant long-term impact. In Afghanistan and Nicaragua, U.S. objectives are vague and ill-defined. The only hope for these limited endeavors lies in the framework of a broader and more consistent U.S. policy, which in turn must be based on a stronger public consensus than exists today.

Identify exploitable opportunities

Unrest within the communist-controlled countries noted earlier is alive and unlikely to go away. Indigenous operational assets can be identified and developed, and the staff resources of CIA and DOD are in a position to expand significantly if required for a joint operational effort.

INITIATIVES FOR 1985

1) Employ paramilitary assets to weaken those communist and non-communist regimes that may already be facing the early stages of insurgency within their borders and which threaten U.S. interests.

Cambodia, Laos, and Vietnam reflect such conditions, as do Angola, Ethiopia, Afghanistan, Nicaragua, Iran and Libya. In each of these countries, the U.S. has been challenged. It may not be possible to reverse each of these situations. But it should be possible at the very least to use them for leverage in a larger strategic approach emphasizing that the U.S. no longer will countenance the subversion or overthrow of friendly governments within the developing world.

2) Develop a broad matrix of U.S. strategy.

It is critically important that employment of paramilitary assets not be undertaken in a policy vacuum. To be effective, it must supplement other instruments of policy, overt and covert. As a substitute for policy, it is doomed to fail. Military or paramilitary action in any of the countries named must necessarily be predicated upon a grasp of the political, social, and economic conditions that give impetus to exisiting unrest. It must be, and must appear to be, benevolent and concerned with amelioration of those conditions. Further, the U.S.

must be particularly sensitive to the dangers that flow from ill-thought-out involvement in local strife in which the U.S. develops assets and presses them beyond their capacities to survive without the U.S.

* * *

COUNTER/ANTI-TERRORISM

The terrorist threat the U.S. faces in the 1980s is unprecedented. There is much that should have been learned about contemporary terrorism since it escalated in the 1960s. Unfortunately, the U.S. has often overlooked these developments and underestimated the threat. Of all the lessons that should have been learned, offensive flexibility in planning and initiating is critical. The U.S. anti-terrorist program has been primarily defensive and reactive in nature. If terrorism is to be combatted, the U.S. must be prepared to deal with a variety of terrorist incidents, both international and domestic, and to instill into the terrorist the same fear he represents to innocent citizens.

With respect to terrorism, the Administration has taken important first steps. On April 3, 1984, President Reagan signed National Security Decision Directive (NSDD) 138, endorsing the principle of preemptive strikes and reprisal raids against terrorists abroad. Thus, the initiative for an offensive U.S. anti-terrorist program was established but much remains to be done.

THE NEXT FOUR YEARS

Strengthen offensively oriented anti-terrorist capabilities.

Such capabilities include the ability to strike preemptively and carry out reprisal raids, to deal with more than one major terrorist action at the same time, and to use intelligence in a timely fashion.

INITIATIVES FOR 1985

1) Require the appropriate federal agencies (primarily, the Departments of State, Defense Justice, Treasury, Energy, FAA, and CIA) to insure that U.S. anti-terrorist requirements—personnel, equipment,

training—are developed and integrated to maintain readiness.

2) Prepare general guidelines for preemptive strikes and retaliatory raids.

It is important to develop within the policy community a commitment to this anti-terrorist program, as well as sensitivity and appreciation of the U.S. anti-terrorist program and its goals.

3) Establish bilateral agreements with U.S. allies.

These are necessary to resolve potential constraints which may restrict the use of U.S. forces to conduct preemptive strikes and retaliatory raids against terrorists.

Multinational anti-terrorist cooperation among police, military, and intelligence specialists in combatting across-border terrorism through exchange of intelligence, joint training visits, and security personnel exchange programs should be strengthened.

4) Require that the Departments of Defense and Justice maintain a high state of domestic and international counter-terrorist unit readiness.

This can be accomplished through exercises directed by the NSC staff and should include participation by high-ranking U.S. officials and appropriate command and control elements.

5) Develop guidelines on how the news media and government authorities will work together during anti-terrorist/counter-terrorist operations.

THE U.S. AND NATO

by
Manfred R. Hamm

The Reagan Administration took office with a strong commitment to strengthen NATO's collective military posture and the U.S. contribution to the alliance. This entailed Intermediate-range Nuclear Force modernization (absent an arms control agreement with Moscow), improved readiness and sustainability of U.S. forces in Europe, more prepositioned supplies (POMCUS) for U.S. reinforcements, better coordination of weapons development and force standardization, more allied burden-sharing, and full implementation of NATO's 1978 Long-term Force Modernization Program.

The Administration was only partially successful in attaining these objectives. Pershing II and land-based cruise missiles began arriving in November 1983. This must be counted as a major accomplishment given strong public opposition by an intense minority in Europe. Higher readiness and sustainability of U.S. forces in Europe was attained through better force management, the issue of new equipment and the acquisition of 30 days of warfighting supplies, as well as improved maintenance and training. After years of congressional cuts, the Administration won qualified funding for the 5th and 6th POMCUS division sets for storage in the Netherlands and Belgium, thus easing air- and sealift shortages for the total D-day commitment of ten divisions. NATO area air defense will be improved through implementation by 1990 of the model agreement on Patriot/Roland missile deployment with West Germany. Similar agreements also are being negotiated with the Netherlands and Belgium.

But the Administration failed to win European compliance with the implementation of the objectives of the 1978 NATO Long-term Defense Program, particularly with respect to net defense spending increases of 3 percent. Instead European NATO countries average only 1.5 percent, although Britain and West Germany were well above this average. Thus, most force goals could not be reached, especially in the area of sustaining the ability to fight for an extended period. The NATO infrastructure program continued to suffer from serious shortfalls, particularly in the provision of adequate facilities for U.S. reinforcements. Only reluctant agreement was reached on ways to raise the nuclear threshold by the introduction of emerging technologies[1] in new conventional weapons programs. Reacting to this perceived European unwillingness to contribute adequately to the common defense, Congress froze the number of U.S. personnel in Europe and the Nunn Amendment, threatening to cut U.S. troops in Europe unless certain conditions were met by the Europeans, garnered considerable support.

THE NEXT FOUR YEARS

Pressure for increased European defense measures

The U.S. must press the European allies to meet the defense spending increases minimally necessary to rectify the most glaring force posture deficiencies and to avoid structural disarmament. Such increased European burden-sharing is also necessary to avert erosion in the U.S. of support for NATO.

Modernize theater nuclear weapons stockpile

The U.S. should seek agreement on the modernization of the theater nuclear stockpile and obtain funding from Congress for production of the 155mm extended range nuclear artillery shell. In the interim, the U.S. should swap the 8-inch (W-79) enhanced radiation shell (neutron warhead) already in production for forward deployed obsolete munitions.

Accord priority to NATO's chemical warfare resources

NATO's chemical warfare capability is awesomely deficient. Reliance on nuclear weapons to deter the Soviets from using chemical warfare is increasingly unrealistic because of growing Soviet theater nuclear superiority, especially following forward deployment of Soviet SS-22 and SS-23 missiles. Consequently, NATO needs to be prepared to fight and prevail in a Soviet-initiated chemical environment. NATO must purchase improved protective, detection, and decontamination equipment at an accelerated pace and modernize the obsolescent stockpile of U.S. chemical ordnance with new 155mm binary munitions.

Develop a theater-wide conventional surface-to-surface missile capability

---

[1]The "Weinberger Initiative" of May 1982 designated four specific areas in which NATO could make better use of its technological base. The term "emerging technologies" refers primarily to novel applications of advanced information processing to battlefield systems but also includes development of improved conventional munitions with computer-assisted guidance systems. NATO agreed in April 1984 to explore the utility of "emerging technologies" in eleven program areas, mostly in the areas of surveillance, target acquisition as well as electronic C^3I and countermeasures.

Existing NATO tactical air assets are unavailable for deep strike missions against high-value Warsaw Pact targets that are planned under new doctrines, such as Airland Battle 2000. Soviet modernization of aerial defenses also calls into question NATO aircraft ability to penetrate Warsaw Pact airspace at tolerable cost. An extended range Lance II, the first stage of the Trident C-4 or the MX, or a conventionally armed Pershing II could meet this requirement.

Upgrade combat capability of existing forces

The combat-to-support troop ratio of NATO forces is lopsided. Actual fighting power of forces must be enhanced through a more widespread use of civilians in non-combat roles. The declining military-age population in Europe also mandates a judicious and optimized use of manpower for combat assignment.

Enhance static anti-tank defenses

For some time, NATO has been experimenting with various cost-effective types of anti-tank barriers to improve its ability to withstand a linear attack against Soviet armored forces. Without such defenses, the present politically conditioned force posture has little chance of succeeding. The concept of pipelines filled with liquid high explosives and buried in critical sectors of the central and northern fronts recently has received attention. Once detonated, these pipelines would create impassable ditches, thus bringing advancing columns of armored vehicles to a halt and rendering them vulnerable to NATO attacks. These barrier systems would provide NATO with valuable time for forward deployment of its forces, offer targets of opportunity for deepstrike missions against second echelon targets, give time for political contacts, and thus raise the nuclear threshold. The U.S. should perfect such barrier systems in cooperation with the allies and urge NATO to emplace them during peacetime without munitions charges.

Strengthen NATO fire suppression capabilities

Growing Warsaw Pact superiority in field artillery must be checked. The Multiple Launch Rocket System (MLRS) using smart munitions will bolster NATO artillery counterfire and enemy air defense suppression assets and therefore should be procured in large numbers on a priority basis.

Emphasize emerging technologies

There should be a timely implementation of the April 1984 NATO agreement on a thorough investigation of eleven areas of application. In this context, the Administration should encourage early cooperation in weapons development and the removal of existing obstacles to technological cooperation. Joint ventures with European firms, and the formation of consortia will offer a framework for greater U.S.-European cooperation in weapons development and procurement.

Enhance survivability of NATO command, control, communications (C^3), airbases, and logistic modal points

Further attention must be given to NATO air defense and the hardening of C^3 installations and airfields against Soviet attack. Otherwise, improved Soviet forward tactical aircraft and missile forces may nullify the initial strengthening of NATO air defenses through Patriot/Roland air defense missile deployment.

Improve sustainability of European forces

There must be a European commitment to enhance the sustainability of their forces through stepped up munitions and spare part acquisitions, infrastructure improvements, and training. NATO councils should establish an action program to improve sustainability and establish binding schedules for its implementation. The U.S. should continue to improve the sustainability of U.S. forces and procure a 60-day capability by 1988, an improvement from the current 30-day capability.

Improve in-theater mobility

There is an urgent need to upgrade NATO's ability to transport troops and weaponry within the European theater to improve the logistics of resupply near combat areas. This will also allow NATO to deploy or redeploy its forces more flexibly in response to the requirements of a dynamic battlefield. The C-17 transport plane currently under development for initial operational deployment in 1992 is highly versatile. It combines short take-off/landing capability for in-theater mobility with intercontinental range and thus will augment U.S. strategic airlift assets. Its development schedule should be accelerated to meet demands in both areas as early as possible.

Correct maldeployment of U.S. forces in Germany

The U.S. should intensify discussions with West Germany about the Master Restationing Plan involving the redeployment of some 20,000 U.S. troops from rear areas to forward positions near the intra-German and Czechoslovak border. Forward stationing will shorten their response time and ensure their early engagement.

Improve out-of-area capability

Europeans have agreed in principle to make up for shortfalls of manpower and material in the event U.S. troops earmarked for NATO will have to be committed elsewhere. This agreement must be implemented by the Europeans by actions such as: detailed operational planning, mock call-up of reserves, and European civilian substitution for U.S. personnel, specifically in logistical support functions.

Bolster NATO's posture on the Northern Flank

NATO must counter the effects of Moscow's military buildup on its Northern Flank. Soviet control of the Scandinavian peninsula would hamper NATO efforts to contain aggression on the central front and endanger the sealanes of communication in the North Atlantic. The Administration should encourage Norway to proceed with its force modernization program and speed up improvement of its defense infrastructure to optimize the effectiveness of timely reinforcements from the U.S. and other NATO countries. The Administration should also press Denmark to reverse the decade-long trend of declining defense expenditures and strengthen its military capabilities. The Administration must also pay more attention to the implications for U.S. security of the changing geostrategic balance in the Arctic region and North Atlantic and initiate programs to bolster anti-submarine and long-range aviation assets in the area.

Enhance the survivability of NATO forces

The vulnerability of its bases to preemptive Soviet attack remains the Achilles heel of NATO's defense preparedness. Over the years, the Warsaw Pact has upgraded its theater air strike capabilities by deploying advanced aircraft and long-range surface-to-surface missiles that pose a severe threat to the survivability of NATO airfields and vital infrastructure assets. Many NATO aircraft still are parked unprotected for a lack of hardened shelters and could be destroyed easily on the ground. Few bases that are to host reinforcements from the U.S. are designed and equipped to accomodate additional aircraft or service these aircraft in protected facilities. Similar deficiencies exist with respect to the hardening of critical logistics and C^3I installations. NATO thus must give priority attention to a reduction of force vulnerability. This will require substantially larger infrastructure funding and protection of existing assets may offer a more cost effective way to enhance NATO's force posture than the acquisition of more costly but vulnerable weapons systems.

INITIATIVES FOR 1985

The Administration should:

1) Seek restoration by Congress of funding of collective chemical protection equipment for the Bradley M2/3, an infantry fighting vehicle.

2) Request funding for production of the l55mm nuclear artillery shell and the l55 mm binary chemical shell and deployment of a binary warhead for the Multiple Launch Rocket System (MLRS).

3) Request supplemental funding for accelerated procurement of more than the 16 MLRS batteries currently planned for by 1986.

4) Seek supplemental funding for the accelerated development of C-17 transport plane to reach its initial operational deployment by 1991.

This will augment current in-theater mobility assets in Europe earlier than currently planned.

5) Revise domestic content and preferential contracting legislation and rewrite sole-sourcing rules to remove obstacles to cooperation with the European allies in weapons development and procurement.

6) Request additional funding for NATO's infrastructure programs and press the European NATO allies for proportional allocation of additional resources.

STRATEGIC TRADE

by
Wayne A. Abernathy*

President Reagan inherited in 1981 a moribund export control system, starved during three administrations. The system had become a bureaucratic nightmare, lacking direction, plagued with delays and backlog. The enforcement effort existed only in theory (just one officer was assigned to enforce the entire grain embargo). The President established a clear priority to revitalize export controls and stop the hemorrhage of sensitive goods and technology to the Soviet bloc.

This priority developed into a set of policies that regarded trade as an important element of the national security equation. The intelligence community was commissioned to assess the national security trade problem, and produced in April 1982 a valuable summary of the challenges and dangers faced. In October 1981, the Customs Service initiated Operation Exodus, which greatly improved export controls enforcement. The Commerce Department in 1982 also began improving enforcement operations. Negotiations were initiated in the COCOM organization, which coordinates export restriction policy among the U.S., Western Europe, and Japan, to increase the effectiveness of multilateral controls, and COCOM held its first high-level meeting in decades. Agreements since have been reached to improve multilateral controls on items such as computers and computer-related technology. In 1984, the President directed the Department of Defense to become more involved in reviewing exports to Western countries, recognizing that most sensitive items diverted to the Soviet bloc first were exported to a non-communist country. Bulk shipment export licenses, which had not been audited for several years, were reviewed and the regulations tightened by the Commerce Department, although these regulations were again softened in September 1984.

Despite these significant improvements, major policy shortcomings resulted in serious setbacks. Most notably, the Administration opposed legislation to reorganize and consolidate the export control system into an independent Office of Strategic Trade. Instead, export controls continue to be administered by the government's key export promotion agency, the Department of Commerce. Even with security-minded individuals in key policy positions, the Commerce De-

* Task Force members included Hon. Lawrence J. Brady, Manfred Hamm, and William J. Olson. The task force did not examine the use of export controls for foreign policy purposes, which can play an important role as part of a coordinated use of economic incentives and disincentives in promotion of U.S. foreign policy interests. interests.

partment impeded enforcement efforts by the Customs Service, opposed Defense Department involvement in evaluating export license applications, and resisted sharing information with other agencies.

Export controls to the People's Republic of China, for example, were greatly relaxed without any adequate assurances that sensitive exports would not be diverted to unauthorized uses, and with little regard for the security interests of U.S. friends in the region. The United States received no *quid pro quo* from the Chinese for this major concession.

Large scale diversions of controlled goods and technologies have continued to occur. Even the celebrated interception in 1983 of more than 30 tons of goods and technology—including a VAX 11/782 computer system—on its way to the Soviet Union revealed continued inadequacies: less than half of the total shipment was caught, and nearly all of the items had been licensed for export by the Commerce Department.

As the Congress took up consideration of the renewal of the Export Administration Act during the 98th Congress, Administration lobbying efforts, conducted by the Commerce Department, quickly degenerated into a singleminded effort to preserve Commerce's bureaucratic turf. National security considerations were neglected. In the end, the Commerce Department, in league with high tech opponents of export controls, succeeded in blocking any improvement in the law. The year ended with the President forced to rely on emergency authority to maintain export controls. At the same time, the President had chosen as members of his advisory President's Export Council individuals who not only opposed his policies but who were openly working to restrict presidential export control authority.

There can be no effective export control program without strong, clear leadership and direction from high levels in the Administration. Such leadership is unlikely given the current organizational structure where export controls are institutionally deemphasized and placed in the ambiguous arrangement of being directed by policymakers at the Department of Commerce whose first priority is export promotion. The effectiveness of export controls increases to the degree that this export promoting bias is offset by national security and enforcement influences.

The effectiveness of export controls is also directly related to the degree of multilateral cooperation achieved among the Western allies. The VAX 11/782 case and improvements in COCOM demonstrate that U.S. allies will respond positively—if sometimes reluctantly—to strong and consistently applied leadership from Washington. Conversely, any relaxation in control efforts by the United States will tend to be amplified by the COCOM partners.

THE NEXT FOUR YEARS

Create an Office of Strategic Trade

The President should seek legislation to create an independent Office of Strategic Trade, incorporating within it the Commerce Department's current licensing responsibilities pursuant to the Export Administration Act and the responsibilities of the State Department's Office of East-West Trade under the Arms Export Control Act. Consolidating strategic trade activities would result in enhanced security, and great savings in defense costs as a result of denying or delaying Soviet-bloc acquisition of advanced technology that can be for military purposes.

Apply economic pressure to the USSR

The United States should pursue policies designed to limit—and where possible reduce—Soviet hard currency earnings. This approach can, immediately and over the long term, reduce significantly Soviet bloc acquisition of sensitive goods and technology. Even the most liberal exporter will not give his goods away, and smugglers demand a premium—and neither will take payment in rubles.

Policies putting pressure on the Soviets could include:

- Making all sales to the Soviet bloc on a cash basis only; no credits should be extended. The U.S. already has taken the first step by prohibiting U.S. government credits.
- Eliminating barter transactions with Soviet bloc countries.
- Restricting imports of Soviet products, particularly those produced in part by slave labor.
- Encouraging Western European countries and Japan to renegotiate current energy and raw materials purchase arrangements with the Soviet bloc. At the least, there should be no increase in purchases.
- Prohibiting exports to the Soviet bloc of goods and technology that will enhance Soviet energy production and delivery.

Strengthen allied cooperation

COCOM itself should be strengthened and COCOM countries should continue to be encouraged to improve their export control systems. Current U.S. licensing requirements which restrict U.S. exports to COCOM members and other nations should be reduced, on a country-by-country basis, only to the degree to which each country effectively implements restrictions similar to those of the U.S.

INITIATIVES FOR 1985

The Administration should:

1) Equalize export restrictions.

Export control policy should treat exports to Soviet-bloc countries the same as exports to the USSR. There are no grounds for believing that the Hungarians or other Soviet-bloc nations will (or can) keep sensitive goods or technologies out of Soviet hands.

2) Expand export control coverage.

Afghanistan, Libya, Syria, Iran, and Iraq should be added to the list of proscribed destinations for national security purposes. As a first step, licensing policy should be based on the assumption that sensitive items exported to these countries will be diverted to potential adversaries.

3) Establish a new licensing category.

An intermediate licensing category should be established governing exports to such countries as Yugoslavia, the People's Republic of China, and India. Licenses for exports to these countries should be subject to review by the Defense Department. While these countries are not currently U.S. enemies, many of their policies are far from friendly, and their willingness to cooperate with U.S. controls on re-exports is at best suspect.

4) Prohibit Soviet-bloc joint ventures.

Regulations should prohibit establishment of joint ventures between U.S. firms and Soviet-bloc governments or business entities (which are state-controlled in any event). This is, for the Soviets, one of the most effective means of obtaining technology, especially since even where a Western nation benefits, the Soviets usually benefit more.

In addition, the President should seek authority to condition any Soviet-bloc ownership or operation of U.S. businesses on reciprocal rights for Americans. If the Soviets refuse, as is probable, then a possible source of technology leakage has been plugged; if they agree, then they will have, in effect, allowed a private sector in their economy, which would be a significant development.

5) Strengthen the Pentagon's role.

The President should seek an amendment to the Export Administration Act to assure the right of the Department of Defense to review at its discretion any pending export license application. Currently, the

Pentagon, which has the most expertise concerning the national security impact of technology, does not have the opportunity to review many such transfers. Pending congressional approval, the President should delegate such authority to the Department of Defense.

6) Improve NSC capabilities.

The National Security Council staff should be expanded to include a senior staff member for strategic trade policy.

7) Reform the export advisory committee.

The charter of the Subcommittee on Export Administration of the President's Export Council should not be renewed.

8) Review Asian "leakage" possibilities.

Hong Kong, Taiwan, South Korea and Singapore are all moving into high technology production, but are not a part of COCOM. The ways in which militarily applicable technologies could reach the Soviet bloc should be reviewed and appropriate arrangements negotiated with Asian nations to prevent such leakage.

9) Amend the Export Administration Act.

The 99th Congress will take up again the question of the renewal and amendment of the Export Administration Act of 1979. In addition to supporting legislative efforts to create an Office of Strategic Trade and to increase the license review role of the Defense Department, the President should press for legislation that would

- transfer enforcement authority to the Customs Service;
- authorize the President to ban exports to or from violators of National Security Controls; and
- establish, until creation of an Office of Strategic Trade, an Under Secretary of Commerce for Export Administration.

14

The Department of State

ASSESSING U.S.-SOVIET RELATIONS

by
W. Bruce Weinrod and Manfred R. Hamm

The Reagan Administration came to office after years of Soviet advances during what was called "detente." Western efforts to restrain Soviet expansionism and to control the arms race by offering Moscow a stake in a long-term, cooperative relationship with the West clearly had failed. Given the record of Soviet behavior during this period, it became apparent that detente had rested on false assumptions about the goals of Soviet foreign policy.

SECRETARIES
Alexander Haig, 1981-July 1982
George Shultz, July 1982-Present

PERSONNEL: 23,786

BUDGET (In Billions of Dollars)

1985 Estimate	$2.5
1984 Estimate	$2.6
1983 Actual	$2.3
1982 Actual	$2.2
1981 Actual	$1.9
1980 Actual	$1.9
1975 Actual	$0.8

Established: 1789

Major Programs:
- Administration of Foreign Affairs
- International Organizations and Conferences
- International Commissions

* The authors gratefully acknowledge the comments made on earlier drafts by Nils H. Wessel, William F. and Harriett F. Scott, Robert L. Pfaltzgraff, Jr., Richard Pipes, Charles Fairbanks, Jiri Valenta and Richard V. Allen. They do not necessarily subscribe to all the views expressed here.

The 1970s were a period of rapid Soviet expansion throughout the Third World. Moscow fomented subversion and insurrection and exploited sources of instability, enthroned client governments with the help of proxy forces, and secured military bases that expanded its global military reach. In Africa, Moscow exploited the collapse of the Portuguese colonial empire, gaining important footholds in Angola, where Cuban involvement was decisive, and in Mozambique. Again with the help of Cuban proxies, Moscow gained a new ally in strategically important Ethiopia and exploited regional differences in the Horn of Africa. With Soviet backing, North Vietnam brought all of Indochina under Communist rule and Moscow took over vital former U.S. airfields and naval installations. Soviet expansion was capped by the invasion of Afghanistan in 1979, where over 100,000 troops are still engaged in bloody fighting. In the Caribbean, Moscow took advantage of Marxist seizures of power in Nicaragua and Grenada to extend its influence.

Equally sobering was the unprecedented magnitude of Moscow's military build-up during these years. One cardinal goal of the U.S. arms control community, especially with respect to strategic nuclear weapons, had been to stabilize deterrence and to restrain the arms race. But there was mounting evidence that Moscow did not share this objective and was ignoring arms control to gain military superiority over the West. The Kremlin's strategic nuclear arsenal grew enormously, bringing Moscow from a position of strategic inferiority at the onset of detente to superiority in some critical measures of nuclear deterrent capabilities. Most disturbing has been the mounting evidence that not only had the Soviets violated arms control agreements but that they had been doing so almost from the date of signing.

In Europe and elsewhere, Soviet conventional forces were modernized, closing the qualitative gap that formerly allowed NATO to offset in part the quantitative superiority of Soviet forces. The Soviet Navy, in particular, developed from a coastal defense force into a blue water navy capable of denying to the U.S. its traditional use of sea lanes indispensable to maintaining trade and security with allies. The Soviet air force, meanwhile, is now able to insert troops on short notice virtually anywhere in the world.

Trade, scientific and technical cooperation and loans on concessionary terms that were supposed to promote detente failed to moderate Soviet behavior. To the contrary, in many respects Moscow's military buildup had benefitted from commercial ties with the West, particularly the transfer of technology with military applications. The West, not Moscow and its satellites, became dependent on trade with the Soviet bloc, which was skillfully manipulated by Moscow to sow discord within the alliance.

Thus by the late 1970s, the once fashionable liberal views about the sources of Soviet behavior had been discredited by Soviet actions. The conviction that Soviet obsession with military power grew out of a paranoia with territorial security based on a history of foreign invasions overlooked the fact that Moscow's concept of security always has depended on creating insecurity among its neighbors. The belief that Moscow's invasion of Afghanistan was merely to protect its security showed insufficient understanding of the power vacuum created by the chaos in Iran. The hopeful view that Moscow's gains were at most ephemeral was discredited by the continuing presence of Soviet and Soviet proxy forces throughout the Third World.

Even President Jimmy Carter, whose Administration, with the major exception of Zbigniew Brzezinski, had embraced these views, finally was forced to recognize that they were naive. During Carter's last year in the White House, U.S. foreign policy began turning gradually toward a more realistic approach to dealing with the Soviets.

The Reagan Administration and Relations with Moscow

Ronald Reagan came to power with a cohesive and well-established view of the Soviet Union, its ideology and domestic political system, and its foreign policy objectives. He drew lessons from the failure of U.S. policy to restrain Soviet power. He believed that the overarching objective of Soviet Communism is to maximize the military and political power of the Soviet state and to extend it abroad whenever the opportunity arises. Since expansionism is endemic to Marxist-Leninist ideology and Soviet state interest, the incoming Reagan Administration concluded that it must be checked by countervailing military power combined with Western political will and unity.

Moscow correctly was viewed as the principal, though not exclusive, cause of international conflict and instability. Its past successes in extending its influence threatened to undermine the Free World. As the most powerful free nation, the U.S. has a responsibility to check Soviet aggression, to foster Western unity, and to mobilize liberal democracy to counter Soviet-sponsored Marxist-Leninist subversion.

Central to Reagan's policy toward Moscow was the restoration of U.S. military strength, which had atrophied for more than a decade under Republicans Nixon and Ford as well as Democrat Carter. This involved strengthening the strategic nuclear deterrent, the rebuilding of the Navy to 600 ships and 15 carrier task forces, accelerated procurement of new equipment for the Air Force and Army, and improvements in military pay, maintenence, training and readiness. The Administration has scored major successes in rectifying the nuclear balance with Moscow. Reagan revived the B-1 strategic bomber program, aborted by the Carter Administration proceeded with the development of the Trident II missile and launched a major program to strengthen U.S. C³I assets. Pursuant to the recommendation of the Scowcroft Commission, the Administration also began R&D for a small, mobile, single warhead missile, the so-called Midgetman.

Despite these successes, the Reagan Administration could not devise a survivable basing mode for the MX missile which would reduce the vulnerability of the U.S. landbased nuclear deterent. The Administration eventually halved procurement of the MX to only 100 missiles. Only this seemed to avert complete cancellation of the MX program by Congress.

Regarding arms control talks, the incoming Administration correctly examined the entire range of choices and took the time necessary to formulate clear objectives before returning to the negotiating table. Strangely, however, it pledged to adhere to SALT II (if Moscow also would), but failed to explain why it was observing a treaty that it considered unverifiable and fundamentally flawed. Nevertheless, it recognized that the U.S. arsenal had to be rebuilt, for arms control could not be negotiated from a position of weakness. The Administration correctly did pursue limited, narrowly drawn agreements, such as the "hotline" upgrading and specific confidence-building measures to avoid a surprise attack on Europe.

The Reagan Administration also strengthened NATO, particularly through deployment of Pershing II and cruise missiles in Western Europe. This deployment, in the face of tough Soviet, and some intense public, opposition in Western Europe, has strengthened the NATO alliance. In a broader context, the President also began forging a new strategic consensus among the principal Western countries. At the Williamsburg economic summit of 1983, the participants for the first time referred to the global Soviet threat and included a statement on the need for strategic, in addition to economic, cooperation with Japan.

The President also sought to stop Western subsidies for the Soviet bloc and to revise Western trade policies to restrict the transfer of high technology to Moscow and its satellites. Useful steps were taken in strengthening the Western COCOM strategic trade monitoring agency and in getting allied governments to agree in principle to stop the most visible forms of credit subsidies, although more needs to be done. The President's determination to stem the costly hemorrhage of Western technology was clear from his willingness to risk a divisive row with the NATO allies when he imposed unilateral export restrictions to halt Western participation in building the Siberian gas pipeline. Other unilateral U.S. actions included an improved policing of trade with the Soviet bloc, which eventually won the cooperation of the European allies and Japan. The Administration did not reach all its objectives in curtailing East-West trade and ending Western subsidies of Soviet military power. But the improvements will have a significant impact on Moscow's ability to draw on Western financial and technological resources to sustain its military buildup and forestall domestic economic collapse.

The Administration also spoke out forcefully against human rights violations and oppression in the Soviet Union and Central Europe at the Helsinki Review Conference held in Madrid. Together with the West Europeans, it used that forum to publicize Moscow's systematic disregard of the obligations it assumed by signing the Helsinki Final Act in 1975. U.S. leadership in seeking Soviet compliance with the human rights provisions of the accord had a positive impact on European public opinion.

When necessary, Reagan was willing to use direct military force to halt threatened Soviet expansion. He dispatched U.S. troops to liberate Grenada, a Soviet-Cuban outpost in the Caribbean and a springboard for Communist subversion throughout the region. In Afghanistan, the Administration gave active, but inadequate, support to the vastly outnumbered and outgunned Freedom Fighters who have resisted Soviet forces for five years. These actions represent a decisive reversal of a decade of U.S. retrenchment in the face of the Soviet challenge. The intervention in Grenada in particular shattered spreading notions that Communist advances are irreversible. It thereby encouraged democratic forces resisting Soviet domination elsewhere in the world. Indeed, with Reagan in the White House, Moscow has scored few solid gains and has suffered some reversals. Throughout the Third World, attraction to Soviet-type Communism is diminishing. Recognition also is growing that the West—not the Soviet Union—can help developing nations grow economically. Thus even Marxist Angola and Mozambique have begun to eye closer ties with the West and the U.S. The White House has encouraged these moves.

The Administration also launched the "National Endowment for Democracy" (NED) to compete ideologically with Moscow. NED is to help develop or consolidate democratic ideals and institutions. The Administration developed Radio Marti for broadcasts to Cuba and upgraded and strengthened the Voice of America (VOA), which had received inadequate backing from the Carter Administration. Reagan recognized that VOA is an important and cost-effective asset in U.S. public diplomacy and that the U.S. must use it extensively if it is to parry Communist propaganda and defeat Moscow in the war of ideas.

Overall, while the rhetoric was sometimes strong, relations between the U.S. and the Soviets stayed on a steady course. There were no true crises between the superpowers, as for example the Cuban missile crisis, the Berlin crisis, or the 1973 Arab-Israeli conflict. Given the steady, sustained U.S. military build-up, prospects are reasonably bright at the beginning of the second Reagan Administration that Moscow finally will join in serious discussions on areas of disagreement.

The Anatomy of an Empire in Decline: Challenges and Opportunities

Trends outside and within the Soviet empire raise the possibility that the pursuit of a strategy of containing the Soviet Union could help bring about its transformation. Among the most critical of these trends are:

1) The West is regaining its military strength. This deprives Moscow of the military and political advantages it hoped to reap from its heavy military investments. The Reagan Strategic Defense Initiative could negate the advantage of Moscow's large strategic nuclear arsenal for nuclear war or political blackmail. Similarly, the growing strength of the West's conventional weapons might make Western leaders more willing to confront Soviet aggression in strategically vital regions, such as the Persian Gulf.

2) Moscow now confronts a more cohesive alliance of democratic nations than it has for years.

3) The West is undergoing a fundamental industrial transformation. The revolution in information processing and microelectronics has engendered technological growth and a decentralization of knowledge. This has created promising opportunities in defense technologies that are already decisively favoring the West and will strengthen fundamentally its ability to contain Moscow's quest for military superiority. Moscow will have great difficulty in meeting this Western advance since to join the information revolution could lead to the spread of information beyond the Soviet elite, a development which the Kremlin greatly fears.

By contrast, the Soviet Union is facing a number of serious challenges on the periphery of its empire. These are compounded by severe domestic problems which, unless resolved through bold actions, could undermine it as a global power. Among the challenges faced by Moscow are:

1) Centrifugal pressures for greater autonomy and diversity are growing in Central Europe, where Soviet Communism has never

gained political legitimacy. One after the other of Moscow's allies is trying to effect domestic reforms, gain a greater degree of independence, and influence its own foreign relations. The costs of political control by Moscow are bound to grow. Reliance on outright military repression, while thus far proving effective in suppressing tentative steps toward independence, undermines the Soviet Union's attempt to split the Western alliance.

2) Moscow is also losing economic leverage over its satellites. It has been forced to cut deliveries of subsidized oil, gas, and other raw materials to its satellites in order to sell them for hard currency in the world market. Its satellites' need for hard currency, meanwhile, increases pressures for closer economic relations with the West. Near total economic dependency on the USSR in the past had been a critical source of Soviet economic leverage over Central Europe.

3) The more Moscow may find itself forced to rely on military coercion to stem disintegration on its periphery, the less reliable will be Central Europe in a possible confrontation against NATO. And if Soviet policy toward Central Europe becomes more repressive, it will trigger the kind of reaction in Western Europe that will foster Western unity and make the West increasingly reluctant to help the USSR economically.

4) With the rise of a generation of technocrats in the developing world, the appeal of anti-Western ideology is diminishing. The cultural attractiveness of the West is also reasserting itself. Moscow's primary means of influence, therefore, increasingly will be its own or surrogate military forces.

5) Moscow's repression of Afghanistan increases anti-Soviet feeling in the Muslim world and among Soviet Muslims. And for the first time, sustained challenges to Soviet-backed Marxist regimes exist—in Angola, Nicaragua, Afghanistan, and Kampuchea. Finally, Moscow's subsidization of client states such as Cuba and Vietnam is a continuing drain on its hard-pressed economy.

The Kremlin confronts serious difficulties at home which may impede its military buildup and expansionist policy abroad. Among these difficulties are:

1) Moscow faces continued long-term decline in the growth rate of its economy. After years of labor intensive growth in traditional smoke-stack industries, Moscow must shift to capital intensive sectors to increase productivity in order to cope with the effects of its sluggish labor force and a declining pool of manpower. At the same time, any Kremlin effort to catch up with the microelectronics revolution in the West has profound implications for the ability of political elites to maintain control. It also would require enormous sums of capital. Moscow thus may be confronting a situation in which

the capital required to maintain and expand the existing industrial infrastructure is unavailable without recourse to Stalin's methods of accumulating capital by drastically suppressing living standards. Even increased capital investment may not be able to stem the industrial decline caused by the rigidities and disincentives to innovations imposed by central economic planning. Over the long term, the Soviet resource pie will be shrinking and force stark choices in the allocation of capital and manpower between military needs and civilian goods. This competition for resources has already begun.

2) The Kremlin confronts mounting demographic problems that tend to jeopardize the ability of the Communist Party and the ethnic Russian elite to maintain control over an empire of more than 100 nationalities. These factors may also limit Moscow's ability to man and use its military forces for foreign adventures. Only slightly more than half of the population is ethnic Russian. The non-Slavic nationalities fiercely resist Moscow's attempts at Russification. Moreover, the birthrates of the non-Russian and Muslim nationalities are much higher than Slavic birthrates. Alcoholism among Russians is so extensive that it often is called an epidemic; absenteeism and corruption, meanwhile, undermine economic output and popular morale. For the first time since World War II, the Soviet standard of living is stagnant or falling. The Soviet Union is the only industrialized country with rising rates of infant mortality and epidemic diseases. The USSR, in fact, may be history's first de-industrializing nation.

3) These demographic trends are creating a mismatch between areas of population growth and the industrial heartland. For Moscow to shift industries to the East will require capital outlays beyond the means of the Soviet Union. Since Muslims reject resettlement in the Slavic republics, where in any event they are unwelcome presents no viable solution, demands on a shrinking pool of Slavic manpower will continue to rise. This will intensify competition for manpower between industry and the military services. Whoever will succeed Konstantin Chernenko as Soviet ruler may confront the same choice that Nikita Khrushchev encountered in the early 1960s when he had to cut the strength of Soviet conventional forces due to manpower shortages.

4) Soviet agriculture is a catastrophe. Food shortages are common outside the major metropolitan areas and there have been reports of malnutrition. Meat is unavailable in the winter for months at a time—even in Moscow. Food theft is also on the rise. Only a thorough restructuring of the Soviet agricultural sector, including *de facto* decollectivization, and massive capital investments, especially in food processing and distribution, could remedy this. But the Kremlin appears loath to admit the failure of its agricultural policies;

the needed capital, meanwhile, is unavailable. Unless earnings from natural gas exports offset projected declines in oil exports, Moscow will become ever less able to cover agricultural production shortfalls by buying foreign food. The Soviet diet, which showed some improvement during the past three decades, may well deteriorate.

These corrosive forces do not inevitably lead to the collapse of the Soviet empire or political system. U.S. policy, therefore, should be formulated with the recognition that factors could block such change. Among them are the entrenchment of the Soviet system since 1917, combined with a relatively effective system of internal repression; the Soviet leaders' current perception that any changes in the system are inherently threatening to their ability to control the nation; the Kremlin's perception that successful external expansion is an important way to justify the ideology of Communism and the sacrifices imposed upon the population; the geographical fact that most of the Soviet empire is geographically contiguous to the Russian heartland itself, thereby making it easier for the Kremlin to persuade the dominant Russian nationality that internal changes may threaten the Russian people and not just Communism; and the demonstrated willingness and capability of the Kremlin to use or provide military force to suppress movements for reform or self-determination and to exploit targets of opportunity to impose Soviet-style Communism; and the absence in the Russian culture of the philosophical and cultural experiences which have produced liberal democracy in the West.

Nonetheless, the Soviet Union may be in decline. This presents challenges and opportunities for U.S. foreign policy makers. Soviet leaders could opt for internal, extensive economic reforms, accompanied by devolution of power from the Communist Party and introduction of political liberalization. Yet pursuing this option would erode the Kremlin's power base and grip on the country. As such, a far more likely option is for the entrenched oligarchy to attempt to manage the system's gradual decline, even at the cost of giving up its expansionist ambitions and status as a military superpower. A third option, which may tempt a rising generation of more assertive Communist leaders, is to use Soviet power before it declines.

THE NEXT FOUR YEARS

U.S. policy toward the Soviet Union must understand the protracted nature of the U.S.-Soviet confrontation. The U.S. should not assume that it can calibrate policy in order to cause a specific change in Soviet policy. Rather, it should proceed on the assumption that a consistent, long-term policy can, over time, create a set of external factors to which Soviet leaders must react, and that this reaction can set in motion developments leading to internal reform and a changed foreign policy.

Thus the Administration should:

Encourage Domestic Reform in the Soviet Union

The most crucial long-term U.S. objective should be the modification of the present Soviet system. There are two reasons for this: 1) the current system practices destabilization and global expansion and appears to be willing to risk a major conflict, including possibly nuclear war; 2) the U.S. cannot remain indifferent to the absence of political liberties and human rights in the USSR and its satellites. The U.S. goal should not necessarily be to replicate democratic capitalism and pluralism, but to encourage pluralism in the USSR political system and thereby set in motion developments that could end Soviet expansionism. As recent events in China indicate, when internal energies are turned toward modernization, there usually is less interest in outward expansion.

The present troubled situation in the USSR offers great opportunities for U.S. policy to foster Soviet evolution toward pluralism and peaceful international behavior. At the same time, there is the risk that Moscow could try to externalize its internal crisis through an aggressive foreign policy. As such, Washington should pursue a policy of double containment to encourage a Soviet domestic political change and hedge against Soviet aggression.

Maintain U.S. Military Preparedness

To discourage the Soviet Union from using its military power, the U.S. must maintain perceivably adequate military strength. The Administration must continue strengthening the U.S. strategic nuclear deterrent and modernize and update conventional forces. At the same time, the U.S. should proceed with the strategic defense program designed to protect the U.S. from incoming Soviet missiles should deterrence break down.

Pursue Arms Reductions

The Administration must be willing to negotiate arms reductions with Moscow if such cuts will enhance the chances for superpower strategic stability. Arms reductions must be verifiable and balanced. At the same time, the Administration must have the political courage to resist arms negotiations and agreements that do not meet these criteria. The Administration must learn the lesson of the recent history of detente that negotiating for the sake of negotiating is not always wise.

The Soviet Union pursues different objectives through the arms control process than the U.S. or other Western countries. For this reason, the consequences of such agreements are unequal, even if the terms of these agreements appear equitable. Moscow has a poor track record, moreover, on obeying treaties, and consistently has neglected measures that would ensure treaties' full and timely verification. The U.S. and other democratic countries, meanwhile, typically are inhibited in the arms negotiation process because their leaders are reluctant to disappoint their publics by enforcing compliance or taking decisive steps, such as abrogating a treaty, when evidence of persistent violations has been established. Finally, in the negotiating process the U.S. bargains under continuing public and congressional pressure to reach an agreement; Moscow is not subject to such pressures. For these reasons the U.S. should not negotiate with Moscow unless there is sufficient reason to expect that Moscow will negotiate seriously and that any resulting agreement is effectively verifiable. In addition, more attention should be given to strategic defense and other means by which the goals of arms control may be reached without formal agreements.

Maintain Strong Alliances with Democracies

The Administration should continue close military and political relations with Western Europe and friendly Asian countries and seek new security arrangements when appropriate. Political unity is as important as military strength and the industrialized democracies of Europe and the Pacific make an indispensable contribution to the common security and deterrence of Soviet aggression.

Foster Democratic Developments

The concepts of national self-determination and democracy hold a powerful appeal. Genuine democratic leaders tend to be anti-Marxist and anti-Soviet. Soviet leaders will always be vulnerable to these ideas internally, in Eastern Europe, in the Third World, and among the best educated sectors of Soviet society. As such, the U.S. should continue increasing the resources devoted to the war of ideas. The Soviets understand that ideas ultimately influence political action and the course of events and the U.S. can afford to do no less. The Voice of America, Radio Free Europe (RFE), Radio Liberty (RL), and the National Endowment for Democracy must be bolstered enough to allow them to counter Moscow's propaganda campaigns and to encourage traditional American values, many of which have universal appeal.

Encourage Decolonization of the Soviet Empire

The Soviet Union is in reality a vast empire. Internally, 135 million Russians dominate 130 million other ethnic and religious groupings while externally, the Russian empire controls 150 million people in contiguous areas and many millions more elsewhere. The U.S. should emphasize this point when speaking of the right to national self-determination, a concept which has a powerful appeal around the world. By stressing this theme in public pronouncements and information aimed at various groups inside the Soviet Union, the U.S. may encourage oppressed minorities to seek greater autonomy from Moscow. Growing assertiveness by the non-Russian minorities may force the Kremlin to divert its attention from foreign adventures to the domestic nationality problem.

Break Up Moscow's International Destabilization Coalition

Whenever possible, Moscow tries to use such proxies and satellite forces as Cuban troops, East German internal security specialists, Czechoslovak and Bulgarian intelligence agents, and North Korean operatives to consolidate Marxist control of shaky countries. The U.S. should try to disrupt this so that the Soviets themselves will be forced to become more visibly involved and bear whatever costs are involved in such activities. The U.S. should place this issue on the agenda for talks with Central European nations and with Cuba, if there are any discussions with that nation.

Reject the Permanency of the Soviet Sphere of Influence

The U.S. must not accept as immutable the Soviet sphere of domination. The U.S. also should reject the notion that a Communist regime cannot be replaced by a democratic and pluralist government. Wherever feasible and appropriate, the U.S. should support pro-democratic forces seeking to end Communist rule. The U.S. should also encourage political change in Central Europe by differentiating among the internal practices and foreign policies of these countries. It should reward political liberalization and deny supporters of Moscow access to the benefits of selective cooperation with the West, especially trade, and most-favored-nation status and membership in world financial institutions.

Deny Moscow Access to Western Technology and Credits

Subsidized trade, soft loans, and loose controls on sales of strategic goods have enabled Soviet leaders to allocate resources to the civilian sector without having to curb defense spending or the expansion of the Soviet empire. Washington must try to force Soviet leaders to live within their resources and to pay a price for mistakes in the allocation of resources between the civilian sector and the military. They should also be compelled to bear the costs of their inefficient economic system, thus making the true costs of Soviet policy apparent and limiting Moscow's options. Finally, the U.S. should restrict Soviet access to Western technology of military relevance because the security costs for the West of such transfers can far exceed the commercial gains. This must continue to be a high priority in U.S. dealings with Moscow and in U.S. attempts to forge a common position among NATO members and with Japan.

Seek Cooperation and Agreements in Areas of Mutual Interest

On occasion, the Soviets bargain seriously. One example is the negotiation of the Austrian State Treaty that ended Soviet occupation of part of Austria in 1955. Another is the Quadripartite Agreement on the status of West Berlin, which secured Western rights and laid the foundations for more specific arrangements regarding West Berlin between both Germanies. The U.S. should be prepared to negotiate toughly with Moscow when mutual interests can be served by an agreement.

Maintain Public Support for Policy Toward Moscow

U.S. policies in the 1970s that minimized or even rejected the seriousness of the Soviet military challenge consistently impeded Washington's ability to maintain an active U.S. foreign policy and a strong defense. Given America's democratic system, and its political and moral heritage, combined with an earlier tradition of isolationism, it is unrealistic to assume that the U.S. can conduct policy toward the Soviet Union without the American public being made aware of the nature of the Soviet threat and its attitude toward important security-related agreements. Ronald Reagan wisely has noted the nature and objectives of the Kremlin, thereby reinforcing public awareness of the underpinnings of U.S. policy. This correct policy should be continued.

INITIATIVES FOR 1985

In setting out its policy agenda for the next four years, the Administration should observe the following guidelines: 1) Continue the arms modernization program to give Moscow an incentive to resume arms control negotiations; 2) be ready to negotiate, but refuse to make concessions simply to induce Moscow to resume substantive bargaining; 3) stipulate absolute Soviet non-interference in Central America as a precondition for agreements in other areas; 4) make plain that any significant improvement in U.S.-Soviet relations will depend upon an end to Soviet support for international terrorism and cooperation in efforts to end it; 5) use the treatment of Soviet dissidents as a litmus test to gauge Moscow's intentions; 6) boost U.S. assistance to anti-Marxist liberation movements in the Third World.

Specifically, the Administration should undertake the following initiatives:

1) Reassess U.S. Approaches To Arms Reduction.

The nuclear balance is clearly a crucial element in U.S.-Soviet relations. The Administration must order a complete review of U.S. arms reduction approaches on the basis of the following guidelines: 1) take a fresh and unprejudiced look at traditional approaches to arms reductions to identify their shortcomings; 2) investigate whether U.S. objectives of arms reduction can be accomplished by means other than formal treaties with Moscow; 3) identify the minimum bargaining requirements for verification and compliance which the U.S. cannot compromise; 4) examine possible new options and bargaining approaches that may become feasible if defensive systems are factored into the strategic balance; 5) establish an effective compliance mechanism within the U.S. government to deal with Soviet violations of arms control agreements prior to undertaking negotiations that might lead to further agreements

2) Define a Framework for U.S.-Soviet Relations.

The President should select an appropriate forum, such as a joint session of Congress, to explain at an early point in his term the framework for U.S. policy toward the USSR. His speech should include: 1) a review of the history of U.S. relations with Moscow and its assessment; 2) a discussion of the nature of the Soviet system and its impact on the conduct of Soviet foreign relations; 3) explanation of the problems arising in conducting relations with a power seeking international destabilization and world revolution; 4) an evaluation of Soviet treaty compliance and of its lessons for future agreements with Moscow; and 5) areas where agreements might be reached; and 6) most important, a detailed discussion of those changes required in Soviet policy before the U.S. can achieve a significant and lasting relaxation of East-West tensions.

3) Appoint an Inter-Agency High-Level Working Group.

This group should be coordinated by a senior National Security Council staff member whose only responsibility would be to monitor possible changes in Soviet long-term strategy and developments in East-West relations. Part of the Group's mandate should be to prepare and issue analyses and make specific policy recommendations to the President.

4) Strengthen NATO's Defense Posture.

The President should emphasize consultations with the NATO allies seeking agreement on specific measures and schedules to improve NATO's conventional and theater nuclear force posture. Special emphasis should also be given to enhancing political and military cooperation among the allies to counter the Soviet threat outside the confines of the treaty area.

5) Set Up an Allied Working Group to Study Approaches to Moscow.

Disagreements on the nature and scope of the Soviet threat and optimal ways to counter it have been at the heart of many inter-Allied disputes on East-West policy. To bridge these disparate perspectives, the Administration should seek allied consent to constitute a special working group with the mandate of studying U.S. and European attitudes toward the East-West conflict to evolve a common perspective and policy framework for a unified Western approach to coping with the Soviet threat.

6) Create New Bureaus of Soviet and Central European Affairs at State.

The Bureau of European Affairs at the State Department now is responsible for U.S. relations with its important NATO allies, the Soviet Union and the captive nations of Eastern Europe. Establishing a separate bureau for Western and Central European affairs and one for Soviet affairs would provide increased attention to all of these important areas. It would also raise the level of the senior official responsible for U.S.-Soviet relations to the Assistant Secretary level. Further, it would eliminate the inevitable current tendency for Soviet policy officials to view U.S. policy toward Moscow within the context of Alliance concerns. They are important but should be factored in after initial review of Soviet policy—not as a part of it. If the regional bureaus eventually are abolished, an Under Secretary for Soviet Affairs should be considered.

7) Continue to Increase Resources for the Battle of Ideas.

In the 1970s, the U.S. tended to disregard the role of ideas in the East-West struggle. Yet ideas are taken very seriously by the Kremlin, Marxist rulers, and insurgents world-wide. Moscow understands how vulnerable it and its empire are to information, facts, and truth. This is why it seeks to prevent their entry. Non-official sources of information provide an important means to increase Soviet public questioning of their system and its policies. Thus, the U.S. should allocate more resources for such projects as research and development on ways of getting information into closed societies. One means could be direct broadcast satellites (DBS) and video-cassettes. More funds should be spent translating books articulating the intellectual roots of democratic capitalism and the defects of Communism in practice and Marxism-Leninism in theory. All information relayed should include discussion of the vulnerabilities of the Soviet system, such as the new privileged classes, corruption, and economic and health problems.

8) Create a Commission on U.S.-Soviet Relations.

To remove the issue of U.S.-Soviet relations from partisan politics, it would be useful for the President to appoint a special commission tasked to review the entire range of issues in the bilateral relations. Its mandate should include an examination of the nature of the Soviet system and the scope of the Soviet challenge. The membership should be balanced and include substantial representation of those who take a tough-minded view of the Soviet Union.

9) Encourage the Development of a Permanent, Institutionalized Community of Democratic Nations.

It is unrealistic to plan on such a group agreeing on specific policies *vis-a-vis* the Soviets, but it would be a significant demonstration of the positive vision of democracy and could lead gradually to a perception of a shared community of values. Such an organization could, for example, provide institutional and material reinforcement for a newly consolidating democracies such as the one in El Salvador. Also, in this way the emerging democracies of the Pacific Basin can be integrated into the network of free nations.

10) Improve Soviet Expertise in U.S.

The pool of those knowledgeable of the Soviet Union should be increased. While private sector scholarships and programs must carry most of the burden, the Administration should utilize existing government programs to develop more expertise. The Administration should work to assure that resources allocated under the Soviet/East European Research and Training Act of 1983 are channeled in large part to policy-oriented institutions and individuals conducting, or being trained to conduct, policy-relevant studies and data analyses. Of course, historical and theoretical academic work is of great importance, but these limited taxpayer funds—only about $5 million in FY 1985—should be utilized primarily for efforts which will be of direct relevance to policy matters, such as studies of Soviet ethnic minorities.

CENTRAL EUROPE

by
Manfred R. Hamm

The Reagan Administration took office with a realistic understanding of the nature of Soviet domination of Central Europe.* It recognized that Moscow was determined to maintain control over its periphery by all necessary means, including military intervention, in the event its surrogate regimes failed to suppress domestic unrest. The new Administration understood that Central Europe constitutes for Moscow more than a security buffer against purported Western aggression. It also serves to "validate" Communist ideology, which explains Moscow's resistance to political change that would demonstrate the reversibility of "Socialist progress." Nevertheless the Administration correctly refused to accept as legitimate and irreversible Moscow's subjugation of Central Europe.

The crisis in Poland that came to a head during its first year in office provided an early test for the Administration. The wave of nationwide strikes led by the Solidarity movement demonstrated once again the lack of popular support for Communism in Central Europe. Indeed, the turmoil in Poland underscored that the people of Central Europe even after forty years of Communist governments had not given up their yearning for political and economic freedoms. It also offered tangible evidence of popular unwillingness to put up with, and accept as permanent, the economic hardships inflicted by the inefficiency of state-run economies. Finally, the events in Poland showed once again that Moscow was willing to concede, at least temporarily, marginal domestic changes in its satellites if confronted with intense popular opposition.

U.S. policy under the Reagan Administration rejected the basic premise of 1970s detente—that trade and increased human contacts would produce significant or permanent political change in Central Europe. On the contrary, it rightly contended that such cooperation would only lower Moscow's cost of dominating its empire and diminish internal pressures for economic and political reforms. By virtue of the close integration of the Central European economies with the Soviet economy through COMECON, morever, Moscow would benefit directly from such cooperation.

To rectify past mistakes, the Administration moved swiftly to stop soft loan subsidies to the Central European economies that had

---

* The term Central Europe, rather than Eastern Europe, is used throughout this essay because it better describes the distinct geographical and historical reality of the region.

become a staple of Western trade promotion. It pushed for and reached agreement within the Organization for Economic Cooperation and Development (OECD) and the Paris-based Coordinating Committee (COCOM) to halt trading on concessionary terms, although less visible forms of subsidies, such as government guarantees of commercial loans remain common practice. After the declaration of martial law in Poland, the European allies joined the U.S. in refusing to reschedule Poland's burgeoning government-secured foreign debt. This precluded similar rescheduling by private banks and, in effect, closed Western capital markets to the Jaruzelski regime. While this move was important in terms of political symbolism, it underscored the limited leverage of creditor nations and bolstered the case against future loan commitments to Socialist countries. Unpaid institutions were largely written off and thus carried by Western governments and taxpayers.

The U.S. also initiated a NATO-wide study on ways to improve the COCOM system for restricting trade in strategic commodities, especially high technology with military applications. Such items often were passed on to the Soviet Union from Central Europe. After much discussion, agreement was reached to update, and in the process tighten, the COCOM guidelines. In a major accomplishment, computer software was, for the first time, brought under COCOM rules. The Administration also stepped up enforcement of national export regulations and created a multinational framework to monitor shipments of sensitive technologies in order to prevent their diversion to the Soviet bloc. This will act in the future as a powerful deterrent against attempts by private firms to circumvent COCOM and national restrictions on trade in strategic goods.

The Administration also reversed the tendency of previous U.S. governments to mute criticism of human rights violations by Central European regimes and to deny political support to indigenous democratic forces for fear that doing so would jeopardize detente or lead to even more repression. Although the Administration did not extend direct assistance to the Solidarity movement, it reversed the Carter Administration's policy of discouraging financial support by private organizations, such as the AFL-CIO, which devoted considerable resources to bolster Solidarity's effectiveness. Even after martial law was imposed by General Jaruzelski in December 1981, private Western assistance allowed Solidarity to operate as an effective underground organization and to continue pressure on the regime.

The Administration imposed economic sanctions to express its disapproval of the crackdown on Solidarity and the declaration of martial law in December 1981. When the Polish government gradually removed the vestiges of martial law, the Administration responded properly by rescinding some U.S. sanctions but leaving others in place. A wholesale rescission of all trade restrictions prior to a complete return to the *status quo ante* would have amounted to U.S. acquiescence to General Jaruzelski's policies, and the U.S. would also have lost its residual leverage.

During the crisis, the U.S. stepped up radio broadcasts by Munich-based Radio Free Europe. RFL is highly respected and widely listened to in Central Europe because of its reputation for objective and comprehensive reporting. For the first time in over a decade, the U.S. remained true to its traditional commitment to democracy and national self-determination by speaking out against repression and flagrant violations of human rights.

Unfortunately, the Administration's praise for the courage of the outlawed Solidarity movement was not matched by measures to liberalize immigration rules for Poles fleeing persecution in their country. Many emigres who gained temporary admission to the U.S. are today subject to deportation by the U.S. Immigration and Naturalization Service (INS) unless they leave voluntarily by an appointed deadline. This practice has tarnished the reputation of the U.S. as a haven for political refugees and should be stopped as long as conditions in Poland do not guarantee their safety.

The U.S. also generally stood firm at the second review conference of the 1975 Helsinki Accord, especially with respect to the principles embodied in the human rights section (so-called "basket III"). It used the sessions in Madrid as a forum to assail martial law in Poland, condemn reprisals against members of the Charter 77 movement in Czechoslovakia and similar groups in the Soviet Union, and denounce the incarceration of dissidents throughout the Soviet bloc. This renewed steadfastness was shared to a large extent by Western European countries and did not go unnoticed in Central Europe. However, late in the Madrid session, the U.S. did yield on its earlier requirement that the Soviets take some specific human rights action before there could be agreement on a confidence-building measures meeting in Stockholm.

The White House also failed on occasion to impose unity of purpose and strict discipline on the various government departments. Therefore, U.S. policy was not as consistent as it should have been in implementing overall Administration strategy toward Central Europe. For instance, at the same time the Department of Commerce was promoting trade with Bulgaria, the State Department advised U.S. citizens not to travel there.

The years of detente had tarnished the image of the West as the beacon of freedom and democracy. In fact, Central Europe viewed verbal professions of commitment to their freedom with a fair deal of cynicism. The Helsinki Accord was widely perceived as ratification of the postwar territorial *status quo* in Europe and legitimization of Soviet hegemony over Eastern Europe. U.S. refusal to remain silent on repression in Poland rekindled hopes among Central Europe's democratic forces that their countries had not been written off as irretrievably under Soviet domination and thus strengthened their determination to continue their struggle for political reform.

THE NEXT FOUR YEARS

Without exception, all empires in history have crumbled due to their inability to contain indefinitely the forces of nationalism and desire for self-determination. Moscow's situation is potentially worse. Its Communist ideology is discredited and has few loyal followers in its satellite countries. The chronic inefficiency of the Soviet model has led these countries to the brink of economic collapse and has forced them to look toward Western Europe for help. Widespread economic deprivation has been spawning apprehension and serves as a powerful catalyst to jettison Soviet domination. At the same time, Moscow's own economic problems weaken its ability to assert absolute control over Central Europe short of outright military oppression.

U.S. policy toward Central Europe must continue to encourage the aspirations to national sovereignty and assist those domestic forces that seek to bring about political liberalization and economic reform. This does not mean the U.S. should embolden Central Europeans to engage in self-defeating rebellions against their Communist regimes by raising hopes for direct U.S. assistance. Such a policy would be irresponsible because the U.S. would be unable to live up to such commitment. It would also be counterproductive since the failure to do so would shatter faith in democracy and the West.

U.S. policy thus should be patient but steady during the historic process of the disolution of the Soviet empire and should broadly follow the following guidelines:

Support Democratic Forces in Central Europe

The U.S. should encourage private organizations to provide financial support and maintain contact with the democratic forces of Central Europe. U.S. embassies in these countries should facilitate these activities as much as possible and improve the flow of information to political activists.

Break the State Monopoly of Information

Inasmuch as Soviet-style totalitarianism depends on popular indoctrination through state-controlled media, denial of free access to information is essential to maintaining political control. The U.S. should utilize even more the resources of Radio Free Europe to inform the peoples of Central Europe about their own countries and the West, as well as international events. This will mitigate the debilitating effects of censorship and raise the level of political awareness. It also will impede and counteract attempts of satellite nation leaders to mold their citizens into an amorphous mass of docile, apathetic, and pliable subjects.

Withhold Economic Privileges

The U.S. government should not grant credit and trade concessions to Central European governments merely in return for transient political liberalization. Communist leaders are genuinely committed neither to liberal democratic principles nor to severing ties to Moscow, upon whose military muscle their reign depends. Nevertheless, U.S. policy should not treat Central Europe as monolithic, but must discern the differences among these countries and the policies of their leaders. This will give U.S. policy the flexibility to selectively reward positive domestic political and economic change to encourage these governments to proceed further in that direction. The extent to which Central European governments allow foreign private enterprises to operate should be an important factor in determining economic policy.

Encourage Openings to the West

Despite their current Communist leadership and domination by Moscow, most of these countries have strong national identities and nationalism is on the rise all across Central Europe. Furthermore, most of these countries share a cultural affinity with the West and have had a brief experience with democratic government during the interwar years. The nationalist tide and economic self-interest are exerting growing pressures for an opening to the West and resistance to Soviet demands for complete subordination to Moscow's foreign policy. Moscow confronts serious centrifugal pressures within its orbit. But that its heavy handed insistence forced East German leader Erich Honecker to cancel his September 1984 visit to his native West Germany demonstrates that Moscow can enforce tight discipline whenever Soviet interests appear threatened by independent-minded Central European leaders. The U.S. should welcome Central European attempts to broaden their freedom of action and cautiously encourage them by distinguishing between policies necessary to reassure Moscow and those pursued to further their own national interests.

Curtail Transfer of High Technology

The U.S. should continue to strengthen restrictions on technology transfers in cooperation with COCOM and, where necessary, through unilateral measures. It would be imprudent to draw an artificial distinction between transfers to Central Europe and the Soviet Union as the technology invariably will reach Moscow's military industry. In fact, Central European countries take active part in the legal and illegal acquisition of advanced militarily-useful Western technology. Moscow establishes the priorities based on its military requirements and uses Central Europe as diversionary channels. The decision of the June 1984 COMECON summit to tie Central Europe's economies even more closely to the Soviet Union will strengthen Moscow's hand in utilizing the satellites as conduits for Western technology.

Insist on Full Compliance with the Helsinki Accord

The Helsinki agreement and its provisions regarding human rights embodied in binding international charters are violated incessantly by the Soviet bloc. Nevertheless, the accord represents a useful yardstick by which to judge Soviet treaty compliance and improvements of human conditions in the Soviet bloc. The periodic review conferences offer the West a multinational forum with a European audience. The Madrid conference demonstrated its utility for spotlighting human rights violations by Communist goverments and harnessing moral outrage among the West European people.

Never Accept Soviet Domination as Legitimate or Permanent

Although the U.S. ability to effect change in Central Europe is severely limited, the U.S. must always reject Soviet claims that the Yalta agreement recognized its right to dominate Central Europe. The U.S. must uphold the principle of national self-determination for the Central European people so as to be true to its own ideals, maintain its credibility, and challenge Soviet hegemony. Irrespective of the exigencies of day-to-day politics, the U.S. should not shrink from speaking up against Soviet subjugation of Central Europe and persistent denials of basic human rights.

Encourage Economic and Political Reform in Yugoslavia

Yugoslavia is not a member of the Soviet bloc and has ardently guarded its freedom from Soviet interference since its former leader, Marshall Tito, broke away from Moscow in the late 1940s. After his death in May 1980, the collective leadership with its rotating presidency that had been devised to keep the country from disintegrating under the centrifugal pressures of its many nationalities, proved capable of preserving political independence and maintaining relative internal stability. But the Communist regime has not made any political and economic reforms and has failed to bring the country into closer association with the West.

Economic mismanagement and inefficiency constitute the greatest danger to Yugoslavia's future political stability. Labor unrest is growing throughout the country, especially in the less developed southern part. Despite its two-tiered economic system, the pervasive central government involvement in the economy stifles economic growth and stunts private initiative. Not unlike its Central European neighbors, the country is burdened with a staggering foreign debt and needs continuing financial assistance.

The Administration should encourage Yugoslavia to undertake urgently required economic reforms that will broaden the private sector, remove the shackles of central planning, and restore growth to the country's battered economy. While it is unlikely that Yugoslavia's Communist party will relinquish its dominant position in the near future, the Administration should support political changes that dilute the party's influence and will facilitate a gradual evolution toward a pluralistic, multi-party political system. The U.S. should also prod Yugoslavia's leadership to establish closer ties with the West and recast its role in the increasingly militant and Moscow controlled non-aligned movement.

INITIATIVES FOR 1985

1) Maintain Sanctions and Oppose Poland's Admission to the IMF. Unless the Polish government lifts the vestiges of martial law and fulfills U.S. demands for a dialogue with Solidarity, the U.S. should not remove the remaining economic sanctions. In any event, it should "veto" Poland's entry into the International Monetary Fund, despite pressures of the U.S. banking community. The Administration should also reexamine whether Hungarian and Romanian IMF membership serves U.S. interests.

2) Terminate Trade with Bulgaria.

Bulgaria's implication in the assassination attempt on Pope John Paul II in 1981 caused global consternation and outrage. Bulgaria also is deeply involved in global narcotics and arms traffic. As one of Moscow's most trusted allies, Bulgaria is actively fomenting revolutionary violence in the Third World while maintaining an oppressive Stalinist-style political system at home. The U.S. should halt trade with Bulgaria and make the resumption of economic ties conditional upon Bulgaria's willingness to stop these practices and improve one of the worst human rights records in the world.

3) Seek Legislation on Terrorism and Surrogate Forces.

It is well documented that Central European countries provide sanctuary and training for international terrorists. Furthermore, East Germans, Bulgarians, and Czechs are training insurgents and building up police and internal security forces modelled on the KGB in numerous Third World countries. The Administration should seek legislation that would deny export benefits embodied in Most-Favored-Nation (MFN) status to all countries engaged in these activities. Whenever necessary, existing MFN status should be revoked.

4) Seek Additional Funding for VOA/RFL.

Despite considerable funding increases over the past few years, these vital assets of U.S. policy are still underfunded. Major capital investments in new equipment need to be made in the near future. More powerful transmitters are also required to overcome Soviet jamming. Broadcasting hours must be increased and new language services must be added. Both necessitate staffing increases and more funding.

5) Apply Extended Voluntary Departure Rules to Illegal Poles.

The Administration should direct the Immigration and Naturalization Service to halt immediately all raids against illegal Polish refugees, recall all departure notices, and suspend deportation proceedings. Extended Voluntary Departure rules should be applied liberally until the political situation in Poland permits the refugees' orderly and safe repatriation. The Administration should also grant political asylum to all those Polish refugees who express their desire to remain in the U.S.

WESTERN EUROPE

by
W. Bruce Weinrod*

The Reagan Administration came into office with several objectives concerning Western Europe: first, to improve political solidarity between the U.S. and Western Europe; second, to follow through successfully on the U.S. 1979 commitment to deploy intermediate-range nuclear missiles (Pershing IIs and ground-launched cruise missiles—GLCMs); and third, to strengthen the overall U.S.-European response to the growing Soviet military challenge. While its record is not perfect, the Administration did substantially achieve its goals in all of these areas.

In the latter years of the Carter Administration, West Europeans complained about the vacillation and weakness of U.S. policy around the world. While European leaders have criticized specific Reagan Administration policies, there also has been a general acknowledgement that these policies have been much more consistent and have also demonstrated strength to friend and adversary alike.

U.S. demonstration of strength and decisiveness gradually has prompted many Europeans to accept some U.S. foreign and defense policies that they earlier had rejected. For example, in the case of U.S. intervention in Grenada, and in the instance of the U.S. intention to quit UNESCO membership, initial European reaction was somewhat critical. In contrast to earlier years, however, the U.S. refused to apologize or backtrack and within a short time, the reaction of many European states changed toward neutrality, sympathy, or even support.

This gradual shift can be seen most vividly with respect to Central America. As the Reagan Administration took office, European leaders were almost uniformly critical of U.S. support for the government of El Salvador and were openly sympathetic to the Sandinista government in Nicaragua. Yet, as a result of the Administration's consistent and firm policies in Central America, a growing appreciation evolved in Western Europe for El Salvador's democratic evolution while concern mounted over the movement toward totalitarianism in Nicaragua. Some West European countries have renewed their financial assistance to El Salvador and cut back similar assistance to Nicaragua. There also has been strong European support for the Contadora process, a regional initiative whose 21 points include a call for an end to expansionism and the establishment of genuine democracy in Central America.

---

* Task Force members included Jeffrey Bingham, Jeffrey Bergner, and Stephen Haseler.

Another major Administration success in Europe has been the deployment of U.S. intermediate-range nuclear missiles. Many observers predicted that the attempt to deploy such weapons would create such deep political turmoil that the decision would have to be reversed. Yet the U.S. and the European governments involved remained steadfast. Only the Dutch have chosen to delay deployment. The weapons were deployed as the first important military response to the Soviet intermediate range nuclear build-up in Europe. This has been a significant policy failure for the Soviet Union, which had sought vigorously to divide Western Europe from the U.S. on this issue.

The U.S. has had at least moderate success in developing a more unified, systematic U.S.-European response to the growing Soviet military challenge in Europe. While significant differences remain, efforts have begun to develop common weapons and to assure that European as well as U.S. technologies are utilized in developing new weapons systems. Also, new agreements for U.S. military bases were negotiated with Portugal, Spain, Greece, and Turkey.

Perhaps most significantly, under U.S. pressure, the Europeans have agreed to strengthen the procedures for restricting the transfer of advanced, defense-related technologies to the Soviet bloc. For example, though the timing and implementation of Washington's December 1982 decision to impose stringent export sanctions on sales of pipeline equipment can be questioned, it did convey to Europeans the seriousness of U.S. concern about European strategic trade and credit policies toward the Soviet bloc. Critics of the sanctions were quick to warn that they would seriously damage U.S.-European relations. In fact, much progress has been made in crafting U.S.-West European guidelines restricting strategic trade and credits to the Soviet bloc.

U.S. policy toward Western Europe must be shaped within the context of a number of long-term historical factors, including:

1) Differing perceptions of the nature of the Soviet threat and how to respond to it, with the Europeans appearing less worried about the Soviet military and ideological challenge;

2) Differing views on the appropriate allocation of global responsibilities in dealing with the Soviet challenge, with the Europeans wanting to play a limited regional role and criticizing U.S. global policies;

3) The trend in some European nations and political parties toward pacifism and neutralism (or at least questioning the premises of the U.S.-European political relationship), rejection of the utility of nuclear weapons in deterring Soviet aggression, a perception that morally equates the U.S. and the U.S.S.R., and the decline of the anti-communist left, especially in England and West Germany;

4) The movement by West Germany toward closer ties with East Germany;

5) A desire by many Europeans to preserve the alleged economic and political benefits of the detente era;
6) An intense opposition by a minority within Europe to nuclear weapons, coupled with a contradictory unwillingness to pay for stronger conventional military forces;
7) The eroding credibility of the U.S. nuclear deterrent as Europeans question whether the U.S. will risk its destruction to defend Europe, especially now that the nuclear balance has shifted away from clear U.S. superiority;
8) The growing Soviet military threat to Western Europe;
9) A continuing economic stagnation along with high unemployment; and
10) An increasing awareness in the U.S. that America's future well-being may be determined more by relations with the Pacific nations than with Europe.

The U.S. need not accept the inevitability of a fundamental weakening of the alliance that might be indicated by these trends. An admirable virtue of the Reagan Administration is its rejection of the gloomy Spenglerian pessimism of the 1970s. The Administration has assumed that U.S. actions could make a difference. Indeed, there are a number of trends that can be encouraged to help maintain a solid U.S.-European political relationship. Among them:
1) The apparent interest of some European governments, especially France and Germany, in improved conventional military capabilities and closer military coordination;
2) The strong anti-Soviet position of many European socialists and social democrats, especially in France, Spain and Italy;
3) The growing anti-Soviet and anti-Marxist sentiment among intellectuals, previously a group often sympathetic to Moscow;
4) The fact that the continuing Soviet build-up against Europe serves as a vivid reminder of Soviet intentions; and
5) Internal U.S. developments, especially the growing emphasis upon the Pacific Basin and the apparent political popularity of legislation to reduce the U.S. military role in Europe, which provides leverage for U.S. efforts to urge increased European defense efforts.

THE NEXT FOUR YEARS

Function As The Alliance Leader

This can be done by assuming global responsibilities, pursuing strong and consistent policies and, in particular, not allowing the important objective of "alliance unity" to deflect the U.S. from taking global actions vital to Western security even if there is European criticism. The U.S. also should advise the Europeans that if they continue to argue so strongly that the Soviets no longer constitute a serious military threat to Europe, and are morally no different from other powers such as the U.S., then the American people are likely to start believing them, leading to greater pressures for U.S. troop withdrawals.

Strengthen the Political Credibility of the U.S. Deterrent

Assuming a relatively equal strategic balance between the Soviets and the U.S., the U.S. can best deter a Soviet attack on Europe by: 1) strengthening conventional capabilities via newly emerging technologies and a strategy that takes the offensive after an attack; 2) developing a strategic defense system which at a minimum would deter a Soviet first nuclear strike on the U.S. and could also protect Europe to a substantial degree.

Strategic Trade and Credit Flows

The Administration should work for the institutionalization and strengthening of restrictions on Western strategic trade and credit flows to the Soviet bloc and for the permanent avoidance of Western dependency upon Soviet natural resources.

The U.S. should in particular encourage Norway to increase its natural gas output and marketing as an alternative to Soviet supplies and suggest that Europe as a whole look to the growing economies of free Asia rather than the stagnant economies of the Soviet bloc for trade expansion.

Consolidate the still-shaky Spanish role in NATO

As a first step, Spain must be persuaded, primarily by other Europeans, to remain in NATO. While the U.S. can do little to directly influence the Spanish decision, it can consider offering inducements such as increased U.S. base payments when the current agreement ends. Later, consideration should be given to a possible Spanish military role in NATO.

Convince the Europeans to refrain from actively undercutting U.S. global policies.

This is especially important in the Western hemisphere, where U.S. policies are designed to halt the spread of Soviet control or influence.

Support the important Turkish role in the Western alliance

Turkey has been subjected to an unfair double standard by some Europeans, although it clearly wishes to be a part of the Western democratic community. Its faults should be dealt with constructively, not by ostracism. U.S. military aid should be allocated on the basis of Turkey's legitimate security requirements.

Seek the gradual integration of Asian democratic nations into an international democratic community of nations

The International Democratic Union, a loose alliance of pro-democratic, pro-free market political parties, provides an example of such an effort. The free nations of Europe and Asia should begin to perceive themselves as belonging to a general community of democratic nations.

Encourage the gradual assumption of more military responsibilities for the defense of Europe by the Europeans themselves.

One vehicle for such an effort would be an expanded Western European Union (WEU). Whatever the means, it is crucial for the future health of the alliance that European defense efforts be increased. This also would facilitate agreement on burden-sharing and especially on responsibility for responding to security threats outside of NATO's geographical limits.

Urge Europeans to utilize the private sector and market incentives to emerge from their economic morass.

The U.S. should point out that the fundamental long-term problem with the West European economies is not external, but is related to policies that some of their governments have pursued for decades.

The U.S. should advise the West Europeans to study the dynamic economies of the U.S. and the Pacific Basin in seeking answers to their economic problems. The U.S. should also seek the reduction of trade barriers as much as possible.

France

Encourage the gradual reassumption by France of at least a *de facto* military role in the Western alliance along with increased French-German military and political cooperation.

Personal Contacts

The U.S. should work to maintain and expand contacts among younger American and European leaders in the "successor generation." Personal contacts can reinforce common political and security interests.

INITIATIVES FOR 1985

1) Encourage trends toward increased European defense.

An interagency task force should be designated to recommend how U.S. leverage can be used to spur greater European cooperation and spending on conventional defenses.

2) Work for stronger European support for democratic evolution in Central America.

The efforts of the past several years to convince Europeans of the merits of U.S. Central American policies should be intensified. West Europeans should be encouraged to provide financial assistance and private investment to Central America's emerging democracies, such as El Salvador, Honduras, and Guatemala. The importance of Central America to European security interests must be emphasized in all appropriate forums, and the Europeans must also be advised that the U.S. will not grant them a veto power over actions necessary to protect or encourage democratic evolution in the Western hemisphere.

3) Educate Europeans about strategic defense.

As with other U.S. initiatives, initial European reaction to the Reagan Administration's strategic defense plans was skeptical or even hostile. The Administration must give priority to explaining in every appropriate forum strategic defense's importance and how it might protect Europe and strengthen deterrence. The U.S. should be patient; new systems and doctrines are not accepted at once and it may take some time for a new strategic consensus to take form.

4) Continue tightening credit flows to the East.

Subsidized Western credits to the Soviet bloc have been reduced. Yet, the U.S. should press for the establishment of a permanent institution to monitor credit flows and thus provide warning should the trends reverse. If this fails, then a U.S.-only monitoring bureau should be established. Consideration then should be given to ways of linking benefits that alliance members obtain from subsidized credit agreements with the Soviet bloc to the allocation of defense costs within the alliance (See also the section in this volume on Strategic Trade).

5) Suggest a new Harmel-type Commission.

In the 1960s, a group headed by Pierre Harmel reviewed the state of the alliance. A similar commission is needed now to assess the political, economic, and security aspects of the U.S.-European relationship. It should also examine whether it is wise to tie essentially military actions, such as the deployment of new missiles in Europe, to Soviet negotiating positions on arms control

CENTRAL AMERICA AND THE CARIBBEAN BASIN

by

Esther Wilson Hannon, Virginia Polk, and Georges Fauriol

The major objectives of the Reagan Administration for the Caribbean Basin and Central American region have been to: 1) encourage the democratic process; 2) promote sound long-term economic development based on a strong private sector; 3) search for peaceful resolution of disputes through democratic elections and verifiable international agreements; and 4) strengthen the security of regional states against the threat posed by violent extremes and external forces.

The major focus of Reagan policy inevitably has been El Salvador. Through economic, technical, and military assistance, the Reagan Administration has supported the democratic process in that country and undermined the political and military strength of the predominantly pro-Cuban Marxist guerrillas, as well as anti-democratic forces of the right.

The establishment of a working democracy in El Salvador also has improved the prospects for peace in that country and the region by invalidating the assumption prevalent in the past decade that violent and leftist or Marxist revolutions were historically inevitable in undeveloped and authoritarian countries, and that, in the interest of peace and social justice, such movements should be allowed to gain control. Thus the Reagan Administration's policies supporting real self-determination have greatly improved the prospects for long-term peace and security for the region.

Recognizing that economic growth in the Central American and Caribbean Basin region is vital to U.S. and Western Hemisphere security, as well as necessary for the emergence of stable, democratic governments, the Reagan Administration launched two major initiatives to promote economic growth in the region: the Caribbean Basin Initiative (CBI) and the Central America Democracy, Peace, and Development Act, based on the recommendations of the National Bipartisan Commission on Central America. The original 1982 CBI proposal contained substantial U.S. trade concessions, investment tax credits, and balance of payments support. A predominantly protectionist U.S. House of Representatives, however, diluted the measure, limiting the impact of the program. Although the original CBI plan did not include tax breaks for U.S. corporations remitting profits from Caribbean investments and continued to restrict imports into the U.S. of sugar and textiles, significant gains have been made. Investments already range from agribusiness to assembly manufacturing, and increased U.S. shares of Caribbean exports show promise for the region.

The Administration's foreign assistance package for Central America, which closely follows the Bipartisan (Kissinger) Commissions's recommendations, has been approved in part but is unlikely to be passed in its entirety. In fact, the program was overly ambitious given the limited absorptive capacities of the region's nations. The Administration also has supported targeting U.S. economic assistance to the region through a new Inter-American Investment Corporation.

The Administration has worked toward the peaceful resolution of conflicts between Nicaragua and its neighbors by cooperating with the Contadora negotiations, begun in January 1983, by Colombia, Panama, Mexico and Venezuela, to reach agreement on a regional peace treaty. The Contadora objectives are: national reconciliation through open elections, a ban on foreign military bases, an end to support for insurgencies and terrorism in neighboring countries, and restoration of a military balance among the region's countries. The Administration also began talks with the Sandinista government of Nicaragua on the same points. In both instances, the Administration has emphasized the central importance of realistic verification and control measures to ensure compliance with the treaty. For this reason, the Administration properly rejected the Sandinista acceptance of a draft treaty that did not adequately cover these matters.

In response to the massive, Soviet-Cuban supported military buildup in Nicaragua and the evidence of the Sandinista government's efforts to undermine the stability of its neighbors, the Reagan Administration increased military assistance to Honduras and El Salvador. This has improved greatly these countries' ability to defend themselves against Nicaraguan-supported guerrillas as well as to deter higher levels of hostility such as that posed by Nicaragua's enormous army.

The Administration's success in obtaining congressional approval for increased military and economic aid for the government of El Salvador has enabled the newly elected Duarte government to initiate talks with the guerrillas from a position of strength and without compromising El Salvador's democratic process. President Duarte's willingness to hold talks with the guerrillas, and the support given to him by the Salvadoran military on this initiative, refute the contention of Administration critics that increased aid inevitably would prolong the conflict.

The Administration also provided assistance to democratic forces fighting the Sandinista government. While critics predicted that such support would only stiffen Nicaraguan resistance, the opposite, in fact, has occurred. Since U.S. aid began, the Sandinistas gradually have become more willing at least to discuss changes in their expansionism and internal repression.

The Administration joined with several Eastern Caribbean states in 1983 to restore order and preempt a Cuban takeover in Grenada. This greatly enhanced perceptions of U.S. strength and willingness to act in defense of its allies and neighbors, and may have established a long-lasting basis for cooperation between the U.S. and many pro-democratic states in the Caribbean.

The most important lesson of the past four years is that the crisis in Central America is long-term and systemic, and will require sustained and coherent policies on the part of the next Administration. The complexity of the region's problems, together with the greater presence of external forces, has diminished the capacity of the U.S. to solve such problems quickly and easily. The Caribbean and Central American nations are independent, nationalistic, and outward looking; they have developed close ties with other economic and political centers such as Western Europe and Japan, and also have some ties to the Soviet Union. In addition, the scope of U.S. influence and power is now constrained by the larger roles assumed in the last decade by Venezuela and Mexico, whose actions sometimes conflict with U.S. interests and objectives.

There also were important lessons from the liberation of Grenada: 1) the Soviet Union will not defend its proxies in a region it considers within the U.S. sphere of influence; 2) the call for U.S. action by the Organization of Eastern Caribbean States (OECS) demonstrates that inter-American cooperation against an extrahemispheric power exists and should be strengthened; 3) the Soviet Union will try to exploit opportunities to influence and dominate revolutionary movements to secure military bases of operation against the U.S.; 4) and Cuba militarily will not oppose U.S. military actions in the Western Hemisphere.

THE NEXT FOUR YEARS

Support Economic Development

The U.S. should support Central America's development efforts. Economic growth can best be achieved by using U.S. economic assistance to help countries overcome the problems of excessive foreign borrowing and government intervention in the economy, encourage adoption of policies that favor private sector growth and private investment, and revive intra-regional trade through the Central American Common Market.

Sustained economic growth in Central America will depend on the domestic economic policies adopted by the countries, as well as on U.S. assistance. The U.S. should use its aid to foster private enterprise by encouraging reforms reducing state-owned enterprises, price controls and subsidies, centralized control of credit and foreign exchange, and other forms of government interference in the economy. Efforts should be made to dismantle inefficient state enterprises and return viable ones to private sector management.

Many of the measures aimed at restoring domestic economic growth, such as realistic exchange rates, reduced bureaucratic controls on credit institutions, and nondiscriminatory regulations for foreign investment, also would help establish a hospitable environment for private investment. Central America, until recently, traditionally had enjoyed a high and productive rate of foreign private investment. Sound policies that encourage efficient production and investment in the private sector should be the key to avoiding excessive foreign borrowing and undue reliance on foreign aid in the future.

The objective of economic growth in Central America also should be furthered by stimulating the region's international trade. The U.S. should help to restore the Central American Common Market, and to widen access to U.S. markets for the region's leading exports by reducing U.S. barriers to such important regional products as textiles, beef, and sugar. Restoration of trade financing is also necessary to revive Central American production and trade. A preferable solution to a trade credit guarantee would be an arrangement whereby overseas banks and suppliers would restore credit lines if short-term credits are insulated from debt rescheduling agreements.

Encourage Democracy

In the political arena the preeminent long-term objective should continue to be support for aspiring and existing democracies in the region. Methods include finding ways to assist pro-democratic countries undergoing immense social, political, and ideological changes as they build the institutions necessary for stable, democratic government. This means assisting pro-democratic groups such as labor unions, trade associations, business groups, and educational institutions as a means of strengthening the foundations of a democratic system. Economic assistance to governments that are democratic or leaning in this direction should be viewed as an important component of U.S. support for democracy. The U.S., however, should not attempt to transplant its own institutions, nor interfere directly in the political process. It should also take care that U.S. assistance does not undermine existing political and social structures before new ones have matured.

The long-term objective of promoting democracy in the region should include assistance to genuinely nationalist groups seeking through military and political pressure against Marxist regimes to bring about democratic reform and free elections. Thus the U.S. should continue to help the opposition groups that are pressuring the Sandinista government to abide by its 1979 promises to the Organization of American States: human rights guarantees, representative government, and economic freedom.

Block Marxist Expansionism

A major objective and priority of the next Administration should be to impel Cuba to end its destabilizing activities in the region. This requires clear and unambiguous statements by the U.S. government of the kinds of activities it will not tolerate; it also requires reinforcing U.S. security relations with the regional states and carefully targeting economic and political assistance to prevent regional susceptibility to Cuban-Nicaraguan supported subversion and revolution.

The next Administration should seek from Nicaragua a cessation of its agression against its neighbors El Salvador, Honduras and Costa Rica, a reduction of its military arsenal and foreign military advisors, and progress toward political pluralism.

Promote Human Rights

Democracy is the best guarantor of human rights. Elected governments are held accountable by the people, and thus cannot violate human rights with impunity. Totalitarian regimes are not subject to such constraints, and the Soviets and Cubans never pressure them to respect human rights. The next Administration, as part of its human rights goals, should try to prevent Communist movements from gaining power in the hemisphere. This should include: 1) assisting democratic and nationalist opposition movements; and 2) informing public opinion, domestically and abroad, to counter the considerable ability of Cuban-Soviet supported groups to mobilize political campaigns on a world-wide basis.

Strengthen the Inter-American System

The U.S. should clarify its interest and objectives in the region through stronger and more consistent support for the Organization of American States (OAS), the Central American Democratic Community, Contadora process and the defense treaties and pacts embodied in the Rio Treaty, the multinational Regional Defense Forces of the Eastern Caribbean states, the Inter-American Defense Board, and Condeca. Not only will this underscore the U.S. special relationship with Latin America, it will strengthen the basis for cooperation and communication among American states and increase the chances for the peaceful resolution of potential conflicts. The special U.S. obligations with regard to defending region's nations detailed in the Rio Treaty should be emphasized.

Military Assistance

Enhancing the security of the inter-American system should remain a primary objective of the next Administration. A major objective of the next Administration should be to bolster the ability of those nations to defend themselves, to strengthen existing collective security agreements, and to formulate new ones where they are needed. In addition to providing low cost arms and equipment to the region's nations, the U.S. should offer regional military forces more grants and educational and training opportunities, particularly in modern and humane methods of counter-insurgency and civic action. This broader approach not only will enhance the defense capability of specific nations, but also will broaden the base of understanding and cooperation between U.S. and regional military leaders and help local governments make their armies more professional.

For the U.S. and its allies to succeed in defeating externally supported insurgencies and effectively combat threats to such strategically vital areas as the Panama Canal and the Caribbean sea lanes, there must be a greater emphasis on the development of irregular warfare units such as the U.S. Special Forces, Rangers, Navy Seals, and the Special Air Force units. These can project U.S. power effectively into areas of low-intensity conflicts involving Soviet-bloc trained and supported forces. Even more important is irregular warfare training for Central American forces. The next Administration also must recognize the special needs of such warfare in its military assistance programs so that adequate and appropriate arms, equipment, medical supplies, and training are made available to local armies.

Following the events in Grenada, which highlighted Soviet-Cuban military interests in the area, there has been a renewed regional interest in the Caribbean Basin's security and stability. Part of the overall objective of strengthening this security should be encouragement of closer ties between the larger nations of Colombia, Mexico and Venezuela and the Caribbean states. The U.S. should encourage Venezuela, Mexico, and Colombia to assist in stabilizing and ensuring the independence of these islands. Venezuela, which in the past expressed interest in playing such a role, should be encouraged to take the lead.

Support from Western Europe

The next Administration should encourage U.S. allies and friends to play a more constructive role in the region. West Germany, Spain, Great Britain, France and Portugal have substantial political and economic interests in the Caribbean and Central American region. In particular, Spain, with its special ties to Latin America, should be asked to assist in seeking political solutions; Great Britain should maintain its small but useful troop presence in Belize as symbolic as well as material support for U.S. efforts in the region; and West Germany and France should continue diplomatic and economic support to the beleaguered democracies in the region.

To maintain West European support for U.S. policies in Central America, the next Administration should continue to send regular diplomatic missions to Western Europe to explain U.S. objectives in Central America and the consequences to West European security should U.S. efforts fail.

Make Mexico Policy a High Priority

Mexico's importance to U.S. strategic and economic interest will require greater efforts in dealing with bilateral issues as well as great sensitivity to Mexico's concerns. The unprecedented challenges facing Mexico today due to a severe economic crisis, growing political challenges from the left and the right, overpopulation, and vulnerability to external challenges, pose clear threats to U.S. interests and security. It should be a major long-term objective of the next Administration to assist Mexico in strengthening its security as well as its economic and political stability. The next Administration should, while respecting Mexico's independence, seek to pursue improved bilateral trade and financial agreements, and seek greater cooperation with the Mexican government on narcotics trafficking, and immigration. With respect to Central America, the U.S. should continue seeking to convince Mexico that the democratic model of political and economic development—such as represented by El Salvador—is better for Mexico's interests than is the Soviet-Cuba aligned Marxist model of Nicaragua.

Narcotics-Terrorism Threat

A recent phenomenon threatening the economic, political, and social stability of many countries in the Caribbean-Central American region, as well as certain areas of the U.S., is the linked activities of narcotics trafficking and terrorism. In response to this, governments in the region, among them Mexico and Colombia, have begun cooperating with each other and finally have begun to respond to U.S. appeals for cooperation on drug control, interdiction, and prosecution of drug producers and distributors. The next Administration must increase diplomatic efforts to win continued cooperation and to find ways to help regional governments establish programs for drug education and drug crop substitution. There must be increased coordination between U.S. and regional intelligence and drug control agencies.

Central America and U.S. Oil Security

The next Administration should consider ways to enhance the security of its oil imports from Central America and the Caribbean, which have risen considerably in relation to other sources since 1977. In 1977, the peak import year, 17.3 percent of U.S. oil came from the Arab members of OPEC (AOPEC), and roughly 7.7 percent from Central America and the Caribbean Basin. Today, only 4.7 percent of U.S. oil needs are met by AOPEC members, while 9.4 percent comes from Central America and the Caribbean. When Venezuela's contribution is included, 12.6 percent of total U.S. oil needs, or 37 percent of all U.S. oil imports, comes from Central America and the Caribbean.

The most immediate regional threat to U.S. energy security comes from Marxist insurgent groups. The Panama Canal, through which about 44 percent of Alaskan crude oil passes on its way to U.S. refineries, and the oil fields themselves, are vulnerable to guerrilla attack. Although the Reagan Administration has made some moves to counter the threat from insurgents in Central America, governments have indicated that they need training assistance and equipment to protect oil sources and shipping.

By providing such aid, the U.S. will avoid higher military expenditures in the future to maintain oil security. Furthermore, both U.S. oil security and Central American prosperity can be enhanced in the long term with U.S. technical assistance in oil exploration and development techniques. Moreover, because food production levels tend to decline in countries with new oil revenues, due to the migration of workers to newly created industrial jobs, the U.S. should provide technical assistance aimed at maintaining food production levels with a smaller agricultural labor force.

INITIATIVES FOR 1985

1) Block shift in regional balance.

The U.S. should take whatever actions are appropriate and necessary to prevent a fundamental shift in the regional balance of power through shipments of advanced weaponry to Nicaragua or Nicaraguan subversion of neighboring nations.

2) Proceed cautiously with Contadora Process.

The U.S. should participate in attempts to arrange a regional settlement of the Central American turmoil. To be minimally acceptable, any pact must: 1) prohibit military alliances with the Soviet bloc; 2) require an end to cross-border export of Marxism and the Nicaraguan military build-up; 3) contain ironclad verification procedures; and 4) address the issue of political, economic and social pluralism in Nicaragua.

3) Urge Congress to maintain high levels of U.S. military assistance to El Salvador.

The emphasis should be on low cost, low-technology equipment, such as mortars and pack artillery. A centralized means for coordinating intelligence gathering and dissemination should be developed to penetrate and neutralize insurgency activities and thus minimize the need for military confrontation. In general, the U.S. advisory effort should be directed toward the employment of counterinsurgency techniques stressing selective targeting, minimal violence, and careful separation of the insurgents from the populace. Also essential is improvement of the army's medical care and medical supplies. Additional military assistance should also include more boats and training for the Salvadoran navy, to improve its ability to interdict seaborne supplies from Nicaragua for the guerrillas, and an increase in the size of the U.S. Military Group over the current limit of 55.

4) Support fully El Salvador's 1985 National Assembly and mayoral elections, and encourage the Salvadoran government to draw non-Marxists away from the guerrilla movement into participation in the democratic process.

5) Encourage modernization of the Salvadoran judicial system.

The rule of law, including an honest and independent judicial system, is an essential component of a liberal democracy, and is also important in maintaining support for the Salvadoran government.

The highest priority should be placed upon the allocation of resources to assist the Salvadoran government in achieving this objective. Whenever possible, training and suggestions should be offered by other Latin American democracies rather than the U.S.

6) Urge Congress to authorize funds for the unified anti-Sandinista forces.

This is a means of pressuring the Sandinista government to fulfill its 1979 pledge guaranteeing its people free elections, human rights and economic freedoms, and to hinder Sandinista support for anti-democratic terrorist guerrilla groups in neighboring countries. U.S.-backed pressure has led to the recent willingness of the Sandinista government to negotiate with the U.S.; support for the anti-Sandinista forces is an important bargaining chip that the U.S., in the interest of promoting democracy and regional security, cannot forego.

7) Devote sustained attention to Grenada in order to assure the long-term success of the 1983 rescue mission.

The U.S. should encourage the early holding of a national referendum on the interim advisory council and on future dates for elections and a new constitution. The National Endowment for Democracy can provide material support for this process and the U.S. should also work closely with the Grenadian private sector to develop a market-oriented strategy for economic growth.

8) Urge Congress to approve economic and military assistance to Guatemala.

The strategic significance to regional and U.S. security of this northern flank of Central America, its economic weaknesses, and its recent steps towards establishing a working democracy make the current hands-off approach of the U.S. government inappropriate.

9) Urge Congress to increase levels of military and economic aid to Honduras.

This assistance is particularly important now to balance the concerns of the civilian and democratic government and military leaders that Honduras is getting inadequate aid and attention in Central America. Funds should be increased for the Regional Military Training Center in Honduras; continued access to Honduran facilities is important for U.S. training of regional armed forces. Joint exercises should be continued on a regular basis to maintain pressure on the Sandinista regime and preclude any adventurism on their part.

10) Encourage Congress to 1) support recent efforts by the Caribbean states to develop a regional security system capable of thwarting small-scale insurgencies; 2) eliminate or modify constraints on U.S. foreign security assistance, especially section 660 of the 1961 Foreign Assistance Act, as amended, which prohibits the use of funds to train a

foreign country's police force; 3) increase grant funds for training regional military forces through IMET, the U.S. program for International Military Education and Training, and other programs that stress maximum respect for civilians and human rights in military situations; and 4) increase Economic Support Funds for foreign exchange needs, balance of payment support and other economic stabilization programs.

11) Restore to the Caribbean Basin Initiative the tax incentive provision reducing or eliminating taxes on remitted profits from U.S. equity investments in the Caribbean Basin.

12) Urge Congress to authorize $51 million for U.S. membership in the new Inter-American Investment Corporation within the Inter-American Development Bank.

The IIC has been designed to promote private sector growth in Latin America by providing loan and equity capital to undercapitalized small and medium-sized private enterprises in Latin America and the Caribbean.

13) Promote changes in the programs of the Inter-American Foundation.

These should stress development of the private sector and market economy at all levels of Central American society through loans, credit facilities, technical and educational assistance and, as much as possible, through the efforts and designs of local private groups.

14) Bring in Pacific Basin Nations.

The Administration should encourage free Pacific nations such as Japan, South Korea, and the Republic of China to invest and trade in Central America. In addition to providing new markets and investment capital to the region, the Asian countries also could transfer valuable management and technological know-how to the region's governments and private sector. The Administration should encourage closer economic ties between Central America and the Pacific countries through meetings and conferences aimed at bringing together representatives from the governments and private sectors of both regions.

SOUTH AMERICA

by
Esther Wilson Hannon*

The objectives outlined by the incoming Reagan Administration for South America were: 1) to restore the Western Hemisphere alliance and the special relationship between the U.S. and Latin America; 2) to impede communist advances, and 3) to encourage long-term economic growth through private sector development. The idea of promoting democracy emerged after events in Argentina, Peru, Bolivia, and Ecuador indicated that a democratizing trend was occurring.

Relations between the U.S. and South America have greatly improved in recent years and there is a growing consensus on many political, economic and defense issues. In addition, there is stronger support by some governments for U.S. policies in the region, particularly with regard to Central America.

However, efforts to strengthen the Western Hemisphere alliance system have been impeded by a reluctance on the part of many South American nations to become dependent once again on the U.S. for military and economic assistance. Countries such as Brazil, which welcomes closer ties to the U.S., and to a lesser degree, Chile, have become independent weapons producers and import arms from Europe. Other South American countries have sought and gained new markets for their manufactured goods and commodities. These developments check U.S. ability to exert its influence and promote its policies.

The Administration's efforts to increase the level and number of contacts between governments have been inconsistent. The Andean countries, Venezuela and Colombia for example, have not received the same attention and diplomatic efforts as the Southern Cone nations.

The debt crisis, involving a majority of the South American nations, somewhat reflects U.S. failure to strengthen the private sector and to encourage market oriented policies in these countries. The problem was compounded, moreover, when the U.S. encouraged borrowing from the International Monetary Fund and from other multilateral lending institutions, which in turn encouraged the private banks to lend to governments. This enhanced rather than limited the role of the state in a country's economy and consequently restricted the productive capacity of the private sector. The structural base of

* Task Force members included Rafael Miguel, Christopher Barton, Deborah De Moss, and Max Singer.

South American economics is, as a result, weaker now than at the beginnning of the Reagan Administration.

As for trade, a key to economic growth and stability, the Reagan Administration can boast of important gains. Strategies for countering trade barriers, quotas and other protectionist measures are being addressed continually at summits and bilateral meetings. Earlier, the Administration resisted calls for increased steel quotas against Brazil, which would seriously undermine its economic stability and its ability to pay its foreign debt obligations. Negotiations are now underway, however, to secure from Brazil and Argentina so-called voluntary restrictions on steel exports from these countries to the U.S.

The most notable results of the Administration's South American policy have been seen in improved ties with Brazil. The 1983 U.S.-Brazil Cooperation Pact covered economic, cultural, nuclear and trade issues. It was an important improvement in the two nations' relations and a signal to the rest of Latin America of renewed U.S. interest in the region. Recent increases in economic assistance to the Andean countries are an important step toward stabilizing a region of fragile political and economic structures and responding to increased Soviet presence and influence there.

The Administration also has fostered democracy in South America and has avoided for the most part heavy-handed interference in this process. The support given to the democratic process also has underscored U.S. commitment to human rights, self-determination, national sovereignty, and other commonly shared principles and values. By backing South America's at times fragile democratic movements, the U.S. has been able to deter leftist totalitarian movements in the region without having to prop up unpopular regimes or interfere overtly in the political processes taking place.

The Administration has, for the most part, successfully linked human rights to the overall democratic process. Although less successful in strengthening the role of the private sector in the region and thus promoting long-term and stable growth, the Administration has drifted away from policies that encourage irresponsible lending and state dominated economies.

A questionable Administration action, and one whose effects cannot yet be fully determined, was its support for Great Britain in its war with Argentina. U.S. support of a NATO ally in a war that had little to do with the North Atlantic Alliance, set back relations with Argentina and undermined U.S. credibility as a dependable ally in the Western Hemisphere. Had the U.S. remained neutral, a position acceptable to both sides, it would have been in a better position to negotiate a peaceful solution to the war and at the same time would have strengthened its position throughout the hemisphere.

THE NEXT FOUR YEARS

Promote the Democratic Process

As a long-term strategy, it is not enough simply to support "anti-communist" regimes. The U.S. also must understand the region's political and cultural traditions and identify those national groups that aspire to genuine sovereignty, economic development, and democratic government. The most effective strategy is to support local democratic organizations and institutions such as labor unions, business groups, trade associations, and educational groups. These are the foundations of stable democracies and the U.S. can play an important role in their development.

Human rights cannot be separated from broad U.S. policy objectives in South America. The evolution toward democracy is, overall, favorable to human rights and should be a major reason for the support given to this process.

Emphasize Regional Cooperation and Mutual Assistance

Past emphasis on arms and weapons as the primary means of strengthening security and enhancing U.S. relations with Latin American military establishments and governments must be complemented by emphasizing cooperation and mutual assistance. The growing number of democratically elected governments in Latin America should facilitate U.S.-Latin American cooperation within the Organization of American States (OAS) as well as in bilateral relations. U.S. participation in the OAS should aim at demonstrating a strong and continued interest in the region, and at strengthening the Organization's effectiveness in dealing with potentially divisive political issues.

U.S. goals should be to assist allies and friendly governments to maintain an effective defense against externally supported aggression and subversion, to strengthen alliances and contribute toward a common defense effort, and to make military facilities throughout the region accessible to American forces. In a major world conflict, such an enhanced regional alliance would lessen or eliminate the need to withdraw American forces stationed in Western Europe to defend the Western Hemisphere and U.S. borders. The overall objective of strengthening Western Hemisphere security and the alliance system will require increased military assistance to those friendly countries whose defense needs have been clearly demonstrated and whose defense capabilities affect the security of their neighbors and the entire region. The U.S. should make available low-cost arms and equipment, military grants, and U.S.-sponsored or -assisted educational and training opportunities for South American military personnel.

Western Hemispheric Security and the Pacific Coast

Promoting long-term objectives in the region requires greater recognition of the strategic and geopolitical importance of the Pacific Coast of South America. Should the Panama Canal be blocked by an unfriendly power, U.S. forces and merchant vessels would have to pass through the Straits of Magellan to reach the Atlantic. Access to safe ports in Peru and especially Chile would be essential for refueling and logistical support. At present, the southernmost U.S. Pacific base is San Diego.

Conditions are very favorable for strengthening U.S. relations with Pacific Coast countries. Their governments are democratic or moving in that direction; they are pro-Western and urgently need and desire U.S. economic and security assistance. Moreover, they have shown an increasing willingness to cooperate actively with the U.S. on hemispheric defense matters.

Crack Down on Narcotics and Terrorism

Although generally separate issues, narcotics and terrorism increasingly are linked in South America and pose a double threat to political and economic stability, the security of the region, and to U.S. efforts to curb drug traffic into the U.S. In response to this growing threat, the U.S. should negotiate with all Latin American countries—particularly Colombia, Peru, and Bolivia—to establish mutual assistance programs, better diplomatic and program efforts, and increased coordination of intelligence and drug control agencies throughout the region.

These efforts should be reinforced by diplomatic initiatives to strengthen cooperation between countries on such difficult issues as extradition treaties and drug crop eradication and control programs. Diplomatic efforts should be backed by aid to provide economic alternatives for illicit narcotics crops and programs aimed at reducing demand for drugs. U.S. objectives and interests clearly lie in greater cooperation and mutual understanding on the international narcotics-terrorism link and the danger it represents for every country.

Encourage Long-Term Economic Growth

Long-term and stable growth and wider distribution of wealth via the private sector should be a major U.S. objective. This requires strategies to deal with two fundamental issues of economic growth: trade liberalization and private sector development.

The international debt crisis involving much of South America depends for its resolution on the maintenance of free trade flows between developing and developed countries. This requires political resistance to protectionism and trade barriers. Bilateral and multilateral meetings and agreements are needed to find ways to coordinate the financial policies of the International Monetary Fund and the International Bank for Reconstruction and Development (World Bank) with countries' efforts to maintain free trade flows, and to establish a consultative framework for debtor countries and their industrialized trading partners so that each is kept informed of the others' economic developments and difficulties. In many cases, conditions attached to IMF loans require debtor countries to increase taxes and cut exports in a way that might hinder economic recovery. The U.S. should not tie assistance to acceptance by debtor countries of any economically harmful IMF loan conditions. Since anti-protectionist measures must be reciprocal, the White House must promote legislative proposals to effect commitments made in international meetings. This would mean coordinating any sound IMF debt resolution efforts with trade liberalization goals.

Equally important to long-term growth is improving the framework for U.S. private direct investment in South America. While the investment climate in South America is created mainly by those countries' policies, U.S. agencies such as AID, Commerce and State can provide more information on opportunities to the U.S. private sector and facilitate private investment in South America. This could be accomplished through increased trade and investment missions, Foreign Commercial Service programs, information banks, matching U.S. investors with South American resources and opportunities, and other agency-sponsored projects aimed at fostering cooperation and understanding between U.S. and South American business leaders and business groups. Improved diplomatic relations, and a greater number of bilateral and multilateral negotiations will go a long way toward improving the investment climate.

U.S. economic assistance programs and loans from U.S. and multilateral lending institutions should be targeted to the private sector instead of government projects, which are generally costly to create and maintain, inefficient, and harmful to the productive private sector.

INITIATIVES FOR 1985

1) Ask Congress to authorize U.S. participation in Inter-American Investment Corporation under the aegis of the Inter-American Development Bank.

It would provide loan and equity capital to small and medium-sized private business enterprises in Latin America, as well as technical assistance to help such firms cope with the problems of growth and development. A stronger private sector would help alleviate the debt crisis and further long-term development prospects. The Inter-American Investment Corporation would promote new enterprises, encourage and finance non-traditional exports, and supply local investment costs and risk capital.

2) Resist U.S. domestic pressure to protect industries challenged by South American exports.

Such protection penalizes the American consumer and impairs the ability of South American countries to earn the hard currency needed to repay their debts. The Administration should initiate frequent bilateral and multi-lateral negotiations and summits to discuss and agree on trade liberalization measures and to strengthen political commitments to resist trade barriers and other trade distorting measures.

3) Support Democratization Efforts.

The National Endowment for Democracy should promote democratic institutions and groups in South America that lack resources and require expert guidance, while avoiding direct interference in political elections and parties.

4) Increase the high level diplomatic, economic and military contacts.

This is important to maintain open channels of communication and to avoid the past pattern of ignoring countries until a problem or crisis erupts. The President should, early in the next Administration, visit South America. President Reagan's trip to Latin America in 1981 signalled greater U.S. interest in the region and notably improved inter-American relations.

5) Place higher priority on international narcotics control.

This should include enhanced cooperation among South American states and the U.S., improved joint surveillance and enforcement capabilities, and economic and technical and military assistance where needed. Congress should be pressed to increase the funding of the State Department's Drug Diplomacy Agency to maintain close ties with governments seeking to control narcotics trade and the deleterious effects of this trade on economic political and social stability. The specific and comprehensive recommendations of the

Senate Drug Enforcement Caucus in August 1984 should be considered as part of the Administration's initiatives.

6) Encourage increased South American participation in the International Military Education and Training (IMET) programs authorized under the Foreign Assistance Act of 1961, and other professional military exchange programs.

Declining participation of South America in recent years, due to lack of funds and congressional concern over human rights violations in some South American countries, has reduced the number of South American officers who understand U.S. interests and military doctrine. Further, it has undermined the major objective of such programs to foster a better understanding of the U.S., its people, institutions, and political system. This is particularly important at a time in which the Soviet Union has been increasing substantially its South American military training and exchange programs.

7) Channel IAF Toward Private Sector.

The Administration should promote Inter-American Foundation programs that develop the private sector and market economy at all levels of South American society through loans, credit facilities, technical and educational assistance, and as much as possible, through the efforts and designs of local private groups.

8) Increase military and economic assistance to the democratic government of Peru.

Congress should be urged to approve the $10 million in military assistance and $30 million in economic assistance requested for FY 1985. Military assistance is vital to strengthen the government's ability to defeat the current guerrilla insurgency and to provide an alternative to low cost Soviet arms and equipment sales; economic assistance would help Peru weather the economic crisis and keep the democratic movement from failing.

9) Reassess the prohibitions placed on U.S. foreign security assistance.

Specifically, Congress should be asked to reconsider Section 660 of the Foreign Assistance Act of 1961, as amended, which prohibits the use of funds to train a foreign country's police force in paramilitary skills unless there does not exist a viable defense force in that country. Many governments with small defense forces and serious terrorist threats are relying increasingly on their police forces for paramilitary actions. In such cases where the threat posed by terrorist groups to a government is great, the U.S. should offer assistance for the training of police as well as military personnel.

10) Lift the prohibition against military sales or assistance to Chile and increase its participation in military training and education programs.

This would encourage more cooperative military relations with that country and ensure the protection of the strategically important sea lanes in the Southern Hemisphere. Chile's strategic importance to U.S. security interests, combined with its modest movement toward political liberalization, makes the continuation of a total U.S. arms embargo against Chile inappropriate.

11) Urge Congress to approve a United States Information Agency (USIA) proposal for scholarship programs for disadvantaged but gifted Latin American youths.

These programs should include up to four-year scholarships, graduate and undergraduate, and vocational programs. Not only would these programs improve country to country relations and make available U.S. educational resources and ideas, they would counterbalance the significant grants and scholarships made by the Soviet Union, Cuba, and East-bloc countries.

ASIA

by
John F. Copper*

After years of neglect the Reagan Administration has given unprecedented emphasis to Asia, particularly the Far East. This was long overdue, and is the logical consequence of President Reagan's decision to put an end to the "Vietnam Syndrome" and to reassert the nation's objectives. U.S. interests in Asia and the Pacific are now developing rapidly and are beginning to rival the traditional primacy of Europe and the Atlantic in American policy-making. The economic dynamism of East and Southeast Asia now appears to have more in common with the booming U.S. than does the relative stagnation prevalent in Europe. American trade with Pacific nations long has exceeded in value the more traditional U.S. commerce with European nations.

Paralleling U.S. economic ties to Asia are important security concerns. A major goal of the Reagan Administration was to restore American military strength and diplomatic credibility in Asia, and to urge Asians to assume greater regional responsibilities, Considerable progress has been made toward this goal. This reverses a half-decade of decline in U.S. interests and U.S. presence in Asia, which weakened American credibility and influence. During this period, Soviet military strength increased substantially, upsetting what had been an essential equilibrium in the region.

A dramatic first step by the Reagan Administration was to reverse the Carter White House policy and assure the Republic of Korea that U.S. troops would not be withdrawn from its soil. This boosted confidence in America's commitment throughout Asia, and stabilized relations between South Korea and the United States. Relations with Korea have never been better than under the Reagan Administration.

The Reagan Administration then encouraged Japan to increase its defense budget and assume additional responsibilities for the defense of Northeast Asia, particularly the vital sea lanes within 1,000 nautical miles of Japan. It was also an important Reagan goal to prevent the People's Republic of China from moving back into the Soviet orbit. The U.S. thus has sought to build a strong and lasting relationship with Beijing, one that would counter Soviet military deployments in the region, reduce significantly the possibility that the U.S. will have to confront a Chinese threat, and increase China's stake in regional peace and stability.

---

* Task Force members included Richard V. Allen, Jeffrey B. Gayner, Martin L. Lasater, Burton Yale Pines, Daryl Plunk, and Katsuro Sakoh.

In Southeast Asia, Reagan sought to maintain the status of vital U.S. bases in the Philippines and enhance the diplomatic role of the Association of Southeast Asian Nations—or ASEAN, comprising the Philippines, Malaysia, Singapore, Indonesia, Thailand and Brunei. He also kept economic and diplomatic pressure on Vietnam to withdraw its occupation army in Kampuchea (formerly Cambodia).

The Administration increased security assistance programs, which had fallen behind Soviet arms assistance to such aggressive states as Vietnam and North Korea. Bolstering America's Asian friends militarily offsets some of the increasing difficulty the U.S. faces in deploying military forces quickly — especially to Southeast Asia.

A second major goal of the Reagan Administration has been to expand U.S. trade and economic relations with Asian countries, particularly Japan, the Republic of China (Taiwan), the Republic of Korea (South Korea), and the People's Republic of China. Part of this strategy is related to policies for the U.S. domestic economy. Low American inflation, for instance, makes American products more competitive in Asian markets. So does reduction of U.S. business taxes and government red tape. U.S. companies moreover, are being encouraged to export. The incoming Reagan Administration seemed to understand that either the U.S. must compete more vigorously in international trade—especially in Asia—or succumb to those at home who favored U.S. tariffs, quotas, domestic content legislation and other forms of protectionism.

The Reagan Administration's human rights policies also differed significantly from those of its predecessor. The Carter Administration's policy making human rights the "soul of American foreign policy" clearly had been a failure, particularly in Asia. The fact that Carter did nothing about the deplorable human rights situations in Kampuchea, Vietnam, and to a somewhat lesser extent in the PRC, made Asians view his human rights campaign as hypocritical. By contrast, the Reagan Administration has won back Asians' respect, for it has treated each country as a separate case and has sought improvements in human rights when feasible. It has not forgotten that the worst violations are in communist countries where the U.S. has little leverage to bring about changes.

The Reagan Administration has attempted to spread democratic values in Asia through example and quiet negotiations. As in the case of human rights, rigid policy gave way to a case-by-case approach. In most situations, this has been more effective than the Carter Administration's righteous lecturing, which ignored functional historical and cultural factors in the nations concerned. In the Republic of Korea, for example, "quiet diplomacy" has been far more successful than were the Carter policies in promoting democratic development and respect for human rights.

The major lesson from the Reagan Asia policy is that years of deterioration in American military strength and economic competitiveness cannot be overcome quickly. This requires more than the span of one administration, four years. The U.S. has learned that Asian leaders are very sensitive to America's posture in Asia and that a strong U.S. position clearly preserves and enhances America's positive image, and reassures those leaders. This is essential to keeping peace in the region. Perhaps no U.S. action was more important to Japan, for example, than Reagan's assurance that U.S. troops would remain in South Korea. This was welcomed too by the non-communist southeast Asian nations.

U.S. security cooperation with Japan increased. Under Reagan's prodding, Tokyo agreed to boost its defense spending by more than five percent annually and broaden its area of military responsibility (namely sealane defense). Tokyo has redefined its defense strategy toward the Soviet threat and has agreed to joint training exercises with U.S. forces. In 1985, Tokyo plans to welcome a squadron of U.S. Air Force F-16 fighters to a base in northern Japan. While these changes are significant advances for Japan, they still fall far short of Tokyo adequately confronting the increasing Soviet threat in the region.

The Reagan Administration has been moderately successful through quiet diplomacy and persuasion in preventing other Asian nations, particularly those which suffered at the hands of the Japanese during World War II, from opposing Japan's broadened defense responsibilities. Fear of Japan in Asia remains and has not been replaced completely by recognition of the Soviet threat. Relations with the People's Republic of China have been managed better by President Reagan than any of his predecessors. But a tendency still exists to exaggerate China's ability to counterbalance the USSR in the region. Moscow keeps forces in Asia for at least three reasons: to project Soviet influence and power into Northeast, Southeast, and South Asia; to protect the strategically important Soviet Maritime Provinces and Siberia; and to contain the potential future threat from China. While it is true that more than 50 Soviet divisions are tied down along the Chinese border, most of them would remain in place regardless of the state of Sino-American and Sino-Soviet relations.

Beijing has proved useful in resisting Soviet aggression in Afghanistan. China and the U.S. also have common interests in containing Vietnamese aggression in Southeast Asia and in achieving a peaceful settlement in Kampuchea based on Khmer self-determination. Washington and Beijing disagree, however, on the extent to which Kampuchea's discredited Pol Pot forces should be supported. In Africa, Latin America and the Middle East, China consistently opposes U.S. policies, even when directed against Soviet supported regimes.

The record of China's international actions demonstrates that Washington usually has overestimated Beijing's importance, while underestimating that of Japan and other non-communist Asian nations. Concessions made to China by the Reagan Administration on matters relating to Taiwan, arms sales, technology transfers, textile quotas, and other bilateral issues have not always been reciprocated.

While the U.S. trade deficit with Asia has not yet begun to shrink, the Reagan Administration has taken important steps toward long range solutions, particularly pressing for Japanese markets to open wider to U.S. products. This has helped reduce somewhat the pressure in the U.S. for protectionist measures against Asian imports. Substantial improvements in U.S. trade relations with the region, however, will take time. America's competitiveness has been impaired somewhat by the very strong dollar in the world currency markets. Yet the muscular dollar and attractive U.S. interest rates encourage large capital investment in the U.S. from Asian nations, which reduces U.S. unemployment and enhances productivity of American companies.

Despite the strong dollar, many American exports remain competitive, such as agricultural products. American farm goods already dominate Japan's imported food market and thus sizable further gains for the U.S. products is unlikely. Instead, the U.S. should seek ways to sell Japan other products such as communication equipment, high-tech goods and services, cigarettes and tobacco products.

THE NEXT FOUR YEARS

Security Measures

Greater efforts to offset the Soviet military buildup in the Pacific are needed. This means an increased U.S. military presence and commitment to U.S. friends and allies in the area. It also means persuading Asian nations to upgrade their own military capabilities. In particular, Japan should fufill its commitment to assume additional responsibilities for sealane defense and, in the event of crisis, help close the straits around Japan to prevent Soviet naval vessels from sailing into the North Pacific or to South or Southeast Asia from their bases in the Maritime Provinces. Should Japan assume these responsibilities, the U.S. Seventh Fleet would be able to operate more frequently in the Indian Ocean and offset Soviet power there.

The U.S. should also provide more and better arms to friendly and allied Asian nations. U.S. arms talks with Moscow should continue to include the Asian region, requiring a reduction of Soviet forces in the area, including nuclear missiles and especially those of the SS-20 designation.

Strengthen Free Trade Policies

The Reagan Administration should match its free trade with policies designed to combat protectionism and do all it can to make U.S. businesses more competitive in the world market. Asia probably offers more opportunities for American investment, sales and purchases than any other area of the world. Washington should explore establishment of a regional free trade area that includes most or all of the free market nations in Asia, particularly East Asia. Now that the Administration has taken the initial step of forming a National Committee of Pacific Economic Cooperation, rapid steps should be taken to give high visibility for the purpose of stimulating Pacific area trade. Only with the removal of barriers to the flow of products and investments will the Pacific Basin region realize its maximum economic potential.

Enhance Regional Approaches to Asia

The U.S. should encourage a regional approach to Asian issues and possibly new regional organizations. This must not be at the expense of existing defense treaties or the Association of Southeast Asian Nations. Washington should explore means of tying its relations with East Asia, Australia and New Zealand to relations with the ASEAN states.

Develop a Hong Kong Policy

The U.S. needs to formulate a Hong Kong policy that protects vital U.S. interests as Britain begins to implement the agreement reached with China over the Colony's status prior to and after the 1997 expiration of British authority. Hong Kong's largest trading partner is the U.S. and Americans constitute the largest investors in Hong Kong. The U.S. should express its interest in the fundamental rights of Hong Kong's five million inhabitants and should make every effort to safeguard American interests there by communicating its views to London and Beijing.

Respond to the crisis in the Philippines

The Philippines is suffering from systemic economic problems requiring U.S. assistance. American prestige has more at stake in the Philippines than anywhere else in Asia because of the country's former status as an American dependency. The economic problems that underlie its political problems can be resolved mainly through economic growth in the Philippines. Similarly there is room for the kind of economic and political reforms that could restore the government's credibility and enhance democracy in the Philippines. The U.S. should encourage the Marcos government and its critics to reach workable compromises and the U.S. must be prepared to assist in fulfilling these compromises.

Maintain a Realistic China Policy

American policy towards the People's Republic of China should continue to be formulated on the basis of mutual advantage. "Playing the China card"—using China to trump the Soviet Union—has no part in this policy. It should be recognized that Washington exercises little influence over relations between the two communist giants. Washington should expect eventual limited reproachment between Beijing and Moscow may occur, but Sino-soviet relations are certain to remain strained.

The U.S. should not consider China an ally. Beijing's policies are subject to fluctuations and its leadership succession is uncertain. U.S. policy toward the PRC, therefore, should be friendly but cautious. Dealing with China must be based on fairness, reciprocity, and promotion of U.S. interests.

Further U.S. concessions on Taiwan are unacceptable . They would have demoralizing effect on the people of Taiwan and undermine the democratic and free enterprise institutions built on the island. U.S. credibility as a friend and ally would suffer greatly were Taiwan abandoned. The provisions of the Taiwan Relations Act should be implemented fully. Among other things this means selling Taiwan advanced weapons, including an advanced fighter of the FX designation, such as the F-20; any other defensive weapons systems necessary to offset any military threat from the mainland; supporting Taiwan's participation in international organizations (such as the Asian Development Bank), and preserving all current U.S.-Taiwan bilateral Agreements.

INITIATIVES FOR 1985

1) Emphasize the importance of Asia.

The President should visit Southeast Asia early in the next Administration. Although the Reagan Administration has emphasized the importance of the region, the President cancelled his trip to Thailand, Indonesia and the Philippines in late 1983. By visiting these countries in 1985, the President would draw the most dramatic attention to the area's importance to the U.S.

2) Strongly support South Korea in its determination to keep the 1988 Olympics in Seoul, as now scheduled.

3) Push Congress to grant South Korea the credits to buy the U.S. military equipment needed to modernize its defenses against attack from North Korea.

4) Provide military aid to the non-communist resistance movement in Kampuchea.

The next administration should work in conjunction with ASEAN to increase U.S. assistance to the non-communist elements of the Kampuchean resistance movements headed by Sonn San and Norodom Sihanouk. Because Vietnam has been unwilling to negotiate a withdrawal from Kampuchea, additional military pressure is required to prompt Vietnam to leave. Only then is self-determination possible for Cambodia. Departure of Hanoi's troops would give all nations in the region a greater sense of security.

5) Resist New Zealand's proposed changes in the ANZUS Pact.

The U.S. should refuse to change the 1950 treaty with Australia and New Zealand simply to accommodate the sweeping promises made by the New Zealand Labor Party during its successful election campaign. It vowed to bar ships with nuclear weapons from New Zealand ports. The U.S. Navy apparently has been counting on using these ports in case of emergency in the region. Without the ports, U.S. Navy operational flexibility will be impaired.

6) Increase U.S. economic and military assistance to the Philippines.

In conjunction with continued democratization of the Philippines, as reflected in the 1984 assembly elections, the U.S. should provide economic and military assistance to cope with existing economic problems and confront the guerrilla insurgency.

7) Cautiously improve relations with the People's Republic of China.

The U.S. should expand commercial, cultural and scientific ties with the PRC and press for greater freedom and access to information by American scholars working in China. Military sales should be limited strictly to defensive equipment that would not threaten the security of other nations in Asia.

8) Encourage the PRC to participate fully in the world economic system.

Support PRC membership in the Asian Development bank, but only if Taiwan retains its membership.

9) Sell Taiwan an advanced fighter such as the FX to replace its outdated inventory and to maintain essential parity in the Taiwan Strait.

10) Continue the Generalized System of Preferences for Asian nations.

Economic growth of the ASEAN states, Korea, and Taiwan depends largely on foreign exchange earnings from trade. Thus the United States should continue the Generalized System of Preferences (GSP) scheme in Title V of the Trade Act of 1974 which expires January 3, 1985. The current law should be renewed specifically to include Korea and Taiwan even though they are relatively more prosperous than their Asian neighbors; U.S. strategic interests, and theirs, are served by permitting them to retain GSP status. Existing tariff and non-tariff import barriers should be reduced in 1985 on numerous specific products produced in Asia.

11) Support the repeal of restrictions on timber exports from federal lands.

Public Law 94-373 prevents the export of timber needed in Asian markets. The U.S. timber industry would be stimulated by access to large new markets overseas, thereby becoming less dependent on the wide fluctuations in U.S. demands.

12) Encourage the abolition of state laws which levy the so-called unitary tax on foreign multinational corporations.

THE MIDDLE EAST

by
Daniel Pipes*

The Reagan Administration came to office with an overall foreign policy mandate to strengthen pro-American forces, counter Soviet expansion, and promote free trade. It soon found that these principles translate most readily into policy in regions where local issues are subordinated to the East-West conflict, such as Grenada and El Salvador. It found them hardest to apply in regions where, while there are also Soviet efforts to destabilize, local issues often predominate—most notably in the Middle East. The Administration failed to develop a clear policy on the Arab-Israeli, Lebanese, and Iraq-Iran conflicts, or on relations with Israel and Saudi Arabia. Persistent confusion in policy has been the result. Policy toward Libya has been clearer, but has been difficult to implement.

The Arab-Israeli Conflict

The U.S. seeks a full and just peace in the Middle East—but will settle for stability, as it often does elsewhere. The Koreas are not at peace, nor are India and Pakistan, but they do enjoy more stable relations than the Arab states and Israel. Without losing sight of the ultimate goal of peace, Washington should adjust its sights to stability. Stabilization of the Middle East represents a realistic goal for U.S. diplomacy.

Lines are clearly drawn in the Middle East: The United States gives strongest support to the area's most democratic and pro-Western country—Israel; the Soviet Union gives strongest support to states and organizations that sponsor terrorism against the West—especially Libya, Syria, and the Palestine Liberation Organization (PLO). Other states of the region fit between these poles.

Although Israel explicitly aligns with the West against the USSR, some have feared that close U.S.-Israeli ties could come at the expense of weakened U.S. bonds with the less pro-Western but more numerous Arab states. Yet the U.S. can enjoy healthy relations with both the Israelis and moderate Arabs. For example, although the U.S. signed a military cooperation agreement with Israel in November 1983, it paid no significant price for this with the Arabs, especially not in U.S. relations with the Persian Gulf states threatened by Iran. To the

* Task Force members included Amos Perlmutter, James A. Phillips, and Adam Garfinkle.

contrary, relations with Israel and the Arabs improved simultaneously. An anti-Soviet "strategic consensus" among the U.S., Israel, and strongly anti-Soviet Arab nations can be attained, if approached carefully.

Israel offers special advantages as an American ally. As the only consistently democratic state in the Middle East, it enjoys the most stable system of government in the region. Israel's political continuity sets it apart from neighboring states, many of whose regimes can be overthrown by a coup or a bullet. Israel's freedom of expression and its moral principles make it possible for the U.S., through its support for Israel, to combine geopolitical advantage with morality in its foreign policy.

A strong and secure Israel is in the American interest because it reduces the chances of destabilizing wars in the Middle East and constrains the expansion of Soviet influence. A powerful Israel forces Arab leaders to see the futility of armed struggle and induces them to see the benefits of a negotiated settlement. In having to choose between pursuing their conflict with Israel militarily with Moscow's support or diplomatically with Washington's assistance, one Arab leader after another has chosen the latter and foregone the Soviet route for the American one. Anwar Sadat summed up the situation when he noted that "the United States has 99 percent of the cards." Israel's strength also helps defend Western supplies of Persian Gulf oil. Israel potentially provides the finest military infrastructure in the area, or it could, as the local state most capable of projecting power, act on its own.

The Iraq-Iran War

American policy has been consistent through four years of war: condemn both sides' aggression, maintain strict political neutrality, and quietly give military help to whichever side is losing. This stance is proper in a conflict where both belligerents are governed by anti-Western regimes. The U.S. interest continues to be that neither side wins but that the parties negotiate a settlement and eventually return to their old borders.

In the long term, good relations with Iran remain far more important than with Iraq. With a population of 45 million and borders on the Soviet Union and the Persian Gulf, Iran undeniably is a strategic prize. Yet, an Iranian victory over Iraq would have very serious consequences. It probably would lead to a fundamentalist regime in Baghdad, which could threaten Kuwait, Bahrain, Jordan, and Saudi Arabia. On the other hand, an Iraqi victory would be even more troublesome; Iraqi dominance of the region not only would endanger those same countries, but could lead to the dismemberment of Iran and this could prompt Soviet intervention.

Lebanon

The U.S. military effort in Lebanon from August 1982 to February 1984 was probably the darkest foreign policy experience of the Reagan Administration. Washington's policy in Lebanon was hamstrung by: 1) uncertain domestic political backing for an ambitious military assignment; 2) deployment of troops without a specific mission; 3) inadequate understanding of the factions within Lebanon and the reasons for their conflict, as well as the goals of the Syrian government; and 4) re-orientation of interest away from Lebanon at the moment of greatest opportunity in September 1982. The Reagan Initiative on the West Bank and Gaza was proposed exactly when a breakthrough in Lebanon might have been within reach.

However unfortunate the U.S. experience there, Lebanon remains an important battleground where Washington must continue an active political involvement. Lebanon historically has had a key role in the intellectual, political, and economic life of the Middle East; its population includes some of the region's most pro-Western elements, and its location makes it an important concern of the United States. There is much yet to be won or lost in Lebanon and the U.S. must not abdicate its role there.

U.S. Relations With Saudi Arabia

Relations with Riyadh bear a striking resemblance to those with Peking. In both cases, America goes out of its way to prove sincere friendship in a relationship that both sides know to be purely expedient. Unnecessary gestures to retain good will characterize relations with Saudi Arabia. This explains why the U.S. has sold sophisticated arms to Riyadh that the Saudis are incapable of maintaining by themselves, why it bowed to the Saudi request and held back on filling the Strategic Petroleum Reserve, and why it has not pressed the Saudis for greater military cooperation.

Although the U.S. often looks to the Saudi government to exert political influence in the region on such matters as the peace process, Syria, and Lebanon, it is in fact a defensive and weak regime. Expecting Saudi help not only is wishful thinking, but it also puts pressures on the Saudi government for actions that sometimes cannot be taken, thereby possibly endangering the regime.

Libya

Libya, led by the obsessively anti-American Colonel Muammar Qadhafi, continues to sponsor terrorism on a worldwide scale. While Libya is a weak military power, its growing strategic cooperation with the Soviet Union greatly concerns its neighbors and the West. American attempts to isolate Libya have been undermined by West Europe's eagerness for trade and by the August 1984 announcement of a "union" between Libya and Morocco, an important American ally. While it remains to be seen how durable this "union" will prove to be, Washington should make it clear to the Moroccans that closer Libyan-Moroccan relations will threaten seriously the harmony of American-Moroccan relations.

THE NEXT FOUR YEARS

Arab-Israeli Conflict

Refrain from imposing solutions: Neither the U.S. nor any combination of outside powers can on their own solve the Arab-Israeli conflict. This is beyond any outside power's capacity, and incautious optimistic rhetoric can raise dangerous expectations and lead to unhealthy dependence. Instead, the U.S. should respond to local initiatives by facilitating communication, serving as an honest broker, and helping to ease the burden of those Middle East nations that take risks for peace.

Maintain Israeli military superiority: Provide Israel with the arms necessary to assure its military predominance over Syrian forces in particular and any likely combination of Arab forces in general. Make clear to all states of the region that the U.S. does not intend to arm both sides of a conflict. This means providing only strictly defensive weapons to governments in a state of war with Israel (such as Jordan and Saudi Arabia).

U.S. Relations With Israel

Deepen and extend the strategic relationship with Israel as it relates to the Soviet Union and its proxies: The U.S. should consider the prepositioning of material, coordination of battle plans, joint maneuvers, and shared intelligence.

Deemphasize the West Bank: While the disposition of the West Bank and Gaza Strip are of great importance to the Arabs and to Israel—indeed it may have mortal significance for Israel—it is not an issue central to the Arab-Israeli conflict, and it is not a vital issue for the U.S. It thus need not overly concern Washington. Arabs and Israelis fought for many years before the West Bank and Gaza came under Israeli rule in 1967; there is no reason to assume that return of these territories to the Arabs would end the conflict. Settling the status of the West Bank and Gaza, often referred to as solving the "Palestinian problem," while important, is in reality but a minor aspect of the overall Arab-Israeli relationship.

Encourage recognition of Israel: The essence of the Arab-Israeli problem lies in the Arab refusal to recognize Israel. On this issue the U.S. can most effectively marshall its influence. Of the Arab League's 21 member states, only the four bordering on Israel—Lebanon, Syria, Jordan, and Egypt—can make war on Israel. Three of these four have resigned themselves to come to terms with Israel's existence: Egypt signed a peace treaty in 1979, Lebanon tried to sign one in 1983, and Jordan has often signaled to Israel its willingness to co-exist. Syria alone continues pursuing policies aimed at destroying Israel by force. Not only does Damascus prepare for war against Israel, but exerts great pressure on other Arab nations—including Lebanon, Jordan, Egypt, and the PLO—to prevent them from accommodating to Israel's existence.

For the U.S. fruitfully to address the Arab-Israeli conflict, it must deal, through measures described below, with the problem of Syrian intransigence. Otherwise, Syria will try to block progress on a U.S.-backed settlement by intimidating Israel's Arab negotiating partners.

Lebanon

Encourage political reform: The U.S. should press the Lebanese government to enfranchise those elements that have until now been excluded—especially the Shi'ites.

The Iraq-Iran War

Assist the side in danger of losing: The U.S. should stay out of the conflict except for discreet and minimal support to whichever side is in danger of losing. It should also open backdoor channels to the Iranian government, and take advantage of the Iranian threat to other states of the region by improving U.S. ties with them, particularly the Arab states of the Persian Gulf.

U.S. Relations With Saudi Arabia

Seek quid pro quos: The U.S. should stipulate that facilities for U.S. land-based air power be made available in Saudi Arabia in return for U.S. military protection. The situation that exists today brings all of the problems of a U.S. presence without the advantages of control; this must be changed.

Keep relationships informal: The U.S. should not define the American role in Saudi Arabia in formal statements. Instead, it must take full advantage of the de facto influence that the U.S. currently enjoys, which follows from on-the-ground military involvement.

Libya

Quarantine Libya: The West cannot afford "business as usual" with Colonel Qadhafi. The U.S. should pressure its allies, particularly France, to help contain Libyan adventurism. Military and economic aid to North African states may make them less vulnerable to Libyan subversion. This would reduce Libya's mischief-making capabilities and underscore to the Libyan people the costs of Qadhafi's erratic aggressions.

INITIATIVES FOR 1985

The Arab-Israeli Conflict

1) Encourage quiet discussions between Jordan and Israel.

Practical matters (water rights, currency regulations, and Jordanian influence on the West Bank) can be dealt with more easily with an American offer of help.

2) Take steps to isolate Syria and reduce its influence on the Arab states.

This might involve helping Syria's Arab opponents coordinate policies, taking preventive anti-terrorist action, aiding the anti-regime forces in Syria, or pressuring the Soviet Union to reduce its military aid to Syria.

Lebanon

3) Assist the central government's army generously.

This makes it possible for the U.S. to maintain links to a key power center in Lebanon—and to prevent the country from possibly falling under Soviet influence.

4) Help with the negotiation of security agreements in South Lebanon to expedite a full Israeli withdrawal.

The Iraq-Iran War

5) Maintain a fleet outside the Persian Gulf to protect shipping, to respond in local emergencies, and to counter potential Soviet intervention.

6) Urge the Western allies to coordinate with Washington their policies toward the belligerents, especially with regard to ending arms sales and oil purchases.

U.S. Relations With Saudi Arabia

7) Do not sell weapons to Saudi Arabia that allow it to threaten its neighbors.

In case of emergencies in the Persian Gulf, lease whatever is needed on a provisional basis (as has been the case with the AWACS) to the threatened nation.

8) Do not pressure Saudi Arabia to exert political influence on other states; conversely, do not resort to wholesale appeasement to accommodate its wishes.

AFGHANISTAN

by
James A. Phillips*

Because the Reagan Administration appreciated the geopolitical implications of the Soviet invasion of Afghanistan, it refused to accept Moscow's control as a *fait accompli*. But while Washington has applauded the courageous struggle of the Afghan freedom fighters, it has not done enough to aid them. Not only has the Administration failed to provide adequate military assistance, it has opposed a congressional resolution calling for increased assistance to the Afghans.

The Afghans have demonstrated an unshakeable will to resist Soviet domination during almost five years of fighting. They lack the military means, however, to triumph over the Soviet invaders. The U.S. could provide the material necessary for an Afghan victory, but has not done so.

In the absence of sufficient external assistance to the Afghans, Moscow believes that time is on its side. Under Party Chief Yuri Andropov, Moscow sought to isolate and demoralize the Afghan resistance through U.N.-sponsored indirect talks with Pakistan. Moscow apparently hoped that this would furnish a diplomatic figleaf for continued Soviet domination of Afghanistan. Soviet unwillingness to provide a timetable for withdrawal and the Soviet terror bombing campaign unleashed in Spring 1984, after Andropov died, underscored the persistent Soviet refusal to negotiate a settlement. The Soviets will not consider serious negotiations unless the costs of holding Afghanistan exceed the strategic benefits.

The U.S. has stood by too long while Afghans have died by the tens of thousands. If the expansion of the Soviet empire is to be halted, Afghanistan is the place to start.

THE NEXT FOUR YEARS

Secure Soviet Withdrawal

Washington should aim at securing a Soviet withdrawal—not merely a bloodying of the Soviets—by helping the Afghans raise the military, economic, and political costs of continued Soviet occupa-

*With Andy Eiva.

tion. The Soviets are too strong to be driven out solely by military means. Military pressure is but a precondition for an acceptable negotiated solution. Another precondition is fostering greater unity among the rival Afghan resistance groups.

INITIATIVES FOR 1985

1) Provide the Afghan freedom fighters with the military means to sustain their resistance and increase the damage they inflict on the Soviet units.

Weapons supplied by the U.S. should include reliable shoulder-fired anti-aircraft missiles, light anti-tank weapons, mortars, and mines.

2) Provide non-military supplies such as medical equipment and medical training to a cadre of Afghan personnel.

3) Provide portable radios to improve military coordination and to disseminate information to civilian supporters.

4) Send food to those Afghans who have become refugees in their own country when they were forced off their land by Soviet scorched earth policies.

5) Encourage Soviet soldiers in Afghanistan to defect by supporting such groups as Resistance International, which attempt to make it easier for Soviet dissenters to reach the West.

6) Encourage cooperation and solidarity among rival anti-Soviet groups.

PAKISTAN

by
James A. Phillips

The U.S.-Pakistan relations deteriorated steadily during the Carter Administration, a trend that the incoming Reagan Administration immediately sought to reverse. Pakistan had become a front-line state, facing Soviet troops across its border, following the 1979 Soviet invasion of Afghanistan. The Reagan Administration negotiated a six-year $3.2 billion aid package evenly divided between military and economic assistance. This aid, along with the sale of forty F-16 fighter bombers, has gone far toward restoring Pakistani trust in the reliability and durability of the American commitment to Pakistan's independence and territorial intergrity.

The single most disruptive issue in Pakistani-American relations is U.S. opposition to Islamabad's clandestine nuclear weapons program. Pakistan's lack of an indigenous defense industry, its historical inability to secure a reliable source of foreign arms, and the greater size of the Indian army have prompted Islamabad to seek a nuclear option to deter India, which detonated a "peaceful nuclear device" in 1974. In 1979, the Carter Administration suspended aid to Pakistan as required under the terms of the Symington Amendment to the 1961 Foreign Assistance Act, which prohibited aid to countries that were developing nuclear weapons. Although the Reagan Administration successfully sponsored legislation that exempted Pakistan from the Symington Amendment for the life of the current aid package, a Pakistani nuclear explosion would result in the suspension of all American military and economic aid.

Pakistani-American relations have also been troubled by General Zia's cautious approach to restoring democracy in Pakistan and by persistent reports of human rights abuses.

THE NEXT FOUR YEARS

Push For Democracy in Pakistan

Washington should work to foster a stable, secure, pro-Western Pakistan free from Soviet intimidation. The restoration of democracy in Pakistan should be a top priority. This should be a gradual process, perhaps best accomplished along the lines of the Turkish model of limited democracy. The State Department should continue to press for the elimination of human rights abuses in Pakistan, taking care to note that the human rights situation in Pakistan today is far superior to that of neighboring Iran or Afghanistan.

Encourage Pakistan to Forego the Development of Nuclear Weapons

Just as stability is a precondition for Pakistani democracy, security is a precondition for Pakistani acceptance of nuclear nonproliferation. The best way for the United States to persuade Pakistan to forego the development of a nuclear deterrent is for Wahington to prove itself to be a dependable ally sensitive to Pakistan's security concerns.

Encourage an Indo-Pakistani Detente

The United States should also work to reinforce and deepen the tentative detente between India and Pakistan that emerged in 1983, before opportunistic Indian politicians try to make Pakistan a scapegoat for India's sectarian problems in upcoming elections. Only the Soviet Union would profit from another Indo-Pakistani war.

INITIATIVES FOR 1985

The Administration should:

1) Offer its good offices to facilitate a confidence-building process that will relax tensions between India and Pakistan.

2) Seek to restrain the Congress from damaging Pakistani-American relations through legislation that will only accelerate the nuclear proliferation it is designed to prevent.

If the United States should not deliver promised aid, the Pakistanis are much more likely to opt for an immediate nuclear weapons test than if Washington remained a dependable backer. The carrot here is more influential than the stick.

3) Work with Islamabad to reduce Pakistani harassment of Afghan freedom fighters whose political headquarters were recently removed from Peshwar.

Also, Pakistani acceptance of a leakproof arms pipeline to the Afghans must be won if the Afghans are to have a chance of forcing a negotiated Soviet withdrawal from Afghanistan.

AFRICA

by
Jeffrey B. Gayner*

The initial program of the Reagan Administration concerning Africa consisted of six broad approaches: 1) promote peace and regional security and deny opportunities to those who seek to foster instability; 2) support proven friends and become known as a reliable partner in Africa; 3) maintain market opportunities, access to key resources, and contribute to expanding African and American economies; 4) support negotiated solutions to the problems of southern Africa; 5) expand that group of nations whose development policies produce economic growth, which have democratic institutions and respect basic human rights; 6) help meet Africa's humanitarian needs.[1]

Under this very broad, general framework some specific issues were cited as requiring special attention, especially the negotiations aimed at bringing independence to Southwest Africa or, as it is commonly known, Namibia; this required an end to Soviet-Cuban military intervention in Angola. In dealing with South Africa the Administration sought "to encourage purposeful, evolutionary change. . .toward a non-racial society." And finally, in dealing with the region's enormous economic problems, the U.S. pledged "to help those who help themselves" and "to engage the American private sector more fully in the economic development process."[2]

The objectives outlined in 1981 could be reiterated in 1984. To be sure, there have been significant gains. The United States policy of "constructive engagement" with South Africa has played a role in a modest but important liberalization of the political system to include the coloreds (people of mixed racial backgrounds) and Asians. Although a significant percentage did not participate in the September 1984 election, a beginning was made toward a more representative system. More significant, perhaps, have been the successful negotiations, backed by Washington, between South Africa and Mozambique in which they have pledged to cease interfering in each other's internal affairs. Mirroring this, movement has begun toward a mutual disengagement of forces agreement between Angola and South Africa regarding the Namibian border region.

Although the White House in 1981 sought a repeal of the Clark

---

*Task Force members included Samuel T. Francis, Kevin Callwood, Ian Butterfield, and James Potts.

[1]Points excerpted from Chester A. Crocker, "Strengthening U.S.-African Relations," *Department of State Bulletin*, August 1981, p.57.

[2]*Ibid.*

Amendment, which bars U.S. assistance to the black nationalist UNITA movement in Angola, Congress balked. The Administration regrettably has not pursued the matter. While the Namibia negotiations remain stalled, the U.S. has continued to seek a comprehensive solution involving withdrawal of foreign forces and self-determination for both Namibia and Angola.

In contrast to these gains, success with other political objectives in the region remains largely elusive. Despite large scale U.S. financial support for the Zimbabwe Development Fund, neither free enterprise nor democracy has developed in the country. Instead, the government of Zimbabwe's president Robert Mugabe has proclaimed publicly its objective of creating a one-party socialist state, and civil strife and government oppression have plagued the country. U.S. generosity, moreover, did not prevent Zimbabwe from denouncing U.S. action in Grenada and from refusing to condemn the Soviet attack on the civilian Korean Airlines flight 007.

In the Horn of Africa the U.S. has provided enough assistance to help secure the Somalia border against Ethiopian attacks, but not enough to allow Somalia to confront its serious economic and social problems. The U.S. contributed vital air surveillance and logistical support to stem the Libyan invasion of Chad, leading eventually to an apparent Libyan withdrawal. However, indications that Ethiopia would extricate itself from its Cuban advisors have not been borne out by events, and Ethiopia now has officially adopted a Communist system. Overall, less progress has been made in Africa in the promotion of democracy and human rights than in any other non-communist area of the world—although this certainly is not the fault of the Reagan Administration.

The greatest disappointment in Africa—the deterioration of the economies of nearly all African countries—also cannot be blamed on the Administration. As Secretary of State George Shultz told Congress in 1984: "Pervasive state controls, bloated state enterprises and bureaucracies, over-valued currencies, and disincentives for agriculture [in Africa] have all had the effect of stifling the private sector and individual initiative." Fundamentally, many African governments have been unwilling or unable to take the steps necessary to allow incentives for private sector growth.

THE NEXT FOUR YEARS

Restructure Foreign Assistance

To promote the private sector approach to economic development, the FY 1985 Foreign Assistance Request included a new $500 million five-year Economic Policy Initiative (EPI) that would provide flexibility in aid programs. The EPI was designed to reward sound economic and social initiatives, such as the privatization of agriculture. While laudable, the amount was far too small; most U.S. money still is going to traditional government-to-government programs. Much more of the AID program should be targeted to boost private sector approaches rather than to discredited existing programs.

Washington should use the economic crisis in Africa as an opportunity to recommend the kinds of fundamental changes in African government policies that will spur economic growth. Only governments that use the market to encourage food production in rural areas and allow private industry and investment to operate should receive significant American assistance. Drought relief and other emergency humanitarian assistance programs should continue to all nations.

End Marxist Influence in Africa

The United States must encourage the countries of Africa to abandon Marxist dogma. But while Marxist theories have worked havoc with economies throughout Africa, the more important Marxist threat to Africa derives from the presence of military forces from such Communist regimes as Cuba, East Germany, Bulgaria, the Soviet Union and North Korea. The United States stations no military forces in Africa and should not accept the continuation of Eastern bloc forces meddling in the affairs of African countries. Thus the U.S. should press for removal of such forces from all countries in Africa.

Focus More Attention and Support on Friendly Governments

The goal of working with friendly governments that pursue sound social and economic policies has not been reflected in U.S. actions. In 1981, for example, Assistant Secretary of State for African Affairs, Chester A. Crocker, praised Malawi, Cameroon and Kenya as governments that have pursued sound political and economic policies. Yet, neither programs for them nor political ties with them have been augmented substantially. The U.S. should know by now that attempts to use aid and other incentives to make marginal gains with generally hostile nations should not take priority over improving ties with more friendly governments.

Coordinate Central African Policy with European Allies

Given the existing close relations and historical connections betweeen many central and west African countries and European nations, the U.S. should closely coordinate political and economic policies with Britain, France, Germany, and other Western nations that provide significant assistance to Africa. The U.S. has neither the resources nor the expertise to provide assistance tailored to the needs of all countries in Africa. Consequently, the U.S. needs to rely on other Western countries to assume primary responsibility for assisting some African countries in their development. Through the competition of different nations pursuing modestly different formulas for development, the U.S. should continue to draw general lessons that might be beneficial throughout the African continent.

Promote Democracy in Africa

While the promotion of democracy and human rights often have received enormous attention in Latin America, Asia, and other areas of the world, Western nations have been unwilling to promote these same values as vigorously in Africa. A general acceptance of the notion of "one man, one vote, one time" has led to benign acquiescence in the development of one-party political systems in Africa, dominated by either the military or one tribal group; and massive abuses of human rights in countries such as Ethiopia, Uganda, Zimbabwe or Angola often have been ignored or dismissed as "internal affairs." In Africa, the Administration and especially the U.S. Congress have been unwilling, in general, to confront seriously the problems of democratic development in Africa. The recently created National Endowment for Democracy, which was designed to encourage the development of democratic institutions, should become deeply involved in Africa in the next decade.

Expand Constructive Engagement With South Africa

To encourage the continued liberalization process within South Africa, Washington should work more closely with South Africa to improve the status of non-white groups. The inclusion of coloreds and Asians in the Parliament should be viewed as significant steps toward the eventual expansion of rights to urban blacks and residents of the homelands—the independent black states being created by South Africa out of parts of its territory. The U.S. should encourage South Africa to repeal the Mixed Marriages and Group Areas acts and all other aspects of apartheid; it should press for these changes through quiet diplomacy.

On the other hand, the U.S. should recognize that South Africa already has made changes that should be rewarded by loosened restrictions on the export to South Africa of such goods as surveillance aircraft and other non-lethal security equipment. U.S. assistance programs designed for the benefit of South African blacks should be expanded to include them regardless of where they live in South Africa, including the homelands. Moreover, the next Administration should oppose vigorously any interference in U.S. private investment and other economic relations with South Africa; such relationships expand economic opportunities for blacks in South Africa and accelerate the liberalization process in racial policies. Nearly all black leaders in South Africa adamantly oppose so-called disinvestment campaigns.

INITIATIVES FOR 1985

1) Encourage Mozambique to Abandon Marxism.

In 1984 the United States designed an economic assistance program for Mozambique that will supplement existing U.S. food assistance for this drought-stricken nation. In general, a coordinated approach is underway by Western nations and South Africa to wean the Mozambique government away from its Marxist heritage. It appears that President Samora Machel may be willing to abandon gradually much of his Marxist dogma and compromise with his political opponents. The U.S. should encourage this process.

One of the principal reasons Machel may be willing to change is due to pressure against his regime by the Movement of National Resistance (MNR) in Mozambique. In recent years, the MNR clearly has represented the growing dissent in the country to a wide range of disastrous economic and political policies initiated by Machel. If, by early 1985, Machel is not decisively moving away from Marxism, then a clear alternative exists through support for the MNR by the United States.

2) Take a Tougher Approach Toward Angola.

Thus far, the Marxist-oriented regime of Jose Eduardo dos Santos in Luanda has given no indication that it is willing to reach a broad solution to the political and security problems in Angola by negotiating with Jonas Savimbi, the leader of the pro-Western UNITA forces. Moreover, the Cuban and other Eastern bloc forces in the country probably have the military power to veto any such agreement. If attempts to reach agreement with the present Angolan regime do not succeed by early 1985, then the U.S. should consider recognition of UNITA as the legitimate government of Angola, especially in view of its continuing success in its guerrilla war. The Administration also should seek legislation to repeal the Clark Amendment and open up assistance programs, especially scholarship programs, to supportors of UNITA. At the same time, the U.S. should encourage other Western governments to at least adopt the current U.S. policy of nonrecognition of Luanda.

3) Settle the Namibian Conflict.

Washington must continue to strive for a settlement in Namibia. The Southwest Africa People's Organziation (SWAPO), like the Marxist regime in Luanda, remains largely dependent on foreign guidance and support. SWAPO should be offered one last chance to agree to a Namibian settlement. During the same period in which Luanda can agree to a plan for the withdrawal of Cuban and other foreign military forces from Angola, SWAPO could agree to a plan which includes the withdrawal of South African forces from Namibia. The failure to reach such an agreement with SWAPO should lead the U.S. to pursue a settlement of the Namibia conflict through other means. Initially, the U.S. should approach other Western nations involved to reach an agreement for internationally supervised elections, even without the participation of SWAPO. In any event, should self-determination in Angola lead to a UNITA government, SWAPO quickly may become a largely irrelevant force in Namibia.

HUMAN RIGHTS

by
Juliana Geran Pilon*

Human rights remain at the core of America's foreign policy. Yet the proper role of human rights in U.S. policy has not always been articulated consistently by the U.S. government. The Reagan Administration has made significant advances in this regard, and spelled out that role as follows: The U.S. seeks elimination of human rights violations, and the furthering of democratic institutions as the surest guarantor of human rights.

The Administration's approach has been to use political and economic pressures or incentives as appropriate. While public denunciation of violations at times may be effective, quiet diplomacy often is preferable, particularly in the case of friendly governments susceptible to U.S. influence. At the Conference on Security and Cooperation in Europe (the Helsinki Conference) whose latest session concluded in September 1983, the U.S. criticized the human rights record of the Soviet Union and its European satellites. Ambassador Max Kampelman severely chastised Moscow in both open and closed meetings at the last session for its treatment of dissidents, prospective emigrants, and for other human rights abuses. Because of the perceived need for consensus among the Western nations, the U.S. unfortunately did not press all of its demands in the final conference resolution. In particular, absent from that resolution was a condemnation of Soviet jamming of radio broadcasts from the West, which deprives its citizens of the right to know what is happening not only outside its borders but also internally.

The Reagan Administration has demonstrated that it understands several important points:

1) There is an inter-relationship between democracy and human rights. Nations with democratic institutions are more likely to respect human rights. Therefore, a pro-democratic policy is also a pro-human rights policy.

2) There is an inter-relationship between the expansion of Soviet and Soviet-proxy control or influence and the loss of human rights. And there is a relationship between the expansion of U.S./Western influence and the protection of human rights. Therefore, a strong policy against Soviet expansion is a pro-human rights policy.

---

* Task Force members included Charles Lichenstein, Max Kampelman, Charles Fairbanks, and Ernest Lefever.

3) The U. S. occasionally will have to work with a friendly authoritarian government that has an unpalatable human rights record in order to protect U.S. security and perhaps prevent a Marxist takeover of that country. Because such regimes can and often do evolve into democracies which respect human rights, while no Marxist regime ever has, this policy, too, ultimately is pro-human rights.

4) There is an important difference between human needs, such as food, and housing, and human rights, which ultimately can be preserved only if the state power is restrained. Failure of many policymakers to understand this fundamental distinction leads to confused and contradictory policies, such as concluding that "socialist" nations automatically behave better in the human rights area than authoritarian governments.

When a nation, such as El Salvador, is under serious military threat from Marxist revolutionaries, the human rights situation should be evaluated keeping in mind: that 1) it takes time for non-Western nations to achieve the U.S. standards of human rights; 2) this is particularly difficult in wartime conditions; 3) there are important distinctions between the residual authoritarianism of Salvador and similar friendly nations and the totalitarianism of Sandinista-ruled Nicaragua; and 4) the U.S. can use its influence only when a nation is open to it. Sandinista Nicaragua has closed itself to U.S. influence while inviting the influence of the Soviet Union and Cuba, systematic violators of human rights. This would be the case also with other nations falling under Marxist-Leninist control.

The Reagan Administration has made some impressive practical human rights advances. A number of free elections and peaceful transfers of power have taken place since 1981. In El Salvador, the U.S. provided technical assistance, international observers, and helped with voter registration for the 1982 and 1984 Salvadoran elections. Indeed, those elections may well have failed to take place had it not been for the vigorous support of the Reagan Administration. "Death squad" activities, moreover, have been curtailed.

Administration policies had a generally positive impact upon human rights in Latin America. In numerous nations, quiet U.S. pressure played a role in preserving or stimulating democratic institutions. For example, in Bolivia, U.S. pressure thwarted a military coup. Only when absolutely necessary did the Administration support nondemocratic regimes. While hoping to advance the cause of democracy everywhere, this desire was nevertheless tempered by practical circumstances and by the knowledge that the most serious enemy of human rights is totalitarianism.

Using quiet diplomacy, the U.S. successfully encouraged several countries to improve their human rights records. South Korea has relaxed its policy on political dissent. South Africa has taken an historic step away from exclusive white rule by including Asians and "coloreds" in the political process. Rather than isolate South Africa, with the result that fear and frustration would have forced it into intransigence and reluctance to risk liberalization, the U.S. continued to allow commercial interaction and pressed for discussions on the future of Nambia. Finally, the establishment of the National Endowment for Democracy could boost the chances of democracy taking root abroad. The NED is an important symbol, a reaffirmation of the American commitment to the advance of democracy and human rights.

The Administration has improved the country reports on human rights practices submitted annually to the Congress by the Department of State. The reports have been valuable and thorough, using improved categories of analysis. By downgrading the questionable categories of "economic and social rights," the reports no longer mislead by implying that such "rights" are similar to civil and political liberties.

One weakness of the Reagan Administration human rights policy has been in dealings with some communist regimes such as Romania and China. Because Bucharest at times defies Moscow's lead on foreign policy issues, the U.S. has extended credits and most-favored-nation status to Romania. Yet this country now is probably the most repressive Eastern bloc nation except for the Soviet Union. U.S. policies have given Romania no incentive to ease its near total suppression of human rights. In China, Administration enthusiasm for political relations has largely obscured the still massive violation of civil and political rights by Beijing. It is estimated that in the past year over 10,000 alleged criminals were executed with little resembling due process of law, and that tens of thousands still remain in political prisons.

Another Reagan Administration weakness concerns the U.S.S.R. To be sure, the Kremlin's current crackdown on dissent began in Summer 1979, well before Reagan took office. The Administration has not used, however, one of the tools provided by law that could penalize Moscow for its human rights abuses. The Department of the Treasury did not follow the advice of Congress and of Customs Commissioner William von Raab to enforce the 1930 Smoot-Hawley Tariff Act that prohibits the importation of goods made by slave labor, which would bar a number of items from the Soviet Union.

The lessons of the Reagan human rights record are: 1) it pays to promote democracy in areas where there is hope for success, notably in Latin America. 2) Bilateralism, consistently applied, can work well, as it did in South Korea. By contrast, such multilateral efforts as the U.N. Human Rights Commission and the Helsinki Conference, seem doomed to be mostly an exercise in futility. 3) The use of force, skillfully applied, in an area of manageable size and in well understood circumstances, can be an effective means to promote conditions for democracy, as was the case in Grenada. 4) Economic inducements, such as granting most-favored-nation status, without proper monitoring techniques, probably will fail to promote human rights. 5) At the Commerce and State Departments, some staffers are less concerned about furthering the human rights policy than in promoting trade with communist governments. 6) The success of totalitarianism (which in the contemporary world almost invariably means Marxism-Leninism) is always a setback for human rights, while a success for U.S. or Western democracy is an advance—either actually or potentially—for human rights.

THE NEXT FOUR YEARS

Emphasize consistently the importance of human rights and bring up the issue whenever possible.

It is important that the U.S. emphasize its moral principles, and remind the world of what distinguishes the U.S. from its totalitarian opponents.

Encourage Democratic Capitalism throughout the world.

It is within a democratic type of framework that human rights are most likely to be observed.

INITIATIVES FOR 1985

1) Enforce the Tariff Act of 1930, and halt the import of goods made by slave labor in the USSR.

2) Consider ending Romania's most-favored-nation trading status.

3) Continue sanctions against Poland and block its admission to the International Monetary Fund until there are greater signs of genuine liberalization.

4) Highlight the systematic human rights violations of such Marxist states as the Soviet Union, Cuba, Angola, Nicaragua, Vietnam, North Korea and the People's Republic of China.

5) Reconsider U.S. participation in the Helsinki process: evaluate the benefits as against the disadvantage of participation in a forum that allows Soviet-bloc governments to perpetuate the illusion that their human rights problems are being seriously addressed by the West.

6) Encourage the National Endowment for Democracy to channel whatever resources it may obtain into projects strengthening the future of democracy. AID funds also should be used in the effort.

7) Raise the issue of Andrei Sakharov's fate.

One major forum should be a formal meeting of the Stockholm Conference on Confidence and Security Building Measures and Disarmament in Europe (CDE). The linkage between CDE and the Helsinki process should be maintained.

INTERNATIONAL ORGANIZATIONS

by
Juliana Geran Pilon*

The United Nations now costs the U.S. taxpayer more than $1 billion annually. This comprises 25 percent of the ever-escalating U.N. budget. In addition, the U.S. provides support services which, according to former U.S. Permanent Representative to the U.N. Andrew Young, may add another billion dollars to the total. Such an enormous burden justifies American taxpayers asking whether the U.N. serves any U.S. interests. The answer, on balance, is not encouraging. Almost all U.N. bodies and agencies are dominated by a coalition of Third World developing countries and Soviet-bloc nations. As a result, nearly all U.N. programs and resolutions are antagonistic to the U.S., the West, and the free enterprise system. To make matters worse, the Manhattan-based U.N. headquarters serves as a valuable cover, complete with diplomatic immunity, for Soviet and similar intelligence agents who spy on U.S. security and technology developments.

The Reagan Administration set clear goals for the U.S. role in the U.N. As articulated by Ambassador Jeane Kirkpatrick, U.S. Permanent Representative to the U.N., in her confirmation hearings and later, the U.S. delegation to the U.N. would attempt "to articulate the legitimate aspirations of the American people" in behalf of freedom, government by consent, and the enhancement of human rights.

Secretary of State Alexander Haig told the U.N General Assembly in 1981 that "the ideals of the U.N. are . . . also American ideals. The Charter embodies American principles." The Reagan Administration has taken the original U.N. mandate very seriously in its assessment of the U.N.

"Success" and "failure" in the U.N. context is always a matter of judgment. Indeed, some successes have been invisible to the public, involving prevention of outcomes that might have damaged U.S. interests. Others have been well publicized.

In December 1983, for example, the Administration gave the required one-year notice that the U.S. will withdraw from UNESCO at the end of 1984 unless the organization undertakes fundamental reforms. This action, privately backed by such key Western states as Britain and the Netherlands, was another important sign of U.S. resolve and of concern that UNESCO, like other U.N. bodies, had strayed from its original purpose.

---

* Task Force members included Charles Lichenstein, Owen Harries, Melanie Merkle, and Burton Yale Pines.

The clear, forceful articulation of American interests in all U.N. fora by Ambassador Kirkpatrick and the U.S. delegation, notably in the area of human rights, was a positive policy. On December 8, 1983, for example, Ambassador Kirkpatrick delivered a devastating criticism of several resolutions dealing with Central America that were unbalanced. Another success in the fall of 1982, was the turning back by an absolute majority of U.N. members of a resolution declaring that Puerto Rico is a "colony" of the U.S.

The decision by the Reagan Administration on December 10, 1982, not to sign the United Nations-sponsored Law of the Sea Treaty signaled that the U.S. would not be intimidated by the U.N. majority into signing agreements and treaties that do not serve U.S. interests. Following Washington's lead, in repudiation of those who warned that the U.S. would be isolated, 46 other nations, representing more than half of the world's GNP, are balking at signing the treaty.

P.L. 98-164, enacted with Administration support on November 22, 1983, further demonstrates U.S. concern about what is happening at the U.N. Section 114, of this law requires the U.S. to withhold the proportion of U.S. contributions to U.N. funds that aid the Palestine Liberation Organization and the South West-Africa People's Organization; Section 115 commits the U.S. to leaving the U.N. should Israel be denied participation or membership in the U.N.; Section 116 requires the President to report to Congress assessing whether the U.N. benefits the U.S., with special emphasis on U.N Charter violations and departures from the original spirit of the U.N.; Section 117 requires the State Department to review the voting patterns at the U.N. to determine how often each member nation supports the U.S. This dramatically demonstrates that Washington now pays attention to how nations vote at the U.N.

Also important is passage of the 1984 law introduced by Senator Nancy Kassebaum to roll back U.S. financial contributions to the regular budget of the U.N. and that of several U.N. agencies by 4 percent. The measure not only will trim U.S. outlays to the U.N., but puts the spendthrift U.N. on notice that the Congress at last is closely watching what goes on at the U.N. and is concerned about the way the U.N. spends its money. This constitutes a precedent for further action in response to U.N. fiscal irresponsibility.

At the same time as these U.S. actions, the dismal isolation of the U.S. in the U.N. system continued. In 1983, for example, the U.S. was in the minority on 81 percent of final votes in the General Assembly. It has not been unusual for the U.S. to be joined in the voting by only a half-dozen states. Even in matters of critical interest to America, the U.S. has been unable to get majority support. Resolution 38/7 of November 3, 1983, for example, condemning the U.S. intervention in

Grenada, was opposed only by Antigua and Barbuda, Barbados, Dominica, El Salvador, Israel, Jamaica, Saint Lucia, and Saint Vincent alongside the U.S.

U.N. funding of such terrorist organizations as the Palestine Liberation Organization and the South West Africa People's Organizations has continued despite efforts to curtail it.

Espionage activities by Soviet-bloc employees at the U.N. and at the bloc missions also continued. At least 350 Soviet-bloc employees connected with the U.N. are involved in outright espionage. All 1,100 are expected to spy upon their U.N. colleagues to some extent.

The Law of the Sea and UNESCO decisions have shown that the U.S. will receive substantial support from its allies if it acts firmly, decisively and provides leadership. Not only are 46 other nations joining the U.S. in not signing the Law of the Sea Treaty, but some of the most important industrial states will probably sign a U.S. alternative treaty.

Similarly, after the U.S. gave its notice of withdrawal from UNESCO, 24 Western countries joined in drawing up a document outlining the urgent need for reform. Had the State Department been more forthright and explicit about the reasons for the U.S. scheduled withdrawal from UNESCO, the U.S. might be enjoying even greater allied support for the move.

When the State Department even actively lobbies against such initiatives as the September 1983 Kassebaum amendment, the result is both failure and a certain amount of confusion as to what U.S. policy should be toward the U.N.

Ambassador Kirkpatrick and her staff have played a strong role in bringing to the attention of the American public the extent to which the U.N. has strayed from its original Charter and intentions. The U.S. delegation also has articulated successfully the American position in the U.N. This reversed the policies of previous Administrations that sought only to "lose gracefully at the U.N." The U.S. condemnation of the Soviet downing of KAL Flight 007 on September 1, 1983 at the Security Council was a dramatic and successful use of that forum. The subsequent failure of the Security Council to pass even a mildly worded resolution condemning that crime, however, provided a vivid indication of the flawed nature of that organization.

THE NEXT FOUR YEARS

The Administration should work for an end to the politicization of U.N. agencies, the double standard on human rights, the support for terrorist movements committed to the overthrow of member states (in violation of the U.N. Charter), and the excessive salaries and pension benefits for U.N. career bureaucrats.

It also should end or sharply curtail the espionage activities of Soviet-bloc employees employed by the U.N. Secretariat and by bloc missions in New York. These activities violate the U.N. Charter and threaten U.S. national security.

Finally it should press for more efficient and economical U.N. operations as well as a 35 percent real reduction in the U.N. budget, and work to end the U.N.'s opposition to the free enterprise system as a model for the development of Third World nations.

INITIATIVES FOR 1985

1) Enforce P.L. 47-357 to deny unlimited travel privileges in the U.S. to those U.N. employees who are nationals of states on the Department's restricted list. Those privileges significantly facilitate espionage and subversive activities.

2) Enforce P.L. 47-357 to bar the U.N. Secretariat from hiring staffers whom the U.S. believes serve in their nations' intelligence agencies.

3) Seek added funds for the FBI for counterintelligence of U.N.-based espionage and for monitoring the activities of U.N. staffers.

4) Ask Congress to tie future U.S. assessed and voluntary contributions to the U.N. to GAO-approved or GAO-conducted audits.

These audits should be as rigorous as those imposed on U.S. departments and agencies and U.S. domestic grant recipients. Programs found by the audit to benefit movements or that are harmful to U.S. security and foreign policy objectives should be denied U.S. support.

5) End U.S. participation in U.N. technical agencies which have become overly politicized and thus do not adequately address technical issues.

In 1985, the U.S. should withdraw from U.N. Conference on Trade and Development (U.S. contribution for 1984-1985 targeted at $14.1 million) and the Center for Transnational Corporations (U.S. contribution for 1984-1985 targeted at $2.5 million). It should also review its participation in the Food and Agriculture Organization, the International Labor Organization, and the U.N. Relief and Works Agency for Palestine Refugees in the Near East (U.S. contribution for 1984-1985 targeted at $140.5 million). These agencies have a long record of sacrificing technical programs while devoting increasing resources to political matters.

6) Continue to monitor and publicize the voting behavior of all U.N. member states, and especially recipients of U.S. foreign assistance.

7) Continue to require periodic and rigorous cost-benefit analyses of U.S. participation in the U.N.

8) Continue the Kassebaum initiative to reduce total U.S. contributions to the U.N. budget.

9) Ask the State Department to determine the cost of support services to the U.N., which has been estimated at about a billion dollars.

10) Propose that the General Assembly sessions should rotate annually from country to country, including the Soviet Union.

THE AGENCY FOR INTERNATIONAL DEVELOPMENT

by
Doug Bandow*

Upon entering office, the Reagan Administration set four major objectives for AID: technology development and transfer; institutional development; economic policy reform; and private sector participation.

Technology Development and Transfer. According to AID, American development assistance was to help other nations "to develop and apply a continuing stream of innovations designed to increase productivity, employment and incomes, and to evaluate and adapt technologies transferred from industrialized countries."

Institutional Development. AID planned to promote the private and public institutions that underlie economic progress. These organizations were intended to have broad local participation and eventually to become self-sustaining.

Economic Policy Reform. Because the value of any foreign assistance depends fundamentally on the soundness of economic policies of the recipient country, the Administration promised to promote a market-oriented approach abroad.

Private Sector Participation. Based on the development experience of the last two decades, along with America's economic heritage, Reagan policymakers pledged to strengthen the private sector in Third World nations by encouraging the sort of policy reform "that will foster a free and open climate in trade, private financial flows and LDCs domestic market."

All four goals are worthy, but the Administration's success in meeting them has varied widely.

AID's greatest achievement probably has been its support for the development of new technologies, involving, for example, oral rehydration therapy for babies who suffer from dehydration and a malaria vaccine. Reagan appointees also made some progress in redirecting Agency efforts to longer lasting institutional programs. They have revised internal bureaucratic incentives to reward career employees, particularly new directors of programs for particular countries, for implementing as well as developing programs. In the past, officials had little to gain from carrying out someone else's project. Now they have a greater responsibility in seeing ideas through to completion.

The Administration proposed the Economic Policy Initiative for

---

* Task Force members included Roy Childs, John Bolton, and Morris Goldman.

Sub-Saharan Africa, which would establish a $500 million fund to aid countries that adopt market policies, and AID claims major credit for convincing Kenya, Senegal, Niger and other nations to adopt a number of worthwhile economic reforms, such as the elimination of price controls and subsidies. AID takes partial credit, along with organizations like the World Bank, for promoting market-oriented changes in Gambia, Ghana, and elsewhere.

Some of the reforms in these nations, however—the creation of advisory committees, freezes on civil service salaries, and so on—are relatively minor, especially given the severity of the nations' economic circumstances. Moreover, AID had backed one policy that is very unlikely to spur economic growth: tax increases. Example: AID cites Niger as one of America's successes, for it "has tightened procedures for tax exemptions, increased penalties for non-compliance, and has introduced new taxes or increased tax rates on imports, profits, and property income." Yet higher taxes reduce individual incentives and stifle economic growth.

Finally, the Administration has sought to promote private enterprise in Third World nations, especially through its Private Enterprise Bureau. The Bureau has had at least one notable success—convincing the Bangladesh government to rely on existing venders and entrepreneurs to distribute contraceptives, instead of creating a separate government delivery apparatus. Ironically, this success is in an area—population control—where a growing body of opinion is concluding that a reassesment would be useful and that large or growing populations are not necessarily a significant cause of underdevelopment. Overall, however, there have been too few systematic efforts to break down the many obstacles inhibiting indigenous private enterprises in developing nations; in fact, much of AID's attention has been focused on subsidizing U.S. businesses.

The problems faced by the Administration do not result from any deficiencies in its objectives. As British developmental expert P.T. Bauer and others have argued, no foreign aid program, no matter how well-administered and favorable the circumstances, is likely to achieve significant positive results. Further, if the recipient nation carries out economic policies that inevitably dampen economic growth, foreign aid will reinforce the negative impact of misguided policies. Thus, the truly effective U.S. policies are those that prompt Third World economic reform and encourage private enterprise. Underwriting technological research tailored to meet the needs of poor nations is superior to general economic aid, which simply subsidizes local government activities. Finally, to the extent that the U.S. sets up programs in other countries, it should establish activities that eventually will become self-sufficient. It is not in the U.S. or the recipient nation's interest to foster permanent dependency or to create temporary institutions that collapse once American money is withdrawn.

Another reason for the Reagan Administration's limited success is that some senior AID officials, appointed by Reagan, have lacked sufficient philosophical commitment to the Reagan agenda. Political officials have also been unwilling to cut off funding for some ineffective private voluntary organizations (PVOs), which continue to receive millions in federal funds every year. While there are some PVOs that have attempted to foster real economic progress in developing countries and to work effectively with the private sector, others have not promoted such cooperation and remain opposed to the Administration's attempts to revamp AID's programs.

Conflict with other departments, particularly State and Agriculture, has limited the Administration's chances in reforming AID. The State Department generally opposes any reduction in the aid level to any nation for two reasons—either bilateral relations are improving or they are worsening. Such resistance to adjustment in U.S. assistance levels makes it particularly difficult to encourage economic reforms abroad.

The Agriculture Department, in contrast, responds to a powerful U.S. political constituency—farmers. It tends to oppose any reform of food aid programs, such as the "Food for Peace" program (Public Law 480), that will reduce the amount of food going overseas. Unfortunately the current program is undercutting Third World agricultural development by reinforcing policies that do not adequately compensate local farmers, thereby reducing their incentive to produce. Current Administration initiatives to improve the "Food for Peace" program by encouraging developing country governments to make politically sensitive policy changes that would increase overall food production deserve further support.

Finally, the Administration's goals are, in an important sense, too subtle to be easily understood within the political community. Many observers, including Congresssmen serving on appropriations committees, tend to judge the success and failiure of AID efforts by the amount of dollars flowing overseas. Thus, the Agency is continually pushed to send more money abroad.

The Administration has been unable to counteract this bias, in part because AID officials have pushed for their appropriations just as hard as all other bureaucracies. But more important, even had the Administration's goals been fully implemented, thereby improving the use of existing aid, it would have had little, if any, measurable effect. American foreign aid is unlikely to have a major impact, if for no other reason than it consititutes a very small percentage of the total resources available to developing nations. In the long run, overall U.S. economic policies, especially keeping an open market for imports from developing nations, will do more for economic growth than will government programs.

THE NEXT FOUR YEARS

Review the Fundamental Basis of Economic and Development Assistance

The Administration, led by the White House, needs to reconsider the very assumption that the U.S. should provide this form of aid. Money should not be proposed, appropriated, and spent if previous outlays have achieved little or nothing, or have even been counterproductive.

Consider Abolishing AID as a Separate Agency

Merging AID into a Mutual Development and Security Administration, as proposed by the Commission on Security and Economic Assistance (the so-called Carlucci Commission), for instance, would better integrate America's economic, military, and political goals.

Even the best designed and administered economic aid program can do little to promote long-term development, given the transcendent importance of local factors. Most U.S. assistance, such as Economic Support Funds, actually furthers other foreign policy goals, particularly that of supporting allied governments. A new organization would make explicit many of the policy conflicts and trade-offs that now are masked by AID's humanitarian and development rubric.

Educate the Public, Foreign Aid Community, and Congress About the Limitations of Development Assistance

Appropriations are now based more on the wishful thinking of well-meaning activists than the observed results of real-world experience.

INITIATIVES FOR 1985

1) Press Congress to amend the law authorizing AID.

If AID is to continue as a separate agency, its statutory authority, objectives, and focus should be changed to reflect the fact that much of its work is really security-related.

2) Loosen the congressional restrictions on AID appropriations.

Congress now establishes the specific accounts, such as health and education, as well as listing the countries in which funds must be spent. This reduces the flexibility of the Agency to adjust assistance levels, promotes the inefficient allocation of resources and weakens its ability to promote policy reforms and private enterprise.

3) Offer legislation to explicitly tie AID assistance to countries' votes in the U.N. and their overall support for the U.S.

Since most economic aid has political or security purposes, levels of assistance should be set with those goals in mind.

4) Establish a better mechanism for screening the large number of Private Voluntary Organizations (PVOs) undertaking development projects.

Many PVOs are not truly private, receiving the bulk of their funds from AID; they should seek increased support from the private sector rather than the taxpayer. In particular, the Administration should urge Congress to remove the requirement that a fixed percentage of the developmental assistance funds be allocated through grants to PVOs. The Administration could still, where appropriate, channel even more funding of development projects through PVOs rather than governmental bureacracies.

5) Assure that AID and the Peace Corps coordinate their respective priorities on an agency-wide basis.

As both agencies have the same goals, their programs should be targeted accordingly.

6) Encourage open flows of capital.

A free international market is the best and most cost-effective form of foreign assistance. It is also better for both American taxpayers and consumers. The U.S. should also encourage governments to permit the free flow of capital into and out of developing nations. Foreign equity participation is particularly important for providing needed capital to those nations with debt problems. The U.S. should also simultaneously lower barriers to goods produced by developing nations and aid levels.

7) Ask Congress to deemphasize loans and loan guarantees and rely more heavily on outright grants, at reduced levels.

A recent General Accounting Office report, for example, found a number of countries to be "consistently in arrears on their loan repayments" for AID's housing guarantee program. Overall, the U.S. has some $24 billion in loans owed to it for economic aid alone, and another $15 billion for military assistance. Since many of these loans will turn out to be gifts, the U.S. would be better off relying on grants in the first place. Doing so would promote honesty in accounting and give the U.S. greater leverage over the recipient nation.

THE MULTILATERAL DEVELOPMENT AGENCIES*

Since 1970, the percentage of America's development assistance going through multilateral instead of bilateral channels has more than doubled. As part of its original budget-cutting package, the Reagan Administration reduced America's total planned expenditures on multilateral development organizations by roughly $100 million annually.

This year, however, the U.S. will contribute slightly more than Carter last proposed—in excess of $1.5 billion—to the major international lending institutions of which it is a member: the World Bank Group (which includes the International Development Association), the Inter-American Development Bank, the Asian Development Bank, the African Development Fund, and the International Fund for Agricultural Development.

Unfortunately, these multilateral organizations do not adequately protect America's economic and political interests. Nor do they significantly advance international development, at least not to a degree commensurate with their cost.

In particular, the World Bank and the other global lending agencies do too little to promote free market policy reforms in Third World countries and rely too heavily on state energy and industrial projects when making loans. And though the U.S. carries roughly one-fourth of the financial burden of the World Bank, for example, it has little influence in the lending process. Between 1981 and 1984 the U.S. opposed, for economic reasons, some 46 loans proposed by the World Bank and the other lending institutions; only one was not approved.

Morever, international aid provides the U.S. with few political or security benefits. At least the bilateral assistance programs administered by the Agency for International Development can be used to serve non-economic ends.

THE NEXT FOUR YEARS

Work to reduce steadily America's financial role in the multilateral banks.

Despite past Administration opposition to large funding increases, total lending will continue to rise and will hit $26.5 billion in 1986.

---

* U.S. participation in these agencies is not under AID jurisdiction, but since their objectives are similar to those of AID, they are reviewed here.

Undertake a comprehensive review of the international development agencies and America's participation in them.

There is no reason to believe *a priori* that the citizens of this nation are better off because America belongs to the multilateral organizations and contributes billions every year to them.

INITIATIVES FOR 1985

1) Continue to resist pressures to further expand or replenish the capital of the various multilateral institutions.

In 1984, for example, the Administration successfully reduced America's share of the the seventh replenishment of the International Development Association, which makes concessional loans to developing nations, from $3.24 billion to $2.25 billion.

2) Oppose all proposals to hike the so-called gearing ratio, that is, the amount of money that can be loaned based on the capital possessed by the institution.

The ratio is now one-to-one, but some countries have proposed increasing that ten-fold or more.

3) Press the organizations to rely more heavily on market-rate lending instead of concessional assistance.

If projects are economically viable, developing countries can afford to borrow at market rates. If the projects are not cost-effective, they should not be funded.

4) Continue to oppose multilateral loans to state enterprises and push for a stronger market orientation to institutional lending policies.

The fundamental problem facing the developing world is not inadequate financial resources, but perverse economic policies. As the World Bank itself concluded in its 1984 Development Report, "domestic policy improvements are essential in enhancing the prospects of low-income countries."

Unfortunately, the international lending organizations, if anything, have done more to subsidize the failures of Third World governments than to eliminate them. There is little material evidence that the billions in loans from the multilateral banks have materially aided development around the globe; the Administration should scrutinize strictly U.S. participation in these institutions, and reduce its financial commitment accordingly.

15

The Intelligence Community

by

Roger A. Brooks and Angelo M. Codevilla*

President Reagan inherited in 1981 an intelligence community that had suffered drastic functional changes during the preceding decade and a purge of its senior professionals during the previous four years. As a result, the intelligence community's ability to perform its major functions had deteriorated.

Human intelligence collection had been cut back by leaders who assumed that technical intelligence means could fulfill the needs of the United States. Morever, use of non-governmental identification for agents ("unofficial cover") was almost eliminated. Technical intelligence collectors were not improved to meet new requirements, and they were designed to focus disproportionately on monitoring the minutiae of arms control treaties.

All of this resulted in the U.S. ignoring important Soviet actions, such as anti-ballistic missile preparations. In addition U.S. capability to react to foreign intelligence operations (counterintelligence) had been nearly eliminated. Covert action, when used at all, was reduced to quiet failures and inconsequential successes. Results of intelligence analysis often were presented in consensus documents that reflected the lowest common denominator of opinion in the intelligence community, and often obscured both real issues and real gaps in collection. This deficiency stemmed in part from political decisions within the Carter Administration to withhold and suppress key intelligence data.

While the Reagan Administration has sought to improve intelligence capabilities, the results have been mixed. Morale within the intelligence community, and respect for and confidence in the capabilities of the intelligence agencies at home and abroad are vastly improved. Yet American intelligence continues to fall short of the extensive improvements envisioned by the Reagan Administration in 1981. At least part of the reason for this is that the Administration made only a handful of political appointments to the CIA, not nearly enough to re-invigorate or re-orient the agency. Problems persist.

---

* Task Force members included Ray Cline, Samuel T. Francis, and David S. Sullivan.

Human intelligence, for example, still has an inadequate number of individuals who can pass as non-Americans, or as Americans unconnected with the U.S. government. More carefully planned human intelligence collection, for example, might have provided military and diplomatic leaders a better picture of the terrorist threat in Beirut prior to the 1983 and 1984 bombings of the U.S. Embassy and Marine Corps barracks in that city. More extensive human intelligence collection in Grenada in 1983 might have provided a better estimate of the threat to the government of Maurice Bishop and the size and capabilities of the Cuban force on the island.

Technical collection, on which so much has been spent, continues to be ill-focused. In October 1983, for example, only a few days before the U.S. rescue mission in Grenada, the National Security Council discovered that aerial photographic coverage of the island was significantly out of date, and had to request new coverage immediately.

There also continue to be considerable shortcomings in the detection of new weapons systems and ways that the Soviets are basing those systems, particularly those that appear to be in violation of U.S.-Soviet arms control agreements. Recent government reports of violations that have taken place over a decade (for example, a missile defense battle management radar under construction for some years near Abalakova in Central Siberia, outlawed by the U.S.-Soviet Anti-Ballistic Missile Treaty, was not discovered until July 1983,) raise questions about the usefulness of continued attempts at verification. This is especially so since the use of scarce intelligence resources for that purpose precludes other, more urgent ones.

The Reagan Administration also vowed in 1981 to improve U.S. capabilities to respond to foreign intelligence operations in the U.S. But the intelligence bureacracy has only just begun to bend to direct presidential orders and congressional mandates to take counterintelligence seriously. One success was the cooperation between the Foreign Counterintelligence section of the FBI and non-U.S. intelligence organizations. This led to the arrest in January 1984 of a Norwegian diplomat on charges of spying for the Soviets, particularly during his almost eight years at the United Nations in New York City. The FBI, however, does not have the capability to protect U.S. citizens, government officials and businesses from the great number of political espionage agents and terrorists who have footholds in the U.S. FBI counter-espionage operations must be strengthened, particularly in Washington and New York City, where large numbers of Soviet citizens work.

The quality of analysis has improved marginally primarily because the volume of recent failures has sobered many analysts. The U.S. could not or would not contribute to untangling the plot on the life of

Pope John Paul II because the CIA lacks both the sources and the will. When Marshal Ogarkov was relieved of his post at the head of the Soviet armed forces—an epochal event in the USSR—American intelligence did not forewarn and could not explain. The production of three new Soviet missiles of the fifth generation surprised U.S. intelligence, which had expected only one. The Soviets built six huge Pechora-class radars before U.S. intelligence figured out they are for anti-ballistic missile battle management.

The Reagan Administration has reemphasized the importance of covert action, the secret, sometimes paramilitary exercise of influence on foreign situations in a manner that is unattributable to, or plausibly deniable by, the U.S. government. There are still considerable problems, however, in the way that the Administration has managed covert action. In particular, covert action has not been integrated with overall policy. Further, some intelligence officials have lobbied against significant prospects both in the interagency process and with the Congress.

Covert action must not be used indiscriminately and should be integrated with overall foreign policy. The Reagan Administration should support covert action as a foreign policy instrument when important U.S. interest are involved and where U.S. direct military involvement is either very difficult or impossible. The Administration should explain to the public and to Congress why covert action may prevent the need for direct U.S. military involvement in certain situations and how it can provide an effective counter to Soviet and Cuban actions.

Since the final product of most intelligence activity is analysis based on a mosaic of collected data, such assessments must be of high quality. To achieve this, the Reagan Administration insisted that intelligence estimates be intellectually honest and accurate, and demanded that conclusions drawn from the analysis be demonstrated by hard evidence. This is in contrast to the often inaccurate and unsubstantiated analysis of the Carter Administration.

There have been positive results. The intelligence community, for example, produced in 1982 an excellent summary of the challenges and dangers posed by Soviet attempts to steal sensitive material and advanced technology products from corporations in the U.S. and their licensees overseas.

There remain several significant problems, however, particularly with the intelligence community's inability to analyze properly and assess a wide range of often conflicting data from many different sources. Pressure within the intelligence community, particularly within the CIA, to achieve a consensus view among the various components of their community, including the Defense Intelligence

Agency (DIA), the military services and the Department of State,substitutes bureaucratic power plays for the honest competition of ideas and thus often produces lower quality intelligence products. There also is not enough input from analysts who specialize in counterintelligence. The principle of competitive analysis by separate teams having equal access to information has not been implemented. Competitive analysis could raise the quality of intelligence products and help to identify whether data that the U.S. receives are genuine or part of the Soviet effort at political and military deception.

THE NEXT FOUR YEARS

In the next four years, the United States must place greater emphasis on the kind of intelligence that would enable foreign policy planners to predict the political and strategic intentions of actual and potential adversaries of the United States. The U.S. must also place greater emphasis on intelligence that provides better knowledge and foresight of potential terrorist activities directed against the United States. Finally, the Administration should develop intelligence that provides U.S. military planners with a better picture of the threat faced by U.S. forces in areas of potential confrontation with either the Soviets or their surrogates in the Third World.

Long-range objectives should focus on five major areas:

Human Intelligence ("HUMINT") Collection

The Administration should seek to hire and train as human intelligence collectors those who can pose as non-Americans or as Americans unconnected with the U.S. government. It should move toward this type of "unofficial cover" and away from placing individuals in positions of "official cover."

The Administration also should improve operational security for human intelligence collectors working for U.S. agencies and thus make their positions more attractive and less vulnerable. This can be done by reducing the number of personnel who have prior and current knowledge of clandestine collection operations; eliminating unjustified access to CIA operational files through Freedom of Information Act law-suits; and improving the expertise and experience of personnel engaged in clandestine collection overseas.

Technical Collection

It is necessary to improve the physical protection and to ensure the modernization of existing technical collection systems. Their numbers should be increased as well. These systems should provide rapid coverage of wide areas to find targets in quickly changing situations, as well as occasional very high resolution spotting and unexpected collection. Technical collection should be augmented with counterintelligence procedures to deal with advances in Soviet deception techniques.

Counterintelligence (CI)

It is essential to establish strong CI representation in each of the intelligence agencies, particularly the CIA and the National Security Agency. Information from CI sources needs to be weighed against all other intelligence data which the U.S. collects and receives to allow U.S. decision-makers to assess better how an enemy may use knowledge of U.S. collection systems to influence what the U.S. receives.

Covert Action

Covert action should be used, when necessary, as an instrument of U.S. foreign policy, addressed to clearly established objectives of that policy. It is important to present covert action to the public and Congress as an integral part of an explicit, comprehensive policy—one that is designed to succeed. Covert action must be shown as a means of achieving U.S. objectives without direct military intervention.

Analysis and Intelligence Estimates

The Administration should institute competitive analysis that allows the major intelligence agencies and the armed forces to present their own analysis to the President and his top advisors, and reduce the tendency to construct only a consensus analysis. It also ought to subject intelligence analysis to the same "counterintelligence-scrutiny" that should be used to detect potential Soviet deception in U.S. technical collection.

INITIATIVES FOR 1985

1) Educate the public.

The President has both the singular responsibility and the capacity to focus the attention of the American people on the fundamental importance to U.S. national security of a strong intelligence capability, the broad legal guidelines within which it should operate, and the necessary limits on public oversight of these operations. The President ought to make this "constituency-building" for U.S. intelligence an early and urgent priority.

2) Improve Intelligence Community leadership.

The Administration should appoint capable, professional and highly-motivated individuals to top leadership positions in the intelligence community, particularly the CIA. Most important, there is a need to appoint more individuals who share the foreign policy and national security goals of the Administration and who share a common perception of the nature of the Soviet challenge.

3) Grant the DIA Director hiring direction.

The Administration should support enactment of a law designed to give the Director of the Defense Intelligence Agency the same flexibility regarding personnel management in DIA that the other intelligence agencies have. A bill to this effect has already passed the Senate.

4) Tighten the focus of technical intelligence.

Technical collection must move away from the large, *sui generis* systems devoted to arms control that consume so much of its budget. Collection of signals must be much better focused. Imagery must increase low-resolution broad area search, occasional very high resolution spotting, and unexpected collection. New technical systems must pass the test of relevance to political-military operations.

5) Improve human collection techniques.

The proportion of case officers able to pass as private U.S. citizens—or, better, as non-Americans—should increase radically. By their cover such case officers must also have access to social strata not normally reached by official representatives of the U.S. government, i.e. scientific personnel, religious circles, small business, or unobtrusive service workers.

6) Allow the PFIAB presidential access.

The President's Foreign Intelligence Advisory Board (PFIAB), a group of wise, independent and disinterested citizens, is carrying on the honorable tradition established by its predecessors over a generation. It has given the President excellent advice on intelligence. The bureaucracy has successfully stifled PFIAB's initiatives. The President should listen to his Advisory Board.

7) Establish Competitive Analysis.

To overcome pressure within the intelligence community, particularly within the CIA, to achieve a consensus view among the various components of their community, including the Defense Intelligence Agency (DIA), the military services and the Department of State, new leaders must institute competitive analysis. They also must offer policymakers a wider variety of perspectives in the integration of data from counterintelligence to help solve the question of whether data the U.S. receives is intended to deceive the U.S.

Part 3

Institutional Reforms

16

The Congressional Budget Process

by
John M. Palffy*

Not even Ronald Reagan has been able to harness the forces pushing up federal spending. Since 1981 federal expenditures have outpaced inflation by 3.9 percent age points and the Congressional Budget Office estimates that spending will balloon from $856 billion in FY 1984 to more than $1.3 trillion by FY 1989.

Despite the pressures of balanced budget campaigns, public opinion polls and despite the fiscally austere rhetoric from Congress and the White House, spending multiplies because of underlying political and institutional incentives, which prevent Congress from controlling the budget. These incentives must be changed. The new Administration, therefore, must give top priority to working with Congress to provide incentives for fiscal responsibility in the budget process.

THE PROBLEM

Why Budgets Grow

In democracies, a political bias favors government spending. Spending is a kind of political currency that buys votes.

Public opinion polls reveal that voters want lower aggregate spending—but they generally want other people's benefits cut, not their own. As do all "economic men," every Congressman makes rational decisions based on costs and benefits. In the political calculus, the costs and benefits of federal spending are manifested in votes lost and gained. The costs of federal spending to Congressmen are often understated because taxpayers seldom are organized as are special interest groups. The result: legislators are under great pressure to bring home the pork, while district support for specific budget cuts tends to be weak.

The Grace Commission neatly characterized the spending paradox in a hypothetical interview:

---

* Task Force members included Robert Tollison, David Hoppe, Bill Hoagland, Marvin Phaup, and Bill Orzechowski.

Interviewer: What do you think of Congress?
Joe Mainstreet: They are a bunch of big spenders.
Interviewer: What do you think of your own Congressman?
Joe: Oh, him, he's a pretty good guy.
Interviewer: Why?
Joe: When the Air Force wanted to close the base outside of town, he wouldn't let them. Same with the Amtrak train. They wanted to shut down the line, said it cost too much. But he pulled some strings to keep it here, because this town would be nothing without it. And he got the Feds to build us a new lake where we can take the kids and swim for free now. He gets things done for the district.
Interviewer: What do you think of the tax rate?
Joe: Way too high! We won't be able to send our kids to college if they go any higher.
Interviewer: What do you think about government spending?
Joe: Out of control! Those big spenders in Congress are going to bankrupt me.

There is a structural political interest, in other words, for Congressmen to satisfy parochial or special interest votes at the expense of the nation and the taxpayers. A Congressman cannot win many votes by cutting spending at home: benefit losers (his constituents) will not vote for him, while the "winners" (voters in other states) cannot. And if he tries to cut spending in other states his colleagues are quick to join a logrolling coalition to preserve their own programs. This logrolling was demonstrated last August in a move to extend the present pricing policy of Hoover Dam electrical power. Western Senators, obviously reluctant to slice away their own pork, voted in a unified bloc to continue the subsidy. Several Eastern Senators, no doubt looking forward to a favor in return, voted with their Western colleagues to continue the subsidy, ensuring its passage.

There are few institutional checks and balances to encourage congressional spending constraint. The congressional budget process, a product of the Congressional Budget and Impoundment Control Act of 1974 (The 1974 Budget Act), was designed explicitly to ensure spending neutrality. In practice, the Act fails to control spending because it allows significant spending to remain outside its purview and its mechanisms allow Congress easily to evade its intent.

There are several specific ways in which the Act has tended to boost spending, and a number of other ways in which legislators have been able to avoid constraints.

1. When buying votes on the unified budget became expensive, Congress found methods to hide spending: the off budget and credit budget. In 1974 Congress began with $1.4 billion in off-budget spending. Since then Congress' petty cash drawer has grown to $14

billion. The amount of outstanding direct and guaranteed loans has more than doubled in the last ten years to over $364 billion.

2. Congress has abdicated regular control over three quarters of total spending—the "uncontrollable" expenditures mandated by existing law and cost of living adjustment (COLA) increases, rather than budgetary decisions. Thus, even if Congress whittles down discretionary spending, aggregate spending continues unabated.

3. At the same time that Congress abdicated its own responsibility to control spending, it tied the hands of the President. The 1974 Budget Act severely limited the President's power to impound funds—that is, to refuse to spend money voted by Congress. The limited powers of rescission and deferral he does retain generally are ignored by Congress. Deferrals are presidential requests to delay temporarily the budget authority. A deferral may be overturned if either House votes against it. Rescissions are presidential requests to cancel budget authority. Both houses must approve of the rescission within 45 days.

4. Not only does Congress ignore the President's budget at will, but it also busts its own—by failing to make policy changes to meet its budget resolution and by passing supplemental bills.

The congressional budget process and the accounting procedures have failed to restrain spending. This does not necessarily mean that the congressional budget process is fundamentally unsound; yet, it argues that the process is incomplete. Given the political and institutional incentives Congress is under to maintain and increase federal spending—and the failure of the current system to achieve a dispassionate assessment of competing claims on federal coffers—major reforms and strengthening of the budget process and structure are needed if the broad fiscal objectives of the new Administration are to be achieved.

How the Budget Process Works

Prior to the 1974 Budget Act, total federal spending was determined by adding up the individual appropriation bills passed by congressional subcommittees. There was no mechanism for considering a target for total spending as such, or for making tradeoffs between competing priorities. In addition, the executive branch controlled the principal sources of budget information and analysis. It also reserved the threat of budget impoundment—of not spending money appropriated by Congress. Consequently, the President's budget was the benchmark for all budgetary decisions, and budgetary power rested primarily in the White House.

In response to this, and in particular to President Richard Nixon's attempts to use impoundment as a means of controlling spending, Congress enacted the Congressional Budget and Impoundment Control Act of 1974. This measure created the budget resolution, the budget committees, and the Congressional Budget Office (CBO). The new budget committees and the CBO provide Congress with a wealth of information on which to base analysis and budget decisions. The Budget Act also created "reconciliation," the process used by Congress to force its committees to comply with the fiscal policy of the budget resolution. The Act significantly restricted the President's budget-making and impoundment powers.

The concurrent budget resolutions emanating from the new budget committees were intended to set targets for aggregate levels of spending and revenues. Under this procedure, the second concurrent budget resolution, due September 15, is meant to be a binding limit on total spending. The Budget Act also established a schedule for budgetary activities and mechanisms to enforce that schedule.

In many ways, the Congressional Budget Act improved federal budgeting. But the immense growth of the budget since 1974 has demonstrated flaws in the Act that may not have been anticipated by its framers. These flaws are now obvious: the process is too time consuming, its control limited, and its bias favors those who wish to maintain or increase federal spending.

The Administration should work with congressional leaders to correct these deficiencies. Agreement should take the form of a new, bipartisan "Truth-in-Spending" Act.

REFORMING THE BUDGET PROCESS

Improving Budget Structure and Accounting Information

When information on the costs of programs is not available, or when the methods that are available underestimate that cost, Congress is inclined to overspend. If voters and legislators are to have the information to assess the costs of federal spending in order to relay efficiently their votes to their representatives it is imperative that the accounting methods of the budget be reformed to provide accurate information.

There are several reasons why spending tends to be underestimated:

1. The federal budget hides billions of dollars in spending each year in the form of off-budget expenditures, offsetting receipts, loans, and

unfunded liabilities. The accounting procedures allow Congress to authorize spending programs without acknowledging their true cost. These loopholes are a major impediment to rational budgeting and to any effective spending limitation rule.

Offsetting receipts such as user fees, for instance, are deducted from budgetary authority and outlays. But this understates total federal spending and the government's use of the nation's resources. Beginning with the Export-Import Bank in 1971, Congress systematically has moved various federal agencies off the unified budget—the entire Social Security program is scheduled to be moved off-budget in 1993. Such off-budget outlays, now amounting to about $14 billion per year, do not appear in budget outlays or the deficit, and are not subject to the ceilings set by congressional budget resolutions. Similar to a company conducting business "off the books," Congress is able to hide large amounts of spending from normal public scrutiny.

The use of offsetting receipts and off-budget outlays should be ended. All outlays should be reported in gross terms, and all accounts reported within the unified budget.

2. Much of the $365 billion in outstanding federal direct and guaranteed loans appears only in the off-budget credit budget. Moreover, loan outlays are represented as the difference between loans tendered and debts collected. This distorts the true cost to the government by hiding the interest and bad debt subsidies. To expose the true cost, departments should continue to secure loans through the Federal Financing Bank (FFB), but the FFB should sell all direct and guaranteed loans to private investors. The loss incurred by the FFB by discounting these subsidized loans would be equal to the government subsidy and should be charged to the original loaning agency as an on-budget appropriation item. This openness would restrain such lending by providing Congress with an explicit account of the costs of the loans.

3. During the past two decades, Congress has been attracted to legislation improving pension and insurance programs to satisfy constituent desires while avoiding responsibility for the cost of the programs. The unfunded liabilities in civil service and military pensions, disability, and Social Security programs measure just how much promised future expenditures exceed receipts. But they do not appear in the budget. The U.S. government has already made spending commitments in excess of projected revenues of $3.05 trillion. If the present trend continues, by 1990 the accumulated unfunded liability will reach almost $7 trillion, and almost $28 trillion by the year 2000.

The present value of unfunded and insurance liabilities should be accounted as an accrued budget expenditure.

Managing the Budget Process

Entitlements are the largest and one of the fastest growing segments of the federal budget. The CBO estimates that entitlements grew from $66 billion in 1970 to $396 billion in 1984. They are projected to reach $551 billion—or 42 percent of the budget—by 1989. Social Security and Medicare make up the bulk of entitlements, most of which are not regularly reviewed in the budget process but benefit from automatic increases in the cost of living. Effective budgeting, regardless of a spending objective, requires that Congress regain control over entitlement spending.

Because entitlements enjoy permanent authorizations that require Congress to spend any amount necessary in order to meet legislated benefits, they do not come within the appropriation process. Unless Congress explicitly restricts the legal benefits, spending continues year in and year out, in spite of and regardless of the budget resolution.

Several reforms would bring entitlement spending within the purview of the budget process, and force Congress to consider their cost. Some experts, for instance, propose that all programs be subject to one year authorizations—that is, an annual sunset. If Congress failed to renew the entitlement legislation before it expired, the program would become discretionary. Alternatively, authorization could remain permanent if the trust fund status of the programs were ended. This would require annual appropriations. Unfortunately such a practice could clog an already crowded budget calendar. Worse still, Congress might simply give automatic increases every election year.

Entitlements should be subject to periodic control and review. Authorizations should be long enough to avoid burdening the process, generally two to five years, but short enough for Congress to take into account changing demographics and budget priorities.

A major reason why federal spending is out of control is that the indexing of entitlements cost of living adjustments (COLAS) will add $170 billion to federal spending between 1985 and 1989. Indexing benefits requires Congress to increase spending without taking any explicit action or responsibility for its cost. In essence, because all spending must be offset by taxes, this indexing imposes "hidden" tax increases. De-indexing entitlements would not prohibit Congress from making periodic adjustments in benefits, but would require that legislators vote for benefit and tax increases explicitly, not simply allow inflation to push up spending. Total de-indexing, however, would burden beneficiaries with uncertainty over their future benefits, and it would crowd the congressional calendar.

To resolve this, non-means tested entitlements should be indexed only partially. This might be accomplished by limiting automatic increases to two-thirds of the rise in the consumer price index, or to the index minus a certain percentage. This would assure relatively stable benefits, but it would restrain the built-in momentum for benefit increases.

Over the past 20 years Congress has passed more than 74 continuing resolutions because appropriations bills have not been completed on schedule. These last-minute funding bills are a sorry and inefficient way of making public policy, legislating spending based on irrational rules and heightening budgetary uncertainty at agencies and state and local governments.

The major reason for these delays is Congress' excessive work load. Not only has the federal budget—and thus the areas of congressional purview—grown immensely, but review also has intensified. At the end of World War II, for instance, 95 percent of federal spending was permanently authorized; today less than 80 percent is so authorized.

Repeated and unnecessary authorizations have three major ill effects on budgeting: They are time-consuming, thus diverting Congress from more substantive policy review; they encourage Congress to "micro-manage" agency budgets, since the shorter review cycle allows Congress greater control over item-by-item spending; and they result in continuing resolutions.

The Defense budget is one area where the defects of single-year authorizations and appropriations are most burdensome. Efficient planning and weapons procurement require multi-year horizons and commitments, but under the present authorization and appropriation cycle most defense plans beyond the current fiscal year must be somewhat tentative.

Congress must find a balance between repeated single-year authorizations that encourage micro-management and clog the congressional calendar, and permanent authorizations that allow unnecessary spending to continue uncriticized. Such a balance can be met with the implementation of a biennial budget cycle, as proposed in separate bills by Senators Dan Quayle (R-Indiana) and William Roth (R-Delaware).

Opponents of the two-year budget cycle contend that it would not save Congress any time because changing economic conditions would require repeated budget supplementals. Though supplemental bills may indeed be required in times of significant economic changes, this will not require the same time commitment from Congress as the usual budget cycle. Moreover, Congress would be forced to give agencies and departments greater leeway in making detailed budget allocations. By locking in aggregate spending figures for two years, the biennial budget would reduce in half the opportunities Congress has to raise spending levels. Most important, a two-year cycle would streamline the process; allowing for longer and more certain planning horizons by eliminating annual authorizations and reducing the likelihood for continuing resolutions.

Enforcing the Budget Act

No budget works without procedural discipline. The 1974 Budget Act provides the basis of an adequate framework, but little discipline or control. As a result, deadlines and constraints are ignored, bills and amendments are introduced late, and figures distorted and manipulated.

A number of steps could be taken to amend the process to avoid these problems.

1) As prescribed by the Budget Act, congressional budget resolutions now include three-year targets and the CBO provides five-year cost estimates of legislation. But the budget targets and cost estimates are not linked together in an effective system of control. As a result, Congress can enact legislation resulting in massive spending increases in the outyears without violating the budget resolution.

These future budget targets should be enforced through points of order (that is, challenging attempts by legislators to "stretch" the procedural rules). Congress, of course, could revise its future spending by passing a new budget resolution. This would be better than the current practice of simply violating the pending resolution.

2) Budget items are arranged in two ways. The President's budget and the budget resolutions are arranged by functional category. Congressional spending bills, on the other hand, are arranged according to appropriation subcommittee responsibilities. This procedure makes it difficult to track budget decisions from the resolution to the appropriations bills, thus allowing the appropriations committee considerable discretion. This confusing approach was adopted in 1974 under pressure from the appropriations committees, which did not want to be bound by the budget resolutions.

Congress should make up its mind which arrangement to use. It either should realign committees along budget function lines or allocate the budget resolution along committee lines.

3) Although the budget resolutions provide for aggregate as well as functional allocations, only the aggregates are enforced by congressional rules. And while points of order can be used only to halt consideration of bills that exceed stipulated aggregate levels, Congress easily evades this constraint. Low priority bills, for instance, tend to be presented early in the session, when they will not be subject to points of order, while popular or high priority bills are held back until

very late in the session, when media and constituent support for key spending measures allows Congress to withstand points of order.

Points of order, therefore, should be permissible against both 302(a) and 302(b) subcommittee allocations (302 allocations refer to Section 302 of the Budget Act, which requires Congress to allocate budget authority and outlays) if Congress continues to appropriate spending by committee, rather than just aggregates. A two-thirds majority waiver vote should be required if Congress wishes to override. If overridden, bills still should be subject to delayed enrollment (that is, not released to the President until all other bills are passed.)

4) Points of order against subcommittee allocations are intended to enforce the budgetary priorities of the whole Congress as determined by and expressed in the first concurrent budget resolution. Enforcement of points of order demonstrates Congress' will that the appropriations committee will allocate limited spending among their programs.

Such priorities might be better enforced if, instead of multiple appropriations bills, Congress voted on only one omnibus appropriations bill. This would require that the subcommittees report their bills to the floor before the beginning of the fiscal year. The omnibus nature of the bill would emphasize the Congress' role of designating spending priorities.

An omnibus bill of this kind would achieve several goals:

- It would require Congress to set spending priorities by forcing tradeoffs between programs when the budget resolution aggregates are violated.
- It would provide only one avenue on which to pass congressional pork barrel. The current method, passing 13 separate bills, gives congressional vote-seekers 13 bills through which to grease their special-interest pork barrel.
- By concentrating debate on spending on one appropriations bill, the congressional schedule would be less crowded.

5) Congress has become expert at underfunding appropriated entitlement programs to meet White House demands for cuts, in the knowledge that program requirements force additional spending later in the year. This budget maneuver allows the appropriations committee to boost spending in either of two ways. By consciously underestimating the cost of mandatory programs in the appropriation bill, it leaves more spending for discretionary items without running into the aggregate limits of the budget resolution. By the time Congress has to vote more money for the mandatory program in the next fiscal year, it is too late to reduce the discretionary allocations.

Another way in which the ploy is used is to avoid enacting cost-cutting legislation recommended by the President. For instance, suppose the President proposed a 2.5 percent cut in food stamp benefits based on a new eligibility requirement. Rather than break the President's budget or change the law, the appropriations committee can simply allocate his request. But if the authorizing committees refuse to change the eligibility requirements, appropriations will last only a portion of the year and a supplemental will be required.

Emergencies do arise, and so Congress must be allowed to supplement earlier funding. A two-thirds majority should be required for approval, however, so that supplementals would be less subject to abuse. Mandatory and discretionary spending should be distinguished clearly from each other in all spending bills. Moreover, budget committee cost estimates and all relevant economic and programmatic assumptions should be included in the final bill report, so that systematic underestimates of funding requirements can be detected and challenged.

6) Congress constantly evades the requirements of the Budget Act by allowing procedural waivers and ignoring deadlines. Since 1976, noted Senator Goldwater last year, the Senate has approved over 250 waivers of just one section of the Budget Act. Congress also regularly ignores deadlines for the first concurrent budget resolution and reconciliation.

Waivers should require a two-thirds majority so that deadlines become much harder to evade.

7) Appropriations committee members wield great power to pass "pork barrel" projects. State and local projects are often "lost" among lines and lines of individual appropriations in larger spending bills and then rushed to the floor before lobbyists and members have time to scrutinize the bill. One common committee tactic is to limit the amount of time between bill mark-up and a floor vote by purposefully delaying mark-up until just before a congressional recess.

A rule requiring that appropriation bills be marked-up and subject to public scrutiny for seven days before a floor vote would allow interested parties time to spot the pork.

8) The First Concurrent Budget Resolutions have become political documents encouraging delays in the congressional calendar. They are not binding, waivers are common, and restraining points of order rare. As a result, spending is largely determined by the effects of changes in demographics and of prices on entitlements, and by the discretionary actions of the appropriation committees.

Effective budgeting requires a "top-down" method of allocation. Aggregate figures and subcommittee allocations, which reflect general congressional spending priorities, should be made by the full Congress. This allocation should be binding on all committees and the bill subject to presidential approval. Concurrent resolutions should require a two-thirds majority. This procedure would limit the appropriations committees to making detailed allocations within predetermined limits.

Restoring the Balance of Power

When Congress passed the Budget Control and Impoundment Act of 1974 it significantly weakened presidential budget power. The democratic process, however, makes Congress susceptible to special and parochial interests. Consequently, in the tradition of American constitutional government, there should be external spending checks and balances—either by the executive branch, which tends to represent general rather than narrow parochial interests, or by an effective institutional rule.

1) The Budget Act severely restricts the President's ability to control federal spending. The President must now either approve or disapprove entire appropriations bills, and so Congress is able to pass special interest spending by incorporating it into major or last-minute funding bills. If the President refuses to sign such "Christmas tree" bills, he usually must shut down the government agencies covered by the legislation, as President Reagan has done. The President, of course, can petition Congress to cancel any spending plans, but unless both Houses of Congress approve the rescission by a two-thirds vote within 45 days, the President must spend the funds. Since the Budget Act went into force in 1975, 41 percent of such presidential rescission requests have been ignored by Congress. None of President Reagan's 1983 rescissions were approved.

A line-item veto would allow the President to rescind individual appropriations items without turning back the entire bill. The rescission then would stand unless Congress explicitly overrode the veto. A line-item veto would subject the federal budget to detailed presidential review, while maintaining Congress's right to initiate and determine spending. There would be less pressure for the President to agree to special interest programs. Senator Mack Mattingly (R-GA) introduced two bills in 1984 that would allow for a modified item veto.

A line-item veto should be enacted by Congress. To avoid political maneuvering and presidential fiat it is important that such a veto allow the President to reduce, as well as to veto, individual spending items, and for Congress to be granted the power to override such a veto by a simple majority.

2) Reconciliation could provide the most potent means of budgetary control under the terms of the 1974 Budget Act. When used effectively as part of the first concurrent resolution, such as during the

1981 budget process, it can enable the general members of Congress to override excessive spending decisions of the authorizing and appropriating committees. Reconciliation is powerful because it allows Congress to bundle numerous spending cuts (often affecting special interests) into one package. Such bundling reduces the power and incentives for individual members to vote down the bill merely to protect their own special interest. Reconciliation, in effect, leads to "reverse logrolling," when one member accepts a cut if another does likewise.

Unfortunately, the fear of offending powerful committee members, combined with a lack of will on the part of Congress to tackle necessary spending cuts, has trimmed the size and scope of spending reconciliation in recent years. Moreover, committees are often late or fail to deliver on their reconciliation instructions.

The reconciliation process should be strengthened and its use expanded. The President and members of the budget committees should take the lead in developing a wide reaching budget-cutting reconciliation bill early in the budget calendar, that affects entitlements and out-year programs. If the committees do not meet the requirements of reconciliation instructions, the budget committee should be vested with the power and duty to substitute their own provisions for consideration by the Congress.

Section 305(b)2 of the Budget Act should be changed, to make alternative proposals germane in achieving cuts required in reconciliation. Section 301(b)2, the "elastic clause" that gives the budget committees wide discretion to interpret the Budget Act, must be preserved to assure that the budget committees have the power and flexibility to control spending.

3) The balanced budget amendment has gained popularity in recent years as a means of reducing budget deficits. Unfortunately, the focus on deficits, and not on the real problem—government spending—gives encouragement to those in Congress who wish to raise taxes. But raising taxes does not reduce the burden of government spending on the economy, it merely takes the pressure off Congress to take serious action to cut spending. For this reason, a constitutional amendment that aims solely at balancing the budget would be of little value. Efforts should concentrate instead on tax and spending limitations.

Under the present accounting system, however, even a spending limitation amendment would be ineffective. Congress has already at its disposal a half-dozen ways to increase spending "off the record." In response to a spending limitation Congress could simply spend billions of dollars off-budget, increase its use of loans, or merely increase its regulatory powers. Consequently, a prerequisite to the enactment of any spending limitation must be a revision of these accounting measures.

Restructuring Congressional Committees

1) The distinction between the authorization and appropriations committees has nearly vanished. Authorizing legislation once dealt solely with substantive matters; authorizations were for raising "such sums as may be appropriate." But authorization committees now recommend specific spending levels, rather than laying out the objective of spending. Often these recommendations are set at unrealistically high levels in order to encourage large appropriations.

The appropriations committees were designed to set funding levels for each authorized program. But there has been a significant increase in the number of legislative riders contained in appropriations bills and in unauthorized funding tacked on to such bills. Moreover, the separate authorization and appropriation cycles, plus the budget resolution process, often require Congress to debate the same program during several committee hearings and at least three times on the floor in any session. This system represents an unreasonable burden on congressional time and detracts from the opportunity to perform effective oversight and negotiate realistic compromise.

The two committees could be combined into program committees, as suggested in 1973 by then Budget Director Charles Schultze. Each "program committee," aligned perhaps along current appropriation subcommittee jurisdiction, could produce authorization and appropriation bills, per current practice, but with considerable reduction in staff expenses, committee hearings, special interest leverage, time, and money.

2) The primary purpose of the House and Senate Budget Committees is to report a first budget resolution in the early spring. But, in recent years, partisan politics have dominated the committee meetings, delaying the committee report and polarizing House and Senate resolutions. In 1983, the Senate failed to report even a first budget resolution.

Senator Pete Domenici (R-New Mexico) has proposed to eliminate some of this confrontation through the creation of a Joint Budget Committee. "Such a joint committee," he says, "might help speed up the budget process by reporting the same budget resolution to each house and then, following floor action in each body, providing the means to work out a conference compromise in a more efficient manner."

A New Form of Budget Process

These reform proposals would streamline the budget process, hold Congress accountable for its spending, and help to ensure fiscal restraint.

The new process would lead to the following budget procedure. In the first year of a congressional session, the joint budget committee would report a first concurrent budget resolution in each chamber:

- The resolution would include the aggregate limits, including credit transactions, of the newly formed program committees.
- The resolution would distinguish between and set limits on mandatory and discretionary spending.
- The resolution would include necessary reconciliation instructions to the program committees necessary to meet these spending targets.
- The resolution would be sent to the President for his signature, and thus become the binding law.

Also during the first year, the program committees would hold hearings and debates on authorizing legislation aimed at achieving these spending goals, and report out such authorizing bills before the year's end.

In the second year of the session, Congress' primary budgetary objective would be to report out the appropriations bills.

Any bill violating the first concurrent resolution would be subject to a point of order, and a two-thirds majority would be needed to override it. If reconciliation were not successful, the budget committee would submit its own proposal on the floor.

CONCLUSION

There is no shortage of ideas on Capitol Hill when it comes to reducing federal spending. Yet, there is little consensus as to whose spending should be cut and a shortage of political will and abilities to overcome the institutional obstacles that confront those few who do attempt to enforce spending discipline and reduction.

The current budgetary system is not neutral. Inherent political and institutional incentives favor status quo or baseline spending and discourage reform.

Reform must focus on five issues:

1. Congress must close its own spending loopholes, such as the credit budget and off-budget expenditures. The American public requires a truthful accounting of its tax dollars and Congress should not be allowed to buy votes with hidden spending.

2. Congress must regain control over entitlement spending by bringing such spending within the purview of the budget process.

3. The Budget Act must be enforced by making violations of its constraints more difficult.

4. Congressional committee structure must be improved and the authorization and appropriations cycle reexamined to balance efficiency and control.

5. The balance of power between Congress and the President and between the special interest and fiscal interests of Congress must be realigned in favor of austerity. Spending priorities must be set early in the budget cycle and committees disciplined to abide by this plan.

The extant structure: the budget process, the accounting system, the balance of power and the committee structure require significant reform to counter the institutional bias toward spending.

Many on Capitol Hill dismiss institutional reform as impossible. They note the vested interests of senior members in preserving their powers under the existing system. Such skeptics ignore powerful examples of major congressional reform—including the Congressional Budget Act of 1974. They also ignore the prevailing feeling among members that the current structure demands reform. Dozens of Senators and Congressmen testified before Senator Quayle's Temporary Select Committee on Committees in the summer of 1984—and most pressed for major reform.

Without major reform any intermittent success in constraining spending excesses will be ephemeral, as institutional forces erode the success in the years to come.

17

The Federal Regulatory Process

by
Catherine England*

In his book, *Regulation and Its Reform*, Judge Stephen Breyer lists 30 different regulatory agencies.[1] He divides the group into three categories: "federal regulatory agencies controlling prices and services," "regulatory agencies concerned with health, safety, and the quality of the environment," and "federal agencies concerned with fraudulent practices and the security of financial institutions."

The activities of the first group frequently are referred to as "economic regulation." In addition to setting prices, these agencies often have a voice in determining who may enter an industry. Agencies concerned with economic regulation include the oldest federal regulatory agency—the Interstate Commerce Commission, founded in 1887—as well as the Federal Maritime Commission, the Federal Power Commission, the Postal Rate Commission, and the Copyright Royalty Tribunal.

Breyer's second group of agencies engage in "social regulation." Though the oldest member of this group, the Packers and Stockyards Administration of the U.S. Department of Agriculture, was established in 1916 to oversee plant conditions and practices in livestock and processed meat production, social regulation expanded most rapidly during the 1960s and 1970s. These years spawned such familiar regulators as the National Highway Traffic Safety Administration, the Environmental Protection Agency, the Consumer Product Safety Commission, and the Occupational Safety and Health Administration.

Federal regulatory agencies may also be grouped as they appear on the federal organization chart. The executive branch agencies are contained within larger cabinet departments and answer to the President. Example: The Federal Power Commission within the Department of Energy, the Food and Drug Administration within the Department of Health and Human Services, the Federal Aviation Administration within the Department of Transportation, and the

---

* Task Force members included Hugh Brady, Robert Okun, and Fred Smith.

[1] Stephen Breyer, *Regulation and Its Reform* (Cambridge, Mass.: Harvard University Press, 1982).

Mining Enforcement and Safety Administration within the Department of Interior.

Other regulatory functions are carried out by independent agencies and commissions, answerable directly to Congress. These include the Interstate Commerce Commission, the Federal Communications Commission, the Nuclear Regulatory Commission, the Securities and Exchange Commission, and the Commodity Futures Trading Commission, to name a few.

Sources of Authority and Control

The agencies derive their authority from two basic sources. The most important of these are the enabling statutes enacted by Congress. These are the laws that direct the Consumer Product Safety Commission to "protect consumers from unreasonably hazardous products," for example.

The vague language in many statutes leaves open the door for the second source of agency authority—court interpretations of the underlying laws. In her book, *Regulation by Prosecution,* Roberta Karmel, a former commissioner at the Securities and Exchange Commission, has noted that the future of a young attorney at a regulatory agency may depend on his or her ability to win cases in which agency authority is expanded to new and unique areas.

There are several means of controlling agency behavior. Just as the courts may extend authority, they may limit it. Similarly, as the ultimate source of regulatory power, congressional oversight plays a role in policing agency actions. Riders on budget appropriations bills may forbid explicitly investigations of specific industries, for example. Authorizing statutes may be amended, and some form of legislative veto is sure to return. In addition, executive branch agencies are subject to directives and executive orders from the President.

In FY 1983, the 25 or so agencies identified by Breyer are authorized by Congress to spend approximately $23 billion. They also employ some 110,000 people in their efforts to protect the safety and welfare of citizens. Such statistics, however, cannot convey the economic impact of the agencies. As an understanding of the full costs of regulation has grown, reform has become unavoidable.

The Need for Reform

If the Reagan Administration intends to leave the American economy in a healthier, more productive state than existed in 1980, reform of the regulatory process should receive as much attention as the tax and budget processes. Unnecessary, inefficient, and counterproductive regulation is at least as harmful economically as excessive taxation and government spending—perhaps even more so because the full costs of regulatory programs are often hidden, and imposed on those consumers and workers least able to bear the burden.

The most obvious costs of regulatory policies are increased prices to consumers. Not only are the costs of complying with regulation passed on to consumers, but when regulations reduce competition, prices climb even higher.

There are even more serious costs imposed by regulation. Funds spent by businessmen to meet regulatory requirements cannot be spent on research and development or capital investment. Thus long-run productivity suffers, and new products become available more slowly. This affects the economy in two important ways. First, slowing the pace of innovation delays the introduction of safer or more efficient products. Ironically, such delays can actually undermine the stated goals of many regulators by keeping safer, more efficient products off the market. Second, reduced expenditures on capital investment and R&D costs jobs. Both the rate of new business formation and the expansion of existing industries are slowed by government regulation.

When new products are developed, meanwhile, federal regulators may play an important role in determining when, and even if, consumers see the new products. Consider the Food and Drug Administration. While it hardly can be argued that drug manufacturers should not be subject to some controls, there is ample reason to question the efficacy of current controls. Because of a few adverse reactions to a new drug, thousands of potential beneficiaries often are denied medication while ever more tests and experiments are conducted. As a result, the U.S. routinely lags behind other developed countries in introducing new drugs. In these cases, the costs of regulation is measured in lives lost.

There are instances in which regulation may be counterproductive. At times reduced consumer choice can lead to additional injuries. For example, safer football helmets could be mandated by law. But additional costs involved in producing such helmets might mean some children could no longer afford any protection. The probable result: more injuries. Similarly, removing lower cost alternatives may cause consumers to substitute other products with their own inherent dangers, or to continue using older models past their safe lives. However unintentionally, therefore, regulation can sometimes actually increase risks for those the laws are supposedly designed to protect.

And some regulations do not produce any consumer benefits at all. In a report by the Center for the Study of American Business, former chairman of the President's Council of Economic Advisors Murray Weidenbaum notes that among the 1977 amendments to the Clean Air Act is Section 125 entitled "Measures to Prevent Economic Disruption or Unemployment." This gives the President the power to require major fuel-burning stationary sources to use locally or regionally available coal.[2] The goal is simply to protect some 10,000 jobs in Midwestern coal-producing states — even at the expense of dirtier air for millions of citizens. And even regulations that appear to protect jobs, such as this section of the Clean Air Act, do so only at the expense of other workers throughout the country.

In short, the U.S. no longer can afford to ignore the costs of regulation. Regulatory programs must be reexamined; some important questions should be answered. Are the goals of the program worth the economic costs imposed? Are those goals being achieved through current methods? Can they be achieved in a less expensive or more efficient manner?

As international markets become more competitive, these questions take on increasing importance. The U.S. no longer can assume it will dominate all world markets. Continued economic health will depend, at least in part, on deregulating where possible and undertaking reform when regulatory goals can be achieved more efficiently.

THE FIRST TERM EXPERIENCE

Executive Branch Changes

During his 1980 campaign, Ronald Reagan targeted regulatory reform as one means of reducing the burden imposed on the economy by the federal government. Early in his Administration, Reagan appointed Vice President George Bush to head a Cabinet-level task force on regulatory relief. The Task Force called on the business community, municipalities, and other interested parties to identify the most burdensome regulations with which they had to comply. From the flood of responses, the Bush Task Force identified the "Terrible Twenty"—regulations which, on the basis of information received, appeared to be the most costly.

---

[2] Murray L. Weidenbaum, *Regulation and the Public Interest*, Contemporary Issues Series 4 (St. Louis, MO: Center for the Study of American Business, February, 1982), p. 6.

In addition to establishing the Task Force, Reagan issued Executive Order 12291, the most recent in a series of efforts to introduce more discipline into the regulatory process. Presidents Gerald Ford and Jimmy Carter had issued similar orders, requiring cost/benefit analysis and establishing regulatory review groups within the executive branch. But Reagan's efforts were much more comprehensive.

Executive Order 12291 requires regulatory decisions to be made by agencies on the basis of cost/benefit and cost effectiveness criteria to the extent permitted by law. Reagan also abolished the Regulatory Council, the Council on Wage and Price Stability, and the Regulatory Analysis Review Group. He directed the Office of Management and Budget (OMB) to establish a regulatory review group, known as the Office of Information and Regulatory Analysis (OIRA), and designated the OMB official in charge of the OIRA as Executive Director of the Vice President's Task Force. Furthermore, Executive Order 12291 requires all executive branch agencies to submit proposed and final regulations to the review group 60 days before they are published in the *Federal Register*. OMB may ask for further information or consultations before the rule is published. Finally, Executive Order 12291 requires that executive branch agencies submit a Regulatory Impact Analysis for all rules defined as "major," that is, those expected to have an annual economic impact of $100 million or more.

Budgetary Authority

From 1970 to 1980, federal expenditures for regulatory activities soared from $800 million to almost $6 billion. In constant dollars (adjusted for inflation), this was a 274 percent increase in budgetary outlays. The Reagan Administration reversed this trend. During FY 1982, federal regulatory agencies' expenditures were reduced 3 percent in current dollars, or almost 9 percent in constant dollars. And while current dollar outlays increased slightly in fiscal 1983, the decreases in real terms continued.[3] This downward trend in agency budgets, regrettably, was reversed slightly in FY 1984 and FY 1985.

Statutory Changes

Despite high hopes at the beginning of 1981, as well as extended discussion and debate of both generic and specific regulatory reform

---

[3] Murray L. Weidenbaum, *Regulatory Reform: A Report Card for the Reagan Administration*, Formal Publication Number 59 (St. Louis, MO: Center for the Study of American Business, November, 1983), pp. 10-13.

bills, only two pieces of reform legislation passed Congress.

The first was the Bus Regulatory Reform Act of 1982. Continuing the deregulation of the surface transportation industries, this Act eased conditions for entry into the market and preempted many state regulations that had restricted interstate bus operation. The 1982 law also establishes a "zone of rate freedom" within which fares may be raised or lowered without prior Interstate Commerce Commission approval. Prices are scheduled to be totally deregulated in 1985, except where set collectively through rate bureaus.

Congress also passed the Garn-St. Germaine Depository Institutions Act of 1982. This expanded the powers of banks and other depository institutions. It directed the Depository Institutions Deregulation Committee (DIDC) to devise a means for banks and thrift institutions to compete with money market mutual funds. The result has been the proliferation, to the benefit of consumers, of bank money market accounts. The Act also accelerated the elimination of the statutory difference in the interest rates paid savers by banks and by savings and loan associations. Finally, the Act authorized interstate and interindustry acquisitions of troubled financial institutions.

Increased Regulation

There also were regulatory increases, however. In the view of many market advocates, Reagan's biggest failures probably were in the area of foreign trade restrictions. "Voluntary" Japanese automobile import quotas were introduced in 1981, for example. "Emergency" sugar import quotas and limits on European steel imports were imposed in 1982.

In addition, the Administration did not always remain true to stated goals—such as replacing engineering standards with performance guidelines. In May, 1983, for example, the Bush Task Force overruled OMB's Office of Information and Regulatory Analysis, and allowed the Department of Labor to continue using engineering standards to attempt to reduce textile workers' exposure to cotton dust. Many market advocates have also been troubled by recent efforts at the Department of Transportation to impose guidelines for acceptable drunk driving laws on state legislators.

The Incentive Structure

Before beginning a reform effort it is necessary to understand the incentives of those involved in the process.

Take the regulators. While regulatory attempts sometimes have been misguided and many agencies ultimately have been "captured" by those they were attempting to regulate, most programs were begun with a genuine desire to serve broader public interests. Most agency career employees thus genuinely seek to promote the public interest as they see it. Naturally, the individuals most likely to apply for and accept employment at a government agency are those who believe that inequities and dangers within society can be dealt with through government action. As a result, many permanent agency employees, even when they recognize certain problems, are suspicious of those calling for reforms. It is necessary, therefore, to establish how the public will be protected or made better off as a result of proposed reforms.

Second, employees of regulatory agencies are almost totally ignored when things are going well, but the first to be blamed in the event of a catastrophe. Government inspectors often have found themselves the subject of horror stories and congressional investigations concerning regulatory unreasonableness on one day only to be told soon after that they were too lax when an airplane crash or a mining accident becomes the subject of investigation. Conflicting signals from Congress, the news media, and the public dictate that regulatory staffers will usually tend to choose more control and regulation over less.

A third incentive is identified in *Going by the Book: The Problem of Regulatory Unreasonableness* by two economists at the University of California at Berkeley, Eugene Bardach and Robert Kagan. That is the tendency to "follow things though to their natural conclusion." No law, rule, or regulation can be all-inclusive. Similarly, there are no mechanisms allowing for perfect enforcement. With sufficient time and effort, some business or individual will find a way around any government rule. Others simply will ignore regulations, hoping to avoid detection. Once such "loopholes" are discovered and exploited, cries of "unequal treatment" or lax behavior on the part of the regulators are often raised. The obvious response is to attempt to close loopholes when found, to ask for stronger enforcement powers, to impose more extensive recordkeeping requirements, or to require additional licenses or permits.

Finally, growing regulatory responsibilities are the means by which individuals employed by regulatory agencies gain power, prestige, and career satisfaction. In expanding their range of responsibilities, such career employees are not subject to market tests or profitability requirements. Rather, efforts to grow are fought before Congress, the courts, and in the news media. None of these groups must bear the full costs of their decisions to expand the range of federal intervention.

Groups outside the regulatory agencies, such as labor unions, businessmen, the legal profession and self-styled "consumer advocacy groups," also play an important role in establishing a demand for regulation. They influence, moreover, the way rules are written and enforced and the direction in which federal intervention grows. Naturally, the rhetoric accompanying these attempts to influence government proclaims the "public interest." In truth, however, these individuals are often concerned with protecting their own interests. Indeed, there often is a relatively small band of interests benefitting directly from the existing regulatory system, and willing to expend considerable energy opposing change. Beneficiaries of reform, on the other hand, may be unaware of the opportunities reform would generate. The result is a good deal of inertia within the system. Any serious attempt at reform must recognize this problem, anticipate likely sources of resistance, and make plans to overcome opponents of change through properly framing the issue.

Educating the Public

Perhaps the most important lesson from the Reagan regulatory reform efforts is the need to engage in a careful education process before, during, and even after reform efforts are undertaken. After the Reagan Administration took office, opponents of regulatory reform—particularly in the health and safety areas—recaptured the moral high ground with surprising ease. In a number of cases, advocates of regulation successfully depicted the Reagan Administration in brutally inhumane terms, and suggested that reform efforts would sacrifice helpless women and children to evil business interests. There was almost no rejoinder from Administration officials. White House officials often failed to search for, or create, opportunities to set the tone of the debate. The Reagan Administration too often allowed itself to be maneuvered into a defensive position on regulatory issues rather than taking the initiative, as it had on many tax and budget matters. Hearing only one side of the story, the normal resistance to change grew, and the fear of defeat and its attending bad publicity frustrated many attempts at reform—sometimes even before they were begun.

Administration officials should have exploited every opportunity to affirm their commitment to a clean environment, safe consumer products, and healthy work places. But they should have explained, patiently, that a commitment to these goals of regulation does not necessarily imply an attachment to the current means of achieving them. In fact, many regulations have become counterproductive and these rules should have been used as a starting point for seeking reform.

The Administration also often failed to mobilize its allies. In many cases, research that supported proposed reform did not become a part of the public debate because the academics, research groups, or businessmen in possession of useful evidence were not given advance warning of likely Administration moves. Thus the Administration failed to mobilize individuals and groups less sensitive to public opinion to "take the heat" by advancing arguments ahead of decisions, and by responding to criticisms, allowing the government to adjust its proposals at the design stage—rather than having to engage in "damage control" once an announcement was made.

In addition, the vocabulary used in change proved to be very important. Economists may relish arguments of "increased efficiency," but the public is interested in "lower prices," and "helping the consumer."

Finally, in building the case for reform, advocates of change need to look for successful, concrete examples. These may come from other countries or from innovative states. Indeed, it may be necessary for advocates of reform to accept change at a much slower, more incremental pace than they desire precisely for the purpose of establishing a record of success.

In short, special interests make certain that there are no cases where "the need for change is obvious." The case for any specific reform must be made repeatedly in a positive manner before substantive change can be achieved.

The Role of the Courts

The courts have played a more important role than many expected. In the regulatory arena, the courts often stalled regulatory efforts by finding that agencies had exceeded their authority in making changes or had failed to document and justify their actions properly. It is not enough, however, simply to condemn the courts for these actions. Deregulation or regulatory reform efforts deserve the same careful documentation reform advocates would impose on those seeking expanded regulations. There is a solid, well-researched case to be made against mandatory airbags in automobiles, for example. Unfortunately, the National Highway Traffic Administration did not do so, thus losing the chance to demonstrate that the Reagan Administration was concerned with safety—and with finding a cost-effective means of achieving regulatory goals. Success in the area of regulatory reform during the next four years will depend in large part on the ability of Administration officials to carefully document and sell proposed changes.

In addition, the courts are charged with enforcing the law as it is written. In some cases, nothing can be done without changing the underlying law. This is one reason statutory reform, discussed later, is so crucial.

Dealing with the courts specifically, a useful change would be venue reform. Cases involving regulatory agencies should be tried in the district where the challenge was raised or where the regulation has the most impact. This would make the system more accessible to individuals and businesses directly affected by regulatory activity. Venue reform might also have the added benefit of using judges with a more complete understanding of regulatory impacts than those judges living in Washington, where a disproportionate share of the cases are heard.

Statutory Reform

Without examining the underlying authority from which the regulators draw their power, there can be no assurance of permanent change. Many statutes offer excessively broad authority and discretion through vague directives. This allows for potentially wide swings in policy depending on who is making decisions.

The Federal Trade Commission, for example, has often been touted as representing one of the most dramatic changes in the past four years. Chairman James Miller's FTC has been much less interventionist than the Commission under Chairman Michael Pertschuk. Yet it is important to recognize that both chairmen directed the Commission under essentially the same statutes. As a result, a more activist chairman could return the FTC to its more interventionist ways.

At the other extreme, some statutes offer excessively strict guidelines. The result may be regulatory behavior widely viewed as "unreasonable" but, nevertheless, required by law. The Delaney Amendment to the Pure Food and Drug Act is one example. Written in 1958, at a time when scientific methods were primitive by today's standards, this Amendment requires that no known carcinogen in any amount may be used as an additive in food for human consumption. Furthermore, the Delaney Amendment requires that the only health risks considered are the cancer risks from using an additive, not other health risks that may arise from not using it. But some substances that appear to be carcinogenic in very large doses may actually benefit humans in smaller amounts, or available substitutes may present an even greater danger. Further, scientists are able to detect ever more minute quantities of various natural and man made substances within foods. But the law, as it is currently written, largely forbids the FDA from taking these factors into account when considering the use of a particular additive.

The Administration should also keep in mind that it is important to propose regulatory reform legislation even when "victory" appears unlikely. A legislative battle provides a forum in which the case for reform can be made before the public. And while compromise is almost always necessary, framing the debate properly could provide the first steps toward more significant change. This can allow later reforms to point to successful examples.

The Administration failed to do this. It should have sought, for instance, change of the Clean Air and Clean Water Acts. While undoubtedly politically charged, specific reform proposals would have given the Administration an opportunity to demonstrate a commitment to the goals of the environmental legislation while seeking more efficient means to the broadly accepted end. It is possible that no significant changes would have been made; but at least important gains would have been made educating the public about the weaknesses in the existing statues.

There is a danger of a new surge of regulation. With growing restraints on government spending, regulation may become a new form of "pork barrel," protecting existing producers and their workforce at the expense of new entrants. In addition, the search for additional security in an uncertain world continues. Consumers often are viewed as helpless and unable to make sound choices.

This makes it particularly important that the Reagan Administration more clearly articulate its vision of a safer world and a cleaner environment achieved through an increased reliance on market forces. The next Administration must recapture the moral high ground in this area by establishing clearly which current regulatory methods are inefficient and counterproductive.

THE NEXT FOUR YEARS

Regulatory reforms can be viewed as falling into three broad categories. First are the generic reforms, which deal with the regulatory process. Second is reform of economic regulation. The third group deals with strategies for dealing with social regulation.

The Regulatory Process

"Generic" reform strategies apply to the regulatory process. They deal with the procedures used at all the agencies in promulgating regulations. The goals of generic reform are broad in nature: to make the regulatory process more efficient, to make Congress more accountable, to give the public and their representatives a more direct role in the regulatory process.

Several means for accomplishing these goals have been discussed during the past four years. Omnibus regulatory reform legislation was given serious attention during the past four years, and was passed by the Senate during both the 97th and 98th Congresses. The House, however, was unable to agree on a similar bill.

Strategies for generic reform should be considered during the next Administration. In many cases, a new "regulation" is required to remove existing rules, that is, to deregulate. Because many of the generic strategies discussed involve greater scrutiny of proposed regulations, of course, they unavoidably slow efforts to change specific regulations.

In most cases, however the potential costs seem worth the benefits. Long-term restructuring of the regulatory process is fundamental to providing the needed predictability and greater accountability in the future.

Cost/Benefit and Cost-Effectiveness Analysis

President Reagan's Executive Order 12291 has been acclaimed as an important step in bringing the regulatory process under control. Among its more important features are the cost/benefit and cost-effectiveness requirements. These criteria should be extended by statute to all regulatory agencies.

Cost/benefit tests obviously are subjective to a large degree in estimating expected benefits or costs. Furthermore, the validity of cost-effectiveness analysis depends on the willingness of the agency staff to search for non-traditional means of achieving regulatory goals as well as their creativity in doing so. Thus, cost/benefit and cost-effectiveness requirements are not the comprehensive cure to the country's regulatory ills they first were thought to be. Their value is in raising certain issues for debate.

When cost/benefit tests were first introduced, proponents were denounced unfairly as unfeeling individuals who sought to place a dollar value on human life. For the most part, however, today's debates over particular cost/benefit analyses center around what costs ought to be included, or exactly how far benefits will extend. This sort of debate helps focus attention on the tradeoffs involved in any regulatory effort.

Similarly, cost-effectiveness analysis forces regulators to consider, however superficially, alternative means of meeting regulatory goals.

And while agency employees may conduct these analyses in a way that seems to support traditional command-and-control regulation, the door is opened for other interested parties to question agency decisions and suggest alternative solutions.

Thus, while cost/benefit and cost-effectiveness criteria do not represent a complete solution, they are a key step in the long-term reform of the regulatory process. They raise important questions about the traditional ways of doing the regulatory business.

Legislative Veto

A legislative veto gives Congress the "last word" over the activities of the regulatory agencies. It allows legislators to intervene directly to prevent specific regulations from taking effect, rather than relying on judicial review or waiting for more general oversight or budget hearings to question particular agency actions. Proponents of the legislative veto view it as a means of giving Congress more responsibility for regulations.

In June 1983, the Supreme Court held certain forms of legislative veto unconstitutional. The Court found that the Constitution requires an acceptable congressional veto must involve both Houses of Congress and the President in any decisions to either affirm or overturn agency actions. This still leaves Congress with many questions: Should "major regulations" (generally defined as those having an annual economic impact of more than $100 million) be approved by the Congress and the President before they are allowed to take affect? Or is enough accountability introduced if Congress has the option of disapproving these regulations when proposed by the agencies? Within what time frame should Congress be required to act if it is going to do so? Should there be a single, generic legislative veto applying across the board to all regulatory agencies? Or is it more appropriate to apply different forms of the veto to different regulatory problems?

It is not immediately clear what form of congressional veto would be best. Perhaps Congress should apply different forms of legislative veto to different agencies. It is obvious, however, that elected representatives should shoulder some of the responsibility for tough regulatory choices.

The nation's legislators have become adept at sidestepping this responsibility. They legislate in broad, vague terms—"protect consumers from 'unreasonably hazardous' products," or "provide 'reasonably safe' workplaces." Unelected agency employees then are left to make the decisions and choices necessary to implement stated policies. This allows Congressmen and Senators to enjoy the best of both worlds. They can be for "equality, safety, and a clean environment," but can claim that they never intended that the EPA bureaucrats should interpret their mandate such that the local factory should be forced to close.

One means of placing the responsibility back with elected officials would be to introduce a widespread legislative veto, allowing Congress to intervene on a case-by-case basis.

Reorganizing the OIRA

The Office of Information and Regulatory Analysis is charged with reviewing proposed regulations as a means of attempting to reduce overlapping and conflicting federal requirements. The OIRA is also expected to provide some overall direction to Administration policy toward regulatory reform. Thus the OIRA is presented with potentially conflicting challenges.

In their oversight role, staff members, quite properly, are protected from outside influence. By the time proposed regulations reach the OIRA staff, interested parties have had ample opportunity to comment publicly on anticipated advantages and disadvantages of the rule under consideration. Those comments are available to OIRA staff, and little is added by allowing additional input at this point.

On the other hand, OIRA's role in establishing broad policy directions for the Administration calls for the greatest input possible. Before suggesting the future direction of the regulatory apparatus as a whole, individual agencies, or specific programs, staff members should solicit opinions and consider input from as broad a political spectrum as possible. The interaction of this wide range of interests can lead to innovative solutions to regulatory problems.

Because these two functions are in direct conflict—at least with respect to the interaction between OIRA staff and the outside world—the Office of Information and Regulatory Analysis should be split into two separate groups. Those involved in "regulatory review" could then be protected from external pressure, while staff members attempting to take a more long-term view and set broader "policy development" would be free to solicit advice from a broad range of interested parties.

Economic Regulation

Traditionally, economic regulation has been the most common form of federal intervention. It is usually justified by the perceived existence of "excessive competition" or a natural monopoly. As a result, economic regulation generally deals with entry into the industry and prices charged by firms within it. Thus, the Interstate Commerce Commission was established to deal with the excessive competition thought to exist within the railroad industry.

Throughout its history, economic regulation has been justified with pro-consumer arguments. Excessive competition is said to harm consumers through industry instability, with prices rising and falling as firms exit and enter the market. When only one firm can efficiently serve the market, a natural monopoly is said to exist, and consumers must be protected from the market power assumed to follow. It is becoming increasingly clear, however, that economic regulation is, in fact, almost always pro-business and pro-labor. Government price and entry controls ultimately protect existing firms from new competition and put the force of the government behind industry price-setting. The practical effect of this regulation is, as a result, government-enforced cartelization of the regulated industry.

Deregulation

The simplest answer to these problems is deregulation. As in the case of airline and trucking deregulation, removing government control can lead to lower prices and a wider range of choice for consumers. There are several candidates for such deregulation during the next four years:

1) Decontrol natural gas prices.

Just as gasoline prices rose and then fell when deregulated, the natural gas industry can also be expected to respond to market signals. Rising gas prices will create the incentive to search for and capture more gas, while encouraging consumers to conserve. The result should be increased supplies and lower prices in the long run.

2) Discontinue agriculture marketing orders specifying the quantity of fruits, vegetables, and specialty crops which may be sold.

Some marketing orders allow growers jointly to determine the amount of their crop that will reach the market, which inevitably means higher prices, and place the force of the U.S. Department of Agriculture behind those decisions. This is not in the best interest of the consuming public. The result is, in effect, legalized cartels.

3) Eliminate many of the entry restrictions applied to financial institutions.

Bankers, brokers, and real estate agents sound much like airlines, truckers and California orange growers when they maintain that their industries are "unique in their function within the economy." But every industry is in some way unique. And as with other industries, regulations limiting the number of banks that may serve an area or drawing artificial distinctions along product lines impose their greatest costs on consumers, who enjoy fewer choices and higher prices.

In sum, government regulation of entry and prices almost always benefits industry participants at the expense of consumers. For this reason, labor unions and industry management can be expected to join in claiming that deregulation will be harmful. Their arguments will be couched in pro-consumer terms, but a careful look at the facts reveals an interest in minimizing competition and maintaining higher profits, wages, and salaries through higher prices.

Assigning Property Rights

In some cases, economic regulation has occurred with the stated goal of controlling the use of common public resources. Perhaps the classic example is regulation of the airwaves by the Federal Communications Commission.

When the technology was developed to permit radio transmission and reception, a problem arose. No one "owned" the electromagnetic spectrum. There had been no need to establish property rights in the spectrum before the introduction of radio, but without these property rights, the potential existed for widespread interference as radio broadcasters competed in using the spectrum.

Logically, those interested in using the new technology would have had strong incentives to work out a system of property rights enforceable by the courts. No one would want their transmissions to be subject to interference by others, and accepting limits on oneself would appear to be the only means of successfully imposing limits on others. Rather than allowing the trial and error necessary before a complete property rights system could be established, however, the federal government intervened. Declaring the airwaves a "public good," Congress instructed the Federal Communications Commission (FCC) to allocate use of the spectrum. In return for being licensed to broadcast, the owners of radio, and, later, television stations were asked to comply with just a few simple rules in the "public interest."

The problems with this approach are becoming increasingly apparent. In the first place, government-allocated frequency use has almost certainly delayed research and development that would allow more efficient use of the spectrum—transmitters and receivers, for example, which reduce interference and permit closer spacing of radio and television stations. There is little reason to risk the resources inventing them when spacing is determined by government fiat. Similarly, government involvement has removed the incentive to discover how close stations may be spaced given current technology. With a system of private property rights in the electromagnetic spectrum, "drop-in" stations and low power television would already be operating, to the public's benefit.

Furthermore, evidence indicates that the electromagnetic spectrum is not being efficiently allocated. The FCC has reserved different parts of the spectrum for different types of users. In addition to radio and television stations, frequencies are set aside for microwave transmissions, cellular radios, satellite communications, business use, and many others. As a result, part of the spectrum is hardly used at all while applicants for radio or television licenses, for example, may wait years for an opportunity to apply. In addition, optimal allocation of the spectrum may differ across the country. Large cities may need more room for cellular car radios while less populated areas may find additional "CB" space more useful.

Finally, the competitive hearings through which licenses are issued create problems. When awarding a license, there are few objective tests for determining which of the many candidates will best serve the public interest. As a result of the subjective nature of comparative hearing process, a license candidate may spend thousands of dollars hiring attorneys and consultants who specialize in preparing applications and arguing cases before the Commission, all with no guarantee of success.

The first step toward solving these problems is to allocate remaining licenses through either auctions or lotteries. An auction should be no more costly than the current system of comparative hearings, and it would be more fair in at least one sense: unsuccessful candidates for a license would avoid the expenses incurred during a similarly contested comparative hearings process. If there are strong political objections to auctions, lotteries would accomplish the same fundamental purpose.

Once the spectrum is allocated, with part set aside for the government's use if desired, the FCC and Congress should step aside and let the owners of the electromagnetic spectrum buy and sell their property as they will. If consumers want more spectrum space for cellular car radios, for example, companies providing that service will be able to buy spectrum rights from other uses consumers value less.

Social Regulation

Social regulation is primarily concerned with protecting health, safety, and the environment. Federal regulation in this area mushroomed during the 1960s and 1970s. Two factors appear to explain this rapid growth. First, an increasingly affluent society was able to turn its attention from more basic economic needs to "quality of life" issues. Second, a faster pace of technological change and scientific breakthroughs identifying previously unrecognized dangers led to a growing insecurity and a search for protection.

Central to the growth of social regulation, and hence crucial to any reform effort, is the question of who bears the ultimate responsibility for problems. How far does the federal government's parental role extend? How much responsibility are individuals expected to assume? Are consumers expected to approach used car salesmen with skepticism, for example, and insist on an independent evaluation of the car's condition? Or is it the federal government's responsibility to ensure only used cars of a minimum quality are available? Should factory employees be expected to recognize certain dangers and take reasonable precautions? Or should the government see that careless workers are protected despite themselves?

In short, individuals seeking change must determine where society wishes to draw the line between legitimate protections from unavoidable risks and excessive infringements on the freedom of individuals to make choices in their lives.

Social regulation also has been characterized by the movement of many regulatory responsibilities from state agencies to federal authorities. It is necessary to understand why there has been this increase in federal activity before reform efforts can be successful.

In some cases, the business community has sought federal preemption. It obviously is less costly to comply with one regulation than to comply with 50. It also is less expensive to lobby one legislature or one regulatory body than 50. So businessmen in some cases may find federal regulation more convenient than state. But federal regulation preempts the kind of experimentation at the state level that can lead to the discovery of better ways of meeting regulatory goals.

State officials may also seek federal intervention. State authorities understandably would prefer regulating enforcement costs to be borne by Washington. Furthermore, some state problems may cross state lines—a polluted river, for example—requiring federal coordination of regulatory activity.

Whatever the reasons for growth, many of the goals of social regulation have become widely accepted. Without an ambitious reform effort in this area, regulatory activity can be expected to continue to expand. If they are to have any success, efforts at reforms must, therefore, establish clearly how regulatory goals will be met in the face of change.

Strategies for reforming social regulation fall into two broad categories. In cases where regulation is likely to continue, there is a need to make the regulatory process more efficient. But there are also opportunities for moving government out of the regulatory process altogether by establishing market mechanisms that will work as well, if not better than, command-and-control regulation.

More Efficient Regulation

One of the best ways to make regulation more effective but less costly is to introduce market-like incentives into the system. Among the most widely discussed of these have been proposed taxes and fines applied to firms exceeding specified pollution levels. Critics often question how advocates of incentive-based systems would measure the harm done in order to properly set taxes and/or fines. But Judge Stephen Breyer noted that the principal advantage of an incentive based system has nothing to do with its ability to measure harm. "Rather, the true virtue of a tax, fee, or similar system lies in its power to provide incentives to direct behavior in a socially desirable direction, without freezing current technology and while preserving a degree of individual choice."[4]

Similarly, an increased reliance on performance criteria over design standards carries many of the benefits of taxes and fines. By leaving to affected firms the decision of how to comply with specific workplace safety standards, for example, the government provides a strong incentive for firms to undertake research to devise better, less expensive ways of protecting their employees. New technology is encouraged rather than inhibited, as it is by design standards.

The mandatory disclosure of certain information may also prove an effective means of achieving regulatory goals. Requiring food processors to disclose the use of certain additives, for example, allows consumers to make a more intelligent choice while avoiding an across-the-board ban on chemicals that may be harmful to only a small part of the population. Similarly, publishing information about the relative safety and fuel efficiency of automobiles will allow each consumer to judge what mix best suits his driving needs and habits. In short, informed consumers can provide extremely powerful incentives for firms to remove lower quality or less safe products from the market.

Market alternatives to regulation

In some cases, private means can achieve regulatory goals. Take,

---

[4] Breyer, *op.cit.*

for example, the use of private firms to provide deposit insurance for banks and savings and loan associations.

Private firms would have an even stronger incentive than government agencies to take the steps necessary to ensure prudent behavior of the institutions they insured. Private insurers have an important tool at their disposal that federal regulators do not. They can raise or lower premiums based on changing behavior by the bank. Federal insurance premiums are set by law and do not vary with risk. In "regulating" the depository institutions they insured, private insurers would have the option of adjusting reserve requirements or capital requirements, for example, to changes in bank behavior, like the opening of new branches or an expansion into insurance or real estate. Federal regulators must apply the same standards to all institutions regardless of how aggressive or conservative their management. In short, turning regulatory responsibilities over to private firms could lead easily to a more stable banking system.

Similarly, firms providing workman's compensation insurance have not only the incentives but also the tools to take over much of the task of the Occupational Safety and Health Administration (OSHA) in securing safe workplaces for employees. Since these insurance companies must pay employees in the event of injury, it is in their best interest to determine what characteristics describe a safe workplace in various industries. By measuring individual firms against these criteria, insurance firms are able to set premiums based on the likely injury rate for that firm. The safer the firm, the lower its premiums, so firms tolerating unsafe working conditions are automatically penalized by their insurer. Both the insurer and the insured firm, moreover, have strong incentives to engage in research directed at making inherently unsafe conditions less dangerous. Thus, private insurance firms have every incentive to inspect frequently, to consult with individual firms on better ways of achieving safer workplaces, and to punish less safe firms with higher premiums. In addition, private firms can be expected to exhibit flexibility OSHA does not in adapting to changing technological conditions.

Supporting private rights of action

Direct regulation may be unnecessary if citizens have clear right to take civil action in the event they are harmed.

Product liability laws are one example. Strict liability, now almost universally recognized, holds that if a consumer is injured through no fault of his own in using a defective product, the manufacturer is liable for damages—regardless of the degree of care taken to avoid the sale of defective products. While no firm can ever be certain that it will never sell a defective product, strict liability laws obviously encourage firms to avoid such sales to the greatest degree possible. So, while product liability laws are far from perfect, they do make redundant much of the work of the Consumer Product Safety Commission. Regulators can never hope to be as efficient as a national court system imposing judgments in thousands of potential cases brought by consumers actually using a product. The judgments and attending bad publicity inherent in the use of the legal system represent stronger deterrents than any the CPSC could hope to devise.

Providing a right to private action might also be used effectively in the oversight of toxic torts. Suppose citizens could purchase insurance against such hazards and the insurers were assigned the insureds' legal rights of action. Insurance firms could then be expected to bring suits for negligence against the firms responsible in toxic torts cases. Thus, consumers would receive compensation, and the insurance industry, acting on behalf of insured individuals would have the means to deter negligent waste disposal.

INITIATIVES FOR 1985

During 1985, efforts should center around generic reform efforts. The Administration should:

1) Reorganize the Office of Information and Regulatory Analysis within OMB.

The staff of the OIRA within OMB should be divided into two distinct groups. The first would continue to carry out the function of reviewing proposed regulations and, as it does now, avoid lobbying attempts by individuals or groups seeking to influence regulatory outcomes. The second group would solicit input from a broad range of interests in an attempt to set longer-term policy directives for the Administration.

This step would allow the policy group to begin work on long-range strategies for reform while providing Administration officials with information useful in conducting the all-important public education process.

2) Introduce legislation extending cost/benefit and cost-effectiveness requirements to all regulatory agencies.

This should receive a high priority. While removing inefficiencies within the existing system is important, it is also necessary to ensure that future regulatory efforts are undertaken in a more thoughtful manner.

3) Enact a workable legislative veto.

This should also receive a high priority during the next session of Congress. While this may mean devising different forms of the veto for various regulatory problems, it is important that steps be taken to return the responsibility for regulatory excess to the Congress, where it belongs.

18

The Social Security System

by
Peter J. Ferrara

The Social Security system is operated by the Social Security Administration (SSA), part of the Department of Health and Human Services. It accounts for almost 30 percent of the entire federal budget. It is hard to see how the size and scope of the federal government can ever be reduced without significantly doing something about Social Security. Dealing with the inherent problems of Social Security must be a top priority of the new Administration.

THE FIRST TERM EXPERIENCE

Insecure Security

Despite the 1983 Social Security rescue legislation, based on the report of a 1982 presidential task force on the system, the program remains plagued by enormous problems. In the short run, based on the Social Security Administration's own projections, the program remains vulnerable to yet another financial collapse. This is likely if a serious recession develops soon, particularly if inflation also picks up. Moreover, the SSA projects that the Hospital Insurance (HI) portion of the program in any event will be unable to pay benefits by the end of this decade. If surpluses from the rest of the program bail out HI, then the program as a whole will remain vulnerable to collapse during future cycles of inflation and recession. Indeed, the latest Annual Report of the Social Security Board of Trustees indicates that the program taken as a whole would collapse by the mid-1990s under the so-called pessimistic set of assumptions—assumptions that in the past have always been closest to reality.

Projections based on the most realistic assumptions indicate that to pay the benefits promised to today's young workers, total Social Security tax rates eventually would have to be raised to at least 33 percent of payroll, compared with the combined 14 percent today. This would mean that Social Security tax would take $6,700 from a worker making $20,000. Former Social Security Chief Actuary A.

Haeworth Robertson estimates that paying promised benefits could require payroll tax rates of over 40 percent.

Low and Inequitable Returns

Perhaps most shocking of all is that even if all the benefits promised to today's young workers are somehow paid, the program will still be a bad deal for these workers. The benefits received by retirees soon after the system was created represented a high return on their tax dollars, thanks to the fact that rates were low, and paid for just a few years. But as workers retired who had paid higher taxes for more of their working careers, the return began to fall. Today's retirees are still receiving above market returns through the program, but those now entering the work force will pay Social Security taxes of several thousand dollars a year for their entire working careers. For most of these young workers, their Social Security benefits will mean a real rate of return of one percent or less. For maximum income workers and for most two earner couples, the real return will be practically zero—even negative in many cases. If these workers could invest their Social Security tax funds in an Individual Retirement Account (IRA), by comparison, they could expect several times the benefits promised them by Social Security. In addition, the program's benefits are grossly inequitable. Two workers paying the exact same taxes their entire careers can receive widely differing benefit amounts. Blacks and other minorities with below average life expectancies receive much lower returns through the program than the rest of the population. A black male age 25 can expect to live only long enough to collect full Social Security retirement benefits for 5 months, while a white male age 25 can expect 6 years of full benefits—about 15 times as much.

THE NEXT FOUR YEARS

The solution to the many serious problems plaguing Social Security does not require sacrifices from the elderly. Social Security reform need not equal reduction. Quite the contrary, appropriate reform would strengthen Social Security and assure today's elderly their benefits, while providing new opportunities for today's young workers so that they could look forward to a secure and prosperous retirement.

Social Security Bond

As the first step of a fundamental reform, the next Administration should request Congress to provide all retirees with a Social Security bond contractually entitling them to their promised benefits. This would give each retiree the same legal status as a U.S. Treasury bond holder. It would then be unconstitutional to cut the benefits of someone who had already retired on Social Security, just as it is unconstitutional to refuse to repay a U.S. Treasury bond.

Super IRA

The Administration should combine the proposal for a bond with the submission of legislation to make major reforms in the entire funding system. Starting on a specific date, say January 1, 1986, a second step should be taken by allowing today's workers to contribute to their IRAs each year, in addition to any other amounts they may contribute, an amount up to 20 percent of their Social Security retirement taxes (OASI). Instead of the usual IRA income tax deduction for these contributions, however, workers would receive a dollar-for-dollar income tax credit equal to the amount of such contributions. Workers would also be allowed to direct their employers to contribute up to 20 percent of the employer share of the Social Security tax to their IRAs, with each employer again receiving a full income tax credit for these amounts. Workers who utilized the credit option would have their future Social Security benefits reduced to the extent they chose the option. A worker who opted for the full credit during his entire career, for instance, would have his future Social Security benefits reduced by 10 percent. If the credit option were in effect in the current fiscal year (FY 85), and workers utilized it twice as much as they currently use conventional IRAs, the income tax revenue loss for the year would be $14.5 billion. But this eventually would be offset completely by reduced Social Security expenditures, as more and more workers retired relying to a large extent on IRAs rather than Social Security. Long before this, however, the revenue loss would be cancelled by new revenues generated from the increased investment through IRAs. Starting on a later date, say January 1, 1990, workers would be allowed to contribute further amounts annually to their IRAs (up to another 10 percent of their OASI taxes) for the purchase of private term life insurance. Workers could again direct their employers to match these contributions for such purchases. Both employee and employer would again receive an income tax credit equal to the amount of these contributions.

Social Security currently pays survivors benefits on behalf of a deceased taxpayer who leaves a dependent spouse and young children, or an elderly spouse. For workers under 65, private term life insurance can perform this function entirely. Consequently, a worker dying before 65 would have his or her Social Security survivors benefits reduced to the extent he had used the tax credit option to purchase term life insurance in force when he died. An employee with no dependents, who does not normally need such life insurance coverage, would be allowed to devote the additional IRA contributions under this credit option entirely to retirement. A worker with only one dependent would be allowed to devote half of these funds to retirement rather than insurance. If this credit option were in effect in the current fiscal year, and workers also used it twice as much as they currently use IRAs, the income tax revenue loss for the year would be $7 billion. Again, this loss would be offset rapidly by reduced Social Security expenditures, since starting in the very first year of such a change, all the survivors of those who died while relying on the credit would receive their private insurance rather than Social Security benefits. The investment arising from the fully funded private life insurance system would also produce increased tax revenues.

The credit options could be expanded further in later years, until workers had the freedom to choose how much to rely on IRAs rather than Social Security. Under such a plan, workers would be allowed to purchase life, disability and old-age health insurance through IRAs to cover the full range of benefits offered by Social Security.

Since the tax credit under these options is taken against income taxes rather than Social Security payroll taxes, full Social Security tax revenues would continue to flow into the program, to finance benefits for today's elderly. Indeed, the reform would greatly strengthen Social Security's financing system. While the program's revenues would be maintained in full, expenditures would be reduced substantially as workers relied more and more on IRAs rather than Social Security, thereby closing the long term funding gap. With the credit options eventually expanded to the maximum, Social Security expenditures would be reduced dramatically, allowing room for sharp reductions in payroll taxes.

Nothing in the package proposed would require Americans to depend on a Super IRA. Workers could remain in Social Security if they so desired. But those who opted for the Super IRAs, of course, could expect much higher retirement benefits. These benefits would also be completely equitable, since each worker would receive back in benefits the amount paid in contributions, plus interest, calculated on an actuarial basis.

The Super IRAs, moreover, could increase national savings by many billions of dollars each year, creating new jobs and greater economic growth. Eventual payroll tax reductions would also improve the economy. With workers relying on IRAs rather than Social Security, federal spending could be reduced by as much as 25 to 30 percent, without the pain of benefit cuts.

INITIATIVES FOR 1985

While the Administration prepares legislation to reform Social Security fundamentals, some important immediate and short-term changes are possible.

1) Index Permissible IRA Contributions.

The current, maximum, tax-deductible contribution to an IRA should be raised to equal the maximum employee contributions to Social Security. This would raise the maximum annual IRA contribution immediately from $2,000 per worker to about $2,600. The maximum would increase each year at the rate of growth of average wages, as does the maximum Social Security taxable income. Such indexing would maintain the real value of the IRA deduction.

2) End Discrimination Against Homemakers.

Non-working spouses currently can contribute only $250 per year to an IRA. This should be increased to the same maximum available to working spouses. The law now discriminates against homemakers, yet they need retirement protection as much as, if not more then, spouses who work.

3) Allow IRA Insurance Purchases.

Workers should be allowed to use their IRA funds to purchase life, disability, and old-age health insurance. This step would take some pressure off Social Security and provide workers with additional protection, just as supplemental IRA benefits do. It would also enable workers to become more familiar with IRAs as an alternative to Social Security.

4) Require Social Security Honesty.

The Social Security Board of Trustees should be required to include each year in its annual report a section comparing the typical rate of return paid by Social Security to those retiring that year with the rate of return likely to be paid to those entering the workforce that year. This would force the government to admit publicly that while the program still offers a good deal to today's retirees, it offers little to today's young people. The Social Security Administration should also be required to send each worker a Statement of Account estimating the rate of return he can expect on total Social Security taxes paid for his account. Finally, the employer's share of the payroll tax should be reported on each worker's paycheck, along with the employee share, with the total then broken down into the amount paid for each type of Social Security coverage.

19

Defense Assessment

by
Theodore J. Crackel*

Introduction

An effective U.S. defense capability has two essential components: forces (weapons and personnel) and procedures to assure the most effective and cost-efficient development and implementation of U.S. strategy and tactics. In the first area, the Reagan Administration orchestrated implementation of a program of force modernization and associated spending increases essential to reverse a near decade-long decline in defense capabilities. An immediate budget supplement in 1981 and a subsequent growth in spending—though reduced substantially by the Congress—has reversed that trend.

The next step is for a new administration to implement changes in defense procedures and organization so as to improve the effectiveness of the dollars spent. These changes, however, should not get in the way of continuing the necessary modernization of U.S. forces.

With respect to process, the Reagan Administration has implemented some decentralization within the Department of Defense (DoD). But an emphasis on decentralization of program execution should not be allowed to obscure the necessity of sure, central direction and guidance in the areas of policy/strategy formulation and resource allocation.

To date, the emphasis on central direction has been in the area of resources. Resource allocation and budgeting have been the main instruments of control. To improve effectiveness, the Reagan Administration has revamped the Defense Resources Board (DRB) and has

*The author wishes to acknowledge the very significant contribution of all those who shared their ideas with The Heritage Foundation's Defense Assessment Project. The paragraphs on Defense Acquisition and Logistics, specifically, were written in close coordination with F. X. Livingston who chaired that working group. Particular thanks also go to all the project's working group chairmen, members, and to many others, including: Henry Young, Mackubin T. Owens, Henry Mohr, Carnes Lord, Donald W. Hurta, Robert K. Griffith, Mike Sovereign, Walter Jajko, J. A. Stockfisch, C. J. Tringali, Patrick L. Renehan, David Westerman, Richard D. Webster, C. Lincoln Hoewing, and John A. Mullett.

made some tentative modifications to the budgeting system. This emphasis on resources and budgeting, however, has come at the expense of policy influence. In fact, the military Services are controlled more by the budgeting process than by carefully articulated defense guidance or strategic designs.

The role and influence of the policy formulators must be expanded. Policy and strategy guidance and the mechanisms to produce them must be enhanced or created at every level in the national security apparatus—from the National Security Council to the Joint Chiefs of Staff.

While substantial progress has been made in force modernization in the last four years, more now needs to be done to fix the way America does its defense business and spends its defense dollars. An emphasis on resources can improve the way weapons systems are purchased. An emphasis on policy and strategy can improve the quality of the decisions about what to purchase. Both are essential. Today the influence of policy needs to be brought into balance with the already established emphasis on resources.

National Security Council

When President Reagan took office, there was general agreement to limit the role of the National Security Council Staff and return to a "cabinet government" model for managing the national security process. The Administration in general has accomplished this.

Today, there are three separate but related roles for the NSC and its staff. First, the NSC is an agency for policy coordination. Second, the NSC represents and protects the interests of the President and the integrity of presidential or national-level policy. Finally, the NSC must monitor the formulation and execution of national security policy and enforce overall discipline on the system itself.

Of these three functions, the first has been performed best by the Reagan Administration; the last needs considerably more emphasis. A fundamental error was the decision to transfer from the NSC staff to the agencies the right to chair the inter-agency committees that form the body of the NSC system, such as groups dealing with the Strategic Arms Reduction Talks (START) or conventional force enhancement. It has complicated and impaired the performance of all three NSC functions, but especially the latter two. While some committees indeed have been created under the chairmanship of the National Security Advisor or his staff—including crisis management, technology transfer, and continuity of government—policy formulation in such vital areas as national security continues to be dominated by the agencies themselves. The result has been enhanced institutional resistance to fundamental policy changes, and incoherence and inefficiency in the overall policy process.

The NSC may be weakest in its most critical function, the formulation and execution of national security policy. To a degree this is so because it has no faculty for formal, long-range planning. Morever, there is no inter-agency organization whose specific duty is to identify U.S. national security objectives, formulate the broad strategic designs, and coordinate planning relative to the political, military, economic and other instruments of national power.

Department of Defense

There is ample evidence that the Administration has given serious thought to some fundamental difficulties in the department. Both acquisition and the budgeting process were early targets for change.

Deputy Secretary of Defense Frank Carlucci (and later Paul Thayer) championed a series of acquisition initiatives aimed at bringing order to that process. At the same time, revisions in the Planning, Programming, and Budgeting System (PPBS) were drafted that would put more emphasis on planning and bringing budgets more in line with objectives, policies, and strategies.

Both efforts have fallen far short of their objectives and one reason is the illogical organization of the Defense Department, which sanctions and perpetuates institutionalized parochialisms. These, in turn, are expressed in the programs, forces, and systems of the Defense budget, despite the fact that they may not necessarily constitute the most effective, imaginative, or economical response to the military threat that faces the nation. The current Defense organization also encourages frequent congressional interference and reinforces the kind of advocacy that leads to an inefficient division of both resources and military roles and missions. Creating a more efficient defense structure requires tempering the role of these advocates, placing a new emphasis on policy guidance, and fixing the budgeting and acquisition processes.

Office of the Secretary of Defense

The Department of Defense, and in particular the Office of the Secretary of Defense (OSD), is poorly organized to do its job of preparing for or conducting combined warfare. OSD organization is overly complicated, and, as a result, often inefficient. That it functions at all is largely due to the Herculean efforts of its civilian and military officials. Some expressions of this poor organization are the Secretary's unwieldy over-extended bureaucratic span of control, an illogical division of responsibilities, excessive staffing in the decision making process, and constant conflict over division of labor within and among components.

Currently, two Under Secretaries, a dozen serving Assistant Secretaries (plus, a roughly equal number of others of comparable rank), three Service Secretaries, the Chairman of the Joint Chiefs of Staff, nine field commanders, and a host of Defense Agency heads have the right to report directly to the Deputy Secretary and the Secretary. The plethora of officials reporting to the Secretary must be reduced.

A beginning point would be to reduce the host of current official titles in OSD. In addition to the Under Secretaries and Assistant Secretaries provided for by law, there are Assistant Under Secretaries, Deputy Under Secretaries, Assistant Deputy Under Secretaries, Deputy Assistant Secretaries, and Principal Deputy Assistant Secretaries. These, of course, are in addition to the Assistants to . . . , the Deputies to Assistant to . . . , and the Executive and Special Assistants to. . . Intra- and inter-agency coordination is made unnecessarily difficult by this arrangement.

Next, OSD's functions should be rationalized. Today functions and responsibilities are split (or sometimes shared) by separate chains of command. For example, the Assistant Secretaries of International Security Policy and International Security Affairs (titles that do more to confuse than to clarify the differences in their roles) have divided formerly conjoined geographical responsibilities. There is a Deputy Assistant Secretary for Europe and the Soviet Empire working for one of the Assistant Secretaries, while the rest of the world's regions have been placed under the other. Given the complexity of today's world, this unnecessarily complicates coordination. Nuclear forces have been similarly divided from general purpose forces for inexplicable reasons but with predictable results. Other areas, such as intelligence and logistics, have been artificially divided between the Under Secretaries.

Congress often has been tempted to "help" the Secretary in this area by legislating organizational arrangements. That "help" has almost always been counterproductive. A better tack would be to allow the Secretary of Defense even broader lattitude to organize his office and to make it most responsive to his direction.

Planning, Programming, and Budgeting

Dozens of in-depth, government-sponsored studies during the last 20 years, reinforced by sharp criticism from many retired senior officials, suggest that the present organization of the flow of work in national security planning is not adequate.

Too much of today's defense management is based on a Planning, Programming, and Budgeting System (PPBS) established in the early 1960s. It is through this device that the Office of the Secretary of Defense really controls the Pentagon.

The process begins in January with the release of the Secretary's "Defense Guidance." This contains an estimate of security threats and opportunities; a brief review of national and military policies and strategies by region and priority; and other major issues including needed, high-priority combat and support capabilities. The Services, with advice from the commanders of the combatant commands (CINCs), then proceed to formulate their individual program and budget requests for the upcoming five-year period—the Program Objective Memoranda (POMs). In May the POMs are forwarded for approval to the Defense Resource Board (DRB) composed of the principle OSD officials, the Service Secretaries and the Chairman of the Joint Chiefs of Staff.

During the summer, the DRB intensively reviews the several Service and Defense Agency POM submissions. DRB decisions are then returned to the Services or Agencies to be worked into a five-year budget and then later consolidated into a Pentagon Five-Year Defense Plan.

This system has several deficiencies:

- Throughout the PPBS process, the commanders, who use forces, and the Joint Chiefs of Staff, who are responsible for preparing joint strategic plans for global warfare, function only in an advisory capability. The providers—not the users—make the decisions.
- Several critical decision-making steps—strategy formulation, requirement analysis, and other steps to operating the forces—lay outside the PPBS process.
- The influence of the Services and Agencies on resource allocation far outweighs that of the joint staff and CINCs. The central responsibilities for integrating policy and resources—coordinating the efforts of all the principal actors—are short-circuited.

These long standing deficiencies in the defense management system strongly suggest that, in addition to obvious structural reforms, the programming and budgeting responsibilities of the Services and Agencies should be revised fundamentally. Defense budgets should be shaped by plans that implement strategic designs, not by parochial service interests or bureaucratic politics.

Policy guidance from the Secretary must be brought into balance with resource interests. A Defense Policy Board (DPB) should be established to highlight the Defense Guidance and other policy outputs. It should be headed by the Under Secretary for Policy and constituted similarly to the Defense Resource Board (DRB). The DPB should determine such defense policies as regional and global politico-military missions, the utilization of forces, broad force employment guidance to include the employment of nuclear weapons. These essentially are the "political" decisions relative to the employment of forces.

These "policy" decisions will guide military strategy formulation by the Joint Chiefs of Staff and the Joint Staff, and derivative planning in the combatant commands.

Following this strategic and operational planning, the responsibility for requirements analysis—detailing the resources needed to implement the plans—falls naturally to the Services and agencies are charged to train, equip and support the forces. The resource requirements derived by the separate Services, should then be forwarded to the Joint Chiefs of Staff, where they would be reconciled with joint plans and strategy. Consolidated requirements would then be sent to the Defense Resource Board for approval. In sharp contrast to today's procedure, this Defense Resource Board (DRB) will debate consolidated resource requirements derived from plans prepared by the operators, not the separate Service requirements generated by programmers.

The Joint Chiefs of Staff

Today the Joint Chiefs of Staff (JCS) organization suffers some critical deficiencies and the very limited reforms enacted in 1984 did little to mitigate them. The JCS, as a body, is seen by many civilian leaders as either unable or unwilling to provide useful advice on tough issues. Joint Staff work comes across as superficial, predictable, and of little help in resolving issues.

Several problems are particularly acute. First, the planning and the formulation of national military strategy that should occur in the joint arena is wholly inadequate. The individual military Services have clear views, but some coherent joint military view has been conspicuously absent. Second, the allocation of Service roles and missions is a function that the current organization essentially has abdicated. Last, as discussed above, the JCS plays no meaningful role in the resource allocation and budgeting process.

The roots of these problems are organizational; they lie in the inherent weakness of the joint structure and the overwhelming influence of the separate Services. Some of the weaknesses of the JCS are self-imposed. The Joint Chiefs have agreed to act only in unanimity, but unanimity is hard to achieve. Service parochialism is as ubiquitous as it is legendary, and the Services, which the Chiefs individually represent, cooperate only grudgingly. Often the wording of advice or recommendations that all the Services finally will endorse is so innocuous that it has little value—the fabled "common denominator" advice.

Strategy Formulation

The current U.S. approach to strategy formulation is a prime example of this difficulty. It implies, through the necessity for consensus, a belief that sound intellectual arguments will convince even the most stubborn Service devotee. In fact, good arguments seldom win out when people and organizations seek foremost to protect their own visions and organizational "turf."

The Joint Chiefs of Staff and their Joint Staff are tasked by law and by Department of Defense directive to develop strategies and contingency plans that require unified strategic direction. Yet, the JCS and the Joint Staff have not been an effective force in strategy planning. The reason is that the individual Services dominate the joint process. Today the Army, Navy, Air Force and Marine Corps vie with each other for the resources necessary to carry out their own Service-centered strategies. Each is convinced that its forces and capabilities are the most important in attaining the nation's objectives. Beyond the goal of deterring nuclear war, the Navy has pressed for a Maritime strategy, while the Army has put forward a Continentalist approach in which its forces would play a more central role. Both compete with the Air Force's strategic air power interests. The prize is the resources that would allow them to shape forces in molds of their individual making.

This situation is unsatisfactory. American military strategies must be based on an evaluation of the nation's interests and objectives—and the threats to those interests and objectives. Military strategy formulation should be handled by the Joint Staff, in coordination with the commanders of the combatant commands (CINCs) and Services. Subordinate operational plans should be developed by the CINCs and approved by the JCS. Only then can decisions be made about the force structure—the way the Services organize to fight. Each Service has unique characteristics and capabilities that must be considered and carefully orchestrated in the development of these strategies. By definition, such unified actions means overcoming the parochialism inherent when individual Services develop the strategic concepts. This means the creation of a stronger joint structure.

General John Vessey, the Reagan Administration's Chairman of the Joint Chiefs, has instituted some changes, but a conflict of interest persists between the Joint Staff and the Service staffs in such key areas as force planning and resource allocation. Efforts, for example, by the new Joint Special Operation Agency to influence (or even monitor) the development of special operations forces have been simply rejected by the individual Services. It is clear that before coherent strategy choices can be made, structural and organization reforms will be required to strengthen the joint system relative to power of the Services. This will require legislation.

Roles and Missions

The current assignment of roles and missions to the various services dates back to agreements reached shortly after World War II. New technologies and techniques, however, blur the distinctions. The Army, for example, with its growing number of attack helicopters has usurped much of the close-air-support role from the Air Force. Longer range Naval aircraft, meanwhile, have invaded the manned strategic nuclear bomber role that the Air Force long assumed was its own. Such confusion of roles leads to duplication and redundancy.

Mission definition is equally inadequate. Incongruous boundaries between commands—unified and combined—inevitably lead to inefficiencies and possibly to disaster. Services want missions because they bring increased resources and career opportunities. The JCS, not surprisingly, has proved incapable of altering established role and mission allocations or in making new ones—except to allocate some part of new missions to each Service. Often cited as examples of this are the ill-fated Iranian and the successful Grenada rescues. The solution was, in each case, to assign some role to each Service—despite inadequate joint doctrine or even the ability to communicate effectively. The inability of the JCS to develop a coherent strategy for force employment into Southwest Asia, should such action become necessary, unfortunately is typical of the inadequacies in the current system.

This has led to a rather *ad hoc* force structure based on each Service's independent reading of strategy design and associated roles and missions.

The "ecumenical" approach to defense has other unfortunate effects. When all the Services must be allowed to participate in every operation, the predictable result is overlapping missions and duplication of effort. Each of the Services has special operations forces—and some, like the Army, have several breeds. Each of the Services has its own separate "air force," and in the Air Force itself there are at least three.

The U.S. cannot afford the confusion and duplication inherent in this situation. The military may always have some duplication of capabilities, but there is little excuse for duplicating roles and missions. A new process of assigning roles and missions is required.

Roles and missions should be derived from national military strategies and prescribed joint doctrine; it must be a top down approach. This requires the strengthening of the organization charged with formulating military strategy and joint doctrine—the Joint Staff.

The Joint Staff must be capable of resisting the power of the individual Services. It must be sufficiently independent to be able to insist that, when the situation dictates, an operation can fall fully under the purview of a single Service. That the Marines, for example, with their associated Navy support, could be made responsible for an entire operation; that the Army and Air Force need not play any direct role.

Reorganization

A main cause of the Joint Chiefs of Staff problem is widely acknowledged to be the juxtaposition of a weak joint staff system and strong Service Departments. "The present system," reported a 1978 Defense Department study of the military command structure, "makes it difficult for the Joint Staff to produce persuasively argued joint papers which transcend Service positions."[1]

The lack of influence of the JCS is an institutional problem. Its insistence on unanimity makes the system a prisoner of any one of the Services. General David Jones, a former Air Force Chief and then Chairman of the Joint Chiefs, illustrated the problem for the House Armed Services Committee. "For a substantive paper of some length, each Service action officer may have as many as 100 recommended changes. They quickly learn the art of compromise—each agreeing to support the balance of the changes proposed by the other in return for equal support. . . . In sum, the current Joint Staff process encourages compromise, relies too heavily on Service participation, and depends on staff officers who are well versed in Service interests, but are ill

1. Richard C. Steadman, *National Military Comand Structure [Study]*, July 1978.

prepared to address issues from a joint perspective."[2] The only member no longer beholden to a Service is the Chairman, but he has little independent authority and few resources upon which to draw. The Joint Staff does not even work for him.

At the top, the Chiefs are expected to make decisions for their Service wearing one hat, and then, wearing another, sit in judgment of them. JCS advice on budget matters is a good example. Service pressures are so great that the Chiefs are seldom able to give up popular Service programs. As a result, they cannot set the priorities that could produce a less costly but equally effective defense budget.

Service strategic thinking is motivated more by competition over constrained defense resources than by clear-headed strategic analysis. Bureaucratic politics and parochial service concerns dominate the JCS process.

A 1970 Blue Ribbon Defense Panel concluded that JCS unanimity in recommendations and advice was more often evidence of accommodation of all Service views than of tough, objective thinking. The roots of this Service parochialism, the report found, lay above all in the fact that staff officers' careers were so closely tied "to the prosperity of their Service."

The situation has not improved since that study. Because of its structure, the Joint Chiefs often cannot deal realistically with issues that affect Service interests. These are matters of fundamental importance to national security: the formation of military strategies; the allocation of resources to various defense missions; the assignment of geographical and functional responsibilities among the field commanders; roles and missions of the services; and joint doctrine and training.

Through the years, a number of studies have addressed this problem and have made strikingly similar proposals. Virtually all have recommended strengthening the role of the Chairman of the JCS and of the Joint Staff. This action is long overdue. Only organization change will shift the emphasis from inherent Service interests to essential joint performance. The Congress took some very tentative steps in this direction in 1984 but has not gone nearly far enough. Both houses have pledged to take up again the issues of JCS reform and comprehensive DOD organizational reform with the intent of enacting legislation in 1985.

Most of what could be fixed in the "jointness" arena under existing authority of the President or Secretary of Defense has been attempted, with little effect. The Administration, therefore, should encourage

---

2. General David C. Jones, Written responses to staff questions. "1982 House Hearings on JCS Reorganization," [H.A.S.C. No. 97-47] p. 95.

immediate congressional action to strengthen the role and voice of the Chairman, the Joint Staff, and the combatant commands.

The Service Secretariates

The power and traditional independence of the separate military departments is steeped in U.S. tradition and has its merits. Yet it also makes joint planning very difficult. The current separate department secretariate structure allows circumvention of directives or issues that might work to an individual Service's disadvantage. The Service Secretaries, at the behest of their military leadership, can and often do take such issues around the JCS to the Secretary of Defense, or even around the Secretary to the President or the Congress. Given the political dynamics of the Washington policy process, Congress even encourages such action, allowing a congressional faction and a Service to champion each other. Paradoxically, the more effective the Service Secretaries are, the more difficult cooperation in the joint arena becomes.

Problems created by the Service structure were addressed by the President's Private Sector Survey on Cost Control—the Grace Commission. "Many organizations," it reports, "perform similar functions" throughout the Pentagon. The Commission cites "a number of managers who argued persuasively that the staffs reporting to the Service Secretaries are anachronisms, left over from their days of Cabinet rank. . . . " The Commission recommends "the elimination of the staffs reporting to the Service Secretaries" and the "creation of a Defense Executive Office to include the Secretary of Defense, the Service Secretaries, the Chairman of the JCS, and the Deputy Secretary of Defense."[3]

A number of studies of the role of the Service Secretariates have been conducted, and most have concluded that the Secretaries can play an important role, but that they must be absolutely loyal to and reflect the policies of the Secretary of Defense in addition to championing Service positions.

Extraordinary efforts on the part of the current Service Secretaries and Chiefs have produced two groundbreaking memoranda identifying some limited areas of interservice cooperation. The nation, however, cannot afford to rely forever on such extraordinary efforts. The structure must be altered to facilitate the joint process. The Grace Commission proposal is a step in the right direction and is consistent with the need to retain the Service Secretaries and link them more closely to the Secretary of Defense.

---

3. President's Private Sector Survey on Cost Control, *Report on the Office of the Secretary of Defense*, Spring-Fall 1983, pp.34, 37.

RECOMMENDATIONS

National Security Council

The Administration should:

- Strengthen the role of the NSC staff in the inter-agency process.
- Create a new senior inter-agency group to identify national objectives, formulate national strategy, and coordinate its planning.
- Create a long-range planning group within the NSC staff to support this latter effort.

Office of the Secretary of Defense

The Administration should:

- Reduce the position titles within the Office of the Secretary of Defense to Secretary, Deputy Secretary, Under Secretary, Assistant Secretary, and Deputy Assistant Secretary. All others should be "Assistants to" these officials.
- Reduce the span of control of the Secretary of Defense. The Service Secretaries and the Chairman of the Joint Chiefs of Staff must report to him, and the General Counsel, the Assistant Secretaries for Legislative Affairs, Public Affairs, and Comptroller have unique functions that require that they also should report directly. Others, however, should report through two Under Secretaries—one for Policy and one for Resources.
- Rationalize OSD's functions in light of the recommendation above. The Under Secretary for Policy should coordinate Regional Affairs (to include Security Assistance); Nuclear Policy; Defense Intelligence; Security Affairs (including technology transfer); Reserve Affairs; and Strategic Defense. The Under Secretary for Resources should coordinate Defense Research; Acquisition Management and Logistics; Mobilization Management; Manpower; Command, Control and Communication; and Requirements, Test and Evaluation Policy.
- Create a Defense Policy Board (DPB), to produce the Defense Guidance and other political-military policy outputs. It should be headed by the Under Secretary for Policy and constituted similarity to the current Defense Resource Board.
- Restructure the current budgeting process in order that programming and budgeting by the Services and Agencies is: (1) guided by

requirements for weapons, support systems, forces, and manpower identified by the combatant commands; (2) reviewed and consolidated by the Joint Staff; and (3) approved by the Defense Resource Board. These requirements must reflect both the Defense Policy Board's guidance, and the strategies and plans prepared by the uniformed Joint Staff and field commands.

Joint Chiefs of Staff

The Administration should:

- Strengthen the role of the nation's senior military officer and provide him with a four-star deputy. The Chairman of the Joint Chiefs of Staff should: (1) be authorized to give military advice in his own right to the President, National Security Council and the Secretary of Defense; (2) "supervise" the combatant commands in addition to acting as their "spokesman"; (3) be placed expressly in the national military chain of command; (4) manage the Joint Staff on his own behalf; (5) select officers for assignment not only to the Joint Staff but also to all joint billets; (6) recommend to the Secretary of Defense the promotion (in their service lines) of fitting officers occupying joint billets.
- Strengthen the Joint Staff by: providing that it work for the Chairman (and not the corporate JCS); by enlarging it in accordance with its enhanced role; and by insuring that officers serving on the Joint Staff continue to return to the field at regular intervals for assignment to either Service or joint billets.
- Assign the Chairman of the Joint Chiefs of Staff, the responsibility for formulating military strategies keyed to the political-military policies and objectives articulated in the guidance formulated by the new Defense Policy Board and issued by the Secretary of Defense.
- Assign the Chairman of the Joint Chiefs of Staff the responsibility for allocating Service roles and missions based on guidance of the Defense Policy Board and the military strategies developed from it.

Service Secretariates

The Administration should:

- Create a Defense Executive Office, as recommended by the Grace

Commission, containing the Secretary of Defense, the Service Secretaries, the Chairman of the Joint Chiefs of Staff, and the Deputy Secretary of Defense.
- Assign the Service Secretaries a larger role in assisting the Secretary of Defense as the Secretary's primary advisors on Service matters.
- Insure that presidential nominations to all positions in DoD (including the Service Secretaries) are reviewed by the Secretary of Defense.

* * *

Defense Acquisition and Logistics

With the key modernization programs in both the strategic and conventional arenas well underway, the Secretary of Defense must now personally undertake a new effort to make significant cost and performance improvements in the acquisition process and the bureaucratic culture within which it operates. The nation must move beyond the volatile and dangerously unpredictable defense spending cycles of the past.

The United States has chosen to rely on technological superiority, but that edge must be real, not just theoretical. In an era when major weapon system development—from concept to fielding—often takes fifteen years or more, and when the effective life of key technologies comes in three to five year cycles, the U.S. appears to be approaching the point when systems will be increasingly outdated even as they roll off the assembly lines. With Soviet weapon system development on a substantially shorter cycle, the U.S. technological edge might soon be in jeopardy.

Virtually every study on the acquisition process in the last ten years has come to the same conclusions. The U.S. must:
- Establish program stability.
- Install realistic budgeting and cost estimating.
- Improve weapon system availability (or readiness) and the ability to support those systems.
- Make capabilities match planned performance.
- Make contracting more effective through multi-year procurement, competition based on quality, and economic rates of production.
- Make managers and companies accountable for their actions, decisions, policies, and contracts.

These are likewise the conclusions of this study and also are found in the acquisition initiatives sought by the Reagan Administration. This latter effort, however, has not proved particularly effective. The problem is not what to do—here there is much agreement—but how to do it. All of the functional elements of the process must be attacked simultaneously, and borrowing from the military lexicon, the principle of mass must be observed. This principle indicates that overwhelming force should be applied at the critical points and at the critical moment. This "mass" can only be created by the Secretary of Defense; lesser forces are demonstrably inadequate. The history of DoD suggests that real reform requires the concerted effort of the Secretary himself.

Five phenomena—five points of attack—are key to any reform of the system:

- Acquisition Policy;
- Organizational Structure;
- Management Information Systems;
- People Policies; and
- Acquisition Strategies and Contracting.

Acquisition Policy

Current Pentagon acquisition policies are confusing, time consuming, and costly. For example, the "milestone" approach has created the misconception that there is some point when research, developmental engineering, test and evaluation (RDTE) is completed and when production begins. This has led to ill-advised rules dictating that "production funds" cannot be expended before a particular milestone, or that RDTE funds will not be authorized afterward, or that production lines will be established only with production funds. The fact is that money needs to be spent on producibility engineering, manufacturing planning, tooling, and maintenance and test equipment from the start. New guidance is needed to insure that funds for these activities are available early in the process. Some projects might be scrapped after early production money was spent, but the savings in both time and money on the majority would far offset any losses.

Organizational Structure

The functional elements of the acquisition and logistics process are currently misaligned. For example, combining Research, Development, Test and Evaluation creates internal contradictions and diametrically opposed objectives. The basic acquisition functions should be realigned as follows:

- Requirements Identification; Test and Evaluation. The agency that defines the functional requirements should play a key role in insuring that they are met in the final product.
- Research. "Research" is linked by habit with "development"—the term "R&D" is ingrained. Research, however, is most effective when freed from specific development and "development" is better treated in train with "production."
- Development; Production; Acquisition Logistics. Hard experience reinforces the notion that production considerations need to be treated early in the development process. The same is true of logistics or considerations of reliability, availability and maintainability.

The current Pentagon organizational layering causes repetitious staff program reviews. This must be minimized. This means increasing staff accountability at some levels, particularly in the planning phases, while reducing staff interference in others. A better management information system would reduce the need for so many reviews.

Management Information Systems

Today numerous data bases are used by managers throughout the Pentagon, with little interaction among them. It is a near certainty that what emerges as total costs or unit costs (or any other specific factor) for any given program will differ markedly from one data base to another. To develop clear audit trails, to ensure that adequate resources are committed at the time of a decision, and to force cost discipline in the process, the various data bases must function as a single system. Changes in one parameter must automatically trigger the appropriate responses in all affected areas. An effective management information system must become a high priority.

People Policies

Acquisition management is one of several areas in which personnel policies must be revised so they do not discourage highly qualified people from seeking Pentagon careers. Military officers must be allowed to specialize at mid-career. Uniformed project managers average less than three years in their positions, and many come to the jobs with no prior experience in that field. The longer tours prescribed in legislation in 1984 are desirable, but a strong professional background in acquisition management is even more essential. After some ten or fifteen years' service, after having qualified in an entry specialty, and after demonstrating an aptitude for acquisition management, selected officers should be invited to specialize in that area and assigned to work in that field for the balance of their careers. They should not suffer significant career penalities for doing so.

More also needs to be done to attract successful mid-career corporate executives and professionals to temporary government service. Current rules requiring divestiture of stock holdings in defense industries should be modified to provide roll-over into other investments without tax penalty. Under today's rules, a successful executive and wise investor could pay as much in capital gain taxes as he would make in a government salary, simply for the privilege of serving the country.

Acquisition Strategies and Contracting

Competition is the key to changes in the acquisition process, but competition should be based on quality. Today's system focuses on price. There is even a "best and final" bidding process through which prices are auctioned down. The net results are lower quality and artificially low prices that firms expect to raise in the process of the inevitable contract changes.

The objective should be to create a "competition culture" built around quality, and effective, "win-win" concepts of business. To do this the concept of "profit" must be shifted from one based on a percentage of cost, to one based on a realistic return on investment. At the same time it must be recognized that there are cases where competition can be effectively initiated only at the sub-contractor level. Market forces, allowed to operate in an environment as free of regulation as possible, are the best insurance of an effective, competitive contract process. The new Federal Acquisition Regulations (FAR) establish such an environment. They are much less detailed than the older guidelines and their utilization will require professional growth in the acquisition and contracting community. That growth needs to be fostered and encouraged. The opposite, in fact, seems to be taking place. The Services are beginning to encumber this process by attaching their own more extensive set of "interpretations." These add an unnecessary layer of regulation and should be abolished.

RECOMMENDATIONS

Defense Acquisition and Logistics

The Administration should:

- Revise Department of Defense Directive 5000.1 to state explicitly that approval for full scale development carries with it the authority to program and obligate funds for critical production engineering and associated activities.

- Realign the organizational structures—both at the policy-making and execution levels—to reflect new functional linkages:
  —Requirement Identification; and Test and Evaluation.
  —Research.
  —Development; Production; and Acquisition Logistics.
- Reduce the level or number of program reviews.
- Install an effective and interactive Information Management System and make it the sole source of program and budget data.
- Install personnel policies that encourage competent professionals—from the military services and from the private sector—to seek appointments to careers in defense acquisition management without incurring excessive career or financial penalties.
- Revise acquisition policies to encourage: competition based on quality instead of cost; and profit based on return on investment instead of cost.
- Fully implement the new Federal Acquisition Regulations (FAR) in Defense by: encouraging professional growth among defense contracting personnel to allow them to work in an environment more free of detailed regulation; and discouraging the individual Services from issuing their own more detailed "interpretations" of the FAR.

20

Regaining Control of The Department of State

by
James T. Hackett

The election of a conservative president in 1980 provided a rare opportunity to make the State Department more responsive to the will of the American people. Over the years, foreign policy-making has been abdicated generally to liberal, internationalist academics, lawyers and foreign policy "experts." They have run American foreign policy, regardless of whether a Democrat or Republican occupied the White House. For them, continuity in foreign policy became an end in itself and a permanent goal.

The election of Ronald Reagan signalled changes in foreign policy, conflicting with the pervasive desire for continuity. The prospect of major policy and personnel changes made the career bureaucrats gravely apprehensive. Secretary of State Alexander Haig, Jr., later described the situation in his book *Caveat:* "The most difficult management problem faced by any incoming Administration is the inertia of the bureaucracy. It is like an asteroid, spinning in an eccentric orbit, captured by the gravity of its procedures and its self-interest, deeply suspicious of politicians who threaten its stability by changing its work habits . . . I found no great enthusiasm in the Department of State for the Reagan Administration."

The trouble is, while Haig understood the problem, he did not correct it. A career Army officer, he mistakenly chose to work through the career bureaucracy. He set the tone of his tenure the day after his arrival in Washington as Secretary-designate, when he met with and dismissed the Reagan transition team. By this, he earned the enthusiastic support of the career foreign service and much of the media. After that, the White House and members of Congress encouraged the appointment of conservatives to State Department policy-making positions, but had only limited success. As a result, the State Department has been staffed at the policy level mainly by senior career officers and relatively liberal non-career appointees, few of whom are dedicated to the Reagan agenda.

The problems faced by the new Administration were compounded by congressional passage, just a month before the election, of the

Foreign Service Act of 1980. This was a major revision of the legislation governing the career foreign service. It had been drafted by the Carter Administration and re-written by liberal congressional staffs working with the foreign service labor unions. By limiting the authority of agency management over career personnel, the Act seriously handicaps the President's appointees in trying to manage the foreign affairs agencies (primarily the State Department, the U.S. Information Agency, and the Agency for International Development).

This new legislation, combined with restrictive labor-management agreements, has produced a foreign service bureaucracy almost totally removed from the oversight of the Administration elected by the people. The U.S. foreign service has become a self-governing bureaucracy. Its members decide who gets in, who gets promoted, who gets bonuses and who can be extended beyond mandatory retirement, with little interference from the President's appointees. When management tries to exercise authority, the unions cry "politicization" to their friends in Congress and the press, putting a political connotation on efforts to exercise good management.

Unlike the laws governing the civil service, the Foreign Service Act does not define senior officers as management officials. As a result, career officers appointed by the President to top policy jobs remain members of the union bargaining unit. The conflict of interest is obvious, but more important, career officers in senior management positions can influence personnel appointments and assignments, including State Department nominations sent to the White House for ambassadorships and top-level Department positions. The State Department currently has about 110 career officers serving as presidential appointees in slots which, by statute, may be filled by non-career political presidential appointees. In all other government agencies combined, there are only about 25 career officers serving as presidential appointees, and eleven of those are inspectors general.

With such a large number of career officers in top-level positions, the foreign service bureaucracy exerts a powerful influence on staffing levels (they want more), the State Department budget (always higher), foreign policy recommendations (liberal and cautious), and implementation of the Administration's foreign policy directives (slowly).

To assure effective management and needed oversight of the foreign service, and the fulfillment of the President's agenda, the State Department's top positions must be filled by dedicated supporters of the President and his policies. Foreign policy can be more responsive to the will of the electorate. It is standard practice in most government agencies to fill policy-making positions with non-career supporters of the President. The State Department should not be an exception.

The structure of the State Department intensifies policy problems. The Department's division of the world into five geographic regions handled by geographic bureaus leads to parochialism and regional advocacy. As each bureau fights for the interests of the countries for which it is responsible, the interests of the United States, or of American citizens or businesses, may be accorded only incidental concern. The top management of the State Department, instead of developing policy from a global perspective, often serves as referee between competing regional bureaus, with the most powerful bureau, or bureau head, determining policy. Recommendations frequently are watered down to accommodate the narrow concerns of a regional bureau.

The State Department lacks adequate oversight. By law, both the Chairman of the Board and Director General of the Foreign Service must be senior members of the career service. Similarly, the Inspector General of the Foreign Service traditionally has been a career officer. The State Department has opposed a 1983 General Accounting Office recommendation that the Department should be brought under the Inspector General Act. This would improve oversight by requiring inspections by professional inspectors, not members of the foreign service. Because career foreign service officers frequently change assignments and in the future may be subordinate to an officer they have to inspect, they cannot be expected to produce fully candid inspection reports. Regardless of good intentions, the conflict of interest is too great for the foreign service to police itself. In addition, many in the Department have a cavalier attitude toward federal expenditures that warrants careful review. Most of the Federal Government is subject to the oversight of the Office of Personnel Management (OPM). There is no good reason for the foreign service to be exempt from either the Inspector General Act or OPM's oversight.

Another conflict of interest exists in the Bureau of International Organization Affairs, which is responsible for submitting to the United Nations the names of United States citizens to fill positions in the U.N. Secretariat and U.N. specialized agencies. The Department frequently submits the names of retired or retiring foreign service officers to fill these positions, with the result that U.S. appointees are not drawn from the population at large.

INITIATIVES FOR 1985

1) Take charge of Presidential Appointments.

The President should exercise his constitutional authority to name supporters of his policies to all presidential appointments, including ambassadorships. He should authorize the White House Office of Presidential Personnel to overrule agency heads when necessary to assure that supporters of the his policies are placed in all policy-determining positions.

2) Require the Office of Presidential Personnel to limit strictly the practice of placing career foreign service officers in non-career, policy-determining positions.

3) Direct the Office of Personnel Management to assume oversight review of the foreign service, as it does for the civil service.

4) Order that the White House, rather than the State Department, forward to the U.N. all recommendations for the appointment of U.S. citizens to the U.N. Secretariat and specialized agencies.

5) Ask Congress to amend the Foreign Service Act.

Specifically, Congress should add "members of the Senior Foreign Service" to the categories of management officials listed in Section 1002(12), thereby designating senior officers as part of management rather than labor.

6) Request Congress to amend Sections 208 and 210 of the Foreign Service Act.

This would be to remove the requirements that the Director General and Chairman of the Board of the Foreign Service be selected from the career service. In addition, to provide adequate oversight, the Chairman of the Board of the Foreign Service should be a presidential appointee *not* drawn from the career service.

7) Comply with the 1983 GAO recommendation to place the State Department under the Inspector General Act, and staff its inspection corps with professional inspectors who are not members of the foreign service.

8) Consider a reorganization of the State Department.

The reorganization should abolish the five regional bureaus and reassign their responsibilities to bureaus with functional responsibilities, such as political, economic, military and scientific affairs. Such a change would break up the Department's regional fiefdoms and permit a substantial reduction in chronic overstaffing.

21

The War Powers Resolution

by
Mark Greenberg*

The War Powers Resolution, enacted at the height of concern about the war in Vietnam and the "Imperial Presidency," was meant to protect the nation from initiation of hostilities by the Executive. The Resolution states that it is intended to define and limit the constitutional power of the President to commit troops "into hostilities or into situations where imminent involvement is indicated by the circumstances to situations in which . . . 1) there has been a declaration of war, 2) there is specific statutory authorization, or 3) there is a national emergency created by an attack upon the United States, its territories or possessions, or its armed forces."[1]

Prior to the introduction of troops, the President is required to consult with Congress in every possible instance, and the Resolution requires that the President sustain this consultation until such time as "American forces are no longer engaged in hostilities, or have been removed from such situations."

Should a President introduce troops into a situation covered by the Resolution, the Resolution requires him to submit to Congress a report within 48 hours setting forth the circumstances necessitating the introduction and the scope and duration of American involvement.

Under the Resolution, the President must terminate American military involvement within 60 to 90 days after the introduction of troops. An extension of this is permissible only if Congress declares war, passes legislation authorizing it, extends the period by statute, or is unable to meet.

At any time, Congress has the authority to terminate U.S. involvement by means of a Concurrent Resolution—a congressional action that must be approved by a majority vote of both Houses of Congress but which is not sent on to the President for approval or veto.

The constitutional and practical dilemmas created by the Resolution have become ever more obvious. The June 23, 1983, decision by the Supreme Court in *I.N.S. v. Chadha*[2] raised serious constitutional

---

*The author would like to acknowledge the assistance of Professor Robert Scigliano. He is in no way responsible for the views expressed here.

[1]Public Law 93-148, 85 Stat 555, 50 USC 1541-1548.

[2]*I.N.S. v. Chadha*, June 23, 1983 (103 S. Ct. 2764).

questions about the ability of Congress by Concurrent Resolution to direct unilaterally the withdrawal of troops committed by the President from a potentially hostile environment. In that case, the Court held that nullification of Executive action by the Congress—a "legislative veto"—was unconstitutional unless it was submitted to the President for his signature or veto. Therefore, the requirement that the President withdraw U.S. troops in compliance with a Concurrent Resolution by the Congress would appear to be unconstitutional.

The Resolution also is constitutionally flawed because it fails to take into account the full extent of the President's powers as Commander-in-Chief.[3] While no President has the authority to take the U.S. from a state of peace into war, there are situations that may require the use of the armed forces, many of which do not require a formal declaration of war or other formal legislative authorization.

"Foreign War" was legally defined in 1800 by the Supreme Court case of *Bas v. Tingy*.[4] The Court held that war is a "contention by force between two nations, in external matters, under the authority of their respective governments." The Constitution recognizes that there are hostilities which are "less than" war and the President has the authority to use troops to protect the nation and its citizens. Yet the War Powers Resolution, unlike the Constitution, fails to take these circumstances into account. Any commitment of troops not formally authorized by Congress, unless as a result of "a national emergency created by an attack on the United States, its territories or possessions, or its armed forces" would appear to be a violation of the Resolution. Certain presidential actions, however, may be essential to U.S. safety and fully consistent with the Constitution.

Perhaps the most obvious instance is the use of troops to protect Americans abroad from danger. In fact, in the Slaughterhouse Cases,[5] the court specifically identified one of the privileges and immunities granted to citizens under the Constitution as "the protection of the Federal government over his life, liberty and property when on the high seas or within the jurisdiction of a foreign government." There have been a number of recent instances of this legitimate use of force. For example, while Congress was debating authorizing legislation that he had requested, President Gerald Ford acted quickly and used force to evacuate American troops from Cambodia and Vietnam in April

---

[3]For an insightful discussion of this issue see Robert Scigliano, "The War Powers Resolution and the War Powers" in J. Bessette and J. Tullis, *The Presidency in the Constitutional Order* (Baton Rouge: Louisiana State University Press, 1981), pp. 124-143.

[4]Dallas 37,43 (1800).

[5]16 Wall 36 (1873).

1975. A legally more cautious, if irresponsible, President might have abandoned U.S. citizens to their fate. One month later, President Ford used troops to rescue the crew of the U.S. freighter Mayaguez, again without authorization. President Carter, recognizing the necessity for secrecy and dispatch, took similar action in his ill-fated attempt to rescue the hostages held in Iran.

The constitutional authority of the President extends to other actions as well. A President, generally speaking, is not in violation of the Constitution if, for example, he sends troops into other nations at the request of that nation, if he uses the armed forces against terrorist groups, or when he sends the Navy into international waters; nor does he violate the Constitution when he responds to the hostile acts of other nations. The shooting down of two Libyan warplanes in the Gulf of Sidra on August 19, 1981, was a clear exercise of a President's constitutional authority.

The War Powers Resolution ignores the constitutional authority of the President as Commander-in-Chief, and it substitutes congressional judgment of, and control over, Executive action.

The Administration should seek to amend the Resolution to make it conform with the Constitution:

1) The purposes and policy section should be rewritten explicitly to permit the President to exercise his constitutional authority.

It should specify clearly that there are hostilities short of war, and that the President can engage U.S. forces in these under his authority as Commander-in-Chief.

2) The section providing that Congress can terminate a troop commitment by concurrent resolution should be amended.

The decision in *Chadha* mandates that legislation (requiring the withdrawal of troops) be submitted to the President for his signature or his veto. In addition, other procedural changes would improve the Resolution.

3) Consultation should be limited to specified members of Congress.

These should include the Speaker and Minority Leader of the House, the Majority and Minority Leaders of the Senate, and the Chairmen and ranking members of the Foreign Affairs and Foreign Relations Committee.

While the War Powers Resolution requires that the President "in every possible instance shall consult with Congress," such consultation is a logistical impossibility. For practical purposes, it is irrelevant whether or not the Resolution means seeking the advice of every member or merely letting them know; even the notification of 535 members is a herculean task. More important, the secrecy surrounding an American operation might be compromised. Further, Congressmen not consulted could use this as a convenient rationale for opposing a particular presidential action, rather than having to take a position only on the merits.

4) The requirement that the President report to the Congress within 48 hours should be modified.

The Commander-in-Chief may well be involved not only in planning and overseeing a military operation, but also in sensitive negotiations. To require a report within 48 hours places too stringent a limitation on the President. Section 4a should be amended to modify the 48-hour period with "whenever possible."

5) The requirement that the President must withdraw troops within 60 days if Congress fails to authorize their continued commitment must be reviewed.

Whether or not this is constitutional is debatable, but it is bad public policy.[6] A 60-day limitation guarantees the intransigence of opponents who have the slightest military reason to stay the course. In the hope—some might say the expectation—that Congress will act to reverse the commitment, U.S. enemies have every reason to resist. In some instances, moreover, the 60-day clause may prompt a President to escalate U.S. involvement rapidly. Rather than restrain an Executive, therefore, the Resolution as currently written might well force him to more extreme military measures.

Conclusion

Debate of the War Powers Resolution to date has been limited and has lacked a serious examination of the constitutional implications and the practical consequences of the measure.

The War Powers Resolution has in practice made procedure, rather than principle or prudence, the standard for judging presidential action. Deployment of troops abroad allows members of Congress to remain silent on the merits of deployment, while assailing the President for ignoring procedural requirements. They are able to avoid association with military action while standing up for "the law." In this way, Congressmen take the safest possible political stance for themselves, at the cost of possibly endangering the lives of U.S. soldiers and U.S. security. A serious debate over the War Powers Resolution is overdue and is a necessary first step toward improving the overly restrictive doctrine.

---

[6] For a persuasive argument that this provision is unconstitutional see Robert F. Turner, *The War Powers Resolution: Its Implementation in Theory and Practice.* (Philadelphia: Foreign Policy Research Institute, 1983) pp. 107-109.

Part 4

Implementing the Mandate

by

Michael Sanera

Introduction

Policy change in Washington is exceedingly difficult. Assuming a will to implement the policy recommendations contained in the previous parts of *Mandate II*, President Reagan and his political appointees must find a way. This part of *Mandate II* will discuss why policy change is so difficult and describe techniques which political appointees can use to overcome the difficulties. This part will, therefore, focus on the role of political appointees—secretaries, under secretaries, deputy secretaries and assistant secretaries—in producing policy change. These officials will be referred to as "political executives." Particular emphasis will be placed on the largely unheralded duties of assistant secretaries, who may rightly be considered the front line troops of policy change. In addition, it is hoped that the advice presented here will benefit all political appointees, including non-career SES and Schedule C appointees, and be of interest to students of the political process.

Following a presidential election, Americans expect implementation of the electoral mandate. In some cases this requires legislative changes and the cooperation of Congress. In other cases, the administrative and policy-making powers of the President can be used. While the political executive plays a vital role in both processes, it is the latter which is the greater concern in this discussion. Political executives have a great deal of latitude within which they can change policy without going to Congress for changes in statutes. This part of *Mandate II* is intended to show the new political executive how to make policy changes within present statutory provisions by making administrative and regulatory changes.

Failure of the political executive to make and implement policy through administrative, regulatory, and policy-making actions is not just a failure to implement the President's program, it is a failure of the democratic process. Administrative discretion and policy-making powers continue to exist and are used by non-elected players in the policy process to implement their objectives. The bureaucracy and special interest groups are very adept at filling the vacuum left by weak and ineffective political leadership. Thus, for the democratic process to operate, the will of the electorate that is expressed in a presidential election must be passed through the President to his political executives to become effective policy change.

No mere list of administrative "dos" and "don'ts" will enable political executives to carry out their responsibilities for policy change. Rather, a broad-based understanding of the political environment in the federal government is necessary. The following chapters will pursue that end through a discussion which adapts knowledge taken from the literature of public administration to the job of the Reagan political executive.

The first chapter discusses the role of the political executive and how that role differs from the role of the typical business manager; the second discusses the political, bureaucratic, and policy environment of the political executive. The third chapter focuses on the specific difficulties or "constraints" faced by the political executive. The fourth chapter describes how the political executive plans and implements effective strategies for positive policy change. The final chapter presents three case studies that illustrate the ideas contained in the previous chapters.

22

Background[1]

The Role of the Political Executive

> Assuming the leadership of an established bureau was thus in many respects like first stepping into a large, fast-flowing river.[2]

Most political executives come to Washington with expectations of making changes. They are fresh from the campaign trail and ready to implement the mandate produced by the election. Often this enthusiasm is followed 18 to 24 months later by a departure from Washington with feelings of frustration and disillusionment.[3] Why does this occur? Or an even better question is, why should it not occur? Most political executives have little relevant experience for the complex political and administrative environment in Washington.[4] Yet they are expected to be able to make major changes in that environment in a short period of 18 months. Turnover is high and repeat performances are fewer than popularly believed.[5] To expect political executives to do anything but be swept along with the current is to expect too much. To avoid this, they must know what they want to do and how to do it. The first and most important step in this process is for the political executive to have a clear understanding of his role and his new political environment.

The principal role of the political executive is not simply to manage the government efficiently, but to produce "policy change." In order to master the process of policy change, the political executive must understand two concepts: the complex nature of public policy and the reality of bureaucratic discretion. Public policy exists on two levels: macro policy, which consists of legislation passed by Congress; and micro policy, that is, regulations issued to implement legislation and administrative actions taken within strictures of existing regulations. Thus, public policy is not merely a bill passed by the Congress and signed into law by the President; policy is what is actually produced by the bureaucracy. It is critical for the political executive to understand that policy exists in the actual operation of his organization and that much of that policy was determined by previous administrations and/or the career bureaucracy acting on its own judgment. The political executive must become deeply involved in the actual administrative operation of his organization in order to recognize existing policy, understand the policy machinery, and develop strategies for change.

The political executive will produce policy change by exercising bureaucratic discretion, which is defined as "the ability of an administrator to choose among alternatives—to decide how the policies of the government should be implemented in specific cases."[6] Bureaucratic discretion is used in the transformation of legislated (macro) policy into actual administrative actions (micro) policy. Bureaucratic discretion exists at all levels of government from the "street level" decisions of a policeman who decides whether or not to issue a ticket, to the management decisions of a mid-level administrator who allocates grant funds among research proposals with different political implications. The following two examples will illustrate the operation of bureaucratic discretion in the determination of public policy of considerable importance.

- In 1974, the state of Utah imposed a work requirement on welfare mothers in the Aid to Families with Dependent Children Program. HEW, using its bureaucratic discretion, declared Utah's program illegal and demanded that Utah abolish the work requirement. The state of Utah refused; the federal government responded by terminating all federal AFDC funding to Utah, which proceeded to run its AFDC program entirely on state funds for two years. In 1976, after extensive negotiations, the regional HEW administration ruled that work requirements were in compliance with existing law; federal funding was resumed. However, when the state of Virginia attempted to enact an identical requirement, it was ruled illegal by HEW administrators in the eastern region. (This anomolous situation was ultimately resolved only by sweeping regulatory and legislative reform during the Reagan Administration.)
- The Professional and Administrative Career Exam (PACE) was a written exam of verbal and mathematical skills designed to select recent college graduates for entry level professional and administrative positions in the government. Those personnel selected for federal positions based on their performance on the PACE formed a select pool from which the overwhelming number of mid-level career executives were recruited. Black interest groups sued the government, alleging that the PACE was discriminatory because the number of blacks hired under the PACE system was not proportional to the number of blacks taking the test.

  Carter Administration officials, not wanting to upset a significant Democratic interest group, decided to settle the case out of court by signing a consent decree with the plaintiffs. The consent decree required that the federal government stop using the PACE, even though the Office of Personnel Management (OPM) had spent millions of dollars developing the exam, and OPM could prove the results of the exam were valid. These officials thus used their bureaucratic discretion to abandon the PACE and promote hiring based on race rather than merit, thereby taking another substantial step in converting federal employment from the merit system to an ethnic-based patronage system.

The amount of bureaucratic discretion in government has increased over the last fifty years. This is due to the extremely vague nature of much legislation in the "Great Society" period and after. Legislation of this sort provides only general statements of purpose and leaves the actual programs to be shaped largely by the bureaucracy.[7] The growth of discretionary power exercised by the bureaucracy often is criticized in the United States because it has shifted policy-making authority from elected officials to unelected bureaucrats, undermining the basic tenets of democratic government.

It is the role of the political executive to bring the actions of bureaucracy into conformance with the electoral mandate. That is to say, the role of the political executive is to exercise bureaucratic discretion to produce policy change in accordance with the political will of the President. If the political executive fails to exercise his bureaucratic discretion, it will simply remain in the hands of bureaucrats who will exercise it as they see fit, not as the political system dictates. As one student of bureaucratic discretion has put it:

> If there is one factor that contributes more than any other to bureaucratic dominance in the political system, it is inattention by the other actors or participants in the policy making, who have the potential capacity to limit the influence bureaucrats can exert over government actions or decisions.[8]

In order to prevent the career bureaucracy from using bureaucratic discretion, the political executive must properly conceive his own role and control the roles of the career bureaucrats below him. In other words, since career personnel "enjoy discretion when their roles are left ambiguous by policy makers, clear definitions of roles and obligations reduce this discretion."[9] Thus, much of the battle over bureaucratic discretion is won when the political executive acts on his definition of his own role as "policy changer" and imposes his definition on that role of the career personnel in the bureaucracy.

To be effective in his role as a "policy changer" the new political executive must develop and implement two sets of skills: political and managerial. The political skills that the political executive needs involve the ability to assess that part of the President's agenda for which he is responsible and to convert that agenda into operational form within his agency. He must be able to develop strategies to implement the agenda, taking existing political constraints into account. An enormous problem of the first Reagan Administration, and for that matter most administrations, is that many political executives tried to operate "agenda free." They failed to work day-in and day-out for the President's agenda. They got side-tracked by management concerns that had nothing to do with policy change. They were captured by the bureaucracy and interest groups.

The successful implementation of the political aspect of the political executive's role is essential for the success for the President and his philosophy. Thus, the success of an administration in large part depends on the appointment of political executives who are deeply committed to the President's philosophy.[10]

The management skills that are required by the political executive are not the same management skills that are used in the average business. They include a knowledge of how to manage the career bureaucracy to produce policy change. These management skills are more difficult than in the private sector because they involve the management of large organizations and the absence of clear information and common purpose. The management problems in government will be discussed more fully in the next section of Chapter I.

The problem of combining political and management skills to produce policy change in a conservative administration is even greater than in most administrations. Although roughly the same environmental conditions exist for every political executive in every administration and most administrations have tremendous difficulty making positive change in policy, the policy agenda of a conservative administration magnifies the problems.[11] An administration that attempts to alter the course of government by introducing conservative philosophy sets for itself a monumental task. Cutting taxes, cutting spending, increasing defense capability, eliminating regulations, establishing a new alignment in federalism, and converting programs to free market approaches, all require extensive change in the status quo. Since the bureaucracy supports the status quo and special interests oppose any change that will reduce the benefits they derive from government programs, they are particularly opposed to the policy agenda of a conservative administration. Both will mobilize and ally with Congress to defeat the positive policy changes proposed by the President and his political executives.

Public Management is not Business Management

The bureaucracy gains a great deal of power because it is difficult to control. Compare a business organization with a governmental agency; the managers attempt to control their respective organizations based on totally different information bases. The business manager has the basic bottom line of the profit and loss statement which provides him with important information about the actions of his organization and subordinates. The political executive, on the other hand, does not have this type of information to use in the management of his agency. This difference provides the basis for different management practices in the two types of organizations.

Public and private management practices, while similar in some respects are not the same. Or as a subtitle of a recent article asks: "Are They Fundamentally Alike in all Unimportant Respects?[12]"

Many businessmen who initially believe public and private management are alike change their minds after working in public life. George Humphrey, President Eisenhower's Secretary of the Treasury, stated: "When I came to Washington in January, I did not realize so clearly as I do now how different government is from business, and how much more difficult it is to get things done. The job of making changes looked a lot easier from the outside.[13]" Many who argue that public and private management are alike also argue that expert business managers appointed to high governmental positions can "straighten out the mess in Washington." As long ago as 1944, Ludwig von Mises, the eminent Austrian economist, argued the opposite, in his book, *Bureaucracy.*

> It is vain to advocate a bureaucratic reform through the appointment of businessmen as heads of various departments. The quality of being an entrepreneur is not inherent in the personality of the entrepreneur; it is inherent in the position which he occupies in the framework of market society. A former entrepreneur who is given charge of a government bureau is in this capacity no longer a businessman but a bureaucrat. His objective can no longer be profit, but compliance with the rules and regulations.[14]

Marver Bernstein of the Brookings Institution came to a similar conclusion after extensive discussions with political executives with former business careers:

> . . . [T]he recruiting process must be based on a recognition that skills of business management are not readily transferable to government and qualities of high competence in business are not necessarily those that earmark the able government executive.[15]

Key differences between the job of the political executive and the business executive have been pointed out by many observers. The political executive: (a) has a shorter time horizon; (b) has less authority; (c) is not a product of a career system; (d) is almost totally exposed to media criticism; (e) has less control over the implementation of policy; and (f) lacks the performance measurement of profitability.[16]

This last point, lacking information produced by a profit and loss statement, is absolutely critical for understanding the difference in the day-to-day operational management of the political executive. Von Mises' analysis makes the importance of this information clear.

> The elaborate methods of modern bookkeeping, accounting, and business statistics provide the enterpriser with a faithful image of all his operations. He is in a position to learn how successful or unsuccessful every one of his transactions was. *With the aid of these statements he can check the activities of all departments of his concern no matter how large it may be.* There is, to be sure, some amount of discretion in determining the distribution of overhead costs. But apart from this, the figures provide a faithful reflection of all that is going on in every branch or department. The books and the balance sheets are the conscience of business. *They are also the businessman's compass. . . . By means of this . . . the businessman can at any time survey the general whole, without needing to perplex himself with the details.*[17]

This superior method of evaluation and calculation provides the business manager with information so that he can delegate broad authority to subordinates who then devise means that produce more efficient operations and earn more profit. Businessmen, therefore, develop management styles which delegate authority to subordinates and hold them responsible for results. They can do this because the information is available to check on the results.

Government, on the other hand, is entirely different. No adequate parallel to the profit and loss statement exists. Political executives find, many times, that career staff have a monopoly over information regarding agency operations. Delegation of authority to career staff often means that they make critical policy decisions. Thus business management practices are generally not possible and, if followed, often produce disastrous results.[18]

In the absence of the information produced by the profit and loss statement, public sector management practices must be able to establish firm control over subordinates. Nothing short of democratic accountability is at stake when broad degrees of operational discretion are granted. As a general rule of thumb, the political executive must delegate less, or at least more carefully, and he must become more involved in the details of the operations of organization than his counterpart in the private sector.

Footnotes

1. This part of *Mandate II* is dedicated to all career federal employees who, by their daily actions, live up to the highest ideals of the civil service. They willingly use their ex-

pertise and knowledge to assist political appointees in the implementation of the Administration's policy objectives. Without them, as every present and past political appointee, myself included, knows, policy change would be impossible. Nothing in this part of *Mandate II* should be construed as reflecting negatively on these career civil servants.

2. Herbert Kaufman, *The Administration Behavior of Federal Bureau Chiefs* (Washington, D.C.: The Brookings Institution, 1981), p. 134.

3. Hugh Heclo cites 22 months as the average term in office for Undersecretaries and assistant secretaries. Hugh Heclo, *A Government of Strangers: Executives Politics in Washington* (Washington, D.C.: The Brookings Institution, 1977), p. 103.

4. Marver H. Bernstein, *The Job of the Federal Executive* (Washington, D.C.: The Brookings Institution, 1958), p. 176.

5. Hugh Heclo, *A Government of Strangers*, p. 102.

6. Francis Rourke, *Bureaucracy, Politics and Public Policy* (Boston: Little, Brown and Co., 1984), p. 36.

7. Theodore J. Lowi, *The End of Liberalism* (New York: W.W. Norton and Co., Inc., 1979) pp. 212-216.

8. Rourke, *Bureaucracy Politics and Public Policy*, p. 210.

9. Robert Nakamura and Frank Smallwood, *The Politics of Policy Implementation* (New York: St. Martin's Press, 1980), p. 33.

10. Although an emphasis will be placed on the importance of political commitment in the work of political executives, a study of the actual techniques for selecting proper political personnel is beyond the scope of this effort.

11. All Presidents have experienced difficulty controlling the executive branch. FDR is quoted as having remarked: "The Treasury is so large and far-flung and ingrained in its practices that I find it is almost impossible to get the action and results I want. . . . But the Treasury is not to be compared with the State Department. You should go through the experience of trying to get any changes in the thinking, policy, and action of the career diplomats and then you'd know what a real problem was. But the Treasury and the State Department put together are nothing as compared with the Na-a-vy. . . . To change anything in the Na-a-vy is like punching a feather bed. You punch it with your right and you punch it with your left until you are finally exhausted, and then you find the damn bed just as it was before you started punching." Theodore Sorenson, *Kennedy* (New York: Harper and Row, 1965), p. 677. President Truman predicted Eisenhower's troubles with policy change when he said "He'll sit here, and he'll say 'Do this! Do that'. And nothing will happen. Poor Ike— it won't be a bit like the Army. He'll find it very frustrating." Nakamura and Smallwood, *The Politics of Policy Implementation*, p.1.

12. Graham T. Allison, Jr., "Public and Private Management, Are They Fundamentally Alike in All Unimportant Respects?" in Barry Bozeman and Jeffrey Straussman, *New Directions in Public Administration* (Monterey, California: Brooks Cole, 1984), p. 32.

13. Quoted in Bernstein, *The Job of the Federal Executive*, p. 200.

14. Ludwig von Mises, *Bureaucracy* (New Rochelle, N.Y.: Arlington House, 1969), p. 49.

15. Bernstein, *The Job of the Federal Executive*, p. 200.

16. See Allison, "Public and Private Management," pp. 36-37.

17. Von Mises, *Bureaucracy*, p. 32. (Emphasis added.)

18. See Donald P. Warwick, *A Theory of Public Bureaucracy* (Cambridge: Harvard University Press, 1975), pp. 199-203, for an analysis of how employee participation in change (participatory management) is different in the public and private sectors. See also Heclo, *Government of Strangers*, p. 193, for a discussion of adaptations of Theory X and Y to the public sector.

23

The Environment of the Political Executive

The inexperienced political executive coming to work for a conservative administration, even a second consecutive conservative administration, is faced with a new and unusual environment. This chapter will acquaint the new political executive with the four principal parts of his new environment: the Constitution, bureaucratic power, the politics/administration dichotomy, and the "real world" of policy-making and implementation.

The Constitution: The Fragmentation of Authority

The single most important instrument shaping the new political executive's environment is the Constitution.

> All legislative Powers herein granted shall be vested in a Congress of the United States which shall consist of a Senate and House of Representatives. (Article I, Section 1)

> The executive Power shall be vested in a President of the United States of America. (Article II, Section 1)

These two sections of the Constitution seem simple enough. They provide the basis for the concept known as the "separation of powers" which divides the legislative, executive and judicial functions into three distinct institutions. This concept is, however, misleading without the corresponding concept of "checks and balances," which involves the President, as the chief executive, in some legislative functions and allows the Congress, as the legislative body, to perform some executive duties. For example, the President signs or vetoes legislation and the Congress confirms executive branch officials. Of course, these concepts also apply to the judicial function embodied in the Supreme Court, but that relationship is less critical to this discussion.

The system of "checks and balances" creates an overlap of functions among the three branches. The purpose of the overlap is not to produce "efficient" government decision-making. Many businessmen entering public service for the first time remark quite correctly that decision-making in the federal government is very inefficient. The purpose is to ensure that power is sufficiently divided and checked so that one person or one institution cannot slowly accumulate power and gain complete control.

The drafters of the Constitution purposely designed an "inefficient" political decision-making system. They did not want political decisions to be made quickly by one institution. They wanted political decision-making to be divided and they wanted the decision-makers to struggle with each other over the power to make decisions. In James Madison's words in *Federalist No. 51,* "Ambition must be made to counteract ambition."[1] This "inefficient" design produces a tension among the three branches and especially between the President and the Congress.

While everyone understands the design of the system intellectually, it is quite another thing to be involved in the daily tensions produced by the system. Although under the Constitution the political executive receives executive power from the President to administer programs through the career civil service, the system is actually more complex. "Checks and balances" ensure that political legitimacy is divided and flows to the bureaucracy, not through the President alone, but also through the Congress.

The political executive becomes the focal point for the constitutionally designed tension between the President and the Congress. The political executive, as the agent of the President for policy change, must work diligently to implement the President's policy priorities. But the Congress, with its own sets of political and policy priorities, can use its political legitimacy to tell the political executive what to do and how to do it.

Although the President hires and fires the political executive, Congress has many tools available to control the political executive and his agency. Congress controls the budget. Congress controls what the agency is authorized to do. Congress can investigate specific actions of the agency. And Congress controls the civil service system which, some argue, is used to prevent effective presidential management of the bureaucracy.

The political executive is thus at the center of the constitutional battle of the two branches. On a day-to-day basis the political executive must deal with conflicts over specific issues derived primarily from the constitutional design. If this were the extent of the complexity, it would still be relatively simple compared to the complexity of the total system. The role of the career bureaucracy further complicates the system.

Bureaucratic Power

The constitutional separation of power between the President and the Congress places the bureaucracy in a unique position. The Constitution gives the President and the Congress enough power to resist the encroachments of the other branch. The bureaucracy represents an additional power center which, if swung to one side or the other, can influence the power balance. The Congress fears presidential control of the bureaucracy and the President fears congressional control of the bureaucracy. This situation puts the bureaucracy in an excellent power position since it can ally with one or the other to further its ends. Much as a child plays one parent against the other to get what it wants, governmental agencies can, at times, play the President and Congress against each other to gain what they want. Career officials who have their own agendas often go to Congress to make appeals for what they want, or seek congressional assistance to stop changes initiated by political executives. Given the constitutionally fomented conflict between the presidency and Congress and the political conflict when the President is a conservative Republican with a liberal Democratic House, the Congress is ready to get involved in the details of the agency operation on the side of the career bureaucracy.[2]

In addition to the power created by its position in the constitutional system, the bureaucracy draws power from other sources. The bureaucracy possesses unique, detailed knowledge about public policies and issues. This knowledge enables the bureaucracy to influence the outlook and decision-making of the political executive.

Moreover, the bureaucracy delivers services to particular client groups. This relationship is mutually beneficial. The bureaucracy forms an alliance with the client groups and can mobilize client groups to oppose any changes that threaten to disrupt their symbiotic relationship. Finally, as indicated in the discussion of bureaucratic discretion above, the bureaucracy draws power from its control over the implementation of policy. These and other aspects of bureaucratic power will be discussed in greater detail in Chapter 24 under "Internal Constraints."

The Policy Process: Politics versus Administration

The reality of bureaucratic power is obscured by the traditional view of the separation of politics and administration. The notion that politics and administration are separated originates in the "classical" theory of public administration, as given expression by Woodrow Wilson.[3] "Classical" theory is the root cause of many of the problems faced by the political executive and in order to understand these problems, the political executive must have a clear understanding of the theory.

"Classical" theory argues that politics and administration are separate fields and should not interfere with each other. Politics is supposed to determine the "ends" of government and once determined, administration is supposed to apply the most efficient technical and professional "means" to implement the "ends." According to "classical" theory, the political executive is not supposed to tell the career staff how to implement a policy and the career staff does not, in any way, influence the policy-making process. Finally the theory argues that any bureaucratic discretion in the system is used to determine "means" not "ends."

A practical example of "classical" theory is the council-manager form of city government. The council is the elected body of legislative office holders. They determine policy for the city and then pass their policy decisions to the professional city manager for implementation. The city manager is the chief executive and he is supposed to administer any policies passed by the council "neutrally" and professionally. Thus, the line separating politics and administration is drawn between the politically elected council and the professional city manager.

"Classical" theory coincided with the growth of government in the late 1800s and early 1900s, and was, indeed, necessary to the creation of the large bureaucratic state which now exists.

> "Classical" theory was a highly useful doctrine late in the nineteenth century and early in the twentieth in the United States, when public bureaucracy was an infant industry that needed a protective ideology behind which it could develop. It made the expansion of bureaucracy much less threatening to American democracy than it might otherwise have appeared to be.[4]

Although the classical theory found great acceptance among public administration theorists through the 1930s, it fell on hard times in the 1940s. Critics recognized that politics and administration cannot be separated and that career staff has a tremendous advantage in influencing the policy-making process.[5] When this influence occurs, it distorts the democratic process because the career staff does not have the political legitimacy to make policy in a democratic system.

Although rejected by the academic community for the last forty years, the classical separation of politics and administration still serves as the basis for common conceptions of the operations of government and greatly influences the public, politicians, and many career bureaucrats.[6] This influence causes four problems for the political executive who is trying to implement fundamental policy change.

First, many career executives feel that the political executive is superfluous because he does not have the professional, technical, or managerial skills necessary to implement policy efficiently. They also believe that he is not needed because career staff "neutrally" implement policy, so the political executive's political legitimacy is not needed. This is especially true in highly technical and scientific agencies.

Second, some career executives, while very protective of their sovereign prerogatives in policy administration, are very aggressive in their attempts to cross the line into policy-making. They usually do this under the guise of giving advice to the political executive. By selectively controlling information, they attempt to influence the policy decisions of the political executive while claiming to maintain the separation between politics and administration.

Third, some career executives have a political agenda that they wish to pursue. These may be former political appointees of Democratic administrations who were converted to career status by that administration before a Republican President assumed office, or they could be ideologues who wish to further their own public policy. In either case, they attempt to use the "classical" theory to cover their political activities. One noted authority in the field of public administration observes:

> For administrators, this presumed separation of administration and politics allows them to engage in politics without the bother of being held accountable politically for the outcomes of their actions. Further, they can engage in policy making—presumably using technical or legal criteria for a decision—without the interference of political actors who might otherwise recognize political or ideological influences on policies and make demands upon them for the modification of those policies.[7]

Fourth, many political executives are influenced by "classical" theory because it relieves them of the hard work associated with learning the details of administration. They gladly leave administration to the "experts" and occupy themselves with the seemingly more prestigious activity of "policy-making." Unfortunately, these political executives are only fooling themselves. Policy-making is meaningless without the follow-through which ensures that implementation is carried out according to the dictates of the political executive. Policy and administration are not separated and "to get control of policy, one must get control of administration."[8] Political executives must get involved in the implementation of the policies they make. Policy development must be followed by policy management in order to implement a President's policies effectively.[9]

These four problems indicate how "classical" theory influences the political executive's relations with his career staff. The political executive must endeavor to reverse the typical pattern where the political executive is limited to policy-making and the career staff is active in both policy-making and administration. The political executive must establish working relationships which make it clear that he will be involved in both policy-making and administration,and that the career staff will be limited to policy administration. This is not to say that the political executive cannot seek advice from career personnel, but as will be discussed more fully in Chapter 25, the political executive must control the relationship so that the career staff does not monopolize the policy-making process.

In addition to separating the notions of "politics" and "administration," classical public administration theory also makes an analogous distinction between "policy formation" and "policy implementation." According to this view, policy is seen as a linear process with distinct phases: policy formation, policy legitimation, policy implementation, and policy evaluation.[10] In the first phase, various political actors compete over policy goals and values. Compromise is reached; policy goals are set and legitimized by law or regulation. Bureaucrats then implement the policy through neutral administration. In the final phase, the effectiveness of the policy and its implementation are evaluated.

In the real world, those things generally regarded as aspects of the policy formation phase—judgments, the weighing of diverse social values, the allocation and application of values, and the determination of goals—permeate all phases of the policy process. Furthermore, in "classical" theory the competition of competing actors with diverse interests generally is restricted to the first, "formation" stage. In reality, competition over policy ends among various actors (politicians, bureaucrats, interest groups, outside experts, courts) continues throughout the process.

"Policy formation," far from being the predominant stage of the process, may in fact be of lesser importance. The real world frequently turns the traditional model on its head.

> There are many contexts in which the latitude of those charged with carrying out a policy is so substantial that studies of implementation should be turned on their heads. In these cases, policy is effectively "made" by those people who implement it.[11]

Finally, the entire notion of a linear process is misleading. According to the linear view, values and ends are determined in the first phase and the "neutral administrator" marches off in a straight line implementing policy in accord with those ends. In reality, any given policy generally will contain diverse ends and values that never are fully reconciled, so the neutral administrator has no clear directions to follow. In addition, actors who "lost" in the policy formation stage will intrude on the implementation stage to alter policy in their interests. Since ends and values of policy never are fully resolved, it is better to conceive of the policy process as a circle in which the boundaries of the phases are indistinct and in which discretion and competition over goals and values exist in all phases.[12]

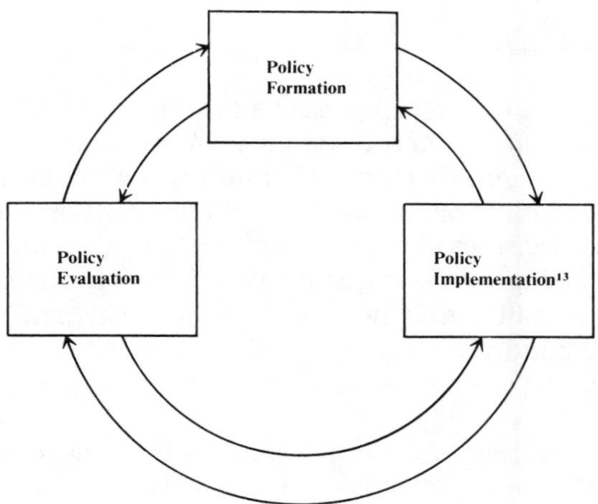

This circular picture of the policy process is more useful for the political executive because it warns him that political opponents will have many different opportunities to defeat his policy objectives. A political executive following "classical" theory will relax once the policy is formally made. The political executive who is aware of the implications of the circular model will place greater efforts in policy implementation and policy evaluation to ensure that the President's policy objectives are implemented fully. The political executive's responsibility for follow-through on policy decisions in the implementation stage cannot be emphasized enough.

The Real World: Political Executives and Bureaucracts[14]

The concept of the separation of politics and administration, although discredited, still formally dominates the working world of the political executive. In reality the political executive finds his relations with his bureaucratic "subordinates" differ greatly from the "classical" world of policy-makers and neutral administrators. The primary interactions between the political executive as policy-maker and his career staff as policy-implementers cannot be captured in a single concept. Five concepts provide a more accurate model of how political executives and career bureaucrats interact in the policy formation and implementation processes. These five concepts have the following descriptive labels:

Classical Technocracy	Instructed Delegation	Bargaining	Discretionary Experimentation	Bureaucratic Entrepreneurship

Together these concepts represent a continuum based on the degree of political executive control over the policy-making process. "Classical" Technocracy, on the extreme left side, represents the separation of policy and administration, as discussed above. Political executives make policy decisions and career staff implement them. Bureaucratic Entrepreneurship, on the extreme right side, represents an interaction where career staff formulate specific policy goals and try to "sell" them to the political executive.

The following chart elaborates on these concepts.[15]

Interactions of Political Executives and Career Staff in the Policy Formation and Implementation Processes

Political Executives	Career staff	Potential Breakdowns
	1. "Classical" Technocracy	
Political executives formulate specific goals and instruct career staff to implement.	Career staff support political executives' goals and devise "neutral" means to achieve these goals.	Neutral means fail to accomplish goals.
	2. Instructed Delegation	
Political executives formulate specific goals and delegate administrative authority to career staff.	Career staff support political executives' goals and negotiate among themselves to achieve goals.	Negotiations fail. (Complexity, Stalemate)
	3. Bargaining	
Political executives formulate goals, but must bargain with career staff over both goals and/or means to achieve goals.	Career staff bargain with political executive over goals and/or means to achieve goals.	Bargaining failures. (Cheating)

	4. Discretionary Experimentation	
Political executives support abstract (undefined) goals and delegate broad discretionary authority to career staff to refine goals and means.	Career staff refine goals and means for political executives.	Ambiguity, Cooptation, Unaccountability.
	5. Bureaucratic Entrepreneurship	
Political executives support goals and means formulated by career staff.	Career staff formulate policy goals and means to carry out goals and persuade political executives to accept their goals.	Cooptation, Unaccountability, Policy-Preemption.

Classical Technocracy is based on the traditional theory of separation of politics and administration. The political executive has a specific policy goal which he gives to the career staff. They apply their technical skills to the accomplishment of the goal. For example, the political executive wants a regional office in Denver closed. That goal is given to the career staff to accomplish. They work out the technical details of transferring or RIFing the personnel, moving continuing operations, and disposing of the building and equipment. This linkage involves little policy development and none that requires career staff involvement. Unfortunately, this concept is discussed the most, but is perhaps the rarest in actual practice. Very few policy goals can be specified to the implementation level by the political executive without some participation of career staff. As noted by the table, the breakdowns that can occur are determined by a technical failure of neutral means and are relatively easy for the political executive to detect.

Instructed Delegation involves delegation of administrative authority to the career staff. A specific goal is given to the career staff, but the goal requires the action of several units within the organization. This results in several groups of career personnel negotiating over the details of the implementation. It appears that policy formation is still in the hands of the political executive, but he must be cautious because the delegation of administrative authority can cause several difficulties.

First, as the diagram illustrates, there can be failures in the negotiation process which produce stalemate and inaction. Often the inaction is not apparent to the political executive for many weeks or months. These delays are one of the principal reasons why the implementation of policy takes so long in government.

Second, the delegation of administrative authority allows the career staff enough leeway to adopt administrative procedures which change the original thrust of the policy. In view of this possibility, the political executive must check to see that the intentions of the policy are actually being carried out by the career staff.

Bargaining comprises the vast majority of the political executive's dealings with the bureaucracy. The political executive formulates goals, but the goals which are formulated are rather broad and lack the administrative content necessary to be implemented directly by the career staff. Instead of closing a regional office, for example, the goal is to cut unnecessary spending or to ease the regulatory burden on small business.

Bargaining usually starts out like the instructed delegation process, with the political executive giving the career staff a goal to be implemented. The career staff usually comes back with questions about means, but during the discussion of means the political executive finds himself discussing the basic goal and finally the discussion turns into bargaining over both ends and means.

While there are always legitimate items for discussion when a broad policy is given to the career staff for implementation, the discussion as it actually develops provides an opportunity for the career staff to insert its own policy preferences or, even worse, for career staff to sabotage the political executive's policy directive. The result of this policy formation process can be a policy that serves the bureaucracy first and the administration second or, in the worst case, serves the opponents of the administration. As two experts in the politics of the policy process observe:

> Since the implementers [career staff] do not necessarily agree with the policy makers [political executives] on goals, they can circumvent policies, and coopt resources, to serve their own ends. In other words, they can pay lip service to a policy goal while actually "cheating" in order to take the money and use it to serve their own policy objectives.[16]

The fourth concept is *Discretionary Experimentation.* In this situation the political executive has vague and abstract goals that he wants to implement. He must grant broad discretion to the career staff to work on both the means and ends. "Vagueness in policy statements means that the responsibility for more specific definition is shifted from policy makers [political executives] to implementers [career staff]."[17] While the political executive might never intentionally allow career staff the amount of discretion implied in this concept, he is at times forced by circumstances to allow it to happen. Political executives are constrained by the time that they can devote to the clarification of goals. When they are short on time, the tendency is to let more discretion slip away. In addition, their own technical shortcomings cause them to allow more discretion over the formulation of policy.

Finally, political executives are forced to form coalitions to push certain policies, which means that policy objectives are compromised by making the goals vague enough to win acceptance by the members of the coalition.

The fifth concept is *Bureaucratic Entrepreneurship*, which completely transfers the initiative for policy formation to career staff. In this case career staff formulate the policy proposal and attempt to gain the support (or legitimation) for the policy from the political executive.

Obviously, much damage comes from the political executive who supports the bureaucratic entrepreneur who is working against the President's policies. At times the bureaucratic entrepreneur is exceedingly difficult to detect because he knows policy details and can mask his personal policy recommendations as routine administrative matters or conceal them within a proposal which the political executive is likely to support. The activities of the bureaucratic entrepreneur will be more fully discussed in Chapter III.

These five concepts give a much more realistic picture of the day-to-day experiences of the political executive than the "classical" theory does. Together they serve as a guide for the political executive to survey his environment. The new political executive in his first month will likely experience situations corresponding to all five concepts. How the political executive handles these situations is the key to his success in policy change.

First, the political executive must recognize and identify each situation as it arises. Next, depending on how the situation fits the five models presented above, the political executive must decide how he can gain more control over the policy-making process. Confronted with a bureaucratic entrepreneur, the political executive can simply make it clear that policy objectives not consistent with the President's agenda will not be considered and that the pursuit of separate covert agendas will not be tolerated. The bargaining situation, perhaps the most common situation, requires the political executive to limit the scope of discussion. The political executive must work personally to move more policy situations from right to left on the five-part continuum. By clarifying policy goals and monitoring details, the political executive can shift his career staff into a situation which more closely resembles the ideal of the classical model in which careerists are restricted to matters which are truly "administrative." Techniques to accomplish this end will be presented in Chapter 25.

Footnotes

1. Alexander Hamilton, James Madison, and John Jay, *The Federalist Papers* (New York: Mentor Books, 1961), p. 322. (Originally published in 1787.)

2. For an excellent discussion of how Congress gets involved in the details of executive branch administration see: Allen Schick, "Congress and the 'Details' of Administration," in *Public Administration Review*, September/October 1976, pp. 516-527.

3. The basis for "classical" theory was first developed by Wilson in his 1887 essay, "The Study of Administration." Wilson's article applied his basic political philosophy of positive government to the field of public administration. This philosophy was in direct opposition to the political philosophy of the writers of the Constitution, who viewed government as a negative influence on personal freedom and a force which must be limited and controlled. See Donald Devine, "American Culture and Public Administration," *Policy Studies Journal*, 11 (December 1982), p. 255-260.

As "classical" theory developed, two additional ideas were added to Wilson's concept of separation of politics and administration. First was Max Weber's concept of a bureaucratic organizational structure based on a centralized, hierarchical pyramid. Weber argued that this structure operated more efficiently than other organizational structures. Second, Frederick Taylor argued that through scientific management techniques, in particular time and motion studies, organizations could greatly improve their efficiency. Woodrow Wilson, "The Study of Administration," *Political Science Quarterly*, 2 (June 1887). Max Weber, *Essays in Sociology*, ed. H.H. Gerth and C. Wright Mills (New York: Oxford University Press, 1946). Frederick W. Taylor, *The Principles of Scientific Management* (New York: Harper and Row, 1911).

4. Rourke, *Bureaucracy, Politics and Public Policy*, p. 36.

5. Charles E. Lindblom, *The Policy Making Process* (Englewood Cliffs, N.J.: Prentice Hall, 1968), p. 75.

6. While the critics of the classical model have dominated, no comprehensive replacement theory has been accepted by the public administration community. This lack of theory creates a great deal of confusion in the field so that, lacking a theoretical foundation, proposals for improvements are hard to evaluate. Several recent proposals to decrease the number of political executives seem to conform to the "classical""theory and do not adequately explain how democratic accountability is to be achieved. See Vincent Ostrom's critical analysis of public administration theory in *The Intellectual Crisis in American Public Administration*, Revised Edition (University, Alabama: The University of Alabama Press, 1974).

7. B. Guy Peters, *The Politics of Bureaucracy*, 2nd ed. (New York: Longman, 1984), p. 147.

8. Herbert Kaufman, "Reflections on Administrative Reorganization," in *Setting National Priorities: The 1978 Budget* (Washington, D.C.: The Brookings Institution, 1978). p. 305.

9. The involvement of the political executive in the "details" of agency administration will be stressed throughout this part of *Mandate II*. This involvement is necessary to successfully change policy, but it does not mean that the political executive tries to get involved in the details of all agency policies. This is impossible. The political executive must select only the politically important policy areas within his agency and get deeply involved in the details.

10. The details of the policy-making process are outlined in Charles O. Jones, *An Introduction to the Study of Public Policy* (North Scituate, Mass: Duxbury Press, 1977).

11. Michael M. Lipsky, "Implementation on its Head," in Walter D. Burnham and Martha W. Weinberg, eds., *American Politics and Public Policy* (Cambridge: MIT Press, 1978), as quoted in Nakamura and Smallwood, *The Politics of Policy Implementation*, p. 19.

12. Nakamura and Smallwood, p. 27.

13. This diagram is a modification of Figure 2-1 in Nakamura and Smallwood, p. 27.

14. This section is based primarily on Nakamura and Smallwood, pp. 111-145.

15. This table is a modification of a table presented in Nakamura and Smallwood, pp. 114-115.

16. Nakamura and Smallwood, p. 122.

17. Nakamura and Smallwood, p. 128.

24

Understanding the Constraints on Policy-Making

Fifty years ago on a Chicago streetcar I heard a woman explain to a child, "The President lives in the White House in Washington, where he signs bills they bring him, and he can do anything he wants to so long as they don't stop him."—Carl Sandberg[1]

The political executive, like the President, "can do anything he wants to so long as they don't stop him." This chapter will illustrate how the other actors in the policy-making process try to constrain the political executive's policy-making. Constraints restrict and limit the political executive, but as every successful political executive knows, they cannot stop him. In order to minimize the restrictions, the political executive must have a realistic understanding of the difficulties he will face. Dramatic change is possible, but only if the political executive develops policy change strategies based on a detailed knowledge of the constraints.

INTERNAL CONSTRAINTS

Internal constraints originate from bureaucratic institutions and processes within the executive branch. The internal constraints listed below are closely interrelated aspects of a single phenomenon that might be called "the bureaucratic problem." Any effort to sub-divide this problem into specific categories must be, to a degree, arbitrary.

Professionals, Decision Making, and Information

The information used in the policy-making process is, perhaps, the most critical factor in determining the quality of the decision. Therefore, whoever controls the information that is used in policy decisions controls the decision. Much of the public administration literature analyzes the ability of the bureaucracy to control information and therefore control policy decisions.

... [T]he contact of the bureaucracy with the environment of the organization, as well as the concentration of technical expertise in the lower echelons of organizations, tends to give bureaucracies a substantial control over information and expertise crucial for policy making.... [T]he ability to control information is a major influence over policy in the hands of the bureaucrat.[2]

In addition, the work of the public sector is much more professional in occupational mix than the private sector. Because of this fact, the political executive leads an organization which, if not dominated, is heavily populated by, professionals. These professionals are indispensable to the operation of government. Without their expert training and knowledge, government would be less efficient and more expensive. But along with those great benefits to government, professionals at times hamper the political executive in his efforts to produce policy change. Professionals' expertise concerning programs enables them to control information, influence policy decisions, and become potential obstacles to policy changes proposed by the administration.[3]

The classic analysis of professionals in the bureaucracy comes from Frederick C. Mosher in his book *Democracy and the Public Service.*[4] Based on Mosher's analysis, the political executive should recognize that professionals operate to control information and constrain the political executive in three ways. First, professionals represent a force that tends to be external to the governmental organization. This external force is created by the interaction of a number of elements. Professionals are trained by professional schools which provide them with an outlook that carries over to influence their behavior inside their agency. The way the professional looks at a problem, selects and analyzes data, and formulates recommendations is, to a great extent, influenced by his educational background. Once a professional leaves his school, he usually joins a professional organization or association which influences his agency behavior by establishing codes of ethics, professional standards, and general outlook.

Because of background and associational similarity, a professional elite can establish itself within an agency and control much of the policy. For example, foresters within the Forest Service constitute a professional elite.[5] This elite, influenced through an interlocking network with the professional schools and the professional associations, exercises substantial control over policy decision-making in the agency. Social workers within government form a similar "professional" caste. Professional associations such as the National Association of Social Workers accept an activist political philosophy and are directly committed to liberal redistributionist goals.[6]

In addition to these specialized professions, generalist managers look to professional associations such as the American Society for Public Administration (ASPA) and the National Academy of Public

Administration (NAPA). These organizations are significant because they greatly influence the senior career executives with which the political executives directly work. ASPA and NAPA are particularly influential in advocating that career officials should be involved in policy-making.[7]

Second, professionals attempt to insulate themselves from politicians by establishing professional control over their personnel system. The professional elite in an agency attempts to obtain authority over personnel actions so that they can establish "self-government in deciding policies, criteria, and standards for employment and advancement, and in deciding individual personnel matters."[8] Actions such as recruitment, assignments, work content, and promotions are targets of control. Specific examples of this principle are personnel boards made up only of members of the profession, and the movement from written exams to "unassembled" exams which consist of a review of the educational and experience record of the candidate. Perhaps the most professionally controlled personnel system in the federal government is the Foreign Service system in the State Department. Career Foreign Service officers have almost total control over the personnel system within their department. This may be the most important reason all recent Presidents have complained that they have difficulty controlling and changing the foreign policy of the country.

The third way professionals operate to control information and influence policy is based on the inherent conflict between the professionals and politicians. Professionals are trained to attack and solve problems by applying science and rationality. Politicians, on the other hand, approach problem-solving through bargaining, negotiation, and compromise. Therefore professionals tend to view politicians as untrained amateurs who do not know the "right" way to solve problems "efficiently." In addition, professionals view government as the agent that violates their professional autonomy and freedom by forcing them to conform to the decisions produced by the "irrational" political process. This tension between politicians and professionals causes professionals to become very active participants in the policy-making process by pushing the process toward their perception of "rationality." Thus, professionals influence the information which they supply to the policy decision process in ways which they believe will provide the "correct" outcome.

Professionals tend to define the mission of their agency in ways which conform to the standards and outlook of their profession. Thus professionals may resist policy changes even if they are to the long run benefit of the profession and the agency. During the late 1950s the Air Force put a low priority on the development of the Intercontinental

Ballistic Missile (ICBM) because it saw the strength and function of the Air Force in terms of pilots flying planes. (Some ranking Air Force Generals actually gave the ICBM a lower status than the Nuclear Powered Airplane.) Similarly, it is very difficult for someone with a social worker background to think of "helping the poor" in ways other than those that expand the social work empire.

Thus, the political executive who sets out to change policy is constrained by the professionals in his organization, unless, of course, the policy change corresponds with the desires of the professional elite. This elite behavior can, in extreme cases, pose a serious challenge to democratic principles.[9] The political executive can develop two general strategies to counteract professional control over information and decision-making. First, political executives can attempt to gain control over the personnel systems that recruit, assign, and reward professionals. Second, the political executive can attempt to develop competing sources of information to break any monopoly that professionals have over information. The specifics of these strategies will be discussed in Chapter 25.

Bureaucratic Ideology[10]

The viewpoint of professionals within an organization will tend to correspond to the overall "bureaucratic ideology" of the organization. While the daily influence of professionals over information provided to the political executive is an obvious obstacle to political control, the "bureaucratic ideology" of an institution constitutes a more subtle, but nonetheless important, constraint with which the political executive must deal. Political executives manage large governmental organizations and these organizations derive their legitimate authority to act from the authorizing statutes passed by Congress. These statutes are usually limited statements of goals and objectives that provide a general framework on which the organization is built. The organization develops a more detailed image of itself by developing a bureaucratic ideology.

In his classic work on the theory of public administration, *Inside Bureaucracy*, Anthony Downs defines bureaucratic ideology as: "a *verbal image* of that portion of the good society relevant to the functions of the particular bureau concerned, plus the chief *means* of constructing that portion."[11] Note that this is a verbal image; thus, in order to develop an understanding of it, the political executive, must pick up the bits and pieces of the bureaucratic ideology through discussions and briefings. This is a difficult process because not all the pieces are of equal importance. Also note that the concept includes the means. The EPA has as part of its bureaucratic ideology the idea that pollution standards are the means of solving a pollution problem. The political executive who wishes to change the means is not just suggesting a simple change in the means to the same objective, clean air and water, but is attempting to make a fundamental change in the bureaucratic ideology of the organization.

Bureaucratic ideologies in all agencies have certain common characteristics. As might be expected, bureaucratic ideologies emphasize the positive benefits of the agency and de-emphasize the costs. They tend to show that the agency benefits the whole society and not a special interest group and they put a stress on the agency's efficient operations. In addition, bureaucratic ideologies attempt to show the necessity to at least maintain current activities and often show the need to expand agency activities. Finally, the precision with which bureaucratic ideologies are developed depends on whether the agency's jurisdiction is being invaded by another agency or whether the agency is attempting to expand through "bureaucratic imperialism."

Agency characteristics, as defined by its ideology, do not necessarily correspond to actual agency behavior. As Downs points out: "It is an idealized version of what the bureau's top leaders would like it to do—tailored to act as a public relations vehicle for them."[12] Therefore, the primary importance of bureaucratic ideology is its efficiency as a communication device, both internal and external. Top officials use bureaucratic ideology to influence Congress and the public to support the agency, to gain a stronger degree of goal consensus from agency personnel, to recruit selectively new members of the organization (those candidates who believe in the ideology are more likely to get a job), and to make decisions.[13]

Finally, "bureaucratic ideology" becomes a prism through which the organization views the external world. In the late 1940s and early 1950s U.S. defense policy was shifting toward an emphasis on deterrence through use of atomic weapons on enemy cities and industrial capacity. For the Air Force, the new emphasis was in accord with its basic self-concepts and offered a larger role: the Air Force supported the shift to the new doctrine. For the Army, the change violated basic concepts concerning defense and provided a diminished role: the Army tended to question the effectiveness of the plan and came to attach an increasing importance to more limited warfare.

How does bureaucratic ideology influence the political executive's efforts at policy change? Bureaucratic ideology creates an organizational environment that allows the members of the organization a quick and easy way to evaluate proposed policy changes. If the change is consistent with the bureaucratic ideology, the change is deemed beneficial. If the change is inconsistent with the bureaucratic ideology, then the change is to be opposed. And finally if the change strikes at the foundation of the bureaucratic ideology, the change is to be fought at all costs.

The political executive, therefore, faces a difficult task in trying to implement policy goals or operational procedures that change part of the agency's bureaucratic ideology.[14] Although bureaucratic ideology presents significant problems for the political executive, it is not all-powerful. The political executive must learn the specific characteristics of the bureaucratic ideology of his agency as quickly as possible. Once learned, he compares his policy change proposals to the bureaucratic ideology in order to predict the degree and nature of the bureaucratic resistance. The political executive must never be deterred from making changes that directly challenge the bureaucratic ideology of his agency.

Administrative Procedures and Structures[15]

One bit of advice is essential for all political executives: they should never overlook the obvious. Government agencies are large organizations made up of large numbers of people. In order for these organizations to accomplish their stated missions, they must coordinate large numbers of people efficiently. Coordination requires that the behavior of the bureau work force be pre-programmed in formal patterns or "bureaucratic routines." Graham Allison, a Harvard political scientist, decribes how this is done in his pathbreaking book, *The Essence of Decision:*

> To perform complex routines, the behavior of large numbers of individuals must be coordinated. Coordination requires standard operating procedures: rules according to which things are done. Reliable performance of action that depends upon the behavior of hundreds of persons requires established "programs." Indeed, if eleven members of a football team are to perform adequately on any particular down, each man must not "do what he thinks needs to be done" or "do what the quarterback tells him to do." Rather, each player must perform the maneuvers specified by a previously established play, which the quarterback has simply called in this situation.[16]

Running a large organization is similar to the quarterback calling plays. Political leaders can call certain plays to trigger certain bureaucratic routines and procedures and thus produce given outputs. Attempting to change the routines is more difficult. "The overriding fact about large organizations is that their size prevents any single central authority from making all important decisions or directing all important activities."[17]

The Cuban Missile Crisis provides an example of the importance of established routines. As the leader of American foreign policy, President Kennedy wanted the blockade of Cuba established in such a way that it would maximize the time available for the Soviets to decide to turn their ships around and minimize the chance that violence would break out unnecessarily when and if a Soviet ship was stopped and boarded. These goals in part conflicted with the Navy's "standard operating procedures" for conducting a blockade.

At one point Secretary of Defense Robert McNamara quizzed Admiral George Anderson, Chief of Naval Operations, about the procedures for the blockade. He asked detailed questions about the first interception of a Russian ship. He asked if Russian-speaking officers were aboard the American ships. He asked about the Russian submarines. Frustrated with McNamara's questions, Anderson picked up the *Manual of Naval Regulations* and waved it in McNamara's face and shouted, "It's all in here!" McNamara responded, "I don't give a damn what John Paul Jones would have done. I want to know what you are going to do now." The engagement ended with Anderson informing McNamara "Now, Mr. Secretary, if you and your Deputy will go back to your offices, the Navy will run the blockade."[18] This confrontation between the President and his advisors on one side and the Navy's "standard operating procedures" on the other did not always result in a clear victory for the President and his policy objectives. The important point here is that, despite McNamara's efforts, routines are largely invisible, i.e., all the details that affect the implementation of broad policies cannot be foreseen. Nevertheless the presence of "invisible" routines is a major reason why in government policies "what goes in at the top doesn't come out at the bottom."

Even in relatively mundane areas, routine procedures can have large political implications. This is particularly clear in the case of government agencies with responsibility for compiling or generating "statistical information." In these cases minute decisions concerning "technical" procedures can have a large impact on social perceptions and policies.

One obvious such case is the Census Bureau's mis-estimates of "poverty" in the United States. Because of technical decisions made long ago, at a low level in the bureaucracy, food stamps, government rent subsidies, and Medicaid payments are excluded from the household questionnaires with which the Census Bureau collects data. Although additional techniques exist for estimating the distribution of these payments among the poor, the Census Bureau ignores these techniques as well, and continues to follow its traditional practices, churning out publications year after year which overestimate the number of persons below the "poverty level" by as much as 75 percent.[19] At the behest of Congress, the Census Bureau has begun collecting some statistics on "non-cash" benefits but has not integrated these statistics with its "poverty" statistics.

These examples relate to very specific sets of routine procedures with political implications. In fact, however, routines exist nearly everywhere in a bureaucracy. Indeed, bureaucracy may be conceived of as a given set of organizational structures and routines. These organizational patterns combine to influence policy output in an automatic manner. To produce policy change, the political executive must understand the existence of the internal dimensions of bureaucracy which shape policy output. The routines and structures of a bureaucracy may be analyzed in terms of five organizational levels that influence decision-making and policy output.[20]

The first level consists of specific actions or decisions taken by an organization. The second level consists of the rules used in decision-making. The third level is comprised of the processes in which the decision-making rules are applied. The fourth level is the institutional structure which generates both the decision-making rules and the processes of the second and third levels, and the fifth, deepest level is the sense of general purpose or mission of the organization. In a small sub-unit of a bureaucracy, the fifth level will consist of the implicit priorities of the office; for larger organizations, the fifth level will correspond to the notion of bureaucratic ideology discussed in the preceding section.

These five structural levels may be illustrated through the operation of the grants program of the Women's Educational Equity Act Program (WEEAP) at the Department of Education. At the first level are specific actions taken in the disposition of a particular grant, for example, a study on "A Model of Inter-Institutional Collaboration for Minority Women." The second level consists of a set of rules by which grant applications are formally "rated." The third level, or the decision-making process, consists of a set of academic reviewers who "rate" the various grant applications. The fourth level is the institutional structure of the WEEAP Program Office which established the rating system and selects the individual reviewers. The fifth level is the sense of mission or purpose of the women's organization. In this case a number of purposes are possible: to exercise constraint in the use of taxpayers' money or to spend money as fast as posssible to justify larger budget requests in the future; to raise the quality of education in the U.S. or to promote liberal "women's" causes and organizations. (The grants program at the Department of Education will be discussed in more detail in Chapter 26.)

Traditionally, much of a political executive's time has been spent with decisions made at the first level. Needless to say, if he restricts himself to this level, he probably will not accomplish much real policy change. However, if he seeks to make changes at the lower levels, he will encounter strong resistance. The lower the structural level to be changed, the greater will be the resistance. Part of this resistance will result from simple bureaucratic inertia or the preference which bureaucracy has for established ways of doing things.

> Like most large organizations, bureaus have a powerful tendency to continue doing today whatever they did yesterday. The main reason for this inertia is that established processes represent an enormous previous investment in time, effort, and money. This investment constitutes a "sunk cost" of tremendous proportions.[21]

Changes require time and effort on the part of a bureaucracy. The greater the "sunk cost" invested in existing routines and structures, the greater will be the resistance to changing them.

In addition, resistance will come from ideological factors. As the political executive seeks changes in the lower structural levels, he nears and then encroaches on the purpose, or bureaucratic ideology, of the institution. The agenda of an administration like the Reagan presidency requires cutbacks in the size and scope of government as well as a philosophical re-orientation of many government programs. The Reagan political executive should seek deep structural changes in the deeper "structural levels" of the bureaucracy affecting the "mission" of the institution. Even though those changes are difficult and demand the highest levels of political skill, they are necessary. Failure to pursue structural change in the bureaucracy will be a failure to carry through the President's electoral mandate.

Bureaucratic Politics and Bureaucratic Entrepreneurs

Bureaucracies are held together by administrative structures and routines but they are also infested with "bureaucratic politics." Bureaucratic politics represents competition for power and political bargaining. This perspective of bureaucracy emphasizes that government policies are more likely to be the result of a compromise between competing political players and interest groups than to be a single integrated strategy produced by a unified group of decision makers. The bureaucracy is seen not as a uniform institution forming and carrying out a single set of policies but rather as a competitive arena where a variety of players—political appointees and career staff—seek to further diverse policy goals.[22]

Bureaucratic politics can be divided into intra-bureaucratic politics, which consists of political competition and bargaining between offices and actors within a given government department or agency, and inter-bureaucratic politics, which consists of interactions between players at various levels in the hierarchy of a given department and various external organizations such as the White House, OMB, other agencies, congressional committees, and the press. In both cases, players will seek to have a determining role in the policies of the department in question. Whereas bureaucratic routines and structures may serve as automatic obstacles to the political executive's plans, bureaucratic politics represents the conscious struggle for control of policy.

When a new political executive enters an agency, he automatically becomes a key player in the on-going political games being played both internal and external to that agency. It is like an American visiting England being invited to play cricket without knowing the rules or the skill levels of the players. The political executive must learn the rules by observing the actions of the players. In addition, he must deduce the object of the game by how the game is played. This process is aided by the initial briefings given the political executive by the career staff, but at the same time these briefings are the first opportunity of the players in the games to attempt to enlist the new political executive to support their side. Therefore, the political executive faces a very strange and unusual environment of games and must immediately begin play. Obviously, the political executive who is totally unaware of these games will be greatly constrained and fall victim to the manipulation of other, more skillful players. The political executive must particularly avoid becoming embroiled in organizational competition that is irrelevant to the President's agenda.

The world of bureaucratic politics is the antithesis of the civics textbook vision of the structure of the executive branch, with its hierarchy of command descending in an orderly manner from the central authority of the White House. Although hierarchic control is never totally absent in government, in general the real world of bureaucracy more closely resembles "a conglomerate of semi-feudal, loosely allied organizations, each with a substantial life of its own."[23]

The competitive semi-feudal nature of the bureaucracy can be clearly illustrated by an incident from the Nixon presidency. Facing a growing national drug problem, the White House sought to centralize anti-drug programs by creating a new Drug Enforcement Administration (DEA). This reorganization entailed the transfer of certain functions and personnel from the Bureau of Customs to the proposed DEA. The Office of Management and Budget advocated the plan and took partial responsibility for pushing it through Congress. Needless to say, the Bureau of the Customs, from the Commissioner on down, resented the reorganization and, contrary to the President's instructions, lobbied strongly against the proposal in Congress. The Customs Bureau lost its fight against the reorganization, but the blood feud did not end at that point. Frustrated by their defeat, pro-Customs forces in the House Appropriations Committee subsequently retaliated against OMB, cutting the funding request for OMB itself by 20 percent.[24]

The political executive who is promoting significant policy change within his department should not be surprised by career bureaucratic subordinates engaging in this type of covert inter-bureaucratic struggle to block his initiatives. Bureaucratic opponents will lobby vigorously against the proposed policy change to client groups, professional interest groups, congressional committee staffs, and the press. The bureaucracy's resources for defending its viewpoint, leaking discrediting material, and mustering outside allies are such that it could be correctly called "the ultimate lobby."

The degree and overtness of bureaucratic sabotage of administration initiatives will vary from agency to agency and from one period to another. Sabotage can range from the covert leaking of highly classified materials in order to discredit the administration or cause the resignation of certain officials to relatively low-key lobbying efforts. For example, many career bureaucrats lobby by responding to a congressional inquiry by saying, "Well the agency policy on this issue is such and such; however, some within the agency believe that. . . . " and then plugging their own viewpoint.[25]

During the Nixon Administration, a number of initiatives were developed which clashed with bureaucratic interests, including the proposed termination and consolidation of a large number of Great Society programs. Nixon political appointees, visiting the office of a congressional committee to explain a given legislative initiative, often would find that the committee staff already had received a briefing from careerists within the agency who were known to have "reservations" about the administration's plans.[26] Political appointees in HEW tackled this problem by installing a "chaperone system." Career bureaucrats were not permitted to visit Capitol Hill without clearance and then were to be chaperoned on each such outing by a political appointee. Congress, however, objected strongly to this system and HEW was forced to abandon it.

The bureaucratic entrepreneur is a close cousin to the bureaucratic opponent who sabotages administrative initiatives. In fact, the dividing line between the two generally will be unclear. The bureaucratic entrepreneur is the diametric opposite of the image of the public servant who executes faithfully policies set by politicians. The bureaucratic entrepreneur will not be content merely to block administration proposals; he wishes to impose his policy agenda on an unwary administration. His power over policy will be an outgrowth of his legitimate responsibility, as an expert on a given issue, to propose policy options and offer advice to political appointees.

The natural victim of the bureaucratic entrepreneur is the "agenda-free" political executive. Appointees arriving in Washington without a clear idea of what they are going to do will have their interior void politely filled by the bureaucrats around them. The objective of the entrepreneur will be to reverse roles with the political executive and have the political appointee promote and implement policies the careerist has formulated. If the bureaucratic entrepreneur is skillful in his approach, the political appointee will not even know that roles have been reversed.

The resources available to the bureaucratic entrepreneur to achieve role reversal are threefold: an extensive amount of information concerning programs and policy issues which will generally exceed that of the political executive; control of a sizable staff of loyal careerists; and a well-established network of influential persons connected to the policy area both inside and outside of government.

Martin Anderson, in his book *Welfare*, provides an excellent example of bureaucratic entrepreneurship in the long history of "guaranteed income" or the "negative income tax" in the government.[27] According to Anderson, high-level bureaucrats at Health, Education and Welfare (HEW) and the Office of Economic Opportunity (OEO) in the mid-sixties, developed a detailed scheme for guaranteed income for the nation. President Johnson thought the idea was too radical and rejected it. In 1968, President Nixon arrived in office having promised "radical welfare reform" in his presidential campaign. Nixon brought with him Daniel Patrick Moynihan as director of his Urban Affairs Council.

Moynihan had an extensive network of contacts throughout the liberal welfare bureaucracy who backed his efforts to take control of Nixon's domestic policy with a flood of research data and proposals. When Nixon indicated that he wished to carry through on his campaign pledge of welfare reform, Moynihan quickly was provided with a proposal by his fellow Democrats in the bureaucracy; the old guaranteed income scheme which had been rejected by Johnson was pulled out of the file cabinets.

By this time, the Nixon presidency was in its fourth month. The press was clamoring for action on the President's welfare reform promise. In other parts of the executive branch, political appointees were laboring to produce a more conservative variant of reform, but these efforts were overwhelmed by the thoroughly prepared, well-documented Moynihan plan which had been gestating in the bureaucracy for years. The President felt a need for something "now," and the Moynihan proposal, rechristened the "Family Assistance Plan" (FAP), became the basis for Nixon's welfare strategy.[28]

FAP was rejected by Congress, but an idea so favored by the bureaucracy would not simply die there. As a Nixon official stated concerning relations with the bureaucracy: "No decision in government is made only once."[29] In keeping with this maxim, the bureaucracy later resold its guaranteed income plans to HEW Secretary Weinberger, who presented it to President Ford as the "Income Supplement Plan" (ISP). Ford rejected the proposal but a variant was remodelled and introduced by President Carter in 1977 as the Program For Better Jobs and Income (PBJI), only to die in Congress.

The history of guaranteed income clearly illustrates the concept of bureaucracy as an autonomous "permanent government." The fact that the FAP/ISP/PBJI scheme was rejected four times by the President or by Congress over nearly twenty years has no effect on the popularity or promotion of the idea within the permanent government, nor does the fact that the public rejects the concept by nearly two to one. The guaranteed income concept is almost certain to enjoy a resurrection in the future, like a phoenix adorned in new acronymal plumage.

The best defense against bureaucratic entrepreneurs is for an administration to have a clear agenda when it takes office. The agenda should be in the form of detailed policy proposals, not merely general principles. This idea will be discussed more fully in the section on "The Political Agenda" below.

EXTERNAL CONSTRAINTS

The political executive faces not only opposing forces within his own agency but constraints stemming from other agencies and from the other branches of the federal government: Congress and the courts. Additional constraints consist of state and local government and non-governmental institutions, such as public employees unions.

Congress

Congress is motivated to limit the discretion of the President and the political executives in the executive branch for two reasons. First, the Constitution sets up a struggle between the branches in which the

Congress uses limits on the political executive as its chief weapon. Second, congressional committees are subject to intense pressure from interest groups. When the policy changes advocated by the political executive conflict with the interest group, the congressional committee is pressed to use its political power to limit the political executive. The former topic will be taken up in this section and the latter will be the subject of the next section, on interest groups.

Congress acts to constrain the political executive because if it does not, it loses some power in the constitutionally prescribed battle between the President and the Congress. It must be remembered that the purpose of the constitutional provisions of "separation of powers" and "checks and balances" is to prevent the consolidation of power in the hands of any one person or institution. Thus the battle between the executive and legislative branches. History illustrates the see-saw nature of the battle. In time of war or national crisis, the presidency has been paramount. Following a war, the Congress moves to reassert its power and restore the balance. This pattern occurred after the Civil War with the congressionally controlled reconstruction, and after World War I, with the congressional battle over the League of Nations. In each case, Congress moved to assert its power by passing measures to constrain and limit the President and his political executives. Recent history also illustrates the concept. After Vietnam and Watergate, the Congress moved to limit the executive branch. Measures passed by Congress include a stronger Freedom of Information Act, the War Powers Act, and the Congressional Budget and Impoundment Control Act. These measures not only limit the President, but also influence the day-to-day activities of public administrators, both political and career.[30]

Congressional power over the operations of the executive branch is such that, given a weak political executive, actual control over policy in an agency may be seized by a coalition of career bureaucrats and congressional committee staff. Morever, in theory it could be argued that congressional control over executive branch operations exceeds that of the President's. Any federal regulation and most administrative actions can be overruled by legislation passed by a majority vote in both Houses. The only formal defense the President has against this type of congressional assertiveness is a very awkward weapon, the veto.

In reality, congressional control is limited by four factors. First, Congress is not a unified actor, but is instead a collection of competing parties and factions with diverse concerns. Second, even if the political executive has limited knowledge of the operations in his bureau, Congress as a whole generally will have even less. In this respect, the flow of information between disaffected bureaucrats and sympathetic Congressmen plays an absolutely crucial role in the struggle between Congress and the presidency. Third, congressional control will generally be "after the fact"; it is more suitable for blocking initiatives than for directing them. The political executive will always have far greater control over the daily activities of his staff than Congress.

Fourth, congressional assertiveness is dependent on the overall political context. Confronted by a popular President with firm policy goals, congressional power over executive branch operations will be diminished. In this regard, the leadership skills of President Reagan compared to his immediate predecessors have worked to shift the balance of power between the branches.

Interest Groups and Iron Triangles

> The regulation of these various and interfering interests forms the principal task of modern legislation and involves the spirit of party and faction in the necessary and ordinary operations of government.
>
> —James Madison, *Federalist No. 10*[31]

At this point of the discussion, several of the factors previously discussed converge with the topic of interest groups to constrain the political executive. One particularly strong form of constraint has been termed the "iron triangles" or "issue networks." These represent political alliances consisting of three parts: a government agency, or bureau, the congressional committee which oversees that agency or bureau, and the specific clientele within the general public who are served by the agency.

"Iron triangles" or "issue networks" are established when interest groups pressure the Congress to establish a new agency or to add to an existing agency responsibilities which serve that interest group.[32] Once legislation is passed, the Congress establishes responsibility for the agency through the committee system. Congressmen who have that interest group in their district in substantial numbers push to serve on the congressional committee. Thus, they are in a strategic position in the Congress to oversee the agency's budget and activities and therefore serve the interest group. If the congressman does a good job of securing higher budgets for the agency and more services to the interest group, the interest group rewards the Congressman by supporting his reelection. As Marver Bernstein notes:

> A major aim of the interest groups is to induce Congress to create agencies in their own image to the greatest degree possible. They aim to have established in the government autonomous organizations whose jurisdictions correspond to the interest of the pressure groups. They

> endeavor to make it possible for these agencies to remain relatively independent of the executive branch as a whole and therefore subject more readily to their influence.[33]

In turn, the Congressman comes to regard the agency not as something he oversees and controls but as a political asset to be protected.

In its pure form an "iron triangle" will consist of a relatively limited and stable group of participants in the public and in government. This group will unify to control a fairly narrow set of government programs in such a way as to benefit all members of the group at the expense of the general taxpayer. The notion implies the creation of a petty bureaucratic fiefdom which has, due to a tight coalition of interests, attained a considerable degree of autonomy not only from presidential power within the executive branch but also from the normal tugging and hauling which characterize the ordinary legislative competition over larger issues such as the level and structure of taxes, and the defense budget. The related concept of an "issue network" implies a broader set of interest groups and government programs as well as less unity and less resistance to ordinary political pressures.

A classic example of a pure "iron triangle" is the Public Health Service hospital system. In 1798, the federal government established a network of hospitals to care for merchant seamen. The rationale at the time was that seamen were poorly paid, there was a shortage of hospitals, and seamen posed a public health hazard by way of the hard-to-cure contagious diseases they habitually contracted in their travels. As early as 1836, attempts were made to terminate the program—without success. By the 1970s the nearly 300,000 merchant seamen in the United States had average incomes twice the national average, scientific advances virtually had eliminated the contagious disease problem, and there was a surplus of hospital facilities in the country. Nonetheless the federal government continued to run eight Public Health Service hospitals and thirty-four outpatient clinics, staffed by over five thousand federal employees providing free health care to merchant seamen.[34] The double irony of this and other "iron triangle" type programs is that due to the inefficiency of the public sector, the seamen would be better served if they simply were provided with direct cash subsidies of equal value. However, iron triangles are not invincible. In 1981, after 183 years, the Reagan Administration successfully terminated the Public Health Service system.

The strength of an iron triangle will vary with the strength of the interest group pressure on, and control over, the congressional committee. Some agencies are part of triangles which are very strong, such as the U.S. Army Corps of Engineers. The Corps provides large "pork barrel" water projects that certain powerful Congressmen protect because they can be translated directly into votes. The Corps knows this and proposes projects that maximize their clout in Congress by building dams in key congressional districts. This quid pro quo relationship makes it difficult for the President and his political executives to control the Corps of Engineers.

Other agencies such as the Federal Emergency Management Administration (FEMA) have relatively weak triangles. FEMA, which deals with natural disasters, cannot target its benefits and thus has difficulty serving the re-election desires of the congressional committee members who supervise the agency's operations. It should be noted that even very small interest groups can have an effective iron triangle system. It took President Carter several years to end subsidies to American beekeepers through the Beekeepers Indemnity Fund.

Finally, the role of the bureaucrat in the iron triangle should be noted. An iron triangle situation intensifies most of the forms of bureaucratic behavior described in the "Internal Constraints" section above. A bureaucrat who is making a comfortable living providing services to a specific interest group has every reason to resist the political executive's efforts to change or curtail his program. Such a bureaucrat will generally have close ties to the congressional committee staff which oversees his program and very little loyalty to the transient political executive. Typical "sabotage" activities such as leaking materials to the press and to Congress or inciting lobbying by the client group have been discussed in the section on "Bureaucratic Politics."

The conservative political executive seeking to change policies controlled by an "iron triangle" will always have a very tough nut to crack. Thus, if the political executive expects to get any policies changed he must constantly heed the remark by a participant in a panel study of political appointees conducted by Marver Bernstein:

> It is the duty of the federal executive not to be so subservient to a constituency that he is afraid to stand up to interest groups served by his agency.[35]

Federalism: State and Local

Federalism, the concept of dividing power between the state and federal governments, influences the way many political executives conduct their daily business. Many programs managed by political executives are joint efforts of federal, state and local governments. Thus, change in these programs requires that the political executives have the ability to work not only with the constraints within the federal system, but also with additional constraints at the state and local levels.

The concept of federalism has created intergovernmental relations (IGR) between units of government that have changed throughout U.S. history. Several metaphors, including the layer cake, the marble cake and the picket fence, have been used to describe these historical periods. The layer cake, of course, indicates that the three levels—federal, state, and local—have distinct boundaries and functions. The marble cake, on the other hand views IGR as a mixture of the three levels with the three levels cooperating to implement policy. The present period, which started around 1965, has been described as "picket fence" federalism. This metaphor means that federal, state, and local governments are linked by specialized programs which each participates in operating. Each of these specialized programs represents a a picket which touches all three levels. Combined, they form a picket fence. Examples of the specialized programs which form the pickets include: highways, welfare, mental health, higher education, urban renewal, agriculture, and public housing.[36] An expert in the area describes the policy change problem for the political executive when he states:

> Each vertical picket represents an alliance among like-minded program specialists or professionals, regardless of the level of government in which they serve. As early as the mid-1950s these inter level linkages of loyalties were identified and criticized as "vertical functional autocracies." Other epithets used against these patterns are: balkanized bureaucracies, feudal federalisms, and autonomous autocracies. These terms emphasize not only the degree of autonomy that the program specialists have from policy control by political generalists [political executives], but also the separateness and independence that one program area has from another.[37]

Federal political executives are faced with not only the problems of professionals within their agencies, but the alliances their agency professionals make with similar program professionals at the state and local levels of government.

In addition, federal funding of functions performed by state and local governments converts those governments into a unique form of special interest group. Posing as "public interest" groups, organizations such as the National Governors Conference, the National League of Cities and the National Association of County Officials became vociferous lobbyists for the continuation of federal programs and financing.[38] In order to create policy change, political executives must develop effective strategies to deal with these "public sector interest groups" as well as the interlocking network of program professionals at various levels of government.

The Courts

The court system, in at least one respect, operates in ways similar to the administrative process. Administrators, both political and career, take a statute which by its very nature is a general authority to do something and develop administrative routines which specifically implement the law. The courts take the same general statute and compare it to a specific case which has been brought before it. In many cases the judge is in the position of deciding whether the general language of the statute permits or prohibits the action that occurred in the specific case. In other words, if the statute prohibits the parking of a vehicle in a particular place at a particular time and a police officer has issued a ticket to a man who parked his horse-drawn carriage in the spot, the judge's job is to determine if the carriage is a vehicle under the law. Thus it is not usually the legislature that specifies what a vehicle is but a series of administrative actions and court decisions. In the first instance, it is the police officer who decides whether to issue a ticket or not and then, if this decision is challenged, it is the job of the judge to make the final decision.

It should be the political executive who makes the initial determination of what the statute means, not the career executive. The political executive has the legitimacy from the people and plays the role of risk-taker within the system. The career executive should provide his advice as to the possible consequences of a particular interpretation of a statute, but it is up to the political executive to make the final decision. This point is important because the political executive's interpretation may be challenged in court, expecially if it is one that changes the course of the existing policy.

The courts act as the ultimate constraint on the political executive's bureaucratic discretion, his power to determine the precise meaning of the law. The implicit power of the court often acts as a greater constraint on a political executive's actions than is necessary. In order to avoid being excessively constrained, the political executive should bear five principles in mind.

First, litigation concerning agency actions and regulations is a natural part of the policy process. Congress deliberately passes vague legislation which needs to be filled in by the policy implementation process. Various political interest groups will try to shape the final policy output by challenging administrative decisions in court; this is an intrinsic part of the process and cannot be avoided. In the same manner, Congress habitually passes statutes embodying incompatible principles. For example in the snail darter case, Congress passed laws protecting endangered wildlife, but at the same time passed laws providing for the building of dams, the generation of power, and so forth. The nasty problem of determining where one principle would leave off and the other start was left to the executive branch and the courts. This enables the Congress to be all things to all people; it also makes continuing litigation inevitable. The political executive who avoids litigation abdicates his proper role in shaping policy.

Second, the political executive who comes from a business background must recognize the fundamental difference between litigation in the private and public sector. In the business world, litigation concerns an allocation of assets and liabilities. Moreover, litigation places a financial drain on both parties. Therefore the businessman's instinct is always to avoid litigation and settle out of court. Litigation in the public sector is different; it is, as stated, quite simply a continuation of the policy-formation process. The political executive who carries the businessman's instinct to avoid litigation into government with him cannot function effectively in his role as policy-maker.

Third, the political executive must recognize the nature of legal advice he receives from career counsel. The career counsel is a risk avoider; he has no reason to go out of his way to help the political executive implement his agenda and every reason to avoid giving advice to his superiors which may end in litigation and a loss in court. Therefore, he will interpret the constraints of existing rulings as broadly as possible and will be reluctant to challenge precedent. As one political counsel puts it: "a career counsel will treat an article in a legal journal like a district court ruling; a district court ruling is treated like an appellate court ruling; and a verdict by an appellate court is treated as if it came from the Supreme Court." The political executive must understand the conservative bias of career government counsel. Whenever possible it is desirable for the political executive to have the support of counsels who are political appointees.

Fourth, the political executive must recognize that a loss in court is not always a political loss. If the administration presents a reasonable case and is overruled by a judge in a decision that is egregious and arbitrary, such a decision reflects badly on those who appointed the judge and those who drafted the law in the first place. Thus a loss in a court of law can become a victory in the court of public opinion, and a spur to more fundamental political change.

Fifth, the political executive must recognize the value of persistence. Policy formation through litigation is a process with many phases. The political executive must expect to lose his case in some stages. If the federal district court in one area rules against him, he may obtain a favorable ruling in another district, or the case may be taken to an appellate court or even in some situations to the Supreme Court.

In summary, the court system, at first glance, appears as a formidable constraint on the bureaucratic discretion of the political executive.

However, if the principles outlined above are borne in mind, the constraints will be discovered to be more malleable than they seem at first glance, and in some cases may actually afford opportunities.

The White House and the Executive Office of the President (EOP)

The new political executive might think it odd that a section on the White House is included in the chapter on Constraints. After all, the political executive works for the President. The distinction to be made is that the White House and the EOP are not the President. These are large organizations which take on bureaucratic characteristics which are intensified because of their close proximity to the power of the President. Political executives are confronted with two major problems when dealing with the White House and the EOP: lack of policy guidance and difficulty in communication.

The new political executive, counter to his expectation, learns that his contacts with the White House are few and that specific guidance concerning the policies and operation of the agency is close to nil.[39] It would seem that this lack of guidance would provide the political executive with considerable freedom rather than restriction. But it must be remembered that political executives serve at the pleasure of the President and that fact produces a feeling that they will be held accountable even if there is no specific guidance from the White House. Thus, a kind of "dog law"[40] is produced which punishes the political executive for actions which have not been specified as unacceptable in advance.

A political executive operating in this environment tends to become very cautious and unwilling to take risks. Policy change demands that the political executive take risks and engage in a certain amount of controversy surrounding the policy debate. Thus, this lack of guidance from the White House produces an overly cautious set of political executives who do not engage in policy change and who leave the President's electoral mandate unimplemented. The White House acts as a policy constraint on its own policy implementation agenda.

Second, when the political executive tries to communicate with the White House, the process is difficult and frustrating. Trying to get questions on policy answered by the White House takes an exceedingly long time. The internal "bureaucracy" of the White House causes policy questions to be coordinated and reviewed almost to death. At times, the delay makes the answer irrelevant when it is finally produced. The cautious nature of the White House in taking policy stands sends the signal to the political executive that the White House is not serious about dramatic policy change.

Public Employee Unions

Under the current law, Congress has asserted that the presence of labor unions in the federal government "safeguards the public interest; contributes to the effective conduct of public business; and . . . encourages the amiable settlement of disputes between employers and employees."[41] In reality, unions in the federal government impede efficiency and raise costs to taxpayers. Moreover, federal unions have sought to become public lobbyists for bigger, more expensive government, and for liberal causes in general.

In a formal sense, current law restricts the role of unions in the federal government by stipulating a broad range of issues which are barred from labor-management negotiations. These reserved "management rights" include: pay and job classification; the mission, budget size, and organization of an agency; and the hiring, promotion, assignment, and laying off of employees. In addition, management may at its discretion refuse to bargain over the method of performing the work it assigns. This formidable array of "management rights" is, however, largely negated by the fact that the law paradoxically requires federal managers to negotiate with unions over the "implementation and impact" of any management decision even if it pertains to the above-mentioned rights.

The unions' right to bargain over "implementation and impact" means in effect that unions can and will have some form of involvement in virtually any decision that has administrative implications within an agency. This unrestricted range of labor-management bargaining becomes yet another obstacle contributing to the fact that it takes forever to get anything done in the government. Negotiations may be used to delay even the most trivial management decision for several months, eventually putting the decision in the hands of the Impasses Panel of the Federal Labor Relations Authority. Moreover, as a general bargaining tactic, unions may adopt a nit-picking, go-slow attitude on all routine administrative actions until management displays a more "cooperative" attitude on more important issues ostensibly removed from the labor-management forum.

The influence of federal employee unions is felt not only in internal agency bargaining, but in the broader political process as well. While existing law prohibits federal employees from lobbying Congress on behalf of particular legislation, this restriction does not apply to the unions of federal employees. Federal unions have become significant lobbyists on all issues pertaining to the management of the federal government. Recently, federal unions have condemned efforts to make government managers more responsive to political direction as a return to "patronage." The unions have resisted proposals to integrate the federal employee retirement system with Social Security, and have blocked plans to link pay to the performance of federal employees. They have advocated boosting federal pay by 20 percent to achieve alleged "equality" with the private sector, and backed "comparable worth" as a means of raising the wages of female federal employees. Federal unions will have particular influence over Congressmen who represent large numbers of federal workers as well as those who generally are "pro-union." In addition, federal unions are provided with a more pervasive political influence through their links with the AFL-CIO.

Federal employee unions are at present widening the scope of their lobbying activities beyond issues relating to internal government affairs and are becoming partisan advocates of larger domestic spending programs and liberal causes. For example, when the Reagan Administration cut back staffing at the Department of Housing and Urban Development, the union local did not hesitate to identify the interests of its employees with liberal policy goals. The survival of liberal social policies and the interest of union employees were deliberately entwined to the extent that the union proclaimed itself the new custodian of the "public interest."[42] In other words, what is good for the American Federation of Government Employees (AFGE) is good for the country. Similarly AFGE President Ken Blaylock has asked union employees in the Defense Department to leak information (possibly including classified materials) pertaining to cost overruns and inefficiencies in military procurement in an effort to thwart the administration's proposed defense build-up.[43]

Federal employee unions also play a political role by serving as an information conduit between the bureaucracy and Congress. Confronted with proposed cutbacks or unwanted policy changes, federal unions will help prepare congressional opposition by providing detailed questions for congressional critics to use during public hearings. Another tactic is for the union to demand documents pertaining to policy-making by way of a Freedom of Information Act request and then to provide those documents to its allies in Congress and in the bureaucracy. Finally, like any organized special interest, the federal employee unions intervene in the electoral process to further their own ends. During the 1982 elections the political action committee of AFGE poured $450,000 into the campaigns of "liberal and progressive Democrats" who shared its goals of greater federal employment and spending.[44]

Under existing law, the political executive must simply accept the opposition of most federal unions in the general political arena. However, on questions pertaining to the impact of unions on government productivity, there is much that can be done. Conventional wisdom holds that the impact of unions in federal government is limited in comparison to their role in the private sector—they cannot bargain over pay or strike, for example. This view ignores the fact that the stalling tactics often employed in public sector labor-management disputes would quickly drive most private firms out of business entirely. This negative influence is compounded by the fact that real cost considerations have little direct impact on a mid-level federal sector manager while the laborious realities of labor-management relations are unavoidable.

This asymmetry creates a tendency to avoid trouble by going easy on the unions—for example, by imposing lower performance standards even though there is no lawful obligation to do so. Most activity of this sort will occur at lower levels in the organization with which the political appointee has little direct experience and will often take forms that are hard to detect, e.g., management proposals that are never made because of fear of union reaction. Nevertheless, the affect on the efficiency of the organization will be quite real. To counteract these tendencies political management must make it very clear to lower level career managers that it will support and reward those managers who stand firmly by their "management rights" in the face of union hostility.

CAPTURE

It should be clear from this discussion of constraints that the job of the political executive is extremely demanding and complex. The image of the political executive stepping into the fast moving river and getting caught up in the current is very apt. It is difficult for the political executive to make his own way in the river. An understanding of the constraints on the political executive provides some realization of the difficulties of promoting policy change, but a closer look at the process by which even the most determined political executive may be "captured" by the system is necessary to fully prepare the new political executive to resist it.

Capture is the process by which the political executive is converted from an agent of the President and his policies to an agent of the career bureaucracy and its policies. The conversion process starts at the time of the initial selection and appointment. As previously discussed, political executives lead agencies dominated by professional staffs. The selection of a political executive is, in part, based on the professional qualifications which are necessary to understand and run a specific agency. This results in the selection of political personnel who often have similar training and experience to that of personnel in the agency. While the political executive may have participated in political party activities and supported the President in the election campaign, these activities are often secondary compared to his professional qualifications. Most will be Assistant Secretary "for" housing development or wildlife, for example, and as such are clearly linked to specific government functions and the corresponding professional groups.

The political executive who does not have professional credentials linked to a certain issue area, is likely to base his qualifications on general "managerial" skills which have little bearing on political loyalties or political agenda. As such, the "manager" is likely to be naive concerning policy issues and the political aspects of his job. "I'd be offended to see these management techniques used for overtly political purposes," one politically appointed "manager" said. "I mean, my personal feeling is that all politicians should have the same objectives and differ on the amount of resources and means to achieve them."[45] Therefore the capture is very likely because the appointee from the start either is sympathetic with the goals and objectives of the agency and reluctant to initiate fundamental change, or lacks the knowledge necessary to resist the bureaucracy's viewpoint on given issues.

From the moment the political executive first walks through the door and is met by sixty pounds of "briefing books," all lobbying quietly for the bureaucracy's viewpoint, he is confronted with a very strong *socialization process* imposed by the organization. One authority has described this process as the ability which organizations have "to implant behavioral templates . . . in their members."[46] The political appointee should never underestimate the power that a large organization has in forcing its definition of roles and goals onto an individual even if that individual is nominally its leader. If the agency is successful in its socialization efforts, the political executive ends up accepting career goals and providing what the bureaucracy lacks—political legitimacy for the implementation of those goals.

Two aspects of the agency socialization process contribute to the process of capture. First, as previously discussed, the initial orientation of the new political executive to the agency passes on the bureaucratic ideology of the agency to the new political executive. If during the initial briefings or during his tenure in office the political executive accepts the bureaucratic ideology and if that ideology runs counter to the political objectives of the administration, then the political executive is essentially captured and loses his effectiveness as an agent of the President.

The second aspect of the socialization process is that of role definition. The initial briefing process and the initial flow of decisions to the political executive helps to determine the role of the political executive within the organization. If the bureaucracy defines the political executive's role so as to segregate him from the "administrative" aspects of policy and the political executive accepts this role definition, then he effectively is captured. In other words, if the political executive attempts to manage by setting broad policy and leaving the details of management "implementation" and "administration" to the career staff, the political executive will lose the ability to control the policy change process.

An additional factor which contributes to capture proceeds from the desire of the political executive to remain out of political controversy. The last thing most political executives want is to make negative headlines in the *Washington Post* or be called before a congressional committee for a tongue-lashing. It is often assumed, quite incorrectly, that a political executive is doing a good job if he stays out of the press. On the contrary, the political executive who is doing a good job at policy change causes controversy that appears in the press. Thus, the desire to keep out of the press pushes the political executive to accept the goals of the career bureaucracy. Since these usually correspond to the goals of the client interest groups of the bureaucracy, there is little criticism.

This acceptance of career goals also means that there is no need for bureaucratic sabotage of the sort described in the section on "Bureaucratic Politics and Bureaucratic Entrepeneurs." Therefore the world of that political executive is relatively quiet, but little policy change takes place.

Finally, the political executive has infrequent contacts with the other members of the administration. He lives in close contact with the members of his agency and it is quite natural that this daily contact causes him to identify with the goals of his agency and to lose the initial fervor of the strongly held political goals of the administration. One of the best descriptions of this situation uses the metaphors of the "native village" and "big city life."

> Weaknesses among political executives lead inevitably to White House complaints about their "going native" in the bureaucracy. The image is apt. To a large extent the particular agencies and bureaus are the native villages of executive politics. Even the most presidentially minded political executive will discover that his own agency provides the one relatively secure reference point amid all the other uncertainties of Washington. In their own agencies, appointees usually have at least some knowledge of each other and a common identity with particular programs. Outside the agency it is more like life in the big city among large numbers of anonymous people who have unknown lineages. Any common kinship in the political party or a shared political vocation is

> improbable, and in the background are always the suspicions of the President's "true" family of supporters in the White House. Political appointees in the larger Washington environment may deal frequently with each other, but these are likely to be the kind of ad hoc, instrumental relations of the city, where people interact without truly knowing each other.[47]

The process of capture is not confined to any single political party. For example, during the Carter Administration, the Secretary of the Department of Housing and Urban Development, Patricia Harris, became a fierce advocate of the Department she was supposed to oversee. Harris submitted budget requests 40 percent over OMB guidelines and mobilized outside interest groups to lobby the White House against its own budget. HUD employees were so delighted with Harris's performance as Secretary that they voted her an honorary member of their union local; presumably, President Carter was somewhat less pleased.[48]

At the beginning of the Reagan Administration, Cabinet appointees were warned about the "capture process." Despite the warning, capture occured quite early on. Within eight days after Reagan took office, Secretary of Transportation Drew Lewis called a meeting for Cabinet secretaries. Reagan officials were astonished to find themselves listening to a proposal for imposing import quotas on Japanese cars—an issue pushed by a deputy assistant secretary held over from the Carter Administration. Despite private DOT assurances that it was not serious about quotas and was merely trying to appease its internal bureaucracy, DOT continued to promote the protection issue. Within a few weeks the efforts of conservatives in the administration were diverted from the positive agenda of cutting taxes into a defensive action to stave off increased protectionism.[49]

Not only was the administration committed to free trade in principle, the promotion of the auto import issue was a no-win proposition for President Reagan politically, imposing costs no matter which side of the issue was taken. Most importantly, political momentum during the crucial first three months of the administration was disrupted; an inordinate amount of attention at the top levels of government was absorbed by the auto import question—attention which should have been devoted to the real economic goals of the adminstration. As Paul Craig Roberts stated: "a government that was supposed to be bringing a policy revolution was deflected from its goal by a deputy assistant secretary of transportation."[50]

Situations of this sort where the political administration collaborates in replacing its own agenda with that of the bureaucracy are not at all uncommon. The environment in which political executives are placed is so powerful that they are almost inevitably swept along with the current. Perhaps the right question is not why so many political executives are captured by the bureaucracy; the more relevant question is, given the pressures of the environment, how does a minority resist the raging current of the stream and produce real changes?

Footnotes

1. Quoted in David T. Stanley, "*Changing Administrations: The 1961 and 1964 Transitions in Six Departments*" (Washington D.C.: The Brookings Institution, 1965), p. 127.
2. Peters, *The Politics of Bureaucracy*, p. 182.
3. Bernstein, *The Job of the Federal Executive*, p.89.
4. The remainder of this section is based on Frederick C. Mosher, *Democracy and the Public Service* (New York: Oxford University Press, 1968), pp. 99-133.
5. See Herbert Kaufman, *The Forest Ranger: A Study in Administrative Behavior* (Baltimore: John Hopkins Press, 1960).
6. Walter I. Trattner, *From Poor Law To Welfare State* (New York: Free Press, 1984), p. 320.
7. In a letter to Senator Ted Stevens (September 9, 1981), David T. Stanley of NAPA recommends that the Reagan administration ". . . fully involve and utilize the talents of career executives in *policy-making* and policy implementation." (Emphasis added.)
8. Mosher, *Democracy and the Public Service*, p. 124.
9. ". . . [D]emocratic morality asserts that responsiveness to the people's will is the ultimate test of public policy. It rejects the right of any elite to *impose* its will." Emmette S. Redford, *Democracy in the Administrative State* (New York: Oxford University Press, 1969), p. 32.
10. This section is based on Anthony Downs, *Inside Bureaucracy* (Boston: Little, Brown and Co., 1967), pp.237-246.
11. *Ibid*., p. 237 (emphasis added).
12. *Ibid*., p. 243.
13. Francis Rourke agrees with Downs. The development of an appropriate ideology is important ". . . both as a method of binding outside supporters to the agency and as a technique for intensifying its employees' loyalty to its purposes." Rourke, *Bureaucracy, Politics and Public Policy*, p. 107. Rourke goes on to argue that bureaucratic ideology contributes significantly to the establishment of the agency esprit and to the mystique which at times surrounds an agency. He cites the EPA as an example of an organization which has developed a strong conservationist mystique around its efforts at pollution control. Rourke, *Bureaucracy, Politics and Public Policy*, p. 107. Thus, an agency develops a strong sense of mission or program loyalty which it is willing to defend by the use of politics. Bernstein concludes that: "The politics of the spoilsman has been replaced by the politics of program loyalty featuring the employee's dedication to the welfare of his agency." Bernstein, *The Federal Executive*, p. 88.
14. ". . . [O]rganizations may have goals of their own and consequently may not accept the goals of their nominal political superiors. Opposition to the policies of politicians is rarely overt as this might violate the formal relationships between elective and permanent officials in government. More commonly, bureaucrats defeat politicians by obfuscation, delay, and the use of rules, regulations, and procedures. . . . Politicians, being short-term occupants of their positions, rarely understand either the procedural mechanisms or the substance of policy as well as their nominal servants and consequently are frequently at the mercy of civil servants." Peters, *The Politics of Bureaucracy*, pp. 185-186.
15. This section is based on Allison, *The Essence of Decision*, pp. 67-100.
16. Allison, *The Essence of Decision*, pp. 67-68.
17. Allison, *The Essence of Decision*, p. 80. In addition, Ban, Goldenberg, and

Marzotto observe that even professionals adopt and defend administrative routines. "They become wedded to tried and true standard operating procedures and strongly held 'wisdom' born of experience about what will and will not work. These perspectives are often difficult to set aside when a new political appointee embarks in a different direction." Carolyn Ban, Edie Goldenberg, and Tony Marzotto, "Controlling the U.S. Federal Bureaucracy: Will SES Make a Difference?" in G.E. Caiden and H. Siedentopf, eds. *Strategies for Administrative Reform* (Lexington, Mass: D.C. Heath, 1982), pp. 211. And finally, in the extreme case, as Francis Rourke points out, bureaucratic momentum "manifests itself in the continuing performance of routines that are no longer required because the problem to which they were addressed no longer exists." Rourke, *Bureaucracy, Politics and Public Policy*, p. 34.

18. Quoted in Allison, *The Essence of Decision*, p. 131.

19. Martin Anderson, *Welfare* (Stanford California: Hoover Institution Press, 1978), pp. 24-25.

20. This section is based on Downs, *Inside Bureaucracy*, pp. 167-168.

21. *Ibid.*, p. 195.

22. Allison, *The Essence of Decision*, p. 144.

23. *Ibid.*, p. 67.

24. This story is provided in Frederic V. Malek, *Washington's Hidden Tragedy: The Failure to Make Government Work* (New York: Free Press, 1978), pp. 222-224.

25. Francis Rourke provides an excellent description of bureaucratic sabotage in the most recent edition of his book *Bureaucracy, Politics and Public Policy*: "Usually, bureaucratic opposition to official policy is covert rather than open—guerrilla warfare rather than frontal assault. Career officials will confide their doubts about the wisdom of the policies being followed by their political superiors to friendly groups with which they have an intimate relationship that policy changes being contemplated by the administration in power are adverse to their interests. They thus convert disputes with political executives into conflicts between their superiors and outside organizations. In this way, they can pursue their objectives without jeopardy to the forms of bureaucratic life of the safety of their own position. Moreover, by avoiding an open break with their superior, they can continue to pass ammunition to a political executive's critics from the security of their intimate participation in the affairs and deliberations of the agency. In this surreptitious way, career officials can incite political conflict in the outside world without risking their own safety by directly participating in the combat. Many of these tactics were used by career employees at the EPA in their struggles with political appointees during the early years of the Reagan administration." pp. 128-129.

26. Richard P. Nathan, "The Administrative Presidency," *The Public Interest*, No. 44 (Summer 1976), p. 44.

27. Anderson, *Welfare*, pp. 1-13, 67-85, 169-207. This example of bureaucratic entrepreneurship is also cited in Nakamura and Smallwood, *The Politics of Policy Implementation*, pp. 134-135.

28. Outside the government, conservatives such as Milton Friedman had supported the idea of a negative income tax, Friedman, however, rejected the government-generated FAP.

29. Nathan, *The Administrative Presidency*, p. 44.

30. For a full discussion of how Congress gets involved in the details of administration see Schick, "Congress and 'Details' of Administration."

31. Hamilton, Madison and Jay, *The Federalist Papers*, p. 79.

32. See Hugh Heclo, "Issue Networks and the Executive Establishment," in Anthony King,ed. *The New American Political System*, (Washington D.C.: American Enterprise Institute, 1978), pp. 87-124.

33. Bernstein, *The Job of the Federal Executive*, p. 127.

34. Malek, *Washington's Hidden Tragedy*, p. 172.

35. Quoted in Bernstein, *The Job of the Federal Executive*, p.134.

36. Deil S. Wright, "Intergovernmental Relations: An Analytical Overview," *The Annals of the American Academy of Political and Social Science* 416 (1974), pp. 14-15.

37. Deil S. Wright, "Intergovernmental Relations," p. 14 and 16.

38. These three, plus the Council of State Governments, National Legislative

Conference, U.S. Conference of Mayors, and International City Management Association, represent what is called the "Big Seven" in the area of intergovernmental relations.

39. Bernstein, *The Job of the Federal Executive*, p. 35.

40. Dogs are punished for acts that are not specified in advance as undesirable. See Gordon Tullock, *The Politics of Bureaucracy* (Washington, D.C.: Public Affairs Press, 1965), p. 182.

41.Federal Labor Relations Authority, *A Guide to the Federal Service Labor Management Statute*, FLRA Doc. 1213 (Washington D.C.: U.S. Government Printing Office, 1981), p. 4

42. *Washington Post*, September 29, 1982.

43. *Washington Times*, May 18, 1983.

44. *Washington Times*, May 15, 1984, p. 4A. Not only the unions but all federal employee and professional groups seem to have become politicized and partisan. For example, the National Association of Retired Federal Employees runs its own PAC. NARFE-PAC gave out over $400,000 to sympathetic Congressmen in 1983-84, ninety percent of the money going to Democrats. *Washington Times*, August 7, 1984, p. 4A.

45. Quoted in Heclo, *A Government of Strangers*, p. 67.

46. Kaufman, *The Administrative Behavior of Federal Bureau Chiefs*, p. 194.

47. Heclo, *A Government of Strangers*, p. 111.

48. *Washington Post*, September 29, 1982.

49. This story is related in Paul Craig Roberts, *The Supply Side Revolution: An Insider's account of Policymaking in Washington* (Cambridge Massachusetts: Harvard University Press, 1984), pp. 122-124.

50. *Ibid.*, p. 123.

25

Techniques for Managing Policy Change

The Political Agenda

> In government the executive does not have the same measuring sticks to help him manage his affairs that the business executive has. He has nothing he can box and crate and put on the loading platform to be sold competitively. Lacking a familiar standard to appraise the real value of his management, he wonders how well he is managing his program.[1]

Political agendas serve an extremely important function in policy-making and politics. Candidates and parties develop elaborate strategies to influence and control the political agenda and the political debate because they know that the agenda often has a significant impact on the policy-making of the country. For the policy-making of the political executive, the development and control of a political agenda is just as important.

Since the public sector does not have a simple measuring device like profits or sales in the private sector, the political agenda serves this purpose. The political executive constantly must compare the daily operations of his organization to the agenda in order to guide his decisions. Successful political executives know that the political agenda is the most important part of their operations; every action, every activity is measured against how it advances the accomplishment of the agenda. On the other hand, political executives who flounder and fail often do so because they fail to develop and implement an agenda.

Failure to establish a political agenda was carried to extremes by the Carter Administration. Carter arrived in Washington with few specific plans in any area. Even after he was in office, there was little discussion of substance among the White House staff and that there was very little idea of how or what to change in governmental programs.[2] While the Carter presidency was plagued with many problems, this was probably one of the more significant ones and it is certainly one that gave the country a sense of drift and lack of leadership.

As previously discussed, the political appointee without an agenda is a ready victim for the bureaucracy. Indeed the "agenda free" political executive may compound this problem; since he is expected to produce results, he may accept eagerly the career policy agenda for lack of an alternative. The "agenda free" political executive, therefore, looks as if he is doing his job because he is "getting things done" while all he is really doing is implementing the bureaucracy's policy goals. Ironically, because a political appointee operating in this mode will generate less internal and external opposition, he may appear to be more "productive" than a political appointee who is actually trying to do his job.

Planning and the Political Agenda

A new administration will arrive in Washington with an agenda marked by different degrees of preparation. In one area, it may have an "off the shelf" policy in the form of a coherent, detailed set of proposed changes in regulations and legislation. In other areas, it may have certain general principles which need to be elaborated into specific legislative and regulatory proposals by the political executive. Worse, in certain areas it may have no more than campaign slogans, with no substance.

The first alternative, "off the shelf," pre-developed policies, is by far the most desirable. A new administration arrives in office with political momentum which lasts three to four months. This is the period in which the chances for major legislative and regulatory changes are optimal. However, this period is almost always too short to develop feasible legislative proposals, even if there is consensus within the administration over general goals.

Martin Anderson comments on this point with respect to his experiences during the first three months of the Nixon Administration:

> Once in office there is not time during the first year to develop the kind of comprehensive legislative proposals that are necessary to cope with the complex, detailed issues they purport to deal with. But the public, and especially the media, is not disposed to waiting much beyond 100 days before clamoring for results. . . . In this situation there is only one thing a newly elected administration can do. It must choose "off the shelf" from among the legislative plans that are available.[3]

The political executive who must work up specific policies from scratch after the administration is in office is greatly disadvantaged. The initial period of momentum will be lost. Political opponents within the administration and careerists in the bureaucracy will have a lengthier opportunity to water down any initiative; external opponents in Congress and in the media will have time to prepare their defenses. In this respect, the success of President Reagan's initial tax cutting was enhanced by the fact that he arrived in office with concrete proposals instead of a vague commitment to "cut taxes."

When the political executive does not come into office equipped with detailed "off the shelf" policy proposals, he will be forced to develop a policy agenda while in office. He must attempt to integrate the general political principles which the administration stands for with specific policy options, and he must bear in mind the inherent informational bias of his position. That is, once inserted into the bureaucracy, he will be subject to a daily torrent of institutionally generated "information" but will have little contact with external political groups, the White House, and other outside forces. To prevent himself from being inundated by the bureaucratic perspective as he formulates a policy agenda, the political executive must make a deliberate effort to remain in contact with other political appointees, to seek information from outside sources on a regular basis, and to use external consultants for guidance.

In developing a policy agenda, the political executive generally will concentrate on legislative and regulatory changes which may be politically feasible to enact within a year or two, but he should not neglect the prospect of long-run policy change as well. The case of Nixon's "Family Assistance Plan" demonstrates the longevity of certain policy proposals. Work on a current policy proposal may bear fruit as much as a decade later. The political executive must understand that fundamental policy change can seldom be an "off the cuff" affair, but is instead an expensive, laborious, and long-run process. Given this understanding, the political executive must use the resources of the executive branch not merely to make short-term policy adjustments but to prepare for and justify more basic long-run change—even if the immediate chances for such change are slight. In doing this the political executive creates "off the shelf" policy options for subsequent officials. Moreover, the act of developing long-run conservative policy options eventually may alter the political climate and make change more feasible.

Discovering Discretion

While pre-planned policy options are very important, particularly for major changes, it is of course impossible to foresee all opportunities for policy change upon entering office. In addition to implementing "off the shelf" plans and initiating long-run planning, the political executive must develop new policy initiatives by making a deliberate effort to "discover discretion" in his immediate political setting. This is particularly important because the implementation of many major policy goals that the political executive has brought to his job with him may be thwarted by powerful internal and external constraints. Large amounts of political capital may be expended on these major policy goals with no results. However, as the political executive learns about the details of his agency's operations, he may discover lucrative "targets of opportunity" for policy change which are more politically feasible than his initial policy goals. These "targets of opportunity" may consist of potential changes in administrative procedures or regulations which have a significant meaning for the President's broad agenda with little accompanying political cost.

One means by which the political executive may facilitate the discovery of discretion or "targets of opportunity" is through a detailed review of statutes and regulations governing the operation of his agency. In this process, he will discover a certain disparity between what the career bureaucrats say about a given regulation or law and what the regulation or law actually says. (Similarly, he will find that his bureaucratic staff will inform him that he cannot take a certain action because it violates regulations, while they routinely ignore dozens of regulations when it serves the interest of the institution to do so.) By discovering the difference between an actual regulation or law and the bureaucracy's interpretation of it, the political executive can find he has more room for maneuver than he had assumed. Moreover, his review will reveal areas of potential policy change which he had not foreseen. Thus, by linking the general political principles of the administration with a knowledge of the agency, the political executive can create a new operational agenda and implement it through his powers of bureaucratic discretion.

Jigsaw Puzzle Management

Whether he is implementing a planned agenda or formulating a new one, the political executive will be involved in politically controversial subjects. This means that control over the process must be retained by the political executive and his immediate political staff. Very little information will be put in writing. Career staff will supply information, but they should never become involved in the formulation of agenda-related policy objectives. Similarly, once controversial policy goals are formulated, they should not be released in total to the career staff. Thus, the political executive and his political staff become "jigsaw puzzle" managers. Other staff see and work on the individual pieces, but never have enough of the pieces to be able to learn the entire picture.

By operating in this fashion, the political executive maintains control over his political agenda and his political opponents can only guess what the political executive is after. Or they ascertain the true intention at a point in the process when it is too late to mobilize effective counter efforts.[4] However, balance in the application of the principles of information control is necessary. Secrecy should be reserved only for truly controversial policies. If information is overly controlled, it can only intensify bureaucratic opposition needlessly.

Mastering the In-Box

Finally, it is very imporant for the political executive to maintain his focus on the political agenda in the midst of his daily routine. Many political executives are swept away in the day-to-day flow of decisions, crisis management, meetings and in-box paperwork. This confusion can be more easily understood by remembering that the political executive has under him hundreds and often thousands of bureaucrats, all carrying out their own bureaucratic routines. They generate an enormous volume of material to be reviewed and material requiring decisions, most of which proceeds from the agenda of the institution as opposed to that of the political executive. Add to this the fact that, as stated before, attempting policy change is difficult because it mobilizes internal and external opposition, while maintaining the institution in its existing course is relatively effort-free—and it becomes possible to understand why many political appointees end up being controlled by their in-boxes rather than vice versa.

To avoid this fate, it is especially important that the political executive gain control over the allocation of his time. The time the political executive has available to him to formulate and implement policy change is short; while bureaucrats operate from a much longer time perspective. It is in the interests of the bureaucracy to delay change, and to take up as much of the political executive's time as possible with the concerns of the bureaucracy. To resist this process, the political executive may instruct his secretary to set aside certain periods in a day which are to be free of meetings, appointments, and interuptions. During those periods, the political executive will be free to work on items he initiates as opposed to those the institution initiates for him. Similarly, it is necessary periodically to pull the entire political staff out of the paperwork flow and get it to re-focus on the political agenda. Here again, a formal procedure is best: for example weekly planning and strategy sessions or two-day out-of-town strategy retreats.

Managing Personnel

Proper management of subordinate bureaucratic personnel is indispensable if the political executive is to be successful in his role. If the political executive handles personnel problems correctly, he will be able to reduce the degree of difficulty he will experience subsequently with the internal constraints discussed earlier. Moreover, effective personnel management can, to a lesser degree, mitigate bureaucratic opposition and thus dampen the forcefulness of the alliance between disaffected bureaucrats, interest groups, the liberal media, and Congress.

In his relations with the bureaucracy beneath him, the political executive must avoid the two extremes of "capture" and the "fortress mentality." Capture, which seems to have been the more prevalent problem in the first Reagan Administration, has already been discussed fully. In the opposite case of the fortress mentality, the political executive adopts a paranoid attitude, seeing the bureaucracy around him as a solid phalanx of political and institutional hostility. Relations between the political executive and bureaucrats are frozen into an adversary format. Communication ceases.

This paranoid attitude is usually unnecessary, particularly if the political executive is sure of his political agenda and unafraid of contamination from bureaucratic lobbying. Although the bureaucracy presents innumerable obstacles to policy change, it is also a resource which, within limits, may be used by the political executive. Indeed, since the tiny handful of political appointees in the executive branch cannot manage the government by themselves, efforts to establish a constructive relationship with career personnel are an absolute necessity.

Although it is not always attainable, the political executive who has the active support of some part of his career staff is always in a much stronger position than the political executive who does not. In this respect, it is important to note that the bureaucrat does not have to engage in active opposition in order to sabotage the political executive. Often he merely has to withhold critical advice and allow the political executive to founder and sink on his own.[5]

A particular problem with respect to this issue is the political executive who arrives in Washington with years of pent-up resentment toward bureaucrats who have "made the mess in Washington." Even though the political executive will soon be face-to-face with a number of first-class "mess makers," he should keep his legitimate hostility in check. The political executive will encounter enough bureaucratic resistance to policy change itself. Attempts to deliberately "pay back" the bureaucracy will only exacerbate opposition needlessly.

The Personnel System

> To institute a civil service system is to accept the idea that competent personnel managing the government machinery should be available for the use by—but not at the absolute disposal of—any political group arriving in office through legitimate means.[6]

Unfortunately, the civil service ideal, as stated above, is not always reality. Political executives will have, in certain circumstances, great difficulty managing the career staff who control the machinery of government. For example, if a political executive wishes to demote or dismiss a career employee, the employee is entitled to:

> (1) a written notice stating reasons, at least 30 days before the proposed action, (2) representation by an attorney or union agent, (3) opportunity to answer orally and in writing within a reasonable time, (4) written decision by an administrative level higher than the one initiating the action, and (5) final agency decision within 30 days after the end of the notice period.[7]

After the termination decision is made, the affected employee may then appeal the agency decision to the Merit Systems Protection Board (MSPB) and, if he claims discrimination, to the Equal Employment Opportunity Commission (EEOC). These protections, as elaborate as they are, are simplified from the protections that existed before 1978.

Such protection is afforded career civil servants because the federal personnel system embodies the merit concept. This concept is based on three essential and interrelated ideas: selection of career personnel based on merit, tenure in position regardless of political changes, and willingness to be responsive to legitimate political leaders.[8] Together, these three principles produce a tension which causes the personnel system to be in conflict with itself.

On the one hand, political control should be maintained so that policies legitimated by the voting public are implemented. On the other hand, the career civil servants must have a degree of formal protection and insulation from the political appointees, to prevent a wholesale return to a political patronage system where employees would be promoted or fired on the basis of political beliefs and loyalty. A career bureaucrat has the same right to his personal political beliefs as any other American citizen. The upper level of the career bureaucracy cannot be purged on an ideological basis every four years. But still, the simple expectation that the private political beliefs of bureaucrats will not interfere with the political executive's control of the government is naive.

Since the start of the merit system in the federal government in 1883, the tension between formal protection of careerists and the need for political responsiveness led to the creation of rules and regulations that attempted to produce, although unsuccessfully, a balance between the two extremes. During the 1960s and 1970s there was a renewed emphasis on the need for political responsiveness; this criticism led to the Civil Service Reform Act of 1978 (CSRA).

One way this Act sought to alter the relationship between political executives and career bureaucrats was to create a new personnel system for high-level career executives. As part of this Act, Congress established the Senior Executive Service (SES) to be composed of the personnel who previously held "super grade" positions of grades 16-18 in the General Schedule. Responsiveness and accountability to political officials was increased by giving the political executive greater control of the hiring, assignment, reward and punishment of these senior career executives.

In addition, the CSRA created a formal process by which the political executive's policy and administrative priorities could be communicated to SES officials and "merit pay managers" (GS 13-15) and by which the performance of those career officials could in turn be rated. Finally, the SES section of CSRA sought to reduce the vested interest which key bureaucrats have in particular programs and clients by encouraging greater government-wide mobility in the higher levels of the bureaucracy and by making it easier to bring outside personnel with fresh perspectives into senior career positions in the government.[9] The specific provisions of CSRA as they relate to the political executive's management of personnel will be discussed below.

The Political Values of Bureaucrats

In order to be effective, the political executive must not only understand the personnel system, but the nature of the bureaucrats around him as well. In this respect, the conservative political executive who pushes for policy change in his agency will find he has less than ideal relations with many of his bureaucratic subordinates; this is not only because the political executive's agenda will threaten vested institutional interests but because of the ideological slant of the Washington bureaucracy outside the Pentagon.

A recent study by Stanley Rothman and S. Robert Lichter confirms charges made by the Nixon White House that the bureaucracy is predominantly liberal and pro-Democratic, though perhaps less than one might imagine.[10] Rothman and Lichter interviewed two hundred SES level personnel, excluding political appointees, from thirteen different departments and agencies. Half of the sample came from traditional agencies: the Departments of Agriculture, Commerce, and the Treasury, and the Bureau of Prisons in the Department of Justice. The other half of the sample came from the "activist" agencies of more recent origin: the Environmental Protection Agency, the Federal Trade Commission, the Consumer Product Safety Commission, the Equal Employment Opportunity Commission, ACTION, the Food and Drug Administration, the Department of Housing and Urban Development, the Department of Health and Human Services, and the Civil Rights Division of the Justice Department.

Forty-eight percent of SES personnel in the traditional agencies identified themselves as liberals, nearly two and one-half times the rate for the American population as a whole. On the other hand, only 29 percent identified themselves as conservatives. In the activist agencies 63 percent identified themselves as liberals compared to 23 percent who regarded themselves as conservative. The voting of the group shown in the chart below conforms to this pattern.

Presidential Voting Record of Top Level Bureaucrats, 1968-1980[11] (Percent Voting For)

	Traditional Agencies	Activist Agencies	Combined
1968			
Nixon	33	23	28
Humphrey	67	76	72
1972			
Nixon	51	35	42
McGovern	47	65	57
1976			
Ford	35	24	28
Carter	65	76	71
1980			
Reagan	48	27	36
Carter	34	55	48
Anderson	19	18	18

The votes of top-level bureaucrats are clearly well to the left of the American public. On the other hand, bureaucrats are decidedly less left-wing than the Washington Press Corps or than the "public interest" activists in Washington. It is interesting to note that nearly half of the bureaucrats in traditional agencies and over a quarter of the bureaucrats in activist agencies voted for Ronald Reagan in 1980—although most of this support was probably moderate Republican or anti-Carter as opposed to conservative in nature. Political attitudes reflect the predominant moderate-liberal slant; 80 percent support abortion; half feel the government should substantially redistribute income, and a third want the government to guarantee jobs. On the other hand, two-thirds believe that business is overregulated.

The Lichter and Rothman study provides a number of clues for the political executive in a second Reagan Administration. It should come as no surprise that a majority of bureaucrats are left of center and will be in varying degrees ideologically opposed to a conservative presidency. However, voting patterns (36 percent for Reagan in 1980 and 42 percent for Nixon in 1972) indicate that the bureaucracy is less solidly left-wing than might be supposed. There appears to be a fair sized pool of "moderates" who will not necessarily be implacably opposed to everything on the conservative agenda.[12]

Moreover, the small group of relatively conservative individuals within the top ranks of the bureaucracy should not be overlooked. These persons represent a significant resource for the political executive. Since the political executive cannot operate the government alone and must, to some extent, depend on career staff, efforts should be made to locate those individuals who are in sympathy with, or at least not antipathetic to, a conservative philosophy.

Lest the notion of a moderate bureaucracy be oversold, it should be noted that there is probably a greater tendency to moderation among top-level administrators than among middle-level careerists. Moreover, even if a bureaucrat is "moderate" or "conservative" in his general outlook, this may not apply to policy changes or reductions in his own particular agency, to which he has ties built up over time.

Finally, there is also a definite radical segment in the top level of the bureaucracy. For example, the Lichter and Rothman data indicate that fourteen percent of SES administrators in both activist and traditional agencies wish to move the nation toward socialism. Bureaucratic opponents will be centered in this group, but it will include others as well. Opponents can be expected to leak and generate a steady flow of material concerning "victimization of the poor" and "selling out to the big corporations." Operating in a network with Congress, the liberal media, and the large population of left-wing "public-interest" groups, left-wing bureaucrat opponents will certainly be the noisiest and perhaps the most influential segment of the bureaucracy.

Evaluating Bureaucratic Personnel

To manage bureaucratic subordinates, the political executive must comprehend not only the basic political slant of the bureaucracy, but also the variety of instititutional roles which bureaucrats assume. Thus while any typology of human behavior must be an oversimplification, it remains true that different individuals within organizations tend to respond to events in fairly set psychological patterns.

Proper utilization of bureaucratic personnel requires a recognition of these patterns.

One useful way of analyzing bureaucrats is to study the degree and type of resistance they exhibit to change and political leadership. Four patterns emerge, allowing bureaucrats to be classified as: *opponents; reluctants; critics;* and *autistics.*[13]

Opponents are unalterably opposed to the policies of the political executive; *reluctants* are opposed, but are not immune to persuasion; *critics* will support the political executive as long as they feel their own views are being considered; *autistics* do not support the political executive because they consistently cannot hear—or they hear incorrectly— what the political executive wants.

Upon arriving in his position, the political executive may regard all career staff as opponents. Although a large number of opponents will certainly exist, in reality he will find other types of careerists around him as well. Initial identification and sorting is of critical importance if the political executive is to manage his staff constructively. For example, once identified, the political executive can transfer opponents to routine jobs where they will have little influence over policy. Reluctants will require concerted efforts at persuasion to win over. Critics, on the other hand, can be useful to the political executive if the political executive simply listens to what the critic has to say before making a decision. Finally, the autistics need to be given simple tasks where no discretion is involved. These are necessary reminders to political managers. Too often managers see personnel in dichotomies. Personnel are either good or bad, productive or nonproductive, opponents or supporters. The world is more complex, and a simple four-part typology, if operationalized by the political executive, can increase his management effectiveness many times.

A second way of understanding the behavior of bureaucratic subordinates is to recognize that different individuals within the same institution have widely different motivations. One very intriguing method of analyzing bureaucratic behavior is based on differences in the motivational patterns of high-level bureaucrats.[14] According to this analysis, bureaucrats may be divided into two basic categories: those who are governed by pure self-interest and those who have mixed motives. The latter group differs from the former in that the usual concerns of career advancement and security are balanced by strong loyalties to other factors such as a program, an institution, or a personal notion of the commonwealth.

Self-interested officials can be divided into *climbers* and *conservers.* Climbers seek power, income and prestige; conservers seek convenience and security. Mixed-motive officials can be divided into: *zealots, advocates* and *statesmen.* Zealots are loyal to narrow, sacred policies which they pursue vigorously. Advocates seek power in the organization to advance their area of organizational responsibility. Statesmen are loyal to the general welfare of society as they see it. Each category will be discussed more fully below.

Although this five part typology over-simplifies, it is again a great improvement on the dichotomy of "opponents" and "supporters." It can be used by the political executive to determine more effective task assignments or to transfer personnel as needed.

The political executive has the most potential for motivating the *climber* because he is purely self-interested and motivated by things over which the political executive has some control. Climbers seek power, income and prestige by three methods: promotion, job aggrandizement and jumping to another agency. Once a political executive identifies a hard-working climber, he should be aware that if he does not satisfy the climber's desires, he may jump to another bureau.

The other two methods provide the political executive with considerable latitude to motivate climbers. The political executive does have influence over promotions and pay increases to reward climbers. The motivation of job aggrandizement is also under the control of the political executive. Although a conservative political executive does not want to build "empires" for career executives, the desire for job aggrandizement can be satisfied by allocating greater responsibilities within the existing system. Climbers must be given clear signals regarding how to succeed in the changed environment of the new conservative administration, that is, that advocacy of government expansion will impede rather than further one's career.

Like climbers, *conservers* are motivated by self-interest. They seek to maximize their security and convenience. In doing so, they tend to support the status quo and avoid change. Conservers, therefore, become an obstacle to the conservative political executive who has an agenda of dramatic policy change. Conservers will be overly cautious in giving advice to the political executive on policy matters. They will think of reasons why things ought not to be done instead of telling the political executive how to accomplish policy objectives. Thus, conservers should not be in critical policy development positions.

It is important to note that there is a long-run tendency for agencies to be dominated by conservers.[15] Older officials who remain in the same position in the same bureau for a long time are most likely conservers; this is especially true of the key career executives at the top of an agency who work directly for political executives. Thus, it is important for political executives to recognize that conserver-dominated organizations will be very status quo-oriented and to take special measures, such as reorganization and personnel transfers, to loosen the organization up for policy change.

Zealots are optimistic, energetic, and aggressive. They are particularly characterized by their single-minded devotion to their sacred policies. In the area of domestic policy, zealots will, for the most part, be troublesome for a conservative political executive. Zealots are very likely to be disloyal if the political executive attempts to make unwanted changes in the zealot's policy area. On the other hand, if the political executive and the zealot agree, the zealot can be very important to the accomplishment of the political executive's objectives. This is especially true in making basic changes in the status quo. Zealots are particularly effective in countering bureaucratic inertia because they are willing to lead vociferous attacks on the status quo, and thus are associated with innovation in the bureaucracy.[16] Zealots can thus be extremely important allies for a political executive who wishes to make major changes in the status quo or a major enemy for the political executive if he wants to change policies in areas managed by zealots.

Advocates are interested in the importance of their functional unit in the organization. Their self-interest causes them to push for expansion of that unit and this often causes conflict with other areas. "Bureaucratic imperialism" comes from advocates, not from climbers. The political executive should not expect the advocate to provide recommendations on how to cut his operations. On the contrary, if given that task, the advocate will probably come back with justifications for why the function should be expanded. Also, advocates will view change in the organization as an opportunity to latch on to other functions and activities which may need a home. Advocates tend to be at the high levels of the organization and thus the political executive should expect to have a high proportion of advocates in his immediate staff.

Advocates also favor innovations because they see them as opportunities to expand. But this is a mixed blessing for the political executive.

> Like climbers, they provide a dynamic force in bureaus. However, they are simultaneously more conservative and more radical than climbers. They are more conservative because their loyalty leads them to oppose changes that might benefit them personally but injure their organizations. They are more radical because they are willing to promote views that might antagonize their superiors if doing so will help their organizations. Consequently, in democracies, advocates are continually calling attention to problems, difficulties, and inadequacies that are often embarrassing to the political leaders in power. The leaders wish to present the public with the impression that everything is under control, whereas advocates seek to magnify the problems facing their bureaus so they can procure more resources.[17]

Consistent *statesman*-like behavior is rare in the bureaucracy. The statesman will tend to sacrifice career and institutional interests when they are contrary to his conception of the greater public interest. On issues where there is an overlap between the statesman's notion of the public interest and the political excutive's, the statesman can be a valuable ally. For example, if the statesman recognizes that certain government operations are a waste of taxpayer's money or should be performed in the private sector, he can be safely delegated responsibility for cutting back those functions. On the other hand, if the administration's conception of the public interest clashes with that of the statesman, the statesman's loyalty to the higher ideal will outweigh the principle of the chain of command, and he will oppose administration efforts. Finally, since all careerists espouse a concern for the public good, it is initially difficult to separate the statesman from other bureaucratic types. Real statesmen are rare and often have difficulty being promoted because of the disparity between their ethical code and the demands of an organizational career.

Techniques for Managing Bureaucrats

Despite the limits of the existing personnel system, and the obstacles presented by bureaucratic temperament, the political executive has a number of techniques at his disposal to manage his bureaucratic subordinates effectively. These include: normative control; co-optation; incentives; selection; and mobility. The use of each specific technique will be governed by the situation as well as the political executive's understanding of the characteristics of a particular subordinate.

The most efficient and effective way to control career staff is for the political executive to exercise normative control.[18] *Normative control,* in contrast to remunerative or coercive controls, rests upon the subordinate's perception of the moral authority of the political appointee in his role as the delegated representative of the President, and upon the specific legal authority attendant upon that role. The political executive's use of normative control is thus based on his central function as political decision-maker and as such is linked to the closely related concepts of *political legitimacy* and the *civil service ideal.*

"Political legitimacy" resides in the political executive: every time the political executive signs a paper or makes a decision, he conveys that legitimacy. The bureaucracy is fully capable of making and implementing policy without the political executive, except that they need his political legitimacy. This dependency relationship establishes norms within the organization which the political executive can use as one of his major resources.[19]

How does the political executive use this resource? He simply refuses to sign documents, make decisions, and approve budgets until he is sure they serve the furtherance of his political agenda. This course of action, over a long period of time, will communicate to the career staff that this political executive is different. He expects the organization to respond to the President's mandate and he will use his position in the organization to ensure that the mandate is fulfilled. This process slowly transmits a new set of norms to the career staff. Those career staff who are pushing their own agendas begin to realize that this political executive, unlike those in the past, will see to it that he does not legitimize the career agenda and that their efforts will fail. If the political executive is successful, the career staff will slowly change their behavior and begin to work on the implementation of the political executive's agenda.

The second aspect of normative control is the civil service ideal which specifies that high-level career civil servants are not to be independent policy makers, but are to carry out the policy of others through "neutral administration" as described in Chapter II. As noted previously, nearly all career administrators will seek a far larger role in practice than is awarded them by this scheme; on the other hand all careerists will have been thoroughly exposed to these concepts during their education and the civil service ideal will still have a certain ethical significance for them. Few will have come to the point where they can utterly disregard the values implicit in the ideal of the civil servant who faithfully executes policies established by the legitimately elected political leadership of the nation.

The political executive may thus control his subordinates by insisting that the legitimate role of policymaker belongs exclusively to him; by insisting that the reciprocal role of the careerist must be to execute policy, not to determine its ends; and that all "administrative details" that affect policy outputs must properly be placed under the scrutiny of the political executive as well. There are distinct limits to the responsiveness which bureaucrats will exhibit to this approach; still it will seldom be completely ineffective.

The technique of *co-optation* is closely related to normative control. Like normative control it assumes bureaucrats will accept the leadership of the political executive, but on the other hand it does not expect this process to be automatic. Rather, some bureaucrats must be coaxed into supporting the political executive. The key to co-optation is that involvment in high priority issues and access to the political leadership are both desired objects on the part of careerists. The political executive may exchange involvement and access for increased loyalty on the part of career employees. The obvious drawback to this is that "co-optation" is often a two-way street.[20] By expanding participation the political executive runs the risk that his efforts will be diluted and his policies deflected from his original goals.

In seeking to co-opt subordinates, the political executive must take care not to surrender his actual control over the political agenda on controversial topics. Proper co-optation thus implies a type of controlled participation which heightens the careerist's sense of involvement within a precise context that assures that political leaders remain in full command of policy-making. For example, the political executive may increase the sense an employee has of the importance of his work by fostering contacts between the political executive and lower level subordinates. To career employees who have demonstrated a commitment to work for the administration's policy goals, the political executive can provide greater "access." He can give assignments to important projects; greater opportunities to provide advice; and more information concerning overall policy-making.

Finally, the political executive may employ the "if/then" method of participation. Using this method the political executive asks his career subordinates: "if I had a policy goal of 'x' then what alternative ways of accomplishing this goal exist and which is best?" This provides careerists with a greater sense of involvement while reducing their ability to impose their own objectives.

The third major technique for managing subordinates is the use of *incentives.* While it is part of popular opinion that federal employees cannot be rewarded or punished, they can. It is often more difficult than in the private sector, but positive incentives such as pay, promotions, and cash awards are available. Negative incentives exist as well. Both sorts of incentives are especially important to bureaucratic climbers.

The range of incentives available to the political executive as well as his control over them was deliberately increased by the Civil Service Reform Act (CRSA) of 1978, in an effort to render senior career managers more responsive to political direction. The new incentive structure pertains both to the Senior Executive Service (SES) managers and to "merit pay" managers at the GS-13 to GS-15 level.

With respect to SES personnel, the political executive has the following incentive tools at his disposal:

> . . . [P]erformance bonuses (up to 20 percent of the executive's salary), distinguished and meritorious rank awards ($20,000 and $10,000 respectively), incentive awards and sabbaticals. The negative incentives include reassignment to a position of lesser importance or responsibility or less desirable geographic location, decreases in salary and loss of SES status. SESers whose performance is judged unsatisfactory must be

> reassigned to another position; if the individual receives two or more unsatisfactory performance ratings within a five-year period, he or she must return to a GS-15 position.[21]

With regard to motivating merit-pay level employees, the political executive may provide permanent "step increases" of from zero to three percent of base pay and one time cash awards of two to ten percent of base pay.

Finally, for both SES and merit pay personnel, incentives are tied to a formal performance evaluation process. At least once each year the political executive and his subordinates are to jointly establish performance objectives for the subordinate; the subordinate is then rated on his accomplishment of those objectives and rewarded appropriately. This process provides an ideal vehicle for the political executive to communicate his policy and administrative priorities to his subordinates. It also affords an opportunity for formally changing priorities established by previous administrations. If the political executive ensures that his political priorities are embodied in the performance evaluation elements of his subordinates and then consistently rewards performance which matches those priorities and punishes performance which does not, he will have an effective instrument for controlling personnel as well as a tool for generating policy change.

The fourth critical management technique is *selection*. The political executive must identify those career personnel that he can work with. One leading scholar notes the importance of selection as a resource for the political executive:

> Again the more productive route lies in selectivity. Experienced political executives everywhere try to build strategy resources by selectively managing the various types of career personnel. In practice this means taking personnel actions to acquire officials already in the bureaucracy who show they can be of help.[22]

The political executive must be able to select the key career personnel and then channel important work to them. This can be done by moving personnel or by reorganization (these will be discussed later), but even without these formal moves the political executive can take informal actions to "rewire the boxes." In other words, the political executive who identifies key career personnel can channel important work to them regardless of their formal areas of responsibilities. This obviously is considered sloppy management by some business management standards, but in the world of the political executive it makes perfect sense, given the fact that some career executives are working for their own agendas and not the political agenda of the political executive.

The fifth technique for managing personnel is *mobility*. The political executive must transfer career personnel so that opponents are placed in the least sensitive policy areas, such as operational areas that are routine and are easily checked. The flexibility of the SES provides the political executive with a greater ability to use mobility at that level than at the lower levels of the bureaucracy. The political executive can select and move any SES member within his agency.[23] As noted earlier, among the chief constraints on the political executive are the iron triangles that exist between the agency career staff, the congressional committees, and the interest groups. Intra-agency mobility of SES personnel may help to weaken some of these iron triangles.[24]

Thus a major strategy of a second Reagan Administration could be to encourage a great deal of intra-agency mobility in the SES to break one side of the iron triangles. Critics might argue that this is an inappropriate use of the career system. But strong opponents to policy change in the bureaucracy have had years to build up relationships with other participants in the policy process that give them a tremendous advantage over the new political executive. In many respects transfers just provide a more even footing for both sides.

Finally, the use of transfers will often be undermined by the fact that the number of potential bureaucratic opponents will exceed the number of non-sensitive slots in the agency. (Congress controls the number of slots.) In this case, transfers must be backed up by a formal or informal "rewiring" of boxes on the organizational chart, removing *de facto* control from unreliable persons irrespective of their official positions.

Using Outside Personnel

Despite the techniques outlined above, political executives will always have less than perfect support from the bureaucrats beneath them. This particularly will be the case with respect to policies that are politically controversial or which threaten the institutional interests of the agency. In such cases, political executives should not seek to rely on bureaucratic personnel but instead should mobilize external resources.

One way is to simply bring reliable outside personnel into the agency. The political executive has substantial authority to bring in political appointees at the GS-1 to GS-15 levels as schedule C appointments, up to the limit of available slots. In addition, certain SES slots can be filled by "non-career" SES political appointees, although only one-tenth of all SES positions may be filled in this fashion. Finally external personnel may be brought into the SES by way of "limited term" and "limited term emergency" appointments which last up to three years.

External resources also may be used simply to by-pass political opponents in the bureaucracy. Policy experts in universities, think tanks, and in business often will provide analyses and position papers *pro bono* in exchange for a role in the policy process. Beyond this, the political executive may hire outside consultants for a limited assignment or may simply "contract out" to non-government organizations those policy studies that cannot be performed within the bureaucracy because of institutional and political biases.

Using the Organizational Structure

Organizational structure is in many ways the converse of personnel transfers. If the personnel that the political executive wants in certain positions cannot be transferred, he can reorganize so that personnel can be used effectively. In other words, combining reorganization and personnel transfers produces a more responsive organization for policy change.

The organizational structure of the agency represents one of the primary resources of the political executive. It is an important resource because, unlike the cases of the personnel system or the budget, there are fewer constraints which effectively limit the actions of the political executive. The major reason that this resource is not used more is that many political executives have pre-determined notions about structure and these notions are reinforced by business and conventional public administration doctrines.

Many political executives, and especially those with business experience, believe that organizational structure should be designed to allow the agency to operate in the most efficient and effective ways possible. These individuals are extremely frustrated when they come to Washington to manage large administrative agencies. They observe organizational structures unlike any they have witnessed in business: agencies with overlapping jurisdictions, sloppy structures, and large staffs which seem to serve little purpose. These and other practices cause many businessmen to conclude that the government agencies are very poorly organized and to wonder how they can function at all. What these businessmen fail to recognize is that there are political reasons behind every organizational decision in an agency. These political reasons can be as large as the decision to create a Department of Education or as small as the closing of a service office in Denver. But as one authority on organization structure concludes: "The basic issues of federal organization and administration relate to power: who shall control it and to what ends?"[25]

Once the businessman who comes to Washington understands this fact, the confusing organizational mess of administrative agencies becomes clearer and he can then begin to think about the use of the organizational structure in his own agency as an important resource to aid in the task of policy change. Other participants in the policy process fully recognize the importance of organizational structure. The National Education Association (NEA) understood the power vested in the organizational structure of Department status when they lobbied for separation of education from the Department of Health, Education and Welfare. President Carter and the Democratic Congress knew the importance of organizational structure when they delivered the new Department, with the expectation that the NEA would remember in the next election.

Given a recognition that organizational structure relates to political power and control and thus can be used as a resource for policy change, how does the political executive exploit this resource? Guidance is provided by a leading Brookings Institution expert on bureaucratic organization:

> Thus, a leader who transfers, combines and splits organizations in government for engineering purposes will usually find that nobody can be sure whether any progress has been made toward those goals. All too often the effects on efficiency, simplicity, and cost cannot be determined at all. When they can be assessed, what is successful by one standard may be a failure by another; what improves things in one way makes them worse in another. Real political capital is thus consumed in the pursuit of phantom goals. In contrast, a leader who shifts organizations around to confer power on selected people or remove it from others in order to mold government policies, and to impress on everyone what his or her values and priorities are, will more often be rewarded with a sense of having expended political resources for significant accomplishments. The calculus of reorganization is essentially the calculus of politics itself.[26]

Reorganization can be used to send firm messages about the values and priorities of the political executive and the administration. Organizational units are established to implement policy priorities. Previous Democratic administrations established many units to implement liberal policies. When they took office, the Reagan political executives were confronted with these units busily implementing liberal policies. Some of these units are based on statute while others are based on administrative decisions. The latter are easy to change. The former require analysis and the development of a strategy which will make changes within the limits of the law.

Often reorganization strategies can be combined with personnel transfers and budget decisions to make for an overall change which maximizes the degree of policy change. In addition, reorganization can promote policy change by breaking up or by-passing old bureaucratic routines and structures. It is often easier to change policy by creating a new organization from scratch than by attempting to change established procedures used by old personnel in an existing organization.[27]

A simple example of this principle comes from the Department of Health, Education, and Welfare during the Nixon Administration. Fred Malek, who later became Deputy Director of Nixon's Office of Management and Budget, was saddled with an extremely inefficient department organization which processed grants to local mental health centers. The existing grants processing system was so cumbersome that on occasion the cost of processing a grant actually exceeded the value of the grant itself. Malek found that personnel within the organization, all of whom had a vested interest in some portion of the existing system, were completely incapable of improving the operation. So, Malek created a new management task force staffed with personnel from other parts of HEW who had no connection with the particular grants operation; this task force successfully streamlined the application process, eliminating unnecessary units and substantially cutting costs. Malek notes that if the personnel in the management task force had been asked to perform the same review of the offices from which they had been transfered, they would have failed because they had already absorbed the established viewpoint of their own offices. By creating a new organizational context, the political executive enabled his bureaucratic subordinates to function successfully.[28]

One final comment on the importance of overlapping jurisdictions—both internal to an agency and between agencies—is necessary. "Classical" organization theory argues that overlap is wasteful.[29] Many businessmen who come to Washington observe this overlap and set out as their primary mission to eliminate it. This businessmen's "crusade" not only has the negative aspect of diverting the political executive from the primary task of policy change, but the negative result of changing organizational structures so that the political executive has less control and the career officials have more. Much of the career power is based on the control of information; overlap creates conflict and competition which in turn produces information which is useful for the political executive in controlling policy implementation.[30]

In addition to the overlap within an agency, overlap exists between agencies. While the political executive may recognize the personal benefits to him in producing information from internal overlap, the external overlap appears to be only a nuisance and a cause of frustration in the implementation of policy. Again many scholars of public administration look at this overlap as a positive force which encourages policy innovation.[31] The political executive should not attempt to eliminate this overlap but should use it to aid in his quest for policy change.

Controlling Subordinate Discretion

> Effective control begins with issuing orders. The less ambiguous and general they are, the less discretion is delegated to subordinates.
>
> —Anthony Downs[32]

The political executive and his business counterpart take entirely different views of subordinate discretion. As indicated in Chapter I, the absence of a quantifiable bottom line makes the political executive's management job much more difficult. When the political executive issues instructions to his staff, he is not aided in checking on the results of his subordinate's actions by a profit statement. Knowing this, subordinates realize that they automatically have more discretion. This section will outline ways by which the political executive can control subordinate discretion and thus be more assured that his directives are being carried out.

Specifically, the political executive may control subordinate discretion by: removing delegations of authority; issuing instructions clearly; and checking on the results of instructions effectively.

Delegations of Authority

Agency heads have overall resposibility and authority to operate the agency. In order to prevent administrative overload of the agency head, he distributes specific authority to act in his stead to lower level executives. For example, in order to diminish his daily workload, an assistant secretary may delegate the authority to approve grants and contracts to career SES personnel below him.

Delegations of authority are formal documents which exist at several levels of the agency. They provide the career bureaucrat formal authority to use bureaucratic discretion. Because of them, career staff can, at times, make legitimate decisions which shape the policy of the agency. As political executives of different administrations come and go, they make changes in these delegations based on their management styles and political agendas. Political executives with business backgrounds, who are accustomed to delegating authority, tend to use these formal delegations extensively. Unfortunately, along with the delegation goes the control over policy.

The conservative political executive must recognize this fact and set out to review all delegations. The review must be guided by two considerations. First, the political agenda will dictate which critical policy areas need special attention. Delegations in these policy areas should be withdrawn in order to secure political control. This does not mean the political executive withdraws all delegations. He withdraws only those in the critical policy areas over which he needs direct control.

The second point follows from the first. By withdrawing delegations of authority, the political executive gets more involved in the actual operations of his agency. This means more work for the political executive because he must make personal decisions on matters which formerly were delegated. But as demonstrated earlier in this part of the *Mandate*, the political executive must get involved in the details of administration in order to produce real change.

Morever, there are ways to ease the added burden somewhat. At the Office of Personnel Management (OPM), the Reagan Administration Director withdrew many delegations of authority. This meant he had a tremendous number of decisions to make every day. In order to speed his decision process, he required that every decision, no matter what office originated the decision, conform to a uniform format. This format included not only the specific decision to be made, but also all statutory and regulatory authorities, all background information and a report by the policy office indicating a "second opinion" on the necessity of the decision.A strict formatting of decision packages along these lines enables the agency head to withdraw delegation and yet handle the increased workload that follows.

Issuing Instructions

The second problem for the political executive in controlling subordinate discretion is to issue clear instructions on what he wants done. Every executive, both business and political, knows how to issue instructions, but issuing instructions to a bureaucracy is not a simple process. As one expert observes: "Giving instructions is not an easy task. People seem to possess an almost infinite ability to misunderstand."[33] The degree of goal ambiguity in any given instruction determines the amount of bureaucratic discretion that the career staff will have. If a general task is given to career staff, it can take on any number of meanings as it is communicated down the hierarchy to the actual staff worker. This problem may be called "leakage of authority."[34]

Leakage results from the fact that as orders are passed down the hierarchy they must be expanded. In other words, it is impossible for the political executive to specify in his order every minute detail. He does not have the knowledge or the time. Therefore, some delegation must take place. Because of the general nature of instructions, at every level in the bureaucratic hierarchy, there will be a necessary "discretionary gap," which results in a difference between the orders received by an official from above and those orders he issues downward. Moreover leakage of authority will be intensified "by the fact that such delegation is accompanied by variances in officials' goals."[35] Various positions in the hierarchy cause officials to have different perspectives, to take on different roles, and to adopt different sets of goals. One student of the bureaucracy goes so far as to state:

> . . . In any large, multi-level bureau, a very significant portion of all the activity being carried out is completely unrelated to the bureau's formal goals, or even the goals of its topmost officials.[36]

The wide variation in perspectives and goals deforms general instructions as they travel through the hierarchy. To minimize leakage of authority, it is necessary for the political executive to have a precise and detailed idea of what he wishes to do, that is, to have a definite political agenda, to translate that idea into specific tasks for subordinates, and to issue clear instructions to career staff concerning those tasks.

One way to clarify instructions is through *repetition*. Repetition establishes the importance of specific points and makes it more difficult for subordinates to misread or "forget" the initial intention.

> Persistence and follow-through lie at the heart of efforts to convey accurate messages. . . . Hence for the political executives to say something once is a statement of intention; to show others what is meant and that it cannot be forgotten becomes a strategic resource.[37]

This is especially important since in the lower reaches of the bureaucracy there will often be some form of debate over the meaning of an assignment; timely repetition will strengthen the side which is closer to the political executive's original goals. Since there is a tendency on the part of all political executives to underestimate the amount of repetition that is necessary, one should always err on the side of too much.

In addition to repeating his instructions, the political executive should attempt to reduce subordinate discretion by giving instructions which are *easy to monitor*. One method for doing this is increased specificity: a task can be divided into subtasks which in turn can be subdivided again. The political executive also can create standard operating procedures that govern all instructions of a certain type; doing so will remove discretion on specific instructions and make compliance easier to review. Finally, the instructions may be linked to objective measures of performance such as time deadlines and dollar costs.

There are certain drawbacks to these techniques. Since they increase the rigidity of response in the organization and since the political executive cannot foresee all implications of a given instruction, they may produce unintended results. Moreover, there often is a disparity between easily monitored criteria and the real quality of an output, deadlines being an obvious example. This problem will be discussed more fully below.

Monitoring Results

After the political executive issues instructions, he waits for the staff to produce results. A principal problem for the political executive is time. As noted previously, the political executive works under the time constraint of a four-year term of office while the career staff has a much longer time horizon. This difference usually causes the career staff to be somewhat unconcerned about the amount of time it takes to formulate and implement policy. The political executive must be very specific about the priority of tasks and amount of time that he wants the career staff to take in completing assignments.

Morever, if the career staff opposes the changes suggested by the political executive, they can deliberately delay and stall.[38] These tactics are very effective, since the political executive is usually distracted by the urgency of other business and soon forgets about the project. Therefore, an effective tracking system is necessary for the political executive to track his essential policy projects.

Tracking systems vary from a pencil and paper system kept in a desk drawer to a sophisticated computer-generated system. The form and style of the system depends on the individual manager and what he thinks works best for him. However, since the supervisor is limited in the time he can spend reviewing the activities of subordinates, he must select certain parts of subordinate behavior to review. There are five possible methods for selecting which subordinate activities to review in depth.[39] They are:

- Firefighting; or reviewing only those activities which have stirred up strong negative reactions by parties outside the agency;
- Reviewing only those areas where subordinates fell short of preplanned performance targets;

- Reviewing internal controversies, i.e., those issues on which subordinates cannot agree;
- Reviewing questions of a definite level of significance, usually as expressed in dollar cost;
- Reviewing a certain number of activities that are chosen at random.

Experts regard the last method, selecting matters for review at random, as the most effective review process because it creates the most uncertainty among subordinates. But this method is perhaps the least used by supervisors, because supervisors generally develop greater interests in some areas than in others.[40]

Irrespective of the review method employed, the political executive will always have the problem of assuring that he has accurate information with which to monitor his subordinates. As subordinates communicate the results of their actions up the hierarchy to the political executive, the information must be condensed. When information is condensed, there is a natural tendency for subordinates to select favorable information for transmission upward and to suppress unfavorable information.[41] Since this is done at every level, the more levels that information must pass through, the more the message gets distorted. This is the other side of the "leakage of authority" that occurs when instructions are transmitted downward.

The political executive who receives information on how his subordinates are carrying out his instructions will receive information which has been selected to produce a favorable impression unless the political executive uses *anti-distortion devices.* Anti-distortion devices will tend to reduce the distortion in the messages in the organization but will not eliminate it. There are four anti-distortion devices: redundancy, counter-biases, elimination of middle-men, and distortion-proof messages.[42]

Redundancy includes the seemingly wasteful practice of creating overlapping areas of responsibility. As noted in preceding sections, common organization theory holds that it is wasteful to have two units doing the same thing. But units with sole responsibility for a function create a monopoly over information regarding the functioning of the unit. The supervisor is thus hampered in much the same way as a buyer who is confronted with a monopoly supplier. Competition, the classic solution to monopoly, applies here. Overlapping jurisdictions produce competition and a degree of conflict, which in turn produces information that the supervisor can use to check on the results of subordinate actions.

A second anti-distortion device is to develop *counter-biases.* This is an almost automatic process used by every supervisor. The political executive merely considers the source of the information. If the information comes from a subordinate who is known to want a budget increase, the information will be evaluated on that basis. The essential point for the political executive to remember is that he must have knowledge of the original bias. If he does not know or makes a mistake in evaluating the bias, the application of a counter-bias will not work. The typologies of bureaucrats presented previously should be useful here.

A third way to reduce distortion is to *eliminate the middle-men.* This can be done by creating flat organizations or using various by-pass devices to go directly to the people with the information. Flat organizations, with wide spans of control, work well for tasks which are largely routine because supervisors can easily check on the compliance of many subordinates. However, political executives generally hold positions that are not routine. Therefore, they generally will not want flat organizations with wide spans of control because this ironically will reduce their control and increase the discretion of subordinates. A by-pass device is more suitable for use in government. A superviser uses a by-pass device when he moves around the hierarchy and goes directly to the bottom of the organization to collect information. This can be done by using informal or personal contacts developed by the political executive at the lower levels. The essential point is for the political executive to secure information from the lower levels without it going through the intermediate supervisors first.

The use of by-pass tends to cause dissatisfaction among the intermediate level officials because they feel that the top-level does not have confidence in them. Therefore the frequent use of by-pass may not be appropriate unless the political executive wants to give an intermediate-level supervisor the message that he really does not have confidence in him.

A fourth method is to develop *distortion-proof messages.* This involves establishing definitions or codes which cannot be changed in the transmission process. It is relatively easy with quantifiable information. While the political executive cannot use this technique for gathering information on all of his operations, some of the operations will lend themselves to a fairly straight performance check. Some examples are: backlog reductions, processing of forms or applications, and project completion by certain dates. It should be noted again that when using this technique the qualitative aspect of the information is usually lost and must be checked by the political executive. For example, in the lower levels of the bureaucracy, deadlines often convert operations into a sort of paper factory that churns out timely but meaningless products.

Use of Staff to Control Line

Perhaps the political executive's most common aid in checking on the task accomplishment of subordinates is the use of staff. Staff offices are supposed to be advisory to the political executive and supply him with information regarding the operations of the line organizations. Staff offices tend, however, to grow, and become large organizations which suffer many of the same problems experienced by all large organizations. A large staff office tends to take on all the characteristics of the line organization. The political executive is assisted by the staff organization, not because it is serving the staff function, but from the fact that the political executive is really supervising two line organizations and the result is desirable redundancy.

This redundancy produces beneficial competition and conflict between the "staff" and line which, more importantly, produces information which the political executive can use to manage the organization. Therefore, the political executive must be skilled in recognizing the information produced by the competition and must be skilled in conflict management. He must not strive to eliminate conflict. On the contrary, he must ensure that a degree of conflict or tension is maintained without getting out of control.

There is sometimes a tendency for lower level staff analysts to "take on" the views of the line organization that they analyze. When they do, their effectiveness as an independent source of information is lost. When a degree of conflict exists between the staff analyst and the line personnel, a rich flow of information is produced. And at the other extreme, when the conflict is severe, the staff analyst is cut off from the information about line operations and the flow of information stops. It is in the interest of the political executive to maintain a certain level of conflict between the staff members and the line personnel to ensure essential information for decision making.

Using the Budget

The budgetary process is one of the most important places where conflict over political goals and values takes place. This is true for the conflict between the Congress and the executive branch over the whole agency budget and the conflict within an agency over increases and decreases in various programs and organizations.

The budgetary process within an agency is, as one political executive put it, "potentially the most important but consistently underutilized policy change vehicle." Most political executives do not have the skill or energy to make the budget process live up to its potential. The budgetary process is complex, tedious and time consuming. Many political executives would rather devote their time to flashy policy papers and giving speeches than get involved in the frustrations and hard work of the budget.

Traditionally, the budgetary process has involved programs and agencies making their case for an incremental increase over their last year's budget or their "base." This incremental approach has been widely criticized for contributing to the growth of government, since career staff have the ability to produce tremendous amounts of information justifying increases and very little supporting cuts.

In recent years, efforts have been made to reform the budgetary process with new "objective" methods, such as the planning, programming, and budgeting system (PPBS) and zero based budgeting (ZBB). These methods were intended to give the political official more control over budget decisions. However, in many respects these "objective" methods have strengthened the position of the bureaucracy against the position of legislatures and political executives.

There are three reasons for this:

First, these methods require more information, and as previously shown, the bureaucracy draws its power from the control of information. Second, these methods decentralize the budget process and push it lower into the bureaucracy, where career personnel dominate. Thus, political control at the higher levels of the bureaucracy is weakened. And finally, the political forces do not have the time required to process the information which is generated by these budgeting methods.[43]

If changes in the budget process have not increased the potential for political control over governmental budgets, what will? The political executive must do four things: learn the process; alter traditional games and roles; get involved in the details; and avoid turf battles.

The budget process is complicated because at any given point a political executive is operating in several different budget cycles. The political executive who is preparing the Fiscal Year 1986 budget is operating in the Fiscal Year 1985, and evaluating the results of the Fiscal Year 1984 budget. Information from the evaluation of the last year's budget is essential for the preparation of the next year's budget. Too often, evaluation data are not utilized. Follow-through on the past year's budget decisions is essential for the "fine tuning" of the present budget and decison-making on the next year's budget. Political executives, given their usual short tenure, are often concerned with the future budget cycle and do not take advantage of the information produced by the implementation of the present budget and the evaluation of past budgets.

Once the budget process is mastered, the political executive must learn to control his own role in the budget process. A leading expert on the budgetary process says that the traditional role of the agency is to ask for a larger budget; the role of the Office of Management and Budget is to restrain such requests.[44]

In conformance with this ritual, the agency head is expected to support the request for "more" against the White House/OMB challenge. Surprisingly, this traditional pattern was perpetrated to a large degree even in the Reagan Administration. During the last four years, most agencies have submitted budget requests over the target levels given by OMB. In part, this is a result of capture; in part, it is a result of a game in which each agency assures that cuts fall proportionally by padding their own requests. Though understandable, this type of game disrupts a conservative administration's agenda. Political executives at all levels should work strenuously to avoid falling into the customary role of advocating more spending to their superiors.[45]

Political executives must also change the expectations of career staff beneath them concerning the budget game. SES and merit pay supervisors will often be rated in part on a "performance element" which requires some form of cost effectiveness; nevertheless, the pattern of the bottom asking for more is still almost universal at all levels in the budgeting process. The political executive must disrupt these patterns by firmly signalling a change in role expectations to his subordinates, and then acting to enforce the new roles. Supervisors who follow the old patterns should be rated poorly, supervisors who produce meaningful proposals for cutting their budget should be rewarded strongly.

Controlling a budget also requires a mastery of its technical details. This is a long-term process and requires the insertion of political appointees into the lower level operations of the budget office. Without a detailed knowledge it is difficult to find where the fat is stored and to cope with variants of the "fireman first" gambit in which the bureaucracy responds to austerity by threatening to cut its most vital or popular functions first. The classic example of this technique occured when the National Park Service responded to budget cuts by eliminating elevator service to the top of the Washington Monument; Congress quickly restored the money.[46]

Finally, the political executive must guard against the budget causing turf battles among the political appointees in an agency or department. Disputes between political appointees are always a problem, but budget decisions usually make the problem much worse. To avoid these turf battles the political executives in an agency or department need to agree on the general goals and philosophy which will govern their decisions. This agreement is best worked out by producing a political agenda, as described above. Once determined, potential disputes are settled infomally (not in writing) among the political appointees without career staff involvement. Prevention of major disputes is critical because career staff are quick to act in ways which aggravate these disputes to gain advantage for themselves, their policy goals, or their organization.

For the policy change potential of the budget process to be fulfilled, political executives must recognize that success will result only from a long-run, detailed, and forceful effort to control the process. One political executive sums it up: "There is no substitute for hard work."

Using Policy Evaluation

Policy evaluation at first glance appears to have less strategic importance than policy formulation or discretionary policy implementation. In fact, policy evaluation is a key instrument, uniquely suited to the purposes of conservative government, but it currently is underutilized. Properly employed, policy evaluations can be used for two purposes: to bring about policy change within government programs; and to combat the growth of government by demonstrating the wasteful and destructive nature of expansive government.

Using Policy Evaluation to Change Government Programs

Policy evaluation within an agency usually is employed to evaluate the effectiveness of specific programs and is often called program evaluation. Many political executives overlook this potential resource to aid in producing policy change. This failure leaves this important information-producing activity in the hands of the bureaucrats. As indicated in Chapter 24, the control over information is perhaps the single most important resource of the career bureaucracy. When the career staff control the imformation produced by program evaluation, the political executive finds he is bombarded with "objective" information which the career staff has developed and which justifies the implementation of career policy goals.

As argued throughout this part of *Mandate II*, changing government programs is always difficult. Anthony Downs analyzes organizational change and comes to the conclusion that change is often initiated only after the recognition of a "performance gap."

> . . . [N]o bureau will alter its behavior patterns unless someone believes that a significant discrepancy exists between what it is doing and what it ought to be doing.[47]

The political executive can use program evaluation as a principal way to find and objectively document performance gaps. Once documented, the political executive can use the evidence to initiate fundamental program changes. In other words, the political executive must ensure that the information-producing resources of his agency are gathering information which is useful for the development and implementation of his political agenda.

The specific context of the program evaluation function is more complicated. Program evaluation staff are usually attached to a staff policy office. As previously indicated, staff personnel must maintain a degree of conflict with the line personnel in order to do their job effectively. The evaluation process takes place in a highly charged political context since the program officials will always try to secure reports which justify continuation or expansion of their programs. The last thing the program official wants is an evaluation report that demonstrates a "performance gap" which causes a political executive to question the existence of the program.[48] Program evaluation personnel within the government also tend to work from a fairly narrow range of assumptions. In order to render policy evaluation more effective, political executives must change and broaden the implicit assumptions which underlie much of the evaluation process.

Using Policy Evaluation to Halt the Growth of Government

The conservative outlook on government holds that big government is not merely inefficient but is in many respects destructive in its consequences. The impact of big government on the economy is especially striking. A recent cross-national study by the World Bank of the link between taxation and economic growth has suggested that each additional $1.00 in government taxation and expenditure today may cut the standard of living of Americans by nearly $5.00 (measured in constant dollars) only ten years in the future.[49] If that is so, the growth of government domestic spending in the Great Society and its aftermath—from 1960 to 1975—will result in a reduction of the GNP of the United States by over 50 percent by the year 2000.[50] The double tragedy of this development is that, even in the short run, despite the extravagant promises of liberals, many expanded government programs have delivered little or have actually damaged society.

A conservative government clearly must seek to halt the growth of government and then bring about real reductions. Unfortunately, efforts to cut back government often will be thwarted in Congress by the timidity of moderates and the active opposition of liberals.

However, even if immediate efforts to cut government are blocked, the political executive has other long-run political tools at his disposal. Policy evaluation is such a tool.

Policy evaluation can underscore the general fraudulence of liberal asumptions and promises concerning the effects of affirmative government. Wasteful and ineffective programs can be identified and cost savings of more efficient service through privatization can be revealed.[51] For example, the General Accounting Office and other external evaluators repeatedly have belied the false claims of success of government job training programs. Serious evaluation shows these programs do not improve the employability or earning capacity of "trainees"; in some cases earnings levels actually are reduced by participation.

Certainly, facts and analysis are far from all-powerful in political debate. Still, serious evaluation can in the short run swing moderate votes in Congress and in the long run shift the context of debate incrementally. Such evaluations are best carried out by contracting studies to responsible parties outside government. Since repetition is an essential ingredient of politics, the political executive should not think in terms of a single study on an issue but of an on-going process of critical review.

Expansion of research and critical evaluation is in some respects opposed to the budget-conscious style of management of Republican administrations. A point which has been raised more than once in this study is that traditional "green eye shade" Republicanism with its emphasis on shaving the costs of programs at the margin or in creating cost-efficiency in government spending often can end up costing more in the long run when it results in a failure to marshall the resources needed to generate basic policy change. As Edgar O. Olsen wrote in a previous volume in this series, concerning sharp cutbacks in research funding at Housing and Urban Development:

> While the current level of spending may accurately reflect the value to taxpayers of the research produced by this office in the past, the amount currently spent on studies of the effects of existing programs represents a gross underestimate of the importance of such studies in achieving lasting reductions in the size of government.... Studies done by competent researchers who are adequately supported and not strongly biased towards these programs will demonstrate their many flaws. The dissemination of this research will contribute to an environment in which eliminating programs permanently is less difficult.[52]

Footnotes

1. A political executive with a business background quoted in Bernstein, *The Job of the Federal Executive*, p. 35.

2. James Fallows, "The Passionless Presidency," *Atlantic Monthly*, May 1979, p. 42.
3. Anderson, *Welfare*, p. 8.
4. Eugene Bardach in his excellent book *The Skill Factor in Politics* notes the importance of secrecy in the policy design stage. "In the initial stages of designing the proposal . . . secrecy is nearly always the norm, since it is assumed that a proposal in its incubation period is unusually vulnerable to attack by its presumptive opponents. Preserving secrecy imposes costs on the proposal designers themselves, however, and for that reason secrecy is almost never perfect." *The Skill Factor in Politics: Repealing the Mental Commitment Laws in California* (Berkeley: University of California Press, 1972), p. 237.
5. Heclo makes this point clear when he states: "Compared with the saboteur's negative acts the top bureaucrats' power derived from withholding positive help is enormous. . . . It is a power that can consist simply of waiting to be asked for solutions by appointees who do not know they have problems." *A Government of Strangers*, p. 172.
6. Heclo, *Government of Strangers*, p. 21.
7. O. Glenn Stahl, *Public Personnel Administration*, 8th ed. (New York: Harper and Row, 1983), p. 302.
8. Heclo, *Government of Strangers*, p. 20.
9. Ban, *et al.*, "Controlling the U.S. Federal Bureaucracy," p. 205-220, and Stahl, *Public Personnel Administration*, pp.61-62.
10. Data in this section are from Stanley Rothman and S. Robert Lichter, "How Liberal are Bureaucrats?" *Regulation*, November/December 1983, pp. 16-22. Additional data were provided directly by Rothman and Lichter. The author greatly appreciates their assistance.
11. Lichter and Rothman, "How Liberal are Bureaucrats?" p. 17. Reprinted by permission of *Regulation* Magazine.
12. In the view of one Reagan Assistant Secretary: "Bureaucrats are not so much ideological as uninformed; they have little understanding of the real world of business and economics and a distorted belief in the efficacy of affirmative government; they can be to a degree 'reeducated,' especially if they are shifted out of old functions, but the process is time-consuming."
13. This typology is a slight modification of concepts presented in Heclo, *A Government of Strangers*, pp. 204-205.
14. This discussion is based on Downs, *Inside Bureaucracy*, pp. 79-111.
15. Down's Law of Increasing Conserverism: "In every bureau, there is an inherent pressure upon the vast majority of officials to become conservers in the long run." *Inside Bureaucracy*, p. 99.
16. Downs, *Inside Bureaucracy*, pp. 206-207.
17. Downs, *Inside Bureaucracy*, p. 109.
18. Carl J. Friedrich, "Public Policy and the Nature of Administrative Responsibility," in Friedrich and Mason, ed. *Public Policy* (Cambridge, Mass: Harvard University Press, 1940). Also see Peters, *The Politics of Bureaucracy*, pp. 259-261.
19. In fact, B. Guy Peters recognizes this when he lists political legitimacy as the number one resource available to political agents (the President and the Congress). *The Politics of Bureaucracy*, p. 190.
20. See Bardach, *The Implementation Game*, p. 105.
21. Ban, *et al.*, "Controlling the U.S. Federal Bureaucracy," p. 209.
22. Heclo, *A Government of Strangers*, p. 215.
23. The SES system does not permit involuntary moves between agencies. Also, involuntary transfers within agencies are prohibited during the first 120 days of a new administration.
24. Ban, *et al.*, "Controlling the U.S. Federal Bureaucracy," p. 212.
25. Harold Seidman, *Politics, Position, and Power*, 3rd ed. (New York: Oxford University Press, 1980), p. 29.
26. Kaufman, "Reflections on Administrative Reorganization," in *Setting National Priorities*, pp. 405-406.
27. FDR was the master of this technique. See Arthur M. Schlesinger Jr., *The Coming of the New Deal* (Boston: Houghton Mifflen Co., 1959), pp. 521-28, 533-37.

28. Malek, *Washington's Hidden Tragedy,* pp. 91-94.
29. Weber, *Essays in Sociology*, pp. 196-198.
30. In addition to Downs, other authors such as Tullock, *The Politics of Bureaucracy*; B. Guy Peters, *The Politics of Bureaucracy*; William A. Niskanen, *Bureaucracy and Representative Government* (Chicago: Aldine/Atherton, 1971); and Ostrom, *The Intellectual Crisis in American Public Administration*, note the positive benefits of overlapping jurisdictions both administratively and in levels of government.
31. See Peters, *The Politics of Bureaucracy*, p. 180, and Downs, *Inside Bureaucracy*, pp. 198-99.
32. Downs, *Inside Bureaucracy*, p. 144.
33. Tullock, *The Politics of Bureaucracy*, p. 183.
34. Downs, *Inside Bureaucracy*, p. 134.
35. *Ibid.*, p. 134.
36. *Ibid.*, p. 136.
37. Heclo, *A Government of Strangers*, pp. 206-207. Gordon Tullock illustrates this point with the following story: "The Chinese maritime Customs, an international service organized by Sir Robert Hart, was justly renowned for its efficiency. Sir Robert was an excellent administrator, and his subordinates were mostly men of exceptional merit. Yet if one reads the circular instructions that were sent by Sir Robert to his various offices, one cannot help but be struck by the frequency with which he repeats ideas. Either he was wasting his time, or else he felt that this amount of repetition was necessary to implant his ideas into the thinking patterns of his subordinates. The latter explanation is more likely to be correct, and it seems probable that even more repetition would be required in a less 'elite' organization." *The Politics of Bureaucracy*, p. 183.
38. Eugene Bardach devotes a major part of his book to "Delay in the Game." See *The Implementation Game: What Happens After a Bill Becomes a Law* (Cambridge: The MIT Press, 1978), pp. 179-248.
39. Downs, *Inside Bureaucracy*, pp. 146-147.
40. *Ibid.*, p. 147.
41. Tullock, *Politics of Bureaucracy*, pp. 137-141.
42. This section is based on Downs, *Inside Bureaucracy*, p. 118-127.
43. Peters, *The Politics of Bureaucracy*, p. 194-195.
44. Aaron Wildavsky, *The Politics of the Budgetary Process*, 3rd ed. (Boston: Little, Brown and Co., 1979).
45. William A. Niskanen, Jr. provides an intriguing recommendation when he states that political appointees should be able to pocket a small percentage of the overall savings they produce within their agency. *Bureaucracy and Representative Government.*
46. Charles Peters and Michael Nelson, *The Culture of Bureaucracy* (New York: Holt, Rinehart and Winston, 1979), p. 12.
47. Downs, *Inside Bureaucracy*, p. 191.
48. See Nakamura and Smallwood, *The Politics of Policy Implementation*, pp. 67-84.
49. Keith Marsden, "Links Between Taxes and Economic Growth," *World Bank Staff Working Papers*, No. 605 (Washington D.C.: The World Bank, 1983.) The Marsden study indicates that an increase of one percentage-point in the tax/GNP ratio decreases the rate of economic growth by 0.36 percentage points. Assuming a one percentage point increase in the tax/GNP ratio and an intital growth rate of 3.5 percent, each dollar in increased taxes will reduce GNP by $4.84 ten years later.
50. Government non-defense spending as a percentage of GNP increased from around 21 percent in 1960 to 30.6 percent in 1975.
51. It is also possible to use resources for prophylactic evaluation, that is, critical evaluations of policy proposals that may become important in the future (for example, national health insurance.)
52. Edgar O. Olsen, "Housing Subsidies for Low-Income Families," in R.N. Holwill, ed., *Agenda 83* (Washington D.C.: The Heritage Foundation, 1983), p. 177.

26

Case Studies in Public Adminstration

1) The Management-By-Objective System at The Department of the Interior[1]

As Secretary of the Interior, James Watt installed a department-wide Management-by-Objective (MBO) system which incorporated a great number of the management principles discussed in the preceding chapters. The particular strength of this system lay in its ability to clarify the political agenda and to integrate this agenda with the activities of the bureaucracy. This was accomplished through a formal four-stage process in which general principles were broken out into a broad range of discrete tasks.

As a first step in this process, Watt and his staff, during their first months in office, set about formulating a guiding political philosophy; from this endeavor emerged seven long-term political "goals" for the Department of the Interior. These goals were in turn translated into about a dozen broad-based policy "objectives" relevant to the next four years. It should be noted that this initial process was not merely rhetorical, but instead represented painstaking effort to establish a conceptual foundation for future policy choices.

Once the policy "objectives" were established, the career staff in each of the Department's bureaus was brought in to formulate a sequence of "tasks" to implement the "objectives." A task, for example, might be to prepare a report, to develop a legislative proposal, or to seek passage of the proposal. In the final stage, "tasks" were broken down into "subtasks." Target dates were set for the completion of each "subtask," and a specific careerist (generally on the GS-13 to GS-15 level) was assigned responsibility for its completion. The performance evaluation plan for the responsible careerist was then linked to the assigned "subtask," each official signing a performance agreement with his supervisor which made his pay in part dependent on the accomplishment of the assignment. The entire MBO system thus took the form of a pyramid in which the seven initial "goals" devolved into the final level of hundreds of "subtasks," each tied to the performance evaluation of a single responsible official.

Once the initial formulation process was completed, steps were taken to implement the system. Each bureau of the Department prepared an MBO briefing book containing the objectives, tasks, subtasks, responsible officials and target dates assigned to it. Within most bureaus, the MBO system was reproduced on a more detailed scale. At all levels the system operated as a on-going process; completed tasks were removed from the system; new tasks were added within the consistent framework of the orginal objectives.

Finally, the Department established a monthly review structure to monitor the implementation of "tasks." At the center of this system was the Departmental Office of Policy Analysis (OPA), which monitored the progress of the bureaus; each bureau was in addition subject to a brief monthly MBO review meeting before the Secretary.

Prior to these monthly meetings, the Office of Policy Analysis would develop a short list of issues where problems had developed or where special progress had been achieved. OPA would inform the bureau of its list; the bureau would in turn produce a list of issues it wished to discuss. The two lists would be combined to produce an agenda for the meeting. OPA would brief the Department Undersecretary on the agenda and the Undersecretary would then present OPA concerns at the meeting. A unique feature of these meetings is that the bureau would bring the career official directly responsible for a given task or subtask to the meeting to speak directly about his program for two or three minutes. This brought careerists from the mid-level of the hierarchy (at times as low as grade 12) into direct contact with the Secretary to be cross-examined or commended.

Far from being a "paperwork" exercise, an MBO system of this type (which is still in operation at Interior) provides numerous concrete advantages to political administrators in the areas of policy formation and implementation. First, in contrast to MBO systems proposed under President Nixon, this system is based explicity on the political goals and values of the administration. If the "goals" are correctly formulated, there will be an inevitable shift in administrative emphasis from policy "maintenance" to policy change.

Second, such a system takes initiative away from the bureaucracy, which is quickly set to work developing the administration's agenda instead of its own. The existence of specified "objectives" acts as a barrier to the activities of bureaucratic entrepreneurs. Rather than operating in a void, the entrepreneur must either modify his agenda to conform to the system's objectives or at a minimum seek to camouflage his proposal so that it appears to do so.

Third, the initial formulation of enduring policy objectives helps the political staff maintain its original post-election enthusiasm and sense of direction through four years of bureaucratic grind and frustration. Finally, such a system in the long run makes the political appointees more accountable to the American people, by clarifying their policy goals and linking their actions to those goals. Reagan appointees who have found pretexts for expanding their agency budgets would presumably have greater difficulty in justifying their actions within such a system.[2]

The monthly MBO review process also exemplifies a number of sound management principles. The most obvious of these is the use of dual channels of communication. An appropriate level of constructive tension is maintained between "line" personnel in the bureaus and "staff" in OPA, but open conflict is avoided by a number of techniques. That is, the bureaus are notified of OPA reports in advance and questioning in the monthly review meeting itself is handled by the Undersecretary and not by OPA staff. The monthly review system also permits "by-pass" communication directly into the lower levels of the bureaucracy. Department heads speak directly to the mid-level personnel most knowledgeable on a given issue; this direct contact also opens future informal by-pass channels of communication.[3]

The presence of lower-level staff in the review meeting also serves as an excellent motivational instrument. The prospect of having one's performance reviewed, criticized, or commended by the Secretary himself is a clear motivator. Beyond this, staff are co-opted by being given a broader sense of participation, in that recognition is implicitly being given to the value of their contribution. (One should never overlook the fact that it is the mid- and lower-levels that actually do the work.)

There are, of course, certain drawbacks and limits to the effectiveness of this MBO system. The unavoidable involvement of the career staff in formulating specific "tasks" will result in a certain deflection of purpose, as well as difficulties in coordinating formal MBO statements with real world activities.

These problems can only be corrected over time as the political staff gains experience with specific programs. For example, in the Bureau of Reclamation, one task called for the phasing out of a particular grant program. Over a year's time, each month, the administrator of the program faithfully reported his progress: after 3 months the task was 25 percent complete; after 6 months, 50 percent. When this administrator left for another job, political appointees discovered he merely had been reporting the passage of time; each week that passed was counted as a portion of the job completed. An MBO system thus does not relieve a political executive of the need to involve himself in the details of "administration." It does, however, provide a framework for that involvement.

An MBO system also makes target dates or deadlines quite prominent. Deadlines provide a dynamic tension within an organization.

However, the difficulties of estimating time requirements, changes in the scope of tasks, and the impact of external circumstances demand common sense and flexibility in modifying time limits. Priority must always be placed on the quality of outputs as opposed to mere timeliness, or the system will degenerate into a cynical game. Finally MBO systems require a vast amount of time and paperwork at every level of the organization. This cost must be recognized to prevent the system from swelling to the point where it becomes counter-productive.

Overall, however, this type of MBO system and review process is a strong organizational asset. It provides a coherent mechanism for the following purposes:

—formulating the political agenda;
—maintaining the agenda over time;
—linking the agenda to operations;
—monitoring implementation;
—developing an information base;
—managing personnel through its links with performance evaluation;
—and motivating personnel through the review meetings.

2) Political Agenda and Bureaucratic Power in NOAA

A study of the National Oceanic and Atmospheric Administration (NOAA) yields two themes. First, NOAA is a classic example of entrenched bureaucratic power in all its aspects: entrepreneurialism; professionalism; iron triangle relationships; and information control. Second, NOAA reflects the tendency of political leadership in the face of powerful internal and external constraints to be captured, especially in the absence of a political agenda or of a strong personal commitment to that agenda.

NOAA's effectiveness in resisting political control stems from a number of factors. NOAA has an excellent public image; the scientific agency that provides weather news and hurricane warnings and conducts "monk seal research" has a great many natural friends and practically no enduring enemies. NOAA has extensive ties to its professional communities: meteorologists and oceanographers. Not only are these groups to a degree dependent on NOAA for employment, but NOAA provides many millions of dollars for research in universities around the country. As a result, the larger professional community remains very supportive of the interests of NOAA as an institution.

In Congress, NOAA acts as a suitable "pork barrel," offering benefits which representatives can take back to their constituents. These range from local weather stations, of which there is nearly one for every congressional district, to extensive regional grant programs. This "cookie jar" function renders Congress sympathetic to NOAA's broader organizational interests. Finally, NOAA is itself split into separate scientific fiefdoms which defy central control; the fiefdoms may offer overlapping or even competing services, but there has never been any real success in harmonizing their activities.

NOAA's close ties to Congress greatly strengthen the power of the career bureaucracy vis-a-vis its nominal leaders in the executive branch. This is especially true with respect to the budget. While NOAA budgeting follows the traditional pattern—NOAA personnel, including political appointees, lobbying their supervisors for more money—even this is something of a paper exercise. The real budget is prepared by congressional staffers and NOAA careerists on the Hill, a fact which is tacitly admitted by the NOAA bureaucracy. The NOAA budget is normally replete with detailed line item expenditures which have been added in this fashion. If a political appointee evokes the hostility of the NOAA bureaucracy, he will find himself hauled before Congress and subject to hostile questions prepared for the Congressmen by NOAA careerists and NOAA unions.

NOAA's defiance of central executive control can be seen in the case of budgeting for its polar orbiting meteorological satellites. These are an older form of satellite with functions that have to a degree been taken over by geostationary satellite programs. In consequence, the Reagan White House and OMB determined the program should be cut from two satellites to one with savings of over $300 million during a five-year period. However, for three years running, Congress put funds for the second satellite back into the budget.

To secure the permanent survival of its program, the NOAA bureaucracy decided to add search and rescue missions to the polar orbiting satellites. Then, without clearance from higher authority, it negotiated a cooperative treaty with the U.S.S.R. and other countries, stipulating that the U.S. would keep two such satellites in orbit for search and rescue purposes, despite the existing administration position that the U.S. government would fund only one satellite. When Office of Management and Budget Director Stockman issued a memo pointing out the contradiction between NOAA's actions and the administration's budgetary policy, NOAA staff quickly leaked the memo, resulting in stories in the *New York Times* and the *Washington Post* criticizing Stockman as a menace to human life and international cooperation. When OMB suggested that there were cheaper ways of meeting search and rescue needs, NOAA protested that the treaty should require the use of NOAA's traditional satellites.

To confront the internal and extenal forces controlling NOAA requires considerable resolve on the part of a political appointee. Unfortunately, the position of NOAA Administrator traditionally has been regarded as apolitical and scientific in nature. The Reagan Administration adopted this view, appointing a university professor with admirable scientific credentials, but little political experience and reportedly ties at least as strong as to the Democratic party as to the Republican party. In contrast, in the position of Associate Administrator, the Reagan Administration placed a private sector meteorologist with strong personal beliefs concerning privatization and cutting government spending. The contrast in the relationship of these two individuals to the NOAA bureaucracy demonstrates the importance both of bureaucratic discretion and commitment to a political agenda in the use of that discretion.

These two principles are clearly exemplified in the decision-making pertaining to the modernization and restructuring of NOAA's National Weather Service (NWS). NWS provides data collection and analysis for most weather forecasting in the United States. By the early 1980s, NWS equipment was aging and in need of replacement with newer technology. Because of the substantial estimated cost (up to $1 billion) of technological modernization, OMB had stipulated that the costs of new equipment be offset in part by savings in other areas. In addition, OMB held that certain forecasts tailored to meet the needs of specific interest groups should be turned over to the private sector.

Because of the complexity of the issues involved, the Associate Administrator determined little could be done by a few political appointees. On the other hand, the NWS bureaucracy was clearly incapable of the task. Therefore, the Associate Administrator contracted with an outside consultant group to study NWS modernization with a special emphasis on cost savings and eliminating unnecessary functions.

The report prepared by the outside contractor concluded the following: 1) The cost of new technology should be partially offset by a streamlining of NWS organization, eliminating all regional centers and over 90 percent of the 334 existing local offices. 2) The national network of 367 weather radio stations (which serve as the primary source of weather news to less than 2 percent of the public) should be eliminated. 3) Services beyond weather forecasts for the general public and severe weather warnings were not a proper NWS function and should be privatized or provided on a reimbursable basis only. In fact, according to the report, NWS had been required by law to seek reimbursement for such specialized services since 1970, but had ignored the requirement.

Although NOAA's "apolitical" Administrator had originally supported the consultant's study, finding hostility both within the bureaucracy and the professional community, he performed an about face. Despite the Associate Administrator's advice that NOAA begin implementing the study's recommendations, the Administrator took the remarkable step of establishing an in-house group of NOAA and Commerce Department careerists to re-study the consultant's work and develop its own plans.

The in-house study, not suprisingly, conformed to the bureaucratic ideology of NWS, viz. to preserve existing structures and expand its functions as much as possible. (NWS hostility to private sector competition is so great that it sought legislation banning the activities of a private firm which provided tornado warning services in Oklahoma.) The in-house report recommended new expenditures on new technology one-third greater than the amounts recommended by the external consultant. All NWS weather radio stations would be maintained and no local or regional offices would be closed. Finally, the report discovered that NWS should comply with the law and require reimbursement for specialized services, but no substantial services would be privatized. The NOAA Administrator then chose to forward the in-house report, in lieu of the consultant's report, to the Department Secretary for approval.

In return for his efforts on behalf of cost cutting and privatization, the Associate Administrator found himself subject to harassment by NOAA unions, and attacks in the press and on the Hill. When the Associate Administrator proposed a new engineering consultant study on the feasibility of modernizing NWS radars by way of currently available commercial technology that was vastly cheaper than the equipment NWS proposed to develop (an issue which had not been addressed in the original consultant's report), NOAA's Administrator blocked the effort, stating that such issues should be left to NWS staff. The Associate Administrator found himself increasingly channelled out of power by the Administrator and by the NOAA bureaucracy; relevant mail was routed around him; he was excluded from important meetings and decisions. On the other hand, the Administrator of NOAA plans to leave office soon to assume the presidency of his former university; Senator Lowell Weicker, Jr.—who has fought the White House tooth and nail over NOAA issues—recently complimented the Administrator for his leadership and lamented that his departure would be a "great loss."

3) Discretionary Grants at the Department of Education

The Department of Education (ED) is authorized by Congress to fund grants for the improvement of education. Grants are issued in many program areas for such diverse purposes as "Domestic Mining, Mineral and Mineral Fuel Conservation" and "Fund for the Improvement of Post-Secondary Education." In fact, in 1982, ED funded over 10,000 grants for a total of three-quarters of a billion dollars. These grant programs represent a tremendous potential for the political executive to advance a president's agenda.

When Reagan political executives entered the Department in 1981 they conducted a thorough analysis of the grants process. This was later supplemented by the work of external consultants. The following discussion draws from these analyses. It illustrates many of the concepts discussed in this part of *Mandate II,* including: the importance of getting involved in the details of administration; discovering discretion; and the over-riding importance of commitment to a political agenda.

Grant Program Analysis

Grant programs at ED represent a particularly interesting problem for Reagan political executives because they are fragmented throughout the Department. Program offices for each grant program are composed of the expert professionals in each field who administer the programs. The Office of Management, on the other hand, attempts to provide centralized management of all grant programs in order to produce efficiencies based on economies of scale and to provide some uniformity in procedures to prevent grantee confusion. The grant cycle contains the following formal steps.

1. Grant announcements are issued by the program office.
2. Grant applications are received and logged by the Office of Management.
3. Program offices review the applications by using panels of experts called "field readers."
4. A ranking of applications is sent to the appropriate Assistant Secretary for review, final ranking and approval.
5. The Office of Managment reviews the applicant's budget and negotiates final budget amounts. Applicants are funded from the top of the ranking down until all funds are expended.
6. Supervision of grantees during the period of the grant is split, with the program office checking to see that the grantees fulfill the terms of the grants and the Office of Management checking on the financial aspects of the grants.
7. At the end of the grant period, a closeout takes place which includes a program office review of reports and an Office of Management audit of the expenditures to ensure they are appropriate.

These seven steps are designed to ensure that grant funds are allocated by fair competition and that once grants are awarded, the grantees meet the agreed terms. These steps are all contained in ED regulations and formal administrative procedures.

The informal operations of the grant programs tell a much different story. These programs are characterized by many small "iron triangles." Educational interest groups have pressured Congress to pass grant programs which fund their pet projects. The ED bureaucracy, if not part of the interest group, is strongly supportive of the special interests behind the programs. This problem is compounded by a field reader selection process that is dominated by interest group networks so that grants are rated and ranked in ways which advance the ideology of a small elite. Typical of the iron triangle relationship is the Bilingual-Bicultural Education Program.

Other programs serve a generalized pork barrel function; for example, the College Library Resources Program, contrary to the purpose expressed in its authorizing statute, dispenses money to college libraries by automatically dividing the appropriation among the eligible applicants. In 1982 this program funded 2,200 college libraries.

The ED career bureaucracy, both in the program offices and in the Office of Management, have a "bureaucratic ideology" which controls the administrative procedures of the Department. The short version of this ideology is: "get the money out the door to the appropriate groups as fast as possible." Administrative procedures and bureaucratic routines concentrate on the pre-award steps (1 through 5 above) of the grant cycle, so that every program meets its deadlines and awards all the money before the end of the fiscal year. Very little time or effort is spent on the post-award steps (6 and 7 above) which are designed to ensure grantee accountability.

Bureaucratic routines established to implement the last few steps in the grant cycle are minimal and ineffective. Grantee drawdowns on grant funds for the purpose of collecting interest on federal funds is a major problem. Monitoring of grantee performance is very weak with very few on-site visits and very little checking on the quality and quantity of grantee reports. The closeout backlog is of monumental proportions.[4] Finally, grantees receive new awards without completing final reports on previous grants because administrative procedures to report on grantee performance are virtually non-existent. In fact, career bureaucrats have named grants "conditional gifts" because once the grant is awarded, they argue that little or nothing can be done to hold grantees accountable.

In keeping with institutional imperative to "get the money out the door," the bureaucracy followed the customary practice of violating its own regulations—neatly illustrating the principle that while the bureaucracy will use law and regulation to fence in an "unreliable" political executive, it will exhibit a less dogmatic attitude when its own concerns are involved. For example, a detailed review by political appointees of the computer records of specific grants revealed that funding amounts in the "amount appropriated" column were occasionally higher than amounts in the "funds requested" column even though only the second figure had been included during the original evaluation and authorization of the grant. Some offices gave increases to almost all grantees, indicating that program officials may have been influenced by the necessity to spend funds by the end of the year.

Since the regulations state that the Department "may fund up to 100 percent of the allowable costs in the budget," this seemed to be a violation of the regulations.[5] When asked, Office of Management career personnel stated that during the grant negotiation process, negotiators increased amounts above the budget requests. This was done to compensate grantees for increases in costs which had taken place between the time the grant application was submitted and the grant was awarded. When asked about a possible violation of the regulations, career staff remarked that in their interpretation of the regulations the increases were part of "allowable cost" even though they had not been included in the original grant budget.

Since senior career officials had their own interpretation of the regulations, the question of the meaning of the term "budget" and "allowable costs" was turned over to the Office of General Counsel (OGC). After several months of study the OGC confirmed that the term "budget" means the budget submitted by the grantee in the original grant application. And if grantees needed more funds, they must follow specific methods stated in regulation to receive supplementary funds. This latter process requires a higher level of administrative review and obviously takes the bureaucratic discretion away from the lower-level officials who previously were exercising it. Even in the face of a clear-cut OGC opinion, career officials in the Office of Management continued to fight the "war of memos" trying to protect their power of administrative discretion. It took over six months of struggle before the career bureaucrats finally agreed that following the regulations was a good idea. And unless a political executive occasionally checks, they will certainly drift back into previous patterns.

Discovering Discretion

However, the review of existing laws, regulations, and procedures was not limited to a mere repudiation of violations by the bureaucracy. Such a review led also to the "discovery of discretion" within the existing regulatory framework. Such discretion would assist the administration in getting control over the grants process—if it so desired. From the review of political appointees and outside consultants it was learned:

- That the Secretary can establish his priorities for funding grants. This includes an "absolute preference" which will exclude applications not furthering his priorities.
- That regulations require a detailed cost analysis and that grantees must relate performance to costs. Grants could be tightened up by establishing rigorous cost analysis.
- That the Secretary could use discretion in requiring a detailed status report before the successive years of multi-year grants are approved.
- That excessive drawdowns of grant funds for the purpose of earning interest on federal funds violates the regulations and that violators are subject to suspension or termination of their grant.
- That existing procedures enabled the Department to take action against applicants who are considered "high risk."

Losing Track of the Agenda

In 1983, external consultants provided three separate reports concerning the ED grants process.[6] The reports complemented the efforts of political appointees within the Department, documenting much of the above analysis. They provided massive evidence of "performance gaps" in existing programs and provided many additional recommendations that would increase the Department's ability to ensure grantee accountability.

Unfortunately, report recommendations are not self-implementing. Washington is undoubtedly the world's leading producer of reports, but is at the same time notoriously resistant to change. The bureaucracy has inertia on its side and opposes change, not only when there is a threat to vital organizational interests, but also because of the simple fact of its "sunk costs" in existing systems.

Proposals for change, whether emanating from political appointees or external consultants, will not succeed unless there is a consensus among political appointees and guidance from higher political officials. Unfortunately, most of the potential for change in the grants program—as outlined above—went unrealized. While bureaucratic opposition played a part in this, the greatest impediment to real change was the lack of leadership support from the Secretary and Undersecretary and the fact that several political executives at the Assistant Secretary level were effectively captured.

As noted in Chapter 24, Assistant Secretaries are often appointed because they have specialized experience or training in the field they supervise. This fact alone tends to make capture more likely because they have more in common with the bureaucracy and the interest groups than with the President's agenda. Several Assistant Secretaries in the Department of Education fit into this pattern. They were unwilling to take actions which would tighten up the administration of grants in their program areas.

For example, as stated above, the field reader review process is critical in the grant selection process. Assistant Secretaries have final approval power over the selection of field readers. Many Assistant Secretaries allow program officials to exercise this power and program officials rely on members of a small elite of field readers who ensure that grants supporting the prevailing program "ideology" get the funds. This incestuous relationship was a major target for change. Reagan political executives suggested that the pools of readers be expanded, and that instead of the existing selection process, with its potential biases, the Department use a computerized selection process.

This change to an objective selection of field readers was resisted by the career program officials who enlisted the support of their Assistant Secretaries. Thus, the Reagan political executives not only had to fight bureaucratic resistance, but other political executives who had the power to make changes, but would not. While it is difficult to discover the exact motivation of these Assistant Secretaries, whether it was lack of interest or ideological agreement with the program officials, the result was the same. A simple change that would have improved the fairness of the grants process was effectively resisted; a great deal of unnecessary time and effort was expended by political executives fighting other political executives—while the career staff maintained their operational control over programs which, in too many cases, worked against President Reagan's political agenda.

The lack of political leadership by the Secretary and Undersecretary is harder to explain. Speculation regarding their motives range from suggestions that they are "agenda free" political executives, to charges that they are active supporters of the public education establishment represented by the NEA and other interest groups which support increased federal aid to education. What is certain is that due to lack of commitment on their part, opportunities for change were ignored, and the discretionary grant program continues largely as it was when President Reagan first took office.

Footnotes

1. Actual details of this system have been simplified slightly to facilitate the presentation.

2. The MBO system must inevitably be classified "for internal use only" and thus available to the general public only in retrospect. This reduces but does not eliminate its utility in producing accountability.

3. This latter point is especially true at the bureau level, where the monthly review meeting is generally reproduced on a smaller scale. Direct contact between political appointees heading bureaus and low-level careerists opens up future by-pass communication. Significant information will be passed from the lower levels of the organization directly to the political appointee by way of a phone call or a passing contact in the hallway. Such events would be virtually impossible without the initial direct contact provided by the monthly review meeting.

4. The Grace Commission reported that 80,000 grants, dating back to 1973 had not been closed. These grants contained one-half billion dollars in unexpended funds. The President's Private Sector Survey on Cost Control (PPSSCC) Task Force Report, Section ED-4 "Contracts and Discretionary Grants," p. 50.

5. 34 CFR 75.233

6. (1) "The Flow of Management Information to Executives of the Department of Education," McManis Associates, March 1983;(2) The President's Private Sector Survey on Cost Control (PPSSCC) Task Force Report, Section ED4, "Contracts and Discretionary Grants'"; and (3) Michael Sanera, "Review of Discretionary Grant Administrative Procedures at the Department of Education," August 1983.

Conclusion

This part of *Mandate II* began by stating that policy change is very difficult to accomplish in Washington. Its last five chapters have attempted to explain why change is so difficult and to demonstrate strategies that will bring about real policy change.

Measuring the political executive's success at policy change is always problematic. Perhaps the best method to measure success is to compare actual change with the potential for change. The potential for change that exists in bureaucratic discretion is enormous. If every Reagan political executive controlled only ten percent of the bureaucratic discretion in his area of responsibility, the federal government could be turned upside down. Much of the President's conservative mandate could be implemented without legislative changes.

Unfortunately, the first Reagan Administration failed to exploit this potential. As in most presidential administrations, many political executives in the first Reagan Administration were captured, worked for narrow interest group goals, and, at times, fought among themselves. The lack of action on the part of the political executives allowed the bureaucracy to maintain its power and continue to grind out the expansion of the federal government. On the administrative level, the first Reagan Administration was "business as usual."

The second Reagan Administration must be different. *Mandate for Leadership II*, particularly this last part, is an attempt to contribute to that difference. The political executives in the second Reagan Administration have an opportunity actually to control, for the first time since the major expansion of the federal government in the New Deal, the federal bureaucracy and to produce fundamental policy change. To do this they must not get caught in the current of the river. They must chart a course and then skillfully navigate the swift current to reach the distant river bank. If, instead of a tiny minority, the majority of political executives are successful, they will contribute to the success of the Reagan presidency, which will be noted in history for reversing the course of the expansionist federal government.

Contributors

Wayne A. Abernathy is an economist with the Subcommittee on International Finance and Monetary Policy of the Senate Committee on Banking, Housing, and Urban Affairs. He also has served as assistant to the Republican Staff Director of the Senate Banking Committee and assistant to the Director of Legislation for Senator Jake Garn (R-UT).

Mark Albrecht is the legislative assistant for national security affairs to Senator Pete Wilson (R-CA).

Steven M. Antosh is Executive Director of the Center on National Labor Policy, a public-interest legal foundation.

Doug Bandow is a Senior Fellow at the Cato Institute. He previously served as a special assistant to President Reagan.

Roger A. Brooks is the Roe Fellow in United Nations Studies at The Heritage Foundation, and a former intelligence officer in the United States Army.

Nolan E. Clark is Deputy Assistant Director for Planning, Bureau of Competition, Federal Trade Commission. He also served as Associate Administrator for Policy and Resource Management of the U.S. Environmental Protection Agency at the beginning of the Reagan Administration.

Angelo M. Codevilla is a member of the staff of the Senate Select Committee on Intelligence. He also serves as legislative assistant to Senator Malcom Wallop (R-Wyoming) on foreign and defense matters, including space policy and weaponry.

John F. Copper is the president of the consulting firm of Copper and Associates. He formerly was director of The Heritage Foundation's Asian Studies Center.

Milton R. Copulos is a Senior Policy Analyst at The Heritage Foundation.

Theodore J. Crackel (Lt. Col., U.S. Army, Ret.) is a Senior Fellow and Director of the Heritage Foundation's Defense Assessment Project.

Ronald F. Docksai is the staff director of the United States Senate Committee on Labor and Human Resources. He authored the 1980 *Mandate for Leadership* chapter on the Department of Education.

George S. Dunlop is Chief of Staff of the U.S. Senate Committee on Agriculture, Nutrition and Forestry. He has been active in staff work for the Republican Party Platforms since 1976.

Catherine England is a Senior Policy Analyst at the Cato Institute. Previously she was a Policy Analyst at The Heritage Foundation.

Georges Fauriol is a Senior Research Fellow and Director of Carribean Basin Studies at the Georgetown University Center for Strategic and International Studies (CSIS).

Peter J. Ferrara is an attorney practicing in Washington, D.C. He formerly was a member of the White House Office of Policy Development and special assistant to the Assistant Secretary for Policy Development and Research at HUD.

Eileen M. Gardner is a Policy Analyst at The Heritage Foundation and edits the Foundation's quarterly newsletter, *Education Update.*

Jeffrey B. Gayner is Counselor for International Affairs at The Heritage Foundation.

Brian Green is a Policy Analyst at The Heritage Foundation.

Mark Greenberg is Legislative Director to Senator Paul Trible (R-Virginia).

James T. Hackett is editor of The Heritage Foundation's monthly *National Security Record.*

Manfred R. Hamm is a Senior Policy Analyst at The Heritage Foundation.

Esther Wilson Hannon is a Policy Analyst at The Heritage Foundation.

Edward L. Hudgins is a Policy Analyst at The Heritage Foundation.

Gordon S. Jones is Vice President for Government and Academic Affairs at The Heritage Foundation.

Paul D. Kamenar is Executive Legal Director of the Washington Legal Foundation, a conservative public interest law firm which has litigated numerous cases concerning constitutional law, regulatory issues, criminal justice matters, and national security and defense.

Lou Kriser, a former Naval Aviator and Professional Staff Member with the House Armed Services Committee, is president of the consulting firm of Snyder, Ball, Kriser and Associates.

Carnes Lord is a political scientist specializing in political theory and international relations/national security. He is a consultant to the National Security Council, the Department of Defense, and the Arms Control and Disarmament Agency.

Joseph T. Mayer is a Professional Staff Member of the Senate Select Committee on Intelligence. He also is Assistant for National Security Affairs to Senator Jake Garn (R-UT).

Richard B. McKenzie is Professor of economics at Clemson University and a Senior Fellow at The Heritage Foundation.

Mackubin T. Owens is the National Security Assistant to Senator Robert Kasten (R-WI), and a ten-year veteran of the Marine Corps.

John M. Palffy is Chief Economist for Senator Dan Quayle (R-Indiana).

James A. Phillips is a Senior Policy Analyst at The Heritage Foundation.

Juliana Geran Pilon is a Senior Policy Analyst with The Heritage Foundation's United Nations Assessment Project.

Daniel Pipes, a specialist on the Middle East and Islamic Affairs, is Associate Professor at the Naval War College.

Virginia Polk is a Policy Analyst at The Heritage Foundation.

Richard Shultz is an Associate Professor of International Politics at the Fletcher School of Law and Diplomacy. He is also a Research Associate at the National Strategy Information Center.

Fred L. Smith Jr. heads the Competitive Enterprise Institute, a pro-market public interest group. He has been an environmental policy analyst for the U.S. Environmental Protection Agency and a Senior Research Economist at the Association of American Railroads.

Norman B. Ture is president of the Institute for Research on the Economics of Taxation. He formerly served as Under Secretary of the Treasury for Tax Policy.

Paul D. Kamenar is Executive Legal Director of the Washington Legal Foundation, a conservative public interest law firm which has litigated numerous cases concerning constitutional law, regulatory issues, criminal justice matters, and national security and defense.

Lou Kriser, a former Naval Aviator and Professional Staff Member with the House Armed Services Committee, is president of the consulting firm of Snyder, Ball, Kriser and Associates.

Carnes Lord is a political scientist specializing in political theory and international relations/national security. He is a consultant to the National Security Council, the Department of Defense, and the Arms Control and Disarmament Agency.

Joseph T. Mayer is a Professional Staff Member of the Senate Select Committee on Intelligence. He also is Assistant for National Security Affairs to Senator Jake Garn (R-UT).

Richard B. McKenzie is Professor of economics at Clemson University and a Senior Fellow at The Heritage Foundation.

Mackubin T. Owens is the National Security Assistant to Senator Robert Kasten (R-WI), and a ten-year veteran of the Marine Corps.

John M. Palffy is Chief Economist for Senator Dan Quayle (R-Indiana).

James A. Phillips is a Senior Policy Analyst at The Heritage Foundation.

Juliana Geran Pilon is a Senior Policy Analyst with The Heritage Foundation's United Nations Assessment Project.

Daniel Pipes, a specialist on the Middle East and Islamic Affairs, is Associate Professor at the Naval War College.

Virginia Polk is a Policy Analyst at The Heritage Foundation.

Richard Shultz is an Associate Professor of International Politics at the Fletcher School of Law and Diplomacy. He is also a Research Associate at the National Strategy Information Center.

Fred L. Smith Jr. heads the Competitive Enterprise Institute, a pro-market public interest group. He has been an environmental policy

The Heritage Foundation

The Heritage Foundation is one of the country's leading public policy research institutes. With offices just two blocks from the United States Capitol. The Heritage Foundation's research and studies programs are designed to make the voices of responsible conservatism heard in Washington, D.C., throughout the United States, and in the capitals of the world.

The key to Heritage's research effort is timeliness—providing the policy-making community with up-to-date research on the important issues of the day. Heritage publishes its findings in a variety of formats for the benefit of decision makers, the media, the academic community, businessmen, and the public at large. Over the past five years The Heritage Foundation has published more than 400 books, monographs, and studies, ranging in size from the 1,093-page government blueprint, *Mandate for Leadership: Policy Management in a Conservative Administration*, to more frequent "Critical Issues" monographs and the topical "Backgrounders" and "Issue Bulletins" of a few thousand words. Heritage's other regular publications include *National Security Record, Policy Digest, Education Update*, and *Policy Review*, a quarterly journal of analysis and opinion.

The Heritage Foundation's 100-member staff—which includes several internationally recognized scholars and former government officials—concentrates on four areas of general study: domestic and economic policy; foreign policy and defense; the United Nations; and Asian studies. With some 1,600 individual scholars and research organizations working with its Resource Bank, The Heritage Foundation is uniquely equipped to provide U.S. policy makers with the intellectual resources needed to guide America into the 21st century.

In addition to the printed word, Heritage regularly brings together national and international opinion leaders and policy makers to discuss issues and ideas in a variety of formal and informal settings. Through a continuing series of seminars, lectures, debates, and briefings. The Heritage Foundation provides a forum for the exchange of ideas and a laboratory for developing these ideas into practical public policy proposals.

The Heritage Foundation was established in 1973 as a nonpartisan, tax-exempt policy research institute dedicated to the principles of free competitive enterprise, limited government, individual liberty, and a strong national defense. Heritage is classified as a Section 501(c)(3) organization under the Internal Revenue Code of 1954, and is recognized as a publicly supported organization described in Sections 509(a)(1) and 170(b)(A)(vi) of the Code. Individuals, corporations, companies, associations, and foundations are eligible to support the work of The Heritage Foundation through tax-deductible gifts.

The Heritage Foundation
214 Massachusetts Avenue, N.E.
Washington, D.C. 20002
(202) 546-4400